SO-BFI-626

WITHDRAWN

WHO WAS
WHO
IN
AMERICAN SPORTS

WHO WAS
WHO
IN
AMERICAN SPORTS

by Ralph Hickok

HAWTHORN BOOKS, INC.

Publishers

New York

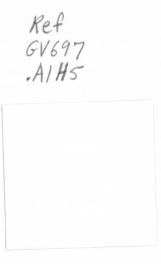

WHO WAS WHO IN AMERICAN SPORTS

CONTENTS

ACKNOWLEDGMENTS

I must acknowledge assistance in gathering information from the following people:

Ed Alsene, director of publicity and sports information, Illinois Wesleyan University; Tom Appenzeller, sports publicity, Presbyterian College; Ron Barnes, sports information director, Vanderbilt University; Tom Bennett, of the Atlanta Braves; Al Bloemker, director of public relations, Indianapolis Motor Speedway Corp.; Steve Brown, assistant director of sports information, Harvard University; Charles Buffum, of the Akron *Beacon-Journal;* Gary Cavalli, assistant sports information director, Stanford University; Michael Cohen, sports information director, Manhattan College; Hal Cowan, sports information director, University of Oregon; Bob Cusumano, assistant director of sports information, University of Michigan.

Frank C. Daniel, secretary, National Rifle Association; Robert Daniel, student assistant for sports information, University of Maryland; Tom Doherty, sports information director, University of Rhode Island; Jim Dynan, sports information director, Bradley University; Otis Dypwick, sports information director, University of Minnesota; Peter Easton, assistant director of sports information, Yale University; Bob Ecklund, sports information director, Kansas State Teachers College; Molly Eigen, National Football Foundation Hall of Fame; David Estridge, director of sports information, Tufts University; Pat Etter, of Los Angeles; Joyce L. Eyler, Western Maryland College Office of Publications and Publicity.

John P. Foster, Central Washington State College; Betty Ann Foxworthy, editor, *Trap and Field;* Anne Gallagher, Northwestern University Office of Sports Information; Jack Geyer, director of public relations, Los Angeles Rams; Ed Given, assistant public relations director, Western Kentucky University; Shep Goldberg, University of Pittsburgh Department of Athletics; Tom Grimes, director of public relations, Oakland Raiders; David J. Grote, director of public relations, National League of Professional Baseball Clubs; Len Harlow, sports information director, University of Maine; Bud Harvey, editor, Professional Golfers Association; Allan R. Heim, public relations director, Cincinnati Bengals; Frances M. Henderson, Morgan State College; Brent Hislop, assistant sports information director, Utah State University; Jay

Horwitz, sports information director, New York University; Jerry Huston, of New Bedford, Massachusetts.

Willie Jacobs, sports publicity director, Austin College; Ed Kiely, director of public relations, Pittsburgh Steelers; Norma Kirkendall, Women's International Bowling Congress Forms and Literature Department; Dick Kubik, sports information director, University of Chicago; Chuck Lane, Green Bay Packers; William J. Latzko, Amateur Fencers League of America; Arthur G. Lentz, executive director, U.S. Olympic Committee; Richard R. Lewis, director of sports information, Holy Cross College; Larry Liddell, assistant director of athletic publicity, University of Mississippi.

Edward L. Marcou, editor, *Bowling* magazine; Tom Miller, athletic publicity director, University of Indiana; Frank Morgan, director of sports information, Ohio University; Eddie Mullens, sports information director, University of Texas at El Paso; Bert Nelson, publisher, *Track and Field News;* William T. Odeneal, State University of New York, New Paltz, New York, for volleyball information; John D. O'Hern, assistant director, Bowdoin College News Service; Hugh F. Ortman, sports information director, Villanova University; Jack Pitzentaylor, St. Bonaventure University; Dick Polen, assistant athletic publicity director, West Virginia University; Joe Pollack, director of public relations, St. Louis Football Cardinals.

Jones Ramsey, sports news director, University of Texas; Steve Roberts, director of sports information, Monmouth College; Robert M. Salter, Trinity (Connecticut) College News Bureau; Mrs. Robert Sanders, De Pere, Wisconsin; W. R. "Bill" Schroeder, executive director, Helms Athletic Foundation; Paul S. Shearn, director of public information, Washington and Jefferson College; Jay Simon, University of Kansas; Don Smith, director of public relations, New York Giants; Don Smith, director of public relations, Professional Football Hall of Fame; R. E. Smith, sports information director, Rutgers University; Fred W. Stabley, director of sports information, Michigan State University; W. C. Stryker, director of sports information, Princeton University.

James I. Tarman, athletic public relations director, Pennsylvania State University; Clement F. Trainer, of Philadelphia, for information on billiards; Elliott Trumbull, assistant director of public relations, Detroit Lions; Jack H. Van Praag, American Badminton Association; Linda L. Walgreen, Purdue University sports information; Frank Weedon, sports information director, North Carolina State University; Don Weiss, director of public relations, National Football League; Ned West, director of sports information, Georgia Tech University; Joe Whritenour, sports information director, Lehigh University; Jack E. Williams, sports information director, North Carolina University; Mike Wilson, sports information director, Washington State University.

In a number of cases, I received unsigned replies containing information I needed, so I can't credit specific people. Such replies came from: The American Greyhound Track Operators Association, the Baltimore Colts, Baylor University, Carnegie Institute of Technology, the Cleveland Browns, the University of Connecticut, Cornell University, Dartmouth College, Dayton University, the University of Georgia, Grambling College, the University of Illinois, the University of Iowa, the U.S. Military Academy, the U.S. Naval Academy, Notre Dame University, the University of Oklahoma, the University of Pennsylvania, the Philadelphia Eagles, the University of Southern California, Syracuse University, the University of Tennessee, the Washington Redskins, and Williams College.

And, of course, I must thank my wife, Cathy, who not only helped with preparing lists, with alphabetizing, and with proofreading, but who also made her usual significant contributions to my mental and emotional health while I was working on this book.

R. H.

INTRODUCTION

Certain guidelines are needed by someone who sets out to do a book like *Who Was Who in American Sports*. The problem is, Who should be included? Or put the other way around, of all the people who might be included, who should be left out?

In facing this problem I was able to do some selecting in advance, at least for the major sports—baseball, basketball, boxing, football, golf, tennis, and track—because they all have halls of fame. With a very few exceptions, I have listed all deceased members of the major sports' halls of fame. (One exception, for example: Morgan Bulkeley, the first president of the National League and a member of the Baseball Hall of Fame, isn't included, because he served for only one year and did virtually nothing for baseball; however, I have included William A. Hulbert, who really founded the National League, ruled it for many years after Bulkeley, and who is not in Cooperstown.)

Minor sports are more difficult. Many of them have more people in their halls of fame than do the major sports, and they can't all be included. So I had to pick and choose, which wasn't easy; I tried in each case to get guidance from someone connected with the sport, though not always successfully. I have used certain rules of thumb, rather than rigid guidelines, for selection. For example, I began with the idea that I would list all players who appeared in one thousand or more major-league baseball games (or for pitchers, those who had one thousand or more innings). Most people meeting that criterion are here, but a number of them have been omitted to make way for those who had to be included for other reasons: Neal Ball, for instance, who had the first unassisted triple play in major-league history, though he appeared in only 496 games.

With all major sports I proceeded in this way, setting up standards but occasionally knocking them down when it seemed necessary. A certain amount of subjectivity has to enter in; there are athletes who, for one reason or another—illness, injury, or just plain bad luck—may not meet arbitrary standards but who simply have to be included.

In boxing, for example, I have listed all deceased former champions who could be considered Americans; there are some boxers listed who never held titles but who had outstanding records, and some of those who held pieces of a title or who claimed titles without actually winning them have been left out.

Although the emphasis in this book is on athletes and coaches, others—inventors, founders, rules-makers, officials, and other "contributors," to use the pet phrase of those who maintain sports halls of fame—have been included if it seems that they did make some very genuine contribution.

All sorts of considerations enter in: Between the fine player and the fine coach is the person who was both a fair player and a fair coach and who, perhaps, ought to be included. Drawing such lines is never easy. Compiling a book like this one is like drawing up a list of the hundred greatest books; any two people will agree on perhaps fifty of them, but the other fifty introduce disagreements.

Sports research is difficult and often frustrating. Many whom I asked for help replied sadly and politely that they would really like to help but just didn't have the information I needed. Dates and places of birth are particularly hard to get. Moreover, quite a few of the basic reference books contain inaccuracies or omissions. One can find as many as three different spellings of a name (Pete Cawthon's name, for example, is spelled "Cawthron" or "Cawthorn" more often than it is spelled correctly); as many as three different birthdates for the same person; and Jackson Haines, according to reliable sources, was born either in Chicago or in Troy, New York.

I have tried to keep from guessing at anything, but in about 10 percent of the entries I have had to "guess" at the year of birth. If a person died in the first half of 1950, at the age of fifty, for example, I have listed the birthdate as 1899, with a question mark; if he died in the second half of 1950, at the age of fifty, I have listed the birthdate as 1900, with a question mark, simply to give some idea of how old he was at various stages of his career.

In a few cases, I have also guessed at a birthplace, again using a question mark; this means either that an obituary or other source referred to this as his "hometown" or that he obviously spent his very early years there.

A good deal of the research was done through query letters to colleges and professional teams. Of nearly three hundred requests for information, I received replies to all but fifteen or twenty, but surprisingly often, even a college or a pro team for which a player starred, or which he coached, is unable to furnish a date and place of birth. In several cases, I was able to find surviving relatives who could supply the information.

Even identifying a sports figure by name poses a problem. The name William Hamilton may not mean much, but the name "Sliding Billy" Hamilton is familiar to many baseball fans. I have tried to present names in such a way that the reader can easily find the entry he is looking for. Thus, Hamilton is listed: **HAMILTON, "SLIDING BILLY" (William R.).**

I haven't ordinarily used obvious nicknames, such as "Bill" for William, "Dick" for Richard, "Tom" for Thomas; but where the nickname takes any sort of unusual form, as "Billy," "Richie," "Tommy," I have used it. In some cases, a person was occasionally called by a nickname, but it is not well known; in those cases, he is listed under his real name, with the nickname following it. Nicknames all appear in quotation marks.

Name changes were common, especially in the early days of baseball and boxing. If a person changed his name, I have listed his real name before his birthdate. Thus, the entry for Barney Ross, whose real name was Barnet Rasofsky, reads: **ROSS, BARNEY** boxing: b. Barnet Rasofsky, Dec. 23, 1909, Chicago. In deciding whether to use a woman's maiden or married name, I have tried to pick the one by which she was best known. Miriam Burns Horn is listed: **BURNS, MIRIAM (Mrs. Horn, Mrs. Tyson);** but "Babe" Didrikson Zaharias is listed under her married name, with her maiden name indicated in parentheses.

If a person belongs to a hall of fame, this is indicated at the end of his entry. The Helms Athletic Foundation maintains halls of fame for basketball, boxing, pro football, college football, golf, tennis, and track and field, among the major sports. The Basketball Hall of Fame is the James A. Naismith Memorial Basketball Hall of Fame, Springfield, Massachusetts; the Boxing Hall of Fame is maintained by *Ring* magazine; the Auto Racing Hall of Fame by the Indianapolis Motor Speedway Corp.; the Tennis Hall of Fame by the U.S. Lawn Tennis Association at Newport, Rhode Island. The National Racing Hall of Fame is at Saratoga, New York; the Jockey Hall of Fame at Pimlico Race Course; the National Football Foundation Hall of Fame for college football at New Brunswick, New Jersey; the Professional Football Hall of Fame at Canton, Ohio; and the Baseball Hall of Fame at Cooperstown, New York.

Other halls of fame are identified by the organizations that maintain them; for example, the American Bowling Congress Hall of Fame and the Professional Golfers Association Hall of Fame.

In baseball entries, I give for everyone a list of the teams he played for and the years in which he played for them; the number of seasons he played, the number of games in which he appeared, and his lifetime batting average (or, for pitchers, lifetime won-lost record and earned-run average). If a player had an unusual number of career home runs, runs batted in, stolen bases, shutouts, strikeouts, etc., during his career, this is also included; so are years in which he led the league in any major category, years in which he hit over .300 or won twenty games or more, and important records that he holds. In listing a player's position, I have chosen the one at which he played the most games; if he played an appreciable number of games at other positions, I have listed those afterward.

If a player is among the top ten all-time in any major category, this is indicated in parentheses after the total figure. Babe Ruth's home-run total, for example, is given as "714 home runs (1st)."

Teams are listed by name of city, with an abbreviation for the league. (See pages xli–xlii for the league abbreviations and all others used in this book.) Chicago NL, for example, would be the National League team now known as the Cubs, Chicago AL the team known as the White Sox. There were other leagues, now defunct, that are considered major leagues: The American Association (1882–91), the Union Association (1884), the Players' League (1890), and the Federal League (1914–15). The National Association of Professional Baseball Players, though not considered a major league, was the first professional league; I have listed National Association records separately before listing major-league affiliations. It was in existence from 1871 through 1875.

Major-league baseball franchises have been fairly stable until recent years, but there have been a few changes that affect listings in this book. Three franchises moved in midseason, and in those cases the cities are listed together, with a hyphen, to make it clear that a player wasn't traded: Brooklyn-Baltimore, in the American Association, 1890; Cincinnati-Milwaukee, in the American Association, 1891; and Chicago-Pittsburgh, in the Union Association, 1884.

It should be pointed out that the New York NL team up until 1958 was the Giant franchise, now in San Francisco, and is not to be confused with the present New York Mets. The Boston NL team moved to Milwaukee in 1953, the Brooklyn NL team to Los Angeles in 1958. American League franchise shifts: Milwaukee to St. Louis in 1902, to Baltimore in 1954; Baltimore to New York in 1903; Philadelphia to Kansas City in 1955, to Oakland in 1968; Washington to Minnesota in 1961; Los Angeles to Anaheim in 1965.

I have listed managerial records for anyone who managed one full season or more, and playing records, however brief, are included for all managers.

With pro football, I haven't indicated that a team was in the National Football League, since it was the only dominant league for such a long time, but other leagues are identified in parentheses. There have been four American Football Leagues, in 1926, 1936–37, 1940–41, and 1960–69; the last of them, of course, has now merged with the National Football League. The only other major professional league was the All-American Football Conference, formed in 1946 and absorbed by the NFL in 1950. The Cleveland Browns and San Francisco 49ers were in the AAFC until 1950, when they became NFL teams. The New York Yanks also moved from the AAFC into the NFL, becoming the Dallas Texans in 1952 and the Baltimore Colts in 1953. The old Baltimore Colt franchise had also moved into the NFL in 1950 but was dissolved after one season.

Major franchise shifts in the NFL: The Frankford Yellowjackets became the

Philadelphia Eagles in 1933; the Portsmouth Spartans became the Detroit Lions in 1934; the Boston Redskins moved to Washington in 1937; the Philadelphia and Pittsburgh franchises traded places in 1941; the Cleveland Rams moved to Los Angeles in 1946; the Brooklyn Dodgers jumped from the NFL to the AAFC in 1946 and merged with the New York Yanks in 1949; the Boston Yanks, formed in 1944, became the New York Bulldogs in 1949, but after one season the franchise was dissolved.

More recently, in the AFL, the Dallas Texans became the Kansas City Chiefs in 1963, the Los Angeles Chargers moved to San Diego in 1961, and the New York Titans' name was changed to the Jets in 1963.

Among books that have been good general sources of information for all sports are: *The Encyclopedia of Sports,* Frank G. Menke; *The Encyclopedia of Jews in Sports,* Bernard Postal and Jesse and Roy Silver; the four volumes of the Marquis *Who Was Who in America; The Dictionary of American Biography* and its two supplements; and *The New York Times Obituary Index, 1858–1968,* used in conjunction with microfilm files of the *Times* in The Free Public Library, New Bedford, Massachusetts.

The weekly obituary column in *The Sporting News* was most valuable in helping to keep the book up to date.

Most basic biographical information and statistics were drawn from either *The Baseball Encyclopedia,* published by Macmillan and Information Concepts, Inc., or *The Sporting News'* publication, *Daguerreotypes.* Information on individual records comes largely from *Baseball's One for the Book,* also a publication of *The Sporting News.* Also of assistance were *The American League Story* and *The National League Story,* both by Lee Allen, and *Baseball's Hall of Fame,* by Robert Smith.

For information on the several Negro-league players who are included, I am indebted to *Only the Ball Was White,* by Robert W. Peterson. Quotes from Sam Crawford about Ty Cobb, "Chief" Myers about John McGraw, and Harry Hooper about Babe Ruth are from Leonard Ritter's *The Glory of Their Times.*

My major source for basketball information was the Hall of Fame at Springfield, Massachusetts, whose executive director, Lee Williams, assisted me greatly during a visit there.

The ultimate authority on boxing is *The Ring Encyclopedia and Record Book,* published annually in a limited edition by *Ring* magazine. Any time that I say that a boxer is, for example, ranked seventh or ranked among the top ten in his weight class, I am using ratings prepared by *Ring*'s editor and publisher, Nat Fleischer, for the 1970 edition of that book. John Lardner's *White Hopes and Other Tigers* and Stanley Weston's *The Heavyweight Champions* were also of assistance.

Three basic football reference books are Roger Treat's *The Official Encyclopedia of Football,* which covers only pro football; Dr. L. H. Baker's *Football Facts and Figures,* a source of much information on college football; and *The Ronald Encyclopedia of Football.* Also useful were the National Football League's *Record Manual,* Alexander M. Weyand's *Football Immortals,* Arthur Daley's *Pro Football's Hall of Fame,* and Robert Smith's *Pro Football: The History of the Game and the Great Players.*

The *Encyclopedia of Golf,* edited by Robert Scharff and the editors of *Golf* magazine, is a basic reference to that sport. Will Grimsley's *Golf: Its History, People and Events* and Herbert Warren Wind's *Story of American Golf* were useful supplements.

For information on tennis I benefited greatly from a visit to the Tennis Hall of Fame at Newport, through the courtesy of Robert H. Van Alen, president, and Grace Haire. I also drew on Parke Cummings's *American Tennis.*

R. H.

LIST OF PERSONALITIES BY SPORT

AIRPLANE RACING

Curtiss, Glenn H.

AUTO RACING

Bettenhaus, "Tony"
Bourque, "Pit"
Cooper, Earl P.
Daywalt, James E.
DePalma, Ralph
Frame, Fred
Harroun, Ray
Hepburn, Ralph
Horn, Ted
Jenkins, "Ab"
Marshmann, "Bobby"
Mays, Rex
Miles, Kenneth
Miller, Chester J.
Milton, "Tommy"
Mudersbach, Allen
Murphy, Jimmy
Myers, "Pop"
O'Connor, Patrick J.
Oldfield, "Barney"
Robertson, George H.
Sachs, "Eddy"
Shaw, Wilbur
Unser, Jerry H.

Vanderbilt, William K.
Vukovich, William
Wallard, Lee
Weatherly, Joseph

BADMINTON

Davidson, Kenneth R.
Hill, Virginia

BALLOON RACING

Curtiss, Glenn H.
Upson, Ralph Hazlett

BASEBALL

Adams, "Babe"
Agganis, Harry
Alexander, Grover Cleveland
Allen, "Johnny"
Altrock, "Nick"
Ames, "Red"
Anderson, John J.
Anson, "Cap"
Archer, "Jimmy"
Armour, William R.
Austin, "Jimmy"
Ayers, "Doc"

Baseball *(cont.)*

Bagby, James C. J., Sr.
Bailey, William F.
Baker, "Home Run"
Baldwin, "Lady"
Ball, Neal
Bancroft, Frank C.
Barnes, Jesse L.
Barnes, "Ross"
Barnes, "Zeke"
Barnie, "Billy"
Barrow, Edward G.
Barry, "Jack"
Barry, "Shad"
Beaumont, "Ginger"
Beck, Frederick T.
Beckley, "Jake"
Beebe, Frederick L.
Bender, "Chief"
Bennett, "Charlie"
Benton, Lawrence J.
Benton, "Rube"
Benz, Joseph L.
Bernhard, William H.
Bescher, Robert W.
Bezdek, Hugo F.
Bickford, Vernon E.
Bierbauer, Louis W.
Bigbee, Carson L.
Birmingham, Joseph L.
Bishop, Max F.
Blaeholder, George F.
Blankenship, Theodore
Blanton, "Cy"
Blue, "Lu"
Bodie, Ping
Bond, Thomas H.

Bonham, "Ernie"
Bottomley, "Sunny Jim"
Bowerman, Frank E.
Boyle, "Jack"
Bradley, George W.
Bradley, William A.
Brain, David L.
Brandt, Edward A.
Bransfield, "Kitty"
Braxton, E. Garland
Breitenstein, Theodore P.
Bresnahan, Roger P.
Bridges, "Tommy"
Bridwell, "Al"
Brodie, "Steve"
Brouthers, "Dan"
Brown, "Buster"
Brown, Clinton H.
Brown, Thomas T.
Brown, "Three-Finger"
Browne, George E.
Browning, "Pete"
Buckenberger, "Al"
Buffington, "Charlie"
Burdock, "Jack"
Burke, "Jimmy"
Burkett, Jesse C.
Burns, George J.
Burns, "Oyster"
Burns, Thomas E.
Byrne, "Bobby"

Cadore, Leon J.
Caldwell, "Slim"
Callahan, "Nixey"
Camnitz, "Howie"
Cantwell, Benjamin C.
Carlson, Harold G.

Baseball *(cont.)*

Davis, Harry H.
Delahanty, "Big Ed"
Delahanty, James C.
Demaree, "Al"
Demaree, "Frank"
DeMontreville, "Gene"
DeMoss, "Bingo"
Denny, Jerry
Devore, Joshua
Dinneen, William H.
Doak, William
Donahue, "Red"
Donlin, Michael J.
Donovan, "Patsy"
Donovan, "Wild Bill"
Dooin, "Red"
Doolan, "Mickey"
Doubleday, Abner
Dougherty, "Patsy"
Douglas, "Shuffling Phil"
Dowd, Thomas J.
Doyle, "Jack"
Dressen, "Chuck"
Dreyfuss, Barney
Duffy, Hugh
Dunlap, Frederick C.
Duryea, "Jesse"
Dwyer, "Frank"
Dyer, "Eddie"

Ebbets, Charles H.
Ehmke, Howard J.
Ehret, "Red"
Elberfeld, "Kid"
Eller, "Hod"
Elliott, Robert I.

Ely, "Bones"
Engel, Joseph W.
Ens, Jewel W.
Esper, "Duke"
Evers, John J.
Ewing, "Bob"
Ewing, "Buck"
Ewing, John

Falkenberg, "Cy"
Farrell, "Duke"
Felsch, "Happy"
Ferguson, Charles J.
Ferguson, Robert V.
Ferris, "Hobe"
Finney, Louis K.
Flick, Elmer H.
Fletcher, Arthur
Fohl, Lee A.
Force, "Davy"
Ford, Russell W.
Foreman, Francis I.
Foster, "Kid"
Foster, "Rube"
Fothergill, "Fats"
Foutz, David L.
Fox, "Pete"
Foxx, "Jimmy"
Fraser, "Chick"
Freeman, "Buck"
Friberg, "Barney"
Fromme, Arthur H.

Galloway, "Chick"
Galvin, "Pud"
Gandil, "Chick"
Gastright, "Hank"
Gehrig, "Lou"

Baseball *(cont.)*

Hutchinson, Frederick C.
Hutchinson, "Wild Bill"

Irwin, Arthur A.
Isbell, William Frank

Jackson, "Shoeless Joe"
Jacobs, Elmer
James, William H.
Jamieson, "Chuck"
Jennings, Hugh
Johnson, "Ban"
Johnson, Walter P.
Johnston, "Doc"
Johnston, James H.
Jones, Fielder A.
Jones, "Sad Sam"
Jones, Thomas
Joss, "Addie"
Joyce, William M.
Judge, Joseph I.

Karger, Edwin
Keane, John J.
Keefe, Timothy J.
Keeler, "Wee Willie"
Kelley, Joseph J.
Kelly, "King"
Kennedy, "Brickyard"
Kerr, "Dickie"
Killefer, "Reindeer Bill"
Killen, Frank B.
Killian, Edwin H.
Kilroy, Matthew A.
Kinder, Ellis R.
King, "Silver"

Kitson, Frank R.
Kittredge, Malachi J.
Klein, "Chuck"
Klem, William J.
Kling, John G.
Knabe, Otto
Kolp, Raymond C.
Konetchy, Edward J.
Kremer, "Ray"
Kress, "Red"

LaChance, "Candy"
Lajoie, "Larry"
Lake, Joseph H.
Landis, Kenesaw Mountain
Laporte, Frank B.
Larkin, Henry E.
Latham, "Arlie"
Lavender, James S.
Lazzeri, "Tony"
Leach, "Wee Tommy"
Leever, Samuel
Leonard, Andrew J.
Leonard, "Dutch"
Lewis, "Ted"
Lloyd, "Pop"
Lobert, "Hans"
Loftus, Thomas J.
Long, Herman C.
Lovett, Thomas J.
Lowe, "Bobby"
Luderus, Frederick W.
Lumley, Harry G.
Lundgren, Carl L.
Luque, "Dolf"
Lush, John C.
Lynch, "Jack"
Lyons, Dennis P. A.

Mack, Connie
Maddox, Nicholas
Magee, "Lee"
Magee, "Sherry"
Mahaffey, Lee Roy
Malone, "Pat"
Mamaux, Albert L.
Mann, Leslie
Manning, "Jack"
Maranville, "Rabbit"
Martin, "Pepper"
Mathewson, "Christy"
Matthews, Wid C.
Maul, Albert J.
May, "Jakie"
Mayer, Erskine
McAleer, James R.
McCarthy, "Jack"
McCarthy, "Tommy"
McCormick, James
McFarland, Edward W.
McGann, "Dan"
McGeary, Michael H.
McGill, "Willie"
McGinnity, Joseph J.
McGraw, John J.
McGuire, "Deacon"
McGunnigle, William H.
McInnis, "Stuffy"
McIntire, "Harry"
McIntyre, Matthew W.
McJames, "Doc"
McKean, Edwin J.
McKechnie, William B.
McLean, "Scooter"
McMahon, "Sadie"
McManus, Martin J.
McNair, Eric

McPhee, "Bid"
McQuillan, George W.
McQuillan, Hugh A.
McVey, Calvin A.
Meadows, Lee
Meekin, Jouett
Meine, "Heinie"
Melillo, Oscar D.
Mercer, "Win"
Merkle, Frederick C.
Mertes, Samuel B.
Meusel, "Irish"
Meyer, "Billy"
Milan, J. Clyde
Miller, "Bing"
Miller, "Doggie"
Miller, "Dots"
Milligan, "Jocko"
Mitchell, Michael F.
Mogridge, George A.
Moore, Earl A.
Moore, W. Wilcey
Moran, Patrick J.
Moran, "Uncle Charlie"
Morgan, "Cy"
Moriarty, George J.
Morrill, John F.
Morris, Edward
Morrison, John D.
Morton, Guy, Sr.
Mullane, Anthony J.
Mullin, George J.
Murphy, Daniel F.
Murphy, John J.
Murray, "Red"
Mutrie, James J.
Myatt, Glenn C.
Myers, "Hy"

Baseball *(cont.)*

Nash, William M.
Nehf, Arthur N.
Nelson, "Jack"
Newsom, "Bobo"
Nichols, "Kid"
Nicol, Hugh N.
Niggeling, John A.
Nunamaker, Leslie G.

O'Connell, Daniel F.
O'Connor, "Jack"
O'Day, "Hank"
O'Doul, "Lefty"
Oldring, Reuben H.
Olson, "Ivy"
O'Neill, Stephen F.
O'Neill, "Tip"
O'Rourke, James H.
Orsatti, Ernesto R.
Orth, Albert L.
Ostermueller, "Fritz"
Ott, Melvin T.
Overall, Orval
Owen, Frank M.

Packard, "Gene"
Paskert, "Dode"
Patterson, Roy L.
Pelty, Barney
Pennock, Herbert J.
Perritt, "Pol"
Perry, H. Scott
Pfeffer, "Fred"
Pfeister, "Jack"
Phillippe, "Deacon"
Phillips, William C.

Piatt, Wiley H.
Picinich, Valentine J.
Pike, "Lip"
Pinckney, George B.
Pipp, "Wally"
Pittinger, "Togie"
Plank, "Eddie"
Posey, "Cum"
Powell, "Jack"
Powell, "Jake"

Quinn, "Jack"
Quinn, Joseph J.

Radbourn, "Old Hoss"
Radcliff, "Rip"
Radford, Paul R.
Ragan, "Pat"
Ramsey, "Toad"
Reilly, John G.
Reulbach, Edward M.
Rhem, Flint
Rhines, William P.
Richardson, Daniel
Richardson, "Hardy"
Richie, Lewis A.
Richmond, Lee
Rickey, W. Branch
Ring, James J.
Ripple, James A.
Ritchey, Claude C.
Rixey, Eppa
Robinson, "Uncle Robbie"
Rogan, "Bullet Joe"
Rolfe, "Red"
Root, Charles H.
Rowe, "Jack"
Rose, "Schoolboy"

Rowland, "Pants"
Rudolph, Richard
Ruel, "Muddy"
Ruether, "Dutch"
Rusie, Amos W.
Ruth, "Babe"
Ryan, James E.

Sallee, "Slim"
Scanlan, "Doc"
Schaefer, "Germany"
Schalk, Raymond W.
Schang, "Wally"
Schmelz, Gustavus H.
Schneider, Peter J.
Schulte, "Wildfire"
Scott, "Deacon"
Scott, "Jack"
Scott, James
Seaton, Thomas G.
Selbach, "Kip"
Selee, Frank G.
Sevareid, "Hank"
Seward, Edward W.
Seybold, "Socks"
Seymour, "Cy"
Shanks, "Hank"
Shaughnessy, "Shag"
Shaute, Joseph B.
Shaw, "Dupee"
Shaw, James
Sheckard, "Jimmy"
Sheely, Earl H.
Sherdel, "Wee Willie"
Shindle, William
Shocker, Urban J.
Shotton, Burton E.
Shoun, "Hardrock"

Siever, Edward T.
Simmons, "Bucketfoot Al"
Slagle, James F.
Smith, Earl S.
Smith, Elmer E.
Smith, Frank E.
Smith, "Germany"
Smith, "Pop"
Smith, "Red"
Smith, "Sherry"
Snyder, Frank E.
Snyder, "Pop"
Sothoron, Allen S.
Southworth, "Billy"
Spalding, Albert G.
Sparks, Tully F.
Speaker, Tristam E.
Stahl, "Chick"
Stahl, "Jake"
Staley, "Harry"
Stallings, George T.
Stanage, Oscar H.
Start, Joseph
Stein, Edward F.
Steinfeldt, Harry M.
Stenzel, Jacob C.
Stephens, "Junior"
Stewart, William
Stirnweiss, "Snuffy"
Stivetts, "Jack"
Stone, George R.
Stone, John T.
Stovall, George T.
Stovey, Harry D.
Stratton, C. Scott
Street, "Gabby"
Suggs, George F.
Sullivan, "Billy"

Baseball *(cont.)*

Summa, Homer W.
Summers, "Ed"
Sutton, Ezra B.
Sweeney, Charles J.
Sweeney, William J.
Swift, Robert V.

Tabor, James R.
Tennehill, Jesse N.
Taylor, C. I.
Taylor, "Dummy"
Taylor, "Jack" (John B.)
Taylor, "Jack" (John W.)
Tebeau, "Patsy"
Tenney, Fred
Terry, "Adonis"
Tesrau, "Jeff"
Thevenow, Thomas J.
Thomas, Roy A.
Thompson, "Hank"
Thompson, L. Fresco
Thompson, Samuel L.
Thorpe, James F.
Tiernan, Michael J.
Tinker, Joseph B.
Titus, John F.
Tobin, James A.
Tobin, John T.
Toney, Frederick A.
Trautman, George
Tucker, Thomas J.
Turner, "Terry"
Tyler, "Lefty"

Vance, "Dazzy"
Van Haltren, George E. M.

Vaughan, "Arky"
Vaughn, "Hippo"
Veach, Robert H.
Viau, Leon
Vitt, "Ossie"

Waddell, "Rube"
Wagner, "Honus"
Walker, "Curt"
Walker, "Tilly"
Walker, William H.
Wallace, "Bobby"
Walsh, Edward A.
Waner, Paul G.
Ward, Aaron L.
Ward, "Monte"
Watkins, George A.
Watkins, William H.
Weaver, "Buck"
Weaver, Samuel H.
Webb, W. Earl
Weidman, "Stump"
Weilman, Carl W.
Weimer, Jacob
Welch, Curtis B.
Welch, "Mickey"
Weyhing, "Gus"
White, "Deacon"
White, William H.
Whitehead, John H.
Whitehill, Earl O.
Whitney, "Long Jim"
Whitted, "Possum"
Wicker, Robert K.
Wilhelm, "Kaiser"
Willett, "Ed"
Williams, James T.
Williams, Kenneth R.

Williams, "Lefty"
Williamson, "Ned"
Willis, Victor G.
Wilmot, Walter R.
Wilson, "Hack"
Wilson, James
Wilson, J. Owen
Wiltse, "Hooks"
Wingo, Ivy B.
Winter, George L.
Wise, Samuel W.
Wood, George A.
Wright, George
Wright, "Harry"

Yde, Emil O.
York, Rudolph P.
York, Thomas J.
Young, "Cy"
Young, Irving M.
Youngs, Ross M.

Zabel, "Zip"
Zachary, "Tom"
Zimmer, "Chief"

BASKETBALL

Anderson, W. Harold

Benington, John
Blackburn, Thomas L.
Blood, Ernest A.
Brown, Walter A.
Buntin, William

Carlson, "Doc"
Case, Everett N.

Cohalan, "Neil"
Crisp, "Hank"

DeBernardi, "Red"
Diddle, Edgar A.

Estes, Wayne

Farley, Richard L.

Gill, "Slats"
Greer, Hugh S.
Gulick, Luther H.

Hapac, William J.
Hepbron, George T.
Hickox, Edward J.
Hoyt, George H.

Jordan, Phil
Julian, "Doggy"

Keaney, Frank W.
Kennedy, "Pat"
Keogan, George E.
Kirsch, Donald
Krebs, James

Lambert, "Piggy"
Lapchick, Joseph

McCracken, Branch
McCracken, Jack D.
Meanwell, Walter E.
Morgan, Ralph
Morgenweck, Frank
Mundorf, Roy M.

Basketball *(cont.)*

Naismith, James A.
Nicholson, Leo

O'Brien, John J.
Olsen, "Ole"

Page, "Pat"

Quigley, Ernest C.

Reid, William A.

Sachs, Leonard
St. John, Lynn W.
Saperstein, Abraham
Schommer, John J.
Sedran, Barney
Smith, Dwight
Steinmetz, Christian W.
Stokes, Maurice

Tatum, "Goose"
Taylor, "Chuck"
Torrence, Walter
Tower, Oswald
Trester, Arthur L.

Wachter, Edward A.

BICYCLING

Bardgett, Walter A.
Curtiss, Glenn H.

BILLIARDS

Cochran, Welker
Greenleaf, Ralph
Hoppe, "Willie"
Kavanagh, Dudley
Layton, John
Lee, Edward L.
Peterson, Charles C.
Schaefer, Jacob, Sr.
Slosson, George F.

BOBSLEDDING

Benham, Stanley
Eagan, Edward P. F.
Stevens, "Hub"

BOWLING

Blouin, James
Bodis, Joseph
Carlson, "Swede"
Daw, Charles
Easter, "Ed"
Gibson, Therman
Knox, William
Koster, John H.
Lindsey, Mortimer J.
McCutcheon, Floretta
Nagy, Steve J.
Sielaff, Louis A.
Smith, James
Steers, Harry H.
Wilman, "Buck"
Wolf, Phil
Young, George
Zunker, Gilbert

BOXING

Aaron, "Young Barney"
Attell, "Abe"

Baer, Max
Barry, Jimmy
Barton, George
Bimstein, "Whitey"
Brady, William A.
Britton, Jack
Buff, Johnny
Burns, Frankie
Burns, Tommy
Burston, Lewis

Campi, Eddie
Canzoneri, Tony
Carnera, Primo
Casey, "Doc"
Chandler, Tom
Chaney, George
Chip, George
Choynski, Joe
Coffroth, James W.
Collyer, Sam
Corbett, "Gentleman Jim"
Corbett, Young

Dade, Harold D.
Delaney, Jack
Dempsey, "The Nonpareil"
Dillon, Jack
Dixie Kid
Dixon, George
Donovan, Mike
Duffy, "Paddy"

Dundee, Johnny
Dundee, Vince

Eagan, Edward P. F.
Eaton, Calvin
Erne, Frank

Ferns, Jim
Fitzsimmons, Robert L.
Floris, "Dan"
Flowers, "Tiger"
Forbes, Harry
Fugazy, Humbert J.

Gans, Joe
Gardner, George
Genaro, Frank
Gibbons, Mike
Gibbons, Tom
Goldman, Charles
Greb, "Harry"

Harris, Harry
Hart, Marvin
Heenan, John G.
Hyer, Tom

Jacobs, Joe
Jacobs, Michael S.
Jeannette, Joe
Jeffries, James J.
Johnson, "Jack"
Johnston, James Joy

Kansas, "Rocky"
Kearns, "Doc"
Kelly, Tom
Kelly, Tommy "Spider"

Boxing *(cont.)*

Ketchel, Stanley
Kilbane, Johnny
Kilrain, Jake
Klaus, Frank

Langford, Sam
Latzo, Pete
Lavigne, George "Kid"
Leonard, Benny
Lesnevich, Gus
Levinsky, Battling
Lewis, Harry
Lewis, Willie
Liston, "Sonny"
Lynch, Joseph

Mandel, Sammy
Marciano, Rocky
Marino, Tony
Matthews, "Matty"
McAuliffe, Jack
McCarthy, "Cal"
McCarty, Luther
McCoy, Al
McCoy, "Kid"
McGovern, "Terry"
McTigue, Michael F.
Mellody, "Honey"
Miller, Freddie
Miskie, Billy
Mitchell, Young
Molineaux, Tom
Moore, Davey
Morrissey, John C.
Muldoon, William A.

Nardiello, Vincent J.
Nelson, "Battling"
Norris, James D., Jr.

O'Brien, Philadelphia Jack
O'Dowd, Mike
Olin, Robert
Ortiz, Manuel
Overlin, Ken

Papke, "Billy"

Richmond, Bill
Rickard, "Tex"
Risko, Eddie "Babe"
Root, Jack
Ross, Barney
Ryan, Paddy
Ryan, Tommy

Sharkey, Thomas J.
Singer, Al
Slattery, Jimmy
Smith, Jeff
Smith, "Mysterious Billy"
Smith, Solly
Stillman, Louis
Sullivan, John L.
Sullivan, Mike "Twin"

Taylor, "Bud"
Thompson, "Cyclone"
Thompson, "Young Jack"

Villa, Pancho

Walcott, Joseph
Walsh, Jimmy

Weill, Al
Welsh, Freddy
Willard, Jess
Williams, Kid
Wills, Harry
Wolgast, Ad
Wolgast, Midget
Wright, "Chalky"

BROADCASTING

McCarthy, "Clem"
McNamee, Graham

CANOEING

Friede, Leo

COLLEGE SPORTS

Griffith, John L.
Houston, Clarence P.
Johns, Wilbur
St. John, Lynn W.

DIVING

Coleman, Georgia

DOG RACING

Lobel, Louis
Smith, Owen P.

FENCING

Calnan, George C.
DeCapriles, José R.

Dow, Warren A.
Hammond, Graeme M.
Lloyd, Marion

FIGURE SKATING

Haines, Jackson
Merrill, Gretchen
Owen, Laurence
Vinson, Maribel

FOOTBALL

Adams, "Tree"
Agannis, Harry
Alexander, William A.
Ames, "Snake"

Bach, Joseph
Baker, "Eddie"
Baker, "Hobey"
Baker, L. H.
Barni, Roy B.
Barrett, Charles
Barwegan, Richard J.
Basca, Michael
Bell, "Bert"
Bezdek, Hugo
Bidwill, Charles W.
Black, "Cupe"
Blazine, Anthony
Blozis, Albert C.
Booth, "Albie"
Borries, "Buzz"
Bowditch, "Pete"
Boynton, Ben Lee
Bradlee, Frederick J.

Football *(cont.)*

Bray, Maurice
Brickley, Charles E.
Brito, "Gene"
Brown, "Babe"
Brown, F. Gordon, Jr.
Bruder, "Hank"
Brumbaugh, Carl L.
Buck, Kenneth
Buncom, Frank, Jr.
Bunker, Paul D.
Busler, Raymond
Byrd, "Curley"

Calac, Peter
Caldwell, "Charlie"
Calhoun, George Whitney
Camp, Walter C.
Campanella, Joseph
Campbell, David C.
Cannon, "Jack"
Carr, Joseph
Casey, Edward L.
Cavanagh, Frank W.
Cawthon, Pete
Chamberlain, Guy
Chevigny, Jack
Christman, Paul J.
Christy, Richard
Cochems, "Eddie"
Conzelman, "Jimmy"
Cooney, James L.
Corbin, "Pa"
Cowan, Hector W.
Coy, "Ted"
Cravath, "Jeff"
Crowther, George M.

Daly, Charles D.
Davis, Ernest
DeGroot, Dudley S.
DesJardien, Paul R.
DeWitt, John R.
Dietz, "Lone Star"
Dilweg, "Lavvie"
Doane, "Dinger"
Dobie, Gilmour
Dorais, "Gus"
Doyle, Edward J.
Driscoll, "Paddy"

Earp, "Jug"
Eckersall, Walter H.
Ehrhardt, Clyde W.
Erdelatz, "Eddie"
Erickson, Harold A.

Farrington, "Bo"
Feeney, Albert J.
Fleming, Donald
Frankian, "Ike"

Galimore, Willie
Gelbert, Charles
Gentry, Dale Lee
Getzein, Charles H.
Gipp, George
Gladchuck, Chester
Glass, "Ned"
Grigg, Cecil

Hagberg, Robert
Hagberg, "Swede"
Handler, Philip
Hardwick, "Tack"
Hare, Cecil

Football *(cont.)*

McEwan, John J.
McGovern, John E.
McGugin, Daniel E.
McLaren, "Tank"
McMillin, "Bo"
McWhorter, Robert L.
Mercer, E. Leroy
Milstead, Century A.
Minds, "Jack"
Molesworth, Keith F.
Mooney, James
Moore, Wilbur
Moran, "Uncle Charlie"
Muller, "Buck"

Nesser, Alfred
Newell, "Ma"
Neyland, Robert R.
Niemi, Laurie

Oberlander, "Swede"
O'Dea, Patrick J.
O'Neill, "Buck"
Owen, Benjamin G.
Owen, Stephen

Peck, Robert D.
Peden, Donald C.
Pennock, Stanley B.
Phillips, Henry D.
Piccolo, Brian
Pierce, Donald
Pierotti, "Al"
Poe, Arthur
Poe, Edgar A.

Ray, "Shorty"

Rockne, Knute K.
Rodgers, "Rat"
Roehnelt, William
Roper, William W.
Ruthstrom, Ralph

Sachs, Leonard
Salmon, "Red"
Sanders, "Red"
Schulz, "Germany"
Schwab, "Dutch"
Shaughnessy, Clark D.
Sheldon, James M., Sr.
Shellogg, "Alec"
Shepherd, William L.
Shevlin, Thomas L.
Slater, "Duke"
Smith, Bruce P.
Sonnenberg, Gustave
Spears, "Doc"
Stagg, Amos Alonzo
Stahlman, Richard F.
Steffen, Walter P.
Stein, Russell F.
Steinback, Laurence J.
Stevenson, "Steve"
Strader, "Red"
Stuldreher, Harry A.
Susoeff, Nicholas
Sutherland, "Jock"

Tatum, James M.
Thomas, Frank W.
Thornhill, "Tiny"
Thorpe, James F.
Torrance, Jack

Walker, "Peahead"
Warner, "Pop"

Weaver, James A.
Weekes, Harold H.
Welch, Francis G.
Wharton, "Buck"
Wheeler, Arthur L.
Wilce, John W.
Williams, Henry L.
Williamson, "Ivy"
Wilson, George
Withington, Paul W.
Wood, "Barry"
Woodruff, George W.
Wray, "Lud"
Wyant, Andrew R. E.
Wyatt, Bowden

Yost, "Hurry Up"
Young, George D.
Young, "Waddy"

Zuppke, Robert C.

GENERAL

Helms, Paul H.

GOLF

Anderson, Willie
Armour, "Tommy"
Barnes, "Long Jim"
Burns, Miriam
Congdon, "Chuck"
Curtis, Margaret
Diegel, Leo
Dudley, Edward
Espinosa, Al
Goodman, Johnny G.
Hagan, Walter C.

Homans, Eugene V.
Hoyt, Beatrix
Lema, "Champagne Tony"
Little, W. Lawson, Jr.
McFarlane, Willie
Miley, Marion
Oliver, "Porky"
Ouimet, Francis D.
Ross, Donald J.
Smith, Alex
Smith, Horton
Smith, MacDonald
Travers, Jerome D.
Travis, Walter J.
Turpie, Marion
Von Elm, George
Ward, "Bud"
Wood, Craig
Zaharias, "Babe"

GYMNASTICS

Preiss, Emil K.

HANDBALL

Casey, Phil
Platak, Joseph

HARNESS RACING

Blake, Octave
Geers, "Pop"
Maybury, William T.
Palin, Septer F.
Parshall, H. M.
Shively, Bion
White, Benjamin F.

HOCKEY

Baker, "Hobey"
Brown, Walter A.
Jeremiah, Edward
Norris, James D., Jr.
Stewart, William

HORSE RACING

Balaski, Lee
Belmont, August, Jr.
Bierman, Carroll
Bradley, Edward R.
Bruce, Saunders D.
Cassidy, Marshall
Fitzsimmons, "Sunny Jim"
Garrison, "Snapper"
Hertz, John D.
Hirsch, Maximiliion
Jacobs, Hirsch
Johnson, William R.
Jones, Ben A.
Kurtsinger, Charles E.
Lindheimer, Benjamin F.
Mayer, Louis B.
Morgan, Justin R.
Morrissey, John C.
Murphy, Isaac
Riddle, Samuel D.
Sande, Earl H.
Shilling, Carrol H.
Sloan, "Tod"
Smith, "Silent Tom"
Vanderbilt, William K.
Westrope, "Jackie"
Whitney, Harry Payne
Winn, Matt J.

Woodward, William F., Sr.
Woolf, George
Workman, "Sonny"
Wright, "Tennessee"

HORSESHOES

May, George W.

LACROSSE

MacLaughlin, Donald C., Jr.

MARATHON

DeMar, Clarence

MOTORBOAT RACING

Herreshoff, Charles F.
Mendelson, Herbert A.
Thompson, "Chuck"

MOTORCYCLE RAC-ING

Curtiss, Glenn H.
Weatherly, Joseph

POLO

Hitchcock, "Tommy"
Keene, Foxhall P.
Milburn, Devereux
Stevenson, Malcolm
Whitney, Harry Payne

PROMOTER

Pyle, "Cash and Carry"

RACQUETS

Pell, Clarence C.

ROWING

Callow, "Rusty"
Carlin, John J.
Comibear, Hiram
Courtney, Charles E.
Curtis, William B.
Gardiner, John
Goodwin, "Goody"
Greer, Frank B.
Kelly, John B.
Love, Harvey
Plaisted, Frederick A.
Ten Eyck, James A.
Ten Eyck, "Ned"
Weed, "Cy"

SHOOTING

Bogardus, Adam H.
Carver, "Doc"
Crosby, "Tobacco Bill"
Elliott, James A. R.
Frederick, Karl T.
Gilbert, Fred
Heikes, Rolla A.
Jacoby, Philo
Kimble, Fred
Marshall, Thomas A.
McCarty, George S.

Oakley, Annie
Topperwein, "Plinky"
Young, Charles A.

SKIING

Proctor, Charles A.
Schneider, Hannes
Tokle, Torger
Werner, "Buddy"

SOCCER

MacLaughlin, Donald C., Jr.

SPORTSWRITING

Corum, Bill
Lardner, "Ring"
Rice, Grantland
Taylor, William H.
Ward, Arch

SQUASH

Sears, Eleonora R.

STEEPLECHASE

Roby, Thomas

SWIMMING

Bachrach, "Bach"
Kahanamoku, Duke P.
Kiphuth, Robert J. H.
Kruger, "Stubby"

Swimming *(cont.)*

Ross, Norman
Wenck, Frederick A.

TENNIS

Bell, Berkeley
Campbell, Oliver S.
Clark, Joseph S.
Clothier, William J.
Connolly, "Little Mo"
Crane, Joshua
Davis, Dwight F.
Dickey, James B.
Dwight, James
Hunt, Joseph R.
Johnston, William M.
Larned, William A.
Mallory, Molla
McLoughlin, Maurice
Murray, R. Lindley
Pell, Theodore R.
Pettitt, Thomas
Richards, Vincent
Sears, Eleonora R.
Sears, Richard D.
Slocum, Henry W., Jr.
Stoefen, Lester R.
Tilden, "Big Bill"
Ward, Holcombe
Whitman, Malcolm D.
Williams, R. Norris, II
Wrenn, Robert D.
Wright, Beals S.
Wright, Irving C.
Wright, William C., Jr.

TRACK

Adams, Platt

Baxter, Irving K.
Blozis, Albert C.
Bonhag, George V.
Bremer, John L., Jr.

Carr, "Billy"
Cartmell, "Nate"
Clark, Ellery H.
Connolly, James B.
Copeland, Lillian
Cregan, John F.
Curtis, Thomas P.
Curtis, William B.

Dewitt, John R.

Efaw, Forest
Ewry, Ray C.

Garrett, Robert S.
Grant, Alexander
Gutowski, Robert A.
Gutterson, Albert L.

Hahn, Archie
Harris, Archie
Harris, Elmore R.
Hayes, John J.
Hickok, William O.
Hillman, Harry L.

Johnson, Cornelius
Johnson, Stone

Jones, John Paul
Jones, Samuel S.

Kraenzelein, Alvin C.

Lee, Horace H.
Locke, Roland A.

Magee, "Jack"
McDonald, "Babe"
McGrath, Matthew J.
Meredith, "Ted"
Myers, "Lon"

Orton, George W.

Paddock, "Charlie"
Pilgrim, Paul H.
Pores, Charles
Prinstein, Myer

Richards, Alma W.
Robertson, Lawson N.
Ryan, Patrick J.

Saling, George J.
Sheppard, Melvin W.
Sherrill, Charles H., Jr.
Sullivan, Bartholomew J.
Sullivan, James E.

Templeton, "Dink"
Tewksbury, J. W. B.
Thorpe, James F.
Tolan, Edward

Torrance, Jack

Wefers, Bernard J.
Welch, Francis G.

Zaharias, "Babe"

VOLLEYBALL

Fisher, George J.
Idell, "Pop"
Laveaga, Robert E.
Morgan, William G.

WALKING

Weston, Edward Payson
Zinn, Ronald L.

WRESTLING

Gotch, Frank
Jenkins, Thomas
Lewis, Ed "Strangler"
Muldoon, William A.

YACHTING

Burgess, W. Starling
Herreshoff, Nathaniel G.
Nichols, George
Steers, George
Stevens, John Cox
Vanderbilt, Harold S.
Vanderbilt, William K.

ABBREVIATIONS

AA	American Association (baseball)
AA	Athletic Association (with identifying name)
AAFC	All-American Football Conference
AAU	Amateur Athletic Union
ABC	American Bowling Congres
AFL	American Football League
AL	American League (baseball)
AP	Associated Press
ATA	American Trapshooting Association
b.	born
BA	batting average
BPAA	Bowling Proprietors' Association of America
d.	died
ERA	earned-run average
Fed L	Federal League (baseball)
IBC	International Boxing Club
IC4A	Intercollegiate Association of Amateur Athletes of America
KO	knockout
L	left-handed
LPGA	Ladies' Professional Golf Association
ML	major league (baseball)
NAIA	National Association of Intercollegiate Athletes
NASCAR	National Association for Stock Car Auto Racing
NBA	National Basketball Association; National Boxing Association
NCAA	National Collegiate Athletic Association
NFF	National Football Foundation
NFL	National Football League
NIT	National Invitation Tournament (basketball)

NL   National League (baseball)
PGA   Professional Golfers Association
PL   Players' League (baseball)
R   right-handed
RBI   runs batted in
Sw. hit switch hitter
TD   touchdown
TKO   technical knockout
UA   Union Association (baseball)
UPI   United Press International
USAC   United States Auto Club
USGA   United States Golf Association
USLTA   United States Lawn Tennis Association
WBA   World Boxing Association
WIBC   Women's International Bowling Congress

WHO WAS
WHO
IN
AMERICAN SPORTS

A

AARON, "YOUNG BARNEY" boxing: b. 1836, London; d. June 15, 1907. His record: 4 wins, 1 loss, 1 draw. The son of an English welterweight, Aaron came to the United States when he was nineteen. He won the American lightweight championship Sept. 2, 1857, by beating Johnny Moneghan in 80 rounds. He lost it on a 10th-round foul to Patrick "Scotty" Brannagan on Oct. 18, 1858, then retired until June 20, 1866, when he fought Sam Collyer for the title, losing in 47 rounds. But he won the title from Collyer in 67 rounds on June 13, 1867, and then retired for good.

ADAMS, "BABE" (Charles B.) baseball: b. May 18, 1882, Tipton, Ind.; d. July 27, 1968. Bat L, throw R; pitcher. St. Louis NL, 1906; Pittsburgh NL, 1907, 1909–16, 1918–26. Nineteen years, 194–140, 2.76 ERA; 44 shutouts; 22–12 in 1911, 21–10 in 1913. Led NL in shutouts, 1920 (8).

Adams had excellent control: In 1920, he set an ML record for fewest walks in a season, 250 or more innings pitched, with only 18; on July 17, 1914, he set an ML record by pitching a 21-inning game without a walk. He is one of twelve pitchers to win three games in one World Series; in 1909, he pitched three complete games and had a 1.33 ERA as the Pirates beat the Tigers, 4 games to 3.

ADAMS, PLATT track: b. ?; d. Feb. 27, 1961. Adams was AAU outdoor champion in the broad jump, 1908, 1911–13, and in the hop, step, and jump, 1907–08, 1912. He won the standing high jump in the 1912 Olympics and finished second in the standing broad jump. His brother Ben was second in the high jump.

ADAMS, "TREE" (John W.) football: b. Sept. 22, 1921, Charleston, Ark.; d. Aug. 20, 1969. Notre Dame tackle, Washington Redskins, 1945–49. One of the first of the modern mammoth tackles, Adams was 6'8" and weighed 275 pounds.

AGGANIS, HARRY baseball, football: b. April 20, 1930, Lynn, Mass.; d. June 27, 1955. "The Golden Greek" had a difficult decision to make after

1

completing his eligibility at Boston University. He was the Cleveland Browns' first draft choice, and he was being offered bonuses by several major-league teams. He chose the Boston Red Sox and a $60,000 bonus and seemed well on his way to stardom when he was suddenly stricken with pneumonia, from which he never recovered.

At BU, he set a school record by throwing 15 TD passes in his sophomore year, 1949, then joined the Marines. The left-handed quarterback returned to BU for the 1951 and 1952 seasons. In 26 games he completed 226 of 418 passes for 2,930 yards and 34 TDs, besides averaging better than 40 yards as a punter. He was voted New England's top player in 1951.

With the Red Sox, 1954–55, he played first base for 157 games, hitting .261. He was hitting .313 after 25 games in 1955 when sidelined by the illness that killed him.

ALEXANDER, GROVER CLEVELAND ("Pete") baseball: b. Feb. 26, 1887, St. Paul, Nebr.; d. Nov. 4, 1950. In 1916, Alexander had what might have been the greatest year any pitcher ever had. Pitching in Philadelphia's Baker Bowl, known as a hitter's park because of its short fences, he set a modern ML record with 16 shutouts, leading the NL in victories (33–12), ERA (1.55), complete games (38), and strikeouts (167). That was one of three consecutive years in which he won 30 or more; he was 31–10 in 1915 and 30–13 in 1917, leading in victories both years and in percentage in 1915 (.756). He holds NL records for complete games, shutouts, most career victories by a right-hander, and lowest career ERA.

His playing record: Philadelphia NL, 1911–17; Chicago NL, 1918–26; St. Louis NL, 1926–29; Philadelphia NL, 1930. Twenty years, 374 wins (3rd), 208 losses, 2.56 ERA; 696 games, 598 starts (7th), 439 complete, 4,189⅓ innings (5th), 4,868 hits (5th), 953 walks, 2,199 strikeouts, 88 shutouts (2nd).

In 1911, he set a modern ML record for most victories by a rookie (28–13), leading the league in wins, complete games (31), innings (367), and shutouts (7). He led in innings (310⅓) and strikeouts (195) in 1912; in shutouts (7) in 1913; in victories (27–15), complete games (32), innings (355), and strikeouts (214) in 1914; in ERA (1.22), complete games (36), innings (376⅓), strikeouts (241), and shutouts (12) in 1915; in ERA (1.86), complete games (35), innings (387⅔), strikeouts (201), and shutouts (8) in 1917; in ERA (1.72) and shutouts (9) in 1919; in victories (27–14), ERA (1.91), complete games (33), innings (363⅓), and strikeouts (173) in 1920; and in shutouts (3) in 1921.

Alexander pitched in only three games in 1918, entering military service soon after the season began. He returned from World War I with a drinking problem that helped decrease his effectiveness in the twenties. Nevertheless, he was 22–12 in 1923 and 21–10 in 1927. Other 20-victory seasons were 20–17 in 1912 and 22–8 in 1913.

He holds or shares NL records for most years leading in innings (7), most years leading in ERA (5), most years leading in strikeouts (7), and most strikeouts as a rookie (227). In three different seasons, 1913, 1916, 1919, he shut out every opposing team at least once.

In three World Series, 1915, 1926, 1928, he was 3–2 with a 3.35 ERA, pitching 4 complete in 5 starts and striking out 29 in 43 innings. His greatest moment—one of the most fabled in baseball—came in 1926, when the Cardinals beat the Yankees, 4 games to 3. Alexander had won the sixth game. Suffering from a hangover, he was called in from the bullpen in the seventh inning of the seventh game to face Tony Lazzeri, a great clutch-hitter, with the bases loaded and two out. He struck out Lazzeri on three pitches and pitched hitless ball the rest of the way for a 3–2 victory and the Series.

Baseball Hall of Fame.

ALEXANDER, WILLIAM A. football: b. June 6, 1889, Mud River, Ky.; d. April 23, 1950. The first coach to take his team to all four major bowl games, Alexander spent his entire football career at Georgia Tech, first as a player, then as an assistant to John W. Heisman, and then as Heisman's successor as head coach, 1920–44. He served as athletic director from 1945 until his death.

His 1928 team had a 10–0–0 record and won the national championship, then beat California 8–7 in the Rose Bowl. His teams beat Missouri 21–7 in the 1940 Orange Bowl, lost 14–7 to Texas in the 1943 Cotton Bowl, and beat Tulsa 20–18 in the 1944 Sugar Bowl. He won Southern Conference titles in 1922 and 1927–28 and Southeastern Conference championships in 1939 (tie) and 1943–44. His overall record was 133–95–8.

Alexander was Coach of the Year in 1942 and won the National Touchdown Club Award in 1948.

National Football Foundation Hall of Fame.

ALLEN, "JOHNNY" (John T.) baseball: b. Sept. 30, 1904, Lenoir, N.C.; d. March 29, 1959. Bat, throw R; pitcher. New York AL, 1932–35; Cleveland AL, 1936–40; St. Louis AL, 1941; Brooklyn NL, 1941–43; New York NL, 1943–44. Thirteen years, 142–75, 3.75 ERA. Led AL in percentage, 1932 (17–4, .810). Two World Series, 1932, 1941: 6.23 ERA in 4⅓ innings.

Allen holds AL records for highest percentage in season (15–1, .938 in 1937) and for most consecutive victories (17, 2 of which were in 1936 and the rest the following year).

ALTROCK, "NICK" (Nicholas) baseball: b. Sept. 15, 1876, Cincinnati, Ohio; d. Jan. 20, 1965. Sw. hit, throw L; pitcher. Louisville NL, 1898; Boston AL, 1902–03; Chicago AL, 1903–09; Washington AL, 1909, 1912–15, 1918–19, 1924. Sixteen years, 87–75, 2.67 ERA; 20–15 in 1904, 22–12 in 1905, 21–12 in 1906. One World Series, 1906: 2 complete games, 1–1, 1.00 ERA.

Despite some fine pitching performances, Altrock was most famous as a clown. Once, pitching in the Pacific Coast League, he walked a player and picked him off first and was so delighted with himself that he proceeded to walk seven men deliberately, picking off six of them. After retiring, he teamed with baseball clown Al Schacht in a vaudeville act.

AMES, "RED" (Leon K.) baseball: b. Aug. 2, 1882, Warren, Ohio; d. Oct. 8, 1936. Sw. hit, throw R; pitcher. New York NL, 1903–13; Cincinnati NL, 1913–15; St. Louis NL, 1915–19; Philadelphia NL, 1919. Seventeen years, 179–165, 2.63 ERA; 22–8 in 1905. No-hitter, Sept. 14, 1903, against St. Louis NL (5 innings); April 15, 1909, against New York NL (9⅓ innings; lost 3–0 in 13 innings). Three World Series, 1905, 1911–12: 4 games, 0–1, 2.45 ERA.

AMES, "SNAKE" (Knowlton L.) football: b. 1868; d. Dec. 23, 1931. Princeton fullback, 1886–89; All-American, 1889. Ames's nickname came from his broken-field running ability; he scored on runs of 89 and 65 yards against Harvard in his senior year. Ames was also an excellent punter. He reintroduced the spiral punt, which for some reason had fallen out of use in the early eighties.

He coached Purdue to 12 victories in as many games, 1891–92.

National Football Foundation Hall of Fame.

ANDERSON, JOHN J. baseball: b. Dec. 14, 1873, Sasbourg, Norway; d. July 23, 1949. Sw. hit, throw R; outfield, first base. Brooklyn NL, 1894–98; Washington NL, 1898; Brooklyn NL, 1899; Milwaukee AL, 1901; St. Louis AL, 1902–03; New York AL, 1904–05; Washington AL, 1905–07; Chicago AL, 1908. Fourteen years, 1,627 games, .290 BA; hit .302 in 1894, .314 in 1896, .325 in 1897, .330 in 1901. Led NL in triples, 1898 (19).

ANDERSON, W. HAROLD basketball: b. Sept. 11, 1902, Akron, Ohio; d. June 13, 1967. A four-sport star at Otterbein College, Anderson coached basketball at Toledo, 1935–43, and Bowling Green State University, 1944–67. His overall record was 411–170. One of his Toledo teams and six of his Bowling Green teams were invited to the National Invitation Tournament.

ANDERSON, WILLIE golf: b. May 1880, North Berwick, Scotland; d. 1910. Two years after arriving in the United States, Anderson finished second in the 1897 U.S. Open. He was seventeen. He won the Open in 1901, 1903–05; his record of four victories in the event has been matched by Bobby Jones and Ben Hogan but not surpassed. No one else has ever won three in a row. Six other times Anderson finished among the top five. He also won the Western Open four times, in 1902, 1904, 1908–09.

He died of arteriosclerosis when he was thirty.

Professional Golfers Association Hall of Fame.

ANSON, "CAP" (Adrian C.) baseball: b. April 17, 1851, Marshalltown, Iowa; d. April 14, 1922. Bat, throw R; first base. Anson was baseball's first great national hero, the Babe Ruth of the premodern era, the first baseball player to write an autobiography. His career spanned twenty-seven seasons (including five in the National Association); he hit over .300 in twenty-four of those seasons, and along the way he also managed five pennant-winners. His twenty-two years in the NL, all with Chicago, is a league record for most consecutive seasons played and most seasons with one team, and he also holds the NL record for most seasons over .300 (19). When he was forty-five, he hit .335 in 108 games.

His playing record: National Association, Rockford, 1871; Philadelphia As, 1872–75. Five years, 245 games, .352 BA; hit .352 in 1871, .381 in 1872, .353 in 1873, .367 in 1874, .318 in 1875.

Chicago NL, 1876–97. Twenty-two years, 2,276 games, 9,101 at-bats, 2,995 hits (10th), 528 doubles, 124 triples, 96 home runs, 1,719 runs, 1,715 RBI (10th), 218 stolen bases (eleven years not included), .329 BA; hit .356 in 1876, .337 in 1877, .341 in 1878, .317 in 1879, .339 in 1880, .362 in 1882, .308 in 1883, .335 in 1884, .310 in 1885, .371 in 1886, .347 in 1887, .311 in 1889, .312 in 1890, .314 in 1893, .388 in 1894, .335 in 1895, .331 in 1896. Led NL in BA, 1881 (.399), 1888 (.344); in doubles, 1877 (19), 1885 (35); in RBI, 1881 (82), 1886 (147), 1888 (84), 1891 (120); in hits, 1881 (137).

On Aug. 6, 1884, he became the second player in history to hit 3 home runs in a game; on Aug. 24, 1886, he set an NL record for most runs in a game, 6.

Anson is generally credited with inventing the hit-and-run play.

Managed Chicago NL, 1879–97; New York NL, 1898 (part): 1,297–957, .575 (10th). Pennants, 1880–82, 1885–86.

Baseball Hall of Fame.

ARCHER, "JIMMY" (James P.) baseball: b. May 13, 1883, Dublin, Ireland; d. March 29, 1958. Bat, throw R; catcher. Pittsburgh NL, 1904; Detroit AL, 1907; Chicago NL, 1909–17; Brooklyn NL, Cincinnati NL, Pittsburgh NL, 1918. Twelve years, 846 games, .250 BA. Known for his strong arm,

Archer on May 24, 1918, tied the NL record for most assists by a catcher in a 9-inning game, 7.

ARMOUR, "TOMMY" (Thomas Dickson) golf: b. Sept. 24, 1895, Edinburgh, Scotland; d. Sept. 11, 1968. Serving with the Black Watch regiment during World War I, Armour suffered a serious head wound that blinded him for six months. After recovering, he emigrated to the United States.

His first big victory came in the 1927 U.S. Open, when he beat Harry Cooper in a playoff. He beat Gene Sarazen in the finals of the PGA tournament in 1930 and won the British Open in 1931. In 1935 he gained the finals of the PGA but lost to Johnny Revolta. Armour also won the Canadian Open in 1927, 1930, and 1934 and the Western Open in 1929.

A classic stylist, he became a successful teaching pro after retiring from competition.

Armour is credited with hitting the longest measured drive ever: Playing the 5th hole in the 1933 British Open at St. Andrews, Scotland, he belted one 430 yards, aided by a strong following wind.

Professional Golfers Association Hall of Fame.

ARMOUR, WILLIAM R. baseball: b. Sept. 3, 1869, Homestead, Pa.; d. Dec. 2, 1922. Managed Cleveland AL, 1902–04; Detroit AL, 1905–06: 382–347, .524.

ATTELL, "ABE" (Abraham W.) boxing: b. Feb. 22, 1884, San Francisco; d. Feb. 6, 1970. His record: 89 wins, 46 by KO; 10 losses, 3 by KO; 17 draws, 40 no-contests. Some have called Attell the greatest fighter ever, pound for pound; others have called him the greatest ever, inch for inch. Such things are hard to prove, but it is certain that he often fought much bigger men to a standstill. Featherweight champion for several years at 5'4" and no more than 118 pounds, he beat most of the best lightweights of his time (135 pounds was the limit then) and came close to winning the lightweight title from Battling Nelson in 1908. Nelson kept his title on an unpopular and much criticized draw. Attell also took on welterweights—145 pounds—and usually won.

He had a remarkable knockout record for his weight class. Later on, he was inspired by James J. Corbett and George Dixon to become a more scientific boxer, but he KOed 15 of his first 16 opponents and 24 of his first 28.

It has been written that Attell won the featherweight title in 1901 by beating Dixon, but there was much confusion about the championship then. Attell was claiming the title as early as 1901, but Brooklyn Tommy Sullivan was also claiming it, and in 1904 Sullivan won from Attell on a 5th-round foul. Not until 1908 did Attell officially win the title by KOing Sullivan in the 4th. (Many people did consider Attell champion throughout this period, however, since losing on a foul wasn't really considered losing in a title fight.)

Attell lost the title on his birthday, Feb. 22, 1912, when Johnny Kilbane won a 20-round decision.

After retiring, Attell was involved in baseball's Black Sox scandal of 1919, probably as payoff man for gambler Arnold Rothstein. According to Eliot Asinof's *Eight Men Out,* Attell had plans to doublecross not only the eight players who were supposedly being bribed to throw the World Series, but also Rothstein himself. When a Chicago grand jury began investigating the case, Attell fled to Canada to avoid subpoena.

Boxing Hall of Fame, Helms Hall of Fame.

AUSTIN, "JIMMY" (James P.) baseball: b. Dec. 8, 1879, Swansea, Wales; d. April 6, 1965. Sw. hit, throw R; third base. New York AL, 1909–10; St. Louis AL, 1911–23, 1925–26, 1929. Eighteen years, 1,580 games, .246 BA. He managed St. Louis AL for parts of 1913, 1918, 1923.

AYERS, "DOC" (Yancy W.) baseball: b. May 20, 1890, Fancy Gap, Va.; d. June 26, 1968. Pitcher. Washington AL, 1913–19; Detroit AL, 1919–21. Nine years, 70–77, 2.84 ERA. In relief, 24–19, 2.72 ERA, 10 saves.

B

BACH, JOSEPH football: b. Jan. 17, 1901, Tower, Minn.; d. Oct. 24, 1966. A tackle at Notre Dame, Bach was one of the Seven Mules who played in front of the Four Horsemen.

He spent two 2-year sessions as Pittsburgh Steeler coach. They were 10–14 in 1935–36 and 11–13 in 1952–53. He also coached Duquesne University in 1934, Niagara University, 1937–41, and St. Bonaventure University, 1950–51. He was an assistant pro coach for seven years and a pro scout after retiring from coaching.

BACHRACH, "BACH" (William) swimming: b. May 15, 1879, Chicago; d. July 15, 1959. As coach at the Illinois Athletic Club, 1912–54, Bachrach developed many great swimmers, among them Norman Ross and Johnny

Weismuller. The IAC team won the 800-meter relay in the 1924 Olympics; Bachrach was Olympic swimming coach that year and again in 1928.

His IAC teams won the AAU 880-yard or 800-meter freestyle relay, 1923, 1925–28; the 300-yard medley relay, 1927–28; and the 400-yard freestyle relay, 1913–18, 1920–25, 1928. They were AAU team champs in 1925, 1927–28.

Bachrach also coached the IAC teams that won the national water-polo championship in 1914–17, 1921, 1923–24, 1930, 1932–34, 1939–41, and 1948–51.

Helms Hall of Fame.

BAER, MAX boxing: b. Feb. 11, 1909, Omaha, Nebr.; d. Nov. 21, 1959. His record: 65 wins, 50 by KO; 13 losses, 3 by KO; 1 no-decision. In a battle of giants during the transition period between the reigns of Gene Tunney and Joe Louis, Baer won the heavyweight championship on a TKO of Primo Carnera in the 11th round on June 14, 1934. Baer knocked Carnera down 12 times before the fight was stopped. He lost the title not quite a year later, June 13, 1935, on a 15-round decision to James J. Braddock, who was the fifth champion in a five-year period.

BAGBY, JAMES C. J., SR. baseball: b. Oct. 5, 1887, Barnett, Ga.; d. July 28, 1954. Sw. hit, throw R; pitcher. Cincinnati NL, 1912; Cleveland AL, 1916–22; Pittsburgh NL, 1923. Nine years, 128–88, 3.10 ERA; 23–13 in 1917. In relief, 22–12, 3.05 ERA, 27 saves. Led AL in victories and percentage (31–12, .721) and complete games (30) in 1920. One World Series, 1920: 1–1, 1.80 ERA. He hit a 3-run homer during an 8–1 victory in the fourth game.

BAILEY, WILLIAM F. baseball: b. April 12, 1889, Fort Smith, Ark.; d. Nov. 2, 1926. Bat, throw L; pitcher. St. Louis AL, 1907–12; Baltimore Fed L, 1914–15; Chicago Fed L, 1915; Detroit AL, 1918; St. Louis NL, 1921–22. Eleven years, 34–78, 3.57 ERA.

BAKER, "EDDIE" (Dr. Edward B.) football: b. Aug. 22, 1909, Nanticoke, Pa.; d. Dec. 22, 1959. A senior quarterback for Pittsburgh in the 1930 Rose Bowl, Baker went on to get a degree in dentistry but turned to football coaching. He coached at Carnegie Tech, 1940–42, 1949–59, compiling a 58–23–4 record. His 1959 team was 7–1, winning him the title of Western Pennsylvania Small College Coach of the Year.

BAKER, "HOBEY" (Hobart A. H.) hockey, football: b. Jan. 15, 1892, Bala-Cynwyd, Pa.; d. Dec. 21, 1918. F. Scott Fitzgerald recalled Hobey Baker: "An ideal worthy of everything in my enthusiastic admiration, yet consum-

mated and expressed in a human being who stood within ten feet of me."
Fitzgerald went to Princeton, where Baker is still a legend, though he isn't
as well known elsewhere—chiefly because hockey, not football, was his best
sport.

But Baker did make 3rd team All-America in 1912–13 and captained the
football team in 1913. He was rated by some sportswriters as the outstanding breakaway runner of the season. He ran back a punt 85 yards in a 22–7
defeat of Dartmouth. He was also a pretty fair drop-kicker; his 44-yard field
goal meant a 3–3 tie with Yale in 1913.

When one reads about Baker's sort of hockey, one irresistibly thinks of
Bobby Orr. Baker was not big, but he was solidly built, at 5'9", 160 pounds.
It was seven-man hockey in those days, with the seventh player known as
the rover, a role similar to that of a rushing defenseman like Orr. Baker's
end-to-end rushes were famous. He would get the puck, and his teammates
would wait to see what he was going to do with it. But he was never selfish;
he would always pass to someone else who had a chance to score.

In his first game at Princeton in 1911, he scored 6 goals in a 14–0 rout
of Williams. Princeton won the intercollegiate title that season, and Baker
was elected captain for his junior year. He played at a unique time. Few
colleges had their own rinks, so most college and amateur hockey was
played in large big-city arenas, and Baker got wide exposure before New
York hockey crowds. After leaving Princeton, he played for the amateur
team representing St. Nicholas Arena in New York. This was that era's
equivalent of modern pro hockey. Arenas put up signs saying "Come See
Hobey Baker Play Hockey," and the crowds came. He scored 5 goals and
had 2 assists in his first game, a 7–5 win over Toronto. He scored 3 in his
second game, a 6–1 victory over the defending Canadian champions. Teams
went after him; he took advantage of the fact to set up teammates or to draw
penalties that helped St. Nick's to victory. The team won the American
league championship in 1914 and beat the Ontario champs 5–1, with Baker
getting 5 assists.

St. Nick's and Baker were so impressive that in 1915 the team was chosen
to play for the Ross Cup, amateur hockey's Stanley Cup, against defending
champion Montreal. St. Nick's won the first of the three-game series, 6–2,
Baker collecting 3 goals and 2 assists. The second game was a 2–2 tie, but
St. Nick's players and fans insisted for years afterward that Baker had
scored a goal late in the game that bounced out of the net so fast the goal
judge never saw it. A tie counted as a victory for the defending champion
at the time, and Montreal held onto the cup with a 2–1 win in the third
game.

Nevertheless, Canadian fans were impressed. A Montreal sportswriter wrote, "A few minutes of Baker on the ice convinced the most skeptical. He could catch a place, and a star's place, on any of our professional teams. The blond-haired boy was a favorite with the crowd."

St. Nick's lost the American playoff to the Boston AA in 1915–16, with Baker severely hampered by an arm injury. In the meantime, he had been taking flying lessons. When the United States entered World War I, Baker was with the first group of American pilots sent overseas. He shot down three German planes, became commander of a squadron, and won the Croix de Guerre. He found aerial combat exhilarating and was disappointed when the war ended.

Scheduled to leave for home on Dec. 21, 1918, he decided to take one last flight, testing a plane that had been having carburetor trouble. It crashed; Baker died in an ambulance.

International Hockey Hall of Fame.

BAKER, "HOME RUN" (John Frank) baseball: b. March 13, 1886, Trappe, Md.; d. June 28, 1963. Bat L, throw R; third base. Philadelphia AL, 1908–14; New York AL, 1916–22. Thirteen years, 1,575 games, 235 stolen bases, .307 BA.

Baker won his nickname by hitting two home runs in two consecutive games in the 1911 World Series for the Athletics; that was also the first of four years in which he led the AL in home runs (9 in 1911, 10 in 1912, 12 in 1913, 8 in 1914).

The idea of someone leading the league with only 10 home runs or so seems funny today, but Baker was a good all-around hitter, particularly dangerous in the clutch. His .347 in 1912 is the highest average ever for an AL third baseman. He hit .305 in 1909, .334 in 1911, .337 in 1913, .319 in 1914, .306 in 1918. He led the AL in RBI in 1912 (130) and 1913 (117) and in triples 1909 (19).

Six World Series, 1910–13, 1921–22: 25 games, 15 runs, 18 RBI, .363 BA. One of his 1911 home runs won a Series game and the other tied a game, sending it into extra innings, as the Athletics beat the Giants, 4 games to 2.

Baker was also an excellent fielder. He led AL third basemen in chances eight times, in putouts seven times, and in fielding average twice.

Baseball Hall of Fame.

BAKER, L. H. football: b. April 9, 1883, New Haven, Conn.; d. May 27, 1960. A Yale graduate but not a football player, Dr. Baker became interested in the game and, about 1934, began collecting material on football. He eventually had a library of 30,000 books and magazines, 20,000 programs, and 150,000 press clippings, with material on more than 70,000 players and coaches, completely cross-indexed. One result was his book, *Football Facts and Figures* (1945), a basic reference book of college football.

BALASKI, LEE horse racing: b. 1915(?), New Orleans; d. Sept. 1, 1964. During his career as a jockey, Balaski rode 1,549 winners. He never won one of the Triple Crown events but was 2nd in the Kentucky Derby in 1935, 3rd in 1938. During the late thirties and early forties, he won such major races as the American Derby, Arlington Futurity, Saratoga Cup, and Coaching Club American Oaks. After World War II, he did most of his riding at Caliente, Mexico.

He died of a broken neck and severed spinal cord after his mount went down on Aug. 22, 1964.

BALDWIN, "LADY" (Charles B.) baseball: b. April 10, 1859, Ormel, N.Y.; d. March 7, 1937. Bat, throw L; pitcher. Milwaukee UA, 1884; Detroit NL, 1885–88; Buffalo PL, Brooklyn NL, 1890. Six years, 73–41, 2.85 ERA. Led the NL in wins (42–13), strikeouts (323 in 487 innings), and shutouts (7) in 1886; the 42 victories is an ML record for left-handers.

BALL, NEAL baseball: b. April 22, 1881, Grand Haven, Mich.; d. Oct. 15, 1957. Bat, throw R; shortstop, second base. New York AL, 1907–09; Cleveland AL, 1909–12; Boston AL, 1912–13. Seven years, 496 games, .251 BA.

On July 19, 1909, Ball came up with the first unassisted triple play in ML history. Playing shortstop for Cleveland against Boston, Ball made a leaping catch of a line drive with runners on first and second. He stepped on second to double off one runner and tagged out the other between first and second.

BANCROFT, FRANK C. baseball: b. May 9, 1846, Lancaster, Mass.; d. May 31, 1921. Managed Worcester NL, 1880; Detroit NL, 1881–82; Cleveland NL, 1883; Providence NL, 1884–85; Philadelphia AA, 1887 (part); Indianapolis NL, 1889 (part); Cincinnati NL, 1902 (part): 371–329, .530. Pennant, 1884.

BARDGETT, WALTER A. bicycling: b. 1879(?), Buffalo, N.Y.; d. Feb. 8, 1953. For nearly twenty years, until World War I, Bardgett raced bicycles in this country and in Europe. After the war, he became an editor of *American Bicycle* magazine, later *American Bicycle and Motorcycle.*

BARNES, JESSE L. baseball: b. Aug. 26, 1892, Perkins, Okla.; d. Sept. 9, 1961. Brother of Zeke. Bat L, throw R; pitcher. Boston NL, 1915–17; New York NL, 1918–23; Boston NL, 1923–25; Brooklyn NL, 1926–27. Thirteen years, 153–149, 3.22 ERA, 26 shutouts; 20–15 in 1920. No hitter, May 7, 1922, against Philadelphia NL. Led NL in wins, 1919 (25–9); in losses, 1917

(13–21) and 1924 (15–20); in shutouts, 1924 (4). Two World Series, 1921–22: 2–0, 1.71 ERA. Both victories came in relief in 1921, when the Giants beat New York AL, 5 games to 2. Barnes hit .444 and scored 3 runs in that Series.

BARNES, "LONG JIM" (James M.) golf: b. 1887, Lelant, Cornwall, England; d. May 24, 1966. The 6'3" Barnes came to the United States when he was nineteen. His first major victory came eight years later, in the 1914 Western Open; he had been the almost-unnoticed fourth-place finisher, behind Francis Ouimet, Harry Vardon, and Ted Ray in the famous 1913 U.S. Open.

Barnes won the first PGA, in 1916, and repeated in 1919 (the event wasn't held during World War I). Twice more, in 1921 and 1924, he got into the PGA finals, but he lost to Walter Hagen both times. He finished 9 strokes ahead of the field in the 1921 U.S. Open. In 1922 he finished second to Hagen in the British Open, but he won that event in 1925, at the age of thirty-eight. Other major victories for Barnes came in the 1917 and 1919 Western Opens and the 1916 and 1919 North and South Opens.

Professional Golfers Association Hall of Fame.

BARNES, "ROSS" (Roscoe C.) baseball: b. May 8, 1850, Mount Morris, N.Y.; d. Feb. 8, 1915. Bat, throw R; second base. National Association, Boston, 1871–75. Five years, 266 games, .379 BA; hit .378 in 1871, .404 in 1872, .402 in 1873, .339 in 1874.

Chicago NL, 1876–77; Cincinnati NL, 1879; Boston NL, 1881. Four years, 234 games, .319 BA. Led NL in hits (138), doubles (21), triples (14), runs (127), BA (.429), and slugging (.590) in 1876.

BARNES, "ZEKE" (Virgil J.) baseball: b. March 5, 1897, Ontario, Kan.; d. July 24, 1958. Brother of Jesse. Bat, throw R; pitcher. New York NL, 1919–28; Boston NL, 1928. Nine years, 61–59, 3.66 ERA. Two World Series, 1923–24: 0–1, 4.15 ERA.

BARNI, ROY B. football: b. Feb. 15, 1927, San Francisco; d. Aug. 15, 1957. University of San Francisco defensive back. Chicago Cardinals, 1952–53; Philadelphia Eagles, 1954–55; Washington Redskins, 1955–56.

BARNIE, "BILLY" (William H.) baseball: b. Jan. 26, 1853, New York City; d. July 15, 1900. Bat, throw R; catcher, outfield. National Association, Hartford, 1874; New York, Keokuk, 1875. Two years, 65 games, .176 BA. Baltimore AA, 1883, 1886. Two years, 19 games, .180 BA. Managed Baltimore AA, 1883–89; Baltimore-Brooklyn AA, 1890 (part);

Philadelphia AA, 1891 (part); Washington NL, 1892 (part); Louisville NL, 1893–94; Brooklyn NL, 1897–98 (part): 578–768, .429.

BARRETT, CHARLES football: b. Nov. 3, 1893, Bellevue, Pa.; d. May 21, 1924. Cornell quarterback; All-American, 1915; 2nd team, 1914.
National Football Foundation Hall of Fame.

BARROW, EDWARD G. baseball: b. May 10, 1868, Springfield, Ill.; d. Dec. 15, 1963. Though he never played professional baseball, Barrow has three chief claims to fame in the sport: He discovered and signed Honus Wagner, he switched Babe Ruth from the mound to the outfield, and he built up the New York Yankee dynasty of the 1920s and 1930s.

Barrow began in baseball as manager of a semipro team in Des Moines, Iowa, where he was city editor of a newspaper. Eventually he became a minor-league manager. He was president of the International League from 1911 to 1917.

He managed the Red Sox, 1918–20, winning the world championship in his first season, the year in which he began playing Ruth in the outfield periodically. After the World Series win, owner Harry Frazee, in financial trouble, began selling his best players, most of them to the Yankees. Ruth went to the Yankees in 1920. After his first season there, Yankee owner Jake Ruppert hired Barrow because he was known as a man who could handle the Babe. Once, when Ruth was causing trouble, Barrow challenged him to a fight, and Ruth backed down; Barrow was a big man who had been a good amateur boxer.

Barrow served as general manager until taking over the team presidency in 1939, after Ruppert's death. He retired early in 1945. During his twenty-five years, the Yankees won 14 pennants and 10 world championships.

His managerial record: Detroit AL, 1903–04 (part); Boston AL, 1918–20: 310–320, .492.
Baseball Hall of Fame.

BARRY, "JACK" (John J.) baseball: b. April 26, 1887, Meriden, Conn.; d. April 23, 1961. Bat, throw R; shortstop, second base. Philadelphia AL, 1908–15; Boston AL, 1915–17, 1919. Eleven years, 1,222 games, .243 BA. A member of the Athletics' "$100,000 infield," he played in five World Series, 1910–11, 1913–15: 25 games, .241 BA; 9 doubles (2nd). He had an outstanding Series in 1911, hitting .368 with 4 doubles, 2 runs, 2 RBI, as the As beat the Giants, 4 games to 2.
Managed Boston AL, 1917: 90–62, .592.

BARRY, JIMMY boxing: b. March 7, 1870, Chicago; d. April 5, 1943. His record: 59 wins, 39 by KO; no losses; 9 draws, 2 no-contests. After his forty-third consecutive victory, Barry claimed the bantamweight title in 1894. He didn't officially become champion until Dec. 6, 1897, when he KOed Walter Croot in 20 rounds. Croot died of a brain injury after the fight.

Barry had two more victories and a succession of draws before retiring undefeated in 1899.

BARRY, "SHAD" (John C.) baseball: b. Sept. 28, 1876, Newburgh, N.Y.; d. Nov. 27, 1936. Bat, throw R; outfield. Washington NL, 1899; Boston NL, 1900–01; Philadelphia, NL, 1901–04; Chicago NL, 1904–05; Cincinnati NL, 1905–06; St. Louis NL, 1906–08; New York NL, 1908. Ten years, 1,099 games; .267 BA; hit .304 in 1905.

BARTON, GEORGE boxing: b. 1884(?); d. May 8, 1969. As a fighter, Barton once defeated Terry McGovern, who later became bantamweight and featherweight champ. Barton went on to referee more than 12,000 fights. He was president of the World Boxing Association, 1952–53, and received the James J. Walker Award in 1953. At the time of his death, he was secretary of the Minnesota Athletic Commission.

BARWEGAN, RICHARD J. football: b. Dec. 25, 1921, Chicago; d. Sept. 2, 1966. Purdue guard. New York Yanks (AAFC), 1947; Baltimore (AAFC), 1948–49; Chicago Bears, 1950–52; Baltimore Colts, 1953–54; All-Pro, 1950–51.

BASCA, MICHAEL football: b. Dec. 4, 1916, Phoenixville, Pa.; d. Nov. 11, 1944. Villanova back. Philadelphia Eagles, 1941. A good passer and outstanding breakaway runner, Basca had three runs of better than 60 yards in 1938 and two others of better than 30 yards.

He died in France, serving with Patton's Third Army.

BAXTER, IRVING K. track: b. 1876(?); d. June 13, 1957. Baxter was Olympic high-jump and pole-vault champion in 1900. He won the AAU high-jump title, 1897–1900 and 1902, and the pole-vault title in 1899. Representing Pennsylvania, he won the IC4A high jump in 1899.

BEAUMONT, "GINGER" (Clarence H.) baseball: b. July 23, 1876, Rochester, Wis.; d. April 10, 1956. Bat L, throw R; outfield. Pittsburgh NL, 1899–1906; Boston NL, 1907–09; Chicago NL, 1910. Twelve years, 1,463 games, .311 BA; hit .352 in 1899, .332 in 1901, .341 in 1903, .301 in 1904, .328 in 1905, .322 in 1907. Led NL in BA (.357) and hits (193) in 1902; in hits (209) and runs (137) in 1903; in hits, 1904 (185) and 1907 (187). Two World Series, 1903, 1910: 11 games, .250 BA.

Beaumont is a coholder of these NL records: most consecutive years leading league in hits, 3; most runs scored in game, 6, on July 22, 1899, when he went 6-for-6; most years leading league in singles, 4; and most consecutive years leading in singles, 3.

BECK, FREDERICK T. baseball: b. Nov. 17, 1886, Havana, Cuba; d. March 12, 1962. Bat, throw L; first base, outfield. Boston NL, 1909–10; Cincinnati NL, 1911; Philadelphia NL, 1911; Chicago Fed L, 1914–15. Five years, 635 games, .252 BA. Led NL in home runs, 1910 (10).

BECKLEY, "JAKE" (Jacob P., "Eagle Eye") baseball: b. Aug. 4, 1867, Hannibal, Mo.; d. June 25, 1918. Bat, throw L; first base. Pittsburgh NL, 1888–89; Pittsburgh PL, 1890; Pittsburgh NL, 1891–96; New York NL, 1896–97; Cincinnati NL, 1897–1903; St. Louis NL, 1904–07. Twenty years, 2,386 games, 9,526 at-bats (9th), 2,930 hits, 473 doubles, 242 triples (4th), 88 home runs; 1,600 runs, 1,575 RBI; .308 BA; hit .343 in 1888, .301 in 1889, .324 in 1890, .303 in 1893, .343 in 1894, .328 in 1895, .330 in 1897, .333 in 1899, .341 in 1900, .307 in 1901, .330 in 1902, .327 in 1903, .325 in 1904. Led PL in triples, 1890 (22).

Beckley holds ML records for most years played, most games played, and most putouts (23,696) for first basemen; most years leading the league in putouts, 6; most career chances (25,000); and most years leading in chances, 6.

Baseball Hall of Fame.

BEEBE, FREDERICK L. baseball: b. Dec. 31, 1880, Lincoln, Nebr.; d. Oct. 30, 1957. Bat, throw R; pitcher. Chicago NL, 1906; St. Louis NL, 1906–09; Cincinnati NL, 1910; Philadelphia NL, 1911; Cleveland AL, 1916. Seven years, 63–84, 2.86 ERA. Led NL in strikeouts, 1906 (171).

BELL, BERKELEY tennis: b. Nov. 8, 1908, Austin, Tex.; d. June 15, 1967. Bell won the boys' junior doubles title in 1926, the national intercollegiate singles championship in 1929 (from the University of Texas), and the national indoor singles in 1935.

BELL, "BERT" (DeBenneville) football: b. Feb. 25, 1895, Philadelphia; d. Oct. 11, 1959. It was tragically appropriate that Bert Bell should die of a heart attack in Franklin Field during the last two minutes of a game between the Philadelphia Eagles and Pittsburgh Steelers. He was, at his death, commissioner of the National Football League. He had been closely associated with both of the teams as head coach and part owner, and though he belonged to a wealthy family and could have done almost anything he wanted, he had chosen to devote his life to professional football.

Bell played football at the University of Pennsylvania, 1920, then became its backfield coach. In 1933, he and Lud Wray bought the Frankford Yellowjacket franchise and moved the team to Philadelphia. The same year, Art Rooney was granted a franchise for Pittsburgh. Wray coached the team for its first three years, Bell taking over in 1936 and continuing through 1940; his teams had a woeful 10–44–2 record during that span.

In the meantime, Bell had been instrumental in one of the most important moves ever made by the NFL. At the annual meeting of owners in 1935, he proposed the league begin a draft of college players in order to help maintain some sort of balance among the teams instead of giving the richest teams the best opportunities to sign college stars. His idea was adopted, and the first draft took place in 1936.

Philadelphia and Pittsburgh swapped franchises in an unusual move in 1941. Bell coached his transplanted team for the first two games of the season. The war caused a severe player shortage, and for the 1943 season the Philadelphia and Pittsburgh clubs merged their rosters.

In 1946, Bell was chosen to succeed Elmer Layden as NFL commissioner. He was given a three-year contract, the first of four contracts he signed with the owners. He never saw one run out, because the owners kept tearing them up well before expiration and giving him new, longer-term pacts. At his death, he had seven years to go on a twelve-year contract.

He served as commissioner during a crucial period and must get a good deal of credit for the NFL's postwar prosperity. He cracked down hard during the NFL's first gambling scandal, in 1946, barring two New York Giant players because of an alleged bribe attempt before that year's title game. Under Bell, the league faced its first really major challenge from another league, the All-American Football Conference. In 1950, Bell announced the merger of the leagues; actually, it was a virtual surrender by the AAFC. Three of its teams were added to the NFL; its other four franchises were dissolved and the players put into a pool for redrafting.

Perhaps Bell's major contribution to NFL success, however, was the television policy he worked out. Basic to Bell's policy was the idea that a team's home games should not be televised in the immediate area of its home city. He also felt that the league itself should sell rights for all games to one network, splitting the money equally among all teams. This policy was not realized until after his death; it took a new federal law and considerable litigation to make it legal.

The NFL Player Pension Plan, which went into effect in 1962, was named for Bell, and rightly so. He once told a sportswriter, "We can't forget that this game was built and made popular by the players. We owe them everything."

Professional Football Hall of Fame, Helms Hall of Fame.

BELMONT, AUGUST, JR. horse racing: b. Feb. 18, 1853, New York City; d. Dec. 10, 1924. August Belmont, Sr., was a cofounder of Jerome and Monmouth Parks and the leading money-winning owner from 1889 to 1890. His son was even more deeply immersed in horse racing. He was probably most famous as the breeder of Man O'War. But he was also a founder of the New York Jockey Club, serving as its president from its founding in 1895 until his death, and he built Belmont Park.

The younger Belmont was interested in other sports, too: He brought the first pair of spiked track shoes to the United States from England in 1870, and he played in one of the first polo matches in this country.

BENDER, "CHIEF" (Charles Albert) baseball: b. May 5, 1883, Brainerd, Minn.; d. May 22, 1954. Bat, throw R; pitcher. Philadelphia AL, 1903–14; Baltimore Fed L, 1915; Philadelphia NL, 1916–17; Chicago AL, 1925. Sixteen years, 208–127, 2.46 ERA, 3,017 innings, 1,711 strikeouts, 41 shutouts; 21–10 in 1913. In relief, 20–14, 2.66 ERA, 36 saves. No-hitter, May 12, 1910, against Cleveland AL (4–0). Led AL in percentage, 1910 (22–5, .815), 1914 (17–3, .850).

A Chippewa Indian, Bender was a fine clutch pitcher. Connie Mack chose him to start the first game in four of the five World Series he played in, even though the Athletics had other outstanding pitchers with better overall records. In World Series play—1905, 1910–11, 1913–14—he had 10 starts (3rd), 9 complete (2nd), 6 wins (3rd), 4 losses (3rd), 59 strikeouts (5th) in 85 innings (4th). In 1905, he got the As' only victory with a 4-hit, 3–0 job in the second game; he lost 2–0 to Mathewson in the fifth and final game. He got his team off to a good start with a 4–1 win over the Cubs in 1910, as the As won in five. After losing to Mathewson 2–1 in the 1911 opener, he beat him 4–2 in the fourth game, then came back after two days' rest to win the sixth and deciding game on a 4-hitter.

He also won two games in Philadelphia's 5-game victory over the Giants in 1913.

Baseball Hall of Fame.

BENHAM, STANLEY bobsledding: b. 1912(?); d. April 22, 1970. Benham was driver of the world-champion four-man team in 1949–50 and finished second in the 1952 Winter Olympics. He also drove to the following championships: North American two-man, 1951, 1954, 1956; four-man, 1948, 1951, 1953, 1956, 1959; AAU senior two-man, 1954, 1956–57; four-man, 1948, 1951, 1953–54, 1956–57.

BENINGTON, JOHN basketball: b. Dec. 31, 1921, Findlay, Ohio; d. Sept. 10, 1969. Benington played on the University of San Francisco team that won the 1949 National Invitation Tournament.

He coached at Drake, 1956–58 (21–28); St. Louis University, 1958–65 (118–71, including a 20–6 mark in 1958–59); Michigan State, 1959–69 (56–38).

BENNETT, "CHARLIE" (Charles W.) baseball: b. Nov. 21, 1854, New Castle, Pa.; d. Feb. 24, 1927. Bat, throw R; catcher. Milwaukee NL, 1878; Worcester NL, 1880; Detroit NL, 1881–88; Boston NL, 1889–93. Fifteen years, 1,062 games, .256 BA; hit .301 in 1881, .301 in 1882, .305 in 1883. His career was ended when he lost both legs in a train accident in 1894.

BENTON, LAWRENCE J. baseball: b. Nov. 20, 1897, St. Louis, Mo.; d. April 3, 1953. Bat, throw R; pitcher. Boston NL, 1923–27; New York NL, 1927–30; Cincinnati NL, 1930–34; Boston NL, 1935. Thirteen years, 127–128, 4.03 ERA. Led NL in percentage in 1927 (17–7, .708); in wins and percentage (25–9, .735) and complete games (28) in 1928.

BENTON, "RUBE" (John C.) baseball: b. June 27, 1887, Clinton, N.C.; d. Dec. 12, 1937. Bat R, throw L; pitcher. Cincinnati NL, 1910–15; New York NL, 1915–21; Cincinnati NL, 1923–25. Fifteen years, 155–144, 3.09 ERA. Led NL in games (50) and starts (39) in 1912. One World Series, 1917: 1–1 record, though he didn't give up an earned run in 14 innings.

BENZ, JOSEPH L. baseball: b. Jan. 21, 1886, New Alsace, Ind.; d. April 23, 1957. Bat, throw R; pitcher. Chicago AL, 1911–19. Nine years, 73–76, 2.42 ERA. No-hitter, May 31, 1914, against Cleveland (6–1). Led AL in losses, 1914 (15–19).

BERNHARD, WILLIAM H. baseball: b. March 15, 1871, Clarence, N.Y.: d. March 30, 1949. Sw. hit, throw R; pitcher. Philadelphia NL, 1899–1900; Philadelphia AL, 1901–02; Cleveland AL, 1902–07. Nine years, 116–82, 3.04 ERA; 23–13 in 1904. Led AL in percentage, 1902 (18–5, .783).

BESCHER, ROBERT W. baseball: b. Feb. 25, 1884, London, Ohio; d. Nov. 29, 1942. Sw. hit, throw L; outfield. Cincinnati NL, 1908–13; New York NL, 1914; St. Louis NL, 1915–17; Cleveland AL, 1918. Eleven years, 1,228 games, 427 stolen bases, .258 BA. Led NL in stolen bases, 1909 (54), 1910 (70), 1911 (80), 1912 (67); in runs, 1912 (120).

BETTENHAUSEN, "TONY" (Melvin E.) auto racing: b. Sept. 12, 1916, Tinley Park, Ill.; d. May 12, 1961. Bettenhausen was USAC national driving champion 1951, 1958. He was killed in a crash during a test run at the Indianapolis Speedway.

Auto Racing Hall of Fame, Helms Hall of Fame.

BEZDEK, HUGO F. football, baseball: b. April 1, 1884, Prague, Czechoslovakia; d. Sept. 19, 1952. The only man who ever both coached major college football and managed a major-league baseball team, Bezdek was a 3rd-team All-American fullback at the University of Chicago in 1905.

He coached Oregon to a 4–0–1 season in 1906, then coached at Arkansas from 1908 to 1912, producing undefeated, untied teams in 1909–10. Bezdek returned to Oregon, 1913–17. His 1916 team had a 7–0–1 record and beat Penn 14–0 in the 1917 Rose Bowl. At Penn State, 1918–29, his teams had a 29-game undefeated streak, 1919–22, with undefeated teams in 1920 and 1921. He was athletic director at Penn State, 1930–37, then coached the Cleveland Rams, 1937–38, compiling a 5–17–0 record. Bezdek managed Pittsburgh NL, 1917–19: 166–187, .470.

Helms Hall of Fame, National Football Foundation Hall of Fame.

BICKFORD, VERNON E. baseball: b. Aug. 17, 1920, Hellier, Ky.; d. May 6, 1960. Bat, throw R; pitcher. Boston NL, 1948–52; Milwaukee NL, 1953; Baltimore AL, 1954. Seven years, 66–57, 3.71 ERA. No-hitter, Aug. 11, 1950, against Brooklyn NL (7–0). Led NL in complete games (27) and innings (311⅔) in 1950. One World Series, 1948: 1 game, 0–1, 2.70 ERA.

BIDWILL, CHARLES W. football: b. Sept. 16, 1895, Chicago; d. April 19, 1947. Bidwill bought the NFL Chicago Cardinal franchise from Dr. David D. Jones in 1933. He clung to it through some lean years and a couple of near misses but died eight months before the team won its first NFL championship. His family still controls the franchise, which was moved to St. Louis in 1960.

Professional Football Hall of Fame.

BIERBAUER, LOUIS W. baseball: b. Sept. 28, 1865, Erie, Pa.; d. Feb. 1, 1926. Bat, throw R; second base. Philadelphia AA, 1886–89; Brooklyn PL, 1890; Pittsburgh NL, 1891–96; St. Louis NL, 1897–98. Thirteen years, 1,383 games, .267 BA; hit .304 in 1889, .306 in 1890, .303 in 1894.

On July 12, 1890, he became the second player to hit two home runs in one inning; on June 22, 1888, he set an ML record, since tied, for most putouts by a second baseman in a 9-inning game, 12.

BIERMAN, CARROLL horse racing: b. 1918(?), Centralia, Ill.; d. March 22, 1970. Bierman rode Gallahadion to victory in the 1940 Kentucky Derby. Other major races he won included the Arlington Classic, Arlington Matron Handicap, Dwyer Handicap, Kentucky Oaks, and Washington Park Futurity.

BIGBEE, CARSON L. ("Skeeter") baseball: b. March 31, 1895, Waterloo, Iowa; d. Oct. 17, 1964. Bat L, throw R; outfield. Pittsburgh NL, 1916–26. Eleven years, 1,147 games, .287 BA; hit .323 in 1921, .350 in 1922.

BIMSTEIN, "WHITEY" (Morris) boxing: b. 1897, New York City; d. July 13, 1969. After 70 professional fights as a bantamweight, under the name of Johnny White, he became a successful trainer, primarily in partnership with Ray Arcel. Among the champions handled by Bimstein were Gene Tunney, Max Baer, Jim Braddock, Primo Carnera, Rocky Graziano, and Barney Ross.

BIRMINGHAM, JOSEPH L. ("Dode") baseball: b. Aug. 6, 1884, Elmira, N.Y.; d. April 24, 1946. Bat, throw R; outfield. Cleveland AL, 1906–14. Nine years, 771 games, .253 BA; hit .304 in 1911.
Managed Cleveland AL, 1912 (part)–15 (part): 170–191, .471.

BISHOP, MAX F. baseball: b. Sept. 5, 1899, Waynesboro, Pa.; d. Feb. 24, 1962. Bat L, throw R; second base. Philadelphia AL, 1924–33; Boston AL, 1934–35. Twelve years, 1,338 games, 966 runs, 1,153 walks; .271 BA; hit .316 in 1928.
Known as Camera Eye for his ability to work walks, Bishop led the AL in walks, 1929 (128). He holds the ML record for most walks in a double-header, 8, a feat he accomplished twice, and the AL record for most times drawing 5 walks in a game, twice. He had 100 or more walks seven different seasons, and he scored more than 100 runs in four straight years.
In three World Series (1929–31) he hit only .187 but walked 12 times and scored 11 runs in 18 games.

BLACK, "CUPE" (Clinton R., Jr.) football: b. Oct. 3, 1894, New York City; d. Oct. 8, 1963. Yale guard; All-American, captain, 1916; 2nd team, 1915. In 1917, when the All-American team was chosen from the armed services, Black was again first team, representing the Newport, Rhode Island, Naval Reserves.

BLACKBURN, THOMAS L. basketball: b. Jan. 23, 1906, Otway, Ohio; d. March 6, 1964. Blackburn coached at Dayton University, 1947–64, compiling a 352–141 record. Ten of his teams went to the National Invitation Tournament. Dayton won the NIT in 1962, after having been runner-up five times.

BLAEHOLDER, GEORGE F. baseball: b. Jan. 26, 1904, Orange, Cal.; d. Dec. 29, 1947. Bat, throw R; pitcher. St. Louis AL, 1925, 1927–35; Philadelphia AL, 1935; Cleveland AL, 1936. Eleven years, 104–125, 4.54 ERA.
Led AL in shutouts, 1929 (4).

BLAKE, OCTAVE harness racing: b. March 28, 1894, New York City; d. Jan. 8, 1969. Blake owned the Newport Stock Farm, first in Vermont and later in Pinehurst, North Carolina. His first outstanding horse was Forbes Chief, who won the Little Brown Jug in 1947. His Newport Dream was the leading two-year-old money-winner in 1953, with $94,933, and won the Hambletonian in 1954. Blake served several terms as Grand Circuit president.
Harness Racing Hall of Fame.

BLANKENSHIP, THEODORE baseball: b. May 10, 1901, Bonham, Tex.; d. Jan. 14, 1945. Bat, throw R; pitcher. Chicago AL, 1922–30. Nine years, 77–79, 4.32 ERA.

BLANTON, "CY" (Darrell E.) baseball: b. July 6, 1908, Waurika, Okla.; d. Sept 13, 1945. Bat L, throw R; pitcher. Pittsburgh NL, 1934–39; Philadelphia NL, 1940–42. Nine years, 68–71, 3.55 ERA. Led NL in ERA (2.58) and shutouts (4) in 1935; in shutouts, 1936 (4).

BLAZINE, ANTHONY football: b. Jan. 2, 1912, Canton, Ill.; d. July 3, 1963. Illinois Wesleyan tackle. Chicago Cardinals, 1935–40; New York Giants, 1941.

BLOOD, ERNEST A. basketball: b. Oct. 4, 1872, Manchester, N.H.; d. Feb. 5, 1955. The only man in the Basketball Hall of Fame who is known primarily as a high-school coach, Blood turned out the fantastic "Wonder Teams" at Passaic, New Jersey, High School, 1915–24. His Passaic teams won 200 games while losing only 1, boasted a 159-game winning streak, and won 7 state titles.
His earlier high-school teams in Potsdam, New York, 1906–15, had never lost to another high school. He also coached at Clarkson University part of the time while he was at Potsdam, and he coached Army the 1925–26 season. His college record was 56–7. Blood began his coaching career with YMCA teams in New England and New York. He actually spent the bulk of his career at St. Benedict's Prep, Newark, New Jersey, 1924–49; his teams there won 421 games and 5 state championships.
Basketball Hall of Fame.

BLOUIN, JAMES bowling: b. Dec. 21, 1886, Trois Rivières, Quebec, Canada; d. April 6, 1947. An early match-game champion, Blouin, who lived in Blue Island, Illinois, took on challengers from throughout the Chicago area and elsewhere. Winning the match-game title in the 1922 World Open, he defended it against Jimmy Smith, Joe Falcaro, Phil Wolf, Mort Lindsey, and Joe Scribner before retiring. Won ABC all-events, 1909,

with 1885; ABC singles, 1911, with 681. Nineteen-year ABC tourney average, 194.
American Bowling Congress Hall of Fame.

BLOZIS, ALBERT C. football, track: b. ?; d. Jan. 31, 1945. Georgetown tackle. New York Giants, 1942–44; All-Pro, 1943. Blozis dominated collegiate shotput and discus events three consecutive years, 1940–42. During those years, he won the shotput at the NCAA, IC4A, and AAU indoor and outdoor meets and the discus at the IC4A indoor and outdoor meets.
An Army lieutenant, he was killed in France.
Helms Hall of Fame (track).

BLUE, "LU" (Luzerne A.) baseball: b. March 5, 1897, Washington, D.C.; d. July 28, 1958. Sw. hit, throw L; first base. Detroit AL, 1921–27; St. Louis AL, 1928–30; Chicago AL, 1931–32; Brooklyn NL, 1933. Thirteen years, 1,615 games, .287 BA; hit .308 in 1921, .300 in 1922, .311 in 1924, .306 in 1925, .304 in 1931.
Blue tied an ML record for most double plays started by a first baseman in a 9-inning game, 3, on Sept. 8, 1922.

BODIE, PING baseball: b. Francesco S. Pezzolo, Oct. 8, 1887, San Francisco; d. Dec. 17, 1961. Bat, throw R; outfield. Chicago AL, 1911–14; Philadelphia AL, 1917; New York AL, 1918–21. Nine years, 1,049 games, .275 BA.

BODIS, JOSEPH bowling: b. Jan. 16, 1897, Hungary; d. April 26, 1970. Bodis set a record, since broken by George Young, by rolling 8 consecutive 1800s in all-events in the ABC tournament. He had 11 above 1800 during his career. He bowled on the ABC championship team, Herb's Indians, in 1924 and averaged 193 for 33 ABC tourneys. He had four sanctioned 300 games.
American Bowling Congress Hall of Fame.

BOGARDUS, ADAM H. shooting: b. 1833, Albany County, N.Y.; d. 1913. Capt. Bogardus had a flair for the dramatic, often demonstrated in the form of unusual bets. In 1868, he won a bet by trapshooting from a moving buggy at 21 yards and beating a stationary opponent who was at 25 yards. The following year he bet $1,000 that he could kill 500 pigeons in 645 minutes; he did it in 528 minutes. (Trapshooting got its name because the targets were originally live birds released from traps.)
Bogardus was also an inventor of an early glass-ball trap, and his rules for the sport were in general use before the turn of the century. In a Madison Square Garden exhibition, he broke 4,844 of 5,000 glass balls in 8 hours and 20 minutes of shooting. He once broke 501 clay birds in 34 minutes,

7 seconds. In still another unusual competition, he bet that he could break 500 targets before his opponent broke 450. When he reached 500, his opponent had only 361.

American Trapshooting Hall of Fame.

BOND, THOMAS H. baseball: b. April 2, 1856, Granard, Ireland; d. Jan. 24, 1941. Bat, throw R; pitcher. National Association, Brooklyn Atlantics, 1874; Hartford, 1875. Two years, 41–48.

Hartford NL, 1876; Boston NL, 1877–81; Worcester NL, 1882; Indianapolis AA, Boston UA, 1884. Eight years, 193–115, 2.25 ERA (9th); 31–13 in 1876, 43–19 in 1879, 26–29 in 1880. Led NL in wins and percentage (40–17, .702), ERA (2.11), strikeouts (170), and shutouts (6) in 1877; in victories and percentage (40–19, .678), complete games (57), innings (432⅔), strikeouts (182), and shutouts (9) in 1878; in ERA (1.96) and shutouts (12) in 1879.

BONHAG, GEORGE V. track: b. 1881, New York City; d. Oct. 30, 1960. Noted as a distance runner, Bonhag won an Olympic Gold Medal the first time he entered a walking event and is still the only American ever to win an Olympic walking medal. Disappointed at finishing 4th in the 5-mile during the 1906 Olympics, he entered the 1,500-meter walk; the judges were being very strict, disqualifying entrants for improper technique, and there weren't many competitors left when Bonhag crossed the finish line, laughing.

He was U.S. indoor 2-mile champion, 1904–07 and 1911, outdoor 5-mile champ in 1911, and 10-mile champion in 1909.

BONHAM, "ERNIE" (Ernest E.) baseball: b. Aug. 16, 1913, Iona, Cal.; d. Sept. 15, 1949. Bat, throw R; pitcher. New York AL, 1940–46; Pittsburgh NL, 1947–49. Ten years, 103–72, 3.06 ERA. Led AL in percentage (21–5, .808), complete games (22), and shutouts (6) in 1942. Three World Series, 1941–43: 4 games, 1–2, 3.21 ERA.

BOOTH, "ALBIE" (Albert J.) football: b. Feb. 1, 1908, New Haven, Conn.; d. March 1, 1959. "Little Boy Blue," a sophomore halfback, only 5'7" and 144 pounds, didn't even start Yale's third game of the 1929 season, against a powerful Army team. When he got into the game, in the second period, Army was ahead 13–0. By the end of the third quarter, Booth had scored 14 points to give Yale a slim lead. He added an insurance TD on an incredible 70-yard punt return on which he ran through the whole Army team. By the time he crossed the goal-line, the Yale Bowl crowd of 80,000 was giving him a standing ovation. It was a good afternoon: 223 yards on 33 carries, plus his kick-return yardage, and 21 points.

It was only one of several great performances. Against Dartmouth in 1931, he ran 53 yards for one TD, returned a kickoff 96 yards for another, and caught a pass for a third. Against Harvard that year, he kicked a 14-yard field goal with seconds to play for a 3–0 victory. Booth captained both the football and basketball teams as a senior; in baseball he hit a grand-slam home run to beat Harvard, 4–3, in his last athletic appearance for Yale. National Football Foundation Hall of Fame.

BORRIES, "BUZZ" (Fred, Jr.) football: b. Dec. 31, 1911, Kentucky; d. Jan. 3, 1969. Navy halfback; All-American, 1934. An excellent broken-field runner, he had many long runs during his career, including one of 75 yards against Columbia in 1932.

National Football Foundation Hall of Fame.

BOTTOMLEY, "SUNNY JIM" (James L.) baseball: b. April 23, 1900, Oglesby, Ill.; Dec. 11, 1959. Bat, throw L; first base. St. Louis NL, 1922–32; Cincinnati NL, 1933–35; St. Louis AL, 1936–37. Sixteen years, 1,991 games, 7,471 at-bats, 2,313 hits, 465 doubles, 151 triples, 219 home runs, 1,422 RBI, .310 BA; hit .371 in 1923, .316 in 1924, .367 in 1925, .303 in 1927, .325 in 1928, .314 in 1929, .304 in 1930, .348 in 1931. Led NL in hits (227) and doubles (44) in 1925; in doubles (40) and RBI (120) in 1926; in triples (20), home runs (31), and RBI (136) in 1928.

Bottomley set an ML record with 12 RBI on Sept. 16, 1924, going 6-for-6 with a double, 2 home runs, and 3 runs scored; he also went 6-for-6 Aug. 5, 1931, and is one of two players to do it twice. He is coholder of the ML record for most times hitting three triples in a game, twice. In four World Series (1926, 1928, 1930–31), 24 games, he hit .200. He hit .345 with 3 doubles, 4 runs, and 5 RBI in the Cardinals' 7-game victory over the Yankees in 1926.

BOURQUE, "PIT" (Napoleon) auto racing: b. 1885(?), Farnham, Quebec, Canada; d. July 8, 1963. In dirt-track racing, Bourque won 21 of 27 starts in 1913–14, then he retired.

BOWDITCH, "PETE" (Edward, Jr.) football: b. Oct. 29, 1881, Albany, N.Y.; d. April 6, 1965. Harvard end; All-American, 1902; 2nd team, 1901.

BOWERMAN, FRANK E. ("Mike") baseball: b. Dec. 5, 1868, Romeo, Mich.; d. Nov. 30. 1948. Bat, throw R; catcher. Baltimore NL, 1895–98; Pittsburgh NL, 1898–99; New York NL, 1900–07; Boston NL, 1908–09. Fifteen years, 1,045 games, .251 BA.

BOYLE, "JACK" (John A.) baseball: b. March 22, 1866, Cincinnati; d. Jan. 7, 1913. Catcher, first base. Cincinnati AA, 1886; St. Louis AA, 1887–89;

Chicago PL, 1890; St. Louis AA, 1891; New York NL, 1892; Philadelphia NL, 1893–98. Thirteen years, 1,068 games, BA .253; hit .301 in 1894. He went 6-for-6 on July 6, 1893.

BOYNTON, BEN LEE football: b. Dec. 6, 1898, Waco, Tex.; d. Jan. 23, 1963. Williams quarterback; captain, 3rd team All-American, 1919–20. Rochester Jeffersons, 1921–22; Buffalo Bisons, 1924. Boynton tied a collegiate record by running back a punt 110 yards in 1920. He had five other runs of 60 yards or better during his career and was a fine passer as well.

Later, he was amateur golf champion of Texas.

National Football Foundation Hall of Fame.

BRADLEE, FREDERICK J. football: b. Dec. 20, 1892, Brookline, Mass.; d. April 28, 1970. Harvard halfback; All-American, 1914. During his three years as a starter, Harvard was undefeated.

BRADLEY, EDWARD R. horse racing: b. Dec. 12, 1859, Johnstown, Pa.; d. Aug. 15, 1946. The first owner to send four winners to the post in the Kentucky Derby, Col. Bradley was a cowboy, a prospector, and a scout in the Indian Wars before he developed the skill at gambling that brought him a fortune. He made his first money playing poker and betting on Indian pony races in the Southwest, then went into bookmaking and other businesses.

His Idle Hour Stock Farm, founded in 1893, was well named: Bradley was told by a doctor to retire from business, so he decided to devote his idle hours to breeding racehorses. The farm produced these Derby winners: Behave Yourself, 1921; Bubbling Over, 1926; Burgoo King, 1932; and Broker's Tip, 1933. Twice Bradley's horses finished 1–2 in the Derby, Black Servant placing in 1921 and Bagenbaggage in 1926. Bimelech, perhaps his greatest horse, was a two-year-old champion with 6 victories in 6 starts in 1939; he was second in the Derby in 1940 but won the Belmont and Preakness. Burgoo King repeated in the Preakness, which had been won by Bradley's Kalitan in 1917, and his Blue Larkspur won the 1929 Belmont.

BRADLEY, GEORGE W. baseball: b. July 13, 1852, Reading, Pa.; d. Oct. 2, 1931. Bat, throw R; pitcher, third base. National Association, St. Louis, 1875. One year, 33–26, .268 BA.

St. Louis NL, 1876; Chicago NL, 1877; Troy NL, 1879; Providence NL, 1880; Detroit NL, 1881; Cleveland NL, 1881–83; Philadelphia AA, 1883; Cincinnati UA, 1884; Philadelphia AA, 1886; Baltimore AA, 1888. Eight years, 139–125, 2.50 ERA; 45–19 in 1876, 25–15 in 1884. No-hitter, July 15, 1876, against Hartford NL (2–0).

BRADLEY, WILLIAM A. baseball: b. Feb. 13, 1877, Cleveland; d. March 11 1954. Bat, throw R; third base. Chicago NL, 1899–1900; Cleveland AL 1901–10; Brooklyn Fed L, 1914; Kansas City Fed L, 1915. Fourteen years 1,460 games, .271 BA; hit .340 in 1902, .313 in 1903, .300 in 1904.

On Sept. 21, 1901, he tied an AL record for third basemen with 7 putouts in a 9-inning game.

Managed Brooklyn Fed L, 1914: 77–77, .500.

BRADY, WILLIAM A. boxing: b. June 19, 1863, San Francisco; d. Jan. 6, 1950. Brady managed the winning fighter in two of the most famous early heavyweight bouts. He was managing a repertory company when Gentleman Jim Corbett, anxious to get a fight with John L. Sullivan, hired him to help. Brady got him the fight and after the victory took him on tour in a play called, of course, *Gentleman Jim*. Brady was also Jim Jeffries' manager and promoted the fight in which Jeffries won the title from Bob Fitzsimmons, who had beaten Corbett. Later, he became a New York theatrical producer.

BRAIN, DAVID L. baseball: b. Jan. 24, 1879, Hereford, England; d. May 25, 1959. Bat, throw R; third base, shortstop. Chicago AL, 1901; St. Louis NL, 1903–05; Pittsburgh NL, 1905; Boston NL, 1906–07; Cincinnati NL, 1908; New York NL, 1908. Seven years, 679 games, .252 BA. Led NL in home runs, 1907 (10).

BRANDT, EDWARD A. baseball: b. Feb. 17, 1905, Spokane, Wash.; d. Nov. 1, 1944. Bat, throw L; pitcher. Boston NL, 1928–35; Brooklyn NL, 1936; Pittsburgh NL, 1937–38. Eleven years, 121–146, 3.86 ERA. Led NL in losses, 1928 (9–21).

BRANSFIELD, "KITTY" (William E.) baseball: b. Jan. 7, 1875, Worcester, Mass.; d. May 1, 1947. Bat, throw R; catcher. Boston NL, 1898; Pittsburgh NL, 1901–04; Philadelphia NL, 1905–11; Chicago NL, 1911. Twelve years, 1,329 games, .270 BA; hit .305 in 1902, .304 in 1908. One World Series, 1903: 8 games, .200 BA.

He set an ML record for most assists by a first baseman in a 9-inning game with 7 on May 3, 1904.

BRAXTON, E. GARLAND baseball: b. June 10, 1900, Snow Camp, N.C.; d. Feb. 25, 1966. Sw. hit, throw L; pitcher. Boston NL, 1921–22; New York AL, 1925–26; Washington AL, 1927–30; Chicago AL, 1930–31; St. Louis AL, 1931, 1933. Ten years, 50–53, 4.13 ERA. In relief, 26–19, 3.58 ERA, 32 saves. Led AL in games (58), saves (13), and relief appearances (56) in 1927; in ERA, 1928 (2.51).

BRAY, MAURICE football: b. Aug. 27, 1909, Paducah, Tex.; d. Dec. 9, 1966. SMU tackle. Pittsburgh Pirates, 1935–36.

BREITENSTEIN, THEODORE P. baseball: b. June 1, 1869, St. Louis; d. May 3, 1935. Bat, throw L; pitcher. St. Louis AA, 1891; St. Louis NL, 1892–96; Cincinnati NL, 1897–1900; St. Louis NL, 1901. Eleven years, 160–170, 4.04 ERA. No-hitters, Oct. 4, 1891, against Louisville AA (8–0; his first ML start); April 22, 1898, against Pittsburgh NL (11–0). Led NL in ERA, 1893 (3.18); in complete games, 1894 (46); in losses (19–30), complete games (46) in 1895. He was used occasionally in the outfield or as a pinch-hitter; in 1899 he hit .352 in 105 at-bats.

BREMER, JOHN L., JR. track: b. Nov. 3, 1874, New York City; d. Dec. 25, 1959. Bremer, from Harvard, won the IC4A 220-yard low hurdles, 1894–96. His time of 24.6 seconds in 1895 was a world record until 1898.

BRESNAHAN, ROGER P. baseball: b. June 11, 1879, Toledo, Ohio; d. Dec. 4, 1944. Bat, throw R; catcher, outfield. Washington NL, 1897; Chicago NL, 1900; Baltimore AL, 1901–02; New York NL, 1902–08; St. Louis NL, 1909–12; Chicago NL, 1913–15. Seventeen years, 1,430 games, .279 BA; hit .350 in 1903, .302 in 1905.

Bresnahan, known as the Duke of Tralee, is credited with inventing shinguards. He often played centerfield and had occasional turns at first, third, and shortstop.

He was a fine clutch hitter: His lifetime average as a pinch-hitter was .317, and in his only World Series, 1905, he hit .313, scoring 3 and driving in another of the Giants' 15 runs as they beat Philadelphia in 5 games.

Baseball Hall of Fame.

BRESSLER, "RUBE" (Raymond B.) baseball: b. Oct. 23, 1894, Coder, Pa.; d. Nov. 7, 1966. Bat R, throw L; pitcher, outfield. Philadelphia AL, 1914–16; Cincinnati NL, 1917–27; Brooklyn NL, 1928–31; Philadelphia NL, St. Louis NL, 1932. Nineteen years, 1,305 games; hit .307 in 1921, .347 in 1924, .348 in 1925, .357 in 1926, .318 in 1929. After beginning his ML career as a pitcher who was 26–31 and plagued by wildness, Bressler became an outfielder and compiled a lifetime BA of .301.

BRICE, FREDERICK football: b. 1895, Lawrence, Mass.; d. Jan. 10, 1967. Coaching at University of Maine, 1919–37, he compiled an 81–13–6 mark and a .862 won-lost percentage.

BRICKLEY, CHARLES E. football: b. Nov. 24, 1891, Boston; d. Dec. 28, 1949. Harvard halfback; All-American, 1912–13. He is generally credited with 34 career field goals, a record for dropkickers, and his 13 in 1913 is a one-year record. (Some sources credit him with 12 in 1912 and 11 in 1911, which would make his career total 36.) He brought Harvard the "Big Three" championship almost single-footed in 1913: He kicked 5 field goals for a 15–0 win over Yale and kicked another for a 3–0 victory over Princeton.

BRIDGES, "TOMMY" (Thomas Jefferson Davis) baseball: b. Dec. 28, 1906, Gordonsville, Tenn.; d. April 19, 1968. Bat, throw R; pitcher. Detroit AL, 1930–43, 1945–46. Sixteen years, 194–138, 3.57 ERA; 1,674 strikeouts in 2,826⅓ innings, 32 shutouts; 22–11 in 1934, 21–10 in 1935. Led AL in strikeouts, 1935 (163); in victories (23–11) and strikeouts (175) in 1936. Four World Series, 1934–35, 1940, 1945: 7 games, 4–1, 3.52 ERA. In 1935, he was 2–0 as Detroit beat Chicago NL in 6.

BRIDWELL, "AL" (Albert H.) baseball: b. Jan 4, 1884, Friendship, Ohio; d. Jan. 24, 1969. Bat L, throw R; shortstop. Cincinnati NL, 1905; Boston NL, 1906–07; New York NL, 1908–11; Boston NL, 1911–12; Chicago NL, 1913; St. Louis Fed L, 1914–15. Eleven years, 1,250 games, .255 BA.

BRITO, "GENE" (Eugene) football: b. Oct. 23, 1925, Los Angeles; d. June 8, 1965. Loyola of Los Angeles defensive end. Washington Redskins, 1951–53, 1955–58; Los Angeles Rams, 1959–60. All-Pro 1955, 1956, 1958 (UPI). Small for his position at 235 pounds, Brito was exceptionally tough and aggressive. He suffered partial paralysis during the 1961 exhibition season and was in and out of hospitals for the rest of his life.

BRITTON, JACK boxing: b. William Breslin, Oct. 14, 1885, Clinton, N.Y.; d. March 27, 1962. His record: 100 wins, 21 by KO; 25 losses, 1 by KO; 20 draws, 174 no-decisions, 1 no-contest. Between 1915 and 1919, Britton and Ted Lewis, of Britain, more or less alternated as welterweight champ; they fought a dozen times during the period, just about splitting even. Lewis won recognition as champion by beating Britton in 12 rounds on Aug. 31, 1915, but Britton won their last fight with a 9-round KO on March 17, 1919, and held the title until Mickey Walker won a 15-round decision in 1922.

BRODIE, "STEVE" (Walter S.) baseball: b. Sept. 11, 1868, Warrenton, Va.; d. Oct. 30, 1935. Bat L, throw R; outfield. Boston NL, 1890–91; St. Louis NL, 1892–93; Baltimore NL, 1893–96; Pittsburgh NL, 1897–98; Baltimore NL, 1898–99; Baltimore AL, 1901; New York NL, 1902. Twelve years, 1,437 games, .303 BA; hit .325 in 1893, .366 in 1894, .348 in 1895, .309 in 1899, .310 in 1901.

Brodie went 6-for-6, with 2 doubles and a triple, on July 9, 1894. He tied the NL record for most years leading outfielders in fielding average, 4.

BROUTHERS, "DAN" (Dennis J.) baseball: b. May 8, 1858, Sylvan Lake, N.Y.; d. Aug. 2, 1932. Bat, throw L; first base. Troy NL, 1879–80; Buffalo NL, 1881–85; Detroit NL, 1886–88; Boston NL, 1889; Boston PL, 1890; Boston AA, 1891; Brooklyn NL, 1892–93; Baltimore NL, 1894–95; Louisville NL, 1895; Philadelphia NL, 1896; New York NL, 1904. Nineteen years, 1,673 games, 6,711 at-bats, 2,296 hits, 460 doubles, 205 triples (8th), 106 home runs, 1,523 runs, 1,056 RBI (4 years not included), 235 stolen bases (8 years not included), .342 BA.

He led the league in home runs (8) and slugging (.541) in 1881; in hits (129), BA (.368), and slugging (.547) in 1882; in hits (159), triples (17), BA (.374), and slugging (.572) in 1883; in slugging, 1884 (.563) and 1885 (.543); in doubles (40), home runs (11), and slugging (.581) in 1886; in doubles (36) and runs (153) in 1887; in doubles (33) and runs (118) in 1888; in BA, 1889 (.373); in BA (.350) and slugging (.512) in 1891; in hits (197), BA (.335), and RBI (124) in 1892.

Brouthers also had these over-.300 years not already mentioned: .319 in 1881, .327 in 1884, .359 in 1885, .370 in 1886, .338 in 1887, .307 in 1888, .330 in 1890, .337 in 1893, .347 in 1894, .300 in 1895, .344 in 1896.

He went 6-for-6, with 2 doubles and 3 runs, on July 19, 1883; on Sept. 10, 1886, he hit 3 home runs in a game.

Baseball Hall of Fame.

BROWN, "BABE" (John H., Jr.) football: b. Oct. 12, 1891, Canton, Pa.; d. June 10, 1963. Navy guard, tackle; All-American as guard in 1913; 2nd team, 1910; 3rd team, 1912; 3rd team as tackle, 1911.

After retiring from the Navy as a vice-admiral in 1954, he was president of the National Football Foundation until his death.

National Football Foundation Hall of Fame.

BROWN, "BUSTER" (Charles E.) baseball: b. Aug. 31, 1881, Boone, Iowa; d. Feb. 9, 1914. Bat, throw R; pitcher. St. Louis NL, 1905–07; Philadelphia NL, 1907–09; Boston NL, 1909–13. Nine years, 48–105, 3.20 ERA. In 1910 he was 8–22 but had a 2.67 ERA.

BROWN, CLINTON H. baseball: b. July 8, 1903, Blackash, Pa.; d. Dec. 31, 1955. Bat L, throw R; pitcher. Cleveland AL, 1928–35; Chicago AL, 1936–40; Cleveland AL, 1941–42. Fifteen years, 89–92, 4.26 ERA. In relief, 41–35, 4.01 ERA, 64 saves. Led AL in saves, 1937 (18).

BROWN, F. GORDON, JR. football: b. Sept. 6, 1879, New York City; d. May 10, 1911. Yale guard; All-American, 1897–1900.

National Football Foundation Hall of Fame.

BROWN, THOMAS T. baseball: b. Sept. 21, 1860, Liverpool, England; d. Oct. 27, 1927. Outfield. Columbus AA, 1883–84; Pittsburgh AA, 1885–86; Pittsburgh NL, 1887; Indianapolis NL, 1887; Boston NL, 1888–89; Boston PL, 1890; Boston AA, 1891; Louisville NL, 1892–94; St. Louis NL, 1895; Washington NL, 1895–98. Sixteen years, 1,741 games, .264 BA. Led league in hits (189), triples (21), runs (177), and stolen bases (106) in 1891; in stolen bases (66) in 1893.

BROWN, "THREE-FINGER" (Mordecai P. C.) baseball: b. Oct. 19, 1876, Nyesville, Ind.; d. Feb. 14, 1948. Sw. hit, throw R; pitcher. St. Louis NL, 1903; Chicago NL, 1904–12; Cincinnati NL, 1913; Brooklyn Fed L, St. Louis Fed L, 1914; Chicago Fed L, 1915; Chicago NL, 1916. Fourteen years, 229–131, 2.06 ERA (3rd), 56 shutouts (8th); 25–6 in 1906, 27–9 in 1908, 21–13 in 1910, 20–21 in 1911. Led NL in ERA (1.04) and shutouts (9) in 1906; in victories (26–9) and complete games (32) in 1909; in shutouts (7) and complete games (27) in 1910.

In four World Series (1906–08, 1910), Brown appeared in 9 games, 7 starts, 5 complete (6th), 5 wins (4th), 4 losses (3rd), 3 shutouts (2nd), 2.81 ERA; 35 strikeouts in 57⅔ innings; 2 saves. He won two games in the 1908 Series, when the Cubs beat Detroit in 5.

Two childhood accidents gave him his nickname. When he was seven, his right hand got caught in a feed-cutter; the index finger had to be amputated just above the first knuckle, and the little finger was useless for the rest of his life. While the hand was still in a cast, he fell and broke the other two fingers, which became permanently misshapen. But this grotesque hand gave his pitches a natural dip, he once explained.

Baseball Hall of Fame.

BROWN, WALTER A. basketball, hockey: b. Feb. 10, 1905, Hopkinton, Mass.; d. Sept. 7, 1964. President of the Boston Garden and Arena Corp. from 1937 until his death, Brown was a major force in organizing the National Basketball Association in 1946, and his team, the Celtics, became the outstanding team in the league for more than a decade. He also owned the National Hockey League Bruins and served as president of the International Hockey Federation in 1947. In 1933, he coached the first American team to win the world amateur title.

Basketball Hall of Fame, International Hockey Hall of Fame.

BROWNE, GEORGE E. baseball: b. Jan. 12, 1876, Richmond, Va.; d. Dec. 9, 1920. Bat L, throw R; outfield. Philadelphia NL, 1901–02; New York NL, 1902–07; Boston NL, 1908; Chicago NL, 1909; Washington AL, 1909–10; Chicago AL, 1910; Brooklyn NL, 1911; Philadelphia NL, 1912. Twelve years, 1,102 games, .273 BA; hit .313 in 1903. Led league in runs scored in 1904 (99). One World Series, 1905: 5 games, .182 BA.

BROWNING, "PETE" (L. Rogers) baseball: b. July 17, 1858, Louisville, Ky.; d. Sept. 10, 1905. Bat, throw R; outfield. Louisville AA, 1882–89; Cleveland PL, 1890; Pittsburgh NL, 1891; Cincinnati NL, 1891–92; Louisville NL, 1892–93; Brooklyn NL, 1894; St. Louis NL, 1894. Thirteen years, 1,183 games, .341 BA; hit .338 in 1883, .336 in 1884, .340 in 1886, .402 in 1887, .313 in 1888, .317 in 1891. Led league in hits (174) and BA (.362) in 1885; in doubles (40) and BA (.373) in 1890; in BA (.378) in 1882.

BRUCE, SAUNDERS D. horse racing: b. Aug. 16, 1825, Lexington, Ky.; d. 1902. After retiring from the Union Army in 1865, Bruce founded the magazine *Turf, Field and Farm,* which he edited until his death. He began publication in 1868 of *The American Stud Book,* recording the pedigrees of U.S. thoroughbreds. The Jockey Club took over publication in 1898.

BRUDER, "HANK" (Henry) football: b. Nov. 22, 1907, Pekin, Ill.; d. June 29, 1970. Northwestern quarterback; captain, 1930. Green Bay Packers, 1931–39; Pittsburgh Pirates, 1940. Bruder was best known for his defensive play as a linebacker.

BRUMBAUGH, CARL L. ("Brummie") football: b. Sept. 22, 1907, West Milton, Ohio; d. Oct. 25, 1969. Florida quarterback. Chicago Bears, 1930–34, 1936; Cleveland Rams, 1937; Chicago Bears, 1938.

BUCK, KENNETH football: b. 1932(?); d. Sept. 23, 1954. College of the Pacific end; All-American, 1953 (Football Writers).

BUCKENBERGER, "AL" (Albert C.) baseball: b. Jan. 31, 1861, Detroit; d. July 1, 1917. Managed Columbus AA, 1889–90 (part); Pittsburgh NL, 1892 (part)–94 (part); St. Louis NL, 1895 (part); Boston NL, 1902–04: 493–540, .477.

BUFF, JOHNNY boxing: b. John Lesky, June 12, 1888, Perth Amboy, N.J.; d. Jan. 14, 1955. His record: 28 wins, 13 by KO; 16 losses, 7 by KO; 4 draws, 45 no-decisions, 1 no-contest. Buff won the U.S. flyweight title on Feb. 11, 1921, with a 15-round decision over Frankie Mason, and on Sept. 23 became world bantamweight champ by beating Pete Herman in 15 rounds. He lost both titles in a span of two months. Joe Lynch stopped him in 14 rounds on July 10, 1922, for the bantam championship, and Pancho Villa KOed him in 11 rounds on Sept. 14 for the flyweight title.

BUFFINTON, "CHARLIE" (Charles G.) baseball: b. June 14, 1861, Fall River, Mass.; d. Sept. 23, 1907. Bat, throw R; pitcher, outfield. Boston NL, 1882–86; Philadelphia NL, 1887–89; Philadelphia PL, 1890; Boston AA, 1891; Baltimore NL, 1892. Eleven years, 232–152, 2.96 ERA; 1,700 strikeouts in 3,404 innings; 25–14 in 1883, 48–16 in 1884, 22–27 in 1885, 21–17 in 1887, 29–17 in 1888, 28–16 in 1889. Led AA in percentage, 1891 (28–9, .757).

Buffinton pitched consecutive 1-hitters, Aug. 6 and 9, 1887.

BUNCOM, FRANK, JR. football: b. Nov. 2, 1939, Shreveport, La.; d. Sept. 14, 1969. Southern California linebacker. San Diego (AFL), 1962–67; Cincinnati (AFL), 1968–69. Buncom played in three AFL All-Star games and was named outstanding defensive player in the 1965 game.

He died from a blood clot caused by a knee injury.

BUNKER, PAUL D. football: b. May 7, 1881, Michigan; d. March 16, 1943. Army: All-American tackle, 1901; All-American halfback, 1902. He was Army's first All-American.

National Football Foundation Hall of Fame.

BUNTIN, WILLIAM basketball: b. May 5, 1942, Detroit; d. May 9, 1968. Michigan center. Detroit Pistons, 1965–66, 42 games, 7.7 points per game. Three times All–Big Ten, Buntin played for Big Ten championship teams, 1964–65. He was the Pistons' first draft choice in 1965, but a chronic overweight problem limited his effectiveness.

He died of a heart attack.

BURDOCK, "JACK" (John J.) baseball: b. 1851, Brooklyn; d. Nov. 28, 1931. Bat, throw R; second base. National Association, Brooklyn, 1872–73; New York, 1874; Hartford, 1875. Four years, 224 games, .265 BA.

Hartford NL, 1876; Brooklyn NL, 1877; Boston NL, 1878–88; Brooklyn AA, 1888; Brooklyn NL, 1891. Fourteen years, 960 games, .246 BA; hit .330 in 1883.

BURGESS, W. STARLING yachting: b. Dec. 25, 1878, Boston; d. March 19, 1947. The son of Edward Burgess, who had designed America's Cup defenders *Puritan* (1885) and *Mayflower* (1886), he designed the most controversial defender in history. *Enterprise,* which took four straight races from the British *Shamrock V* in 1930, was scorned as a "mechanical yacht" by many sailing veterans. She had a virtually hollow hull containing about two dozen winches operated by "the black gang," a crew of eight who stayed below deck for the entire race. She also had a "tin mast," made of

two Duralumin shells riveted together, and a unique boom, shaped somewhat like a boat, on which the foot of the mainsail could slide to assume
the most efficient aerodynamic curve.

After 1930, such a yacht was, in effect, abolished from competition. But
Rainbow, the Burgess-designed 1934 defender, had a Duralumin mast and
a unique bending boom, which also allowed the most efficient curve on the
mainsail. After losing the first two races to *Endeavour,* she won four
straight to keep the cup.

BURKE, "JIMMY" (James T.) baseball: b. Oct. 12, 1874, St. Louis; d. March
6, 1942. Bat, throw R; third base. Cleveland NL, 1898; Chicago AL, Milwaukee AL, 1901; Pittsburgh NL, 1901–02; St. Louis NL, 1903–05. Six
years, 548 games, .244 BA.

Managed St. Louis NL, 1905 (part); 1918 (part)–20: 189–213, .470.

BURKETT, JESSE C. ("Crab") baseball: b. Dec. 4, 1868, Wheeling, W.Va.;
d. May 27, 1953. Bat, throw L; outfield. New York NL, 1890; Cleveland
NL, 1891–98; St. Louis NL, 1899–1901; St. Louis AL, 1902–04; Boston
AL, 1905. Sixteen years, 2,067 games, 8,421 at-bats, 2,850 hits, 2,273 singles, 320 doubles, 182 triples, 75 home runs, 1,720 runs, 952 RBI, 1,029
walks, 389 stolen bases, .338 BA.

One of only three players in history to hit over .400 two consecutive
seasons (Cobb and Hornsby are the others), Burkett specialized in line-drive
singles. He was also a great bunter and fine base-runner. Six times he had
more than 200 hits in a season and 10 times he stole 20 or more bases. He
led the NL in BA (.409) and hits (225) in 1895; in BA (.410), hits (240),
and runs (160) in 1896; in BA (.376), hits (226), runs (142), and total bases
(314) in 1901. He hit .309 in 1890, .348 in 1893, .358 in 1894, .383 in 1897,
.341 in 1898, .396 in 1899, .363 in 1900, and .306 in 1902.

Baseball Hall of Fame.

BURNS, FRANKIE boxing: b. June 24, 1889, Jersey City, N.J.; d. April 10,
1961. His record: 50 wins, 33 by KO; 5 losses, 1 by KO; 10 draws, 105
no-decisions. A bantamweight, Burns was a spoiler whose KOs of Young
Zulu Kid and Johnny Ertle postponed title fights for them. Burns himself fought for the title three times in a six-year span; he lost twice and the
third time champion Kid Williams held onto his crown with a 20-round
draw.

BURNS, GEORGE J. baseball: b. Nov. 24, 1889, Utica, N.Y.; d. Aug. 15,
1966. Bat, throw R; outfield. New York NL, 1911–21; Cincinnati NL,
1922–24; Philadelphia NL, 1925. Fifteen years, 1,853 games, 2,077 hits,

1,188 runs, 872 walks, 383 stolen bases, .287 BA; hit .303 in 1914, .302 in 1917, .303 in 1919. Led NL in runs (100) and stolen bases (62) in 1914; in runs (105) in 1916; in runs (103) and walks (75) in 1917; in runs (86), walks (82), and stolen bases (40) in 1919; in runs (115) and walks (76) in 1920; in walks, 1921 (80) and 1923 (101). Three World Series, 1913, 1917, 19_ _: 19 games, .257 BA.

In 1921, he hit .333, with 4 doubles, as the Giants beat the Yankees, 5 games to 3.

Burns holds NL records for most years leading in runs, 5, most consecutive years leading in walks, 3, and most years leading outfielders in games played, 6.

BURNS, MIRIAM (Mrs. Horn, Mrs. Tyson) golf: b. 1903(?), Kansas City, Mo.; d. March 19, 1951. She won the USGA Women's Amateur title in 1927, the Trans-Mississippi Amateur the same year, and the Western Amateur in 1923.

BURNS, "OYSTER" (Thomas P.) baseball: b. Sept. 6, 1962, Philadelphia; d. Nov. 16, 1928. Bat, throw R; outfield, shortstop. Wilmington UA, 1884; Baltimore AA, 1884–85, 1887, 1888; Brooklyn AA, 1888–89; Brooklyn NL, 1890–95; New York NL, 1895. Eleven years, 1,186 games, .300 BA; hit .341 in 1887, .304 in 1889, .315 in 1892, .354 in 1894. Led league in RBI, 1890 (128).

BURNS, THOMAS E. baseball: b. March 30, 1857, Honedale, Pa.; d. March 19, 1902. Bat L, throw R; third base, shortstop. Chicago NL, 1880–91; Pittsburgh NL, 1892. Thirteen years, 1,251 games, .264 BA.

He hit 2 doubles and a home run in one inning, Sept. 6, 1883, tying the ML record for most extra base hits in an inning; he also scored 3 runs in the inning, an NL record.

Managed Pittsburgh NL, 1892 (part); Chicago NL, 1898–99: 185–168, .524.

BURNS, TOMMY boxing: b. Noah Brusso, June 17, 1889, Hanover, Ont., Canada; d. May 10, 1955. His record: 46 wins, 36 by KO; 5 losses, 1 by KO; 8 draws, 1 no-decision. Burns won two titles, in a way, in little more than a year but held neither long. On Feb. 23, 1906, he won the world heavyweight championship by KOing Marvin Hart in 20 rounds. He held that title until Dec. 23, 1906, when Jack Johnson, who had been trying to get a match with Burns for some time, finally caught up with him in Australia and beat him on a 14-round TKO. In the meantime, Burns had pared down and won the light-heavyweight crown, in theory, with a 20-round decision from Philadelphia Jack O'Brien on May 8, 1907, but he never seriously claimed that title.

BURSTON, LEWIS boxing: b. 1894(?), New York City; d. March 19, 1969. Burston managed a large number of foreign fighters, among them four champions: Marcel Thil and Marcel Cerdan, both of France, Randy Turpin, of England, and Dick Tiger, of Nigeria.

BUSLER, RAYMOND football: b. Jan. 16, 1916, Watertown, Wis.; d. Oct. 9, 1969. Marquette tackle. Chicago Cardinals, 1940–41, 1945.

BUSSEY, YOUNG football: b. Oct. 4, 1917, Simpson, Tex.; d. October 1944. LSU quarterback. Chicago Bears, 1940–41. He was one of the nation's top collegiate passers in 1937, completing 42.5 percent of his throws for 731 yards.

He was killed leading a landing party in the Philippines.

BUTCHER, "MAX" (Albert Maxwell) baseball: b. Sept. 21, 1910, Holden, W.Va.; d. Sept. 15, 1957. Bat, throw R; pitcher. Brooklyn NL, 1936–38; Philadelphia NL, 1938–39; Pittsburgh NL, 1939–45. Ten years, 95–106, 3.73 ERA. Led NL in losses, 1939 (6–17).

BUTKOVICH, ANTHONY football: b. 1922(?); d. April 18, 1945. Halfback, Illinois, 1941–42, Purdue, 1943. Butkovich starred against Ohio State in 1942, scoring on runs of 82 and 75 yards in a 44–22 loss. He was third among major college runners in 1943 with 833 yards in 142 carries, a 5.9 average.

He was killed in the South Pacific.

BYRD, "CURLY" (Harold C.) football: b. Feb. 12, 1889, Crisfield, Md.; d. Oct. 18, 1970. One of the few football coaches ever to become a university president, Byrd was a three-sport star at Maryland. After winning his doctorate, he returned to his alma ma* as football coach and athletic director, 1913–34. He became vice-presiuent of the university in 1932, and in 1936 he was named its president. His coaching record was 121–85–17

Helms Hall of Fame.

BYRNE, "BOBBY" (Robert M.) baseball: b. Dec. 31, 1884, St. Louis; d. Dec. 31, 1964. Bat, throw R; third base. St. Louis NL, 1907–09; Pittsburgh NL, 1909–13; Philadelphia NL, 1913–17; Chicago AL, 1917. Eleven years, 1,282 games, .254 BA. Two World Series, 1909, 1915: 8 games, .240 BA.

On June 8, 1910, he set an ML record for third basemen with 12 assists (11-inning game).

C

CADORE, LEON J. baseball: b. Nov. 20, 1891, Chicago; d. March 16, 1958. Bat, throw R; pitcher. Brooklyn NL, 1915–23; Chicago AL, 1923; New York NL, 1924. Ten years, 68–72, 3.14 ERA. One World Series, 1920: 0–1, 9.00 ERA in 2 innings.

Cadore pitched all the way in Brooklyn's 26-inning, 1–1 tie with Boston on May 1, 1920. He gave up 1 earned run on 15 hits, walking 5 and striking out 7. He also set an NL record for most chances accepted by pitcher, 13.

CALAC, PETER football: b. 1892(?); d. Jan. 14, 1968. Carlisle back. Canton Bulldogs, 1919–20; Cleveland Indians, 1921; Oorang Indians, 1922–23; Buffalo Bisons, 1924; Canton Bulldogs, 1925–26. For all but two years (1924–25) of his football career, Calac was primarily a blocking back for Jim Thorpe.

CALDWELL, "CHARLIE" (Charles W.) football: b. Aug. 2, 1901, Bristol, Va.; d. Nov. 1, 1957. After playing football at Princeton (1925), Caldwell briefly tried pro baseball—he pitched in three games for New York AL in 1925—and then went into coaching. At Williams, he compiled a 76–37–6 record, winning eight "Little Three" titles in 17 seasons, 1928–44. Then he returned to Princeton, 1945–56, compiling a 70–30–3 record. His teams were unbeaten and untied in 1950–51, putting together a 24-game winning streak, and Caldwell was Coach of the Year in 1950. Princeton won the Lambert Trophy as top team in the East in both undefeated seasons. His teams won 3 Ivy League Titles.

Helms Hall of Fame, National Football Foundation Hall of Fame.

CALDWELL, "SLIM" (Raymond B.) baseball: b. April 26, 1888, Corydon, Pa.; d. Aug. 17, 1967. Bat L, throw R; pitcher. New York AL, 1910–18; Boston AL, 1919; Cleveland AL, 1919–21. Twelve years, 134–120, 3.21 ERA; 20–10 in 1920. No-hitter, Sept. 10, 1919, against New York AL (3–0). One World Series, 1920: 0–1.

Caldwell led the AL in pinch-hit at-bats in 1915 with 33; he had 9 hits for a .300 BA.

CALHOUN, GEORGE WHITNEY football: b. Sept. 16, 1890, Green Bay, Wis.; d. Dec. 6, 1963. When a young man named Curly Lambeau, a dropout from Notre Dame, complained that he really missed playing football, Calhoun suggested he start his own team. Calhoun was, at the time, sports editor of the Green Bay newspaper; he was in a unique position to give the new team the publicity it needed. But he did much more.

In a story he christened the team the Packers after uniforms were donated by a packing company. And for years Calhoun, who had been crippled by a football injury in college, was the team's front office. Without pay he served as secretary, public-relations man, traveling secretary, and fundraiser, and, in days before tickets and gates, he passed the hat among the spectators to raise admission money.

CALLAHAN, "NIXEY" (James J.) baseball: b. March 18, 1874, Fitchburg, Mass.; d. Oct. 4, 1934. Bat, throw R; primarily pitcher, 1894–1902; third base, 1903; outfield, 1904–13. Philadelphia NL, 1894; Chicago NL, 1897–1900; Chicago AL, 1901–05, 1911–13. Thirteen years; as pitcher, 99–73, 3.39 ERA; 20–10 in 1898, 21–12 in 1899; as hitter, 923 games, .273 BA. No-hitter, Sept. 20, 1902, against Detroit AL (3–0).

Managed Chicago AL, 1903–04, 1912–14; Pittsburgh NL, 1916–17: 393–458, .462.

CALLOW, "RUSTY" (Russell S.) rowing: b. Aug. 9, 1890, Kamiichie, Wash.; d. Feb. 22, 1961. Callow coached rowing at the University of Washington, 1923–27; his first varsity eight, in 1923, was undefeated and was the first Washington crew to win the Intercollegiate Rowing Association regatta, at Poughkeepsie; his crews also won it in 1924 and 1926. He coached Pennsylvania, 1927–50, and Navy, 1951–59. His Navy crews set what is still a college record by winning 31 consecutive races, 1952–55. The 1952 crew was undefeated and won the Olympic championship. They won both the IRA regatta and the Adams Cup, 1952–54.

Helms Hall of Fame.

CALNAN, GEORGE C. fencing: b. ?; d. April 3, 1933. Calnan was U.S. foil champion, 1925–28 and 1930–31, and épée champion, 1923. He was an Olympic team member, 1928 and 1932.

A Navy lieutenant, he died when the dirigible *Akron* went down in the Pacific.

Helms Hall of Fame.

CAMNITZ, "HOWIE" (Samuel Howard) baseball: b. Aug. 22, 1881, Covington, Ky.; d. March 2, 1960. Bat L, throw R; pitcher. Pittsburgh NL, 1904,

1906–13; Philadelphia NL, 1913; Pittsburgh Fed L, 1914–15. Eleven years, 132–106, 2.75 ERA; 21–15 in 1911, 22–21 in 1912. No-hitter, Aug. 23, 1907, against New York NL (1–0; 5 innings). Led NL in percentage, 1909 (24–6, .800). One World Series, 1909: 0–1, 12.27 ERA, 3⅔ innings.

CAMP, WALTER C. football: b. April 7, 1859, New Haven, Conn.; d. March 14, 1925. Camp is famous for the All-American team he selected for thirty-six years, until his death, but he made more important contributions to the game. He is credited with proposing the idea of the scrimmage line at the 1880 rules conference of the American Intercollegiate Football Association. Until then, American football was a continuous action game, with play stopping only occasionally.

As a freshman at Yale in 1876, Camp helped organize the football team that won the first AIFA championship. He went on to play for six seasons and part of a seventh—he was attending Yale Medical School, and there were no rules limiting eligibility. A halfback, he captained the team, 1878–79 and 1881. Yale was 25–1–6 during his playing career.

After graduating, Camp held the rather nebulous position of "chief football adviser" and was also treasurer of the Yale Field Association, a job similar to that of athletic director in modern terms. He resigned both jobs in 1910 because of the pressures of business.

Camp also came up with the yards-in-downs idea, adopted in 1882, and the loss-of-yardage penalty. He proposed the neutral zone for linemen in 1885, but the rule wasn't adopted until 1906. For years he edited the annual *Football Guide,* in which his All-American selections appeared.

Camp died while attending the 1925 meeting of the Football Rules Committee in New York.

Helms Hall of Fame, National Football Foundation Hall of Fame.

CAMPANELLA, JOSEPH football: b. Sept. 3, 1930, Cleveland; d. Feb. 15, 1967. Ohio State tackle. Dallas Texans, 1952; Baltimore Colts, 1953–57.

CAMPBELL, DAVID C. football: b. Sept. 5, 1873, Waltham, Mass.; d. June 30, 1949. Harvard end; All-American, 1899–1901; captain, 1901. Campbell worked for several years before entering Harvard at the age of twenty-five. An intelligent player, he improvised a buck lateral play that went 60 yards for the only TD in a 6–0 victory over Army in 1901.

Helms Hall of Fame, National Football Foundation Hall of Fame.

CAMPBELL, OLIVER S. tennis: b. ?; d. July 11, 1953. Representing Columbia, Campbell won the national intercollegiate doubles title, 1888–89, with two different partners. At eighteen, he won the U.S. outdoor singles title in 1890 and repeated the following two years. He also won the outdoor

---

doubles, 1888 (with Valentine G. Hall) and 1891–92 (with Robert F. Huntington, Sr.)

Tennis Hall of Fame.

CAMPI, EDDIE boxing: b. DeCampus, July 4, 1893, San Francisco; d. June 20, 1918. His record: 63 wins, 19 by KO; 7 losses, 2 by KO; 8 draws, 22 no-decisions, 1 no-contest. Despite a fine record, Campi never got a bantamweight title fight. He was KOed by Kid Williams in a 1914 bout to determine a challenger for then-champion Johnny Coulon. Williams beat Coulon. Later in the year, Campi lost a tough 20-round decision to Pete Herman, who went on to beat Williams for the title.

Campi died in a hunting accident.

CANNON, "JACK" (John J.) football: b. 1908, Columbus, Ohio; d. Nov. 12, 1967. Notre Dame guard; All-American, 1929. A colorful player who refused to wear a helmet, Cannon played brilliantly in the 7–0 victory over Army in 1929. He kicked off three times and made the tackle each time, and he threw the key block on the 96-yard interception return that won the game.

National Football Foundation Hall of Fame.

CANTWELL, BENJAMIN C. baseball: b. April 13, 1902, Milan, Tenn.; d. Dec. 4, 1962. Bat, throw R; pitcher. New York NL, 1927–28; Boston NL, 1928–36; Brooklyn NL, 1937; New York NL, 1937. Eleven years, 76–108, 3.91 ERA. Led NL in percentage, 1933 (20–10, .667); in losses, 1935 (4–25).

CANZONERI, TONY boxing: b. Nov. 6, 1908, Slidell, La.; d. Dec. 9, 1959. His record: 138 wins, 44 by KO; 29 losses, 1 by KO; 11 draws, 3 no-decisions. Canzoneri won the world featherweight title with a 16-round decision over Benny Bass on Feb. 10, 1928. He lost it Sept. 28, 1928, on a 15-round decision to André Routis.

He became a lightweight soon after and won that title by KOing Al Singer in the 1st round on Nov. 14, 1930. On April 3, 1931, Canzoneri moved up to the junior welterweight title, KOing Jack "Kid" Berg in the 3rd round. He lost the junior welterweight crown to Johnny Jadick in 10 rounds, Jan. 18, 1932, and lost the lightweight title to Barney Ross in 10 rounds on June 23, 1933.

After Ross gave up the title in 1935 because he couldn't make the weight, Canzoneri reclaimed it with a 15-round decision over Lou Ambers, but he lost to Ambers in 15 rounds in 1936.

Boxing Hall of Fame.

CARLIN, JOHN J. rowing: b. 1876(?), Philadelphia; d. Nov. 8, 1968. Carlin was president of the National Association of Amateur Oarsmen for more than twenty-five years and served as vice-president of the International Rowing Federation of North America. He helped Mexican officials set up the rowing course for the 1968 Olympics, then went to the Games on a stretcher because of the illness that killed him shortly afterward.

CARLSON, "DOC" (Harold C.) basketball: b. July 4, 1894, Murray City, Ohio; d. Nov. 1, 1964. Pittsburgh, 1918; captained undefeated, untied football team of 1917.

Coaching basketball at Pitt, 1922–53, he compiled a 370–246 record. His 1928 team had a 21–0 record and won the national championship; his 1930 team, 23–2, was also named national champion. Carlson designed the "Figure Eight," basketball's first patterned offense.

Basketball Hall of Fame, Helms Hall of Fame.

CARLSON, HAROLD G. baseball: b. May 17, 1894, Rockford, Ill.; d. May 28, 1930. Bat, throw R; pitcher. New York NL, 1917–23; Philadelphia NL, 1924–27; Chicago NL, 1927–30. Fourteen years, 114–120, 3.97 ERA. Led NL in shutouts, 1925 (4). One World Series, 1929: 0–0, 6.75 ERA in 4 innings of relief.

CARLSON, "SWEDE" (Adolph D.) bowling: b. June 23, 1897, Konserum, Sweden; d. Jan. 16, 1967. Arriving in the United States at fifteen, he took up bowling a year later. In 1928, he won the match-game title from Charley Daw, defended it once, then lost it to Joe Scribner in 1929. He was second in all-events and doubles in the 1927 ABC tourney. He averaged 195 in 40 ABC tourneys. He had two sanctioned 300 games.

American Bowling Congress Hall of Fame.

CARNERA, PRIMO boxing: b. Oct. 26, 1906, Sequals, Italy; d. June 29, 1967. His record: 86 wins, 66 by KO; 12 losses, 5 by KO; 1 no-contest (both fighters disqualified). One of the most paradoxical of sports careers was that of the 6'6", 260-pound "Ambling Alp," who was briefly heavyweight champion. As champion, he was jeered at by fight fans and observers; but, in that most laughable of sports, professional wrestling, he won more respect than he could ever have hoped to win in the boxing ring.

A wrestler and weightlifter with a small circus in Europe, he was discovered by a French promoter in 1928 and came to the United States in 1929. Within four years, he was fighting for the title. But many suspected, with some reason, that many of his opponents had taken dives. Still, he won the crown with an uppercut that KOed champion Jack Sharkey in the 6th round on June 29, 1933. He lost it in his third defense, being knocked down 12 times before Max Baer was declared the new champion on an 11th-round TKO. Now he was abandoned by the large syndicate that had been formed to guide him to the title, and that had also collected almost all of the money along the way.

Back in Italy, Carnera joined anti-Fascist forces, was captured, and spent most of World War II in a forced-labor camp. He returned to the United States after the war and took up wrestling. At least he made money, and the generally known story of his victimization, first by the syndicate and then by the Fascists, won him a new measure of sympathy and, finally, respect. He became a citizen but returned to his native Italy to die.

CARPENTER, "HICK" (Warren W.) baseball: b. Aug. 16, 1855, Grafton, Mass.; d. April 18, 1937. Bat R, throw L; third base. Syracuse NL, 1879; Cincinnati NL, 1880; Worcester NL, 1881; Cincinnati AA, 1882–89; St. Louis NL, 1892. Twelve years, 1,118 games, .259 BA; hit, .342 in 1882. Led AA in hits, 1882 (120). He went 6-for-7 and scored 5 runs, Sept. 12, 1883.

CARR, "BILLY" (William A.) track: b. Oct. 24, 1909, Pine Bluff, Ark.; d. Jan. 14, 1966. In the 1932 Olympics, Carr raced to a world record of 46.2 seconds in the 400-meter run, setting such a pace that two other runners broke the Olympic record. The time was a world record until 1936, an Olympic record until 1952. Representing Pennsylvania, he won the event in the IC4A and the outdoor AAU championships that year.

Just eight months after his Olympic victory, Carr broke both legs in an auto accident, ending his career.

CARR, JOSEPH F. football: b. Oct. 22, 1880, Columbus, Ohio; d. May 20, 1939. The second president of the National Football League (he replaced Jim Thorpe in 1921), Carr demonstrated his farsightedness when he insisted, in the first year of his presidency, that teams should not sign a college player until his class had graduated. (The rule was not formally adopted by the league until 1926, but Carr enforced it.) When a Milwaukee team in 1925 used four high-school players in a game, Carr demonstrated that he could be tough. He threw the team out of the league, barred the manager for life, and fined the Chicago Cardinal owners for playing against the Milwaukee team.

Carr, who had been manager of the Columbus Panhandles before the NFL was formed, served as president until his death.

Professional Football Hall of Fame.

CARRASQUEL, "ALEX" (Alejandro A. A. E.) baseball: b. July 24, 1912, Caracas, Venezuela; d. Aug. 19, 1969. Bat, throw R; pitcher. Washington AL, 1939–45; Chicago AL, 1949. Eight years, 50–39, 3.73 ERA. In relief, 26–15, 3.50 ERA, 16 saves. Carrasquel was the first South American to play

ML baseball. He was banned from 1945 to 1949 for playing in the outlawed Mexican League.

CARRICK, WILLIAM M. baseball: b. Sept. 5, 1873, Erie, Pa.; d. March 7, 1932. Throw R; pitcher. New York NL, 1898–1900; Washington AL, 1901–02. Five years, 63–89, 4.14 ERA. Led NL in complete games, 1899 (40); in losses, 1900 (19–22).

CARRIGAN, WILLIAM F. ("Rough") baseball: b. Oct. 22, 1883, Lewiston, Maine; d. July 8, 1969. Bat, throw R; catcher. Boston AL, 1906, 1908–16. Ten years, 706 games, .257 BA. Carrigan tied an ML record by catching 3 no-hitters.

Managed Boston AL, 1913–16, 1927–29: 489–500, .494. Pennants, World Series, 1915–16.

CARSEY, "KID" (Wilfred) baseball: b. Oct. 22, 1870, New York City; d. ? Bat, throw R; pitcher. Washington AA, 1891; Philadelphia NL, 1892–97; St. Louis NL, 1897–98; Cleveland, New York, Washington NL, 1899; Brooklyn NL, 1901. Ten years, 116–138, 4.95 ERA; 20–15 in 1893, 24–16 in 1895. Led AA in losses, 1891 (14–37).

CARTMELL, "NATE" (Nathaniel J.) track: b. Jan. 13, 1883, Uniontown, Ky.; d. Aug. 23, 1967. Cartmell swept both short dashes for three consecutive years for the University of Pennsylvania in IC4A competition, winning the 100 and 200 both in 1906–08.

CARTWRIGHT, ALEXANDER J. baseball: b. April 17, 1820, New York City; d. July 12, 1892. If baseball can be said to have had an inventor, it was Cartwright, not Abner Doubleday. A surveyor, Cartwright belonged to the Knickerbocker Club, the first formally organized baseball club in the United States. Late in 1845, the team's first year, Cartwright designed the baseball diamond. The only changes since then are that the pitching distance is now 60 feet, 6 inches, instead of 45 feet, and home plate has moved back into a corner of the diamond; Cartwright had located it out toward the pitcher.

Cartwright headed the committee that drew up the rules of baseball for the Knickerbockers, then umpired the first game played under those rules. In 1849 he joined the gold rush to California and evidently taught the Knickerbockers' version of baseball along the way. He spent most of the rest of his life in Hawaii, where he also popularized the game.

Baseball Hall of Fame.

CARUTHERS, ROBERT L. baseball: b. Jan. 5, 1864, Memphis, Tenn.; d. Aug. 5, 1911. Bat L, throw R; pitcher, outfield. St. Louis AA, 1884–87;

Brooklyn AA, 1888–89; Brooklyn NL, 1890–91; St. Louis NL, 1892; Chicago NL, Cincinnati NL, 1893. Ten years, 705 games, .282 BA; hit .334 in 1886, .357 in 1887; as pitcher, 218–99, 2.83 ERA; 30–14 in 1886, 29–9 in 1887, 29–15 in 1888, 23–11 in 1890. Led league in wins and percentage (40–13, .755), ERA (2.07), and shutouts (6) in 1885; in percentage (29–9, .763) in 1887; in wins and percentage (40–11, .784) and shutouts (7) in 1889.

CARVER, "DOC" (W. F.) shooting: b. 1840, Winslow, Ill.; d. 1927. Carver began his shooting on the plains and as a buffalo hunter. In 1877, he issued a challenge to shoot glass-ball and live-bird matches against anyone in the world. He beat every challenger in the United States and in Europe. During a performance for the Prince of Wales, he broke 14 of 15 glass balls in 15 seconds, broke 100 in a row, then broke 28 out of 30 from a running horse. Carver later became Buffalo Bill's partner in establishing the Wild West Show.

American Trapshooting Hall of Fame.

CASE, EVERETT N. basketball: b. June 21, 1900; d. April 30, 1966. Case built North Carolina State into a basketball power, compiling a 377–133 record, 1947–64. He retired in midseason, right at the end of 1964, because of fatigue.

CASEY, DANIEL M. baseball: b. Oct. 2, 1865, Binghamton, N.Y.; d. Feb. 8, 1943. Bat R, throw L; pitcher. Wilmington UA, 1884; Detroit NL, 1885; Philadelphia NL, 1886–89; Syracuse AA, 1890. Seven years, 96–90, 3.18 ERA. Led NL in ERA (2.86) and shutouts (4) in 1887.

CASEY, "DOC" (Edward) boxing: b. Bridgeport, Conn.; d. March 16, 1966. After playing football at Villanova, Casey became a fighter, then went into training. Among the better-known boxers he handled were Jack Delaney, Battling Battalino, Max Schmeling, Freddie Miller, and Frankie Genaro.

CASEY, EDWARD L. football: b. May 16, 1894, Natick, Mass.; d. July 26, 1966. Harvard halfback; All-American, 1917 (Service Team, Boston Navy Yard), 1919; 2nd team, 1916. Buffalo All-Americans, 1920. Casey coached Tufts, 1922–25, compiling a 15–16–2 record; he moved to Harvard as freshman coach in 1926, then was head coach, 1931–34, compiling a 20–11–1 record.

He coached the Boston Redskins, 1935 (2–8–1), and the Boston Bears, 1940 (AFL; 5–4–1).

National Football Foundation Hall of Fame.

CASEY, HUGH T. baseball: b. Oct. 14, 1913, Atlanta, Ga.; d. July 3, 1951. Bat, throw R; pitcher. Chicago NL, 1935; Brooklyn NL, 1939–42, 1946–48;

New York AL, Pittsburgh NL, 1949. Seven years, 75–42, 3.45 ERA. Primarily a relief pitcher, Casey never had a losing season. In relief, he was 51–20, with 55 saves and a 3.14 ERA. In 1947, he had 18 saves and was 10–4 in relief. Two World Series, 1941, 1947: 2–2, 1.72 ERA. The Dodgers lost, 4 games to 3, to the Yankees in 1947 despite Casey, who appeared in 6 of the games, won 2 of them and saved another, and had an 0.87 ERA.

CASEY, JAMES P. ("Doc") baseball: b. March 15, 1871, Lawrence, Mass.; d. Dec. 30, 1936. Bat L, throw R; third base. Washington NL, 1898–99; Brooklyn NL, 1899–1900; Detroit AL, 1901–02; Chicago NL, 1903–05; Brooklyn NL, 1906–07. Ten years, 1,114 games, .258 BA.

CASEY, PHIL handball: b. Ireland; d. July 12, 1904. Casey came to the United States in 1882 and built the first U.S. handball court in New York City. He won the first informal championship in 1888 by beating Bernard McQuade. Then he won the world title, and a $1,000 side bet, by beating Irish champ John Lawler. Casey defended his title many times before retiring in 1900.

CASSIDY, MARSHALL horse racing: b. Feb. 21, 1892, Washington, D.C.; d. Oct. 23, 1968. Starting as an amateur jockey in 1906, Cassidy worked his way through a variety of jobs to one of the most important of all, as executive secretary of the Jockey Club. He invented the stall starting gate, perfected the photo-finish camera and the film patrol that has made it almost impossible for a jockey to get away with a foul, installed the first electric timing device in the United States, and established the Jockey Club's school for racing officials.

In 1966, he was given the National Turf Writers' award for meritorious service to thoroughbred racing.

CASTER, GEORGE J. baseball: b. Aug. 4, 1907, Colton, Cal.; d. Dec. 18, 1955. Bat, throw R; pitcher. Philadelphia AL, 1934–35, 1937–40; St. Louis AL, 1941–45; Detroit AL, 1945–46. Twelve years, 76–100, 4.54 ERA. In relief, 33–26, 3.78 ERA, and 39 saves. Led AL in losses, 1938 (16–20) and 1940 (4–19), in saves, 1944 (12). One World Series, 1945: 0.00 ERA in ⅔ inning.

CAVANAGH, FRANK W. football: b. April 28, 1876, Worcester, Mass.; d. Aug. 29, 1933. After playing football as an end at Dartmouth, Cavanagh coached Cincinnati, 1898, upsetting his alma mater, 17–14. He received his law degree, then coached Holy Cross, 1903–05, and Dartmouth, 1911–16. His 1913 team was 7–0–1 and the 1914 team was 8–1–0.

He won his nickname, "The Iron Major," during World War I, when he was severely wounded by shrapnel. The injury was to help bring about his relatively early death.

Cavanagh then coached Boston College, 1919–26, producing an undefeated team (8–0–0) in 1920. But his greatest fame came at Fordham, 1927–32. The 1929 team was tied once, and the 1930–31 teams each lost a game; the overall record for those three seasons was 23–2–2. The strong defensive line of 1929–30 won the name The Seven Blocks of Granite, a phrase that was revived for the 1936 Fordham line.

Though listed as coach in 1932, Cavanagh was ill, and the coaching was actually done by his assistant, Hiker Joy.

National Football Foundation Hall of Fame.

CAWTHON, PETE football: b. March 24, 1898, Houston; d. Dec. 30, 1962. A baseball-basketball star at Rice, Cawthon made his name as a football coach. At Austin College, 1923–27, he had a 22–19–4 record. At Texas Tech, 1930–41, he was 70–27; his 1932 team was the highest scoring in the country, rolling up 382 points while winning 10 of 12 games. Texas Tech lost the 1939 Cotton Bowl, 20–13, to St. Mary's.

Cawthon coached the Brooklyn Dodgers, 1943–44 (2–18).

CHADWICK, HENRY baseball: b. Oct. 6, 1824, Exeter, England; d. April 20, 1908. Baseball was played under different rules in different places until 1858, when 25 teams formed the National Association. Chadwick, a New York newspaperman, compiled the first official rule book and, until 1870, served as chairman of the association's rules committee. In 1881 he became editor of *Spalding's Baseball Guide*. Chadwick is also credited with inventing the scorer's system still in use.

Baseball Hall of Fame.

CHAMBERLAIN, "ICE BOX" (Elton P.) baseball: b. Nov. 5, 1867, Warsaw, N.Y.; d. Sept. 24, 1929. Bat, throw R; pitcher. Louisville AA, 1886–88; St. Louis AA, 1888–90; Columbus AA, 1890; Philadelphia AA, 1891; Cincinnati NL, 1892–94; Cleveland NL, 1896. Ten years, 157–120, 3.57 ERA; 25–11 in 1888, 32–15 in 1889, 22–23 in 1891. No-hitter, July 23, 1893, against Boston NL (6–0; 7 innings). Led AA in shutouts, 1890 (6).

CHAMBERLIN, GUY (Berlin Guy) football: b. Jan. 16, 1894, Blue Springs, Nebr.; d. April 4, 1967. Nebraska halfback. Pro end, Decatur Staleys, 1920; Chicago Staleys, 1921; Canton Bulldogs, 1922–23; Cleveland Indians, 1924; Frankford Yellowjackets, 1925–26; Chicago Cardinals, 1927.

Chamberlin spent five years as a playing coach and won championships 4 times. His Canton teams won titles, 1922–23, without ever losing a game; they were 10–0–2 and 11–0–1. The franchise moved to Cleveland in 1924 and again won the NFL championship, with a 7–1–1 record. In 1925–26, Chamberlin coached Frankford; they were 13–7–0 his first year and won the title with a 14–1–1 record in 1926. After retiring as a player, Chamberlin coached the Chicago Cardinals in 1928; they were 1–5–0, his only losing season. His overall professional coaching record was 66–14–5, an .825 percentage.

Helms Hall of Fame, National Football Foundation Hall of Fame, Professional Football Hall of Fame.

CHANCE, FRANK L. ("Husk") baseball: b. Sept. 9, 1877, Fresno, Cal.; d. Sept. 14, 1924. Bat, throw R; first base, catcher. Chicago NL, 1898–1912; New York AL, 1913–14. Seventeen years, 1,285 games, 4,294 at-bats, 1,272 hits, 194 doubles, 79 triples, 20 home runs, 797 runs, 596 RBI, 401 stolen bases, .296 BA; hit .327 in 1903, .310 in 1904, .316 in 1905, .319 in 1906. Led NL in runs, 1906 (103); stolen bases, 1903 (67) and 1906 (57).

Chance was moved from behind the plate to first base in 1902 and he stayed there for the rest of his career. He became famous as the third man in the Tinker-to-Evers-to-Chance double-play combination, but he was also known as the Peerless Leader for guiding the Cubs to 4 pennants in a five-year span as playing manager. He got the job in the middle of the 1905 season because of his leadership ability on the field. He managed the Cubs through 1912, winning pennants, 1906–08 and 1910, and the World Series, 1907–08. He also managed New York AL, 1913–14 (part) and Boston AL, 1923. His overall record: 932–640, .593 (6th).

In those four World Series, 20 games, he hit .310, with 10 stolen bases (3rd). In the Cubs' 5–game win over Detroit in 1908, he hit .421, stole 5 bases, scored 4 runs, and had 2 RBI. After 1912, he played very little, partly because of chronic headaches caused by having been beaned several times.

Baseball Hall of Fame.

CHANDLER, TOM boxing: b. Nov. 6, 1842, Waterford, Ireland; d. Aug. 11, 1938. Chandler, who had only four recorded fights, KOed Dooney Harris, April 13, 1867, for the middleweight title. However, he refused to face challenger George Rooke and never fought again. He won 3 of his fights, drew the other.

CHANEY, GEORGE ("Kayo") boxing: b. 1893, Baltimore; d. Dec. 20, 1958. His record: 109 wins, 86 by KO; 17 losses, 8 by KO; no draws, 55 no-decisions. Though he began as a bantamweight and was never more than a lightweight, Chaney was a powerful puncher, as his nickname implies. He had 86 KOs in 181 bouts. He fought once for a title, Sept. 4, 1916, but was KOed by featherweight champion Johnny Kilbane in the 3rd round.

CHAPMAN, "JACK" (John C.) baseball: b. May 8, 1843, Brooklyn; d. June 10, 1916. Throw R; outfield. National Association, Brooklyn, 1874; St. Louis, 1875. Two years, 96 games, .253 BA. Louisville NL, 1876. Seventeen games, .239 BA.

Managed Louisville NL, 1877; Milwaukee NL, 1878; Worcester NL, 1882 (part); Detroit NL, 1883–84; Buffalo NL, 1885 (part); Louisville NL, 1889 (part)–92 (part): 306–428, .417. Pennant, 1890.

CHAPMAN, RAYMOND W. baseball: b. Jan. 15, 1891, Beaver Dam, Ky.; d. Aug. 17, 1920. Bat, throw R; shortstop. Cleveland AL, 1912–20. Nine years, 1,050 games, 233 stolen bases, .278 BA; hit .302 in 1917, .300 in 1919, .303 in 1920. Led AL in runs and walks, 1914 (84 of each).

Chapman was the only player ever killed in a major-league game; he died after being hit in the head by a pitch from the New York Yankees' Carl Mays.

CHASE, "HAL" (Harold H.) baseball: b. Feb. 13, 1883, Los Gatos, Calif.; d. May 18, 1947. Bat R, throw L; first base. New York AL, 1905–13; Chicago AL, 1913–14; Buffalo Fed L, 1914–15; Cincinnati NL, 1916–18; New York NL, 1919. Fifteen years, 1,917 games, 2,158 hits, 363 stolen bases, .291 BA; hit .323 in 1906, .315 in 1911, .314 in 1914. Led league in hits (184) and BA (.339) in 1916; in home runs, 1915 (17).

Prince Hal holds the record in both leagues for most chances accepted in a doubleheader (AL, 38 in 1905; NL, 35 in 1919) and is a coholder of the ML record for most putouts in a 9-inning game, 22.

Managed New York AL, 1910 (part), 1911: 85–78, .521.

Acquitted of a charge of attempted bribery to fix a game in 1919, Chase was implicated in another, similar case the following year. Though not formally banned, he never played major-league baseball again.

CHENEY, LAURANCE R. baseball: b. May 2, 1886, Belleville, Kan.; d. Jan. 6, 1969. Bat, throw R; pitcher. Chicago NL, 1911–15; Brooklyn NL, 1915–19; Boston NL, Philadelphia NL, 1919. Nine years, 115–100, 2.70 ERA; 20–14 in 1913, 20–18 in 1914. Led NL in percentage (26–10, .722) and complete games (28) in 1912; in saves (11) in 1913.

CHESBRO, "HAPPY JACK" (John D.) baseball: b. June 5, 1874, North Adams, Mass.; d. Nov. 6, 1931. Bat, throw R; pitcher. Pittsburgh NL, 1899–1902; New York AL, 1903–09; Boston AL, 1909. Eleven years, 196–131, 2.68 ERA; 332 games, 261 complete, 35 shutouts, 1,265 strikeouts in 2,897 innings; 21–10 in 1901, 21–16 in 1903, 20–15 in 1905, 22–16 in 1906. Led NL in shutouts, 1901 (6), and in shutouts (8), victories, and percentage (28–6, .824) in 1902; led AL in victories and percentage (41–13, .824), starts (51), complete games (48), and innings (454 ⅔) in 1904.

Chesbro was the only pitcher ever to lead both leagues in percentage. His 41 wins in 1904 is the modern ML record. He also set AL records for most starts, 51, and most complete games, 48, that season.

Baseball Hall of Fame.

CHEVIGNY, JACK football: b. near Hammond, Ind.; d. Feb. 19, 1945. Notre Dame halfback, 1928. Coached Chicago Cardinals, 1932 (2–6–2); University of Texas, 1934–36 (14–14–2).

Chevigny was killed during the invasion of Iwo Jima.

CHILDS, "CUPID" (Clarence A.) baseball: b. Aug. 14, 1868, Calvert County, Md.; d. Nov. 8, 1912. Bat L, throw R; second base. Philadelphia NL, 1888; Syracuse AA, 1890; Cleveland NL, 1891–98; St. Louis NL, 1899; Chicago NL, 1900–01. Thirteen years, 1,455 games, .306 BA; hit .345 in 1890, .317 in 1892, .326 in 1893, .353 in 1894, .355 in 1896, .338 in 1897. Led league in doubles, 1890 (33); in runs, 1892 (136).

Childs set an ML record for second basemen by handling 18 chances in a 9-inning game on June 1, 1890.

CHIP, GEORGE boxing: b. George Chipulonis, Aug. 25, 1888, Scranton, Pa.; d. Nov. 6, 1960. His record: 38 wins, 34 by KO; 16 losses, 3 by KO; 3 draws, 97 no-decisions, 1 no-contest. Chip won the middleweight title, Oct. 11, 1913, with a 6-round KO of Frank Klaus. He lost it, April 6, 1914, when Al McCoy KOed him in the 1st.

CHOYNSKI, JOE boxing: b. Nov. 8, 1868, San Francisco; d. Jan. 25, 1943. His record: 50 wins, 25 by KO; 14 losses, 10 by KO; 6 draws, 8 no-decisions, 1 no-contest. Choynski turned pro in 1888 after winning the Pacific Coast amateur title. He quickly became a stepping stone for Jim Corbett, who KOed him and won a decision from him in two 1889 fights. Choynski's biggest victory was a 3rd-round KO of Jack Johnson in 1901. He also fought, at one time or another, Bob Fitzsimmons, Tom Sharkey, Jim Jeffries, Marvin Hart, and Philadelphia Jack O'Brien.

Boxing Hall of Fame.

CHRISTENSEN, "CHRIS" (George W.) football: b. Dec. 1909, Pendleton, Ore.; d. July 1, 1968. Oregon tackle. Portsmouth Spartans, 1931–33; Detroit Lions, 1934–38.

CHRISTMAN, PAUL J. football: b. March 5, 1918, St. Louis; d. March 2, 1970. Missouri tailback; All-American, 1939 (Rice). Quarterback, Chicago Cardinals, 1945–49; Green Bay Packers, 1950.

In 1938, Nebraska kicked a field goal early in the game and seemed to be on its way to a twelfth straight victory over Missouri. Then a blond sophomore tailback took over. In four plays, three of them completed passes, he took Missouri 75 yards to a TD and to an eventual 13–10 upset. The following year, Nebraska was again favored in the traditional game. Now a junior, Paul Christman told a sportswriter beforehand, "I'll pass the bums out of the stadium by the half."

He threw three TD passes in the first half and Missouri went on to win, 27–13. It was Nebraska's only defeat in 1939.

The story is typical of Christman, the "Merry Magician." He could be brash and cocky, but he was at his best in the big games. Despite an injury in his senior year, he set what was then a conference record of 4,133 yards in total offense, averaging 4 yards a carry and completing 195 of 426 passes.

His pro career was delayed by World War II. At Chicago, he was one-fourth of the Cardinals' "Dream Backfield": Elmer Angsman and Charlie Trippi at the halves, Marshall Goldberg at fullback. In 1947, the Cards won their first NFL championship. In 1948, they won the division but lost the title playoff to the Philadelphia Eagles, 7–0.

Christman's 6-year NFL record: Completed 504 of 1,140 passes, 44.2 percent, for 7,294 yards and 58 TDs, a 6.40-yard-per-attempt average.

National Football Foundation Hall of Fame.

CHRISTOPHER, RUSSELL O. baseball: b. Sept. 12, 1907, Richmond, Cal.; d. Dec. 5, 1954. Bat, throw R; pitcher. Philadelphia AL, 1942–47; Cleveland AL, 1948. Seven years, 54–64, 3.37 ERA. Led AL in saves, 1948 (17).

CHRISTY, RICHARD football: b. ? Chester, Pa.; d. Aug. 7, 1966. North Carolina State halfback. Pittsburgh Steelers, 1958; Boston Patriots (AFL), 1960; New York Titans (AFL), 1961–62; New York Jets (AFL), 1963. In four AFL years, he carried the ball 299 times for 1,166 yards, a 3.9 average, and 10 TDs; he returned 125 punts for 1,400 yards, an 11.2 average, and 6 TDs.

He was killed in a car crash.

CICOTTE, "EDDIE" (Edward V.) baseball: b. June 19, 1884, Detroit; d. May 5, 1969. Sw. hit, throw R; pitcher. Detroit AL, 1905; Boston AL, 1908–12; Chicago AL, 1912–20. Fourteen years, 207–147, 2.37 ERA; 35 shutouts; 21–10 in 1920. Led AL in percentage, 1916 (15–7, .682); in victories (28–12) and ERA (1.53) in 1917; in losses (12–19) in 1918; in victories and percentage (29–7, .806) and complete games (29) in 1919. Two World Series, 1917, 1919: 2–3, 2.42 ERA. Cicotte won the opener 2–1 in 1917 but lost the third game 2–0 as the White Sox beat the Giants 4 games to 2. He struck out 13 in 23 innings, including 6 innings of relief. His downfall came in 1919. He gave Cincinnati 5 runs in the fourth inning of the opener for a 9–1 loss, then made 2 errors in the fifth inning of the fourth game, allowing both runs in a 2–0 loss. He pitched well in a 4–1 victory in the seventh game, but the Reds beat Chicago, 5 games to 3. Cicotte was one of eight Chicago players banned from baseball after the 1920 season for allegedly conspiring to throw the 1919 series in what is known as the Black Sox Scandal.

CISSELL, "BILL" (Chalmer William) baseball: b. Jan. 3, 1904, Perryville, Mo.; d. March 15, 1949. Bat, throw R; second base, shortstop. Chicago AL, 1928–32; Cleveland AL, 1932–33; Boston AL, 1934; Philadelphia AL, 1937; New York NL, 1938. Nine years, 956 games, .267 BA; hit .315 in 1932.

CLAPP, JOHN E. baseball: b. July 17, 1851, Ithaca, N.Y.; d. Dec. 17, 1904. Bat, throw R; catcher. National Association, Middletown, 1872; Philadelphia, 1873–75. Four years, 163 games, .284 BA; hit .306 in 1872, .331 in 1874.

St. Louis NL, 1876–77; Indianapolis NL, 1878; Buffalo NL, 1879; Cincinnati NL, 1880; Cleveland NL, 1881; New York NL, 1883. Seven years, 425 games, .283 BA; hit .305 in 1876, .318 in 1877, .304 in 1878.

Managed Indianapolis NL, 1878; Buffalo NL, 1879; Cincinnati NL, 1880; New York NL, 1883: 137–177, .436.

CLARK, ELLERY H. track: b. Mar. 13, 1874, West Roxbury, Mass.; d. July 27, 1949. Shortly after graduating from Harvard, Clark became a member of the Boston AA team that went to the first modern Olympics, in Greece in 1896. He won the running broad jump and running high jump. He was all-around champion of the United States in 1897 and 1903.

CLARK, JOSEPH S. tennis: b. ?; d. April 15, 1956. Representing Harvard, Clark won the first national intercollegiate singles championship in 1883, teaming with H. A. Taylor to win the doubles as well. In 1885, he and Richard D. Sears won the U.S. outdoor doubles.

Tennis Hall of Fame.

CLARKE, "BOILERYARD" (William J.) baseball: b. Oct. 18, 1868, New York City; d. July 29, 1959. Bat, throw R; catcher. Baltimore NL, 1893–98; Boston NL, 1899–1900; Washington AL, 1901–04; New York NL, 1905. Thirteen years, 950 games, .256 BA; hit .315 in 1900.

CLARKE, FREDERICK C. baseball: b. Oct. 3, 1872, Winterset, Iowa; d. Aug. 14, 1960. Bat L, throw R; outfield. Louisville NL, 1894–99; Pittsburgh NL, 1900–11, 1913–15. Twenty-one years, 2,242 games, 8,568 at-bats, 2,672 hits, 361 doubles, 220 triples (7th), 67 home runs, 1,619 runs, 506 stolen bases, .312 BA; hit .347 in 1895, .325 in 1896, .390 in 1897, .307 in 1898,

.342 in 1899, .324 in 1901, .316 in 1902, .351 in 1903, .306 in 1904, .309 in 1906, .324 in 1911. Led NL in doubles (32) and slugging (.532) in 1903; in triples, 1906 (13). Two World Series, 1903, 1909: 15 games; 2 doubles, 1 triple, 2 home runs, 10 runs, 4 stolen bases, 9 RBI; .245 BA.

Clarke got 5 hits in his first ML game, the only player ever to do so. On Aug. 23, 1910, he set an NL record for most assists by an outfielder in a 9-inning game with 4.

He managed Louisville NL, 1897–99; Pittsburgh NL, 1900–15: 1,602 wins (9th), 1,179 losses, .576 (9th). Pennants, 1901–03, 1909; world championship, 1909.

Baseball Hall of Fame.

CLARKSON, JOHN G. baseball: b. July 1, 1861, Cambridge, Mass.; d. Feb. 4, 1909. Bat, throw R; pitcher. Worcester NL, 1882; Chicago NL, 1884–87; Boston NL, 1888–92; Cleveland NL, 1892–94. Twelve years, 327 wins (9th), 177 losses, 2.81 ERA; 518 starts, 485 complete (8th), 4,536 innings, 4,295 hits, 1,191 walks, 1,978 strikeouts, 37 shutouts; 36–17 in 1886, 25–18 in 1890, 33–19 in 1891, 25–16 in 1892. No-hitter, July 28, 1885, against Providence NL (4–0). Led NL in wins (53–16), complete games (68), innings (623), strikeouts (308), and shutouts (10) in 1885; in wins (38–21), complete games (56), innings (523), and strikeouts (237) in 1887; in wins (33–20), innings (483⅓) in 1888; in wins and percentage (49–19, .721), ERA (2.73), complete games (68), innings (620), strikeouts (284), and shutouts (8) in 1889.

Clarkson was one of the strongest-armed pitchers in an era full of strong arms. Six times he won more than 30 games, including five years in a row; in one of those seasons he won 49, in another 53. Yet his secret was not really a strong arm but a curve ball; he had such long fingers that throwing a curve put less strain on the rest of his arm than it would on another pitcher's.

Clarkson had a problem with temperament. When his arm finally gave out, despondency set in. He died in a mental hospital.

Baseball Hall of Fame.

CLEMENTS, "JACK" (John T.) baseball: b. June 24, 1864, Philadelphia; d. May 23, 1941. Bat, throw L; catcher. Philadelphia UA, 1884; Philadelphia NL, 1884–97; St. Louis NL, 1898; Cleveland NL, 1899; Boston NL, 1900. Seventeen years, 1,157 games, .286 BA; hit .315 in 1890, .310 in 1891, .394 in 1895.

CLOTHIER, WILLIAM J. tennis: b. 1882(?); d. Sept. 5, 1962. Clothier won the national outdoor singles title in 1906; he had lost in the finals in 1904.

In 1902, representing Harvard, he was intercollegiate singles champion and teamed with E. W. Leonard to win the doubles. He was the first president of the Tennis Hall of Fame at Newport, Rhode Island.

Tennis Hall of Fame.

COAKLEY, "ANDY" (Andrew J.) baseball: b. Nov. 20, 1882, Providence, R.I.; d. Sept. 27, 1963. Bat L, throw R; pitcher. Philadelphia AL, 1902–06; Cincinnati NL, 1907–08; Chicago NL, 1908–09; New York AL, 1911. Nine years, 61–58, 2.36 ERA. He led the AL in wins and percentage (20–6, .769) in 1905. One World Series, 1905: 0–1, 2.00 ERA.

COBB, "TY" (Tyrus R.) baseball: b. Dec. 18, 1886, Narrows, Ga.; d. July 17, 1961. Bat L, throw R; outfield. Detroit AL, 1905–26; Philadelphia AL, 1927–28.

Only Cobb or Honus Wagner could possibly challenge Babe Ruth for the title of baseball's greatest player. The man you choose would depend on your taste: For power, you would pick Ruth; for versatility, Wagner. But if your criterion is the drive to win, Cobb might well be your man. He combined sheer native ability with an incredible desire to win. His long-time teammate Sam Crawford once said of him, "He came up from the South, you know, and he was still fighting the Civil War. . . . Well, who knows, maybe if he hadn't had that persecution complex, he would never have been the great ballplayer he was. He was always trying to prove he was the best."

Cobb's record, like Ruth's, almost defies analysis. He led the AL in every major hitting category at one time or another. In 1911, he led in 12 of them, the only AL player ever to do so. He won the triple crown in 1909. After hitting only .240 (in 41 games) in his rookie year, he hit over .300 in 23 consecutive seasons, a record; no other player has done it more than 17 years in a row. He holds all-time ML records for games, 3,034; at-bats, 11,437; runs, 2,245; hits, 4,192; singles, 3,052; and BA, .367. His 890 stolen bases is the modern record. He is second all-time in doubles (725), triples (294), and total bases (5,863) and fourth in RBI (1,933). He tied an ML record by hitting over .400 three times, twice in a row. His 26 steals of home is also a record; he did it 6 times in 1915, an AL record broken in 1969 by Rod Carew, and he did it 3 times in 1925, when he was forty.

He is holder or coholder of the following ML records: most years 200 or more hits, 9; most years led league in hitting, 12, most consecutive, 9; most years led league in hits, 8, most consecutive, 3; most consecutive years led in RBI, 3; most times 5 hits in a game, 14, most times in one season, 4 (1922); most years 20 or more triples, 4; most times stealing from first to home, 3; most times stealing home in one game, 2 (June 18, 1915); most consecutive years with one team, 22.

He is also holder or coholder of these AL records: most years played 100 or more games, 19; highest BA over 5-year period, .397 (1909–13); most total bases in game, 16 (May 15, 1925, when Cobb went 6-for-6 with a double and 3 home runs); most years leading in total bases, 6, most consecutive, 3.

His year-by-year BA record, 1906–28 (L indicates led league): .313, .350 (L), .324 (L), .377 (L), .385 (L), .420 (L), .410 (L), .390 (L), .368 (L), .369 (L), .371, .383 (L), .382 (L), .384 (L), .334, .389, .401, .340, .338, .378, .339, .357, .323. Other categories in which he led the league: hits (212), RBI (119), stolen bases (49), slugging (.468), in 1907; hits (188), doubles (36), triples (20), RBI (108), slugging (.475), in 1908; hits (216), home runs (9), runs (116), RBI (107), stolen bases (76), slugging (.517), in 1909; runs (106), slugging (.554), in 1910; hits (248), doubles (47), triples (24), runs (147), RBI (127), stolen bases (83), slugging (.621), in 1911; hits (227), slugging (.586), in 1912; slugging (.513) in 1914; hits (208), runs (144), stolen bases (96), in 1915; runs (113), stolen bases (68), in 1916; hits (225), doubles (44), triples (23), stolen bases (55), slugging (.571), in 1917; triples (14) in 1918; hits (191) in 1919.

Three World Series, 1907–09: 17 games, .262 BA. Cobb had one outstanding World Series, in 1908, when the Tigers lost to Chicago; he hit .368, with 3 runs and 4 RBI (the Tigers had only 15 runs).

Cobb managed Detroit, 1921–26: 479–444, .519.

Baseball Hall of Fame.

COCHEMS, "EDDIE" (Edward B.) football: b. 1876(?), Madison, Wis.; d. April 9, 1953. Cochems starred as a halfback at Wisconsin; he turned in a 100-yard run against Chicago in 1901. He coached at Clemson, 1904–05, then won his nickname, the Father of the Forward Pass, at St. Louis University in 1906, the first year the pass was legal. Cochems took full advantage of it, way ahead of most coaches. He did it so well that St. Louis had an 11–0 record and rolled up 407 points that year, an average of 37 a game. In beating Kansas, St. Louis scored on passes of 48 and 45 yards.

COCHRAN, WELKER billiards: b. Oct. 7, 1896, Manson, Iowa; d. July 28, 1960. Cochran was world professional champion in three-cushion billiards, 1933, 1935, 1937–38, 1944–46, and in 18.2 balkline, 1927 and 1934. In 1926 he set an exhibition record for 18.2 with a run of 684. The following year, he set 18.1 balkline exhibition records for high run (353), high single average (150), and high grand average (61). He also set a three-cushion record, in a 1945 match, of 60 in 20 innings.

COCHRANE, "MICKEY" (Gordon S.) baseball: b. April 6, 1903, Bridgewater, Mass.; d. June 28, 1962. Bat L, throw R; catcher. Philadelphia AL,

1925–33; Detroit AL, 1934–37. Thirteen years, 1,482 games, 5,169 at-bats, 1,652 hits, 333 doubles, 64 triples, 119 home runs, 1,041 runs, 832 RBI, .320 BA; hit .331 in 1925, .338 in 1927, .331 in 1929, .357 in 1930, .349 in 1931, .322 in 1933, .320 in 1934, .319 in 1935.

Cochrane tied an ML record by getting 2 hits and scoring 2 runs in a single inning as a pinch-hitter on Aug. 8, 1932. He hit 3 home runs in a game on May 21, 1925.

Five World Series, 1929–31, 1934–35: 31 games, 17 runs, 25 walks (6th), .245 BA. He hit .400 in the Athletics' 5-game win over Chicago in 1929. In 1930 he hit home runs in both the first and second games during the As' 6-game triumph. In 1935 he singled and scored the winning run in the ninth inning of the sixth and deciding game as Detroit beat the Cubs.

Like many of the playing managers, he was a fiery field leader. He managed Detroit, 1934–38: 413–297, .582. Pennants, 1934–35; world championship, 1935.

Baseball Hall of Fame.

COFFROTH, JAMES W. boxing: b. Sept. 12, 1874, Sacramento, Calif.; d. Feb. 6, 1943. One of boxing's first real promoters, Coffroth was instrumental in bringing major bouts to the West Coast. As a young lawyer he saw some fights in New York and decided to become a promoter in San Francisco. Among his major fights were the second Jim Corbett–Jim Jeffries bout, 1903; Philadelphia Jack O'Brien's win over Bob Fitzsimmons, 1905; Stanley Ketchel's championship victory over Jack "Twin" Sullivan, 1908; and his defense of the title against Billy Papke in the same year.

COHALAN, "NEIL" (Cornelius J.) basketball: b. ?, New York City; d. Jan. 22, 1968. An 11-letter man in four sports at Manhattan College, Cohalan coached basketball there, 1929–42, compiling a 165–80 record. He served in the Navy during World War II, then coached the New York Knickerbockers, 1946–47, with the understanding that Joe Lapchick would take over the following season. He had a 33–27 record with the Knicks.

COLE, "KING" (Leonard L.) baseball: b. April 15, 1886, Toledo, Iowa; d. Jan. 6, 1916. Bat, throw R; pitcher. Chicago NL, 1909–12; Pittsburgh NL, 1912; New York AL, 1914–15. Six years, 56–27, 3.12 ERA. Led NL in percentage, 1910 (21–4, .840). One World Series, 1910: 0–0, 3.38 ERA in 8 innings.

COLEMAN, GEORGIA diving: b. 1912, Los Angeles; d. Sept. 14, 1940. The 1932 Olympic springboard champion, Miss Coleman won the U.S. outdoor springboard and platform titles, 1929–31. She was indoor 10-foot springboard champ, 1929–32, 3-foot champion, 1931. Miss Coleman contracted polio in 1937 but learned to swim all over again before her death, which was caused by pneumonia.

Helms Hall of Fame, Swimming Hall of Fame.

COLLINS, "EDDIE" (Edward T., "Cocky") baseball: b. May 2, 1887, Millerton, N.Y.; d. March 25, 1951. Bat L, throw R; second base. Philadelphia AL, 1906–14; Chicago AL, 1915–26; Philadelphia AL, 1927–30. Twenty-five years, 2,825 games (3rd), 9,949 at-bats (6th), 437 doubles, 187 triples, 47 home runs, 1,817 runs (7th), 1,299 RBI, 1,503 walks (8th), 743 stolen bases (5th), .333 BA.

Connie Mack called Collins "the greatest second baseman who ever lived." Another second baseman, Frank Frisch, went further: "Eddie Collins was the greatest infielder I ever saw." Collins's hitting figures help bear out Frisch; so do his fielding records: He holds the ML record for most times leading league in fielding at his position, 9, and for most career putouts and assists at second base. On Sept. 11, 1912, he set a modern record by stealing 6 bases in a game. He holds the record for most career sacrifices, 511, and was also an expert at using the bunt to get on base.

Collins led the AL in runs, 1912 (137), 1913 (125), and 1914 (122); in walks, 1915 (119); in stolen bases, 1910 (81), 1919 (33), 1923 (47), and 1924 (42). He hit over .300 in 17 seasons, including nine in a row: .346 in 1909, .322 in 1910, .365 in 1911, .348 in 1912, .345 in 1913, .344 in 1914, .332 in 1915, .308 in 1916, .319 in 1919, .369 in 1920, .337 in 1921, .324 in 1922, .360 in 1923, .349 in 1924, .346 in 1925, .344 in 1926, .338 in 1927.

In six World Series, 1910–11, 1913–14, 1917, 1919, 34 games, he hit .328. His 14 stolen bases is a record, his 7 doubles is 4th, his 42 hits 8th; he walked 10 times, scored 20 runs, and drove in 11. In Philadelphia's 5-game win over Chicago in 1910, he hit .429 with 4 doubles, 4 stolen bases, 5 runs, and 3 RBI; in their 5-game win over the Giants in 1913, he hit .421 with 5 runs, 3 RBI, and 3 stolen bases.

Managed Chicago AL, 1925–26: 160 wins, 147 losses, .521.

Baseball Hall of Fame.

COLLINS, "JIMMY" (James J.) baseball: b. Jan. 16, 1870, Buffalo, N.Y.; d. March 6, 1943. Bat, throw R; third base. Louisville NL, 1895; Boston NL, 1896–1900; Boston AL, 1901–07; Philadelphia AL, 1907–08. Fourteen years, 1,728 games, .294 BA; hit .346 in 1897, .328 in 1898, .304 in 1900, .332 in 1901, .322 in 1902. Led NL in home runs, 1898 (15).

Collins got an even 2,000 hits during his career. He holds ML records at third base for most career putouts and most putouts in a season (252 in 1900), he holds the NL record for most chances in a season (601 in 1899), and he tied the AL record for most chances in a game, 14 (15 innings).

Managed Boston AL, 1901–06 (part): 469–389, .544. Pennants, 1903–04. His team won the first World Series in 1903, over the Pittsburgh Pirates. (There was no 1904 Series.)

Baseball Hall of Fame.

COLLINS, PHILIP E. baseball: b. Aug. 27, 1900, Rockford, Ill.; d. Aug. 14, 1948. Bat, throw R; pitcher. Chicago NL, 1923; Philadelphia NL, 1929–35; St. Louis NL, 1935. Eight years, 80–85, 4.66 ERA.

COLLINS, RAYMOND W. baseball: b. Feb. 11, 1887, Colchester, Vt.; d. Jan. 9, 1970. Bat, throw L; pitcher. Boston AL, 1909–15. Seven years, 89–62, 2.51 ERA; 20 shutouts; 20–8 in 1913, 20–13 in 1914. One World Series, 1912: 2 games, 0–0, 1.88 ERA.

Collins had great success pitching to Ty Cobb; he once walked another hitter in order to pitch to Cobb.

COLLINS, "RIP" (Henry W.) baseball: b. Feb. 26, 1896, Weatherford, Tex.; d. May 27, 1968. Sw. hit, throw R; pitcher. New York AL, 1920–21; Boston AL, 1922; Detroit AL, 1923–27; St. Louis AL, 1929–31. Eleven years, 108–82, 3.99 ERA. One World Series, 1921: 0–0, 54.00 ERA in ⅔ inning.

COLLINS, "RIPPER" (James A.) baseball: b. March 30, 1904, Altoona, Pa.; d. April 16, 1970. Sw. hit, throw L; first base. St. Louis NL, 1931–36; Chicago NL, 1937–38; Pittsburgh NL, 1941. Nine years, 1,084 games, .296 BA; hit .310 in 1933, .333 in 1934, .313 in 1935. Led NL in home runs (35) and slugging (.615) in 1934. Three World Series, 1931, 1934, 1938: 13 games, .277 BA. He hit .367 with 4 runs and 4 RBI in 1934, as the Cardinals beat Detroit in 7 games.

COLLINS, "SHANO" (John F.) baseball: b. Dec. 4, 1885, Charlestown, Mass.; d. Sept. 10, 1955. Bat, throw R; outfield. Chicago AL, 1910–20; Boston AL, 1921–25. Sixteen years, 1,695 games, .262 BA; hit .303 in 1920. Two World Series, 1917, 1919: 10 games, .270 BA.

Managed Boston AL, 1931–32 (part): 73–136, .349.

COLLYER, SAM boxing: b. Walter Jamieson, 1842, England; d. Dec. 7, 1904. Collyer served with the Union Army during the Civil War, winning the Congressional Medal of Honor. He turned to boxing after the war, winning the lightweight title in a 47-round bout with Young Barney Aaron, June 20, 1866. On June 13, 1867, Aaron regained the title in 67 rounds but then retired, and Collyer claimed it again. After one defense, he lost to Billy Edwards in 47 rounds on Aug. 24, 1868.

Boxing Hall of Fame.

COMISKEY, CHARLES A. ("Commy") baseball: b. Aug. 15, 1889, Chicago; d. Oct. 26, 1931. The founder of the Chicago White Sox began his ML career as a right-handed first baseman for St. Louis AA in 1882. He was player-manager in 1883 and 1885–89, winning 4 straight pennants, 1885–88. In 1890 he joined the Chicago entry in the Players League, moving back to St. Louis in 1891 and then joining Cincinnati NL, 1892–94, serving as player-manager at all these stops. As a player, he compiled a .264 BA in 13 seasons and 1,390 games. He hit .335 and stole 117 bases in 1887 and had a career total of 378 stolen bases, not counting the 1882–86 period, when such statistics weren't compiled. His managerial record for eleven years was 824 wins, 533 losses, .607 (3rd).

After retiring as a player, "The Old Roman" acquired the St. Paul franchise in the Western League, working closely with Ban Johnson to gain major-league status for that circuit. In 1900, when the name was changed to the American League, Comiskey moved his franchise to Chicago. He remained as owner and president of the Chicago White Sox until his death.

Baseball Hall of Fame.

COMORSKY, ADAM A. baseball: b. Dec. 9, 1904, Swoyersville, Pa.; d. March 2, 1951. Bat, throw R, outfield. Pittsburgh NL, 1926–33; Cincinnati NL, 1934–35. Ten years, 813 games, .285 BA; hit .321 in 1929, .313 in 1930. Led league in triples, 1930 (23).

His two unassisted double plays, on May 31 and June 13, 1931, tied an ML season record for outfielders.

CONGDON, "CHUCK" (Charles) golf: b. Nov. 12, 1909, Blaine, Wash.; d. Feb. 28, 1965. One of the few club professionals to win a major tournament, Congdon was Canada Open champion in 1948. He also won the Portland Open in 1947 and the National Senior Open in 1960.

CONIBEAR, HIRAM rowing: b. ?; d. Sept. 9, 1917. Though he knew little or nothing about rowing until he became coach at the University of Washington in 1908, Conibear was highly successful. His crews won the Pacific Coast Regatta, 1908, 1910–11 (in each of those years, there were two regattas, and Washington won one), 1913–14 (won two races each year), and 1916–17.

Helms Hall of Fame.

CONNOLLY, JAMES B. track: b. 1868, South Boston, Mass.; d. Jan. 20, 1957. Connolly, later to become famous as a writer of sea stories, was a Harvard student when the first modern Olympics were being organized in Greece in 1896. The college refused to give him a leave of absence, but he went, anyway, and became the first modern Gold Medal winner in the hop, step, and jump. He never got his degree.

CONNOLLY, "LITTLE MO" (Maureen, Mrs. Norman Brinker) tennis: b. Sept. 17, 1934, San Diego; d. June 21, 1969. In 1953 Miss Connolly became the first, and still the only, woman to score a grand slam, winning the Australian, French, Wimbledon, and U.S. titles in a single year. She had won at Wimbledon in 1952, and she repeated in 1954 for her third consecutive title. She also won the U.S. outdoor title three years in a row, 1951–53, and the French title two years in a row, 1953–54. Yet she was not even twenty when her career ended abruptly. She was thrown from a horse at her California home and her right leg was shattered. It never healed properly, and she retired.

Miss Connolly was the youngest girl ever to win the national junior title, in 1949, and she repeated in 1950 (she also won in junior doubles both years, with two different partners). At sixteen, she was the youngest member ever of the U.S. Wightman Cup team, and she won her match in straight sets.

At 5'4", 130 pounds, Miss Connolly played a powerful game but not a flashy one. She was deadly accurate and made very few errors.

Helms Hall of Fame, Tennis Hall of Fame.

CONNOLLY, THOMAS H., SR. baseball: b. Dec. 31, 1870, Manchester, England; d. April 28, 1961. Connolly came to the United States when he was thirteen and quickly learned to play baseball, then became an umpire. By 1898, he was umpiring in the NL; in 1901, he joined the AL for its first season as a major league, and umpired the first game played that year. He remained active as an umpire until June of 1931, an AL record. He then became chief of staff for AL umpires, serving until January of 1954, when he ended fifty-six years of service to baseball.

Baseball Hall of Fame.

CONNOR, ROGER baseball: b. July 1, 1857, Waterbury, Conn.; d. Jan. 4, 1931. Bat, throw L; first base. Troy NL, 1880–82; New York NL, 1883–89; New York PL, 1890; New York NL, 1891; Philadelphia NL, 1892; New York NL, 1893–94; St. Louis NL, 1894–97. Eighteen years, 1,997 games, 7,794 at-bats, 2,467 hits, 441 doubles, 233 triples (5th), 136 home runs, 1,620 runs, 1,078 RBI (four years not included), 227 stolen bases (seven years not included), .317 BA; hit .332 in 1880, .330 in 1882, .357 in 1883, .317 in 1884, .355 in 1886, .317 in 1889, .349 in 1890, .305 in 1893, .316 in 1894, .329 in 1895. Led league in hits (169) and BA (.371) in 1885; triples in 1882 (18) and 1886 (20); walks in 1888 (73); RBI (130) and slugging (.528) in 1889; home runs (13) and slugging (.541) in 1890; doubles (37) in

1892. Connor went 6-for-6 on June 1, 1895, with 2 doubles, a triple, and 4 runs. On May 9, 1888, he hit 3 home runs in a game.

CONROY, "WID" (William E.) baseball: b. April 5, 1877, Camden, N.J.; d. Dec. 6, 1959. Bat, throw R; shortstop, third base, outfield. Milwaukee AL, 1901; Pittsburgh NL, 1902; New York AL, 1903–08; Washington AL, 1909–11. Eleven years, 1,377 games, .248 BA. He tied the ML record for third basemen by handling 13 chances in a 9-inning game on Sept. 25, 1911.

CONWAY, PETER J. baseball: b. Oct. 30, 1866, Burmont, Pa.; d. Jan. 14, 1903. Bat R; pitcher. Buffalo NL, 1885; Kansas City NL, 1886; Detroit NL, 1886–88; Pittsburgh NL, 1889. Five years, 61–61, 3.59 ERA; 30–14 in 1888.

CONZELMAN, "JIMMY" (James G.) football: b. March 6, 1898, St. Louis; d. July 31, 1970. Conzelman played football, baseball, and basketball at Washington University, St. Louis, then was quarterback and halfback for the Great Lakes Navy team that won the 1919 Rose Bowl. He played for the Decatur Staleys, 1920; Rock Island Independents, 1921–22; Milwaukee Badgers, 1923–24; Detroit Panthers, 1925–26; Providence Steamrollers, 1927–29.

He coached Rock Island, 1922 (4–2–1); Milwaukee, 1923–24 (15–10–3); Detroit, 1925–26 (9–14–2); Providence, 1927–29 (20–12–5). His 1928 Steamrollers won the NFL championship, and Conzelman was named most valuable player.

He owned the Detroit franchise during the two years he coached and played there. It had cost him $50, but he lost $30,000 and sold out. Two years later, the franchise was sold for $300,000.

Conzelman coached Washington University, 1934–39, winning the Missouri Valley Conference title in 1939, then returned to pro coaching with the Chicago Cardinals, 1940–42, 1946–48. His teams won division titles, 1947–48, and the NFL championship in 1947. His record with the Cardinals was 34–31–3, giving him an overall pro mark of 82–69–14.

A colorful, versatile figure, Conzelman at one time or another was also a writer for the *Saturday Evening Post,* a member of the board of directors of the St. Louis baseball Cardinals, a newspaper publisher, a songwriter, a radio commentator, an advertising and public-relations executive, and the middleweight boxing champion of the Navy.

Pro Football Hall of Fame.

COOLEY, DUFF C. baseball: b. March 29, 1873, Leavenworth, Kan.; d. Aug. 9, 1937. Bat L, throw R; outfield. St. Louis NL, 1893–96; Philadelphia NL, 1896–99; Pittsburgh NL, 1900; Boston NL, 1901–04; Detroit AL, 1905.

Thirteen years, 1,318 games, .294 BA; hit .339 in 1895, .307 in 1896, .329 in 1897, .312 in 1898.

COOMBS, "JACK" (John W.) baseball: b. Nov. 18, 1882, LeGrande, Iowa; d. April 15, 1957. Sw. hit, throw R; pitcher. Philadelphia AL, 1906–14; Brooklyn NL, 1915–18; Detroit AL, 1920. Fourteen years, 158–110, 2.78 ERA; 35 shutouts, 1,052 strikeouts in 2,320 innings; 20–10 in 1912. Led AL in victories (30–9) and shutouts (13) in 1910; in victories, 1911 (29–12).

Coombs's 13 shutouts in 1910 is an AL record; in that year he shut out every other team in the league. A good hitter, he was primarily an outfielder in 1908, after suffering arm trouble the year before. He had a lifetime pinch-hitting average of .306 and a World Series BA of .333.

Three World Series, 1910–11, 1916: 5 wins (4th), no losses, 2.70 ERA; 34 strikeouts in 53⅓ innings. He won 3 games in the Athletics' 5-game victory in 1910.

COONEY, JAMES L. football: b. Feb. 3, 1878, Pine Brook, Pa.; d. Oct. 27, 1964. Princeton tackle; All-American, 1904, 1906.

COOPER, EARL P. auto racing: b. 1886; d. Oct. 22, 1965. Cooper was national driving champ, 1913, 1915, 1917. In 12 races at Indianapolis, his best finish was second.

National Racing Hall of Fame, Helms Hall of Fame.

COOPER, MORTON C. baseball: b. March 2, 1913, Atherton, Mo.; d. Nov. 17, 1958. Bat, throw R; pitcher. St. Louis NL, 1938–45; Boston NL, 1945–57; New York NL, 1947; Chicago NL, 1949. Eleven years, 128–75, 2.97 ERA; 32 shutouts, 913 strikeouts in 1,840⅔ innings; 22–7 in 1944. Led NL in wins (22–7), ERA (1.78), and shutouts (10) in 1942; in wins and percentage (21–8, .724) in 1943; in shutouts (7) in 1944. Three World Series, 1942–44: 2–3, 3.00 ERA; 6 starts, 2 complete, 1 shutout.

Cooper pitched consecutive 1-hitters on May 31 and June 4, 1943.

COPELAND, LILLIAN track: b. Nov. 25, 1904, New York City; d. Feb. 7, 1964. At the University of Southern California she won every intercollegiate event she entered. She won a number of AAU championships in the weights: the 8-pound shot, 1925–28, 1931; discus, 1926–27; javelin, 1926–31. When she learned the shotput was not a women's Olympic event, she took up the discus, winning a silver medal in the 1928 Games, a gold medal in 1932.

Helms Hall of Fame.

CORBETT, "GENTLEMAN JIM" (James J.) boxing: b. Sept. 1, 1866, San Francisco; d. Feb. 18, 1933. His record: 20 wins, 9 by KO; 5 losses, 3 by

KO; 6 draws, 2 no-decisions. The first man to win the heavyweight championship under the Marquis of Queensbury rules drifted into professional boxing almost by accident. He was a college graduate working as a bank clerk when he joined the Olympic Athletic Club in San Francisco. Shortly afterward, he won the club boxing championship. Taking the name of Jim Dillon, Corbett then went to Salt Lake City, where he KOed one professional and fought a draw with another, Don McDonald, whom he fought a number of times during an exhibition tour in 1886.

Corbett became a pro in 1889 and quickly became known as the Dancing Master for his speed and agility. On Sept. 7, 1892, for a purse of $25,000 and side bet of $10,000, Corbett completely outboxed John L. Sullivan at New Orleans in the first heavyweight fight with gloves and three-minute rounds.

After winning virtually every round, he KOed Sullivan in the 21st. As champion, Corbett interspersed fights with tours on the vaudeville circuit and in a play, *Gentleman Jim.* He lost his title to Bob Fitzsimmons on a 14th-round KO, March 17, 1897. Corbett retired, tried a comeback against James J. Jeffries, who had won the title from Fitzsimmons, but was KOed in the 23rd round on May 11, 1900.

Boxing Hall of Fame, Helms Hall of Fame.

CORBETT, YOUNG boxing: b. William H. Rothwell, Oct. 4, 1880, Denver; d. April 10, 1927. His record: 53 wins, 34 by KO; 14 losses, 8 by KO; 12 draws, 25 no-decisions. Corbett won the featherweight title with a 2nd-round KO of Terry McGovern on Nov. 28, 1901. He vacated the title at the end of 1902 because he couldn't make the weight. Actually, he and McGovern had both been above the weight limit in the title fight. Corbett continued to fight in higher classes until 1910.

Boxing Hall of Fame.

CORBIN, "PA" (William H.) football: b. July 20, 1864, Union, Conn.; d. April 14, 1943. Yale center, 1886–88; captained undefeated (13–0) team in 1888 that outscored opponents 698–0.

National Football Foundation Hall of Fame.

CORCORAN, LAWRENCE J. baseball: b. Aug. 10, 1859, Brooklyn; d. Oct. 4, 1891. Throw R; pitcher. Chicago NL, 1880–85; New York NL, 1885–86; Indianapolis NL, 1887. Eight years, 177–89, 2.36 ERA; 23 shutouts, 1,103 strikeouts in 2,392⅓ innings; 43–14 in 1880, 34–20 in 1883, 35–23 in 1884. No-hitters, Aug. 19, 1880, against Boston NL (6–0); Sept. 20, 1882, against Worcester NL (5–0); June 27, 1884, against Providence NL (6–0). Led NL in strikeouts, 1880 (268); in wins 1881 (31–14); in percentage (27–12, .692); and ERA (1.95) in 1882.

Corcoran was the first pitcher in history to throw 3 no-hitters. The first was when the rubber was 45 feet from home plate, the other two when it was 50 feet away. He is also credited by some with being the first pitcher to work out a system of signals with his catcher; supposedly, he let the catcher know when he was going to throw a curve by shifting his chaw of tobacco to the other side of his mouth.

CORCORAN, THOMAS W. baseball: b. Jan. 4, 1869, New Haven, Conn.; d. June 24, 1960. Bat, throw R; shortstop. Pittsburgh PL, 1890; Philadelphia AA, 1891; Brooklyn NL, 1892–96; Cincinnati NL, 1897–1906; New York NL, 1907. Eighteen years, 2,200 games, 387 stolen bases; .256 BA; hit .300 in 1894.

His 14 assists in a 9-inning game on Aug. 7, 1903, is the ML record for shortstops.

CORKHILL, "POP" (John S.) baseball: b. April 11, 1858, Parkersburg, Pa.; d. April 4, 1921. Bat L, throw R; outfield. Cincinnati AA, 1883–88; Brooklyn AA, 1888–89; Brooklyn NL, 1890; Cincinnati NL, Philadelphia AA, 1891; Pittsburgh NL, 1891–92. Ten years, 1,086 games, .254 BA; hit .311 in 1887.

CORRIDON, FRANK J. ("Fiddler") baseball: b. Nov. 25, 1880, Newport, R.I.; d. Feb. 21, 1941. Bat, throw R; pitcher. Chicago NL, 1904; Philadelphia NL, 1904–05, 1907–09; St. Louis NL, 1910. Six years, 72–69, 2.81 ERA.

CORUM, "BILL" (Martene William) sportswriting: b. July 20, 1895, Speed, Mo.; d. Dec. 16, 1958. Nicknamed the Little Major because at twenty-three, he was the youngest major in the American Expeditionary Force during World War I. He became a reporter for *The New York Times* in 1920, then moved to the *Journal-American* as a baseball writer, where he was such a hit that he became a columnist two years later. He quickly became one of the best-known sports columnists in the country, and his fame led to frequent appearances on radio and television.

In 1949, after the death of Matt J. Winn, Corum became president of Churchill Downs and took annual leaves of absence to work on preparations for the Kentucky Derby.

COURTNEY, CHARLES E. rowing: b. 1849, Union Springs, N.Y.; d. 1920. Courtney won the Association single sculls championship in 1875, the doubles, 1875–76. He was Cornell crew coach, 1885–1920; during that time, his crews won the Intercollegiate Rowing Association regatta, 1896–97, 1901–03, 1909–12, 1915; the Childs Cup sprint, 1885, 1887, 1889; and the Carnegie Cup race, 1911–12, 1914, 1916, 1919–20.

Helms Hall of Fame.

COVELESKI, HARRY F. baseball: b. Kowalewski, April 23, 1886, Shamokin, Pa.; d. Aug. 4, 1950. Sw. hit, throw L; pitcher. Philadelphia NL, 1907–09; Cincinnati NL, 1910; Detroit AL, 1914–18. Nine years, 81–57, 2.39 ERA; 13 shutouts, 511 strikeouts in 1,248 innings; 21–13 in 1914, 23–13 in 1915, 22–11 in 1916.

The brother of Hall of Fame pitcher Stan Coveleski, Harry acquired the nickname the Giant Killer when, called up to the Phillies from the minors in September, 1908, he beat the Giants three times in a week to knock them out of the pennant race.

COWAN, HECTOR W. football: b. July 12, 1863, Hobart, N.Y.; d. Oct. 19, 1941. Princeton guard, 1885–87; tackle, 1888–89; All-American, 1889; captain, 1888–89. It would be unusual, to say the least, for an interior lineman to score 79 TDs in his college career nowadays, but Cowan did it. In his day, of course, guards-back and tackles-back plays were frequently used. But Cowan was an outstanding runner; today he might be a back.

A divinity student, 5'10" and 190 pounds, he was a rough but not dirty player. His greatest moment came in 1889, when Princeton beat Yale 10–0, snapping a 49-game winning streak. He ran 5 yards with a fumble, dragging Yale players all the way, for one of Princeton's TDs.

National Football Foundation Hall of Fame.

COY, "TED" (Edward H.) football: b. May 24, 1888, Andover, Mass.; d. Sept. 8, 1935. Yale fullback; All-American, 1908–09; 2nd team, 1907; captain, 1909. Some of Coy's runs—105 yards in his first game, 80 yards in another, 60 in another—might lead one to believe that Coy was a breakaway speedster, but actually he was a 200-pound pile-driving runner. He was also a great all-around performer and a particular nemesis of Princeton.

In 1907, he scored two TDs to wipe out a 10–0 Princeton halftime lead and give Yale a victory. The following year, he scored the only TDs in wins over Syracuse and Army and kicked a field goal to gain a 10–10 tie with Brown. Yale went into the Princeton game undefeated, and Coy was shifted to end. With Princeton ahead 6–0, he moved back to fullback in the second half and again scored two TDs for a Yale win.

An appendectomy kept Coy out of the first four games of the 1909 season. He went into the Army game in the second half with orders not to run, and he threw a 30-yard pass for the winning TD. His TD and field goal led Yale to a 17–0 win over Princeton. In the climactic game against Harvard, his punts kept Yale out of trouble; his two field goals and a safety led to an 8–0 victory.

Helms Hall of Fame, National Football Foundation Hall of Fame.

CRANDALL, "DOC" (James Otis) baseball: b. Oct. 8, 1887, Wadena, Ind.; d. Aug. 17, 1951. Bat, throw R; pitcher. New York NL, 1908–13; St. Louis Fed L, 1914–15; St. Louis AL, 1916; Boston NL, 1918. Ten years, 106–61, 2.92 ERA. In relief, 37–14, 21 saves, 2.77 ERA; 22–14 in 1915. Three World Series, 1911–13: 5 games, 1–0, 1.69 ERA.

CRANE, "CANNONBALL" (Edward N.) baseball: b. May 1862, Boston; d. Sept. 19, 1896. Bat, throw R; pitcher. Boston UA, 1884; Washington NL, 1886; New York NL, 1888–89; New York PL, 1890; Cincinnati NL, Cincinnati-Milwaukee AA, 1891; New York NL, 1892–93; Brooklyn NL, 1893. Eight years, 73–96, 3.99 ERA.

CRANE, JOSHUA tennis: b. ?; d. Dec. 18, 1944. Crane won the U.S. court tennis championship four consecutive years, 1901–04.

CRAVATH, "GAVVY" (Clifford C.) baseball: b. March 23, 1881, Escondido, Calif.; d. May 23, 1963. Bat, throw R; outfield. Boston AL, 1908; Chicago AL, Washington AL, 1909; Philadelphia NL, 1912–20. Eleven years, 1,219 games, .287 BA; hit .341 in 1913. As a pinch-hitter, 32 for 106, .302. Led league in hits (179), home runs (19), RBI (128), and slugging (.568) in 1913; in home runs (19) in 1914; in home runs (24), runs (89), RBI (115), and walks (86) in 1915; in home runs, 1917 (12), 1918 (8), 1919 (12). One World Series, 1915: 5 games, .125 BA.

Managed Philadelphia NL, 1919 (part)–20: 91–137, .399.

CRAVATH, "JEFF" (Newell Jefferson) football: b. Feb. 5, 1903, Breckenridge, Colo.; d. Dec. 10, 1953. Southern California center; captain, 1926.

Cravath coached at Denver University, 1929–31 (14–11–1), then assisted at USC for several years. At San Francisco in 1941, he had a 6–4–0 record, but his team led the Far West in scoring. Then he returned to USC as head coach, 1942–50. His Trojans were Pacific Coast champions, 1943–45, 1947. The 1944 team was unbeaten but twice tied in 10 games. His teams split in four Rose Bowls, beating Washington 29–0 in 1944 and Tennessee 25–0 in 1945, losing to Alabama 34–14 in 1946 and to Michigan 49–0 in 1948. Cravath's overall record at Southern Cal was 54–28–8.

He died of injuries suffered in an auto accident.

CRAWFORD, "WAHOO SAM" (Samuel E.) baseball: b. April 18, 1880, Wahoo, Nebr.; d. June 15, 1968. Bat, throw L; outfield. Cincinnati NL,

1899–1902; Detroit AL, 1903–17. Nineteen years, 2,517 games (9th), 9,570 at-bats (8th), 2,961 hits, 458 doubles, 309 triples (1st), 97 home runs, 1,391 runs, 366 stolen bases, 1,525 RBI, .309 BA.

What Babe Ruth was to home runs, Sam Crawford was to triples. His career record for 3-base hits will probably never be broken. He also holds records for most years leading league in triples, 6; most years leading AL in triples, 5, most consecutive, 3; most years 20 or more triples, 5. His 26 triples in 1914 ties the AL record. Crawford is the only player ever to lead both leagues in home runs.

He led the league in home runs, 1901 (16); triples, 1902 (22), 1903 (25); runs, 1907 (102); home runs, 1908 (7); doubles, 1909 (35); triples (19) and RBI (120) in 1910; triples, 1913 (23); triples (26), home runs (8), and RBI (104) in 1914; triples (19) and RBI (112) in 1915. He hit .330 in 1901, .333 in 1902, .335 in 1903, .323 in 1907, .311 in 1908, .314 in 1909, .378 in 1911, .325 in 1912, .317 in 1913, .314 in 1914. Three World Series, 1907–09: 17 games, .243 BA.

Baseball Hall of Fame.

CREGAN, JOHN F. track: b. Jan. 29, 1878, Schenectady, N.Y.; d. Dec. 20, 1965. Representing Princeton, Cregan won the IC4A one-mile run, 1898–1900, and the half-mile, 1898. In AAU outdoor competition, he won the mile, 1897–98, the half-mile, 1897. He was 2nd in the 800 meters at the 1900 Olympics.

CRIGER, LOUIS baseball: b. Feb. 6, 1872, Elkhart, Ind.; d. May 14, 1934. Bat, throw R; catcher. Cleveland NL, 1896–98; St. Louis NL, 1899–1900; Boston AL, 1901–08; St. Louis AL, 1909; New York AL, 1910; St. Louis AL, 1912. Sixteen years, 1,012 games, .221 BA. One World Series, 1903: 8 games, .231 BA.

He led league catchers in assists, 1903, and in fielding average, 1903–04.

CRISP, "HANK" (Henry G.) basketball: b. Dec. 10, 1896, Crisp, N.C.; d. Jan. 23, 1970. Crisp was Alabama basketball coach, 1924–42, 1946, with an overall record of 266–129. His teams won the Southern Conference title in 1931, the Southeastern Conference title in 1936. He was Alabama athletic director, 1931–39, 1954–57.

Though he lost his right hand in an accident when he was thirteen, he won letters in three sports at Virginia Tech.

CROSBY, "TOBACCO BILL" (William R.) shooting: b. Aug. 27, 1866, O'Fallon, Ill.; d. Nov. 11, 1939. At thirteen, Crosby entered his first trap-shooting tournament and won it in a shoot-off with his father, who had brought him along just to watch. The same year, he had the second high

66   CROSS, "LAVE"

average in the Illinois State meet. He went on to hold, at one time or another, the E.C. Cup, DuPont Cup, Hazard Trophy, Schmelzer Trophy, and Sportsmen's Review Trophy. He set a long-run record of 345 in 1901 —the old record was 114. In 1905, he made it 419.
American Trapshooting Hall of Fame.

CROSS, "LAVE" (Lafayette N.) baseball: b. May 11, 1867, Milwaukee; d. Sept. 4, 1927. Bat, throw R; catcher, third base, outfield. Louisville AA, 1887–88; Philadelphia AA, 1889; Philadelphia PL, 1890; Philadelphia AA, 1891; Philadelphia NL, 1892–97; St. Louis NL, 1898–99; Cleveland NL, 1899; Brooklyn NL, St. Louis NL, 1900; Philadelphia AL, 1901–05; Washington AL, 1906–07. Twenty-one years, 2,275 games, 2,644 hits, 411 doubles, 301 stolen bases, .292 BA; hit .301 in 1891, .386 in 1894, .317 in 1898, .328 in 1901, .342 in 1902. One World Series, 1905: 5 games, .105 BA.
His 15 assists in a 12-inning game, Aug. 5, 1897, is an ML record for second basemen, a position which he played for only 60 games in his entire career.

CROSS, "MONTY" (Montford M.) baseball: b. Aug. 31, 1869, Philadelphia; d. June 21, 1934. Bat, throw R; shortstop. Baltimore NL, 1892; Pittsburgh NL, 1894–95; St. Louis NL, 1896–97; Philadelphia NL, 1898–1901; Philadelphia AL, 1902–07. Fifteen years, 1,681 games, .234 BA. One World Series, 1905: 5 games, .176 BA.
Cross had 14 putouts in an 11-inning game on July 7, 1899, an ML record for shortstops. His .182 BA in 1904 is the lowest ever for a player appearing in 150 or more games.

CROWTHER, GEORGE M. football: b. 1892, Bridgeport, Conn.; d. July 23, 1963. Brown quarterback; All-American, 1912.

CULLOP, "NICK" (Norman A.) baseball: b. Sept. 17, 1887, Chilhowie, Va.; d. April 15, 1961. Bat R, throw L; pitcher. Cleveland AL, 1913–14; Kansas City Fed L, 1914–15; New York AL, 1916–17; St. Louis AL, 1921. Six years, 56–52, 2.73 ERA; 22–11 in 1915.

CUMMINGS, "CANDY" (William A.) baseball: b. Oct. 17, 1848, Ware, Mass.; d. May 16, 1924. Bat, throw R; pitcher. The only records on his performance are from the National Association: New York Mutuals, 1872; Lord Baltimores, 1873; Philadelphias, 1874; Hartfords, 1875. Four years, 124–72; 33–20 in 1872, 28–14 in 1873, 28–26 in 1874, 35–12 in 1875.
Hartford NL, 1876; Cincinnati NL, 1877. Two years, 21–22, 2.78 ERA.
Cummings is generally credited with inventing the curve ball in 1864, while pitching for the Brooklyn Stars, essentially an amateur team. The

claim that he could throw a curve was disputed by some, and the controversy continued for nearly a century. Cummings never put on any kind of controlled demonstration to prove it.
Baseball Hall of Fame.

CUNNINGHAM, "BERT" (Ellsworth E.) baseball: b. Nov. 25, 1865, Wilmington, Del.; d. May 14, 1952. Bat, throw R; pitcher. Brooklyn AA, 1887; Baltimore AA, 1888–89; Buffalo PL, Philadelphia PL, 1890; Baltimore AA, 1891; Louisville NL, 1895–99; Chicago NL, 1900–01. Twelve years, 142–167, 4.22 ERA; 22–29 in 1888, 28–15 in 1898.

CUPPY, "NIG" (George J.) baseball: b. George M. Koppe, July 3, 1869, Logansport, Ind.; d. July 27, 1922. Bat, throw R; pitcher. Cleveland NL, 1892–98; St. Louis NL, 1899; Boston NL, 1900; Boston AL, 1901. Ten years, 162–98, 3.49 ERA; 28–13 in 1892, 24–15 in 1894, 26–14 in 1895, 25–14 in 1896. Led NL in shutouts, 1894 (3).

CURTIS, MARGARET golf: b. ?; d. Dec. 24, 1965. Margaret Curtis and her sister Harriott dominated the Women's Amateur Championship for a number of years. Margaret won the tournament, 1907, 1911–12, beating Harriott in the finals for her first victory. She was runner-up, 1900–05, and she was medalist or comedalist in 1901–02, 1905, 1907, and 1912.
Harriott won in 1906 and was medalist or comedalist in 1904 and 1908. The sisters donated the Curtis Cup, given biennially since 1932 to the winning team in competition between women amateurs from Great Britain and the United States.
Margaret teamed with Eleonora Sears to win the U.S. outdoor doubles title in tennis in 1908.
Ladies Professional Golf Association Hall of Fame.

CURTIS, THOMAS P. track: b. 1871(?), San Francisco; d. May 28, 1944. Curtis won the 110-meter hurdles at the first modern Olympics, in 1896.

CURTIS, WILLIAM B. track, rowing: b. Jan. 17, 1837, Salisbury, Vt.; d. 1900. Curtis won the AAU outdoor hammer throw in 1876, 1878, and 1880, the 56-pound weight throw in 1878. He is better known as the father of American rowing and has sometimes been called the father of American amateurism. In 1872, it was generally assumed that a professional was someone who competed for pay or cash prizes. But the so-called Schuylkill Navy, an organization of rowing clubs in the Philadelphia area, held a rowing regatta that year and rejected many applications from oarsmen on the grounds that they were professionals because they made side bets on their races, a common practice.

The banished oarsmen raised such an uproar that Curtis and a Philadel phia newspaperman, James Watson, were asked to study the problem. I two pamphlets, they basically upheld the Schuylkill ruling; they defined a professional as anyone who competes in the hope of receiving any sort o cash prize, including side bets. That ruling was accepted in 1873, upon th organization of the National Association of Amateur Oarsmen.

CURTISS, GLENN H. airplane, balloon, bicycle, and motorcycle racing: b May 21, 1878, Hammondsport, N.Y.; d. July 23, 1930. Curtiss began with an interest in sheer speed; as a boy, he challenged relay teams of neighbor hood youngsters to race him around the block. Then he turned to bike racing; for three years he was undefeated at meets and fairs. The motorcycle was the natural next step. Curtiss first built engines, then entire motorcy cles; he won a national championship in 1903 at the Empire State track, and in 1904 he set a record at Ormond Beach, Florida, that stood for seven years. In 1907, he averaged 137 miles an hour for one mile, then a record.

In the meantime, he had begun designing engines for airships. That led into designing engines for airplanes, and air racing. In 1909 Curtiss won the Scientific American Trophy by averaging 35 miles an hour over a measured course; the Gordon Bennett Cup in the first National Aviation Meet; the Prix de la Vitesse and other trophies in European meets and races. In 1910, he won the $10,000 New York World Prize for flying from Albany to New York, about 150 miles, in 2 hours, 51 minutes.

The rest of his life was devoted mainly to research and design.

CUSHMAN, EDGAR L. baseball: b. March 27, 1852, Eaglesville, Ohio; d. Sept. 26, 1915. Bat R, throw L; pitcher. Buffalo NL, 1883; Milwaukee UA, 1884; Philadelphia AA, 1885; New York AA, 1885–87; Toledo AA, 1890. Six years, 62–80, 3.86 ERA. No-hitter, Sept. 28, 1884, against Washington UA.

CUYLER, "KIKI" (Hazen S.) baseball: b. Aug. 30, 1882, Harrisville, Mich.; d. Feb. 11, 1950. Bat, throw R; outfield. Pittsburgh NL, 1921–27; Chicago NL, 1928–35; Cincinnati NL, 1935–37; Brooklyn NL, 1938. Eighteen years, 1,879 games, 7,161 at-bats, 2,299 hits, 394 doubles, 157 triples, 127 home runs, 1,305 runs, 1,065 RBI, 328 stolen bases, .321 BA; hit .354 in 1924, .357 in 1925, .321 in 1926, .309 in 1927, .360 in 1929, .355 in 1930, .330 in 1931, .317 in 1933, .338 in 1934, .326 in 1936. Led NL in runs (144) and triples (26) in 1925; in runs (113) and stolen bases (35) in 1926; in doubles, 1934 (42); in stolen bases, 1928 (37), 1929 (43), and 1930 (37).

In 1925, Cuyler twice scored 5 runs in a game, tying an ML record. His 26 triples in 1925 is a modern record for a right-handed hitter. On Aug. 9, 1924, he went 6-for-6, with 3 doubles, a triple, and 3 runs scored.

"Bert" Bell
(*Professional Football
Hall of Fame*)

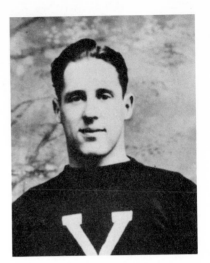

"Albie" Booth
(*Courtesy Yale University*)

"Dan" Brouthers
(*Boston Public Library*)

"Three-Finger" Brown
(*Boston Public Library*)

Walter C. Camp
(Courtesy Yale University)

Edward L. Casey
(Courtesy Harvard University)

Frank L. Chance
(Boston Public Library)

Guy Chamberlin
*(Professional Football
Hall of Fame)*

John G. Clarkson
(Boston Public Library)

"Ty" Cobb

"Jimmy" Conzelman
(*Professional Football
Hall of Fame*)

"Paddy" Driscoll
(*Professional Football
Hall of Fame*)

Hugh Duffy
(*Boston Public Library*)

John J. Evers
(*Boston Public Library*)

"Jimmy" Foxx

"Pud" Galvin
(*Boston Public Library*)

"Lou" Gehrig, right, and "Babe" Ruth
(*Wide World*)

George Gipp
(*Courtesy
University of Notre Dame*)

Walter C. Hagen

"Tack" Hardwick
(*Courtesy Harvard University*)

Percy D. Haughton
(*Courtesy Harvard University*)

"Pudge" Heffelfinger
(*Courtesy Yale University*)

"Fats" Henry
(*Professinal Football
Hall of Fame*)

"Arnie" Herber
(*Green Bay* Press-Gazette)

"Willie" Heston
(*Courtesy
University of Michigan*)

Rogers Hornsby

"Wee Willie" Keeler

Walter Kiesling
(*Professional Football
Hall of Fame*)

Robert J. H. Kiphuth
(*Courtesy Yale University*)

"Larry" Lajoie

"Curly" Lambeau
(*Green Bay* Press-Gazette)

Joseph Lapchick
(*Basketball Hall of Fame*)

"Champagne Tony" Lema
(*New Bedford* Standard-Times)

"Sonny" Liston
(*Ronald Rolo—*
New Bedford Standard-Times)

Vincent T. Lombardi
(*Green Bay* Press-Gazette)

"Bobby" Lov
(*Boston Public Lib*

In three World Series, 1925, 1929, 1932, 16 games, he hit .281, scoring 9 runs and driving in 12, with 5 doubles, 1 triple, and 2 home runs. In 1925, he won the second game for Pittsburgh with a 2-run home run in the eighth inning, and he won the seventh game with a 2-run double in the eighth, as the Pirates beat Washington. A feud with his Pittsburgh manager, Donie Bush, kept him out of the 1927 Series and resulted in his trade to the Cubs the following year. Cuyler wanted to play center field and bat third, but Bush put him in left field and made him bat second. His hitting suffered; then he missed several games with an injury, and after recovering, played very little. He stayed on the bench during the Pirates' 4-game loss to the Yankees in the Series, despite "We want Cuyler" cries.

Baseball Hall of Fame.

D

DADE, HAROLD D. boxing: b. Oct. 9, 1924, Chicago; d. July 17, 1962. His record: 41 wins, 9 by KO; 30 losses, 5 by KO; 6 draws. Dade won the bantamweight title on Jan. 6, 1947, with a 15-round decision over Manuel Ortiz, but he lost it in a rematch on March 11, also in 15 rounds. He retired in 1955.

DAHLEN, "BAD BILL" (William F.) baseball: b. Jan. 5, 1870, Nelliston, N.Y.; d. Dec. 5, 1950. Bat, throw R; shortstop, third base. Chicago NL, 1891–98; Brooklyn NL, 1899–1903; New York NL, 1904–07; Boston NL, 1908–09; Brooklyn NL, 1910–11. Twenty-one years, 2,443 games, 1,589 runs, 547 stolen bases, .272 BA; hit .301 in 1893, .357 in 1894, .352 in 1896. Led NL in RBI, 1904 (80). One World Series, 1905: 5 games, .000 BA.

Managed Brooklyn NL, 1910–13: 251–355, .414.

Dahlen tied the ML record for most seasons as a shortstop, 20, and holds the ML record for most career assists at that position, 7,414.

DAILY, EDWARD M. baseball: b. Sept. 7, 1862, Providence, R.I.; d. Oct. 21, 1891. Pitcher. Philadelphia NL, 1885–87; Washington NL, 1887–88; Columbus AA, 1889; New York NL, Brooklyn-Baltimore AA, 1890; Louisville AA, 1890–91. Seven years, 66–70, 3.39 ERA; 26–23 in 1885.

DAILY, "ONE-ARM" (Hugh I.) baseball: b. 1857, Baltimore; d. ? Bat, throw R; pitcher. Buffalo NL, 1882; Cleveland NL, 1883; Chicago-Pittsburgh UA,

Washington UA, 1884; St. Louis NL, 1885; Washington NL, 1886; Cleve land AA, 1887. Six years, 73–87, 2.90 ERA; 846 strikeouts in 1,415 inning. 23–19 in 1883, 28–28 in 1884. No-hitter, Sept. 13, 1883, against Philade phia NL (1–0). Led UA in strikeouts, 1884 (483).

Daily pitched consecutive 1-hitters, July 7 and 10, 1884, and pitched tw other 1-hitters that year, setting an ML record of 4 in one season. He struc out 19 during the July 7 1-hitter to tie an ML record.

DALRYMPLE, ABNER F. baseball: b. Sept. 9, 1857, Warren, Ill.; d. Jan. 2 1939. Bat L, throw R; outfield. Milwaukee NL, 1878; Chicago NL, 1879 86; Pittsburgh NL, 1887–88; Cincinnati-Milwaukee AA, 1891. Twelv years, 951 games, .288 BA; hit .354 in 1878, .330 in 1880, .323 in 1881, .30 in 1884. Led league in hits (126) and runs (91) in 1880; in home runs, 188. (11).

DALY, CHARLES D. football: b. Oct. 31, 1880, Roxbury, Mass.; d. Feb. 12 1959. Harvard quarterback, 1898–1900; Army, 1901–02; captain, 1900 All-American, 1898–99, 1901; 2nd team, 1900; 3rd team, 1902. The onl man to play for a Harvard team that beat Yale and an Army team that bea Navy, Daly was a fine kicker, an elusive runner, a sure tackler but, abov all, a leader. While he played quarterback, Harvard had a 32-game un defeated streak, losing to Yale in his last game, when he played little becaus of an injured knee.

In Army's 1901 win over Navy, he scored all his team's points, runnin a kickoff 98 yards for a TD, adding the conversion, and kicking a 35-yar field goal in the 11–5 victory. He also averaged more than 40 yards puntin and saved the game by catching a Navy runner from behind, short of th goal line, after a 65-yard punt return.

He coached Army, 1913–16, 1919–22, producing unbeaten teams ir 1914, 1916, and 1922.

Helms Hall of Fame, National Football Foundation Hall of Fame.

DALY, THOMAS P. baseball: b. Feb. 7, 1866, Philadelphia; d. Oct. 29, 1939. Sw. hit, throw R; catcher, second base. Chicago NL, 1887–88; Washington NL, 1889; Brooklyn NL, 1890–96, 1898–1901; Chicago AL, 1902–03; Cincinnati NL, 1903. Sixteen years, 1,564 games, .278 BA; hit .300 in 1889, .341 in 1894, .313 in 1899, .312 in 1900, .315 in 1901. Led league in doubles 1901 (38).

DAUBERT, JACOB E. baseball: b. April 17, 1884, Shamokin, Pa.; d. Oct. 9, 1924. Bat, throw L; first base. Brooklyn NL, 1910–18; Cincinnati NL, 1919–24. Fifteen years, 2,014 games, 7,673 at-bats, 2,326 hits, 250 doubles, 164 triples, 56 home runs, 1,117 runs, 722 RBI, 251 stolen bases, .303 BA hit .307 in 1911, .308 in 1912, .301 in 1915, .316 in 1916, .308 in 1918, .304 in 1920, .306 in 1921, .336 in 1922. Led NL in BA, 1913 (.350), 1914 (.329); triples, 1918 (15), 1922 (22). Two World Series, 1916, 1919: 12 games, .217.

DAUSS, "HOOKS" (George A.) baseball: b. Sept. 22, 1889, Indianapolis; d. July 27, 1963. Bat, throw R; pitcher. Detroit AL, 1912–26. Fifteen years, 223–182, 3.32 ERA; 23–13 in 1915, 21–9 in 1919, 21–13 in 1923. In relief, 41–23, 3.54 ERA, 39 saves.

DAVENPORT, "DAVE" (Arthur D.) baseball: b. Feb. 2, 1892, Alexandria, La.; d. Oct. 16, 1954. Bat, throw R; pitcher. Cincinnati NL, 1914; St. Louis Fed L, 1914–15; St. Louis AL, 1916–19. Nine years, 74–83, 2.93 ERA; 22–18 in 1915. No-hitter, Sept. 7, 1915, against Chicago Fed L. Led Fed L in complete games (30), strikeouts (229), and shutouts (10) in 1915.

DAVIDSON, KENNETH R. badminton: b. Dec. 24, 1905, Headingly, Leeds, England; d. Dec. 25, 1954. After arriving in the United States in 1935, Davidson raised the standard of American play greatly. He was particularly outstanding at doubles; he influenced the switch from side-by-side to front-and-back play. With Lealand R. Gustavson, he coauthored *Winning Badminton.*

Davidson died in a plane crash, returning to the United States from an exhibition tour in Asia.

DAVIS, CURTIS B. baseball: b. Sept. 7, 1903, Greenfield, Mo.; d. Oct. 12, 1965. Bat, throw R; pitcher. Philadelphia NL, 1934–36; Chicago NL, 1936–37; St. Louis NL, 1938–40; Brooklyn NL, 1941–46. Thirteen years, 158–131, 3.42 ERA; 24 shutouts; 22–16 in 1939. One World Series, 1941: 0–1, 5.06 ERA.

DAVIS, "DIXIE" (Frank T.) baseball: b. Oct. 12, 1890, Wilson Mills, N.C.: d. Feb. 4, 1944. Bat, throw R; pitcher. Cincinnati NL, 1912; Chicago AL, 1915; Philadelphia NL, 1918; St. Louis AL, 1920–26. Ten years, 75–71, 3.97 ERA. Led AL in shutouts, 1924 (5).

DAVIS, DWIGHT F. tennis: b. July 3, 1879, St. Louis; d. Nov. 28, 1945. Better known as a politician and public servant, Davis was an outstanding young tennis player who donated the Davis Cup to help spread the sport throughout the world.

As a junior at Harvard, in 1899, he won intercollegiate championships in both singles and doubles (with Holcombe Ward); he and Ward also won national outdoor doubles titles, 1899–1901. In 1900, Davis donated the cup for international team play. He was a member of the first Davis Cup team, winning in both singles and doubles (again with Ward).

Davis won a distinguished-service cross as an officer in World War I became Secretary of War at forty-six, the youngest member of Calvin Coolidge's cabinet, and later served as governor-general of the Philippines Tennis Hall of Fame, Helms Hall of Fame.

DAVIS, ERNEST football: b. Dec. 14, 1939, New Salem, Pa.; d. May 18 1963. Syracuse halfback; All-American, 1960 (UPI), 1961 (AP, UPI); Heis man Trophy, 1961. A runner in the mold of Jimmy Brown—big, powerful fast, and elusive—Davis was recruited for Syracuse by Brown and went on to break most of Brown's school rushing records. Davis was the first Negro to win the Heisman Trophy and he became the first Negro drafted by the Washington Redskins, who had first choice in the NFL. But Davis wa traded to the Cleveland Browns, where he could play next to Jimmy.

Davis never played pro football. Shortly after he joined the Browns, i was discovered that he had leukemia. After one brief remission, the disease returned and killed him.

DAVIS, GEORGE S. baseball: b. Aug. 23, 1879, Cohoes, N.Y.; d. Oct. 17 1940. Sw. hit, throw R; shortstop, third base, outfield, second base. Cleve land NL, 1890–92; New York NL, 1893–1901; Chicago AL, 1902; New York NL, 1903; Chicago AL, 1904–09. Twenty years, 2,363 games, 612 stolen bases, .294 BA; hit .355 in 1893, .352 in 1894, .343 in 1895, .320 in 1896, .353 in 1897, .307 in 1898, .337 in 1899, .319 in 1900, .301 in 1901. Led league in RBI, 1897 (134). One World Series, 1906: 3 games, .308 BA. Davis went 6-for-6 on Aug. 15, 1895, with 2 doubles and a triple and 3 runs scored.

DAVIS, HARRY H. ("Jasper") baseball: b. July 10, 1873, Philadelphia; d. Aug. 11, 1947. Bat, throw R; first base. New York NL, 1895–96; Pittsburgh NL, 1896–98; Louisville NL, 1898; Washington NL, 1898–99; Philadelphia AL, 1901–11; Cleveland AL, 1912; Philadelphia AL, 1913–17. Twenty-two years, 1,768 games, .277 BA; hit .305 in 1897, .306 in 1901, .307 in 1902, .309 in 1904. Led league in doubles, 1902 (43), 1905 (47), 1907 (36); triples, 1897 (28); home runs, 1904 (10), 1905 (8), 1906 (12), 1907 (8); runs, 1905 (92); RBI, 1905 (83), 1906 (96). Three World Series: 16 games, .246 BA. Hit .353, with 3 doubles and 5 runs, in As' victory in 1910.

DAW, CHARLES bowling: b. April 12, 1894, Beloit, Wis.; d. Jan. 19, 1947. The first man to roll two 700 series in ABC tournaments, Daw was a member of a team that gave a special exhibition of bowling during the 1936 Olympics. In 1923, he was on the ABC champion team and won the doubles title; he won the doubles again in 1932. He won the U.S. match-game title from Frank Kartheiser in 1927 but lost it the following year. He had five sanctioned 300 games.

American Bowling Congress Hall of Fame.

DAYWALT, JAMES E. auto racing: b. Aug. 28, 1924, Wabash, Ind.; d. April 4, 1966. Daywalt was named Rookie of the Year for his sixth-place finish in the 1953 Indianapolis 500, his best finish there in eight tries.

He died of cancer.

DeBERNARDI, "RED" (Forrest S.) basketball: b. Feb. 3, 1899, Nevada, Mo.; d. April 29, 1970. At Westminster, Mo., College, DeBernardi was a member of the first All-American team in 1920 and repeated in 1921. He went on to play AAU basketball with, among others, the Hillyards and the Cook Painters, both championship teams. He played in eleven AAU tournaments and was named to the All-Tournament team seven times. In 1938 he was chosen to the All-Time All-American team.

Helms Hall of Fame, Basketball Hall of Fame.

DeCAPRILES, JOSÉ R. fencing: b. Feb. 13, 1912, Mexico; d. Feb. 29, 1969. DeCapriles came to the United States in 1920. He competed for New York University, 1929–33, and for various clubs, 1933–60. He was national épée champion 1938 and 1951 and national foil champ in 1946. A member of 1936, 1948, and 1952 Olympic teams, he was nonplaying captain in 1956. He founded the magazine *American Fencer* in 1949, served as president of the Amateur Fencers League of America, and was chairman of the U.S. Olympic Fencing Committee, 1953–57.

Helms Hall of Fame.

DeGROOT, DUDLEY S. football: b. 1900(?); d. May 5, 1970. Stanford center; captain, 1922. (He was also a member of the U.S. rugby team that won the Olympic championship in 1924.) DeGroot compiled an overall 116–67–9 record, coaching at Santa Barbara State, Rochester University, San Jose State, West Virginia, and New Mexico. At San Jose, he produced two straight unbeaten, untied teams, 1938–39. In winning 25 straight, San Jose scored 635 points, an average of 25.4 per game, giving up just 85.

He coached the Washington Redskins, 1944–45, winning the Eastern Division title in 1945, but his club lost the title playoff 15–14 to the Cleveland Rams. His record at Washington was 14–5–1. Then he moved to the Los Angeles Dons (AAFC), 1946–47, compiling a 14–12–2 record.

DELAHANTY, "BIG ED" (Edward J.) baseball: b. Oct. 30, 1867, Cleveland; d. July 2, 1903. Brother of James. Bat, throw R; outfield, first base. Philadelphia NL, 1888–89; Cleveland PL, 1890; Philadelphia NL, 1891–1901;

Washington AL, 1902–03. Sixteen years, 1,835 games, 7,505 at-bats, 2,59⌐ hits, 522 doubles, 185 triples, 100 home runs, 1,599 runs, 1,464 RBI, 45⌐ stolen bases, .346 BA (5th).

A big, strong hitter, Delahanty became the second man in history to hi⌐ 4 home runs in a game, on July 13, 1896. He is the only player ever to hav⌐ two 6-for-6 games, on June 2, 1890, and June 16, 1894. He is coholder c⌐ the NL record for most consecutive hits, 10, and he hit over .400 thre⌐ times: .407 in 1894, .404 in 1895, .410 in 1899. But 1899 was the only yea⌐ he won the batting title. He led the league in slugging in 1892 (.495), 189⌐ (.583), 1896 (.631), 1899 (.582), and 1902 (.590); in hits, 1899 (238); i⌐ triples, 1892 (21); in home runs, 1893 (19); in doubles, 1895 (49), 1896 (44⌐ 1899 (55), 1901 (38), and 1902 (42); in RBI, 1893 (146), 1896 (126), an⌐ 1899 (137); and in stolen bases, 1898 (58).

He hit .306 in 1892, .368 in 1893, .397 in 1896, .377 in 1897, .334 in 1898⌐ .323 in 1900, .354 in 1901 and .376 in 1902.

Delahanty was hitting .333 in 42 games in 1903 when he was suspende⌐ for heavy drinking. He was taking a train home when he got into a drunke⌐ argument and was put off the train just as it was about to cross the Interna⌐ tional Bridge at Fort Erie, Ontario. He tried to catch up to the train to ge⌐ back on, but the draw was open and he fell into the water. His body wa⌐ carried over Niagara Falls and recovered a week later.

Baseball Hall of Fame.

DELAHANTY, JAMES C. baseball: b. June 20, 1879, Cleveland, Ohio; d⌐ Oct. 17, 1953. Bat, throw R; second base, third base, outfield. Chicago NL⌐ 1901; New York NL, 1902; Boston NL, 1904–05; Cincinnati NL, 1906; St⌐ Louis AL, 1907; Washington AL, 1907–09; Detroit AL, 1909–12; Brooklyn⌐ Fed L, 1914–15. Thirteen years, 1,186 games, .283 BA; hit .317 in 1908⌐ .339 in 1911. One World Series, 1909: 7 games, .346 BA.

James was the brother of Ed.

DELANEY, JACK boxing: b. Ovila Chapdelaine, March 19, 1900, St. Francis⌐ Quebec, Canada; d. Nov. 28, 1948. His record: 70 wins, 42 by KO; 10 losses⌐ 3 by KO; 3 draws, 2 no-decisions, 1 no-contest. Delaney won the light⌐ heavyweight title, July 26, 1926, by decisioning Paul Berlenbach in 1⌐ rounds; he resigned in 1927 to fight as a heavyweight.

Helms Hall of Fame.

DeMAR, CLARENCE marathon: b. June 7, 1888, Madeira, Ohio; d. June 11⌐ 1958. The only American to come close to winning the Olympic marathon⌐ since Johnny Hayes's victory in 1908, DeMar finished third in 1924. He⌐ entered the Boston marathon 25 times, winning 7, and he finished every⌐ time. In his first victory, in 1911, he set a record that was broken the⌐

following year, but his record of 2 hours, 18 minutes, 10 seconds, set in 1922, held up until 1956. His other Boston victories came in 1923–24, 1927–28, and 1930. He won the AAU marathon, 1926–28.

DEMAREE, "AL" (Albert W.) baseball: b. Sept. 8, 1866, Quincy, Ill.; d. April 30, 1962. Bat L, throw R; pitcher. New York NL, 1912–14; Philadelphia NL, 1915–16; Chicago NL, 1917; New York NL, 1917–18; Boston NL, 1919. Eight years, 81–72, 2.77 ERA. One World Series, 1913: 0–1, 4.50 ERA.

DEMAREE, "FRANK" (Joseph Franklin) baseball: b. J. F. Dimaria, June 10, 1910, Winters, Calif.; d. Aug. 30, 1958. Bat, throw R; outfield. Chicago NL, 1932–33, 1935–38; New York NL, 1939–41; Boston NL, 1941–42; St. Louis NL, 1943; St. Louis AL, 1944. Twelve years, 1,155 games, .299 BA; hit .325 in 1935, .350 in 1936, .324 in 1937, .304 in 1939, .302 in 1940. Four World Series, 1932, 1935, 1938, 1943: 12 games, .214 BA.

He went 6-for-7, with 3 doubles, on July 5, 1937.

DeMONTREVILLE, "GENE" (Eugene N.) baseball: b. March 26, 1874, St. Paul, Minn.; d. Feb. 18, 1935. Bat, throw R; second base, shortstop. Pittsburgh NL, 1894; Washington NL, 1895–97; Baltimore NL, 1898–99; Chicago NL, 1899; Brooklyn NL, 1900; Boston NL, 1901–02; Washington AL, 1903; St. Louis AL, 1904. Eleven years, 922 games, .303 BA; hit .343 in 1896, .341 in 1897, .328 in 1898, .300 in 1901.

DeMOSS, "BINGO" (Elwood) baseball: b. Sept. 5, 1889, Topeka, Kan.; d. Jan. 26, 1965. Bat, throw R; second base, shortstop. Negro leagues: Topeka Giants, Indianapolis ABCs, Chicago American Giants, Kansas City Giants, Oklahoma Giants, Detroit Stars, 1905–25.

Managed Indianapolis, Detroit, American Giants, Chicago Brown Bombers, 1925–43. He was rated Negro baseball's outstanding second baseman during the teens and early twenties.

DEMPSEY, "THE NONPAREIL" JACK boxing: b. John Kelly, Dec. 15, 1862, County Kildare, Ireland; d. Nov. 1, 1895. His record: 48 wins, 8 by KO; 3 losses, 2 by KO; 8 draws, 4 no-decisions. A young cooper went to a New York boxing match in 1883 and found himself volunteering to replace a fighter who didn't show up. He gave his name as Jack Dempsey, and he won. Within a year he was considered lightweight champion, but he never claimed that title. In 1884, Canadian George Fulljames declared himself "middleweight" champion—the first time the term was used—and challenged anyone who weighed less than 158 pounds. Dempsey weighed about 130, but KOed Fulljames in 22 rounds on Aug. 30.

Dempsey never did weigh more than 150, but he fought people from all classes without a loss until Aug. 27, 1889, when George La Blanche KOed him in the 22nd round with a "pivot punch." The punch, which had never been used before, was declared illegal shortly afterward, and La Blanche was never considered champion.

Bob Fitzsimmons won Dempsey's middleweight title with a 13-round KO on Jan. 14, 1891. "The Nonpareil" had just three more fights; his health was failing. He went to Oregon early in 1895, hoping to recuperate, but died there.

Boxing Hall of Fame.

DENNY, JERRY baseball: b. Jeremiah Dennis Eldridge, March 16, 1859 New York City; d. Aug. 16, 1927. Bat, throw R; third base. Providence NL 1881–85; St. Louis NL, 1886; Indianapolis NL, 1887–89; New York NL 1890–91; Cleveland NL, Philadelphia NL, 1891; Louisville NL, 1893–94 Thirteen years, 1,237 games, .260 BA; hit .324 in 1887. Led league in strikeouts, 1888 (79).

Denny's 11 assists and 13 chances on May 29, 1890, tied the ML record for third basemen in a 9-inning game. On Aug. 17, 1882, he set an ML record with 16 chances in 18 innings. He went 6-for-6, with a double, a home run, and 3 runs scored, on May 4, 1889.

DePALMA, RALPH auto racing: b. 1883, Italy; d. March 31, 1956. DePalma was national driving champion in 1912 and 1914. He won the Indianapolis 500 in 1915 with an average speed of 89.84 miles per hour, a record until 1922. In 1919 he set a 1-mile record of 149.875 miles per hour at Daytona Beach, Fla.; it stood for only one year.

In 1912, DePalma was leading at Indy with five laps to go when his car began losing oil. It died with less than a mile to go. He and mechanic Rupert Jeffkins pushed the car across the finish line after Joe Dawson had won the race. (Their second-place finish was not allowed, of course, but they won a standing ovation.)

Auto Racing Hall of Fame, Helms Hall of Fame.

DesJARDIEN, PAUL R. ("Shorty") football: b. Aug. 24, 1893, Coffeyville Kan.; d. March 7, 1956. University of Chicago center; All-American, 1913 2nd team, captain, 1914. Guard, Hammond Pros, 1919; Chicago Tigers Chicago Cardinals, 1920; Rock Island Independents, 1921.

Helms Hall of Fame, National Football Foundation Hall of Fame.

DEVLIN, ARTHUR McA. baseball: b. Oct. 16, 1879; d. Sept. 18, 1948. Bat throw R; third base. New York NL, 1904–11; Boston NL, 1912–13. Ten years, 1,300 games, .268 BA. One World Series, 1905: 5 games, .250 BA.

Devlin handled 13 chances on May 23, 1908, tying the ML record for third basemen in a 9-inning game.

DEVORE, JOSHUA baseball: b. Nov. 13, 1887, Murray City, Ohio; d. Oct. 5, 1946. Bat L, throw R; outfield. New York NL, 1908–13; Cincinnati NL, 1913; Philadelphia NL, 1913–14; Boston NL, 1914. Seven years, 601 games, .277 BA; hit .304 in 1910. Three World Series, 1911–12, 1914: 14 games, .204 BA.

He got 5 hits on Aug. 22, 1911, hitting the first pitch each time at bat.

DeWITT, JOHN R. football, track: b. Oct. 29, 1881, Phillipsburg, N.J.; d. July 28, 1930. Princeton tackle, 1901; guard, 1902–03; captain, 1903; All-American, 1902–03. Like many linemen of his day, DeWitt was often used in the backfield to run or kick, and he was outstanding at both. He was a rough player who once told an opponent at the beginning of a game, "There are two ways to play me: Stay out of my way or get hurt."

Against Lafayette in 1901, he scored the winning TD on a 50-yard run with 3 minutes to play. In 1902, his two field goals were the only points in a 10–0 win over Cornell, and he also kicked field goals of 45 and 50 yards during the year.

DeWitt captained an undefeated, untied team in 1903. He scored the only TD against Georgetown, ran 70 yards for a TD against Dartmouth, scored a TD and kicked a field goal of 40 yards against Lafayette. But the greatest victory came against a favored Yale team. After Yale scored the first TD, DeWitt ran 50 yards with a blocked kick and made the conversion to tie the score, then booted a 43-yard field goal into the wind to win the game.

He was IC4A hammer-throw champion for four straight years, 1901–04; his throw of 164 feet, 10 inches, in 1902 was the world record until 1922. He won a Silver Medal in the 1904 Olympics.

National Football Foundation Hall of Fame.

DICKEY, JAMES B. tennis: b. 1892(?), Georgia; d. Oct. 12, 1964. An ardent booster of tennis, Dickey was long-time president of the Eastern Lawn Tennis Association and was elected president of the USLTA in February 1964. He was the first USLTA director to back the idea of an open tournament, permitting amateurs to compete against professionals. It has been adopted since his death.

DIDDLE, EDGAR A. basketball: b. Gradyville, Ky.; d. Jan. 2, 1970. Diddle coached basketball at Western Kentucky State, 1922–64, compiling a 759–302 record. The total of 1,061 games is a record for a coach at one college. His teams won or shared 32 championships in three different conferences and went to the NCAA tournament three times and the National Invitational Tournament eight times.

Diddle was a colorful coach whose sideline prop was a red towel. He would hurl it into the air when one of his players did something exciting, bury his face in it when he saw a mistake, and loop it around his neck, noose style, when things got really bad.

Western Kentucky's $3-million arena is named for him.

DIEGEL, LEO golf: b. April 26, 1899, Detroit; d. May 8, 1951. Three times a finalist in the PGA championship (then match play), Diegel lost to Walter Hagen in 1926 but beat Al Espinosa in 1928 and Johnny Farrell in 1929. He won the Canadian Open four times, 1924–25, 1928–29.

Professional Golfers Association Hall of Fame.

DIETZ, "LONE STAR" (William) football: b. 1886(?); d. July 20, 1964. Carlisle guard; captain 1911.

Coached Boston Redskins, 1933–34 (11–11–2).

DILLON, JACK boxing: b. Ernest C. Price, Feb. 2, 1891, Frankfurt, Ind.; d. Aug. 7, 1942. His record: 91 wins, 60 by KO; 6 losses, none by KO; 15 draws, 127 no-decisions, 1 no-contest. After KOing Hugo Kelly in the 3rd round on May 28, 1912, Dillon claimed the light-heavyweight championship. However, he was not genuinely recognized as the champion until he won a 10–round decision from Al Norton on April 28, 1914. Dillon lost the title to Battling Levinsky in 12 rounds on Oct. 24, 1916.

Boxing Hall of Fame, Helms Hall of Fame.

DILWEG, "LAVVIE" (Lavern R.) football: b. Nov. 1, 1903, Milwaukee, Wis.; d. Jan. 2, 1968. Marquette end. Milwaukee Badgers, 1926; Green Bay Packers, 1927–34; All-Pro, 1931. Dilweg was an outstanding receiver in his era, and the Packers did a lot of passing. It's unfortunate that complete statistics weren't kept while he was playing.

DINNEEN, WILLIAM H. baseball: b. April 5, 1876, Syracuse, N.Y.; d. Jan. 13, 1955. Bat, throw R; pitcher. Washington NL, 1898–99; Boston NL, 1900–01; Boston AL, 1902–07; St. Louis AL, 1907–09. Twelve years, 171–178, 3.01 ERA; 21–15 in 1900, 21–21 in 1902, 21–11 in 1903, 23–14 in 1904. No-hitter against Chicago AL, Sept. 27, 1905 (2–0).

In 1904, Dinneen set AL records by pitching 37 consecutive complete games, 337 consecutive innings, without being relieved.

He was the pitching hero of the first World Series, in 1903, winning 3 and losing 1 as Boston beat the Pirates, 5 games to 3. He had 4 starts, 4 complete games, 2 shutouts, and a 2.06 ERA.

DIXIE KID boxing: b. Aaron L. Brown, Dec. 23, 1883, Fulton, Mo.; d. Oct. 3, 1935. His record: 77 wins, 63 by KO; 16 losses, 3 by KO; 6 draws, 23 no-decisions, 1 no-contest. The Dixie Kid won the welterweight title on

April 30, 1904, when he was fouled by Joe Walcott in the 20th round. A rematch with Walcott on May 12 ended in a draw, and Dixie Kid gave up the title shortly afterward because he could no longer make the weight.

DIXON, GEORGE boxing: b. July 29, 1870, Halifax, Nova Scotia; d. Jan. 6, 1909. His record: 78 wins, 30 by KO; 26 losses, 4 by KO; 37 draws, 9 no-decisions. The first Negro to hold a world title, Dixon is considered one of the great fighters of all time. He won the world bantamweight title by KOing Nunc Wallace in the 18th round, June 27, 1890. Dixon outgrew that class, resigned the title, and became U.S. featherweight champion, March 31, 1891, with a 22-round KO of Cal McCarthy. He won the world title, July 28, 1891, with a 5-round KO of Abe Willis, British champ, and held it until Oct. 4, 1897, when he lost to Solly Smith in 20 rounds. Smith quickly lost to Dave Sullivan, and Dixon regained the crown with a 10-round victory over Sullivan on Nov. 11, 1898.

Dixon was KOed by Terry McGovern in the 8th round on Jan. 9, 1900, but he claimed McGovern was overweight. He fought Abe Attell twice for the crown in 1901, Oct. 20 and Oct. 28; the first fight was a 20-round draw, but Attell won the second in 15 rounds.

Helms Hall of Fame, Boxing Hall of Fame.

DOAK, WILLIAM L. baseball: b. Jan. 28, 1891, Pittsburgh; d. Nov. 26, 1954. Bat, throw R; pitcher. Cincinnati NL, 1912; St. Louis NL, 1913–24; Brooklyn NL, 1924, 1927–28; St. Louis NL, 1929. Sixteen years, 170–157, 2.98 ERA; 36 shutouts, including ten 1–0 victories; 20–6 in 1914, 20–12 in 1920. Led NL in ERA, 1914 (1.72); in ERA (2.59) and percentage (15–6, .714) in 1921.

DOANE, "DINGER" (Erling) football: b. 1897, Natick, Mass.; d. June 5, 1949. Tufts back. Cleveland Indians, 1919–20; Milwaukee Badgers, 1922–24; Detroit Panthers, 1925–26; Pottsville Maroons, Providence Steamrollers, 1927.

DOBIE, GILMOUR football: b. Jan. 21, 1879, Hastings, Minn.; d. Dec. 23, 1948. "Gloomy Gil" was always pessimistic about his teams, and he virtually never complimented a player, but he produced 14 unbeaten teams in 31 teams of coaching. After playing end and quarterback at Minnesota (1902), he coached North Dakota State to two undefeated seasons, 1906–07, then went to Washington, 1908–16. His Huskies never lost a game in his nine years. The undefeated streak of 63 games (including 4 ties), which began the year before he arrived and continued into the following season, is the longest in college football history. Included in the streak were 39 consecutive wins.

He coached Navy, 1917–19, compiling a 17–3 mark, then moved on to Cornell. After his 1921, 1922, and 1923 teams went undefeated, he was given college football's first ten-year contract. He left after the 1935 season for Boston College. His 1936 Boston College team lost only one game and beat archrival Holy Cross. In 1938 BC was unbeaten until its final game, when it lost to Holy Cross. Dobie, still suffering the aftereffects of a serious 1936 auto accident, retired after that season.

Helms Hall of Fame, National Football Foundation Hall of Fame.

DONAHUE, "RED" (Francis R.) baseball: b. Jan. 23, 1873, Waterbury, Conn.; d. Aug. 25, 1913. Bat, throw R; pitcher. New York NL, 1893; St. Louis NL, 1895–97; Philadelphia NL, 1898–1901; St. Louis AL, 1902–03; Cleveland AL, 1903–05; Detroit AL, 1905–06. Thirteen years, 168–175, 3.61 ERA; 21–8 in 1899, 22–13 in 1901, 22–11 in 1902. No-hitter, July 8, 1898, against Boston NL.

His most spectacular season was terrible: He was 10–35 in 1897, setting an ML record for most losses. He led the NL in games (46), starts (42), and complete games (38) that year.

DONLIN, MICHAEL J. baseball: b. May 30, 1878, Erie, Pa.; d. Sept. 24, 1933. Bat, throw L; outfield. St. Louis NL, 1899–1900; Baltimore AL, 1901; Cincinnati NL, 1902–04; New York NL, 1904–06, 1908, 1911; Boston NL, 1911; Pittsburgh NL, 1912; New York NL, 1914. Twelve years, 1,049 games, .333 BA; hit .340 in 1901, .351 in 1903, .329 in 1904, .356 in 1905, .334 in 1908. Led NL in runs, 1905 (124). One World Series, 1905: 5 games, .316 BA.

Donlin went 6-for-6 and scored 5 runs, with 2 doubles and 2 triples, on June 24, 1901.

DONOVAN, MIKE boxing: b. Sept. 27, 1847, Chicago; d. March 24, 1918. His record: 24 wins, 2 by KO; 2 losses, both on fouls; 7 draws. George Rooke claimed the middleweight title in 1872 but refused to fight Donovan and retired from the ring for seven years, and Donovan was generally considered champion. He lost a title fight on a 14th-round foul to W. C. McLellan in April, 1878, but beat McLellan in 7 rounds the following month. When Rooke and Donovan finally fought, in March, 1881, Donovan won in 2 rounds. Donovan retired late in 1884 to become boxing instructor for the New York Athletic Commission.

DONOVAN, "PATSY" (Patrick J.) baseball: b. March 16, 1865, County Cork, Ireland; d. Dec. 25, 1953. Bat R, throw L; outfield. Brooklyn NL, Boston NL, 1890; Louisville AA, Washington AA, 1891; Washington NL, 1892; Pittsburgh NL, 1892–99; St. Louis NL, 1900–03; Washington AL,

1904; Brooklyn NL, 1906–07. Seventeen years, 1,821 games, 518 stolen bases, .301 BA; hit .305 in 1891, .317 in 1893, .302 in 1894, .308 in 1895, .319 in 1896, .322 in 1897, .302 in 1898, .316 in 1900, .303 in 1901, .315 in 1902, .327 in 1903. Led NL in stolen bases, 1900 (45).

Donovan managed Pittsburgh NL, 1897, 1899 (part); St. Louis NL, 1901–03; Washington AL, 1904; Brooklyn NL, 1906–08; Boston AL, 1910–11: 683–878, .438.

DONOVAN, "WILD BILL" (William E.) baseball: b. Oct. 13, 1876, Lawrence, Mass.; d. Dec. 9, 1923. Bat, throw R; pitcher. Washington NL, 1898; Brooklyn NL, 1899–1902; Detroit AL, 1903–12; New York AL, 1915–16; Detroit AL, 1918. Eighteen years, 188–137, 2.69 ERA; 1,552 strikeouts, 35 shutouts, in 2,966⅔ innings. Led league in wins, 1901 (27–14); in percentage, 1907 (26–4, .867) and 1908 (19–7, .731). Three World Series, 1907–09: 1 win, 4 losses (3rd), 2.70 ERA; 6 starts, 5 complete (6th).

Managed New York AL, 1915–17; Philadelphia AL, 1921 (part): 251–310, .447.

DOOIN, "RED" (Charles S.) baseball: b. June 12, 1879, Cincinnati; d. May 14, 1952. Bat, throw R; catcher. Philadelphia NL, 1902–14; Cincinnati NL, 1915; New York NL, 1915–16. Fifteen years, 1,289 games, .240 BA.

Dooin holds the NL record for most career assists by a catcher, 1,593. Managed Philadelphia NL, 1910–14: 392–370, .514.

DOOLAN, "MICKEY" (Michael J.) baseball: b. M. J. Doolittle, May 7, 1880, Ashland, Pa.; d. Nov. 1, 1951. Bat, throw R; shortstop. Philadelphia NL, 1905–13; Baltimore Fed L, 1914–15; Chicago Fed L, 1915; Chicago NL, New York NL, 1916; Brooklyn NL, 1918. Thirteen years, 1,727 games, .230 BA.

He tied the ML record for most years leading shortstops in games played, 6, and holds the NL record for most years leading shortstops in assists, 5.

DORAIS, "GUS" (Charles E.) football: b. July 2, 1891, Chippewa Falls, Wis.; d. Jan. 3, 1954. Quarterback Dorais and end Knute Rockne, of Notre Dame, made football history in 1913. Working at a resort during the summer, the two practiced the forward pass. Against Army that fall, Dorais completed 12 consecutive passes for 3 TDs as Notre Dame came up with a stunning 35–13 upset. The game not only helped to popularize the forward pass but also established Notre Dame as a football power.

Dorais played pro football for several teams before the National Football League was organized. He coached at Columbia College (now Loras), Iowa, 1916–19, Gonzaga, 1920–24, and Detroit, 1925–42, compiling an overall record of 150–70–13. He coached the Detroit Lions, 1943–47, for a 20–31–2 mark. Dorais also coached the College All-Stars to a 6–0 victory over Green Bay in 1937.

Helms Hall of Fame, National Football Foundation Hall of Fame.

DOUBLEDAY, ABNER baseball: b. June 26, 1819, Ballston Spa, N.Y.; d. Jan. 26, 1893. A West Point graduate, Doubleday fired the first gun in defense of Fort Sumter, North Carolina, at the outbreak of the Civil War and was a major-general by the war's end. He was mistakenly credited as the originator of baseball by a commission set up in 1907. A. G. Mills, commission chairman, wrote the report; no other member signed it. Based on unknown evidence, Mills said that as a schoolboy in Cooperstown, New York, Doubleday had diagrammed a baseball diamond in 1839. This was the basis for baseball's "centennial" celebration in 1939 and for the establishment of the Hall of Fame at Cooperstown. Far from being a schoolboy in 1839, Doubleday was already a student at West Point, and there is no known evidence to support Mills's claim. (See Cartwright, Alexander J.)

DOUGHERTY, "PATSY" (Patrick H.) baseball: b. Oct. 27, 1876, Andover, N.Y.; d. April 30, 1940. Bat L, throw R; outfield. Boston AL, 1902–04; New York AL, 1904–06; Chicago AL, 1906–11. Ten years, 1,233 games, .284 BA; hit .342 in 1902, .331 in 1903. Two World Series, 1903, 1906: 14 games, .185 BA. Led AL in hits (195) and runs (106) in 1903; in runs, 1904 (113); in stolen bases, 1908 (47).

DOUGLAS, "SHUFFLING PHIL" (Philips B.) baseball: b. June 17, 1890, Cedartown, Ga.; d. Aug. 1, 1952. Bat, throw R; pitcher. Chicago AL, 1912; Cincinnati NL, 1914–15; Brooklyn NL, 1915; Chicago NL, 1915, 1917, 1919; New York NL, 1919–22. Nine years, 93–93, 2.80 ERA. Led league in shutouts, 1921 (3). Two World Series, 1918, 1921: 2–2, 2.00 ERA. In 1921, he lost the first game, 3–0, but won the fourth game, 4–2, and the seventh game, 2–1, as the Giants beat the Yankees, 5 games to 3.

Douglas was banned from baseball during the 1922 season for writing a letter to a friend on the Cardinals offering to "take a vacation" for the rest of the year if the Cardinals "would make it worth my while."

DOW, WARREN A. fencing: b. 1905(?); d. Nov. 22, 1965. Dow was U.S. men's foil champion, 1942–43; he was a member of the championship foil team, 1937–38, 1941–42, 1947–48.

DOWD, THOMAS J. ("Buttermilk Tommy") baseball: b. April 20, 1869, Holyoke, Mass.; d. July 2, 1933. Bat, throw R; outfield, second base. Boston AA, 1891, Washington AA, 1891; Washington NL, 1892; St. Louis NL,

1893–97; Philadelphia NL, 1897; St. Louis NL, 1898; Cleveland NL, 1899; Boston AL, 1901. Ten years, 1,320 games, .271 BA; hit .323 in 1895.

DOYLE, EDWARD J. football: b. Aug. 17, 1898, New York City; d. Nov. 8, 1942. Army end. Frankford Yellowjackets, 1924; Pottsville Maroons, 1925. Doyle was the first American officer killed in the World War II invasion of North Africa.

DOYLE, "JACK" (John J.) baseball: b. Oct. 25, 1869, Killorgin, Ireland; d. Dec. 31, 1958. Bat, throw R; played every position except pitcher but was primarily a first baseman. Columbus AA, 1889–90; Cleveland NL, 1891–92; New York NL, 1892–95; Baltimore NL, 1896–97; Washington NL, 1898; New York NL, 1898–1900; Chicago NL, 1901; Washington AL, New York NL, 1902; Brooklyn NL, 1903–04; Philadelphia NL, 1904; New York AL, 1905. Seventeen years, 1,564 games, .299 BA; hit .321 in 1893, .367 in 1894, .313 in 1895, .339 in 1896, .354 in 1897, .313 in 1903.

Doyle went 6-for-6 on Sept. 3, 1897, with 2 doubles.

DRESSEN, "CHUCK" (Charles W.) baseball: b. Sept. 20, 1898, Decatur, Ill.; d. Aug. 10, 1966. Bat, throw R; third base. Cincinnati NL, 1925–31; New York NL, 1933. Eight years, 646 games, .272 BA.

Managed Cincinnati NL, 1934 (part)–37 (part); Brooklyn NL, 1951–53; Washington AL, 1955–57 (part); Milwaukee NL, 1960–61 (part); Detroit AL, 1963–66 (part): 1,037–993, .511. Pennants, 1952–53.

Dressen liked to tell his teams, "Stay close through the early innings, and I'll think of something."

He played pro football as a quarterback for the Decatur Staleys, 1920, and Racine Legion, 1922–23.

DREYFUSS, BARNEY baseball: b. Feb. 23, 1865, Freiburg, Germany; d. Feb. 5, 1932. Dreyfuss was a part owner of the Louisville Colonels, 1888–99, then gained full control of the Pittsburgh Pirates in 1901. He was responsible for the beginning of the modern World Series; when the Pirates won the NL pennant, Dreyfuss challenged the AL champion Boston team to a postseason series, which Boston won.

In 1909, Dreyfuss unveiled Forbes Field, the first steel stadium and most modern baseball park of its time. In his thirty-one years of ownership, Pittsburgh won 6 pennants and finished in the first division 26 times.

DRISCOLL, "PADDY" (John L.) football: b. Jan. 11, 1896, Evanston, Ill.; d. June 29, 1968. Northwestern halfback; third team All-American, 1916. Decatur Staleys, 1920; Chicago Cardinals, 1920–25; Chicago Bears, 1926–29. An uncannily accurate kicker, Driscoll had a career total of 377 points on 29 TDs, 56 conversions, and 49 field goals. He holds the NFL records for most field goals by dropkick in a game, 4, on Oct. 11, 1925, and for longest field goal by dropkick, 50 yards, Sept. 28, 1924, and Oct. 11 1925.

He coached the Cardinals, 1921–22 (12–6–3), and the Bears, 1956–57 (14–9–1).

Professional Football Hall of Fame, Helms Hall of Fame, National Football Foundation Hall of Fame.

DUDLEY, EDWARD golf: b. Feb. 10, 1902, Brunswick, Ga.; d. Oct. 25, 1963. At 6'4" and 200 pounds, Dudley was a long-ball hitter, with the inconsistency that often goes with distance off the tee. His only major victory was the 1931 Western Open.

DUFFY, HUGH baseball: b. Nov. 26, 1866, Cranston, R.I.,; d. Oct. 20, 1954. Bat, throw R; outfield. Chicago NL, 1888–89; Chicago PL, 1890; Boston AA, 1891; Boston NL, 1892–1900; Milwaukee AL, 1901; Philadelphia NL, 1904–06. Seventeen years, 1,736 games, 7,042 at-bats, 2,282 hits, 325 doubles, 118 triples, 105 home runs, 1,553 runs, 1,299 RBI, 574 stolen bases, .324 BA. Duffey's .440 BA in 1894 is the highest ever recorded. It was the only year he led the league in hitting, but he hit over .300 nine other times: .320 in 1890, .336 in 1891, .301 in 1892, .363 in 1893, .352 in 1895, .300 in 1896, .340 in 1897, .304 in 1900, .302 in 1901. He led the league in runs, 1890 (161); in hits, (237), doubles (51), home runs (18), RBI (145), and slugging (.690) in 1894; and in home runs, 1897 (11).

On June 18, 1894, he tied an ML record by reaching first base safely three times in one inning.

Managed Milwaukee AL, 1901; Philadelphia NL, 1904–06; Chicago AL, 1910–11; Boston AL, 1921–22: 535–671, .444.

Baseball Hall of Fame.

DUFFY, "PADDY" (Patrick) boxing: b. Nov. 12, 1864, Boston; d. July 19, 1890. His record: 24 wins, 14 by KO; 1 loss, by KO; 11 draws. There was no real title for welterweights, though they fought among themselves, in the late 1880s. But Duffy, having lost only 1 of 36 fights, proclaimed himself champion of his class in 1888 and retired after 1 more fight. William McMillan had claimed the British title; Duffy KOed him in 17 rounds.

DUNDEE, JOHNNY boxing: b. Joseph Carrora, Nov. 22, 1893, Italy; d. April 22, 1965. His record: 113 wins, 19 by KO; 31 losses, 2 by KO; 18 draws, 159 no-decisions. "The Scotch Wop," though rated among the top ten featherweights of all time, was a champion for less than two years. He was nearly thirty when he won the title on July 26, 1923, with a 15-round decision over Eugene Criqui. Early in 1925, Dundee resigned the title because he couldn't make the weight.

DUNDEE, VINCE boxing: b. Vincent Lazzaro, 1904, Italy; d. July 27, 1949. His record: 112 wins, 27 by KO; 19 losses, 1 by KO; 13 draws, 5 no-decisions, 1 no-contest. Dundee fought a 15-round draw with Ben Jeby on March 17, 1933, for the New York Commission middleweight title, then won the American title on Oct. 30 of the same year with a 15-round decision over Lou Brouilliard. He lost it on a 15-round decision to Teddy Yarosz on Sept. 11, 1934.

DUNLAP, FREDERICK C. baseball: b. May 21, 1859, Philadelphia; d. Dec. 1, 1902. Bat, throw R; second base. Cleveland NL, 1880–83; St. Louis UA, 1884; St. Louis NL, 1885–86; Detroit NL, 1886–87; Pittsburgh NL, 1888–90; New York PL, 1890; Washington AA, 1891. Hit .325 in 1881, .326 in 1883. Led NL in doubles, 1880 (27); led UA in hits (185), home runs (13), runs (160), BA (.412), and slugging (.621) in 1884.

DURYEA, "JESSE" (James W.) baseball: b. Sept. 7, 1862, Osage, Iowa; d. Aug. 7, 1942. Bat, throw R; pitcher. Cincinnati AA, 1889; Cincinnati NL, 1890–91; St. Louis AA, 1891; Cincinnati NL, 1892; Washington NL, 1892–93. Five years, 59–66, 3.45 ERA; 32–19 in 1889.

DWIGHT, JAMES tennis: b. ?; d. July 14, 1917. Sometimes called the father of American tennis, Dr. Dwight was one of the genuine pioneers of the sport. He learned to play in 1876 on the second court built in America, on his uncle's property at Nahant, Massachusetts. He was never a singles champion, but he and Richard D. Sears won the U.S. outdoor doubles, 1882–84 and 1886–87. He wrote one of the first books about the game, in 1887, and was president of the U.S. Lawn Tennis Association, which he helped found, from 1891 to 1912.

Tennis Hall of Fame.

DWYER, "FRANK" (John F.) baseball: b. March 25, 1868, Lee, Mass.; d. Feb. 4, 1943. Bat, throw R; pitcher. Chicago NL, 1888–89; Chicago PL, 1890; Cincinnati-Milwaukee AA, 1891; St. Louis NL, 1892; Cincinnati NL, 1892–99. Twelve years, 176–152, 3.85 ERA; 21–18 in 1892, 24–11 in 1896. Managed Detroit AL, 1902: 52–83, .385.

DYER, "EDDIE" (Edwin H.) baseball: b. Oct. 11, 1900, Morgan City, La.; d. April 20, 1964. Bat, throw L; pitcher. St. Louis NL, 1922–27. Six years, 15–15, 4.75 ERA.

Managed St. Louis NL, 1946–50: 446–325, .578. Pennant, world championship, 1946.

E

EAGAN, EDWARD P. F. boxing, bobsledding: b. April 26, 1898, Denver, Colo.; d. June 14, 1967. While still a student at Yale, Eagan was Olympic light-heavyweight boxing champion in 1920. In 1932, he was a member of the Olympic champion four-man bobsled team, becoming one of very few athletes ever to win Gold Medals in two different sports. Active as a fund-raiser for the U.S. Olympic team and other athletic causes for many years, he was New York Athletic Commission chairman, 1945–51.

EARP, "JUG" (Francis) football: b. July 22, 1897, Monmouth, Ill.; d. Jan. 8, 1969. Monmouth center. Rock Island Independents, 1920–21, 1924; Green Bay Packers, 1922–32; New York Yankees, 1927. Earp occasionally played guard or tackle.

EASTER, "ED" (Ebber D.) bowling: b. Nov. 20, 1882, Winston-Salem, N.C.; d. Aug. 14, 1961. A thirty-year Army veteran, Easter came late to serious competitive bowling, when he was nearly sixty. He won the ABC all-events in 1946 and was the oldest member ever of an ABC championship team in 1950. His sixteen-year ABC tourney average was 193. He had four sanctioned 300 games, two of them when he was over seventy years old.
American Bowling Congress Hall of Fame.

EATON, CALVIN boxing: b. 1908(?); d. Jan. 10, 1966. Eaton and his wife, Aileen, were instrumental in making Los Angeles a major boxing city. They promoted boxing and wrestling matches, including 26 world title fights, in LA.

EBBETS, CHARLES H. baseball: b. Oct. 29, 1859, New York City; d. April 18, 1925. Ebbets in 1883 went to work for Brooklyn's first professional team, handling publicity, bookkeeping, and other jobs. In 1890, he invested in the team. He became its president in 1898 and by 1903 he owned a controlling interest; he controlled it until his death. When Brooklyn built a new baseball park in 1913, sportswriters voted to name it Ebbets Field, home of the Dodgers until they moved to Los Angeles.

ECKERSALL, WALTER H. football: b. June 17, 1887, Chicago; d. March 24, 1930. A 150-pound quarterback at the University of Chicago, Eckersall was an All-American, 1904–06, and was named to the pre-1920 All-American team. He is the only college player ever to kick 5 field goals in a game twice, against Illinois in 1905 and against Nebraska in 1906. When Chicago ended Michigan's 56-game winning streak with a 2–0 victory in 1905, Eckersall's great punting was largely responsible for holding the "point-a-minute" team scoreless. Eckersall was also a good breakaway runner—he had a TD of 106 yards against Wisconsin in 1904 and runs of 50, 40, and 30 yards in 1905—and his speed made him an outstanding defensive back. When the forward pass became legal, 1906, Eckersall became an expert at an early version of the option, heading around end with the choice between running or throwing.

After graduation, he became a sportswriter for the *Chicago Tribune,* choosing annual all-Western and All-American teams.

Helms Hall of Fame, National Football Foundation Hall of Fame.

EFAW, FOREST track: b. ?; d. Jan. 31, 1957. Efaw was the AAU 3,000-meter steeplechase champion, 1941–1944, 1947–48, and indoor 3-mile champion, 1945–46.

EHMKE, HOWARD J. baseball: b. April 24, 1894, Silver Creek, N.Y.; d. March 17, 1959. Bat, throw R; pitcher. Buffalo Fed L, 1915; Detroit AL, 1916–17, 1919–22; Boston AL, 1923–26; Philadelphia AL, 1926–30. Fifteen years, 167–166, 3.75 ERA; 20–15 in 1923 (for 8th-place team). Led AL in losses, 1924 (19–17), in complete games, 1925 (22). No-hitter, Sept. 17, 1924, against Philadelphia AL; in his next start, Sept. 11, he pitched a 1-hitter. One World Series, 1929: 1–0, 1.42 ERA; 13 strikeouts in 12⅔ innings.

EHRET, "RED" (Philip S.) baseball: b. Aug. 31, 1868, Louisville, Ky.; d. July 28, 1940. Bat, throw R; pitcher. Kansas City AA, 1888; Louisville AA, 1889–91; Pittsburgh NL, 1892–94; St. Louis NL, 1895; Cincinnati NL, 1896–97; Louisville NL, 1898. Eleven years, 139–167, 4.02 ERA; 25–14 in 1890. Led NL in shutouts, 1893 (4).

EHRHARDT, CLYDE W. football: b. July 4, 1921, Murfreesboro, Tenn.; d. Feb. 4, 1963. Georgia center. Washington Redskins, 1946, 1948–49.

Ehrhardt served as football coach and athletic director at Presbyterian College from spring of 1962 until his death. His record was 1–9–0 in his one season there.

ELBERFELD, "KID" (Norman A.) baseball: b. April 13, 1875, Pomeroy, Ohio; d. Jan. 13, 1944. Bat, throw R; shortstop, third base. Philadelphia NL, 1898; Cincinnati NL, 1899; Detroit AL, 1901–03; New York AL,

1903–09; Washington AL, 1910–11; Brooklyn NL, 1914. Fourteen years, 1,292 games, .271 BA; hit .308 in 1901, .301 in 1903, .306 in 1906.

ELLER, "HOD" (Horace O.) baseball: b. July 5, 1894, Muncie, Ind.; d. July 18, 1961. Bat, throw R; pitcher. Cincinnati NL, 1917–21. Five years, 61–40, 2.62 ERA; 52 complete games, 88 starts, 10 shutouts. In relief, 16–5, 1.88 ERA, 5 saves. Eller was the pitching star of the 1919 World Series, beating the Chicago White Sox twice with 2 complete games, a 2.00 ERA, 15 strikeouts, and only 2 walks in 18 innings.

He struck out 3 hitters on 9 pitches in 1 inning, Aug. 21, 1917, tying an ML record.

ELLIOTT, JAMES A. R. shooting: b. 1874, near Kansas City, Mo.; d. 1924. Elliott was the only man ever to hold all major national live-bird shooting trophies simultaneously. He won permanent possession of the Kansas City Star Cup and the Field Cup by winning each 3 times in a row, and he held the Sportsman's Review Trophy, DuPont Cup, Republic Cup, and Cast Iron Medal twice in succession. In the 1900 Missouri tournament, he killed 214 of 215 birds.

American Trapshooting Hall of Fame.

ELLIOTT, "JUMBO JIM" (James T.) baseball: b. Oct. 22, 1900, St. Louis; d. Jan. 7, 1970. Bat, throw L; pitcher. St. Louis AL, 1923; Brooklyn NL, 1925, 1927–30; Philadelphia NL, 1931–34; Boston NL, 1934. Ten years, 63–74, 4.24 ERA. In relief, 11–11, 3.96 ERA, 12 saves. Led NL in victories, 1931 (19–14).

ELLIOTT, ROBERT I. baseball: b. Nov. 26, 1916, San Francisco; d. May 4, 1966. Bat, throw R; third base, outfield. Pittsburgh NL, 1939–46; Boston NL, 1947–51; New York NL, 1952; Chicago AL, St. Louis AL, 1953. Fifteen years, 1,978 games, 170 home runs, .289 BA; hit .315 in 1943, .317 in 1947, .305 in 1950. Led NL in walks, 1948 (13). One World Series, 1948: 6 games, .333 BA. He hit two home runs off Bob Feller, driving in 4 runs, in fifth game, but Braves lost to Cleveland in sixth.

Managed Kansas City AL, 1960: 58–96, .377.

ELY, "BONES" (Frederick W.) baseball: b. June 7, 1863, Girard, Pa.; d. Jan. 10, 1952. Bat, throw R; began as pitcher-outfielder, became shortstop in 1893. Buffalo NL, 1884; Louisville AA, 1886; Syracuse AA, 1890; Brooklyn NL, 1891; Baltimore NL, 1892; St. Louis NL, 1893–95; Pittsburgh NL, 1896–1901; Philadelphia AL, 1901; Washington AL, 1902. Fifteen years, 1,342 games, .258 BA; hit .306 in 1894.

ENGEL, JOSEPH W. baseball: b. March 12, 1893, Washington, D.C.; d. June 12, 1969. Bat, throw R; pitcher. Washington AL, 1912–15; Cincinnati

NL, 1917; Cleveland AL, 1919; Washington AL, 1920. Seven years, 18–23, 3.38 ERA.

Engel became known as the Barnum of the bushes for his showmanship as head of the Chattanooga team in the Southern Association. He once traded a shortstop for a 25-pound turkey, invited sportswriters to dinner, and complained, "I got robbed. This damn bird is tough." He was also an outstanding scout for the Senators; he discovered Joe Cronin, Bucky Harris, Goose Goslin, and Joe Judge, among others. He signed Cronin for $7,500 when he was hitting .221 in the minor leagues; five years later the Senators sold Cronin to the Red Sox for $250,000.

ENS, JEWEL W. baseball: b. Aug. 24, 1889, St. Louis; d. Jan. 17, 1950. Bat, throw R; second-first base. Pittsburgh NL, 1922–25. Four years, 67 games, .290 BA.

Managed Pittsburgh NL, 1929 (part)–31: 176–167, .513.

ERDELATZ, "EDDIE" (Edward J.) football: b. 1912, San Francisco; d. Nov. 10, 1965. An end at St. Mary's of California (1936), Erdelatz was one of Navy's most successful coaches, compiling a 50–26–8 record, 1950–58. His teams won the Sugar Bowl in 1955, 21–0 over Mississippi, and the 1958 Cotton Bowl, 20–7 over Rice. But his biggest victory came in 1950, when he brought a Navy team that had lost six games against an unbeaten Army team. Army had beaten Navy six straight times, but Erdelatz's team shocked the Cadets, 14–2.

He coached the Oakland Raiders in 1960 (6–8); he was fired after they lost their first two games in 1961.

ERICKSON, HAROLD A. football: b. March 10, 1899, Maynard, Minn.; d. Jan. 28, 1962. Washington and Jefferson end. Minneapolis Marines, 1921–22. Erickson played on two different Rose Bowl teams, with Great Lakes in a 17–0 win over Mare Island in 1919 and with the Washington and Jefferson team that played a scoreless tie with California in 1922.

ERNE, FRANK boxing: b. Jan. 8, 1875, Zurich, Switzerland; d. Sept. 17, 1954. His record: 22 wins, 10 by KO; 6 losses, 4 by KO; 12 draws. Erne began his ring career in the United States in 1894. He fought George Lavigne for the lightweight title on Sept. 28, 1898; Lavigne held onto the crown with a 20-round draw, but Erne won a 20-round decision on July 3, 1899, to become champion. Erne tried to move up to the welterweight title in 1901 but was KOed in the 9th round by Jim "Rube" Ferns on Sept. 23. On May 12, 1902, he lost the lightweight title when Joe Gans KOed him in the 1st round.

ESPER, "DUKE" (Charles H.) baseball: b. July 28, 1868, Salem, N.J.; d. Aug. 31, 1910. Throw L; pitcher. Pittsburgh NL, Philadelphia AA, 1890; Philadelphia NL, 1890–92; Pittsburgh NL, 1892; Washington NL, 1893–94; Baltimore NL, 1894–96; St. Louis NL, 1897–98. Nine years, 102–100, 4.40 ERA; 20–15 in 1891. Led NL in losses, 1893 (12–28).

ESPINOSA, AL golf: b. March 24, 1894, Monterey, Calif.; d. Jan. 4, 1957. Espinosa's only major victory came in the 1928 Western Open. However, the same year he got into the finals of the PGA tournament, losing to Leo Diegel, and in 1929 he was tied for the lead at the end of regulation play in the U.S. Open but lost to Bobby Jones in a 36-hole playoff.

ESTES, WAYNE basketball: b. May 13, 1943, Anaconda, Mont.; d. Feb. 8, 1965. The first Utah State player to score more than 2,000 career points, Estes was the nation's second leading major college scorer at the time of his death, behind Rick Barry. He was listed as a candidate for the AP All-America team. The night of his death, he had scored 48 points in a 91–62 win over Denver. His personal high was 52, a school record.

While trying to help some people who had had an auto accident, he was electrocuted by a high-voltage wire that had been snapped in the crash.

EVERS, JOHN J. baseball: b. July 21, 1881, Troy, N.Y.; d. March 28, 1947. Bat L, throw R; second base. Chicago NL, 1902–13; Boston NL, 1914–17; Philadelphia NL, 1917; Chicago AL, 1922; Boston NL, 1929. Eighteen years, 1,762 games, 324 stolen bases, .270 BA; hit .300 in 1908, .341 in 1912.

When Evers arrived in the majors, his 115-pound frame brought some snickers. But he was the prototype of the second baseman who beats other teams by scrapping, pivoting, and thinking. He was so dedicated to baseball that he went to bed with the rulebook every night. His study of the official rules led to the celebrated, and misnamed, "Merkle boner" of 1908.

The rules say that if a runner is forced out to end an inning, no run can score on the play; they also say that a runner is forced out if the ball reaches the base before he does, if he can't retreat to the base he previously occupied.

Merkle's boner occurred on Sept. 23, 1908. In a game at New York, the Cubs and the Giants, in a fight for the NL pennant, were tied 1–1. The Giants had a runner on third; Merkle was on first. Al Bridwell hit a single to center, and a run apparently scored. Merkle ran off the field and fans ran on, thinking the game was over. But Evers stood at second base, calling for the ball. The Cub center fielder threw it toward him, but the New York third-base coach ran across the diamond, got the ball, and threw it into the stands. Evers got another ball, stood on second, and appealed to Hank O'Day, the plate umpire. O'Day consulted with his base umpire, and Merkle was called out. He had run off the field before touching second base. It was a force play, and the run wasn't allowed. With fans on the field and the sky growing dark, O'Day decided not to continue play.

At the end of the season, the Cubs and Giants were tied for first place, and they had to replay that game of Sept. 23. The Cubs won the game and the pennant, 4–2.

Instead of being remembered as Merkle's bonehead play, the celebrated 1908 incident should be remembered as Evers's heads-up play. Merkle's mistake was routine at the time.

Evers holds the NL record for most steals of home, 21. In four World Series, 1906–08, 1914, 20 games, he hit .316; his 8 stolen bases is 4th. His 2-run single won the finale of the Braves' 4-game sweep of Philadelphia in 1914.

Managed Chicago NL, 1913, 1921, 1924: 196–208, .485.

Baseball Hall of Fame.

EWING, "BOB" (George L.) baseball: b. April 24, 1873, New Hampshire, Ohio; d. June 20, 1947. Bat, throw R; pitcher. Cincinnati NL, 1902–09; Philadelphia NL, 1910–11; St. Louis NL, 1912. Eleven years, 123–119, 2.49 ERA; 20–11 in 1905.

EWING, "BUCK" (William) baseball: b. Oct. 17, 1859, Hoaglands, Ohio; d. Oct. 20, 1906. Bat, throw R. Troy NL, 1880–82; New York NL, 1883–89; New York PL, 1890; New York NL, 1891–92; Cleveland NL, 1893–94; Cincinnati NL, 1895–97. Eighteen years, 1,315 games, 336 stolen bases (7 years not included), .303 BA. Led NL in home runs, 1883 (10), and in triples, 1884 (20).

The greatest catcher of the premodern era, Ewing played every position, including nine turns as a pitcher. Besides 636 games as a catcher, he played 235 at first base, 235 in the outfield, and 127 at third.

Managed New York PL, 1890; Cincinnati NL, 1895–99; New York NL, 1900 (part): 489–395, .553.

Baseball Hall of Fame.

EWING, JOHN baseball: b. June 1, 1863, Cincinnati; d. April 23, 1895. Pitcher. Louisville AA, 1888–89; New York NL, 1890; New York NL, 1891. Four years, 53–63, 3.68 ERA; 525 strikeouts in 1,058⅔ innings. Led NL in percentage (21–8, .724) and ERA (2.27) in 1891. A sore arm ended his career.

EWRY, RAY C. track: b. Oct. 14, 1873, Lafayette, Ind.; d. Sept. 29, 1937. An invalid when young, Ewry was advised by a doctor to begin exercising, and he went on to win 10 Olympic Gold Medals. In the 1900 Games, he won the standing high jump, standing broad jump, and standing hop, step, and jump. He repeated that triple victory in 1904, and in 1906 and 1908 he won the standing broad and high jumps. Those events have been discontinued; Ewry still holds world records in all three.

Helms Hall of Fame.

F

FALKENBERG, "CY" (Frederick P.) baseball: b. Dec, 17, 1880, Chicago; d. April 14, 1961. Bat, throw R; pitcher. Pittsburgh NL, 1903; Washington AL, 1905–08; Cleveland AL, 1908–11, 1913; Indianapolis Fed L, 1914; Brooklyn Fed L, Newark Fed L, 1915; Philadelphia AL, 1917. Twelve years, 128–123, 2.68 ERA; 1,164 strikeouts, 27 shutouts, in 2,275 innings; 21–10 in 1913, 25–18 in 1914. Led Fed L in strikeouts (236) and shutouts (9) in 1914.

FARLEY, RICHARD L. basketball: b. April 13, 1932, Winslow, Ind.; d. Oct. 1, 1969. Farley played on Indiana's 1953 national champions. Syracuse Nats, 1954–56; 142 games, 6.3 points per game.

FARRELL, "DUKE" (Charles A.) baseball: b. Aug. 31, 1866, Oakdale, Mass.; d. Feb. 15, 1925. Sw. hit, throw R; catcher. Chicago NL, 1888–89; Chicago PL, 1890; Boston AA, 1891; Pittsburgh NL, 1892; Washington NL, 1893; New York NL, 1894–96; Washington NL, 1896–99; Brooklyn NL, 1899–1902; Boston AL, 1903–05. Eighteen years, 1,563 games, .275 BA; hit .302 in 1891, .322 in 1897, .314 in 1898, .301 in 1899. As pinch-hitter, 23 for 59, .390 BA. Led league in home runs (12) and RBI (110) in 1891.

FARRINGTON, "BO" (John R.) football: b. Jan. 18, 1936, Dewalt, Tex.; d. July 26, 1964. Prairie View end. Chicago Bears, 1960–63. Farrington caught a 98-yard TD pass from Bill Wade on Oct. 8, 1961, the second longest in history.

He and teammate Willie Galimore were killed in an auto accident.

FEENEY, ALBERT G. football: b. Nov. 12, 1892, Indianapolis, Ind.; d. Nov. 12, 1950. Notre Dame center. Canton Bulldogs, 1919–21.

He was mayor of Indianapolis at his death.

FELSCH, "HAPPY" (Oscar E.) baseball: b. Aug. 22, 1891, Milwaukee; d. Aug. 17, 1964. Bat, throw R; outfield. Chicago AL, 1915–20. Six years, 749 games, .293 BA; hit .300 in 1916, .308 in 1917, .338 in 1920. Two World Series, 1917, 1919: 14 games, .229 BA.

On Aug. 14, 1919, he tied an ML record for outfielders in a 9-inning game with 4 assists. That season, he set an ML record for most double plays by an outfielder, 15. On June 23, he tied an AL record for a 9-inning game with 11 putouts.

Felsch was implicated in the Black Sox Scandal of 1919 and was one of eight players banned from baseball for life as a result.

FERGUSON, CHARLES J. baseball: b. April 17, 1863, Charlottesville, Va.; d. April 29, 1888. Sw. hit, throw R; pitcher, outfield. Philadelphia, 1884–87. Four years, 99–64, 2.67 ERA; 728 strikeouts, 13 shutouts in 1,514⅔ innings; 21–25 in 1884, 26–20 in 1885, 30–9 in 1886, 22–10 in 1887; .288 BA. Led NL in ERA, 1886 (1.98).

FERGUSON, ROBERT V. baseball: b. 1845, Brooklyn; d. May 3, 1894. Sw. hit, throw R; second-third base. National Association: New York Mutuals, 1871; Brooklyn Atlantics, 1872–74; Hartfords, 1875. Five years, 259 games, .243 BA.

Hartford NL, 1876; Brooklyn NL, 1877; Chicago NL, 1878; Troy NL, 1879–82; Philadelphia NL, 1883; Pittsburgh AA, 1884. Nine years, 562 games, .271 BA; hit .351 in 1878.

Managed Hartford NL, 1876; Brooklyn NL, 1877; Chicago NL, 1878; Troy NL, 1879–82; Philadelphia NL, 1883 (part); Pittsburgh AA, 1884 (part); New York AA, 1886 (part)–87 (part): 292–351, .454.

The only active player ever to serve as president of a professional league, Ferguson headed the National Association of Professional Baseball Players from its second year, 1872, to its final year, 1875, after which it succumbed to the newly formed National League.

FERNS, JIM ("Rube") boxing: b. Jan 20, 1874, Pittsburg, Kan.; d. June 11, 1952. Ferns won the welterweight title from Mysterious Billy Smith on a foul in the 21st round, Jan. 15, 1900. He lost it to Matty Matthews on a 15-round decision, Oct. 16, 1900, but regained it by KOing Matthews in 10 rounds on May 24, 1901. On Dec. 18 of the same year he lost the title for good to Joe Walcott on a 5th-round KO.

FERRIS, "HOBE" (Albert S.) baseball: b. Dec. 7, 1877, Providence, R.I.; d. March 18, 1938. Bat, throw R; second base. Boston AL, 1901–07; St. Louis AL, 1908–09. Nine years, 1,286 games, .239 BA. One World Series, 1903: 8 games, 7 RBI, .290 BA.

FINNEY, LOUIS K. baseball: b. Aug. 13, 1910, Buffalo, Ala.; d. April 22, 1966. Bat L, throw R; outfield, first base. Philadelphia AL, 1931, 1933–39; Boston AL, 1939–42, 1944–45; St. Louis AL, 1945–46; Philadelphia NL, 1947. Fifteen years, 1,270 games, .287 BA; hit .302 in 1936, .310 in 1939, .320 in 1940. Led AL in pinch-hit at-bats and hits, 1939 (13 for 40, .325).

FISHER, GEORGE J. volleyball: b. April 2, 1871, Cincinnati; d. April 20, 1960. Fisher was long involved actively in YMCA and Boy Scout work and in volleyball. He received an M.D. from Cincinnati College of Medicine and Surgery in 1898. He was the first president of the U.S. Volleyball Association, 1930–51, and first editor of the *Volleyball Rule Book,* 1916–48.
   Helms Hall of Fame, Volleyball Hall of Fame.

FITZSIMMONS, ROBERT L. boxing: b. June 4, 1862, Halston, Cornwall, England; d. Oct. 22, 1917. His record: 28 wins, 23 by KO; 11 losses, 6 by KO; 1 draw. The frailest-looking heavyweight champion ever, Fitzsimmons was a master at defense and at counterpunching, one of the first fighters to realize that ducking under an opponent's blows to throw punches at the body could be as effective as throwing long-range blows toward the head. His career began in 1880 when he won an amateur tournament in New Zealand by scoring four KOs in one night. He turned pro in 1882, winning his first 14 fights by KO, many of them with the "solar-plexus punch" he was to make famous.
   Fitzsimmons came to the United States in 1890 and in 1891 he won the middleweight title by knocking out Nonpareil Jack Dempsey in the 13th round at New Orleans. In 1897, when he was nearly thirty-five, he won the heavyweight crown, KOing Jim Corbett with a solar-plexus punch in the 14th round on March 17. He lost his first defense when Jim Jeffries KOed him in the 11th round on June 9, 1899.
   In the meantime, the light-heavyweight division for those weighing between 158 and 175 pounds had been formed. Now forty-one, Fitzsimmons won that title on Nov. 4, 1903, with a 20-round decision over George Gardner. He held it until Dec. 20, 1905, when Philadelphia Jack O'Brien KOed him in the 13th round.
   Helms Hall of Fame, Boxing Hall of Fame.

FITZSIMMONS, "SUNNY JIM" (James) horse racing: b. July 23, 1874, Brooklyn; d. March 11, 1966. It's tempting to find something symbolic in the fact that the house in which Fitzsimmons was born was torn down to make way for the Sheepshead Bay Race Track, where he launched his seventy-five years of involvement with horse racing. He started as a water boy, then became a jockey for about ten years, with little success. He turned to training when he became too heavy to keep riding.

Fitzsimmons became the best-known horse trainer of all time, saddling 2,275 winners that brought in $13,082,911. His best years were with William Woodward's Belair Stud Farm, for whom he developed two Triple Crown winners, Omaha (1935) and Gallant Fox (1930). Ten other mounts trained by Fitzsimmons won one or two legs of the Triple Crown. He led all trainers in winnings in 1936 (42 winners, $193,415), 1939 (45 winners, $266,205), and 1955 (66 winners, $1,270,055).

When Belair Stud was broken up after Woodward's death, Fitzsimmons, then eighty-one, joined Wheatley Stable and saddled Bold Ruler, who was Horse of the Year in 1955.

He was the first president of the Horsemen's Benevolent and Protective Association. He retired in 1963.

National Racing Hall of Fame.

FLAGSTEAD, "PETE" (Ira J.) baseball: b. Sept. 22, 1893, Montague, Mich.; d. March 13, 1940. Bat, throw R; outfield. Detroit AL, 1917, 1919–23; Boston AL, 1923–29; Washington AL, 1929; Pittsburgh NL, 1929–30. Thirteen years, 1,217 games, .290 BA; hit .331 in 1919, .305 in 1921, .311 in 1923, .305 in 1924. Flagstead tied an ML record for outfielders on April 19, 1926, by starting 3 double plays.

FLAHERTY, "PATSY" (Patrick J.) baseball: b. June 29, 1876, Carnegie, Pa.; d. Jan. 23, 1968. Bat, throw L; pitcher. Louisville NL, 1899; Pittsburgh NL, 1900; Chicago NL, 1903–04; Pittsburgh NL, 1904–05; Boston NL, 1907–08; Philadelphia NL, 1910; Boston NL, 1911. Nine years, 66–83, 3.10 ERA. Led AL in losses, 1903 (11–25).

FLEMING, DONALD football: b. June 11, 1937, Bellaire, Ohio; d. June 4, 1963. Florida defensive back. Cleveland Browns, 1960–62.

Fleming was electrocuted while working in construction during the off-season.

FLETCHER, ARTHUR baseball: b. Jan. 5, 1885, Collinsville, Ill.; d. Feb. 6, 1950. Bat, throw R; shortstop. New York NL, 1909–20; Philadelphia NL, 1920, 1922. Thirteen years, 1,529 games, .277 BA; hit .319 in 1911. Four World Series, 1911–13, 1917: 25 games, .191 BA.

He managed Philadelphia NL, 1923–26; New York AL, 1929 (part): 237–383, .382.

FLICK, ELMER H. baseball: b. Jan. 11, 1876, Bedford, Ohio; d. Jan. 9, 1971. Bat L, throw R; outfield. Philadelphia NL, 1898–1902; Cleveland AL,

1902–10. Thirteen years, 1,482 games, 5,593 at-bats, 1,750 hits, 268 doubles, 164 triples, 48 home runs, 947 runs, 330 stolen bases, .313 BA; hit .302 in 1898, .342 in 1899, .367 in 1900, .333 in 1901, .306 in 1904, .311 in 1906, .302 in 1907. Led AL in RBI (110) in 1900; in stolen bases (38) in 1904; in hitting (.306), slugging (.462), and triples (18) in 1905; in triples (22), runs (98), and stolen bases (39) in 1906; in triples (18) in 1907.

Baseball Hall of Fame.

FLORIO, "DAN" (Dominick) boxing: b. 1896(?), New York City; d. Oct. 11, 1965. A manager-trainer, Florio handled Jersey Joe Walcott when he became heavyweight champion. He was also Floyd Patterson's trainer during his career as champ.

FLOWERS, "TIGER" (Theodore) boxing: b. Aug. 5, 1895, Camille, Ga.; d. Nov. 16, 1927. His record: 115 wins, 49 by KO; 13 losses, 8 by KO; 6 draws, 14 no-decisions, 1 no-contest. After a long wait, Flowers won the middleweight championship on Feb. 26, 1926, by beating Harry Greb in 15 rounds. After defending against Greb on another 15-round decision, Aug. 19, 1926, he lost the title to Mickey Walker on a 10-round decision, Dec. 3. Flowers fought for one more year; he died after an operation four days after his last fight.

FOHL, LEE A. baseball: b. Nov. 28, 1876, Marietta, Ohio; d. Oct. 30, 1965. Fohl caught 4 ML games, Pittsburgh NL, 1902, Cincinnati NL, 1903.

Managed Cleveland AL, 1915 (part)–19 (part); St. Louis AL, 1921–23; Boston AL, 1924–26: 713–792, .474.

FORBES, HARRY boxing: b. May 13, 1879, Rockford, Ill.; d. Dec. 19, 1946. His record: 80 wins, 30 by KO; 15 losses, 11 by KO; 23 draws, 12 no-decisions. Forbes fought Terry McGovern for the bantamweight title on Dec. 22, 1899, but was KOed in the 2nd round. When McGovern became a featherweight, Forbes and Casper Leon were the top contenders for the bantam crown. They fought a 20-round draw on Sept. 6, 1900, but on April 2, 1901, Forbes won a 15-round decision from Leon. He lost the title to Frankie Neil on a 2nd-round KO, Aug. 13, 1903. Forbes then made a try for the featherweight title but was KOed in 5 rounds by Abe Attell, Feb. 1, 1902. Neil KOed him in 3 rounds in another bantamweight title fight, June 17, 1904.

FORCE, "DAVY" (David W.) baseball: b. July 27, 1849, New York City; d. June 21, 1918. Bat, throw R; shortstop, third base. National Association: Washington, 1871; Troy, 1872; Baltimore, 1872–73; Chicago, 1874; Philadelphia, 1875. Five years, 259 games, .326 BA. Led league in BA, 1872 (.412).

New York NL, Philadelphia NL, 1876; St. Louis NL, 1877; Buffalo NL, 1879–85; Washington NL, 1886. Ten years, 768 games, .211 BA.

FORD, RUSSELL W. baseball: b. April 25, 1883, Brandon, Manitoba, Canada; d. Jan. 24, 1960. Bat, throw R; pitcher. New York AL, 1909–13; Buffalo Fed L, 1914–15. Seven years, 98–71, 2.59 ERA: 710 strikeouts in 1,487⅓ innings; 26–6 in 1910, 21–11 in 1911. Led AL in losses, 1912 (13–21); led Fed L in percentage, 1914 (20–6, .769.)

FOREMAN, FRANCIS I. baseball: b. May 1, 1863, Baltimore; d. Nov. 19, 1957. Bat, throw R; pitcher. Chicago-Pittsburgh UA, Kansas City UA, 1884; Baltimore AA, 1885, 1889; Cincinnati NL, 1890–91; Baltimore NL, Washington NL, 1892; New York NL, 1893; Cincinnati NL, 1895–96; Boston AL, 1901; Baltimore AL, 1901–02. Eleven years, 99–93, 3.94 ERA; 23–21 in 1889.

FOSTER, "KID" (Edward C.) baseball: b. Feb. 13, 1888, Chicago; d. Jan. 15, 1937. Bat, throw R; third-second base. New York AL, 1910: Washington AL, 1912–19; Boston AL, 1920–22; St. Louis AL, 1922–23. Thirteen years, 1,498 games, .264 BA.

FOSTER, "RUBE" (Andrew) baseball: b. Sept. 17,. 1879, Calvert, Tex.; d. Dec. 9, 1930. The founder of genuine organized Negro baseball, Foster was first an outstanding pitcher in Texas and Michigan. He joined the Cuban X Giants late in 1902 and quickly became their top pitcher. In 1903, when they beat the Philadelphia Giants for the Negro championship, he pitched 4 of their 5 victories. Foster joined the Philadelphia team in 1904 and pitched them to the championship in a 3-game series with the Cuban X Giants. He got both Philadelphia's wins, striking out 18 in one game and pitching a 2-hitter in the other.

He remained with Philadelphia until 1907, when he joined the Chicago Leland Giants, where he remained for three seasons. He managed them to a 123–6 record in 1910.

In 1911, Foster and John M. Schorling organized the Chicago American Giants, which became the best Negro team in the Midwest. Foster continued playing occasionally until 1915. The American Giants were well paid for black players in that period, and they took their long trips in a private railroad car.

In 1919, Foster began campaigning for a Negro league. The result was the formation of the National Negro League in February, 1920. Foster hoped eventually to have a single league with two circuits, but a rival league began operation in the East in 1923. Because of Foster's leadership, the NNL was a good deal stronger than its eastern rival. Foster could be extremely harsh when necessary, but he also used his own money to help teams on many occasions when they needed traveling expenses.

He was president and secretary of the NNL until late in 1926, when he was committed to a mental institution, where he died four years later. The NNL survived him by only two years.

FOTHERGILL, "FATS" (Robert R.) baseball: b. Aug. 16, 1897, Massillon, Ohio; d. March 20, 1938. Bat, throw R; outfield. Detroit AL, 1922–30; Chicago AL, 1930–32; Boston AL, 1933. Twelve years, 1,072 games, .326 BA; hit .367 in 1926, .359 in 1927, .317 in 1928, .354 in 1929. A 230-pounder, Fothergill led the AL in pinch-hit at-bats and hits in 1929 (19 for 53). In his career, he pinch-hit 253 times and had 76 hits (7th) for a .300 BA.

FOUTZ, DAVID L. ("Scissors") baseball: b. Sept. 7, 1856, Carroll County, Md.; d. March 5, 1897. Bat, throw R; pitcher, outfield, first base. St. Louis AA, 1884–87; Brooklyn AA, 1888–89; Brooklyn NL, 1890–96. Thirteen years, 1,135 games, .277 BA; hit .357 in 1887, .303 in 1890. As pitcher, led league in victories (41), percentage (.719), and ERA (2.11) in 1886; 33–14 in 1885 and 25–12 in 1887; 147–66 overall.

Managed Brooklyn NL, 1893–96: 264–257, .507.

FOX, "PETE" (Ervin) baseball: b. March 8, 1909, Evansville, Ind.; d. July 5, 1966. Bat, throw R; outfield. Detroit AL, 1933–40; Boston AL, 1941–45. Thirteen years, 1,461 games, .298 BA; hit .321 in 1935, .331 in 1937, .315 in 1944. Three World Series, 1934–35, 1950: 14 games, .327; 9 doubles (2nd). He hit 6 doubles in 1934; in 1935, he hit .385 in the Series.

FOXX, "JIMMY" (James E., "Double X") baseball: b. Oct. 22, 1907, Sudlersville, Md.; d. July 21, 1967. Bat, throw R; outfield. Philadelphia AL, 1925–35; Boston AL, 1936–42; Chicago NL, 1942, 1944; Philadelphia NL, 1945. Twenty years, 2,317 games, 8,134 at-bats, 2,646 hits, 458 doubles, 125 triples, 534 home runs (5th), 1,751 runs, 1,922 RBI (5th), 4,956 total bases (9th), 1,452 walks (8th), 1,311 strikeouts (4th), .325 BA.

Foxx came closer than anyone else to breaking Babe Ruth's record of 60 home runs in a 154-game season; he led the AL with 58 in 1932. He also led in 1933 with 48, 1935 with 36, and 1939 with 35. In 1938 he hit 50 home runs but finished second.

He is holder or coholder of these ML records: most consecutive years 30 or more home runs, 12; most seasons more than 400 total bases, 2; most consecutive years more than 100 RBI, 13; most extra base hits, 6 (a double, a triple, and 4 consecutive home runs), and most total bases (21) in a doubleheader, July 2, 1933; most years leading in strikeouts, 7.

He holds the AL records for most times scoring 5 or more runs in a game, 3; highest slugging percentage for a righthander, .749 in 1932; most career home runs for a righthander, 524; and most total bases in a season for a righthander, 438 in 1932.

Twice Foxx got 6 hits in a game: On May 30, 1930, he went 6-for-7, with 2 doubles and a triple; on July 10, 1932, he went 6-for-9, with a double and 3 home runs. He also hit 3 home runs in a game, June 8, 1933. On June 16, 1938, he went to bat 6 times and walked 6 times, tying records for most walks in a game and most times facing the pitcher without an official at-bat. Foxx won the triple crown in 1933. He led the AL in hitting, 1933 (.356), 1938 (.349); in runs, 1932 (151); in total bases, 1932 (438), 1933 (403), and 1938 (398); in RBI, 1932 (169), 1933 (163), 1938 (175); in slugging percentage, 1932 (.749), 1933 (.703), 1935 (.636), 1938 (.704), and 1939 (.694). In three World Series, 1929–31, 18 games, Foxx hit .344 (10th), with 3 doubles, a triple, 4 home runs, 11 runs scored, and 11 RBI; his .609 slugging percentage is 8th. He hit 2 home runs in the As' 5-game victory over the Cubs in 1929, and his 2-run home run in the ninth inning of the fifth game in 1930 gave the As a 2–0 victory as they beat St. Louis in 6 games.

Baseball Hall of Fame.

FRAME, FRED auto racing: b. 1893(?); d. April 24, 1962. Frame won the Indianapolis 500 in 1932, at what was then a record time of 104.14 miles per hour.

FRANKIAN, "IKE" (Malcolm) football: b. 1907(?); d. April 14, 1963. St. Mary's (California) and California end; All-American, 1928 (AP; with St. Mary's). Boston Redskins, 1933; New York Giants, 1934–35; Los Angeles Bulldogs (AFL), 1937.

FRASER, "CHICK" (Charles C.) baseball: b. March 17, 1871, Chicago; d. May 8, 1940. Bat, throw R; pitcher. Louisville NL, 1896–98; Cleveland NL, 1898; Philadelphia NL, 1899–1900; Philadelphia AL, 1901; Philadelphia NL, 1902–04; Boston NL, 1905; Cincinnati NL, 1906; Chicago NL, 1907–09. Fourteen years, 176–215, 3.68 ERA; 21–12 in 1899, 22–16 in 1901. No-hitter, Sept. 18, 1903, against Chicago NL (10–0).

FREDERICK, KARL T. shooting: b. Feb. 2, 1881, Chateaugay, N.Y.; d. Feb. 11, 1962. Frederick won a Gold Medal for any target pistol at 50 meters in the 1920 Olympics. He was a member of the U.S. Olympic Committee executive committee, 1920–48, and president of the National Rifle Association, 1934–36.

FREEMAN, "BUCK" (John F.) baseball: b. Oct. 30, 1871, Catasauqua, Pa.; d. June 25, 1949. Bat, throw L; pitcher, Washington AA, 1891; outfield, first base, Washington NL, 1898–99; Boston NL, 1900; Boston AL, 1901–07. Eleven years, 1,126 games, .293 BA; hit .318 in 1899, .301 in 1900, .339 in 1901, .309 in 1902. Led league in home runs, 1899 (25), 1903 (13); in triples, 1904 (19); in RBI, 1902 (121), 1903 (104). One World Series, 1903: 8 games, .281; 3 triples.

FRIBERG, "BARNEY" (Gustaf Bernhard) baseball: b. Aug. 18, 1899, Manchester, N.H.; d. Dec. 8, 1958. Bat, throw R; infield, outfield. Chicago NL, 1919–20, 1922–25; Philadelphia NL, 1925–32; Boston AL, 1933. Fourteen years, 1,299 games, .281 BA; hit .318 in 1923, .301 in 1929, .341 in 1930.

FRIEDE, LEO canoeing: b. Aug. 13, 1887, New York City; d. Nov. 6, 1959. Friede won the American canoe-sailing championship, 1914–18, 1920, 1922, and 1925–26, and the International Challenge Cup, 1913–14.

FROMME, ARTHUR H. baseball: b. Sept. 3, 1883, Quincy, Ill.; d. Aug. 24, 1956. Bat, throw R; pitcher. St. Louis NL, 1906–08; Cincinnati NL, 1909–13; New York NL, 1913–15. Ten years, 78–90, 2.90 ERA.

FUGAZY, HUMBERT J. boxing: b. 1884(?), New York City; d. April 7, 1964. Fugazy attained prominence as a promoter when he staged an all-star card at the Polo Grounds on July 2, 1925. The bouts featured were: Harry Greb against Mickey Walker; Harry Wills against Charlie Weinert; Dave Shade against Jimmy Slattery. He also promoted the 1926 light-heavyweight title fight between Paul Berlenbach and Jack Delaney at Ebbets Field. After some years of retirement, Fugazy came back in 1960 to help promote the fight in which Floyd Patterson regained his heavyweight title from Ingemar Johannsen.

G

GALIMORE, WILLIE football: b. March 30, 1935, St. Augustine, Fla.; d. July 26, 1964. Florida A & M halfback. Chicago Bears, 1957–63. A great breakaway runner, Galimore in seven years gained 2,985 yards in 670 attempts, a 4.5-yard average, scoring 26 TDs rushing. He had a total of 37 career TDs for 222 points.

He and teammate Bo Farrington were killed in a car crash.

GALLOWAY, "CHICK" (Clarence E.) baseball: b. Aug. 4, 1896, Manning, S.C.; d. Nov. 3, 1969. Bat, throw R, shortstop. Philadelphia AL, 1919–27; Detroit AL, 1928. Ten years, 1,085 games, .264 BA; hit .324 in 1922.

His career ended prematurely when he was hit in the ear with a ball during a pregame warmup.

GALVIN, "PUD" (James F.) baseball: b. Dec. 25, 1855, St. Louis; d. March 7, 1902. Bat, throw R; pitcher. National Association, St. Louis, 1875. One year, 8 games, 4–2.

Buffalo NL, 1879–85; Pittsburgh AA, 1885–86; Pittsburgh NL, 1887–89; Pittsburgh PL, 1890; Pittsburgh NL, 1891–92; St. Louis NL, 1892. Fourteen years, 359 wins (7th), 307 losses (2nd), 2.87 ERA; 697 games (9th), 682 starts (2nd), 639 complete (2nd), 5,941⅓ innings (2nd), 744 walks, 1,799 strikeouts, 56 shutouts (8th); 37–27 in 1879, 28–24 in 1881, 28–23 in 1882, 46–22 in 1884, 29–21 in 1886, 28–21 in 1887, 23–25 in 1888, 23–16 in 1889. No-hitters, Aug. 20, 1880, against Worcester NL (1–0); Aug. 4, 1884, against Detroit NL (18–0). Led NL in shutouts, 1883 (5) and 1884 (12); in starts (75), complete games (72), and innings (656⅓) in 1883.

In 1884, Galvin shut out every other team in the league. His no-hitters were the 6th and 13th in major-league history.

Baseball Hall of Fame.

GANDIL, "CHICK" (Charles A.) baseball: b. Jan. 19, 1888, St. Paul, Minn.; d. Dec. 13, 1970. Bat, throw R; first base. Chicago AL, 1910; Washington AL, 1912–15; Cleveland AL, 1916; Chicago AL, 1917–19. Nine years, 1,147 at-bats, .277 BA; hit .305 in 1912, .318 in 1913. Two World Series, 1917, 1919: 14 games, .245 BA. Gandil drove in the winning run in two of Chicago's three victories during their eight-game loss to Cincinnati in the 1919 Series, but he was one of eight Chicago players banned from baseball for life for allegedly accepting bribes to throw the Series. Most accounts say Gandil was the ringleader and paymaster for the players involved.

GANS, JOE boxing: b. Nov. 25, 1874, Philadelphia; d. Aug. 16, 1910. His record: 119 wins, 54 by KO; 9 losses, 5 by KO; 10 draws, 18 no-decisions. The "Old Master," ranked as the best lightweight of all time, KOed Frank Erne in 45 seconds of the 1st round to win the lightweight title on May 12, 1901. He held it until July 4, 1908, when he lost to Battling Nelson in 17 rounds. Gans died of tuberculosis.

Helms Hall of Fame, Boxing Hall of Fame.

GARDINER, JOHN rowing: b. 1876, Gravenhurst, Ontario, Canada; d. Jan. 12, 1961. Gardiner was stroke for the University of Pennsylvania three consecutive years, 1899–1901; Penn won the Intercollegiate Rowing Association Regatta the first two years.

Helms Hall of Fame.

GARDNER, GEORGE boxing: b. March 17, 1877, Lisdoonvarna, County Clare, Ireland; d. July 8, 1954. His record: 41 wins, 19 by KO; 11 losses, 5 by KO; 10 draws, 2 no-decisions, 1 no-contest. Gardner won the light-heavyweight title with a 12-round KO of Jack Root on July 4, 1903, but lost it to Bob Fitzsimmons in 20 rounds in his next fight, Nov. 25. He fought Root, the first light-heavyweight champion, 5 times, with 2 KOs, 2 draws, and 1 loss on a foul.

GARRETT, ROBERT S. track: b. June 24, 1875, Baltimore County, Md.; d. April 25, 1961. Garrett became a member of the U.S. team at the first modern Olympics in 1896 simply by paying his own way to Athens. A weight man on the Princeton track team—which he captained in 1897— Garrett had never seen a discus, but he had a friend make one several weeks before the Games so he could get some practice. He won both the shotput and the discus in Athens. He was also IC4A shotput champion in 1897.

Helms Hall of Fame, Helms World Trophy, 1896.

GARRISON, "SNAPPER" (Edward) horse, racing: b. ?; d. Dec. 13, 1944. The phrase "Garrison finish" was born of Garrison's technique of consistently holding his horse back for a dramatic come-from-behind victory. Evidently he was one of the first jockeys to realize the truth of the racing axiom, "A horse has only one sprint per race." He rode from 1882 to 1887. He won the 1891 Belmont aboard Foxford. Other major victories came in the American Derby, Kentucky Oaks, Ladies Handicap, Matron Stakes, Monmouth Handicap, Suburban Handicap, and Withers Stakes.

Jockey Hall of Fame, National Racing Hall of Fame.

GARVIN, "NED" (Virgil L.) baseball: b. Jan. 1, 1874, Navasota, Tex.; d. June 16, 1908. Throw R; pitcher. Philadelphia NL, 1896; Chicago NL, 1899–1900; Milwaukee AA, 1901; Chicago AL, 1902; Brooklyn NL, 1902–04; New York AL, 1904. Seven years, 57–98, 2.72 ERA.

GASTRIGHT, "HANK" (Henry C.) baseball: b. H. C. Gastreich, March 29, 1865, Covington, Ky.; d. Oct. 9, 1937. Bat, throw R; pitcher. Columbus AA, 1889–91; Washington NL, 1892; Boston NL, Pittsburgh NL, 1893; Brooklyn NL, 1894; Cincinnati NL, 1896. Seven years, 72–63, 4.20 ERA; 30–14 in 1890. Led NL in percentage, 1893 (15–5, .750).

GEERS, "POP" (Edward F.) harness racing: b. 1851(?), Tennessee; d. 1924. In the late 1870s, Geers brought a number of Tennessee pacers to the North and helped to popularize them; until then, only trotters were popular among harness fans. One of the outstanding horses he drove was Robert J, the top money-winning pacer in 1894. Geers drove to victories in the Walnut Hall Cup (5 times), the Horseman's Futurity, Kentucky Futurity, Review Futurity, and Transylvania.

He was killed in a racing accident at Wheeling, West Virginia.

Harness Racing Hall of Fame.

GEHRIG, "LOU" (Henry Louis) baseball: b. June 19, 1903, New York City; d. June 2, 1941. Bat, throw L; first base. New York AL, 1923–39. Seventeen years, 2,163 games, 8,001 at-bats, 2,721 hits, 535 doubles, 162 triples, 493 home runs, 1,888 runs (4th), 5,059 total bases (7th), 1,190 extra base hits (5th), 1,991 RBI (2nd), 1,508 walks (7th), .340 BA.

Gehrig spent most of his career in the shadow of Babe Ruth, it has often been said, but he didn't go unappreciated. He became, rather, a symbol of remarkable courage by playing 2,130 consecutive games, an ML record that will probably never be broken. He demonstrated another sort of courage with his ability to come through in the clutch; Ruth may have been the most feared slugger of his time, but Gehrig was probably the most feared clutch-hitter. He holds ML records for most seasons 150 or more RBI, 7, most consecutive, 3; most years 100 or more RBI, 13; most grand-slam home runs, 23; and his 184 RBI in 1931 is an AL record. Unquestionably he helped Ruth to his record of 60 home runs in 1927—often a team would decide to pitch to Ruth rather than walk him intentionally, with Gehrig up next.

With Wally Pipp playing first base, Gehrig appeared in only 23 games for the Yankees in his first two seasons. Early in 1925, however, Pipp was benched after being hit in the head with a pitch, and Gehrig went on to play every game that season and for thirteen more seasons thereafter. During spring training of 1939, it was obvious that something was wrong. Gehrig's strength was gone; he looked clumsy in the field. His manager, Joe McCarthy, wouldn't bench him because of Gehrig's streak, but after eight games of the season Gehrig benched himself. "I'm not helping the team," he told McCarthy. Though in uniform most of the rest of the season, he never played again. At Mayo Clinic, he learned he had amyotrophic lateral sclerosis. There was no cure. From October, 1939, almost until his death, he worked for the New York City Parole Commission.

Gehrig is the only player ever to hit for more than 400 total bases in five seasons (no other player ever did it more than twice, and only 12 have done it once), the only man ever to get 4 or more extra-base hits in a game 5 times, and one of seven players ever to hit 4 home runs in a game. He holds AL records for most years played 150 or more games, 12; most years scoring 100 or more runs, 13; most times scoring 5 or more runs in a game, 3; most times 3 or more home runs in a game, 4; most consecutive games hitting a home run in each game, 6; and most consecutive games getting an RBI in each game, 10 (he had three such streaks). Eight times he had more than 200 hits in a season (2nd); he hit over .300 twelve consecutive years, and 5 times he hit more than 40 home runs. He won the triple crown in 1934.

Gehrig led the AL in hitting, 1934 (.363); runs, 1931 (163), 1933 (138), 1935 (125), 1936 (167); hits, 1931 (211); doubles, 1927 (52), 1928 (47); triples, 1926 (20); home runs, 1931 (46), 1934 (49), 1936 (49); RBI, 1927 (175), 1928 (142), 1930 (174), 1931 (184), 1934 (165); slugging, 1934 (.706), 1936 (.696); total bases, 1927 (447), 1930 (419), 1931 (410), 1934 (409); walks, 1935 (132), 1936 (130), 1937 (127).

His clutch-hitting ability shows up especially in his World Series record. In seven Series, 1926–28, 1932, 1936–38, 34 games (4th), he drove in 35 runs (3rd), scored 30 (4th), had 43 hits (7th), 8 doubles (3rd), 3 triples (2nd), and 10 home runs (5th), with a .361 BA (5th) and .731 slugging percentage (2nd).

Gehrig had two sensational Series. In the Yankees' sweep of St. Louis in 1928, he hit .545, with a double, 4 home runs, 9 RBI, 5 runs scored, and a slugging percentage of 1.727; in 1932, a Yankee sweep over Chicago, he hit .529, with a double, 3 home runs, 8 RBI, 9 runs scored, and a slugging percentage of 1.118. In the 34 games he played, the Yankees won 27, and Gehrig drove in the winning or go-ahead run in 7 of them.

Baseball Hall of Fame.

GELBERT, CHARLES S. football: b. Dec. 24, 1871, Hawley, Pa.; d. Jan. 16, 1936. Pennsylvania end; All-American, 1894–96.

National Football Foundation Hall of Fame.

GENARO, FRANKIE boxing: b. Frank di Gennara, Aug. 26, 1901; d. Dec. 27, 1966. His record: 83 wins, 19 by KO; 22 losses, 4 by KO; 9 draws, 15 no-decisions. Genaro turned pro after winning the Olympic flyweight championship in 1920. He won the U.S. flyweight title by beating Pancho Villa in 15 rounds on March 1, 1923, but Villa went on to win the world title from Jimmy Wilde. After Villa's death in 1925, Genaro claimed the world crown but lost a 10-round decision on Aug. 22, 1925, to Fidel LaBarba, who then called himself world champion.

LaBarba retired in 1927. On Nov. 28, Genaro lost a 10-round decision to Frenchy Belanger for the NBA version of the title. He won it with a 10-round decision over Belanger, Feb. 6, 1928, lost it on a 1-round KO by Spider Pladner on March 2, 1929, then won it back from Pladner on a 5th-round foul, April 18. Finally, on Oct. 27, 1931, Genaro got his first shot at the world title. He was KOed by Young Perez in the 2nd round.

GENTRY, DALE LEE football: b. July 2, 1917, Phoenix, Ariz.; d. Jan. 30, 1966. Washington State end. Los Angeles Dons (AAFC), 1946–48. In three pro seasons he caught 74 passes for 1,001 yards, a 13.5-yard-per-catch average, and made 5 TDs.

GERBER, "WALLY" (Walter "Spooks") baseball: b. Aug. 18, 1891, Columbus, Ohio; d. June 19, 1951. Bat, throw R; shortstop. Pittsburgh NL, 1914–15; St. Louis AL, 1917–28; Boston AL, 1928–29. Fifteen years, 1,521 games, .256 BA.

GETZEIN, CHARLES H. ("Pretzels") baseball: b. Feb. 14, 1864, Chicago; d. June 19, 1932. Pitcher. Detroit NL, 1884–88; Indianapolis NL, 1889; Boston NL, 1890–91; Cleveland NL, 1891; St. Louis NL, 1892. Nine years, 145–139, 3.46 ERA. Led NL in percentage, 1887 (29–13, .690).

GIBBONS, MIKE boxing: b. July 20, 1888, St. Paul, Minn.; d. Aug. 31, 1956. His record: 62 wins, 38 by KO; 3 losses; 4 draws, 58 no-decisions. One of the several outstanding fighters who never won a title, Gibbons, brother of Tom, is ranked among the top 10 all-time middleweights. He was never KOed, although he met some of the top fighters of his day, including Harry Greb, Al McCoy, Jack Dillon, George Chip, and Mike O'Dowd.
Helms Hall of Fame.

GIBBONS, TOM boxing: b. March 22, 1891, St. Paul, Minn.; d. Nov. 19, 1960. His record: 57 wins, 47 by KO; 4 losses, 1 by KO; 1 draw, 43 no-decisions, 1 no-contest. A middleweight turned heavyweight, Gibbons, brother of Mike, fought Jack Dempsey for the title on July 4, 1923, and went the distance, losing a 15-round decision. He was KOed only once, by Gene Tunney, in his last fight.
After turning heavyweight in 1921, Gibbons ran up an amazing string during which, in a single year, he scored KOs in 20 of 24 fights.
Helms Hall of Fame, Boxing Hall of Fame.

GIBSON, JOSHUA baseball: b. Dec. 21, 1911, Buena Vista, Ga.; d. Jan. 20, 1947. Bat, throw R; catcher. Negro leagues: Homestead Grays (Pittsburgh), 1930–31; Pittsburgh Crawfords, 1932–36; Pittsburgh Grays, 1936–39; Vera Cruz (Mexican League), 1940–41; Homestead Grays, 1942–46.
Asked how good Josh Gibson was, Hall of Fame catcher Roy Campanella replied, "Well, when we were on the same team, I played third

base." The "black Babe Ruth" was certainly the hardest hitter Negro baseball ever produced and possibly its greatest all-around player as well. He could hit the ball with awesome strength. He's credited with the longest home run ever hit in Yankee Stadium, a drive that hit 2 feet from the top of the wall in center field, 580 feet from the plate. Had it cleared the wall, it would have gone an estimated 700 feet.

One former teammate says that Gibson hit a home run over the triple deck in the stadium's left field in 1934; if so, it is the only time a ball was ever hit out of Yankee Stadium.

It's a pity that Negro leagues didn't keep better records. Those that exist aren't always reliable, because they often include all games played, including exhibitions against inferior teams. Gibson is credited with 75 home runs in 1931, 67 in 1932, 72 in 1933, and 69 in 1934; he may have played as many as 200 games in each of those seasons. He led the Negro National League in hitting, with marks of .457 in 1936, .440 in 1938, .338 in 1944, and .393 in 1945. He led in home runs in 1944, with 6 (39 games), and in 1945, with 8 (44 games). He was named to the Western All-Star team every year from 1933 to 1946 except for the two seasons he spent in Mexico, and he hit .500 in All-Star play.

There's some difference of opinion about the quality of his catching. The consensus seems to be that he was not very good when he started, but eventually he became an excellent defensive catcher. Campanella said, "Anything I could do, he could do better," and Walter Johnson said of him, "He catches so easy he might as well be in a rocking chair. Throws like a rifle."

Troubled by a brain tumor for four years, Gibson died of a stroke.

GIBSON, "MOONEY" (George) baseball: b. July 22, 1880, London, Ontario, Canada; d. Jan. 25, 1967. Bat, throw R; catcher. Pittsburgh NL, 1905–16; New York NL, 1917–18. Fourteen years, 1,213 games, .236 BA. One World Series, 1909: 7 games, .240 BA.

Managed Pittsburgh NL, 1920–22 (part); Chicago NL, 1925 (part); Pittsburgh NL, 1932–34 (part): 413–344, .546.

GIBSON, THERMAN bowling: b. Jan. 30, 1917, Harbor Springs, Mich.; d. March 28, 1969. Three times a member of the ABC tourney champion team, 1952–53, 1955, he was also three-time winner of Michigan all-events, twice won Elks national all-events titles, and was BPAA doubles champion in 1947 and 1955. His thirty-one-year ABC tourney average was 198, with six 1900s, including a 1991. He had two sanctioned 300 games and four 299s.

American Bowling Congress Hall of Fame.

GILBERT, FRED shooting: b. Spirit Lake, Iowa; d. Aug. 8, 1927. Gilbert was the leading shooter among industry representatives in the early part of the century, leading them in average, 1901–05 and 1907. He won the DuPont Cup in 1895 and the E.C. Cup in 1896; he also held, at various times, the Hazard Trophy, Schmelzer Trophy, Sportsmen's Review Trophy, Republic Cup, Kansas City Star Cup, and Field Cup. He won the representatives' title in the 1908 Grand American Handicap, in a shootoff, and repeated in 1919, when he set what was then a world record by breaking 591 consecutive targets.

American Trapshooting Hall of Fame.

GILL, "SLATS" (Amory T.) basketball: b. May 1, 1901, Salem, Ore.; d. April 5, 1966. After winning All-America honors as a forward at Oregon State in 1924, Gill became a high-school coach until 1928, when he took over as head coach at his alma mater. From 1928 to 1964, his teams were 599–392, with 5 Pacific Coast Conference titles. They finished 4th in the NCAA tournament in 1949 and 1963. He served as Oregon State athletic director from 1964 until his death.

Basketball Hall of Fame, Helms Hall of Fame.

GIPP, GEORGE football: b. Feb. 18, 1895, Lauriam, Mich.; d. Dec. 4, 1920. Notre Dame fullback; captain, All-American, 1920.

Notre Dame football chronicler Francis Wallace aptly described Gipp as "a most peculiar kind of saint." Like many other legendary figures, Gipp was an eccentric personality. While in college he earned his spending money by playing cards and billiards—against hustlers, not other students. A couple of times he vanished from Notre Dame and turned up at other schools; Knute Rockne had to find him and bring him back. Like Jim Thorpe, he was a lazy athlete who played indifferently in unimportant games, but the big games brought out his brilliance.

For three years after graduating from high school, Gipp was a cab driver. A baseball scholarship brought him to Notre Dame. He hadn't played high-school football, but he made the Notre Dame freshman team and quickly gave a sign of what was to come: In one game, he went into punt formation at his own 38-yard line, but instead of punting he drop-kicked a 62-yard field goal.

Early in his sophomore year, he left school and went to Wisconsin, but Rockne persuaded him to return. He became a starter. His runs and passes sparked a 70-yard drive that gave Notre Dame a 7–2 victory over Army. With time running out, he broke up an Army pass in the end zone to save the game.

The war curtailed the 1918 schedule, and that season didn't count against a player's eligibility. In 1919 Rockne produced his first unbeaten, untied team. In the big game, Army took a 9–0 lead, but Gipp scored on a 7-yard run after setting up the TD with passes totaling 75 yards, and then he threw a long pass to Eddie Anderson to set up the winner in a 12–9 victory.

Army was again the chief victim of Notre Dame, and of Gipp, in 1920. After trailing 17–14 at half time, Notre Dame won, 27–17. Gipp gained 96 yards passing, 124 yards running, and 112 yards running back kicks. The following week he had TD runs of 92 and 80 yards against Purdue. A dislocated shoulder forced him out of the Indiana game, but he persuaded Rockne to let him go back in, late in the game, with Notre Dame 5 yards from a TD. He scored in two cracks at the line for a 13–0 win.

He sat out most of the final game that season, with Northwestern, because of his shoulder and a bad cold. But the fans yelled for him, and he went in long enough to throw a 45-yard TD pass.

The cold turned out to be a streptococcus infection of the throat. It turned into pneumonia, and he never recovered.

But death didn't end the George Gipp story. In 1928, Notre Dame was up against an unbeaten Army team. No one scored in the first half. In the dressing room at half time Rockne revealed a "secret": On his deathbed Gipp had told Rockne that some time when a Notre Dame team was losing an important game, he should ask them "to win just one for the Gipper." The aroused Irish went out and beat Army, 12–6.

There is some evidence that Rockne had told his 1921 team the same thing during the half-time intermission of the Indiana game. There is no evidence that Gipp actually made that deathbed request. His early death and the "win one for the Gipper" story have added to the legend and have sometimes obscured the fact that Gipp was a truly great player. Walter Camp said, "He could do anything that any backfield man could ever be required to do, and do it in a well-nigh superlative fashion."

Helms Hall of Fame, National Football Foundation Hall of Fame.

GLADCHUCK, CHESTER football: b. ?; d. Sept. 4, 1967. Boston College center; All-American (AP), 1940. New York Giants, 1941, 1946–47.

GLADE, FREDERICK M. baseball: b. Jan. 25, 1876, Dubuque, Iowa; d. Nov. 23, 1934. Bat, throw R; pitcher. Chicago NL, 1902; St. Louis AL, 1904–07; New York AL, 1908. Six years, 53–69, 2.62 ERA. Led league in losses, 1905 (6–25, despite a 2.81 ERA).

GLASS, "NED" (Edgar T.) football: b. May 24, 1879, Syracuse, N.Y.; d. April 9, 1944. Yale guard; All-American, 1902.

GLASSCOCK, "PEBBLY JACK" (John W.) baseball: b. July 22, 1859, Wheeling, W.Va.; d. Feb. 24, 1947. Bat, throw R; shortstop. Cleveland NL,

1879–84; Cincinnati UA, 1884; St. Louis NL, 1885–86; Indianapolis NL, 1887–89; New York NL, 1890–91; St. Louis NL, 1892–93; Pittsburgh NL, 1893–94; Louisville NL, Washington NL, 1895. Seventeen years, 1,736 games, .290 BA; hit .313 in 1884, .325 in 1886, .352 in 1889, .320 in 1893. Led league in hits, 1889 (205); in hits (172) and BA (.336) in 1890.

Glasscock tied an NL record for most years leading shortstops in assists, 5. He went 6-for-6 on Sept. 27, 1890.

GLEASON, "KID" (William J.) baseball: b. Oct. 26, 1866, Camden, N.J.; d. Jan. 2, 1933. Bat L, throw R; pitcher, Philadelphia NL, 1888–91; St. Louis NL, 1892–94; Baltimore NL, 1894; second base, Baltimore NL, 1895; New York NL, 1896–1900; Detroit AL, 1901–02; Philadelphia NL, 1903–08; Chicago AL, 1912. Twenty-two years, 1,966 games, .261 BA; hit .309 in 1895, .319 in 1897. As pitcher: 38–17 in 1890, 24–22 in 1891, 20–23 in 1892, 21–22 in 1893; overall, 138–130, 3.79 ERA.

Gleason managed Chicago AL, 1919–23: 392–364, .519. Pennant, 1919 (the year of the Black Sox Scandal).

GOLDMAN, CHARLES boxing: b. Dec. 21, 1887, Russia; d. Nov. 11, 1968. Goldman had 137 fights in an eleven-year professional career, then became a trainer in 1914. He handled such fighters as Al McCoy, Lou Ambers, Joey Archibald, and Marty Servo but became genuinely, and deservedly, famous for his handling of Rocky Marciano. Marciano got into boxing late and it was Goldman who gave him the style and boxing sense that, combined with his punching ability, took him to the heavyweight championship.

GOLDSMITH, FRED E. baseball: b. May 15, 1852, New Haven, Conn.; d. March 28, 1939. Bat, throw R; pitcher. Troy NL, 1879; Chicago NL, 1880–84; Baltimore AA, 1884. Six years, 112–68, 2.73 ERA; 16 shutouts. Led NL in percentage, 1880 (21–3, .875).

GOODMAN, JOHNNY G. golf: b. 1910, Omaha, Nebr.; d. Aug. 9, 1970. Goodman, Omaha city champion at the age of fifteen, attracted nationwide attention in 1929 by beating Bobby Jones in the first round of the National Amateur. He reached the finals of that tournament in 1932 but lost to C. Ross Somerville. He won it in 1937.

In 1933, Goodman became the fifth amateur to win the U.S. Open; no amateur has won it since. He won the Trans-Mississippi Amateur, 1927, 1931, and 1935.

GOODWIN, "GOODY" (J. T.) rowing: b. ?; d. Jan. 11, 1913. Goodwin stroked the Columbia four-oared crew that beat all American competition, 1877–78, and went to the Henley Regatta in 1878 to win the Visitors'

Challenge and Steward's Challenge Cups. He later coached the Columbia crew.

Helms Hall of Fame.

GORE, GEORGE F. baseball: b. May 3, 1852, Saccarappa, Maine; d. Sept. 16, 1933. Bat L, throw R; outfield. Chicago NL, 1879–87; New York NL, 1887–89; New York PL, 1890; New York NL, 1891–92; St. Louis NL, 1892. Fourteen years, 1,310 games, .301 BA; hit .319 in 1882, .334 in 1883, .318 in 1884, .313 in 1885, .304 in 1886, .305 in 1889. Led league in BA (.360) and slugging (.463) in 1880; in runs, 1881 (86) and 1882 (99); in walks, 1882 (29), 1884 (61), 1886 (102).

Gore is coholder of three ML records: On June 25, 1881, he stole 7 bases; on July 9, 1885, he got 5 extra-base hits (3 doubles and 2 triples) in a game; and 6 times during his career he scored 5 or more runs in a game. One of those times was on May 7, 1880, when he went 6-for-6.

GOTCH, FRANK wrestling: b. April 27, 1878, Humboldt, Iowa; d. ? At 5'11" and 210 pounds, Gotch was an exceptionally strong, clever wrestler. He was one of the early catch-as-catch-can wrestlers, after Tom Jenkins had popularized the style. He won the title from Jenkins in 1905, and except for one brief period held it until his retirement in 1913, winning 154 of 160 official matches. He lost the title in 1906 to Freddie Beall when, after Gotch was knocked out by banging his head against a ring post, Beall pinned him, but he beat Beall easily in a rematch.

GOWDY, "HANK" (Harry) baseball: b. Aug. 24, 1889, Columbus, Ohio; d. Aug. 1, 1966. Bat, throw R; catcher, first base. New York NL, 1910–11; Boston NL, 1911; Boston NL, 1912–17, 1919–23; New York NL, 1923–25; Boston NL, 1929–30. Seventeen years, 1,050 games, .270 BA; hit .317 in 1922, .325 in 1924. Three World Series, 1914, 1923–24: 14 games, .310 BA. He led the Braves to their 4-game sweep over the Athletics in 1914, hitting .545 with 3 doubles, a triple, a home run, 3 runs scored, and 3 RBI.

GRANT, ALEXANDER track: b. 1874, St. Mary's, Ontario, Canada; d. Oct. 13, 1946. A versatile distance runner, Grant won 13 national championships in five different events through a five-year period. Representing Pennsylvania, he won the IC4A outdoor 2-mile run, 1899–1900. He also won these AAU titles: outdoor mile, 1899, 1901–03; outdoor 5-mile, 1899 (tie with R. Grant); outdoor 2-mile steeplechase, 1900; outdoor half-mile, 1900; indoor 2-mile, 1899–1901, 1903.

Helms Hall of Fame.

GRANTHAM, GEORGE F. ("Boots") baseball: b. May 20, 1900, Galena, Kan.; d. March 16, 1954. Bat L, throw R; second-first base. Chicago NL,

1922–24; Pittsburgh NL, 1925–31; Cincinnati NL, 1932–33; New York NL, 1934. Thirteen years, 1,444 games, .303 BA; hit .316 in 1924, .326 in 1925, .318 in 1926, .305 in 1927, .323 in 1928, .307 in 1929, .324 in 1930, .305 in 1931. Two World Series, 1925, 1927: 8 games, .231 BA.

GRAY, SAMUEL D. ("Sad Sam") baseball: b. Oct. 15, 1897, Van Alstyne, Tex.; d. April 16, 1953. Bat, throw R; pitcher. Philadelphia AL, 1924–27; St. Louis AL, 1928–33. Ten years, 111–115, 4.20 ERA. Led AL in shutouts, 1929 (4); in losses, 1931 (11–24).

GREB, "HARRY" (Edward Henry) boxing: b. June 6, 1894, Pittsburgh; d. Oct. 22, 1926. His record: 111 wins, 46 by KO; 7 losses, 2 by KO; 3 draws, 168 no-decisions, 1 no-contest. Often cited as one of the greatest boxers, pound for pound, of all time—perhaps second only to Sugar Ray Robinson —Greb was the only man ever to beat Gene Tunney. Tunney was American light-heavyweight champion when Greb beat him in 15 rounds on May 23, 1922. Greb lost that title to Tunney on Feb. 23, 1923, but became world middleweight champ on Aug. 31 of the same year by beating Johnny Wilson on a 15-round decision.

He fought Tunney once again for the light-heavy crown on Dec. 10, 1923, losing a 15-round decision, but held the middleweight title until Feb. 26, 1926, when Tiger Flowers won a 15-round decision. Flowers also won a 15-round decision in a rematch, Aug. 19, 1926. It was Greb's last fight; he died of an eye operation little more than two months later.

Helms Hall of Fame, Boxing Hall of Fame.

GREENLEAF, RALPH billiards: b. 1899(?); d. March 15, 1950. Considered by many to be the greatest pocket-billiards player of all time, Greenleaf held the world professional title 19 times, 1919–24, 1926, 1927–28, 1930–32, 1937. In 1929, he set records for high single-game average (63) and high grand average (11.02) in tournament play on a 5′ by 10′ table.

GREER, FRANK B. rowing: b. East Boston, Mass.; d. May 7, 1943. Greer was U.S. championship single-sculls winner, 1903–05, and Association single-sculls champion in 1900. He was Olympic single-sculls champion in 1904. Helms Hall of Fame.

GREER, HUGH S. basketball: b. Aug. 5, 1904, Suffield, Conn.; d. Jan. 14, 1963. After twenty-one seasons as a high-school coach (267–78, with 4 undefeated teams, 5 Connecticut state champions, and winning streaks of 67, 43, and 31 games), Greer took over at the University of Connecticut during the 1946–47 season. During sixteen seasons there, he had 15 winning teams and 12 Yankee Conference champions. His overall record was 286–112.

GREGG, "VEAN" (Sylveanus A.) baseball: b. April 13, 1885, Chehalis, Wash.; d. July 29, 1964. Bat R, throw L; pitcher. Cleveland AL, 1911–14; Boston AL, 1914–16; Philadelphia AL, 1918; Washington AL, 1925. Eight years, 89–65, 2.70 ERA; 20–13 in 1912, 20–14 in 1913; 720 strikeouts in 1,392⅓ innings. Led AL in percentage (23–7, .767) and ERA (1.81) in 1911.

GRIFFIN, MICHAEL J. baseball: b. March 20, 1865; d. April 10, 1908. Bat L, throw R; outfield. Baltimore AL, 1887–89; Philadelphia PL, 1890; Brooklyn NL, 1891–98. Twelve years, 1,511 games, 473 stolen bases, .296 BA; hit .301 in 1887, .358 in 1894, .333 in 1895, .308 in 1896, .316 in 1897, .300 in 1898. Led league in runs, 1889 (152); in doubles, 1891 (36).

Griffin holds the ML record for most stolen bases by a rookie, 98, in 1887.

GRIFFITH, CLARK C. baseball: b. Nov. 20, 1869, Stringtown, Mo.; d. Oct. 27, 1955. Bat, throw R. The Old Fox began as a player in 1891, became a playing manager in 1901, a nonplaying manager in 1915, an executive in 1920, and an owner in 1921. At his death in 1955, he had been directly associated with major-league baseball for sixty-five years. Griffith spent most of his playing career as a pitcher but was a good enough hitter to take some turns in the outfield and at every infield position. He was also used as a pinch-hitter. Boston AA, St. Louis AA, 1891; Chicago NL, 1893–1900; Chicago AL, 1901–02; New York AL, 1903–07; Cincinnati NL, 1909–10; Washington AL, 1912–14. Twenty-one years, 236–145, 3.31 ERA. Led league in percentage (24–7, .774) and shutouts (5) in 1901; in shutouts, 1900 (4); in ERA, 1898 (1.88); 21–14 in 1894, 26–14 in 1895, 23–11 in 1896, 21–18 in 1897, 24–10 in 1898, 22–14 in 1899.

Managed Chicago AL, 1901–02; New York AL, 1903–08 (part); Cincinnati NL, 1909–11; Washington AL, 1912–20: 1,491 wins (9th), 1,367 losses (8th), .522. Pennant, 1901.

He became president of the Washington Senators in 1920 and took over as major owner in 1921. Upon his death, his son, Clark R., succeeded him. The team became the Minnesota Twins in 1962.

Baseball Hall of Fame.

GRIFFITH, JOHN L. college sports: b. 1880(?), Carroll, Ill.; d. Dec. 7, 1944. A 1902 graduate of Beloit College, Wisconsin, Griffith was athletic director at three colleges before World War I, when, as a major, he developed the Army's physical-fitness program. In 1919 he took charge of the physical-education teacher-training program at the University of Illinois and was instrumental in organizing the first annual NCAA track meet in 1921. He

served as commissioner of the Western Conference–Big Ten from 1922 until his death.
Helms Hall of Fame.

GRIFFITH, THOMAS H. baseball: b. Oct. 26, 1889, Prospect, Ohio; d. April 13, 1967. Bat L, throw R; outfield. Boston NL, 1913–14; Cincinnati NL, 1915–18; Brooklyn NL, 1919–25; Chicago NL, 1925. Thirteen years, 1,401 games, .280 BA; hit .307 in 1915, .312 in 1921. One World Series, 1920: 7 games, .190 BA.

GRIGG, CECIL football: b. Feb. 15, 1891, Sherman, Tex.; d. Sept. 5, 1968. Austin College quarterback. Canton Bulldogs, 1919–23; Rochester Jeffersons, 1924–25; New York Giants, 1926; Frankford Yellowjackets, 1927. Coached Rochester, 1924–25 (0–13–1).

GROH, "HEINIE" (Henry K.) baseball: b. Sept. 18, 1889, Rochester, N.Y.; d. Aug. 22, 1968. Bat, throw R; second-third base. New York NL, 1912–13; Cincinnati NL, 1913–21; New York NL, 1922–26; Pittsburgh NL, 1927. Sixteen years, 1,676 games, .292 BA; 308 doubles, 180 stolen bases; hit .304 in 1917, .320 in 1918, .310 in 1919, .331 in 1921. Led NL in hits (182) and doubles (39) in 1917; in runs (88) and doubles (28) in 1918; in walks (84) in 1916. Five World Series (with three different teams), 1919, 1922–24, 1927: 21 games, .264 BA. In 1922, when the Giants beat the Yankees in 4 straight games, he hit .474.

Groh's fielding average of .983 in 1924 is an NL record for third basemen, and he led his position in fielding average six times, but his famous "bottle bat" made him a pesky hitter. He had the original bat whittled to his specifications: He wanted a very thin handle but a solid hitting surface just above it so he could get good wood on inside pitches.

GROOM, ROBERT B. baseball: b. Sept. 12, 1884, Belleville, Ill.; d. Feb. 19, 1948. Bat, throw R; pitcher. Washington AL, 1909–13; St. Louis Fed L, 1914–15; St. Louis AL, 1916–17; Cleveland AL, 1918. No-hitter, May 6, 1917, against Chicago AL (3–0). Ten years, 122–151, 3.10 ERA; 1,159 strikeouts, 22 shutouts, in 2,336⅓ innings; 24–13 in 1912. Led league in losses, 1909 (7–26), 1914 (13–21), 1917 (8–19).

GRUENIG, "ACE" (Robert F.) basketball: b. March 12, 1913, Chicago; d. 1958. A 6'8" center, Gruenig established his reputation as an AAU player. During a twelve-year period, 1937–48, he was an AAU All-Tournament player 10 times, and he led his team to championships in 1937 (Denver Safeways) and 1942 (Denver American Legion).
Basketball Hall of Fame, Helms Hall of Fame.

GULICK, LUTHER H. basketball: b. Dec. 4, 1865, Honolulu; d. Aug. 13, 1918. While physical director at the YMCA training school in Springfield, Massachusetts, Dr. Gulick asked a young man named James Naismith to devise an indoor game that would promote physical fitness. The result was basketball. Dr. Gulick was active in the early development of the sport, helping to organize the Public School League in New York City. He was a longtime member of the Playground Association and the National Recreation Association.

Basketball Hall of Fame, Helms Hall of Fame.

GUMBERT, ADDISON C. baseball: b. Oct. 10, 1868, Pittsburgh; d. April 23, 1925. Throw R; pitcher. Chicago NL, 1888–89; Boston PL, 1890; Chicago NL, 1891–92; Pittsburgh NL, 1893–94; Brooklyn NL, 1895–96; Philadelphia NL, 1896. Nine years, 122–102, 4.27 ERA; 22–12 in 1890, 22–19 in 1892.

GUTOWSKI, ROBERT A. track: b. ?; d. Aug. 2, 1960. Gutowski, from Occidental College, set a world record in the pole vault of 15' 8¼ " in 1957. He tied Don Bragg in the AAU indoor event in 1958; he and Jim Graham tied in the NCAA event in 1956 and Gutowski won it in 1957 with a vault of 15'9¾ ", which would have been a world record, but it was not allowed because the wind blew the pole back into the pit.

He was killed in a car crash.

GUTTERSON, ALBERT L. track: b. 1887(?), Vermont; d. April 7, 1965. Gutterson won the running broad jump in the 1912 Olympics; his jump of 25'11¼ " was an Olympic record until 1928.

H

HADLEY, "BUMP" (Irving D.) baseball: b. July 5, 1904, Lynn, Mass.; d. Feb. 15, 1963. Bat, throw R; pitcher. Washington AL, 1926–31; Chicago AL, 1932; St. Louis AL, 1932–34; Washington AL, 1935; New York AL, 1936–40; Philadelphia AL, New York NL, 1941. Sixteen years, 161–165, 4.25 ERA; 1,442 walks (7th), 1,318 strikeouts in 2,944⅔ innings. In relief, 21–23, 3.81 ERA, 25 saves. Led AL in losses, 1932 (14–21). Three World Series, 1936–37, 1939: 2–1, 4.15 ERA.

HAGBERG, ROGER football: b. Feb. 28, 1939, Rochester, Minn.; d. April 15, 1970. Minnesota fullback. After several years in Canadian football, Hagberg played for the Oakland Raiders, 1965–69, where he was often used at tight end.

He died in a car crash.

HAGBERG, "SWEDE" (Rudolph) football: b. June 18, 1907, Follansbee, W.Va.; d. Nov. 25, 1960. West Virginia center. Buffalo Bisons, 1929; Brooklyn Dodgers, 1930.

HAGEN, WALTER C. golf: b. Dec. 21, 1892, Rochester, N.Y.; d. Oct. 5, 1969. What Francis Ouimet was to American golf and Bobby Jones to amateur golf, Walter Hagen was to professional golf. A flamboyant showman, a shrewd psychologist, a great performer when money was on the table, he might well have been the greatest golfer who ever lived. Bobby Jones beat him out for that honor, with Ben Hogan finishing second and Hagen third, in a 1950 poll of sportswriters. But in the only head-to-head match they ever played, a 72-hole contest in 1926, Hagen beat Jones badly, 11-and-10.

Hagen won the U.S. Open in 1914, when he was only twenty-one, shooting a 68 in the first round and leading all the way. He repeated in 1921. In his first eight tries at the British Open, he won four times, in 1922, 1924, 1928, and 1929. In the eight-year span (not including 1925 and 1927, when he didn't enter), he also finished 2nd once and tied for 3rd once. The 1924 win offered a perfect example of Hagen's showmanship. He needed a 6-foot putt on the final green to win, on a rainy day. He didn't even line up the putt; he simply strode up to the ball, hit it, and turned away, tossing his putter to his caddy. As the putt dropped in, the roar from the gallery told Hagen that he was British Open champion.

Match play was perhaps Hagen's greatest strength. He won the PGA, when it was a match tournament, in 1921 and 1924–27; his four straight victories will probably never be equaled. A fifth time he got into the finals but lost to Gene Sarazen, in the second hole of sudden death, after they were tied at the end of 36.

His ability to "psych" an opponent was demonstrated in the 1926 PGA final, against Leo Diegel. Early in the match, Hagen "graciously" conceded some fairly difficult putts. Then, as the match got further along, Diegel had an easy 2-footer and looked at Hagen to see if he would concede it. Hagen turned his back without a word. Diegel decided it must be tricky; he studied and restudied the green, then missed the putt.

Hagen also won the Western Open in 1916, 1921, 1926–27, 1932; the North and South Open, 1918, 1923–24; and the Canadian Open, 1931.

Sometimes called the father of professional golf, Hagen took advantage of his fame to earn extra money by endorsing clubs, balls, and other equipment. And he insisted that pros—who weren't highly regarded in those days—should be allowed to use the clubhouses and locker rooms of the courses on which they were playing, and he won his point even in England, where amateurism was considered the greatest of virtues.

Helms Hall of Fame, Professional Golfers Association Hall of Fame.

HAHN, ARCHIE track: b. 1880, Milwaukee, Wis.; d. Jan. 21, 1955. Hahn won the 200-meter dash in the 1904 Olympics in 21.6 seconds, which was the world record for seventeen years. He also won the Olympic 100 in 1904 and 1906 and the 60-meter dash (since discontinued) in 1904. The Milwaukee Meteor was AAU outdoor 100-yard champion in 1902, the 220-yard champion in 1903, 1905. In 1901, he tied the world record in the 100, at 9.8 seconds.

Hahn attended the University of Michigan.

Helms Hall of Fame.

HAHN, "NOODLES" (Frank G.) baseball: b. April 29, 1879, Nashville, Tenn.; d. Feb. 6, 1960. Bat, throw L; pitcher. Cincinnati NL, 1899–1905; New York AL, 1906. Eight years, 130–93, 2.55 ERA; 210 complete games in 229 starts, 908 strikeouts, 25 shutouts in 2,012⅓ innings. No-hitter, July 12, 1900, against Philadelphia NL (4–0). Led NL in strikeouts, 1899 (145); in shutouts, 1900 (4); in complete games (41) and strikeouts (239) in 1901.

HAINES, JACKSON figure skating: b. 1840, Troy, N.Y., or Chicago; d. 1879. A ballet master, Haines settled in Vienna, Austria, in 1863. The following year, he moved ballet to the ice and thus invented figure skating. He established schools in many countries, and his pupils took the idea all over the world. He died and was buried in Finland, his tombstone reading, "The American Skating King" (or "The American Ice Master," depending on the translation).

HALL, "SEA LION" (Charles L.) baseball: b. Carlos Clolo, May 6, 1888, Kerrville, Tex.; d. Dec. 6, 1943. Bat, throw R; pitcher. Cincinnati NL, 1906–07; Boston AL, 1909–13; St. Louis NL, 1916; Detroit AL, 1918. Nine years, 51–47, 3.08 ERA. In relief, 22–7, 2.65 ERA, 18 saves. Led AL in relief appearances in 1910 (19) and 1913 (31). One World Series, 1912: 0–0, 3.38 ERA in 10⅔ innings of relief.

HALLMAN, WILLIAM W. baseball: b. March 30, 1867, Pittsburgh; d. Sept. 11, 1920. Bat, throw R; second-third base, shortstop. Philadelphia NL, 1888–89; Philadelphia PL, 1890; Philadelphia AA, 1891; Philadelphia NL,

1892–97; St. Louis NL, 1897; Brooklyn NL, 1898; Cleveland AL, 1901; Philadelphia NL, 1901–03. Fourteen years, 1,503 games, .272 BA; hit .307 in 1893, .309 in 1894, .314 in 1895, .320 in 1896.

HAMILTON, "SLIDING BILLY" (William R.) baseball: b. Feb. 16, 1866, Newark, N.J.; d. Dec. 15, 1940. Bat, throw L; outfield. Kansas City AA, 1888–89; Philadelphia NL, 1890–95; Boston NL, 1896–1901. Fourteen years, 1,591 games, 1,690 runs, 1,187 walks, 912 stolen bases (1st), .344 BA (7th). He led the league in hits, 1891 (179); runs, 1891 (141), 1894 (192), 1895 (166), 1897 (152); walks, 1891 (102), 1894 (126), 1895 (96), 1896 (110), 1897 (105); stolen bases, 1889 (111), 1890 (111), 1894 (98), 1895 (97); BA, 1891 (.340), 1893 (.380). He hit .301 in 1889, .325 in 1890, .330 in 1892, .404 in 1894, .389 in 1895, .365 in 1896, .343 in 1897, .369 in 1898, .310 in 1899, .333 in 1900.

The greatest base-stealer in history, Hamilton is surprisingly little known. He holds the ML record for most consecutive games scoring, 24, and for most runs in a season, 192, both in 1894. On Aug. 31, 1894, he tied an ML record by stealing 7 bases. He also holds the NL record for most seasons scoring 150 or more runs, 4.

Baseball Hall of Fame.

HAMMOND, GRAEME M. fencing: b. Feb. 1, 1858, Philadelphia; d. Oct. 30, 1944. A founder and first president of the Amateur Fencers League of America, serving 1891–1925, Dr. Hammond won the national épée title in 1893, the saber title, 1893–94.

Helms Hall of Fame.

HANDLER, PHILIP football: b. July 21, 1908, Ft. Worth, Tex.; d. Dec. 8, 1968. TCU guard. Chicago Cardinals, 1930–36.

He coached the Cardinals in 1943 and 1945, was co-coach during the merger with Pittsburgh in 1944, and co-coach in 1949. His overall record was 7–34.

HANDLEY, LEE E. baseball: b. July 31, 1913, Clarion, Iowa; d. April 8, 1970. Bat, throw R; third-second base. Cincinnati NL, 1936; Pittsburgh NL, 1937–41, 1944–46; Philadelphia NL, 1947. Ten years, 968 games, .269 BA. Led NL in stolen bases, 1939 (17).

HANLON, "NED" (Edward H.) baseball: b. Aug. 22, 1857, Montville, Conn.; d. April 14, 1937. Bat L; outfield. Cleveland NL, 1880; Detroit NL, 1881–88; Pittsburgh NL, 1889; Pittsburgh PL, 1890; Pittsburgh NL, 1891; Baltimore NL, 1892. Thirteen years, 1,267 games, 279 stolen bases (eight years not included); .260 BA.

He managed Pittsburgh NL, 1889 (part); Pittsburgh PL, 1890; Pittsburgh NL, 1891; Baltimore NL, 1892–98; Brooklyn NL, 1899–1905; Cincinnati NL, 1906–07: 1,315–1,165, .530. Pennants, 1894–96, 1899–1900.

HAPAC, WILLIAM J. basketball: b. Jan. 26, 1918, Cicero, Ill.; d. March 9, 1967. Illinois forward; captain, All-American, 1940. He played professionally with teams in Chicago, Illinois, Anderson, Indiana, and Oshkosh, Wisconsin.

HARDWICK, "TACK" (Huntington R.) football: b. Oct. 15, 1892, Quincy, Mass.; d. June 26, 1949. Harvard halfback, end; All-American, 1914; 2nd team, 1913. A halfback as a sophomore, he moved to end the following year and, as a senior, alternated between the two positions. He was an exceptionally strong player and a fine punter.
Helms Hall of Fame, National Football Foundation Hall of Fame.

HARE, CECIL football: b. March 21, 1919, Glenbush, Saskatchewan, Canada; d. April 14, 1963. Gonzaga back. Washington Redskins, 1941–42, 1945; New York Giants, 1946.

HARE, T. TRUXTON football: b. Oct. 12, 1878, Philadelphia; d. Feb. 2, 1956. Pennsylvania guard, 1897–1900; captain, 1899–1900; All-American, 1897–1900. Walter Camp said Hare was the only player who could have been All-American at any position. At 6'2" and 200 pounds, he was faster than most backs and, like many other early linemen, was often used as a runner. He was also his team's signal-caller, punter, and dropkicker. In an unusual defense designed by George Woodruff, the Penn guards played off the line, operating much like modern linebackers, and Hare was devastating in that role.
He could beat other teams in almost every way possible. His punting saved a 12–6 win over Cornell in 1898; his 25-yard field goal, from a bad angle, was the only score in an 1899 victory over Carlisle; in a losing cause in 1900, he scored on a run of 35 yards, dragging five Harvard players a good part of the distance; he salvaged a 5–5 tie with Chicago in 1899 by stopping three consecutive line smashes from inside the Penn 2-yard line.
He finished second in the Olympic hammer throw in 1900.
Helms Hall of Fame, National Football Foundation Hall of Fame.

HARLOW, RICHARD C. football: b. Oct. 19, 1889, Philadelphia; d. Feb. 19, 1962. After playing for Penn State (1913), Harlow coached there, 1915–17, compiling a 20–8–0 mark; at Colgate, 1922–25, his teams were 24–9–3; at Western Maryland, 1926–34, he had a 61–13–7 record, and his 1929 team was 11–0–0. He then became the first nonalumnus to coach at Harvard,

1935–47, where his teams were 45–39–7. He was Coach of the Year in 1936.
Helms Hall of Fame, National Football Foundation Hall of Fame.

HARMAN, HARVEY J. football: b. Nov. 5, 1900, Selingsgrove, Pa.; d. Dec. 17, 1969. A tackle at Pittsburgh, 1922, Harman coached at Haverford, 1922–29, Sewanee, 1930, Pennsylvania, 1931–37, and Rutgers, 1938–41, 1946–56. He became executive secretary of the National Football Foundation in 1956 and was its executive director from 1958 until his death.

HARMON, ROBERT G. baseball: b. Oct. 15, 1887, Liberal, Mo.; d. Nov. 27, 1961. Sw. hit, throw R; pitcher. St. Louis NL, 1909–13; Pittsburgh NL, 1914–16, 1918. Nine years, 103–133, 3.33 ERA; 23–15 in 1911.

HARPER, HARRY C. baseball: b. April 24, 1895, Hackensack, N.J.; d. April 23, 1963. Bat, throw L; pitcher. Washington NL, 1913–19; Boston AL, 1920; New York AL, 1921; Brooklyn NL, 1923. Ten years, 56–77, 2.87 ERA; 623 strikeouts in 1,256 innings. Led AL in losses, 1919 (6–21). One World Series, 1921: 0–0, 20.25 ERA in 1⅓ innings.

HARPER, "JACK" (Charles W.) baseball: b. April 2, 1878, Franklin, Pa.; d. Sept. 30, 1950. Bat, throw R; pitcher. Cleveland NL, 1899; St. Louis NL, 1900–01; St. Louis AL, 1902; Cincinnati NL, 1903–06; Chicago NL, 1906. Eight years, 76–62, 3.58 ERA; 23–12 in 1901, 23–9 in 1904. Led NL in shutouts, 1904 (6).

HARPER, JESSE C. football: b. Dec. 10, 1883, Pawpaw, Ill.; d. July 1, 1961. After playing football at Chicago, 1904, Harper coached at Wabash College in Indiana, moving in 1913 to Notre Dame. His first team, captained by Knute Rockne, had a 7–0–0 record. Rockne gained his first coaching experience as Harper's assistant.

HARRIS, ARCHIE track: b. July 3, 1918, Urbanna County, Va.; d. Oct. 29, 1965. Harris won the NCAA outdoor discus title, representing Indiana, 1940–41, and the AAU championship in 1941. His throw of 174' 8¾ " was briefly a world record.

HARRIS, ELMORE R. football, track: b. June 3, 1922, Normal, Ala.; d. Dec. 8, 1968. Morgan State back. Brooklyn Dodgers (AAFC), 1947. Harris won the AAU outdoor 200-meter hurdles and the NCAA outdoor 220-yard hurdles in 1944.

HARRIS, HARRY boxing: b. Nov. 18, 1880, Chicago; d. June 5, 1959. His record: 40 wins, 15 by KO; 2 losses; 7 draws, 5 no-decisions. Harris claimed the bantamweight title early in the century. He won the vacant title, March

18, 1901, with a 15-round decision over Pedlar Palmer, then became a featherweight.

HARRIS, JOSEPH ("Moon") baseball: b. May 20, 1891, Coulters, Pa.; d. Dec. 10, 1959. Bat, throw R; first base, outfield. New York AL, 1914; Cleveland AL, 1917, 1919; Boston AL, 1922–25; Washington AL, 1925–26; Pittsburgh NL, 1927–28; Brooklyn NL, 1928. Ten years, 969 games, .317 BA; hit .304 in 1917, .316 in 1922, .335 in 1923, .302 in 1924, .313 in 1925, .307 in 1926, .326 in 1927. Two World Series, 1925, 1927: 11 games, .350 BA.

HARRISS, "SLIM" (William J. B.) baseball: b. Dec. 11, 1896, Brownwood, Tex.; d. Sept. 19, 1963. Bat, throw R; pitcher. Philadelphia AL, 1920–26; Boston AL, 1926–28. Nine years, 95–135, 4.25 ERA. Led AL in losses, 1922 (9–20), 1927 (14–21).

HARROUN, RAY auto racing: b. 1879; d. Jan. 19, 1968. Harroun won the first Indianapolis 500-mile race in 1911, with an average speed of 74.59 miles per hour. He was national driving champion in 1910.
Helms Hall of Fame, Auto Racing Hall of Fame.

HART, EDWARD J. football: b. May 22, 1887, New York City; d. Nov. 28, 1956. Princeton fullback, tackle; captain, 1910–11; All-American, 1911, tackle. Hart was big (5'11", 210 pounds), fast, and exceptionally strong; he was so well muscled, in fact, that he once broke a flange in a neck vertebra and didn't find out about it for three years. He was especially tough on defense but was a good downfield blocker as well.
He captained a team that beat Yale in 1911, after Yale had won seven straight from Princeton. One of the Princeton players said afterward, "We had to win. We were more afraid of Eddie than we were of Yale." They also beat strong Harvard and Dartmouth teams that year; the win over Harvard came when Hart hit a Harvard player who had fielded a punt on his own 5-yard line and carried him into the end zone for a safety.
Helms Hall of Fame, National Football Foundation Hall of Fame.

HART, MARVIN boxing: b. Sept. 16, 1876, Fern Creek, Ky.; d. Sept. 17, 1931. His record: 29 wins, 20 by KO; 7 losses, 4 by KO; 4 draws, 8 no-decisions. Hart won the heavyweight title, which had been vacated by Jim Jeffries, by KOing Jack Root in 12 rounds in 1905. It had simply been decided that the winner of that fight would be the next champion; Jeffries refereed. Hart lost the title to Tommy Burns, Feb. 23, 1906, on a 20-round decision.

HARTSEL, "TOPSY" (Tully F.) baseball: b. June 26, 1874, Polk, Ohio; d. Oct. 14, 1944. Bat, throw L; outfield. Louisville NL, 1898–99; Cincinnati

NL, 1900; Chicago NL, 1901; Philadelphia AL, 1902–11. Fourteen years, 1,354 games, 246 stolen bases, .276 BA; hit .335 in 1901, .311 in 1903. Led league in runs (109), walks (87), and stolen bases (47) in 1902; in walks, 1905 (121), 1906 (88), 1907 (106), and 1908 (93). Two World Series, 1905, 1910: 6 games, .273 BA.

Hartsel tied the ML record for most putouts by a left fielder in a 9-inning game, 11, on Sept. 10, 1901.

HAUGHTON, PERCY D. football: b. July 11, 1876, Staten Island, N.Y.; d. Oct. 27, 1924. Harvard tackle; 2nd team, All-American, 1898.

After graduation, he helped establish a football team at Cornell, coaching, 1899–1900, then went into business. But he returned to Harvard as head coach, 1909–16. His 1909 team won all nine games, outscoring its opponents 225–21. During a stretch from 1911 to 1915, Harvard had a 34-game unbeaten streak, with 3 ties. His overall record at Harvard was 71–7–5.

Haughton headed a syndicate that bought baseball's Boston Braves, and he was president of the team, 1916–18. He returned to college coaching, at Columbia, in 1923 but died early in his second year there. His collegiate record, 96–17–6, in thirteen years, is fourth best in history.

He was national racquets champion in 1906.

Helms Hall of Fame, National Football Foundation Hall of Fame.

HAWLEY, EMERSON P. ("Pink") baseball: b. Dec. 5, 1872, Beaver Dam, Wis.; d. Sept. 19, 1938. Bat L, throw R; pitcher. St. Louis NL, 1892–94; Pittsburgh NL, 1895–97; Cincinnati NL, 1898–99; New York NL, 1900; Milwaukee AL, 1901. Ten years, 167–179, 3.96 ERA; 31–22 in 1895, 22–21 in 1896, 27–11 in 1898. Led NL in shutouts, 1895 (4); in complete games, 1900 (34); in losses, 1894 (19–27).

HAWLEY, JESS B. football: b. March 25, 1887, St. Paul, Minn.; d. March 20, 1946. Hawley went to Minnesota for a year, then moved on to Dartmouth, where he played football for three years. He coached at Iowa, 1910–15, compiling a 24–18–0 record. At Dartmouth, 1923–28, he was 39–10–1. His 1924 team was undefeated but tied by Yale; the 1925 team was unbeaten and untied. From 1923–26, Hawley's teams had a 22-game unbeaten streak.

Hawley was an early advocate of the forward pass.

HAYES, FRANKLIN W. baseball: b. Oct. 13, 1914, Jamesburg, N.J.; d. June 22, 1955. Bat, throw R; catcher. Philadelphia AL, 1933–34, 1936–42; St. Louis AL, 1942–43; Philadelphia AL, 1944–45; Cleveland AL, 1945–46; Chicago AL, 1946; Boston AL, 1946. Fourteen years, 1,364 games, .259 BA; hit .308 in 1940.

Hayes holds ML records for most double plays for a catcher, 29, in 1945, and for most consecutive games played by a catcher, 312, from Oct. 2, 1943, to April 21, 1946. His 155 games in 1944 is an AL record for catchers.

HAYES, JOHN J. track: b. 1889(?); d. Oct. 25, 1968. A New York department-store clerk and the youngest member of the 1908 Olympic team, Hayes won one of the most famous marathons in history. Dorando Pietri, of Italy, was in the lead when he entered the stadium, but he collapsed just yards from the finish line; officials helped him across the line and he was subsequently disqualified, the victory going to Hayes.

HAYNES, JOSEPH W. baseball: b. Sept. 2, 1917, Lincolnton, Ga.; d. Jan. 7, 1967. Bat, throw R; pitcher. Washington AL, 1939–40; Chicago AL, 1941–48; Washington AL, 1949–52. Fourteen years, 76–82, 4.01 ERA. In relief, 27–19, 3.49 ERA, 21 saves. Led AL in relief appearances, 1942 (39).

HAZEL, HOMER H. football: b. June 2, 1895, Piffard, N.Y.; d. Feb. 3, 1968. Rutgers All-American end, 1923, All-American fullback, 1924. Hazel started his football career as a freshman in 1916 but dropped out for six years. He returned to school to become one of the few players ever to make All-American at two positions. He was an excellent punter.

Hazel coached Mississippi, 1925–29, with a 21–22–3 record.

Helms Hall of Fame, National Football Foundation Hall of Fame.

HEALY, "EGYPTIAN" (John J.) baseball: b. Oct. 27, 1866, Cairo, Ill.; d. March 16, 1899. Bat, throw R; pitcher. St. Louis NL, 1885–86; Indianapolis NL, 1887–88; Chicago NL, Washington NL, 1889; Toledo AA, 1890; Baltimore AA, 1891; Baltimore NL, Louisville NL, 1892. Eight years, 79–136, 3.84 ERA; 22–21 in 1890. Led NL in losses, 1887 (12–29).

HEARDEN, "RED" (Thomas F.) football: b. 1904(?), Green Bay, Wis.; d. Dec. 27, 1964. Notre Dame back; co-captain, 1926. Green Bay Packers, 1927-28; Chicago Bears, 1929.

HEATHCOTE, CLIFTON E. baseball: b. Jan. 24, 1898, Glen Rock, Pa.; d. Jan. 19, 1939. Bat, throw L; outfield. St. Louis NL, 1918–22; Chicago NL, 1922–30; Cincinnati NL, 1931–32; Philadelphia NL, 1932. Fifteen years, 1,415 games, .275 BA; hit .309 in 1924. One World Series, 1929: 2 games, 1 at-bat, .000 BA.

HECKER, GUY J. baseball: b. April 3, 1856, Youngville, Pa.; d. Dec. 4, 1938. Bat, throw R; pitcher, first base, outfield. Louisville AA, 1882–89; Pittsburgh NL, 1890. Nine years, 703 games, .283 BA; as pitcher, 173–146, 2.92 ERA; 26–23 in 1883, 30–23 in 1885, 26–23 in 1886. He hit .319 in 1887.

Led AA in victories (52–20), ERA (1.80), complete games (72), and strike-outs (385) in 1884; led in BA, 1886 (.341). No-hitter, Sept. 19, 1882, against Pittsburgh AA (3–1).

Hecker holds the ML record for most runs scored in a game, 7, on Aug. 15, 1886—a day on which he went 6-for-7, with 3 home runs, tying the ML record for most home runs and most total bases in a game by a pitcher. On July 4, 1884, he won both games of a doubleheader, pitching 18 innings without issuing a walk.

Managed Pittsburgh NL, 1890: 23–113, .169.

HEENAN, JOHN G. boxing: b. May 2, 1835, West Troy, N.Y.; d. Oct. 25, 1873. Heenan learned to fight in a mining camp in Benicia, California. In 1858 he got a match with John C. Morrissey, who claimed to be champion. Heenan broke his right hand in the 1st round but managed to go 10 more rounds before giving up. He asked for a rematch, but Morrissey retired. Heenan then claimed the American title and headed for England.

On April 17, 1860, he fought Tom Sayers, who claimed the English title. The fight was stopped without decision when spectators entered the ring in the 42nd round. Americans who were there insisted that Heenan was win-ning, and it seems likely that Englishmen who had bet on Sayers deliber-ately stopped the fight to keep from losing their money. Sayers retired, Tom King took the title, and Heenan, who had been in England all this time, challenged King. They fought on Dec. 18, 1863, and again the outcome was controversial. After the 18th round, King couldn't come "up to scratch" in the allotted time, 30 seconds, but the fight wasn't awarded to Heenan. King was given all the time he needed to recover, and Heenan's seconds threw in the towel after 7 more rounds.

Boxing Hall of Fame.

HEFFELFINGER, "PUDGE" (William W.) football: b. Dec. 20, 1867, Min-neapolis: d. April 3, 1954. A member of the first Walter Camp All-Ameri-can team in 1889, Heffelfinger repeated the next two years. At Yale, he also played baseball, threw the weights, and rowed on the varsity crew.

Gifted with great speed and agility at 6'3" and 210 pounds, he was the first of the running guards, pulling out of the line to lead interference downfield instead of simply blocking straight ahead. It was legal at that time for a lineman to help a runner by grabbing him and hurling him against the opposition or to get behind him and push him through it, both tactics at which Heffelfinger excelled. He was also noted for his ability to defeat the "flying wedge" by hurling himself at its point and tearing apart the linked chain of blockers.

In 1916, when he was forty-eight, he returned to Yale to help the team prepare for its Harvard and Princeton games. He almost wrecked it instead. Getting into a scrimmage to teach by example, he knocked out five starters in two plays, until coach "Tad" Jones ordered him off the field.

Helms Hall of Fame, National Football Foundation Hall of Fame.

HEIKES, ROLLA O. shooting: b. Dec. 25, 1856, near Dayton, Ohio; d. Sept. 23, 1934. Heikes won the first Grand American Handicap at targets, in 1900, and won both the Cast Iron Medal and the E.C. Cup 5 consecutive times. Some of his greatest accomplishments came at rapid-fire shooting. He once broke 500 targets in 37 minutes, 15 seconds, using three guns, and set a world record by breaking 100 flying targets in 2 minutes, 58 seconds, using four guns.

American Trapshooting Hall of Fame.

HEILMANN, HARRY E. baseball: b. Aug. 3, 1894, San Francisco; d. July 9, 1951. Bat, throw R; outfield, first base. Detroit AL, 1914, 1916–29; Cincinnati NL, 1930, 1932. Seventeen years, 2,146 games, 7,787 at-bats, 2,660 hits, 542 doubles (8th), 151 triples, 183 home runs, 1,291 runs, 4,053 total bases, 1,537 RBI, .342 BA (10th); hit .320 in 1919, .309 in 1920, .356 in 1922, .346 in 1924, .367 in 1926, .328 in 1928, .344 in 1929, .333 in 1930. Led AL in hitting, 1921 (.394), 1923 (.403), 1925 (.393), 1927 (.398); in hits, 1921 (237); in doubles, 1924 (45).

Heilmann was one of only eight players to hit over .400 during the modern era, and he was one of only three to hit home runs in all ML parks that were in use during their careers.

Baseball Hall of Fame.

HEISMAN, JOHN W. football: b. Oct. 25, 1869, Cleveland; d. Oct. 3, 1936. Heisman played football at Brown, 1887–89, and at Pennsylvania, 1890–91. He began his thirty-six-year coaching career at Oberlin College in 1892 with an undefeated, untied team that beat Michigan once and Ohio State twice. He went to Akron in 1893, returned to Oberlin in 1894, then settled down at Auburn, 1895–99, producing a 13–3–2 record. He moved to Clemson in 1900, immediately producing an undefeated team (6–0–0); his record in four years there was 19–3–2.

Heisman's longest tenure was at Georgia Tech, 1904–19; he built that school into a football power. He had three straight unbeaten teams, 6–0–1 in 1915, 8–0–1 in 1916, and 9–0–0 in 1917, compiling a 32-game unbeaten streak (including two ties), during which Tech outscored its opposition, 1,592–62. Among the games was a 222–0 defeat of Cumberland in 1916, the highest score ever recorded. He also coached at Pennsylvania, 1920–22; Washington and Jefferson, 1923; and Rice, 1924–27.

He was a founder of the American Football Coaches Association and one of the driving forces behind the legalization of the forward pass. The Heisman Trophy is named in his honor.

Helms Hall of Fame, National Football Foundation Hall of Fame.

HELMS, PAUL H. general: b. Sept. 19, 1889, Ottawa, Kan.; d. Jan. 5, 1957. Helms founded the Helms Athletic Foundation, 1936, and Helms Hall, 1948, the world's largest sports shrine, museum, and library. The nonprofit foundation exists largely to recognize outstanding athletes, coaches, and contributors through various trophies and halls of fame. One of the most important is the Helms World Trophy. Each year six athletes, one from each continent, are chosen to have their names engraved on the trophy. Awards have been made retroactive to 1896, the year of the first modern Olympic Games. Halls of fame have been established in 21 areas of sports.

HEMMING, GEORGE E. baseball: b. Dec. 15, 1868, Carrollton, Ohio; d. June 3, 1930. Bat, throw R; pitcher. Brooklyn PL, Cleveland PL, 1890; Brooklyn NL, 1891; Cincinnati NL, 1892; Louisville NL, 1892–94; Baltimore NL, 1894–96; Louisville NL, 1897. Eight years, 91–82, 4.55 ERA; 20–13 in 1895.

HEMPHILL, CHARLES J. ("Eagle Eye") baseball: b. April 20, 1876, Greenville, Mich.; d. June 22, 1953. Bat, throw L; outfield. Cleveland NL, St. Louis NL, 1899; Boston AL, 1901; Cleveland AL, 1902; St. Louis AL, 1902–04, 1906–07; New York AL, 1908–11. Eleven years, 1,242 games, .271 BA; hit .308 in 1902.

HENDERSON, "HARDIE" (James Harding) baseball: b. Oct. 31, 1862, Philadelphia; d. Feb. 6, 1903. Pitcher. Philadelphia NL, 1883; Baltimore AA, 1883–86; Brooklyn AA, 1886–87; Pittsburgh NL, 1888. Six years, 81–121, 3.50 ERA; 930 strikeouts in 1,788⅓ innings; 27–23 in 1884. Led AA in losses, 1885 (25–35).

HENDRICKS, "JACK" (John C.) baseball: b. April 9, 1875, Joliet, Ill.; d. May 13, 1943. Bat, throw L; outfield. Chicago NL, New York NL, 1902; Washington NL, 1903. Two years, 42 games, .207 BA.

Managed St. Louis NL, 1918; Cincinnati NL, 1924–29: 520–528, .496.

HENDRIX, CLAUDE R. baseball: b. April 13, 1889, Olathe, Kan.; d. March 22, 1944. Bat, throw R; pitcher. Pittsburgh NL, 1911–13; Chicago Fed L, 1914–15; Chicago NL, 1916–20. Ten years, 142–116, 2.65 ERA; 1,092 strikeouts, 27 shutouts in 2,371⅓ innings; 23–9 in 1912. No-hitter, May 15, 1915, against Pittsburgh Fed L. Led Fed L in victories (29–11) and complete games (34) in 1914; led NL in percentage, 1918 (19–7, .731). One World Series, 1918: 0–0, 0.00 ERA, in 1 inning of relief.

HENLINE, "BUTCH" (Walter J.) baseball: b. Dec. 20, 1894, Ft. Wayne Ind.; d. Oct. 9, 1957. Bat, throw R; catcher. New York NL, 1921; Philadelphia NL, 1921–26; Brooklyn NL, 1927–29; Chicago NL, 1930–31. Eleven years, 740 games, .291 BA; hit .316 in 1922, .324 in 1923, .304 in 1925. On Sept. 15, 1922, he hit 3 home runs in a game.

HENRY, "DUTCH" (Frank J.) baseball: b. May 12, 1902, Cleveland; d. Aug. 23, 1968. Bat, throw L; pitcher. St. Louis AL, 1921–22; Brooklyn NL, 1923–24; New York NL, 1927–29; Chicago AL, 1929–30. Eight years, 27–43, 4.39 ERA. In relief, 11–10, 4.36 ERA, 6 saves.

HENRY, "FATS" (Wilbur F., "Pete") football: b. Oct. 31, 1897, Mansfield, Ohio; d. Feb. 7, 1952. Washington and Jefferson tackle; All-American, 1919; 2nd team, 1918. Canton Bulldogs, 1920–23; Akron Pros, 1925; Canton Bulldogs, 1925–26; New York Giants, 1927; Pottsville Maroons, 1927–28; Staten Island Stapletons, 1930.

A great kicker as well as a big, ferocious lineman (5'10", 240 pounds), Henry holds NFL records for longest punt, 94 yards, Oct. 28, 1923; longest dropkicked field goal, 50 yards, Nov. 13, 1942 (tied); and most consecutive conversions by dropkick, 49. He looked deceptively fat but was very agile; Grantland Rice once described him as "bouncing around like a rubber ball."

He was co-coach at Canton, 1925–26, and coach at Pottsville, 1928, for an overall record of 7–21–3.

Helms Hall of Fame, National Football Foundation Hall of Fame, Professional Football Hall of Fame.

HEPBRON, GEORGE T. basketball: b. Aug. 27, 1863, Still Pond, Mo.; d. April 30, 1946. A friend of two other members of the Basketball Hall of Fame, Dr. Luther H. Gulick and James Naismith, Hepbron early saw the need to curb roughness in the sport. He was long active as an official—he refereed the first National AAU Tournament, in 1897—and he developed the first national rules questionnaire.

Basketball Hall of Fame, Helms Hall of Fame.

HEPBURN, RALPH auto racing: b. ?; d. May 16, 1948. Hepburn began his career as a dirt-track motorcycle racer; a number of his records still stand. He once did a mile in 39 3/5 seconds in 1922, and in 1921 he set a 300-mile record of 3 hours, 30 minutes, and 3 seconds. As an auto racer he never managed to win at Indianapolis, in 15 tries; in 1937 he was second, by 2.16

seconds, to Wilbur Shaw, in the closest race ever run at Indy. He was killed there during a practice run.

Helms Hall of Fame, Auto Racing Hall of Fame.

HERBER, "ARNIE" (Arnold) football: b. April 2, 1910, Green Bay, Wis.; d. Oct. 14, 1969. The first of the great long passers, Herber arrived almost too soon, before the long pass was a commonly used weapon. The ball was still fat and hard to throw, and Herber held it wrong, with the laces in his palm. Nevertheless, putting on an exhibition for a movie-maker, he threw 50 yards through a 2-foot-square pane of glass on his first try and then, when a retake was needed, did it again.

After attending both Wisconsin and Regis colleges, he played for the Green Bay Packers, 1930–40, the New York Giants, 1944–45. During his thirteen seasons, he completed 481 of 1,185 passes for 8,033 yards, 66 TDs, and 6.78 yards per attempt. He led the NFL in passing in 1932, 1934, and 1936 and was All-Pro in 1932. In 1936, he became the first man to pass for more than 1,000 yards.

Professional Football Hall of Fame, Helms Hall of Fame.

HERRESHOFF, CHARLES F. motorboat racing: b. May 28, 1876, Nice, France; d. Jan. 30, 1954. Though he made a number of improvements in the auto, Herreshoff is best known as a designer of motor yachts. His *Alabama* was American champion, 1907–09, and his *Vim* won the New York–Poughkeepsie races, 1908–09. *Nevada* won the 1901 International Exposition races in Glasgow. He was a member of a family better known for designing and building sailing ships.

HERRESHOFF, NATHANIEL G. yachting: b. March 18, 1848, Bristol, R.I.; d. June 2, 1938. For twenty-seven years, every America's Cup defender —five of them, conquering a total of six challengers—was designed by Nat Herreshoff. He was born to build ships: A Bristol, Rhode Island, shipyard had been in the family since 1790. After attending MIT, he joined his brother John in the shipyard. He genuinely began to come into his own as a designer of racing vessels in 1890. In that year he turned out *Gloriana* and *Wasp,* both highly successful. Starting in 1890, Herreshoff vessels won 7 of 13 Goelet Cups, 22 of 62 Astor Cups, 4 of 7 Breton Reef Cups, 14 of 24 King's Cups, and 2 of 7 Cape May Challenge Cups.

When the British challenged for the America's Cup in 1893, Herreshoff built *Vigilant,* which whipped *Valkyrie II* in three straight races. His *Defender* did the same to *Valkyrie III* in 1895. Then came Sir Thomas Lipton with his Shamrock line. Herreshoff's *Columbia* won the first two challenges, also in straight races, in 1899 and 1901, and *Reliance* beat *Shamrock IV* in 1903. The aptly named *Resolute,* facing the next British challenge, in 1920, was the first Herreshoff design to lose a cup race, but she came back from an 0–2 deficit to retain the cup for the United States.

HERSCHBERGER, CLARENCE football: b. ?; d. Dec. 14, 1936. Chicago fullback; captain, All-American, 1897. Chicago's first All-American, Herschberger was one of the outstanding punters in college football's early years.

HERTZ, JOHN D. horse racing: b. April 10, 1879, Ruttka, Austria; d. Oct. 8, 1961. The man who founded the Yellow Cab Co. and a car-rental service was also the owner of two great horses. Count Fleet won the Triple Crown in 1943, was named Horse of the Year, and was the top money-winner, with $174,055. He also became the outstanding sire of 1951, when his offspring won 124 races for $1,160,847. His sire, Reigh Count, had won the 1928 Kentucky Derby. Hertz's Stoner Creek Stud Farm produced, in all, winners of 2,955 races and more than $9 million. Hertz owned Arlington Park from 1929 to 1940.

HERZOG, "BUCK" (Charles L.) baseball: b. July 9, 1885, Baltimore; d. Sept. 4, 1953. Bat, throw R; infield. New York NL, 1908–09; Boston NL, 1910–11; New York NL, 1911–13; Cincinnati NL, 1914–16; New York NL, 1916–17; Boston NL, 1918–19; Chicago NL, 1919–20. Thirteen years, 1,493 games, .259 BA. Four World Series, 1911–13, 1917: 25 games, .245 BA. He hit .400 in the 1912 Series, with 4 doubles, a triple, 6 runs, and 4 RBI.
  Managed Cincinnati NL, 1914–16 (part): 165–226, .442.

HESS, OTTO C. baseball: b. Nov. 13, 1878, Berne, Switzerland; d. Feb. 24, 1926. Bat, throw L; pitcher. Cleveland AL, 1902, 1904–08; Boston NL, 1912–15. Ten years, 69–91, 1.98 ERA; 20–18 in 1906.

HESTON, "WILLIE" (William M.) football: b. Sept. 9, 1878, Galesburg, Ill.; d. Sept. 9, 1963. Michigan halfback, captain, 1904; All-American, 1903–04; 3rd team, 1901–02. Heston had everything a coach could ask for in a running back. He weighed only 185 pounds, but it was spread solidly over a 5'8" frame. He could run the 100 in just over 10 seconds and for the first 40 yards could outrun Archie Hahn, the Olympic sprint champion; he had a very quick start, high leg action, and a devastating stiff arm.
  Heston captained the 1900 football team at San Jose, California, Normal School, which hired "Hurry-Up" Yost to coach the last game of the year, for the state normal-school championship. Yost moved Heston from guard to halfback and San Jose won. In 1901, Yost became head coach at Michi-

gan and persuaded Heston to follow him and study for a law degree instead of teaching.

In his second game, he scored four TDs. In Michigan's 49–0 victory over Stanford in the 1902 Rose Bowl, he gained 170 yards in 18 attempts. By the time he was finished, he had scored 93 TDs in four years, and Yost's "point-a-minute" teams had won 43 of 44 games, tying the other, during the period. Statistics weren't carefully kept, and no one knows how much total yardage he gained, but it is known that he ran for 237 of Michigan's 260 yards against Chicago in 1903, and several other times he gained more than 200 yards in a game.

Heston collected $600 from the Canton Bulldogs for one game in 1905. He gained little yardage but played well on defense. In 1906 he played for a college all-star team against the Massillon Tigers, injured a leg, and retired from football.

Helms Hall of Fame, National Football Foundation Hall of Fame.

HEUSSER, EDWARD B. baseball: b. May 7, 1909, Murray, Utah; d. March 1, 1956. Sw. hit, throw R; pitcher. St. Louis NL, 1935–36; Philadelphia NL, 1938; Philadelphia AL, 1940; Cincinnati NL, 1943–46; Philadelphia NL, 1948. Led NL in ERA, 1944 (2.38). Nine years, 56–67, 3.69 ERA. In relief, 19–16, 3.96 ERA, 18 saves.

HEVING, JOSEPH W. baseball: b. Sept. 2, 1900, Covington, Ky.; d. April 11, 1970. Bat, throw R; pitcher. New York NL, 1930–31; Chicago AL, 1933–35; Cleveland AL, 1937–38; Boston AL, 1938–40; Cleveland AL, 1941–44; Boston NL, 1945. Thirteen years, 76–48, 3.90 ERA. In relief, 60 wins (7th), 35 losses, 3.62 ERA, 63 saves. He had fine seasons in 1939, when he was 11–2, with 7 saves and a 3.07 ERA, and in 1944, when he was 8–2, with 10 saves and a 1.74 ERA.

HEWITT, WILLIAM E. football: b. Oct. 8, 1909, Bay City, Mich.; d. Jan. 14, 1947. Michigan end. Chicago Bears, 1932–36; Philadelphia Eagles, 1937–39; Philadelphia-Pittsburgh, 1943; All-Pro, 1933–34, 1936–37. Hewitt, who played without a helmet, was an outstanding pass rusher; he had such a quick start that he often seemed to be offside.

He died in a car crash.

Professional Football Hall of Fame.

HICKMAN, HERMAN M., JR. football: b. Oct. 1, 1911, Johnson City, Tenn.; d. April 25, 1958. Tennessee guard; All-American, 1931 (Rice). Brooklyn Dodgers, 1932–34; All-Pro, 1933.

Hickman was head coach at Yale, 1948–51, compiling a 15–17–3 record.

He was also at one time a professional wrestler, and through television became known as a wit, comic poet, and expert storyteller.

HICKMAN, "PIANO LEGS" (Charles T.) baseball: b. March 4, 1876, Dunkirk, N.Y.; d. April 19, 1934. Bat, throw R; first base, outfield, second-third base. Boston NL, 1897–99; New York NL, 1900–01; Boston AL, 1902; Cleveland AL, 1902–04; Detroit AL, 1904–05; Washington AL, 1905–07; Chicago AL, 1907; Cleveland AL, 1908. Twelve years, 1,081 games, .296 BA; hit .313 in 1900, .361 in 1902. Led AL in hits, 1902 (193).

HICKOK, WILLIAM O. football, track: b. Aug. 23, 1874, Harrisburg, Pa.; d. Sept. 4, 1933. Yale guard; All-American, 1893–94. He was IC4A shotput and hammer-throw champion, 1893–95, and won the AAU outdoor shotput in 1895.

HICKOX, EDWARD J. basketball: b. April 10, 1878, Cleveland; d. Jan. 28, 1966. Hickox had a 209–85 record coaching at Springfield, Mass., College, the birthplace of basketball, 1927–43, and was 21–3 in one season at American International College, 1945–46. He was historian of the National Association of Basketball Coaches for twenty years, a Rules Committee member for eighteen years, and a tireless worker for construction of the Naismith Memorial Basketball Hall of Fame at Springfield.

Basketball Hall of Fame, Helms Hall of Fame.

HIGGINS, MICHAEL F. ("Pinky") baseball: b. May 27, 1909, Red Oak, Tex.; d. March 21, 1969. Bat, throw R; third base. Philadelphia AL, 1930, 1933–36; Boston AL, 1937–38; Detroit AL, 1940–44, 1946; Boston AL, 1946. Fourteen years, 1,802 games, .292 BA; hit .314 in 1933, .330 in 1934, .302 in 1937, .303 in 1938. Two World Series, 1940, 1946: 14 games, .271 BA.

Higgins set an ML record in 1938 by getting 12 hits in 12 consecutive times at bat; he also had two walks in the streak, thus getting on base 14 consecutive times. He hit 3 home runs in a game on June 27, 1935, and again on May 20, 1940.

He managed Boston AL, 1955–59 (part), 1960 (part)–62: 543–541, .501.

HIGHAM, RICHARD baseball: b. 1852, England; d. March 18, 1905. Bat L, throw R; outfield, catcher. National Association, New York, 1871; Baltimore, 1872; New York, 1873–75; Chicago, 1875. Five years, 239 games, .288 BA.

Hartford NL, 1876; Providence NL, 1878; Troy NL, 1880. Three years, 130 games, .323 BA; hit .327 in 1876, .320 in 1878. Led NL in doubles, 1876 (21); in doubles (22) and runs (60) in 1878.

HILL, EDWARD K. football: b. July 9, 1870, Granville, Ill.; d. Nov. 10, 1932. After playing football at Dartmouth, 1892, Hill coached Illinois, 1892–93. He was a long-time member of the Intercollegiate Football Rules Committee. National Football Foundation Hall of Fame.

HILL, MACK LEE football: b. ?; d. Dec. 14, 1965. Southern University fullback, Kansas City Chiefs (AFL), 1964–65. Virtually unknown as a college player, Hill led the AFL in rushing average in 1964 with 567 yards in 105 carries for a 5.4 average. In his two seasons he gained 1,203 yards in 230 carries, also a 5.4 average, and 8 TDs.
He died during routine surgery for a knee injury.

HILL, VIRGINIA (later **Mrs. Mosdale**) badminton: b. Deignan, April 17, 1907, Los Angeles; d. June 8, 1967. Mrs. Hill won the U.S. mixed doubles (with Wynn Rogers) in 1947. She was administrative secretary and treasurer, American Badminton Association, 1960–67; in 1967 she received the Players' Appreciation Cup for her contributions to the sport.

HILLMAN, HARRY L. track: b. ?; d. Aug. 9, 1945. Hillman won the 200-meter and 400-meter hurdles and the 400-meter run at the 1904 Olympics. He was AAU 440-yard champion in 1903 and 1908 and 220-yard hurdle champion in 1906.
He was Dartmouth track coach from 1910 until his death.

HINES, PAUL A. baseball: b. March 1, 1852, Washington, D.C.; d. July 10, 1935. Bat, throw R; outfield. National Association, Washington Nationals, 1872–73; Chicago White Stockings, 1874–75. Four years, 178 games, .302 BA.
Chicago NL, 1876–77; Providence NL, 1878–85; Washington NL, 1886–87; Indianapolis NL, 1888–89; Boston NL, Pittsburgh NL, 1890; Washington AA, 1891. Sixteen years, 1,481 games, .301 BA; hit .331 in 1876, .307 in 1880, .309 in 1882, .302 in 1884, .312 in 1886, .308 in 1887, .305 in 1889. Led league in doubles, 1876 (21), 1881 (27), 1884 (36); in BA (.358), home runs (4), and RBI (50) in 1878; in hits (146) and BA (.357) in 1879. Hines was baseball's first triple crown winner, in 1878. He went 6-for-6 on Aug. 26, 1879.

HINKEY, FRANK A. football: b. Dec. 23, 1871, Tonawanda, N.Y.; d. Dec. 30, 1925. Yale end; All-American, 1891–94. An unlikely looking prospect, only 5'9" and 155 pounds, Hinkey had been warned by doctors to avoid strenuous sports because of lung trouble; he ultimately died of tuberculosis.

But he was a demon, particularly on defense. Both Penn and Harvar
ended athletic relations with Yale during Hinkey's career because of hi
rough play. Other teams tried to retaliate but couldn't seem to faze hin
Only once was he removed from a game because of injury; it was the onl
game Yale lost during his career.

He captained the team in 1893 and 1894; at the time, a captain wa
actually a coach, and Yale had a 26–1 record during his captaincy. He wa
a leader by example; his ferocious play turned the team, as one sportswrite
of the time put it, into a "set of Yale brutes."

Hinkey coached Yale to a 7–3 record in 1914; he was the first coacl
to study game films. He had less success in 1915 and didn't last the sea
son.

Helms Hall of Fame, National Football Foundation Hall of Fame.

HIRSCH, MAXIMILLION horse racing: b. July 12, 1880, Fredericksburg
Tex.; d. April 3, 1969. Hirsch trained winners of 1,933 races, includin;
Assault, who won the 1946 Triple Crown. He also trained Bold Venture
who won the Kentucky Derby and Preakness in 1936; Middleground, wh
won the Derby and Belmont in 1950; and Belmont winners Vito (1928) an
High Gun (1954).

HITCHCOCK, JAMES F. football: b. June 28, 1911, Inverness, Ala.; d. Jun
23, 1959. Auburn halfback; captain, All-American (Rice, AP), 1932. Th
brother of baseball player and manager Billy Hitchcock, he played briefl
with Boston NL, 1938.

National Football Foundation Hall of Fame.

HITCHCOCK, "TOMMY" (Thomas, Jr.) polo: b. Feb. 11, 1900, Long Is
land, N.Y.; d. April 19, 1944. The Babe Ruth of polo was rated at 10 goal:
18 times in his nineteen-year career, 1922–40. The only exception was 1935
when he had a 9-goal rating. He played for the National Open champion:
in 1923, 1927, 1935–36, the winners of the Monty Waterbury Memoria
Cup in 1928, 1932, 1935, and 1939, and for American teams that won th
Westchester Cup matches from Great Britain in 1921, 1924, 1927, 1930
and 1939.

A lieutenant-colonel and commander of a flying group in World War II
Hitchcock was killed in a plane crash.

HOAK, DONALD A. ("Tiger") baseball: b. Feb. 5, 1928, Roulette, Pa.; d
Oct. 9, 1969. Bat, throw R; third base. Brooklyn NL, 1954–55; Chicago NL,
1956; Cincinnati NL, 1957–58; Pittsburgh NL, 1959–62; Philadelphia NL,
1963–64. Eleven years, 1,263 games, .265 BA. Led NL in doubles, 1957
(39). Two World Series, 1955, 1960: 10 games, .231 BA.

OBLITZEL, RICHARD C. baseball: b. Oct. 26, 1888, Waverly, W.Va.; d. Nov. 14, 1962. Bat, throw L; first base. Cincinnati NL, 1908–14; Boston AL, 1914–18. Eleven years, 1,314 games, .278 BA; hit .308 in 1909. Two World Series, 1915, 1916: 10 games, .273 BA.

OFFER, WILLIAM L. baseball: b. Nov. 8, 1870, Cedar Rapids, Iowa; d. July 21, 1959. Bat, throw R; pitcher. Baltimore NL, 1895–98; Pittsburgh NL, 1898–99; Cleveland AL, 1901. Six years, 92–45, 3.75 ERA; 22–11 in 1897. Led NL in percentage (31–6, .838) and shutouts (4) in 1895; in percentage, 1896 (25–7, .781).

OFMAN, "CIRCUS SOLLY" (Arthur F.) baseball: b. Oct. 29, 1882, St. Louis; d. March 10, 1956. Bat, throw R; outfield, Pittsburgh NL, 1903; Chicago NL, 1904–12; Pittsburgh NL, 1912–13; Brooklyn Fed L, 1914; Buffalo Fed L, 1915; New York AL, Chicago NL, 1916. Fourteen years, 1,193 games, .269 BA; hit .325 in 1910. Three World Series, 1906, 1908, 1910: 16 games, .298 BA.

OGAN, JAMES J. football: b. Nov. 1, 1876, Torrington, Conn.; d. March 20, 1910. Yale tackle; All-American, 1902–04.
National Football Foundation Hall of Fame.

OGAN, "SHANTY" (James F.) baseball: b. March 21, 1906, Somerville, Mass.; d. April 7, 1967. Bat, throw R; catcher. Boston NL, 1925–27; New York NL, 1928–32; Boston NL, 1933–35; Washington AA, 1936–37. Thirteen years, 989 games, .295 BA; hit .333 in 1928, .300 in 1929, .339 in 1930, .301 in 1931.
Hogan set an NL record for catchers with 121 consecutive errorless games, May 17, 1933, to Aug. 3, 1934. He tied an ML record for catchers by starting 3 double plays, Aug. 19, 1931.

HOLKE, WALTER H. ("Union Man") baseball: b. Dec. 25, 1892, St. Louis; d. Oct. 12, 1954. Sw. hit, throw L; first base. New York NL, 1914, 1916–18; Boston NL, 1919–22; Philadelphia NL, 1923–25; Cincinnati NL, 1925. Eleven years, 1,212 games, .287 BA; hit .311 in 1923, .300 in 1924. One World Series, 1917: 6 games, .286 BA.
Holke set an NL record for fewest errors by a first baseman in 150 or more games with only 4 in 1921, and his fielding average of .997 tied the NL record. In the famous 26-inning game of May 1, 1920, he set ML records for most putouts, 42, and most chances, 43, for a first baseman.

HOLLEDER, DONALD W. football: b. Aug. 3, 1934, New York; d. Oct. 17, 1967. Army end, quarterback; All-American, 1954 (UPI, Coaches). An All-American end as a junior, Holleder moved to quarterback the following

year and guided Army to a 14–6 win over Navy. He won the Swede Nelso
Award for sportsmanship in 1955.

He was killed in Vietnam.

HOLLENBACK, "BIG BILL" (William M.) football: b. Feb. 22, 1886, Blu
Bell, Pa.; d. March 12, 1968. Pennsylvania halfback; All-American, 1908
2nd team, 1906–07. He captained the undefeated Penn team in 1908. Hol
lenback won a dental degree but coached at Penn, Penn State, Missouri, an
Syracuse in the early part of the century, before going into practice.

Helms Hall of Fame, National Football Foundation Hall of Fame.

HOLLIDAY, "BUG" (James W.) baseball: b. Feb. 8, 1867, St. Louis; d. Feb
15, 1910. Bat, throw R; outfield. Cincinnati AA, 1889; Cincinnati NL
1890–98. Ten years, 928 games, .311 BA; hit .321 in 1889, .319 in 1891
.310 in 1893, .372 in 1894. Led league in home runs, 1889 (19) and 189'
(13).

HOLLOCHER, "CHARLIE" (Charles J.) baseball: b. June 11, 1896, St
Louis; d. Aug. 14, 1940. Bat L, throw R; shortstop. Chicago NL, 1918–24
Led NL in hits, 1918 (161). Seven years, 760 games, .304 BA; hit .316 in
1918, .319 in 1920, .340 in 1922.

HOLMES, "DUCKY" (James W.) baseball: b. Jan. 28, 1869, Des Moines
Iowa; d. Aug. 6, 1932. Bat L, throw R; outfield. Louisville NL, 1895–97'
New York NL, 1897; St. Louis NL, 1898; Baltimore NL, 1898–99; Detroi
AL, 1901–02; Washington AL, 1903; Chicago AL, 1903–05. Ten years, 93'
games, 236 stolen bases, .282 BA; hit .320 in 1899.

HOMANS, EUGENE V. golf: b. ?; d. Oct. 30, 1965. In 1929, Homans tied
Bobby Jones as medalist in the National Amateur with a 149. In 1930, he
lost to Jones in the finals of the event. He won the 1930 North and South
Amateur.

HOPP, HARRY football: b. ?; d. Dec. 22, 1964. Nebraska back. Detroit
Lions, 1941–43; Miami Seahawks, Buffalo Bisons (both AAFC), 1946; Los
Angeles Dons, 1947 (AAFC).

HOPPE, "WILLIE" (William F.) billiards: b. Oct. 11, 1887, Cornwall-on-
Hudson, N.Y.; d. Feb. 1, 1959. In 1905 an eighteen-year-old American had
the effrontery to challenge Frenchman Maurice Vignaux, the world billiards
champion. Vignaux made things difficult: He insisted that there be a $1,000
side bet and that the winner take all the gate receipts. Willie Hoppe some-
how raised the money and went to Paris to meet the "invincible" champion.
The match took place Jan. 15, 1906. The world was stunned when wires

brought the news that Hoppe had won; it was the first of 51 major billiards championships for him.

Hoppe had begun to play billiards when he was six, standing on a chair in order to reach the table in his father's hotel. At sixteen, he won the 18.2 balkline championship for young masters. He went on to win these world professional titles: three-cushion, 1936, 1940–44, 1947–52; 18.2 balkline, 1908, 1910–20, 1923–24, 1927; 18.1 balkline, 1906–07, 1909–11, 1914–26, 1927. He holds records for highest three-cushion runs in American League play (20 in 1927), exhibition play (25 in 1928), and match play (15 in 1936, 20 in 1947, with no safeties and optional cue ball), and in 1950 he set a record of 1.33 for highest grand average in tournament play.

During his career, he walked about 26,000 miles around billiards tables in more than 100,000 hours of play.

ORN, TED auto racing: b. Eylard Theodore Von Horn, Glendale, Cal.; d. Oct. 10, 1948. After eleven years of racing with little success, Horn finished second at Indianapolis in 1936. It began a string of nine consecutive Indy 500s in which Horn never placed worse than 4th, though he never won. He was National and Eastern Sectional driving champion, 1946–48, Midwestern Sectional champion, 1938 and 1946.

Horn was killed at the DuQuoin, Illinois, Speedway.

Helms Hall of Fame, Auto Racing Hall of Fame.

HORNSBY, ROGERS ("Rajah") baseball: b. April 27, 1896, Winters, Tex.; d. Jan. 5, 1963. Bat, throw R; second base, shortstop, third base. St. Louis NL, 1915–26; New York NL, 1927; Boston NL, 1928; Chicago NL, 1929–32; St. Louis NL, 1933; St. Louis AL, 1933–37. Twenty-three years (5th), 2,259 games, 8,173 at-bats, 2,930 hits, 541 doubles (9th), 168 triples, 302 home runs, 1,579 runs, 1,584 RBI, 4,713 total bases, 358 BA (2nd), .577 slugging (8th). He hit over .300 in: 1916 (.313), 1917 (.327), 1919 (.318), 1926 (.317), 1927 (.361), 1929 (.380), 1930 (.308), 1931 (.331).

Led NL in: BA, 1920 (.370), 1921 (.397), 1922 (.401), 1923 (.384), 1924 (.424), 1925 (.403), 1928 (.387); runs, 1921 (131), 1922 (141), 1924 (121), 1927 (133), 1929 (156); hits, 1920 (218), 1921 (235), 1922 (250), 1924 (227); doubles, 1920 (44), 1921 (44), 1922 (46), 1924 (43); triples, 1917 (17), 1921 (18); home runs, 1922 (42), 1925 (39); RBI, 1920 (94), 1921 (126), 1922 (152), 1925 (143); slugging, 1917 (.484), 1920 (.559), 1921 (.639), 1922 (.722), 1923 (.627), 1924 (.696), 1925 (.756), 1928 (.632), 1929 (.681); total bases, 1912 (253), 1920 (329), 1921 (378), 1922 (450), 1924 (373), 1925 (381), 1929 (410); walks, 1924 (89), 1927 (86), 1928 (107).

Two World Series, 1926, 1929: 12 games, .245 BA.

Hornsby's .424 in 1924 is a modern ML record for right-handers. During the 1921–25 period, he compiled an average of .402, an ML record for fi▮ consecutive years. His slugging percentage of .756 in 1925 is an NL recor and is the ML record for right-handed hitters. He hit safely in 33 straigl games in 1922 to set a modern NL record for right-handers, and he is tl only NL player to win the triple crown twice, in 1922, 1925.

He holds these other ML records: most consecutive years leading leagu in hits, 3; most hits in two consecutive years, 485, in 1921–22; most yea▮ led in total bases, 7; most home runs by second baseman, 42, in 1922. H holds NL records for: most consecutive years led in BA, 6; most times le in slugging, 9; most times led in runs, 5; most times led in RBI, 4; most tot: bases, 450, in 1922. Hornsby hit 3 consecutive home runs on April 24, 193

He managed St. Louis NL, 1925 (part)–26; Boston NL, 1928 (part Chicago NL, 1930 (part)–32 (part); St. Louis AL, 1933 (part)–37 (part 1952 (part); Cincinnati NL, 1952 (part)–53 (part): 680–798, .460. Pennar and World Series, 1926.

Aggressive as a player, Hornsby was extremely blunt as a person and ɛ a manager. His bluntness cost him jobs, probably more often because caused difficulties with the front office than because of player problem After managing the Cardinals to their first pennant, in 1926, and to a Worl Series victory over the Yankees, he was traded, largely because he ha▮ thrown Cardinal owner Sam Breadon out of the clubhouse for schedulin▮ an exhibition game during the height of the pennant race.

Baseball Hall of Fame.

HORNUNG, "JOE" (Michael Joseph, "Ubbo Ubbo") baseball: b. June 1▮ 1857, Carthage, N.Y.; d. Oct. 30, 1931. Bat, throw R; outfield. Buffalo NI 1879–80; Boston NL, 1881–88; Baltimore AA, 1889; New York NL, 189(Twelve years, 1,125 games, .257 BA; hit .302 in 1882. Led league in run▮ 1898 (107). Hornung tied NL records for most years leading outfielders i▮ fielding average, 4, and most consecutive, 3. He tied the ML record for mos chances handled by a left fielder, 11, on Sept. 23, 1881.

HOUSTON, CLARENCE P. college sports: b. Jan. 23, 1891, Virgil, S.D.; d Oct. 11, 1965. A football player at Tufts, 1914, Houston became a lawye but maintained his interest in sports. He headed the NCAA complianc committee in 1947, when it drafted the so-called sanity code, tightenin, rules concerning athletic eligibility and scholarships. He was president o the NCAA, 1956–57.

HOWELL, "HANDSOME HARRY" baseball: b. Nov. 14, 1876, Brooklyn d. May 22, 1956. Bat, throw R; pitcher. Brooklyn NL, 1898; Baltimore NL 1899; Brooklyn NL, 1900; Baltimore AL, 1901–02; New York AL, 1903

St. Louis AL, 1904–10. Thirteen years, 131–146, 2.74 ERA; 20 shutouts. Led AL in complete games, 1905 (35).

OY, "DUMMY" (William E.) baseball: b. May 23, 1862, Houckstown, Ohio; d. Dec. 15, 1961. Bat L, throw R; outfield. Washington NL, 1888–89; Buffalo PL, 1890; St. Louis AA, 1891; Washington NL, 1892–93; Cincinnati NL, 1894–97; Louisville NL, 1898–99; Chicago AL, 1901; Cincinnati NL, 1902. Fourteen years, 1,796 games, 2,044 hits, 1,419 runs, 594 stolen bases, .287 BA; hit .304 in 1898, .306 in 1899. Led league in stolen bases, 1888 (82); in walks, 1891 (119) and 1901 (86).

A deaf mute, Hoy was only 5′4″ and 145 pounds. His 82 stolen bases in 1888 is an NL record for a rookie. On June 19, 1889, he set an ML record by throwing out 3 runners at home.

OYT, BEATRIX golf: b. August, 1880, Westchester County, N.Y.; d. Aug. 14, 1963. She dominated women's golf for some years, almost from the beginning of the sport in the United States. She was sixteen when she won the second USGA Women's Amateur, in 1896; she is still the youngest player ever to win the tournament. She was also champion, 1897–98, and she was medalist in the event, 1899–1900.

Ladies' Professional Golf Association Hall of Fame.

OYT, GEORGE H. basketball: b. Aug. 9, 1883, South Boston; d. Nov. 11, 1962. Hoyt was a pioneer of basketball in New England, traveling throughout the region to assist players, coaches, and officials. He organized the first officials' board in eastern Massachusetts. For thirty-four years he was an official or honorary official at the Eastern Massachusetts Tournament.

Basketball Hall of Fame.

UBBS, KENNETH D. baseball: b. Dec. 23, 1941, Riverside, Calif.; d. Feb. 13, 1964. Bat, throw R; second base. Chicago NL, 1961–63. Three years, 324 games, .247 BA. NL Rookie of the Year in 1962, Hubbs set ML records for second basemen in 1964 by going 78 games and handling 418 consecutive chances without an error.

He died in a private plane crash.

UGGINS, MILLER J. baseball: b. March 27, 1879, Cincinnati; d. Sept. 25, 1929. Sw. hit, throw R; second base. Cincinnati NL, 1904–09; St. Louis NL, 1910–16. Thirteen years, 1,585 games, 324 stolen bases, .265 BA; hit .304 in 1912. Led NL in walks, 1905 (103), 1907 (83), 1910 (116), 1914 (105).

"The Mighty Mite"—5′6″, 140 pounds—once drew walks in 11 consecutive games, an NL record; on June 1, 1910, he drew 4 walks, sacrificed once, and hit a sacrifice fly, tying the ML record for most times facing the pitche without having an official at-bat. On July 13, 1911, he handled 16 chance. an NL record for second basemen.

He managed St. Louis NL, 1913–17, New York AL, 1918–29. His grea Yankee teams won pennants, 1921–23, 1926–28, and won the World Serie 1923 and 1927–28; the last two wins were both 4-game sweeps. His recor(1,413–1,134, .555. In World Series play his team won 18 (6th), lost 15 (5th for a .545 percentage (5th).

Baseball Hall of Fame.

HUGHES, JAMES J. baseball: b. Jan. 22, 1874, Sacramento, Calif.; d. Jun 2, 1924. Pitcher. Baltimore NL, 1898; Brooklyn NL, 1899, 1901–02. Fou years, 82–41, 3.00 ERA; 23–12 in 1898. No-hitter, April 22, 1898, agains Boston NL (8–0). Led NL in victories and percentage (28–6, .824) in 1899

HUGHES, "LONG TOM" (Thomas J.) baseball: b. Nov. 26, 1878, Chicage d. Feb. 8, 1956. Throw R; pitcher. Chicago NL, 1900–01; Baltimore AL 1902; Boston AL, 1902–03; New York AL, 1904; Washington AL, 1904 13. Thirteen years, 132–171, 3.09 ERA; 1,368 strikeouts, 24 shutouts i 2,644 innings; 20–7 in 1903. One World Series, 1903: 0–1, 9.00 ERA.

HUGHES, THOMAS L. baseball: b. Jan. 28, 1884, Coal Creek, Colo.; d. No\ 1, 1961. Bat, throw R; pitcher. New York AL, 1906–07, 1909–10; Bostoi NL, 1914–18. Nine years, 58–39, 2.57 ERA; 476 strikeouts in 863 innings In relief, 20–3, 2.32 ERA, 14 saves; 20–14 in 1915. No-hitters, Aug. 3C 1910, against Cleveland AL (9⅓ innings; lost 5–0 in 11 innings); June 16 1916, against Pittsburgh NL (2–0). Led NL in percentage, 1916 (16–3 .842).

HULBERT, WILLIAM A. baseball: b. Oct. 23, 1832, Burlington Flats, N.Y. d. April 10, 1882. Hulbert organized the National League and kept it goin, for its first several years. Ironically, he isn't in the Hall of Fame, but Morgai Bulkeley, president of the league for only one year (the first) and little mor(than a figurehead, is.

In 1875, Hulbert was an executive with the Chicago team in the Nationa Association of Baseball Players. The league was in trouble. Attendance wa down; there was nothing to prevent players from jumping from one tean to another when offered more money. Boston had cornered the top player: and was practically unbeatable: In 1875, Boston won 71 games and los only 8.

Hulbert wanted a strong Chicago team. During 1875, he persuaded fou of Boston's best players—Albert G. Spalding, Calvin McVey, Ross Barnes and Deacon White—to agree to join Chicago the following season. A littl later, he signed two of Philadelphia's top players, Cap Anson and Ezra Sutton. When word leaked out, there was talk that Chicago might be banned from the league. Hulbert decided to beat other owners to the punch by organizing a new league.

He and Spalding wrote the by-laws. In January, 1876, the idea was discussed with owners of semipro teams in Cincinnati, Louisville, and St. Louis. They were interested. Then Hulbert got four eastern teams interested. At a meeting in New York on Feb. 2, 1876, Hulbert got the four eastern owners to join the league; he nominated Bulkeley as president because Bulkeley, owner of the Hartford team, represented the East.

Hulbert's Chicago team won the National League's first pennant. Hulbert served as league president, 1877–81, after Bulkeley had spent one year in the office.

HUMPHREYS, "BERT" (Albert) baseball: b. Sept. 26, 1880, California, Pa.; d. Sept. 21, 1945. Bat, throw R; pitcher. Philadelphia NL, 1910–11; Cincinnati NL, 1911–12; Chicago NL, 1913–15. Six years, 53–43, 2.79 ERA; 10 shutouts. Led NL in percentage, 1913 (17–4, .810).

HUMPHRIES, JOHN W. baseball: b. June 23, 1915, Clifton Forge, Va.; d. June 24, 1965. Bat, throw R; pitcher. Cleveland AL, 1938–40; Chicago AL, 1941–45; Philadelphia NL, 1946. Nine years, 52–63, 3.78 ERA; 12–8, 4.77 ERA, 12 saves in relief.

HUNT, JOSEPH R. tennis: b. Feb. 17, 1919, Calif.; d. Feb. 2, 1945. Hunt won the national boys singles and doubles in 1934, the national boys junior singles in 1937, and the junior doubles in 1936–37. Representing the Naval Academy, he won the intercollegiate singles title in 1941. He was U.S. outdoor singles champion in 1943.

Serving in the Navy during World War II, he was killed in a plane crash.

HURST, "DON" (Frank O'Donnell) baseball: b. Aug. 12, 1905, Maysville, Ky.; d. Dec. 6, 1952. Bat, throw L; first base. Philadelphia NL, 1928–34; Chicago NL, 1934. Seven years, 905 games, .298 BA; hit .304 in 1929, .327 in 1930, .305 in 1931, .339 in 1932. Led NL in RBI, 1932 (143). Hurst started 3 double plays on Sept. 17, 1930, tying an ML record for first basemen.

HUTCHINSON, FREDERICK C. baseball: b. Aug. 12, 1919, Seattle, Wash.; d. Nov. 12, 1965. Bat L, throw R; pitcher. Detroit AL, 1939–41, 1946–53. Ten years, 95–71, 3.73 ERA; 13 shutouts. One World Series, 1940: 0–0, 9.00 ERA in 1 inning.

He managed Detroit AL, 1952 (part)–54; St. Louis NL, 1956–58 (part);

Cincinnati NL, 1959 (part)–64 (part): 830–827, .501. Pennant, 1961. Hutchinson died of lung cancer.

HUTCHISON, "WILD BILL" (William F.) baseball: b. Dec. 17, 1859, New Haven, Conn.; d. March 19, 1926. Bat, throw R; pitcher. Chicago NL 1889–95; St. Louis NL, 1897. Eight years, 183–162, 3.60 ERA; 21 shutouts. Led NL in victories (42–25) and complete games (65) in 1890; in victories (44–19) and complete games (56) in 1891; in victories (37–36), complete games (67), and strikeouts (316) in 1892.

HYER, TOM boxing: b. Jan. 1, 1819, New York City; d. June 26, 1864. His father, Jacob Hyer, won an 1816 grudge fight with Tom Beasley, said he could lick anyone in America, and half-jokingly claimed the title. No one challenged. Tom eventually claimed the title "by inheritance." He was challenged by George McChester and beat him in 101 rounds on Sept. 9, 1841. His major victory came in 1849, when he KOed Yankee Sullivan in 16 rounds. Sullivan was an experienced English boxer on an all-comers tour of the United States. Hyer could find no challengers after that, and he retired.

Boxing Hall of Fame.

I

IDELL, "POP" (A. Provost) volleyball: b. Aug. 31, 1889; d. May 6, 1965. Often called the father of modern volleyball, Idell was an outstanding player, coach, and official. He was one of the first to publish articles on the sport's fundamentals, and he developed its first teaching film. In 1946, when the U.S. Volleyball Association began presenting awards to those who had made contributions to the game, he was one of the first seven people so honored.

Helms Hall of Fame.

INGRAM, JONAS H. football: b. Oct. 15, 1886, Jeffersonville, Ind.; d. Sept. 10, 1952. Ingram participated in track, crew, and football at Navy, 1906. He coached football there, 1914–16, and was director of athletics, 1926–30; in between, he had won the Congressional Medal of Honor. He became a vice-admiral during World War II. Throughout his naval career, he fre-

quently officiated at college football games and judged boat races. Retiring
from the Navy, he became commissioner of the now-defunct All-American
Football Conference, 1946–49.

National Football Foundation Hall of Fame.

IRWIN, ARTHUR A. baseball: b. Feb. 14, 1858, Toronto, Canada; d. July 16,
1921. Bat L, throw R; shortstop. Worcester NL, 1880–82; Providence NL,
1883–85; Philadelphia NL, 1886–89; Washington NL, 1889; Boston PL,
1890; Boston AA, 1891; Philadelphia NL, 1894. Thirteen years, 1,010
games, .241 BA.

Irwin managed Washington NL, 1889 (part); Boston AA, 1891; Washington NL, 1892 (part); Philadelphia NL, 1894–95; New York NL, 1896
(part); Washington NL, 1898 (part)–99: 405–408, .498. Pennant, 1891.

ISBELL, WILLIAM FRANK baseball: b. Aug. 21, 1875, Delevan, N.Y.: d.
July 15, 1941. Bat L, throw R; first-second base, outfield. Chicago NL,
1898; Chicago AL, 1901–09. Ten years, 1,119 games, .250 BA, 253 stolen
bases. Led AL in stolen bases, 1901 (52). One World Series, 1906: 6 games,
.308 BA, 4 runs, 4 RBI; he set a record with 4 doubles in the fifth game.

J

JACKSON, "SHOELESS JOE" (Joseph J.) baseball: b. July 16, 1887, Brandon Mills, S.C.; d. Dec. 5, 1951. Bat L, throw R; outfield. Philadelphia AL,
1908–09; Cleveland AL, 1910–15; Chicago AL, 1915–20. Thirteen years,
1,330 games, .356 BA (3rd), .518 slugging percentage. Led AL in hits (197),
doubles (39), and slugging percentage (.551) in 1913; in triples, 1912 (26),
1916 (21), and 1920 (20); in total bases, 1912 (331) and 1916 (293). It seems
impossible that Jackson never won a batting title. His .408 BA in 1911 was
the highest ever for a man who didn't win it, and three other times he hit
over .380. His over-.300 years: .387 in 1910, .395 in 1912, .373 in 1913, .338
in 1914, .308 in 1915, .341 in 1916, .301 in 1917, .354 in 1918, .351 in 1919,
.382 in 1920. On Aug. 11, 1912, he tied an ML record by stealing home
twice in a game. Two World Series, 1917, 1919: 14 games, .345 BA, 9 runs,
8 RBI. In 1919, he hit .375, with 3 doubles, a home run, 5 runs, and 6 RBI,
as Chicago lost to Cincinnati, 5 games to 3. Despite that record, he was

implicated in the Black Sox Scandal and was banned from baseball after the 1920 season.

JACOBS, ELMER (William Elmer) baseball: b. Aug. 10, 1892, Salem, Mo. d. Feb. 10, 1958. Bat, throw R; pitcher. Philadelphia NL, 1914; Pittsburgh NL, 1916–18; Philadelphia NL, 1918–19; St. Louis NL, 1919–20; Chicago NL, 1924–25, 1927. Nine years, 49–81, 3.55 ERA.

JACOBS, HIRSCH horse racing: b. April 8, 1904, New York City; d. Feb. 13, 1970. Jacobs began by racing pigeons when he was twelve. Ten years later, he saddled his first winning horse, and he went on to saddle 3,596 winners, a record. His horses collected more than $15 million in purses. He never had a Kentucky Derby winner, but he had a Handicap Horse of the Year in 1945 with Stymie. He bought Stymie, a nonwinner at the time, for $1,500; the horse eventually won $914,485, a record until broken by Citation in 1950. Jacobs led trainers in winnings 11 times, 1933–39, 1941–44, and in money won in 1946.

Racing Hall of Fame.

JACOBS, JOE boxing: b. May 7, 1896, New York City; d. April 24, 1940. Jacobs, known in fight circles as Yussel the Muscle, is the only fight manager in *Bartlett's Familiar Quotations*. He managed, among others, Frankie Genaro, Jack Delaney, and Mike McTigue, then handled Max Schmeling during most of the German's fights in New York. The night Schmeling fought Jack Sharkey for the heavyweight title, June 12, 1930, Jacobs leaped into the ring near the end of the 4th round, after Schmeling had been knocked down. "Stay down," Jacobs yelled, "you was fouled." He created such a ruckus that although the bell rang for the 5th round, it was never fought, and the officials gave Schmeling the championship by disqualifying Sharkey.

When Sharkey beat Schmeling in a 15-round decision in 1932, Jacobs came up with the immortal quote, "We wuz robbed." More famous, however, is his statement after he had been talked into going to a World Series game on what turned out to be a cold, wet day. Jacobs complained, "I should of stood in bed."

JACOBS, MICHAEL S. boxing: b. March 10, 1880, New York City; d. Jan. 24, 1953. A newsboy in New York, Jacobs was given two free tickets to a boxing match and found he could sell them. That gave him the idea of becoming a ticket broker. During the Depression, he became promoter of the Milk Fund and Christmas Fund matches. He was so successful that he formed the 20th Century Sporting Club (later the International Boxing Club). Jacobs's greatest coup came when he signed the young Joe Louis to an exclusive contract. After Louis became the hottest fighter around, Jacobs was signed as matchmaker for Madison Square Garden. By 1941, he and his club controlled all the world titles from the lightweight through the heavyweight class.

He sold the 20th Century Sporting Club to James Norris in 1949.

JACOBY, PHILO shooting: b. Dec. 5, 1837, Prussia; d. March 25, 1922. Jacoby learned to shoot after arriving in California in 1859 and was an instant success. In 1868, he was sent to represent the United States at the Berlin Shooting Championships, and he won first prize. In 1873, he returned to Europe, winning a number of titles. He captained the California team that won the world championship at the Philadelphia Centennial Exposition in 1876.

JAGADE, "CHICK" (Harry) football: b. Jan. 1, 1928, Chicago; d. Nov. 24, 1968. Indiana halfback; Baltimore (AAFC), 1949; Cleveland Browns, 1951–53; Chicago Bears, 1954–55. Jagade was fifth in collegiate rushing in 1944, with 398 yards. In his five years in the NFL he gained 1,554 yards on 379 attempts, a 4.1 average, and scored 11 touchdowns.

JAMES, WILLIAM H. ("Big Bill") baseball: b. Jan. 20, 1888, Ann Arbor, Mich.; d. May 24, 1942. Sw. hit, throw R; pitcher. Cleveland AL, 1911–12; St. Louis AL, 1914–15; Detroit AL, 1915–19; Boston AL, Chicago AL, 1919. Eight years, 65–71, 3.21 ERA. One World Series, 1919: 0–0, 5.79 ERA in 4⅔ innings of relief.

JAMIESON, "CHUCK" (Charles D.) baseball: b. Feb. 7, 1893, Paterson, N.J.; d. Oct. 27, 1969. Bat, throw L; outfield. Washington AL, 1915–17; Philadelphia AL, 1917–18; Cleveland AL, 1919–32. Eighteen years, 1,779 games, .303 BA; hit .319 in 1920, .310 in 1921, .323 in 1922, .345 in 1923, .359 in 1924, .309 in 1927, .307 in 1928, .301 in 1930. Led AL in hits, 1923 (222). One World Series, 1920: 6 games, .333 BA.

JEANNETTE, JOE boxing: b. Aug. 26, 1879, North Bergen, N.J.; d. July 2, 1958. His record: 72 wins, 56 by KO; 9 losses, 1 by KO; 9 draws, 64 no-decisions. One of several Negro heavyweights who never got a chance at the title, Jeannette spent a good part of his career fighting other Negroes, including Jack Johnson, Sam Langford, Sam McVey, and Black Bill. When it was suggested to champion-in-exile Johnson in 1914 that he give Jeannette a title fight in Paris, Johnson replied, "On a good night, Joe is just liable to beat me or make it close, and what's the sense of that for the kind of money we'd draw?"

Boxing Hall of Fame.

JEFFRIES, JAMES J. boxing: b. April 15, 1875, Carroll, Ohio; d. March 3 1953. His official fight record: 20 wins, 16 by KO; 1 loss, 1 by KO; 2 draws. Jeffries won the heavyweight title from Bob Fitzsimmons with an 11-round KO on June 9, 1899. He KOed James J. Corbett twice in title fights, the second time in 1903, after which he went into semiretirement, but he didn't actually give up the crown until 1905. After Jack Johnson became the first Negro to hold the championship, the searchers for the "great white hope" talked Jeffries into making a comeback. He wasn't in very good shape. Johnson, after beating him badly throughout, KOed him in the 15th round on July 4, 1910.

JENKINS, "AB" (David Abbott) auto racing: b. Jan. 25, 1883, Spanish Fork, Utah; d. Aug. 9, 1956. Jenkins drove racing cars and motorcycles on dirt tracks until 1926; from that point on, his races were mostly against time. He won nationwide notice in 1926 by driving from New York to San Francisco in a shorter time than it took the fastest transcontinental train. He was among the first to begin speed runs on the Bonneville, Utah, salt flats when they replaced the Daytona Beach sand for high-speed driving. Between 1935 and 1951, he set more than 500 records, at one time holding records for 50 miles and for every sanctioned distance above that mark.

JENKINS, THOMAS wrestling: b. ?; d. Jan. 19, 1957. A one-eyed worker in a Cleveland rolling-mill until he became a professional wrestler, Jenkins did more than anyone to popularize catch-as-catch-can wrestling. He was generally considered the champion—no one could beat him, which was a good reason—until he lost the title to Frank Gotch in 1905.

JENNINGS, HUGH A. baseball: b. April 2, 1869, Pittston, Pa.; d. Feb. 1, 1928. Bat, throw R; shortstop, first base. Louisville AA, 1891; Louisville NL, 1892–93; Baltimore NL, 1893–99; Brooklyn NL, 1899–1900; Philadelphia NL, 1901–02; Brooklyn NL, 1903; Detroit AL, 1907, 1909, 1912, 1918. Seventeen years, 1,285 games, 359 stolen bases, .311 BA; hit .335 in 1894, .386 in 1895, .355 in 1897, .328 in 1898.

Jennings's .401 BA in 1896 is an ML record for a shortstop. He also led his position in fielding for 5 consecutive years, an NL record, and in 1896 he was hit by pitched balls 49 times, an ML record. From 1900 on, he was primarily a first baseman.

He managed Detroit AL, 1907–20: 1,131–972, .538. Pennants, 1907–09. Baseball Hall of Fame.

JEREMIAH, EDWARD hockey: b. Nov. 4, 1905, Worcester, Mass.; d. June 7, 1967. A 1930 graduate of Dartmouth, Jeremiah coached hockey at his alma mater for twenty-nine seasons. His teams once compiled a 46-game winning streak, and he was twice named college coach of the year. Dartmouth won Ivy League championships under his leadership in 1934, 1938–39, 1942–43, and 1947–49.

JESSEE, DANIEL E. football: b. Feb. 22, 1901, Grayson, Ky.; d. April 30, 1970. Jessee won nine letters in three sports at College of the Pacific (1926). He was head football coach at Trinity College, Connecticut, 1932–66, with a 150–76–7 record, producing undefeated, untied teams in 1934, 1949, and 1954–55. He also coached baseball, 1935–67, compiling a 237–156–5 record. In 1966 he became the first small-college coach to be president of the American College Football Coaches Association.

Helms Hall of Fame.

JOESTING, HERBERT W. football: b. April 17, 1902, Minneapolis, Minn.; d. Oct. 2, 1963. Minnesota fullback; captain, 1927; All-American, 1926 (Rice, AP), 1927. Minneapolis Redjackets, 1929–30; Frankford Yellowjackets, 1930–31; Chicago Bears, 1931–32.

Coached Minneapolis, 1929 (1–9–0).

National Football Foundation Hall of Fame.

JOHNS, WILBUR college sports: b. 1903(?); d. July 14, 1967. As basketball coach at his alma mater, Johns produced UCLA's first champions in the Southern Division of the old Pacific Coast Conference, in 1945 and 1947. As athletic director, 1947–63, he was largely responsible for bringing top coaches to the school, among them Red Sanders in football and John Wooden in basketball.

JOHNSON, "BAN" (Byron Bancroft) baseball: b. Jan. 5, 1864, Norwalk, Ohio; d. March 28, 1931. Johnson was a baseball writer in Cincinnati until Charles A. Comiskey, then an executive with the Cincinnati team, persuaded him that he ought to get into the administrative end of the game; in 1893, Johnson became president of the Western League. In 1900, the Western League became the American League. Comiskey by then had taken over the Minneapolis franchise in the league; he moved it to Chicago in 1901. He and Johnson planned a careful campaign, strengthening their league by moving into larger cities and then by raiding the National League for established players. The battle for major-league status was won with a truce: the "Cincinnati agreement," signed in 1903 by club owners from both leagues. Outlined by Johnson, it provided that the two leagues would keep their separate identities but that all of organized baseball, including the minor leagues, would be ruled by a three-man National Commission.

Johnson was AL president until 1927, when he resigned.

Baseball Hall of Fame.

JOHNSON, CORNELIUS track: b. 1916(?); d. Feb. 15, 1946. Johnson was a Los Angeles high-school student in 1932, when he was among four men tied for first place in the Olympic high jump; he finished fourth in the jumpoff. He won the Olympic title in 1936. He also won or tied for first place in AAU outdoor competition, 1932–36, tying in 1934 and 1936 and winning a jumpoff in 1936. He won the indoor title in 1935. His jump of 6'9¾" in 1936 was at the time the world record.

Helms Hall of Fame.

JOHNSON, "JACK" (John A.) boxing: b. March 31, 1878, Galveston, Tex.; d. June 10, 1946. His record: 80 wins, 44 by KO; 7 losses, 5 by KO; 14 draws, 13 no-decisions. The first Negro heavyweight champion was way ahead of his time in some respects. He married four times, and three of his wives were white; he was quick-witted and often outspoken, and he refused to be an Uncle Tom. As a result, bigots called for a "great white hope" who could win the championship from him throughout his seven-year reign.

Johnson began fighting as a Galveston dock worker. When he was seventeen, he won a tournament in Illinois by KOing four men in one night. His first major fight was in San Francisco in 1902, when he beat George Gardner; a year later, Gardner became light-heavy champion. By 1905, Johnson had to be considered a contender for the heavyweight title. He chased the new champ, Tommy Burns, to Europe, then to Australia, where he finally got the title fight by agreeing to let Burns's manager referee. The fight was on Dec. 26, 1908, and it wasn't much of a contest. Johnson was beating Burns so badly that police jumped into the ring to stop it during the 14th round.

Many still considered James Jeffries the champion, since he had retired undefeated. He came back, and Johnson KOed him in 15 rounds on July 4, 1910. Johnson capitalized on the title by getting into vaudeville, only occasionally defending his crown. Then his third mother-in-law had him arrested on charges of abduction and violation of the Mann Act. Sentenced to a year and a day in prison, Johnson entered an appeal—which was eventually successful—and fled the country to avoid prison. His exile finally took him to Havana, where he lost his title to Jess Willard on April 15, 1915, on a 26th-round KO. (Johnson later said he threw the fight because he was promised that if he did, he would be allowed to return to the United States without being arrested. His story isn't generally believed.)

Johnson wrote a revue for the London stage, fought bulls in Spain, wrestled throughout Europe, fought several matches in Mexico, and finally, in 1920, returned to the United States and served his time in federal prison.

After his release, he boxed occasional exhibitions, appeared on the stage, and gave lectures.

Helms Hall of Fame, Boxing Hall of Fame.

JOHNSON, "SMILEY" (Howard W.) football: b. Sept. 22, 1910, Clarksville, Tenn.; d. Feb. 26, 1945. Georgia guard; captain, 1939. Green Bay Packers, 1940–41.

He was killed during the invasion of Iwo Jima.

JOHNSON, STONE football, track: b. April 26, 1940, Dallas; d. Sept. 8, 1963. Grambling halfback. In the 1960 Olympics, he was a member of the 400–meter relay team that finished first but was disqualified because of a faulty baton pass on the last leg.

As a rookie with the Kansas City Chiefs, he died of a fractured spine suffered in an exhibition game.

JOHNSON, WALTER P. baseball: b. Nov. 6, 1887, Humboldt, Kan.; d. Dec. 10, 1946. Bat, throw R; pitcher. Washington AL, 1907–27. Twenty-one years, 413 wins (2nd), 277 losses (3rd), 2.17 ERA (7th), 802 games (4th), 666 starts (3rd), 532 complete (5th), 5,923⅔ innings (3rd), 1,045 walks, 3,499 strikeouts (1st), 110 shutouts (1st). In relief, 42–25, 2.19 ERA, 35 saves. No-hitter, July 1, 1920, against Boston AL (1-0). Led AL in wins, 1913 (34–7), 1914 (28–18), 1915 (28–13), 1916 (25–19), 1918 (23–13), 1924 (23–7); percentage, 1913 (.829) and 1924 (.767); ERA, 1912 (1.39), 1913 (1.09), 1918 (1.27), 1919 (1.49), 1924 (2.72); complete games, 1910 (38), 1911 (36), 1913 (30), 1914 (33), 1915 (35), 1916 (36); strikeouts, 1910 (313), 1912 (296), 1913 (243), 1914 (225), 1915 (203), 1916 (228), 1917 (188), 1918 (162), 1919 (147), 1921 (143), 1923 (130), 1924 (158); in shutouts, 1911 (6), 1913 (11), 1914 (9), 1915 (7), 1918 (8), 1919 (7), 1924 (5). Other 20-win seasons: 24–17 in 1910, 25–13 in 1911, 32–12 in 1912, 23–16 in 1917, 20–14 in 1919, 20–7 in 1924. Two World Series, 1924–25: 6 games, 5 starts, 5 complete (6th), 50 innings, 56 hits, 15 walks, 35 strikeouts, 1 shutout; 3–3, 2.34 ERA.

Hall-of-Famer Sam Crawford compared Johnson to "one of those compressed-air pitching machines. . . . You hardly see the ball at all. But you hear it. Swoosh, and it smacks into the catcher's mitt." Johnson was a tall, big-framed man (6'1", 200 pounds) with unusually long arms that gave him extra leverage. By spending his whole career with Washington, he set an AL record for most consecutive years with one team. Unfortunately, Washington had a weak team during his prime years. In his first seventeen seasons, Washington finished 8th twice and 7th five times. In 1909, with a 2.21 ERA, Johnson had a 12–25 record.

He is the only pitcher to have more than 3,000 strikeouts and the only one with more than 90 shutouts. He holds the AL records for victories, losses, complete games, and innings.

Johnson is holder or coholder of these ML records: most years led in strikeouts, 12, most consecutive, 8; most years 100 or more strikeouts, 18, most years 200 or more, 7; most men struck out in one inning, 4; most opening games started, 13; most shutouts in opening games, 7; most years led in shutouts, 7; longest shutout, 18 innings.

AL records: most games started, 666; most years led in complete games, 6; most years led in innings, 5; most years 300 or more innings, 9; most years led in wins, 6; most years 30 or more wins, 2; most years 20 or more wins, 12; most consecutive wins, one season, 16; most consecutive scoreless innings, 56; lowest season ERA, 1.09, in 1913; most years 300 or more strikeouts, 2.

Johnson was a good all-around player. In 1925, in 36 games (30 as a pitcher), he had a .433 average, an ML record for a pitcher, and on July 29, 1917, he hit 3 doubles in a game, tying the ML record for pitchers. He set AL records for pitchers by handling 103 chances without an error in 1913 and by leading in fielding average 3 times.

Baseball Hall of Fame.

JOHNSON, WILLIAM R. horse racing: b. 1782, Warren County, N.C.; d. Feb. 10, 1849. Johnson was a canny promoter of horse races, especially between the North and the South. He headed a syndicate that offered in 1823 to race a southern horse against the acknowledged northern champion, American Eclipse, who was beating every challenger at every distance. There was a side bet of $10,000 on the three-heat race, at Union Course, Long Island. Johnson plotted the southern strategy. American Eclipse was probably unbeatable. But if the South's horse, Sir Henry, went all out in the first heat, he could win it, since the northern jockey would avoid tiring his horse in order to win the last two heats. The southerners bet heavily on the first heat; Sir Henry romped to victory, American Eclipse won the last two heats, but the southerners took home much more than they had lost on the $10,000 side bet.

Johnson also promoted the race in 1855 between a great horse from the South, John Bascombe, and the North's Post Boy. John Bascombe won easily, in two heats, and the southerners won an estimated $2 million.

JOHNSTON, "DOC" (Wheeler R.) baseball: b. Sept. 9, 1887, Cleveland, Tenn.; d. Feb. 17, 1961. Bat, throw L; first base. Cincinnati NL, 1909; Cleveland AL, 1912–14; Pittsburgh NL, 1915–16; Cleveland AL, 1918–21; Philadelphia AL, 1922. Eleven years, 1,055 games, .263 BA; hit .305 in 1919. One World Series, 1920: 5 games, .273 BA.

JOHNSTON, JAMES H. baseball: b. Dec. 10, 1889, Cleveland, Tenn.; d. Feb. 14, 1967. Bat, throw R; first base, outfield. Chicago AL, 1911; Chicago NL, 1914; Brooklyn NL, 1916–25; Boston NL, New York NL, 1925. Thirteen years, 1,377 games, .294 BA; hit .325 in 1921, .319 in 1922, .325 in 1923. Two World Series, 1916, 1920: 7 games, .250 BA.

JOHNSTON, JAMES JOY boxing: b. 1875, Liverpool, England; d. May 7, 1946. Johnston managed champions Jack Sharkey, Harry Greb, Ted "Kid" Lewis, Johnny Dundee, Pete Latzo, and Mike McTigue. For a while he was a promoter and the matchmaker for Madison Square Garden, with no great success. Despite his list of champions, he was an expert at making money for mediocre fighters.

JOHNSTON, WILLIAM M. tennis: b. Nov. 2, 1894, San Francisco; d. May 1, 1946. Little Bill Johnston and Big Bill Tilden were singles rivals and Davis Cup partners in the late teens and early twenties. Johnston, 5'8" and 120 pounds, was a hustler who won every major U.S. championship. In Davis Cup play, he lost only 3 singles matches in seven years. He and Tilden won the cup from Australia in 1920 and defended it 6 times. In 1915, Johnston won the national singles title. After two years in World War I service, he won the title again, beating Tilden in the 1919 finals, but Tilden then won it 6 straight times, with Johnston the runner-up every year but 1921.

Johnston won the Wimbledon singles in 1923. He teamed with C. J. Griffin to win the U.S. doubles in 1915–16 and 1920, with Mary K. Browne to win the mixed doubles in 1921, and he won the national clay-court singles and doubles (with Sam Hardy) in 1919.

Tennis Hall of Fame, Helms Hall of Fame.

JONES, BEN A. horse racing: b. Dec. 31, 1882, Parnell, Mo.; d. June 13, 1961. He and his son, Horace A., helped make Calumet Farm one of the great stables. Jones trained two Triple Crown winners, Whirlaway (1941) and Citation (1948)—he's listed as trainer of Citation for the Derby, while his son is listed as trainer for the Belmont and Preakness. Citation won 32 of 45 starts, for a total of $1,085,760, including $709,470 in 1948, when he was Horse of the Year. Whirlaway was Horse of the Year twice, 1941–42, and was leading money-winner for his age both years.

Jones saddled three other Kentucky Derby winners: Lawrin, 1938; Pensive, 1944 (also Preakness winner), and Ponder (1949). He was top money-winning trainer, 1941, 1943–44, and 1952.

Racing Hall of Fame.

JONES, FIELDER A. baseball: b. Aug. 13, 1874, Shinglehouse, Pa.; d. March 13, 1934. Bat L, throw R; outfield. Brooklyn NL, 1896–1900; Chicago AL,

1901–08; St. Louis Fed L, 1914–15. Fifteen years, 1,793 games, 359 stolen bases, .284 BA; hit .354 in 1896, .314 in 1897, .304 in 1898, .310 in 1900, .311 in 1901, .321 in 1902. One World Series, 1906: 6 games, .095 BA.

Managed Chicago AL, 1904 (part)–08; St. Louis Fed L, 1914 (part)–15; St. Louis AL, 1916–18 (part): 685–582, .541. Pennant, World Series, 1906.

JONES, HOWARD H. football: b. Aug. 23, 1885, Excello, Ohio; d. July 27, 1941. Brother of Tad. An end at Yale (1908), Jones coached Syracuse to a 5–2–1 record, then returned to Yale to turn out the great 1909 team, which had a 10–0 record and didn't give up a point. He coached at Ohio State, 1910 (6–1–3), then retired briefly. At Yale in 1913, he was 5–2–3. Another brief retirement, and Jones coached Iowa, 1916–23, turning out unbeaten teams in 1921 and 1922. After a year at Duke, he spent the rest of his coaching career at Southern California, 1925–40.

Jones's USC team won or tied for eight Pacific Coast titles in sixteen years and won in all five of their Rose Bowl appearances, in 1930, 1932–33, and 1939–40.

In his twenty-nine years of coaching, he had only one losing season. His overall record was 120–36–13.

Helms Hall of Fame, National Football Foundation Hall of Fame.

JONES, JOHN PAUL track: b. 1881(?); d. Jan. 5, 1970. Representing Cornell, Jones won the IC4A half-mile, 1911–12, the mile, 1911, 1912 (tie), and 1913, and the cross-country, 1910–12. He set a world record of 4:15.4 in the mile in 1911 and lowered it to 4:14.4 in 1913. That mark stood for two years.

Helms Hall of Fame.

JONES, "SAD SAM" (Samuel P.) baseball: b. July 26, 1892, Woodsfield, Ohio; d. July 6, 1966. Bat, throw R; pitcher. Cleveland AL, 1914–15; Boston AL, 1916–21; New York AL, 1922–26; St. Louis AL, 1927; Washington AL, 1928–31; Chicago AL, 1932–35. Twenty-two years, 229–217, 3.84 ERA; 647 games, 487 starts, 250 complete, 3,883 innings, 1,396 walks, 1,223 strikeouts, 35 shutouts; 23–16 in 1921, 21–8 in 1923. No-hitter, Sept. 4, 1923, against Philadelphia AL (2–0; he pitched a 2-hitter in his next start). Led AL in percentage, 1918 (16–5, .762), in shutouts, 1921 (5). Four World Series, 1918, 1922–23, 1926: 6 games, 2 starts, 1 complete; 0–2, 2.05 ERA.

Jones is coholder of the records for most consecutive seasons in the majors, 22, and most AL teams played for, 6.

JONES, SAMUEL S. track: b. 1879(?); d. April 13, 1954. Jones won the Olympic high jump in 1904. Representing New York University, he won the IC4A title, 1900–01, and was AAU outdoor champion, 1901, 1903–04.

JONES, "TAD" (Thomas Albert Dwight) football: b. Feb. 22, 1887, Excello, Ohio; d. June 19, 1957. Brother of Howard. Yale halfback; All-American, 1907; 2nd team, 1906. After coaching Syracuse, 1909–10 (9–9–2), Jones coached at prep schools, then went to Yale, 1916, 1920–27. He produced an unbeaten team in 1923; his teams won the "Big Three" title in 1916, 1923–24, and beat Harvard 6 out of 9 times.
National Football Foundation Hall of Fame.

JONES, THOMAS baseball: b. Jan. 22, 1877, Honesdale, Pa.; d. June 21, 1923. Bat, throw R; first base. Baltimore AL, 1902; St. Louis AL, 1904–09; Detroit AL, 1909–10. Eight years, 1,058 games, .251 BA. One World Series, 1909: 7 games, .250 BA.
His 22 putouts on May 11, 1906, tied the ML record for first basemen in a 9-inning game.

JORDAN, PHIL basketball: b. Sept. 12, 1933, Puyallup, Wash.; d. June 8, 1965. Whitworth College, Washington; New York Knicks, 1956–58; Detroit Pistons, 1958–59; Cincinnati Royals, 1959–61; New York Knicks, 1961–62; St. Louis Hawks, 1962–63; 442 games, 10.9 points per game.

JOSS, "ADDIE" (Adrian) baseball: b. April 12, 1880, Juneau, Wis.; d. April 14, 1911. Bat, throw R; pitcher. Cleveland AL, 1902–10. Nine years, 160–97, 1.88 ERA (2nd); 261 starts, 235 complete, 45 shutouts; 20–12 in 1905, 21–9 in 1906, 24–12 in 1908. Perfect game, Oct. 2, 1908, against Chicago AL (1–0; the second perfect game pitched from the 60' 6" distance); no-hitter, April 20, 1910, against Chicago AL (1–0). Led AL in wins, 1907 (27–10); in shutouts, 1902 (5); in ERA, 1904 (1.59) and 1908 (1.16).
Despite injury and illness, Joss compiled a brilliant, if brief, pitching record. In his first start, April 26, 1902, he threw a 1-hitter; his ERA that year, 2.77, was the highest he ever had. Five times it was under 2.00, including four consecutive seasons.

JOYCE, WILLIAM M. baseball: b. Sept. 21, 1865, St. Louis; d. May 8, 1941. Bat L, throw R; third-first base. Brooklyn PL, 1890; Boston AA, 1891; Brooklyn NL, 1892; Washington NL, 1894–96; New York NL, 1896–98. Eight years, 904 games, 264 stolen bases, .294 BA; hit .355 in 1894, .312 in 1895, .333 in 1896, .304 in 1897. Led league in walks, 1890 (123) and 1895 (96); in home runs, 1896 (14).
Joyce tied an ML record with 4 triples in a game, May 18, 1897; he hit 3 home runs in a game, Aug. 20, 1894.
He managed New York NL, 1896 (part)–98 (part): 177–122, .592.

JUDGE, JOSEPH I. baseball: b. May 25, 1894, Brooklyn; d. March 11, 1963. Bat, throw L; first base. Washington AL, 1915–32; Brooklyn NL, 1933;

Boston AL, 1933–34. Twenty years, 2,166 games, 7,893 at-bats, 2,350 hits, 1,184 runs, 1,034 RBI, 213 stolen bases, .298 BA; hit .333 in 1920, .301 in 1921, .314 in 1923, .324 in 1924, .314 in 1925, .308 in 1927, .306 in 1928, .315 in 1929, .326 in 1930. Two World Series, 1924–25: 14 games, .286 BA. Though only 5'8", Judge was an outstanding fielder at first base. Six times he led his position in fielding average, an AL record. His twenty seasons ties the ML record for longevity at the position. He saved Walter Johnson's only no-hitter, July 1, 1920, by making a diving stab of a line drive for the last putout.

JUHAN, FRANK A. football: b. April 27, 1887, Macon, Ga.; d. Jan. 1, 1968. University of the South center, 1911. He was Southern Intercollegiate Boxing Champion, 1909–10. At his death, he was Baptist Episcopal bishop of Florida.
National Football Foundation Hall of Fame.

JULIAN, "DOGGY" (Alvin T.) basketball: b. April 1, 1901, Reading, Pa.; d. July 28, 1967. Julian began his coaching career at Albright College, after winning 12 high-school and 10 college letters (Bucknell, 1923) in three sports. At Albright, he coached football, 1925–30, basketball, 1927–28, and baseball, 1927–28. He coached football and basketball at Muhlenberg, 1936–45, then settled down as basketball coach with Holy Cross, 1945–48, the Boston Celtics, 1948–50 and Dartmouth, 1950–67.
His overall college record was 386–341. His 1947 Holy Cross team won the NCAA championship.
Basketball Hall of Fame, Helms Hall of Fame.

JUZWIK, STEVE football: b. June 18, 1918, Gary, Ind.; d. June 6, 1964. Notre Dame back. Washington Redskins, 1942; Buffalo Bisons (AAFC), 1946; Buffalo Bills (AAFC), 1947; Chicago Rockets (AAFC), 1948.

K

KAHANAMOKU, DUKE P. swimming: b. Aug. 24, 1890, Honolulu; d. Jan. 22, 1968. When Kahanamoku arrived in California in 1912, many people were surprised to see that he was using the "crawl," still new to American swimmers. But Hawaiians had been using it for centuries. He quickly

---

became this country's outstanding freestyle sprinter, winning the U.S. outdoor title at 100 yards in 1916–17 and 1920, the indoor event in 1913, and the Olympic Gold Medal at 100 meters in 1912 and 1920.

After slowing down, he became a fine water-polo player and a pioneer surfer, as well as sheriff of Honolulu.

Helms Hall of Fame.

KAHN, "EDDIE" (Edwin B., "King Kong") football: b. Nov. 9, 1911, New York City; d. Feb. 17, 1945. North Carolina guard. Boston Redskins, 1935–36, Washington Redskins, 1937. Kahn was killed during the World War II invasion of Leyte.

KANSAS, ROCKY boxing: b. Rocco Tozzo, April 21, 1895, Buffalo, N.Y.; d. Jan. 10, 1954. His record: 64 wins, 32 by KO; 13 losses, 3 by KO; 7 draws, 80 no-decisions. Kansas won the light-heavy championship with a 15-round decision over Jimmy Goodrich, Dec. 7, 1925. He lost it, July 3, 1926, on a 10-round decision to Sammy Mandell.

KARGER, EDWIN baseball: b. May 6, 1883, San Antonio, Tex.; d. Sept. 9, 1957. Bat, throw L; pitcher. Pittsburgh NL, 1906; St. Louis NL, 1906–08; Cincinnati NL, 1909; Boston AL, 1909–11. Six years, 48–65, 2.79 ERA. No-hitter, Aug. 11, 1907, against Boston NL (4–0; 7 innings).

KARILIVACZ, CARL F. ("Kava") football: b. Nov. 20, 1930, Glen Cove, N.Y.; d. Aug. 30, 1969. Syracuse defensive back, Detroit Lions, 1953–57; New York Giants, 1958; Los Angeles Rams, 1959–60. Karilivacz was a member of pro football's first standout defensive backfield at Detroit, with Jack Christiansen, Yale Lary, and Jim David.

KAVANAGH, DUDLEY billiards: b. ?; d. March 12, 1914. In 1858, Kavanagh won an eight-day tournament in New York City for a total purse of $2,000. In the first match open to the public, April 12, 1859, he beat Michael Foley for a $250 side bet. On April 6, 1862, he beat Maurice Daley for a $500 side bet in a match in which push shots were barred for the first time.

KEANE, JOHN J. baseball: b. Nov. 3, 1911, St. Louis; d. Jan. 6, 1967. Managed St. Louis NL, 1961 (part)–64; New York AL, 1965–66 (part): 398–350, .532. Pennant and World Series, 1964.

KEANEY, FRANK W. basketball: b. June 5, 1887, Boston; d. Oct. 10, 1967. A 1911 graduate of Bates College, Keaney came from high-school coaching to Rhode Island State College—now the University of Rhode Island—in 1920. From then until 1948, when he became athletic director, he had a

402–124 record; his teams went to the National Invitation Tournament, 1941–42 and 1945–46.

An early exponent of the fast break, Keaney was known to bench a player who dared to dribble the ball in the back court. He also coached football, 1920–40 (70–84–13), baseball, 1921–48 (197–97–1), and track and cross-country, 1920–25. He served as athletic director until 1956.

Basketball Hall of Fame, Helms Hall of Fame.

KEARNS, "DOC" (Jack) boxing: b. John L. McKernan, Aug, 17, 1882, Waterloo, Mich.; d. July 7, 1963. Kearns discovered Jack Dempsey in 1917. From then until 1926, when they broke up in a series of suits and counter-suits, the pair grossed more than $11 million under an agreement that called for a 50–50 split. (That agreement eventually led to the lawsuits.) Kearns was a great bally-hoo artist and a tireless storyteller. He also handled, at various times, Abe Attell, Benny Leonard, Joey Maxim, and Archie Moore. A sort of third partner in the Kearns-Dempsey alignment was promoter Tex Rickard, whom Kearns had met in Alaska during the gold rush.

KEEFE, TIMOTHY J. baseball: b. Jan. 1, 1856, Cambridge, Mass.; d. April 23, 1933. Bat, throw R; pitcher. Troy NL, 1880–82; New York AA, 1883–84; New York NL, 1885–89; New York PL, 1890; New York NL, 1891; Philadelphia NL, 1891–93. Fourteen years, 336 wins (8th), 225 losses; 2.63 ERA; 594 starts (8th), 557 complete (3rd), 5,061⅓ innings (6th), 2,527 strikeouts (5th), 39 shutouts; 41–27 in 1883, 37–18 in 1884, 32–13 in 1885, 41–20 in 1886, 35–19 in 1887, 28–13 in 1889. Led league in ERA, 1880 (0.86); in strikeouts (361) and complete games (68) in 1883; in ERA, 1885 (1.58); in complete games, 1886 (62); in victories and percentage (33–11, .750), ERA (1.74), strikeouts (333), and shutouts (8) in 1888.

"Sir Timothy" tied an ML record in 1883, winning 19 consecutive games and beating every other team in the league. On July 4, 1883, he won both games of a doubleheader, pitching a 1-hitter and a 2-hitter.

Baseball Hall of Fame.

KEELER, "WEE WILLIE" (William H.) baseball: b. March 3, 1872, Brooklyn; d. Jan. 1, 1923. Bat, throw L; outfield. New York NL, 1892–93; Brooklyn NL, 1893; Baltimore NL, 1894–98; Brooklyn NL, 1899–1902; New York AL, 1903–09; New York NL, 1910. Nineteen years, 2,123 games, 8,591 at-bats, 2,932 hits, 241 doubles, 145 triples, 1,719 runs, 495 stolen bases, .341 BA; hit .371 in 1894, .377 in 1895, .386 in 1896, .379 in 1899, .362 in 1900, .339 in 1901, .333 in 1902, .313 in 1903, .343 in 1904, .302 in 1905, .304 in 1906. Led league in hits (239) and BA (.424) in 1897; in hits (216) and BA (.385) in 1898; in runs, 1899 (140), and hits, 1900 (204).

"Hit 'em where they ain't" was Keeler's sermon, and he practiced what he preached, slapping the ball through and looping it over infields; his 2,512 singles is third in ML history. He set ML records for: most consecutive seasons more than 200 hits, 8; most times 5 or more hits in a game, one season, 4 in 1897; most singles in season, 206 in 1898; most times scored 5 or more runs in a game, 6; highest average for a left-handed hitter, .424 in 1897.

In 1897, he hit safely in 44 straight games, the NL record. Keeler went 6-for-6 on Sept. 3, 1897, and collected 8 more hits in the next two games to set an ML record for most hits in three consecutive games, 14, and added 3 hits the following day to tie the record for most hits in 4 consecutive games.

Baseball Hall of Fame.

KEENE, FOXHALL P. polo: b. about 1866, California; d. Sept. 25, 1941. Keene was America's first 10-goal player, and he won the 10-goal rating 14 times, 1891–92, 1894–95, 1897–1902, 1917–20. He played for the United States in the Westchester Cup matches against England in 1886 and 1902.

KELLEY, JOSEPH J. baseball: b. Dec. 9, 1871, Cambridge, Mass.; d. Aug. 14, 1943. Bat, throw R; outfield, first base. Boston NL, 1891; Pittsburgh NL, 1892; Baltimore NL, 1892–98; Brooklyn NL, 1899–1901; Baltimore AL, 1902; Cincinnati NL, 1902–06; Boston NL, 1908. Seventeen years, 1,834 games, 194 triples (9th), 443 stolen bases, .317 BA. Led league in stolen bases, 1896 (87).

Managed Cincinnati NL, 1902 (part)–05; Boston NL, 1908: 337–321, .512. Baseball Hall of Fame.

KELLY, JOHN B. rowing: b. Oct. 4, 1889, Philadelphia; d. June 21, 1960. He won the Association singles and doubles sculls in 1914 and the Championship singles and quarter-mile singles, 1919–20. Then Kelly went to England to compete in the 1920 Diamond Sculls at the Henley Regatta. But he was ruled out. No official explanation was given, but Kelly was told, unofficially, that the muscles he had developed as a bricklayer gave him an unfair advantage over the "gentlemen" competitors. He did win the Olympic singles and doubles in 1920, and he and Paul V. Costello (his cousin) repeated in the doubles in 1924. Kelly's son, John Jr., won the Diamond Sculls in 1947 and 1949. His daughter, Grace, became a movie star and, later, the Princess of Monaco.

Helms Hall of Fame.

KELLY, "KING" (Michael J.) baseball: b. Dec. 31, 1857, Troy, N.Y.; d. Nov. 8, 1894. Bat, throw R; catcher, outfield. Cincinnati NL, 1878–79; Chicago

NL, 1880–86; Boston NL, 1887–89; Boston PL, 1890; Boston AA, Cincin-nati-Milwaukee AA, 1891; Boston NL, 1891–92; New York NL, 1893. Sixteen years, 1,463 games, 315 stolen bases, .307 BA; hit .348 in 1879, .323 in 1881, .305 in 1882, .322 in 1887, .318 in 1888, .326 in 1890. Led league in doubles, 1881 (27), 1882 (37), 1889 (41); in runs (120) and BA (.354) in 1884; and in runs (155) and BA (.388) in 1886.

Kelly was a colorful and popular player. His sale to Boston for $10,000 after the 1886 season helped touch off the player rebellion known as the Brotherhood War, which resulted in formation of the so-called Players League in 1890. Players had decided they must be worth more than the $2,000 maximum salary if a single contract could be worth $10,000.

Kelly holds the NL record for most consecutive years leading in runs, 3. He tied the NL record with 6 runs on Aug. 27, 1887, a day on which he went 6-for-7, with a double and home run.

He managed Boston PL, 1890; Cincinnati-Milwaukee AA, 1891 (part): 124–105, .541. Pennant, 1890.

Baseball Hall of Fame.

KELLY, TOM boxing: b. Jan. 2, 1839, St. John, New Brunswick, Canada; d. Sept. 6, 1887. His record: 4 wins, 3 losses. Kelly fought Englishman George Seddons for the featherweight title on Oct. 7, 1868, losing in 96 rounds. Seddons refused to fight him again and retired in 1873. Kelly then claimed the title and was generally recognized as champion until late in the 1870s.

KELLY, TOMMY "SPIDER" boxing: b. Sept. 6, 1867, New York City; d. ? His record: 30 wins, 11 by KO; 9 losses, 4 by KO; 4 draws, 1 no-decision. Variously known as Harlem Tommy and the Harlem Spider, Kelly claimed the bantamweight title in 1887, but Hugh Boyle became champ with an 8th-round KO on Dec. 24. After Boyle retired, George Dixon and Kelly claimed the title. Dixon soon became a featherweight, however, and on Dec. 24, 1888, Kelly and Cal McCarthy fought for the U.S. championship. It ended in an 8-round draw. McCarthy also outgrew the division and in the spring of 1889 Kelly beat the British champion, Chappie Moran, in 4 rounds for the vacant world title. He lost to Moran in 10 rounds on June 5 but KOed him in 10 on Jan. 31, 1890, to regain the title.

Kelly lost the championship to Billy Plimmer on May 9, 1892, in a 10-round decision.

KENNEALLY, GEORGE football: b. April 12, 1902, Boston; d. September 1968. St. Bonaventure end. Pottsville Maroons, 1926–28; Boston Braves, 1929; Chicago Cardinals, 1930; Boston Braves, 1932; Philadelphia Eagles, 1933–35. Kenneally was a co-owner of the Boston franchise in 1929.

KENNEDY, "BERT" (Albert R.) football: b. Oct. 24, 1876, Douglas County, Kan.; d. Sept. 3, 1969. Kennedy captained the 1897 Kansas team. He coached at Kansas, 1904–10, compiling a 53–9–4 record. His 1908 team was 9–0–0, and he had a 19-game winning streak during the 1907–09 period. He coached at Haskell Institute, 1911–15, compiling a 32–22–3 mark.

KENNEDY, "BRICKYARD" (William V.) baseball: b. Oct. 7, 1868, Bellaire, Ohio; d. Sept. 23, 1915. Throw R; pitcher. Brooklyn NL, 1892–1901; New York NL, 1902; Pittsburgh NL, 1903. Twelve years, 186–157, 3.96 ERA. One World Series, 1903: 0–1, 5.14 ERA.

KENNEDY, "PAT" (Matthew Patrick) basketball: b. Jan. 28, 1908, Hoboken, N.J.; d. June 16, 1957. Kennedy became a basketball referee almost immediately after graduating from Montclair State College in 1928. For eighteen years he officiated high-school, college, and pro games, serving as supervisor of NBA officials, 1946–50. Then he joined the Harlem Globetrotters as their official for seven years, almost matching the players in showmanship.
Basketball Hall of Fame.

KEOGAN, GEORGE E. basketball: b. March 8, 1890, Minnesota Lake, Minn.; d. Feb. 17, 1943. Keogan spent twenty-four seasons coaching high schools and small colleges in the Midwest before becoming head coach at Notre Dame in 1923, where he remained until his death. His Irish teams won 327 while losing only 96, a .773 percentage. His 1927 (19–1) and 1936 (22–2) teams were chosen Helms national champions. Keogan is credited with inventing the shifting man-for-man defense.
Basketball Hall of Fame.

KERR, "ANDY" (Andrew) football: b. Oct. 7, 1878, Cheyenne, Wyo.; d. Feb. 12, 1969. Kerr combined a perfectionist approach with a love for razzle-dazzle. A 1900 graduate of Dickinson, he was Pop Warner's assistant at Pittsburgh in 1921, when Warner agreed to coach at Stanford but not until 1924. Kerr went on ahead to install the tricky double wing and was head coach at Stanford, 1922–23. He assisted Warner there for two more years, then went to Washington and Jefferson, 1926–28; his second team there was undefeated. Kerr then settled down at Colgate, 1929–46, compiling a 95–50–7 record. His 1932 team was unbeaten, unscored on, and, as Kerr put it, "uninvited"—he felt it should have received a bowl bid. He retired briefly, then coached at Lebanon Valley, Pennsylvania, College, 1947–49.
Helms Hall of Fame, National Football Foundation Hall of Fame.

KERR, "DICKIE" (Richard H.) baseball: b. July 3, 1893, St. Louis; d. May 4, 1963. Bat, throw L; pitcher. Chicago AL, 1919–21, 1925. Four years, 53–34, 3.84 ERA; 21–9 in 1920. One World Series, 1919: 2–0, 1.42 ERA, 1 shutout.

Kerr was often referred to as the "honest hero of the Black Sox Scandal" because in his rookie year he had two of Chicago's three victories in the World Series that Cincinnati won, 5 games to 3. Ultimately, eight Chicago players were suspended for life for allegedly taking bribes from gamblers.

KETCHEL, STANLEY boxing: b. Stanislaus Kiecal, Sept. 14, 1886, Grand Rapids, Mich.; d. Oct. 15, 1910. His record: 49 wins, 46 by KO; 4 losses, 2 by KO; 4 draws, 4 no-decisions. Ketchel won the middleweight title, Feb. 22, 1908, by KOing Jack "Twin" Sullivan in 20 rounds. He lost it on a KO by Billy Papke, Sept. 7, 1908, in 11 rounds, but Ketchel, infuriated by his defeat, came back to regain it from Papke with a brutal 11-round TKO on Nov. 26 of the same year. He held it until his death: He was shot and killed during one of his frequent vacations in the West, at Conway, Missouri.

Ketchel fought heavyweight champ Jack Johnson on Oct. 16, 1909, and knocked Johnson down but was KOed in the 12th round. He is ranked No. 1 middleweight of all time.

Helms Hall of Fame, Boxing Hall of Fame.

KIESLING, WALTER football: b. May 27, 1903, St. Paul, Minn.; d. March 3, 1962. St. Thomas of Minnesota guard. Duluth Eskimos, 1926–27; Pottsville, 1928; Chicago Cardinals, 1929–33; Chicago Bears, 1934; Green Bay Packers, 1935–36; Pittsburgh Pirates, 1937–38; All-Pro 1932.

Kiesling coached Pittsburgh part of 1939, 1940, part of 1941, all of 1942. He was co-coach during the merger with Philadelphia in 1943 and during the merger with the Cardinals in 1944. He coached the Steelers 1954–56. His overall record was 30–55–5.

Professional Football Hall of Fame.

KILBANE, JOHN boxing: b. April 18, 1889, Cleveland; d. May 31, 1957. His record: 46 wins, 22 by KO; 4 losses, 2 by KO; 8 draws, 80 no-decisions, 2 bouts stopped by police. Kilbane held the featherweight title for more than eleven years. He won it Feb. 22, 1912, by outpointing Abe Attell in 20 rounds, and he lost it to Eugene Criqui, of France, on a 6-round KO, June 2, 1923.

Helms Hall of Fame, Boxing Hall of Fame.

KILLEFER, "REINDEER BILL" (William L.) baseball: b. Oct. 10, 1887, Bloomingdale, Mich.; d. July 2, 1960. Bat, throw R; catcher. St. Louis

AL, 1909–10; Philadelphia NL, 1911–17; Chicago NL, 1918–21. Thirteen years, 1,035 games, .238 BA. Two World Series, 1915, 1918: 7 games, .111 BA.

He managed Chicago NL, 1921 (part)–25 (part); St. Louis AL, 1930–33 (part): 523–623, .456.

KILLEN, FRANK B. baseball: b. Nov. 30, 1870, Pittsburgh; d. Dec. 4, 1939. Bat, throw L; pitcher. Cincinnati-Milwaukee AA, 1891; Washington NL, 1892; Pittsburgh NL, 1893–98; Washington NL, 1898–99; Boston NL, 1899; Chicago NL, 1900. Ten years, 163–131, 3.78 ERA. Led NL in wins, 1893 (35–14); in wins (30–18), complete games (44), and shutouts (5) in 1896; in complete games, 1897 (38).

KILLIAN, EDWIN H. baseball: b. Nov. 12, 1876, Racine, Wis.; d. July 18, 1928. Bat, throw L; pitcher. Cleveland AL, 1903; Detroit AL, 1904–10. Eight years, 100–78, 2.38 ERA, 22 shutouts. Led AL in shutouts, 1904 (8). Two World Series, 1907–08: 0–0, 4.26 ERA.

KILPATRICK, JOHN REED football: b. June 15, 1889, New York City; d. May 7, 1960. Yale end; All-American, 1909–10. President, Madison Square Garden, 1939 until his death.

National Football Foundation Hall of Fame.

KILRAIN, JAKE boxing: b. John J. Killion, Feb. 9, 1859, Green Point, N.Y.; d. Dec. 22, 1937. One of sports' famous losers, Kilrain was beaten by John L. Sullivan in 75 rounds on July 8, 1889, in the last major bare-knuckle fight in the United States.

His record: 18 wins, 3 by KO; 5 losses, 2 by KO; 12 draws, 1 no-decision.

KILROY, MATTHEW A. baseball: b. June 21, 1866, Philadelphia; d. March 2, 1940. Bat, throw L; pitching. Baltimore AA, 1886–89; Boston PL, 1890; Cincinnati-Milwaukee AA, 1891; Washington NL, 1892; Louisville NL, 1893–94; Chicago NL, 1898. Ten years, 142–133, 3.47 ERA; 1,170 strikeouts in 2,435⅔ innings. No-hitters, Oct. 6, 1886, against Pittsburgh AA (6–0); July 29, 1889, against St. Louis AA (0–0; 7 innings). Led AL in losses (29–34), complete games (66), and strikeouts (513) in 1886; in wins (46–19), complete games (66), and shutouts (6) in 1887; in complete games (55) in 1889.

KIMBLE, FRED shooting: b. 1846, Knoxville, Ill.; d. 1941. Kimble revolutionized shotguns when he invented the choke-bore in 1868. In 1884 he invented the first composition target for trapshooting. At the Iowa State Shoot in 1880, he was overall champion with 224 out of 226 targets, including live birds, clays, and glass balls. The same year, he broke 735 glass balls in a row during a thirteen-day tour.

American Trapshooting Hall of Fame.

KINDER, ELLIS R. baseball: b. July 26, 1914, Atkins, Ark.; d. Oct. 16, 1968. Bat, throw R; pitcher. St. Louis AL, 1946–47; Boston AL, 1948–55; St. Louis NL, 1956; Chicago AL, 1956–57. Twelve years, 102–71, 3.43 ERA. In relief, 44–30, 2.78 ERA, 102 saves. Led AL in percentage (23–6, .793) and shutouts (6) in 1949, when he had 13 straight wins. After 1950, Kinder was primarily a relief pitcher. In 1951, he was 10–1 in relief with 14 saves and a 2.14 ERA; in 1953, he was 10–6, with 27 saves and a 1.85 ERA.

KING, PHILIP football: b. March 16, 1872, Washington, D.C.; d. Jan. 7, 1938. Princeton; All-American quarterback, 1891, 1893; halfback, 1892; 2nd team halfback, 1890; captain, 1892. King scored 55 touchdowns and 56 conversions during his career.

He coached Princeton, 1894, Wisconsin, 1896–1902, 1906, compiling a 71–14–1 record; his 1901 and 1906 teams were undefeated.

National Football Foundation Hall of Fame.

KING, "SILVER" (Charles F.) baseball: b. Koenig, Jan. 11, 1868, St. Louis; d. May 19, 1938. Bat, throw R; pitcher. Kansas City NL, 1886; St. Louis AA, 1887–89; Chicago PL, 1890; Pittsburgh NL, 1891; New York NL, 1892–93; Cincinnati NL, 1893; Washington NL, 1896–97. Ten years, 204–153, 3.18 ERA; 20 shutouts; 32–12 in 1887, 34–16 in 1889, 30–22 in 1890, 24–24 in 1892. No-hitter, June 21, 1890, against Brooklyn PL. Led league in victories (45–21), ERA (1.64), complete games (64), and shutouts (6) in 1888; in ERA (2.69) and shutouts (4) in 1890; in losses (14–29) in 1891.

KIPHUTH, ROBERT J. H. swimming: b. Nov. 17, 1890, Tonawanda, N.Y.; d. Jan. 7, 1967. Probably the most remarkable coaching record compiled in any sport is Kiphuth's: From 1918 through 1959, his swimming teams at Yale won 527 dual meets, losing only 12. In only two seasons did they lose more than a single meet. When he retired after the 1959 season, Yale had won 182 straight meets; during the 1925–37 span, they had won 172 in a row.

In 1942, Yale won the AAU indoor title and Kiphuth's New Haven Swim Club teams won it in 1949, 1951, 1953–55, and 1957. Yale was NCAA champion in 1942, 1944, 1951, and 1953 and won the Eastern League title, 1939–43, 1947–59. Kiphuth coached the U.S. women's Olympic swimming team in 1928, the men's teams in 1932, 1936, and 1948. He was Yale athletic director, 1949–59.

Helms Hall of Fame.

KIRSCH, DONALD basketball: b. Sept. 29, 1920, Portland, Ore.; d. May 7, 1970. Kirsch coached basketball at Oregon, 1947–69, and compiled a 429–228 record, without a losing season. His Oregon baseball teams, during the period, also never had a losing season but did play .500 ball one year.

He died of Parkinson's disease.

KITSON, FRANK R. baseball: b. April 11, 1872, Hopkins, Mich.; d. April 14, 1930. Bat L, throw R; pitcher. Baltimore NL, 1898–99; Brooklyn NL, 1900–02; Detroit AL, 1903–05; Washington AL, 1906–07; New York AL, 1907. Ten years, 126–123, 3.17 ERA, 20 shutouts.

KITTREDGE, MALACHI J. baseball: b. Oct. 12, 1869, Clinton, Mass.; d. 1927. Bat, throw R; catcher. Chicago NL, 1890–97; Louisville NL, 1898–99; Washington NL, 1899; Boston NL, 1901–03; Washington AL, 1903–06; Cleveland AL, 1906. Sixteen years, 1,215 games, .219 BA.

KLAUS, FRANK boxing: b. Dec. 30, 1887, Pittsburgh; d. Feb. 8, 1948. His record: 49 wins, 25 by KO; 4 losses, 2 by KO; 2 draws, 34 no-decisions. Klaus beat Georges Carpentier on a foul in the 19th round, June 24, 1912, for the European middleweight title. He won the world title from Billy Papke, also on a foul, in 15 rounds on March 5, 1913. He lost it on a 6th-round KO by George Chip on Oct. 11, 1913.

KLEIN, "CHUCK" (Charles H.) baseball: b. Oct. 7, 1904, Indianapolis, Ind.; d. March 28, 1958. Bat L, throw R; outfield. Philadelphia NL, 1928–33; Chicago NL, 1934–36; Philadelphia NL, 1936–39; Pittsburgh NL, 1939; Philadelphia NL, 1940–44. Seventeen years, 1,753 games, 6,486 at-bats, 2,076 hits, 398 doubles, 300 home runs, 1,168 runs, 1,201 RBI, .320 BA, .543 slugging.

Klein is coholder of ML records for most consecutive years 200 or more hits, 5; most consecutive years leading in total bases, 4; most consecutive years 400 or more total bases, 3; most assists by an outfielder in a season, 44, in 1930.

He is a holder or coholder of NL records for most home runs in a season, 58, in 1930; most consecutive years leading in runs, 3; most years 150 or more runs, 2; most extra base hits in a season, 107; most RBI by a left-handed hitter, 170, in 1930. He's the only NL player to get more than 400 total bases in three different seasons. His 445 total bases in 1930 is second highest in NL history. On July 10, 1936, he hit 4 home runs in a game, one of seven players to do so, and on Aug. 21, 1935, he scored 8 runs in a doubleheader, a modern NL record. Klein won the Most Valuable Player award in 1932.

He led the NL in BA, 1933 (.368); runs, 1930 (158), 1931 (121), 1932 (152); hits, 1932 (226), 1933 (223); doubles, 1930 (59), 1933 (44); home runs, 1929 (43), 1931 (31), 1932 (38), 1933 (28); RBI, 1931 (121), 1933 (120); slugging, 1931 (.584), 1932 (.646), 1933 (.602); stolen bases, 1932 (20). He hit .356 in 1929, .386 in 1930, .337 in 1931, .348 in 1932, .301 in 1934, .306 in 1936, .325 in 1937.

One World Series, 1935: 5 games, .333 BA. His 2-run homer won the fifth game for the Cubs as they beat Detroit in 6 games.

KLEM, WILLIAM J. baseball: b. Feb. 22, 1874, Rochester, N.Y.; d. Sept. 1, 1951. Not many umpires become famous, but Bill Klem became a legend. He was a colorful character—but he knew the rule book by heart. When Klem began umpiring in the National League in 1905, players and managers were willing to challenge the umpire to a fight if they had to, and often he didn't get full backing from the league office. In his first year, Klem was faced with an argument from Giant manager John McGraw. Klem drew a line in the dirt with his toe and told McGraw that if he crossed it he would be out of the game. McGraw did cross it; Klem did throw him out. McGraw shouted, "I'll get your job for this." Klem replied, "Mr. McGraw, if *you* can get my job, I don't want it."

He went on to umpire for thirty-seven seasons, an ML record. McGraw still argued with him at times, but he wanted Klem umpiring any important games the Giants played. Klem was famous for his statement, "I never called one wrong." He amplified on it: "When I say I never called one wrong, I mean that in my heart I was right. If I knew a decision was wrong, I would not make it—not for all the men and all the money in the world. Therefore, I never called one wrong."

He supervised league umpires from 1942 until his death.

Baseball Hall of Fame.

KLING, JOHN G. baseball: b. Feb. 25, 1875, Kansas City, Mo.; d. Jan. 31, 1947. Bat, throw R; catcher. Chicago NL, 1900–08, 1910–11; Boston NL, 1911–12; Cincinnati NL, 1913. Thirteen years, 1,260 games, .271 BA; hit .312 in 1906. Four World Series, 1906–08, 1910: 21 games, .185 BA.

Kling is coholder of NL records for most years leading catchers in fielding average, 4, and most years leading in putouts, 6.

Managed Boston NL, 1912: 52–101, .340.

KNABE, OTTO (Franz Otto) baseball: b. June 12, 1884, Carrick, Pa.; d. May 17, 1961. Bat, throw R; second base. Pittsburgh NL, 1905; Philadelphia NL 1907–13; Baltimore Fed L 1914–15; Chicago NL, Pittsburgh NL, 1916. Eleven years, 1,284 games, .247 BA.
Managed Baltimore Fed L, 1914–15: 131–177, .425.

KNOX, WILLIAM bowling: b. April 21, 1887, Philadelphia; d. May 18, 1944. Knox rolled the first 300 game in ABC tournament history in 1913 and won the all-events title in 1923 with 2,019, which was a record for ten years. His twenty-two-year ABC tourney average was 191.
American Bowling Congress Hall of Fame.

KOCH, "BOTCHEY" (Barton) football: b. Aug. 13, 1906, Temple, Tex.; d. April 28, 1964. Baylor guard; captain, All-American, 1930.

KOLP, RAYMOND C. ("Jockey") baseball: b. Oct. 1, 1894, New Berlin, Ohio; d. July 29, 1967. Bat, throw R; pitcher. St. Louis AL, 1921–24; Cincinnati NL, 1928–34. Twelve years, 79–95, 4.08 ERA. In relief, 17–14, 3.67 ERA, 18 saves.

KONETCHY, EDWARD J. ("Big Ed") baseball: b. Sept. 3, 1885, LaCrosse, Wis.; d. May 27, 1947. Bat, throw R; first base. St. Louis NL, 1907–13; Pittsburgh NL, 1914; Pittsburgh Fed L, 1915; Boston NL, 1916–18; Brooklyn NL, 1919–21; Philadelphia NL, 1921. Fifteen years, 2,083 games, 2,148 hits, 255 stolen bases, .281 BA; hit .302 in 1910, .314 in 1912, .314 in 1915, .308 in 1920. Led league in doubles, 1911 (38).
Konetchy got 10 consecutive hits in 1919, tying an NL record.

KOPPISCH, WALTER F. football: b. 1901(?), Buffalo, N.Y.; d. Nov. 5, 1953. Columbia halfback; All-American, 1924; 3rd team, 1923; captain, 1922–24. Buffalo Bisons, 1925; New York Giants, 1925–26. A dangerous runner, Koppisch scored on TD runs of 76, 67, and 55 yards in a single quarter against New York University.

KOSTER, JOHN H. bowling: b. April 21, 1871, New York City; d. Aug. 14, 1945. Koster was the first man to win four ABC titles, a record that stood until 1962. He was on the tournament champion team in 1902 and 1912, won the all-events in 1902 and the doubles in 1913. His twenty-three-year ABC tourney average was 188.
American Bowling Congress Hall of Fame.

KRAENZLEIN, ALVIN C. track: b. Dec. 12, 1876, Milwaukee; d. Jan. 6, 1928. Kraenzlein won four Gold Medals in the 1900 Olympics: in the 60-meter dash, the 110- and 200-meter hurdles, and the running broad

jump. He held world records in all four events at one time. He also had a remarkable record in IC4A and AAU competition: Representing Pennsylvania in the IC4A, he won the 100-yard dash in 1900, the 120-yard high hurdles, 1898–1900, the 220-yard low hurdles, 1989–1900, and the broad jump in 1899. In AAU competition, he won the 100-yard dash in 1899, the 120-yard high hurdles, 1898–99, the 220-yard low hurdles, 1897–99, and the broad jump in 1899.
Helms Hall of Fame.

KREBS, JAMES basketball: b. Sept. 8, 1935, St. Louis; d. May 5, 1965. SMU center; All-American, 1957. Minneapolis Lakers, 1957–60; Los Angeles Lakers, 1960–64. Seven years, 515 games, 8.0 points per game.

KREMER, "RAY" (Remy P.) baseball: b. March 23, 1893, Oakland, Calif.; d. Feb. 8, 1965. Bat, throw R; pitcher. Pittsburgh NL, 1924–33. Led NL in wins and percentage (20–6, .769) and ERA (2.61) in 1926; in wins in 1930 (20–12); in ERA in 1927 (2.47); in shutouts in 1924 (4). Ten years, 143–85, 3.76 ERA. Two World Series, 1925, 1927: 2–2, 3.12 ERA.

KRESS, "RED" (Ralph) baseball: b. Jan. 2, 1907, Columbia, Calif.; d. Nov. 29, 1962. Bat, throw R; shortstop, third-first base, outfield. St. Louis AL, 1927–32; Chicago AL, 1932–34; Washington AL, 1934–36; St. Louis AL, 1938–39; Detroit AL, 1939–40; New York NL, 1946. Fourteen years, 1,391 games, .286 BA; hit .305 in 1929, .313 in 1930, .311 in 1931, .302 in 1938.

KROUSE, RAY football: b. March 21, 1927, Washington, D.C.; d. April 7, 1966. Maryland tackle. Defensive tackle, New York Giants, 1951–55; Detroit Lions, 1956–57; Baltimore Colts, 1958–59; Washington Redskins, 1960.

KRUGER, "STUBBY" (Harold) swimming: b. 1897(?) Honolulu; d. Oct. 7, 1965. Kruger was U.S. indoor 300-yard medley champion in 1924 and was a member of the Illinois AC 400-yard free-style relay team that won national indoor championships, 1923–25. He was named Swimmer of the Year in 1923. Later, he became a movie stunt man, doubling for stars from Douglas Fairbanks, Sr., in *The Black Pirate* to Spencer Tracy in *The Old Man and the Sea.*

KURTSINGER, CHARLES E. horse racing: b. 1906, Shepherdsville, Ky.; d. Sept. 24, 1946. Kurtsinger rode War Admiral to the Triple Crown in 1937; he also won the Kentucky Derby and Belmont Stakes aboard Twenty Grand in 1931 and rode Head Play to a Preakness victory in 1933. He also rode winners in such other major races as the Belmont Futurity, Dwyer Handicap, Flamingo Stakes, Pimlico Special, Saratoga Cup, Suburban Handicap, Widener Handicap, Withers Stakes, and Wood Memorial.

L

LAACK, GALEN football: b. April 3, 1932, Abbotsford, Wis.; d. Jan. 1, 1959. College of the Pacific guard. Philadelphia Eagles, 1958. He died in an auto accident.

LaCHANCE, "CANDY" (George J.) baseball: b. Feb. 15, 1870, Waterbury, Conn.; d. Aug. 18, 1932. Sw. hit, throw R; first base. Brooklyn NL, 1893–98; Baltimore NL, 1899; Cleveland AL,1901; Boston AL, 1902–05. Twelve years, 1,263 games, .280 BA; hit .312 in 1895, .308 in 1897, .307 in 1899, .303 in 1901. One World Series, 1903: 8 games, .222 BA.

LAHR, WARREN football: b. Sept. 5, 1923, Wyoming, Pa.; d. Jan. 19, 1969. Western Reserve defensive back. Cleveland Browns, 1949 (AAFC), 1950–59 (NFL); All-Pro, 1951. Lahr is tied for second with 5 career TDs on interception returns.

LAJOIE, "LARRY" (Napoleon) baseball: b. Sept. 5, 1875, Woonsocket, R.I.; d. Feb. 7, 1959. Bat, throw R; second base. Philadelphia NL, 1896–1900; Philadelphia AL, 1901–02; Cleveland AL, 1902–14; Philadelphia AL, 1915–16. Twenty-one years, 2,480 games, 9,589 at-bats (7th), 3,242 hits (6th), 650 doubles (4th), 162 triples, 83 home runs, 1,503 runs, 1,599 RBI, 380 stolen bases, .338 BA; hit .361 in 1897, .324 in 1898, .378 in 1899, .337 in 1900, .329 in 1905, .355 in 1906, .324 in 1909, .384 in 1910, .365 in 1911, .368 in 1912, .335 in 1913. Led league in hitting, 1901 (.426), 1902 (.378), 1903 (.344), 1904 (.376); in runs, 1901 (145); in hits, 1901 (232), 1904 (208), 1906 (214), 1910 (227); in doubles, 1898 (43), 1901 (48), 1904 (49), 1906 (48), 1910 (51); in home runs, 1901 (14); in slugging, 1897 (.569), 1901 (.643), 1903 (.518), 1904 (.546).

Lajoie's .426 in 1901 is an AL record for hitting. A smooth, graceful fielder as well as a fine hitter, Lajoie was such a drawing card that for several years the Cleveland team was called the Naps. He set an AL record for most chances accepted at second base, 988, in 1908; in 1899 he set an NL record for most putouts for a second baseman in a 9-inning game, 11. Playing out of position in 1910, he set an AL record for most putouts by a shortstop in a 9-inning game, 10.

He managed Cleveland, 1904–09 (part): 397–330, .546. Baseball Hall of Fame.

LAKE, JOSEPH H. baseball: b. Dec. 6, 1881, Brooklyn; d. June 30, 1950. Bat, throw R; pitcher. New York AL, 1908–09; St. Louis AL, 1910–12; Detroit AL, 1912–13. Six years, 61–92, 2.85 ERA. Led AL in losses, 1908 (9–22).

LAMBEAU, "CURLY" (Earl L.) football: b. April 9, 1898, Green Bay, Wis.; d. June 1, 1965. After playing freshman football at Notre Dame in 1917, Lambeau went home to recuperate from tonsilitis and got a job but soon found that he missed football. So he organized his own team in 1919. His employer, the Green Bay Packing Co., bought the uniforms, so the team was christened the Packers. In 1921, Lambeau got an NFL franchise. He played halfback and coached the team through 1929, when the Packers won the first of three straight championships. In 1930 he quit as a player but continued to coach through the 1949 season. His overall record: 212–109–24, with six championships (1929–31, 1936, 1939, 1944). They also won a division title in 1938, losing the title game to the Giants, and in 1941 they tied for the division championship but lost the playoff to the Bears.

Lambeau coached the Chicago Cardinals, 1950–51 (8–16), and the Washington Redskins, 1952–53 (10–13–1).

Lambeau, with George Halas, led the way in scouting for talent at small colleges as well as the major football schools and was among the first to make a determined effort to lure players from the Deep South.

Professional Football Hall of Fame.

LAMBERT, "PIGGY" (Ward L.) basketball: b. May 28, 1888, Crawfordsville, Ind.; d. Jan. 20, 1958. A Wabash College graduate, 1911, Lambert coached high-school basketball for five years and then went to Purdue in 1916. Coaching there through the 1945–46 season, he had a 365–145 record. His teams won 11 Big Ten championships. He was named Coach of the Year in 1945.

Basketball Hall of Fame, Helms Hall of Fame.

LANDIS, KENESAW MOUNTAIN baseball: b. Nov. 20, 1866, Millville, Ohio; d. Nov. 25, 1944. The first commissioner of baseball first gained some measure of fame in 1907 when, as a U.S. district judge, he fined Standard Oil of Indiana a record $29,240,000 in a series of rebate cases (the decision was eventually reversed on appeal).

Until 1921, baseball was run by a three-man commission. But the revelation that eight Chicago White Sox players, offered bribes by gamblers, had evidently conspired to throw the 1919 World Series convinced club owners that they needed one strong man to rule organized baseball. They picked Landis. For twenty-three years, he reigned with an iron hand. His decisions sometimes angered owners, but they respected him, and every seven years they renewed his contract. During his first few years in office, he several times banned players for life to avoid even the suspicion of a scandal. He also attacked the common practice of hiding good young players in the minor leagues, improved players' contracts, and once ordered the entire proceeds of a World Series game be donated to charity when the game was called for no very good reason, when the score was tied.

Baseball Hall of Fame.

LANGFORD, SAM boxing: b. Feb. 12, 1880, Weymouth, Nova Scotia, Canada; d. Jan. 12, 1956. His record: 136 wins, 98 by KO; 23 losses, 4 by KO; 31 draws, 58 no-decisions, 2 no-contests. "The Boston Tar Baby" beat 6 world champions at one time or another and is ranked among the top 10 heavyweights of the century, but he never held a title. A solidly built man with a 44" chest and 73" reach, he began fighting as a featherweight but eventually grew into the heavyweight class.

Helms Hall of Fame, Boxing Hall of Fame.

LAPCHICK, JOSEPH basketball: b. April 12, 1900, Yonkers, N.Y.; d. Aug. 10, 1970. The 6'5" Lapchick was one of the first big men in basketball. He became a pro at seventeen, without graduating from high school, in order to help his immigrant parents support the family, and he starred for twenty seasons, 1917–36. He played for, among others, the Original Celtics, the Brooklyn Visitations, and the Cleveland Rosenblums. He also revived the Celtics as a barnstorming team in 1930.

Lapchick coached at St. John's University, 1936–47 and 1956–66, winning a record four National Invitation tournaments. He coached the New York Knickerbockers, 1947–56, compiling a 300–222 record. His St. John's teams were 335–129.

Basketball Hall of Fame, Helms Hall of Fame.

LaPORTE, FRANK B. baseball: b. Feb. 6, 1880, Uhrichsville, Ohio; d. Sept. 25, 1939. Bat, throw R; second-third base. New York AL, 1905–08; Boston AL, 1908; New York AL, 1909–10; St. Louis AL, 1911–12; Washington AL, 1912–13; Indianapolis Fed L, 1914; Newark Fed L, 1915. Eleven years, 1,193 games, .281 BA; hit .314 in 1911, .311 in 1912, .311 in 1914.

LARABA, ROBERT football: b. May 30, 1933, Niagara Falls, N.Y.; d. Feb. 16, 1962. Texas Western linebacker. Los Angeles Chargers (AFL), 1960; San Diego Chargers (AFL), 1961. Laraba was killed in a car crash.

LARDNER, "RING" (Ringgold W.) sportswriting: b. March 6, 1883, Niles, Mich.; d. Sept. 25, 1933. At a time when most sportswriters were glorifying athletes, Lardner was looking at them ironically—even, at times, sarcastically. As a traveling writer with the Chicago Cubs, he saw many players off the field, and he portrayed them as he saw them. The typical Lardner athlete is an uneducated, semiliterate braggart full of alibis for every error and every defeat. Lardner's remarkable ear for speech earned him a high place in American literature as it was entering its realistic period.

Besides writing newspaper columns and stories, Lardner was a frequent contributor to the *Saturday Evening Post.* His first book, *You Know Me Al,* published in 1916, was supposedly a collection of letters to home from a major-league rookie. His stories are generally humorous, but beneath the humor there is a bitter pessimism that came to the fore in *Champion,* a short novel, later a movie, which portrays a champion fighter as a selfish, brutal sadist.

LARKIN, HENRY E. baseball: b. Jan. 12, 1863, Reading, Pa.; d. Jan. 31, 1942. Bat, throw R; first base, outfield. Philadelphia AA, 1884–89; Cleveland PL, 1890; Philadelphia AA, 1891; Washington NL, 1892–93. Ten years, 1,184 games, .303 BA; hit .329 in 1885, .319 in 1886, .310 in 1887, .319 in 1889, .332 in 1890. Led league in doubles, 1885 (37), 1886 (36).

Larkin twice got 6 hits in a game. On June 16, 1885, he went 6-for-6, with 2 doubles, a triple, a home run, and 4 runs scored. On June 7, 1892, he went 6-for-7, scoring 3 runs.

Managed Cleveland PL, 1890 (part): 27–33, .450.

LARNED, WILLIAM A. tennis: b. Dec. 30, 1872, Summit, N.J.; d. Dec. 16, 1926. Winner of seven national outdoor singles titles, 1901–02, 1907–11, Larned was also inventor of the steel-frame racket. Representing Cornell, he won the national intercollegiate title in 1892. He contracted a rheumatic disease while serving in the Spanish-American War and couldn't resume competition until he was nearly 29. He was on 6 Davis Cup teams.

Helms Hall of Fame, Tennis Hall of Fame.

LATHAM, "ARLIE" (Walter Arlington) baseball: b. March 15, 1859, West Lebanon, N.H.; d. Nov. 29, 1952. Bat, throw R; third base. Buffalo NL, 1880; St. Louis AA, 1883–89; Chicago PL, 1890; Cincinnati NL, 1890–95; St. Louis NL, 1896; Washington NL, 1899; New York NL, 1909. Seventeen years, 1,627 games, 679 stolen bases (five years not included), .269 BA; hit .301 in 1886, .316 in 1887, .313 in 1894, .311 in 1895. Led league in runs, 1886 (152); in stolen bases, 1888 (109).

Latham went 6-for-6 and scored 5 runs on April 24, 1886.

LATZO, PETE boxing: b. Aug. 1, 1902, Coleraine, Pa.; d. July 7, 1968. On May 20, 1926, Latzo won the welterweight title from Mickey Walker on a 10-round decision. He lost it June 3, 1927, to Joe Dundee on a 15-round decision.

His record: 65 wins, 25 by KO; 31 losses, 2 by KO; 3 draws, 50 no-decisions, 1 no-contest.

LAVEAGA, ROBERT E. volleyball: b. May, 4, 1894, Winnemucca, Nev.; d. June 15, 1966. A graduate of George Williams College, Chicago, Laveaga was long associated with the YMCA physical program, through which he was introduced to competitive volleyball. He wrote the first textbook on the sport.

LAVENDER, JAMES S. baseball: b. March 25, 1884, Barnesville, Ga.; d. Jan. 12, 1960. Bat, throw R; pitcher. Chicago NL, 1912–16; Philadelphia NL, 1917. Six years, 63–76, 3.09 ERA. No-hitter, Aug, 31, 1915, against New York NL (2–0).

LAVIGNE, GEORGE "KID" boxing: b. Dec. 6, 1869, Bay City, Mich.; d. March 9, 1928. His record: 35 wins, 16 by KO; 5 losses, 2 by KO; 8 draws, 7 no-decisions. Lavigne won the vacant world lightweight title on June 1, 1896, by KOing Dick Burge in the 17th round. Lavigne, who started his professional career in 1885, was undefeated until March 10, 1899, when he lost to Mysterious Billy Smith in a 14-round nontitle bout. In his next fight, July 3, he lost his title to Frank Erne on a 20-round decision.

Helms Hall of Fame, Boxing Hall of Fame.

LAYTON, JOHN billiards: b. 1886(?), St. Louis; d. Jan. 18, 1956. Layton was world professional three-cushion champion, 1920, 1921–23, 1928–30, 1934.

LAZETICH, MILAN football: b. Aug. 27, 1921, Anaconda, Mont.; d. July 9, 1969. Montana, Michigan, tackle. Guard, Cleveland Rams, 1945; Los Angeles Rams, 1946–50.

LAZZERI, "TONY" (Anthony M.) baseball: b. Dec. 26, 1903, San Francisco; d. Aug. 6, 1946. Bat, throw R; second base. New York AL, 1926–37; Chicago NL, 1938; Brooklyn NL, New York NL, 1939. Fourteen years, 1,739 games, 986 runs, 1,191 RBI, .292 BA; hit .309 in 1927, .332 in 1928, .354 in 1929, .303 in 1930, .300 in 1932.

Lazzeri won the nickname Poosh-'Em-Up for his ability to move runners around the bases. Seven times he had more than 100 RBI in a season. He also had some remarkable streaks. Though he never hit more than 18 home runs in a season, he twice hit 3 in a game, on June 8, 1927, and on May 24, 1936. On the latter date, 2 of them were grand slams and he had 11 RBI, an AL record for one game. On May 23, he had hit 3 home runs in a doubleheader, collecting 4 RBI; he holds the ML record for most RBI in two consecutive games, 15, and he tied the record for most home runs in two consecutive days, 6. On May 25 he hit another to tie the AL record for most home runs in four consecutive games, 7—half his total production for the year.

In seven World Series, 1926–28, 1932, 1936–38, 32 games, he hit .262, with 3 doubles, a triple, 4 home runs, 16 runs scored, and 19 RBI.

LEA, LANGDON ("Biffy") football: b. May 11, 1874, Germantown, Pa.; d. Oct. 4, 1937. Princeton tackle; captain, 1895; All-American, 1893–95.
Helms Hall of Fame, National Football Foundation Hall of Fame.

LEACH, "WEE TOMMY" (Thomas W.) baseball: b. Nov. 4, 1877, French Creek, N.Y.; d. Sept. 29, 1969. Bat, throw R; outfield, third base. Louisville NL, 1898–99; Pittsburgh NL, 1900–12; Chicago NL, 1912–14; Cincinnati NL, 1915; Pittsburgh NL, 1918. Nineteen years, 2,155 games, 1,355 runs, 361 stolen bases, .269 BA; hit .305 in 1901, .303 in 1907. Led NL in triples (22) and home runs (6) in 1902; in runs, 1909 (126) and 1913 (99). Two World Series, 1903, 1909: 15 games, .293 BA, 11 runs, 9 RBI, 4 triples (1st). He hit .320, with 4 doubles and 8 runs, in Pittsburgh's 7-game victory over Detroit in 1909; his great running catch of a long drive by Ty Cobb with two men on saved a 4–1 opening-game win for the Pirates.

LEE, EDWARD L. billiards: b. 1905(?); d. May 18, 1969. Lee was national amateur three-cushion champion, 1931–35, 1946, 1948–56, 1958, 1963–64. He was world champion in 1936.

LEE, HORACE H. track: b. Oct. 23, 1859, Philadelphia; d. April 1, 1933. Lee became the first American to run 100 yards in 10 seconds, in 1877; that was the world record, tied several times, until 1890. He also briefly held the world record in the 220, at 23.5 seconds. Representing Pennsylvania, he won these IC4A titles: 100-yard dash, 1877–79; 220-yard dash, 1877–78; broad jump, 1877.

LEEVER, SAMUEL baseball: b. Dec. 23, 1871, Goshen, Ohio; d. May 19, 1953. Bat, throw R; pitcher. Pittsburgh NL, 1898–1910. Thirteen years, 195–102, 2.47 ERA, .657 percentage (10th); 21–23 in 1899, 22–7 in 1906. Led NL in percentage, 1901 (15–5, .750); in percentage (25–7, .781), ERA (2.06), and shutouts (7) in 1903; in percentage in 1905 (20–5, .800). One World Series, 1903: 0–2, 6.30 ERA.

LEMA, "CHAMPAGNE TONY" (Anthony) golf: b. Feb. 25, 1934, Oakland, Calif.; d. July 24, 1966. Lema burst onto the golfing scene with a brilliant succession of victories in 1964, climaxed by the British Open championship. He had earlier won three major tournaments in a row—the Thunderbird, Cleveland, and Buick Opens—and he rounded out the year by winning the World Series of Golf. In 1965, he repeated in the Buick and the Carling and was second in winnings, with $101,861. He won his nickname by setting up champagne for the press after every major victory.

Lema and his second wife died in a plane crash.

LEONARD, ANDREW J. baseball: b. June 1, 1846, County Cavan, Ireland; d. Aug. 22, 1903. Bat, throw R; outfield, shortstop, second base. National Association, Washington, 1871; Boston, 1872–75. Five years, 286 games, .321 BA; hit .341 in 1872, .340 in 1874, .323 in 1875.

Boston NL, 1876–78; Cincinnati NL, 1880. Four years, 215 games, .267 BA.

LEONARD, BENNY boxing: b. Benjamin Leiner, April 7, 1896, New York City; d. April 18, 1947. His record: 88 wins, 68 by KO; 5 losses, 4 by KO; 1 draw, 115 no-decisions. A very clever boxer, Leonard won the lightweight title six years after turning pro by beating Freddie Welsh on a 9-round TKO, May 28, 1917. He retired in 1924, still champion. He received the Edward J. Neil trophy in 1944, when he was a lieutenant commander in the Maritime Service.

Helms Hall of Fame, Boxing Hall of Fame.

LEONARD, "DUTCH" (Hubert B.) baseball: b. April 16, 1892, Birmingham, Ohio; d. July 11, 1952. Bat, throw L; pitcher. Boston AL, 1913–18; Detroit AL, 1919–21, 1924–25. Eleven years, 138–113, 2.77 ERA, 1,158 strikeouts, 32 shutouts in 2,190 innings. No-hitters, Aug. 30, 1916, against St. Louis AL (4–0); June 3, 1918, against Detroit AL (5–0). Led league in 1914 with 1.01 ERA, an ML record for 200 innings or more. Two World Series, 1915, 1916: 2 games, 2 complete, 2–0, 1.00 ERA, 9 strikeouts in 18 innings.

LESNEVICH, GUS boxing: b. Feb. 22, 1915, Cliffside Park, N.J.; d. Feb. 28, 1964. Lesnevich lost two close 15-round decisions to Billy Conn in his quest for the light-heavyweight title, Nov. 17, 1939, and June 5, 1940. He won the NBA version of the title on May 22, 1941, by beating Anton Chistoforidis in 15 rounds and became recognized as world champ with a 15-round decision over Tami Mauriello on Aug. 26 of that year.

Lesnevich entered the Coast Guard in 1942 and his title was frozen for the duration of the war. He lost it to Freddie Mills on July 26, 1948, in a 15-round decision. In 1949, he tried for the vacant light-heavy title, losing to Joey Maxim, and a little later fought Ezzard Charles for the heavyweight title but was KOed in 7 rounds. That was his last fight.

He was Fighter of the Year in 1947.

LEVINSKY, BATTLING boxing: b. Barney Lebrowitz, June 10, 1891, Philadelphia; d. Feb. 12, 1949. His record: 65 wins, 24 by KO; 19 losses, 4 by KO; 12 draws, 167 no-decisions. Levinsky won the light heavyweight title, Oct. 24, 1916, with a 12-round decision over Jack Dillon. He lost it, Sept. 12, 1920, when he was KOed by Georges Carpentier, of France, in 4 rounds. (Earlier in the year Levinsky had lost by a foul to Boy McCormick, of England, but McCormick never claimed the title and retired shortly afterward.) On Jan. 23, 1922, Levinsky lost the American title to Gene Tunney on a 12-round decision.

Helms Hall of Fame, Boxing Hall of Fame.

LEWIS, ED "STRANGLER" wrestling: b. Robert Friedrich, 1890, Madison, Wis.; d. Aug. 7, 1966. When professional wrestling was a genuine sport, Lewis compiled an incredible record, winning more than 6,200 matches while losing only 33. He earned somewhere around $4 million, often getting guarantees of more than $100,000 for a single match. He won the heavyweight championship in 1920 and lost it to Gus Sonnenberg in 1932.

Lewis became a professional wrestler at fourteen, adopting the name Ed Lewis to keep his parents from finding out. The "Strangler" came later, from his deadly use of the headlock. Lewis once offered to meet Jack Dempsey in a wrestling-boxing match, but Dempsey didn't accept the challenge.

LEWIS, HARRY boxing: b. Sept. 16, 1886, New York City; d. Feb. 22, 1956. His record: 90 wins, 42 by KO; 16 losses, 1 by KO; 11 draws, 56 no-decisions. Though he never held a title, Lewis is ranked among the top 10 welterweights of all time.

LEWIS, "TED" (Edward M.) baseball: b. Dec. 25, 1872, Machynlleth, Wales; d. May 24, 1936. Bat, throw R; pitcher. Boston NL, 1896–1900; Boston AL, 1901. Six years, 94–64, 3.53 ERA; 21–12 in 1897, 26–8 in 1898.

LEWIS, WILLIAM H. football: b. Nov. 30, 1868, Berkeley, Va.; d. Jan. 1, 1949. Amherst center, 1888–91; Harvard, 1892–93; All-American, 1892–93. Lewis, the son of former slaves, came to New England with his family as a youth. He was the first Negro All-American and probably the first Negro to captain a college team (he was temporary captain for the Harvard-Princeton game in 1893). He was also the first Negro admitted to the American Bar Association, in 1911; there was not another until 1943.

Rather small even for his day, at 170 pounds, Lewis was exceptionally fast and was a keen student of football. He surprised coaches and teammates by ranging widely from his defensive center position to make tackles on the flanks and in the backfield.

LEWIS, WILLIE boxing: b. May 21, 1884, New York City; d. May 17, 1949. His record: 81 wins, 57 by KO; 16 losses, 9 by KO; 14 draws, 44 no-decisions. A clever welterweight and middleweight, Lewis often fought men much heavier than himself, which helps account for the number of KOs he suffered. He never got a title fight.

LINDHEIMER, BENJAMIN F. horse racing: b. Oct. 11, 1890, Chicago; d. June 5, 1960. Lindheimer helped Chicago remain a major horse-racing city by buying Washington Park in 1935 and Arlington Park in 1941, refurbishing both. His major contributions as a track-owner were to emphasize comfort for the spectator and boost prize money for second- and third-place finishes. He was named Horseman of the Year by the Jockey Guild in 1955 and by the Horsemen's Benevolent and Protective Association in 1957.

LINDSEY, MORTIMER J. bowling: b. Dec. 20, 1888, Newark, N.J.; d. May 16, 1959. Twice a member of the ABC tournament champion team, in 1912 and 1914, Lindsey won the ABC all-events in 1919 and had four 1900s and a forty-six-year ABC tourney average of 192.
American Bowling Congress Hall of Fame.

LIPSCOMB, "BIG DADDY" (Gene) football: b. Aug. 9, 1931, Detroit; d. May 10, 1963. Defensive tackle, Los Angeles Rams, 1953–55; Baltimore Colts, 1956–60; Pittsburgh Steelers, 1961–62; All-Pro, 1958–59. One of the few players to make it in pro football without college experience, Lipscomb stood 6'6", weighed about 290, and was exceptionally quick and agile for his size.
His death, allegedly from an overdose of heroin, stirred controversy, many of his teammates insisting that Lipscomb had been afraid of needles and had always refused to take shots of pain-killer.

LIPSCOMB, PAUL W. football: b. Jan. 13, 1923, Benton, Ill.; d. Aug. 20, 1964. Tennessee tackle. Green Bay Packers, 1945–49; Washington Redskins, 1950–54; Chicago Bears, 1954.

LISTON, "SONNY" (Charles) boxing: b. 1932 (?) near Little Rock, Ark.; d. about Dec. 29, 1970. His record: 47 wins, 37 by KO; 4 losses, 2 by KO. Liston won the heavyweight championship with a 1st-round KO of Floyd Patterson on Sept. 25, 1962. After again KOing Patterson in the 1st round in a rematch, Liston lost the title to Cassius Clay on Feb. 25, 1964, when he failed to come out for the 7th round because of an injured shoulder. In a rematch, Liston suffered the quickest KO in heavyweight-title history, at one minute of the 1st round.

LITTLE, W. LAWSON, JR. golf: b. June 23, 1910, Newport, R.I.; d. Feb. 1, 1968. Little won both the U.S. and British Amateur championships in 1934 and defended both titles successfully in 1935, an astonishing feat in match play. Only two other golfers (Bobby Jones and Harold Hilton) had ever won both titles in the same year. Little turned pro in 1936. He won the Canadian Open that year. In 1940, he won the U.S. Open in an 18-hole playoff with Gene Sarazen after both finished the regulation 72 holes with 287 scores.

Helms Hall of Fame, Professional Golfers Association Hall of Fame.

LLOYD, MARION (Mrs. Joseph Vince) fencing: b. April 16, 1906, Brooklyn; d. Nov. 2, 1969. National foil champ in 1928 and 1931, she was a three-time Olympics competitor and was the only American woman to reach the semifinals twice in foils, in 1928 and 1936.

LLOYD, "POP" (John H.) baseball: b. April 25, 1884, Palatka, Fla.; d. March 19, 1964. Bat L, throw R; shortstop, first-second base. Negro leagues: Cuban X Giants, 1906; Philadelphia Giants, 1907–09; Leland Giants, 1910; Lincoln Giants (New York), 1911–13; Chicago American Giants, 1914–17. Player-manager, Brooklyn Royal Giants, Columbus Buckeyes, Bacharach Giants, Hilldale Club, Lincoln Giants, 1918–31.

Lloyd was known as the Black Wagner—and Honus Wagner felt honored by the comparison, which was apt. Like Wagner, Lloyd was a big man, with enormous hands that scooped up dirt and pebbles every time he fielded a grounder; he was an excellent hitter, particularly in the clutch; and despite his size, he was deceptively fast and a dangerous baserunner. As usual with Negro league players, complete figures are not available, except for published statements that Lloyd hit .475 in 1911 and .418 in 1923. It is certain that he hit cleanup for the Lincoln Giants—who beat the Philadelphia Phils (and Grover Cleveland Alexander), 9–2, in a 1913 exhibition—and for the American Giants, one of the top Negro teams of the period.

He was also highly rated as a manager, largely for his ability to inspire self-confidence in younger players.

LOBEL, LOUIS dog racing: b. 1911(?), Chelsea, Mass.; d. Nov. 9, 1967. An All–New England tackle at Boston University, Lobel helped build up dog racing as director and general counsel of Wonderland Track, Revere, Massachusetts, and was one of the founders of the Atlantic Seaboard Circuit.

He was long a national vice-president of the American Greyhound Track Operators Association.
Greyhound Hall of Fame.

LOBERT, "HANS" (John B.) baseball: b. Oct. 18, 1881, Wilmington, Del.; d. Sept. 14, 1968. Bat, throw R; third base, shortstop. Pittsburgh NL, 1903; Chicago NL, 1905; Cincinnati NL, 1906–10; Philadelphia NL, 1911–14; New York NL, 1915–17. Fourteen years, 1,317 games, 316 stolen bases, .274 BA; hit .300 in 1913.
He managed Philadelphia NL, 1938 (part), 1942: 42–111, .275.

LOCKE, ROLAND A. ("Gipper") track: b. 1903(?), N. Platte, Nebr.; d. Dec. 22, 1952. Representing Nebraska, Locke won the NCAA 100- and 220-yard-dash titles in 1926; his time of 20.6 in the 220 was a world record until 1935, as was his 200-meter time of 20.6, also set in 1926. Both marks were broken by Jesse Owens.

LOFTUS, THOMAS J. baseball: b. Nov. 15, 1856, Jefferson City, Mo.; d. April 16, 1910. Bat R; outfield. St. Louis NL, 1877; St. Louis AA, 1883. Two years, 9 games, .182 BA.
Managed Milwaukee UA, 1884; Cleveland AA, 1888–89; Cincinnati NL, 1890–91; Chicago NL, 1900–01; Washington AL, 1902–03: 455–583, .438.

LOMBARDI, VINCENT T. football: b. June 11, 1913, Brooklyn; d. Sept. 3, 1970. A guard at Fordham on the great 1935–36 lines, for which the name The Seven Blocks of Granite was revived, Lombardi was a high-school teacher and coach before becoming an assistant at Fordham and then at the U.S. Military Academy. In 1954 he became offensive coach for the New York Giants.
In 1959 he took an unenviable job as head coach for the Green Bay Packers, who had had a 1–10–1 record, their worst ever, the previous season. But Lombardi produced a 7–5 team his first year, a division champion in his second, and NFL champions in 1961–62 and 1965–67, which was the only time since the NFL playoff system began that a team has won three titles in a row. The Packers easily won the first two Super Bowls, pitting the NFL against the AFL. After the 1967 title and 1968 Super Bowl victory, Lombardi retired from coaching but remained as general manager of the Packers for a year. In 1969 he took on another rebuilding job as head coach, general manager, and vice-president of the Washington Redskins. They had a 7–5–2 record in his only season there, their first winning season in fourteen years.
Lombardi, whose slogan was, "Winning isn't a big thing; it's the only

thing," had a .738 percentage as a professional coach, on a 96–34–6 record. He died of cancer. Professional Football Hall of Fame.

LOMBARDO, THOMAS A. ("Lombo") football: b. April 17, 1922, Missouri; d. Sept. 24, 1950. Army quarterback-halfback. He captained the powerful 1944 team that featured Glenn Davis and Doc Blanchard. Lombardo was killed in Korea.

LONG, HERMAN C. ("Germany") baseball: b. April 13, 1866, Chicago; d. Sept. 17, 1909. Bat L, throw R; shortstop. Kansas City AA, 1889; Boston NL, 1890–92; Detroit AL, New York AL, 1903; Philadelphia NL, 1904. Sixteen years, 1,872 games, 2,124 hits, 1,455 runs, 1,052 RBI, 534 stolen bases, .277 BA; hit .324 in 1894, .316 in 1895, .343 in 1896, .322 in 1897. Led NL in runs, 1893 (149); in home runs, 1900 (12).

LOVE, HARVEY rowing: b. Aug. 18, 1910, Seattle, Wash.; d. Jan. 14, 1963. Love was coxswain of the University of Washington crews that won the Pacific Coast Regatta, 1930–31. He coached Harvard, 1952–62; his Harvard crews won the Adams Cup, 1956–59, and the Compton Cup, 1952, 1954–55, 1958–59.

LOVETT, THOMAS J. baseball: b. Dec. 7, 1863, Providence, R.I.; d. March 20, 1928. Bat R; pitcher. Philadelphia AA, 1885; Brooklyn AA, 1889; Brooklyn NL, 1890–91, 1893; Boston NL, 1894. Six years, 88–59, 3.94 ERA; 23–19 in 1891. No-hitter, June 22, 1891, against New York NL (4–0). Led NL in percentage, 1890 (30–11, .732).

LOWE, "BOBBY" (Robert L.) baseball: b. July 10, 1868, Pittsburgh; d. Dec. 8, 1951. Bat, throw R; second base, outfield, third base. Boston NL, 1890–1901; Chicago NL, 1902–03; Pittsburgh NL, 1904; Detroit AL, 1904–07. Eighteen years, 1,820 games, 302 stolen bases .273 BA; hit .346 in 1894, .309 in 1897. Lowe was the first man to hit 4 home runs in a game, on May 30, 1894, when he also hit 2 in an inning. Until 1932, he was the only man to hit 4 consecutive home runs in a game. He had three other memorable days: On June 11, 1891, he went 6-for-6, with a double and a home run, scoring 4 runs; on June 18, 1894, he reached first base safely 3 times in an inning; on May 3, 1895, he scored 6 runs in a game, tying the NL record.

LUDERUS, FREDERICK W. baseball: b. Sept. 12, 1885, Milwaukee; d. Jan. 4, 1961. Bat L, throw R; first base. Chicago NL, 1909–10; Philadelphia NL, 1911–20. Twelve years, 1,346 games, .277 BA; hit .301 in 1911, .315 in 1915. He tied an NL record for most assists by a first baseman, 7, on Aug. 22, 1918.

In his only World Series, 1915, Luderus was virtually the Phillies' only hitter as they lost to Boston in 5 games. He hit .438—the team average was .184—and drove in 6 of their 10 runs.

LUMLEY, HARRY G. baseball: b. Sept. 29, 1880, Forest City, Pa.; d. May 22, 1938. Outfield. Brooklyn NL, 1904–10. Seven years, 730 games, .274 BA; hit .324 in 1906. Led NL in triples (18) and home runs (9) in 1904; in slugging (.477) in 1906.
A severe shoulder injury ended his career prematurely.
He managed Brooklyn NL, 1909: 55–98, .359.

LUMMUS, "JACK" (John) football: b. Oct. 22, 1916, Ennis, Tex.; d. March 8, 1945. Baylor end. New York Giants, 1941. He was killed while leading a tank attack at Iwo Jima.

LUNDGREN, CARL L. baseball: b. Feb. 16, 1880, Marengo, Ill.; d. Aug. 21, 1934. Bat, throw R; pitcher. Chicago NL, 1902–09. Eight years, 90–55, 2.42 ERA; 19 shutouts.

LUQUE, "DOLF" (Adolfo) baseball: b. Aug. 4, 1890, Havana, Cuba; d. July 3, 1957. Bat, throw R; pitcher. Boston NL, 1914–15; Cincinnati NL, 1918–29; Brooklyn NL, 1930–31; New York NL, 1932–35. Twenty years, 193–179, 3.24 ERA; 26 shutouts. In relief, mostly during his last five seasons, he was 33–16, with a 2.86 ERA and 28 saves. Led NL in losses, 1922 (13–23); in wins and percentage (27–8, .771), ERA (1.93), and shutouts (6) in 1923; in ERA, 1925 (2.63); in shutouts, 1921 (3) and 1925 (4). Two World Series, 1919, 1933: 1–0, 0.00 ERA in 9⅓ innings.

LUSH, JOHN C. baseball: b. Oct. 8, 1885, Williamsport, Pa.; d. Nov. 18, 1946. Bat, throw L; pitcher. Philadelphia NL, 1904–07; St. Louis NL, 1907–10. Seven years, 66–87, 2.68 ERA; 16 shutouts. Sometimes an outfielder or pinch-hitter.

LYNCH, "JACK" (John H.) baseball: b. Feb. 5, 1855, New York City; d. April 20, 1923. Bat, throw R; pitcher. Buffalo NL, 1881; New York AA, 1883–87; Brooklyn-Baltimore AA, 1890. Seven years, 110–104, 3.69 ERA; 23–21 in 1885, 20–30 in 1886. Led AA in percentage, 1884 (37–14, .725).

LYNCH, JOSEPH boxing: b. Nov. 30, 1898, New York City; d. Sept. 1, 1965. His record: 42 wins, 29 by KO; 13 losses; 15 draws, 64 no-decisions. Lynch won the bantamweight title, Dec. 22, 1920, in a 15–round fight with Pete Herman. He lost it to Herman, June 15, 1921. However, after Herman had lost the championship to Johnny Buff, Lynch regained it by knocking out

Buff in 14 rounds, July 10, 1922. He held it until Dec. 19, 1924, when Eddie Martin beat him in 15 rounds.
Helms Hall of Fame.

LYONS, DENNIS P. A. baseball: b. March 12, 1866, Cincinnati; d. Jan. 2, 1929. Bat, throw R; third base. Providence NL, 1885; Philadelphia AA, 1886–90; St. Louis AA, 1891; New York NL, 1892; Pittsburgh NL, 1893–94; St. Louis NL, 1895; Pittsburgh NL, 1896–97. He hit .367 in 1887, .329 in 1889, .354 in 1890, .306 in 1893, .307 in 1896. Led AA in slugging, 1890 (.531).
Lyons went 6-for-6, scoring 4 runs, on April 26, 1887.

M

MACK, CONNIE baseball: b. Cornelius A. McGillicuddy, Dec. 22, 1862, East Brookfield, Mass.; d. Feb. 8, 1956. Bat, throw R; catcher. Washington NL, 1886–89; Buffalo PL, 1890; Pittsburgh NL, 1891–96. Eleven years, 723 games, .245 BA.

In 1930 Mack was given the Edward W. Bok Prize for distinguished service to Philadelphia. The honor is usually given only to artists, philanthropists, scientists, and educators. But Mr. Mack's Athletics had just won their 7th pennant and 4th world championship. They repeated as pennant winners and world champions in 1930, and they won the pennant again in 1931—their last under Mack, though he managed them for another nineteen seasons.

Mack began the longest managerial career in the history of baseball late in the 1894 season, when he became playing manager of the Pittsburgh NL team; he was there through 1896. In 1901 he became manager of the Philadelphia team in the AL, which had just won major-league status; he remained there for fifty years, becoming chief owner and president of the team. Mack set records for most years managing, 53, most years with one team and in one league, 50, most games won, 3,776, and most lost, 4,025 (a .484 percentage). In World Series play his teams won 24 (4th) and lost 19 (3rd), a .558 percentage (3rd). His teams won pennants in 1902, 1905, 1910–11, 1913–14, 1929–31, and world championships in 1910–11, 1913, and 1929–30. He also had more last-place finishes than any other manager.

Indeed, Mack had an unusual record. Twice he built up great teams, only to sell many of his best players. After his club lost the World Series in 4 games to the "Miracle Braves" in 1914, Mack sold a number of stars, including the "$100,000 infield." Seven times during the next ten years, the As finished last. In 1925 they again became contenders, but the Yankees were too powerful for them until 1929. After the third straight pennant, in 1931, Mack again broke up a great team by selling players: In a three-year period he sold, among others, Lefty Grove, Jimmy Dykes, Jimmy Foxx, Max Bishop, Mickey Cochrane, and Roger Cramer. During the last nineteen years of his managership, they finished in the 2nd division 16 times, in the cellar 10 times.

To a generation of baseball fans, Mack was a tall, slender man, in hat and suit, standing in the dugout and signaling to his players by waving a scorecard. He never came onto the field to argue with an umpire; his patience with players was also almost unlimited. He was quiet, imperturbable—but his players, and all but a very few good friends, always called him "Mr. Mack."

Baseball Hall of Fame.

MacLAUGHLIN, DONALD C., JR. lacrosse, soccer: b. May 21, 1941, Baltimore; d. Jan. 2, 1966. MacLaughlin was an All-American lacrosse player at Navy in 1963; he was also a fine soccer player. He won the Academy Athletic Association Sword, the highest athletic award given at the school.

He was killed when his plane crashed in Vietnam.

MADDOX, NICHOLAS baseball: b. Nov. 9, 1886, Gavanstown, Md.; d. Nov. 27, 1954. Pitcher. Pittsburgh NL, 1907–10. Four years, 44–20, 2.29 ERA; 23–8 in 1908. No-hitter, Sept. 20, 1907, against Brooklyn NL (2–1). One World Series, 1909: 1–0, 1.00 ERA

MADIGAN, "SLIP" (Edward P.) football: b. 1896(?); d. Oct. 10, 1966. A center at Notre Dame (1919), Madigan in 1921 went to St. Mary's of California to build up football. The school had only seventy-one students; it had dropped football in 1920, after losing 127–0 to California the previous season. Coaching there through 1940, the flamboyant Madigan had a 108–41–11 record. His unbeaten 1929 team was unscored on until the last game of the season, a 31–6 win over Oregon. He also had a unbeaten team in 1926. Madigan was probably the highest-paid coach in the country during the twenties; he got a share of gate receipts, in addition to his salary.

He also coached at Iowa, 1943–44.

Helms Hall of Fame.

MAGEE, "JACK" (John J.) track: b. Jan. 12, 1883, Newark, N.J.; d. Jan. 1, 1968. Magee was track coach at Bowdoin College, Maine, 1914–55. His teams won 20 state championships, including 9 in a row. He was U.S. Olympic track coach in 1924, 1928, and 1932 but turned down the job in 1936 because he felt the games should not be held in Nazi Germany. An all-weather track at Bowdoin has been named for him.
Helms Hall of Fame.

MAGEE, "LEE" (Leo C.) baseball: b. Leopold C. Hoernschemeyer, June 4, 1889, Cincinnati; d. March 14, 1966. Sw. hit, throw R; outfield, infield. St. Louis NL, 1911–14; Brooklyn Fed L, 1915; New York AL, 1916–17; St. Louis AL, 1917; Cincinnati NL, 1918; Brooklyn NL, Chicago NL, 1919. Nine years, 1,034 games, .275 BA. Hit .323 in 1918.
Magee had 4 assists in a game on June 28, 1914, tying an ML record for outfielders.

MAGEE, "SHERRY" (Sherwood R.) baseball: b. Aug. 6, 1884, Clarendon, Pa.; d. March 13, 1929. Bat, throw R; outfield. Philadelphia NL, 1904–14; Boston NL, 1915–17; Cincinnati NL, 1917–19. Sixteen years, 2,084 games, 441 stolen bases (9th), .291 BA; 2,168 hits; hit .328 in 1907, .306 in 1912, .306 in 1913, .314 in 1914. Led NL in RBI, 1907 (85); in BA (.331), slugging (.507), runs (110), and RBI (123) in 1910; in slugging (.513), RBI (104), and doubles (38) in 1914; in RBI, 1918 (76). One World Series, 1919: 2 games, .500 BA (1-for-2).

MAHAFFEY, LEE ROY baseball: b. Feb. 9, 1903, Belton, S.C.; d. July 23, 1969. Bat, throw R; pitcher. Pittsburgh NL, 1926–27; Philadelphia AL, 1930–35; St. Louis AL, 1936. Nine years, 67–49, 5.01 ERA. One World Series, 1931: 0–0, 9.00 ERA in 1 inning of relief.

MALLORY, MOLLA (Bjurstedt) tennis: b. 1893(?), Oslo, Norway; d. Nov. 21, 1959. Molla Bjurstedt was Norway's top woman tennis player when she came to the United States to visit a relative in 1914. She liked the country so much that she got a job and became a permanent resident. She set a record by winning the U.S. outdoor singles title 8 times, 1915–18, 1920–22, and 1926. One of her most famous matches came during the 1921 tournament, when she met the celebrated Suzanne Lenglen at Forest Hills. Miss Lenglen had beaten her earlier in the year, in Paris, and Mrs. Mallory wanted revenge. It came in an unexpected way. She won the first set handily, 6–2, and shortly after the second set began, Miss Lenglen burst into tears and left the court, defaulting because, she said, she was ill.
A believer in a hard, steady, offensive game, Mrs. Mallory also won the indoor singles, 1915–16, 1918, and 1921–22; she teamed with Eleanora

Sears to win the outdoor doubles, 1916–17, and with Marie Wagner to win the indoor doubles in 1916; she and Bill Tilden won the outdoor mixed doubles in 1922–23 and the indoor mixed doubles in 1921–22; she and Irving C. Wright won the outdoor title in 1917.
Helms Hall of Fame, Tennis Hall of Fame.

MALLORY, WILLIAM N. football: b. Nov. 20, 1901, Memphis, Tenn.; d. Feb. 19, 1945. Yale fullback; captain, All-American, 1923.
National Football Foundation Hall of Fame.

MALONE, "PAT" (Perce L.) baseball: b. Sept. 25, 1902, Altoona, Pa.; d. May 13, 1943. Sw. hit, throw R; pitcher. Chicago NL, 1928–34; New York AL, 1935–37. Ten years, 134–92, 3.74 ERA; 1,024 strikeouts, 16 shutouts in 1,915 innings. In relief, 27–16, 3.39 ERA, 26 saves. Led NL in wins (22–10), strikeouts (166), and shutouts (5) in 1929; in wins (20–9) and complete games (22) in 1930. Three World Series, 1929, 1932, 1936: 0–3, 3.05 ERA.

MAMAUX, ALBERT L. baseball: b. May 30, 1894, Pittsburgh; d. Jan. 2, 1963. Bat, throw R; pitcher. Pittsburgh NL, 1913–17; Brooklyn NL, 1918–23; New York AL, 1924. Ten years, 76–67, 2.90 ERA; 625 strikeouts, 15 shutouts, in 1,293 innings; 21–8 in 1915, 21–15 in 1916. In relief, 14–9, 2.79 ERA, 10 saves. One World Series, 1920: 0–0, 4.50 ERA in 4 innings.

MANDELL, SAMMY boxing: b. Samuel Mandella, Feb. 5, 1904, Rockford, Ill.; d. Nov. 8, 1967. His record: 82 wins, 28 by KO; 17 losses, 5 by KO; 8 draws, 60 no-decisions, 1 no-contest. Mandell won the world lightweight title on July 3, 1926, by outpointing Rocky Kansas in 10 rounds. He lost it to Al Singer on July 17, 1930, on a KO at 1:32 of the 1st round.

MANN, LESLIE baseball: b. Nov. 18, 1893, Lincoln, Nebr.; d. Jan. 14, 1962. Bat, throw R; outfield. Boston NL, 1913–14; Chicago Fed L, 1915; Chicago NL, 1916–19; Boston NL, 1919–20; St. Louis NL, 1921–23; Cincinnati NL, 1923; Boston NL, 1924–27; New York NL, 1927–28. Sixteen years, 1,493 games, .282 BA; hit .306 in 1915, .328 in 1921. Led Fed L in triples, 1915 (19). Two World Series, 1914, 1918: 9 games, .241 BA.

MANNING, "JACK" (John E.) baseball: b. Dec. 20, 1853, Braintree, Mass.; d. Aug. 15, 1929. Bat, throw R; outfield, pitcher, infield. National Association, Boston, 1873; Baltimore, Hartford, 1874; Boston, 1875. Three years, 153 games, .282 BA; as pitcher, 17–17.
   Boston NL, 1876; Cincinnati NL, 1877; Boston NL, 1878; Cincinnati NL, 1880; Buffalo NL, 1881; Philadelphia NL, 1883–85; Baltimore AA, 1886. Nine years, 682 games, .257 BA; as pitcher, 19–9, 3.53 ERA.

MARA, TIMOTHY football: b. July 29, 1887, New York City; d. Feb. 16, 1959. Mara, a bookmaker with a natural interest in sports, set out one day in 1925 to try to buy a share of boxer Gene Tunney. He ended up spending $500 for a National Football League franchise for New York City. He named his team the Giants, after John McGraw's popular baseball club. Mara was an excellent promoter, and the strength of his franchise in the nation's biggest city helped the NFL on its way to prosperity. Despite financial losses in the early years, Mara made sacrifices to build friends and fans for his team. The Giants frequently turned game profits over to charities, and Mara started the idea of giving discounts on blocks of tickets to lodges and other organizations, for resale to their members. A likeable, expansive man, Mara was known for keeping his word; it was typical of him that he kept one coach, Steve Owen, for twenty-two years with nothing more than a verbal agreement and handshake.

Professional Football Hall of Fame.

MARANVILLE, "RABBIT" (Walter J. V.) baseball: b. Nov. 11, 1891, Springfield, Mass.; d. Jan. 5, 1954. Bat, throw R; second base, shortstop. Boston NL, 1912–20; Pittsburgh NL, 1921–24; Brooklyn NL, 1926; St. Louis NL, 1927–28; Boston NL, 1929–33, 1935. Twenty-three years (5th), 2,670 games (7th), 10,078 at-bats (5th), 2,605 hits, 2,020 singles, 291 stolen bases, .258 BA.

He has the lowest BA of any nonpitcher in the Hall of Fame, and some teams refused to sign him because they thought he was too small (5'5", 150 pounds), but Maranville holds the NL record for most seasons played, and his nineteen seasons and 2,153 games at shortstop are also ML records. He holds ML records for most chances, 12,471, and most assists, 7,338, at shortstop, and NL records for most putouts, 5,133, most years leading in putouts, 6, and most years 500 or more assists, 5. Two World Series, 1914, 1928: 8 games, .308 BA.

Baseball Hall of Fame.

MARCIANO, ROCKY boxing: b. Rocco Marchegiano, Sept. 1, 1923, Brockton, Mass.; d. Aug. 30, 1969. His official record: 49 wins, 43 by KO; no losses. Marciano came to boxing at a comparatively late age and became something like a self-made champion, with the help of manager Al Weill and trainer Charlie Goldman. He was the only heavyweight champion to retire without having lost a professional fight.

Slow afoot, sometimes even clumsy, Marciano had tremendous punching ability, which earned him the nickname The Brockton Blockbuster. Just as important was his ability to absorb punches. He won all 49 of his professional fights, 43 of them by KOs. In many of those victories, he was well behind on points and taking severe physical beatings before coming up with the KO. (Archie Moore, one of his KO victims, compared himself to a matador, Marciano to a bull.) But his boxing ability is sometimes underrated. Though he often got hit, he didn't often get hit squarely. Under Goldman's guidance, he learned how to slip punches, roll with them, or catch them on his elbows.

After 42 victories, the big one an 8-round TKO of Joe Louis, Marciano won the heavyweight title on Sept. 28, 1952, by KOing Jersey Joe Walcott in the 13th round. He KOed Walcott in the 1st round of a rematch, then defended the title successfully 5 more times, winning 4 on KOs, before retiring in 1956.

Helms Hall of Fame, Boxing Hall of Fame.

MARINO, TONY boxing: b. 1912, Pittsburgh, Pa.; d. Feb. 1, 1937. His record: 26 wins, 7 by KO; 12 losses, 2 by KO; 2 draws. Marino became bantamweight champion by KOing Baltazar Sangchili in the 14th round on June 29, 1936. He lost it, Aug. 31, on a 13th-round KO by Sixto Escobar. He died of a cerebral hemorrhage the day after losing an 8-round decision to Indian Quintana.

MARSHALL, GEORGE PRESTON football: b. Oct. 11, 1896, Charleston, W.Va.; d. Aug. 9, 1969. Marshall headed a syndicate that paid $5,000 for the Boston Redskin franchise in the NFL in 1932. One of his first moves as an owner was to suggest that the league split into two divisions, each to have its own champion, setting up a championship game that would be the equivalent of baseball's World Series. The idea was approved and has been important ever since in keeping fans interested in pro football.

Boston, after four so-so years, won the Eastern Division title in 1936. Unhappy with poor attendance in Boston, Marshall moved the championship game to New York's Polo Grounds. The Redskins lost to Green Bay, 21–6. Marshall moved the team to Washington the following season and signed Sammy Baugh, the great passer from Texas Christian who led the team to 5 division titles and 2 NFL championships, in 1937 and 1942.

Marshall promoted his team the way he promoted his chain of laundries. His second wife, Corinne Griffith, of silent-movie fame, wrote the lyrics to pro football's first fight song, and Marshall hired the sport's first marching band.

Professional Football Hall of Fame.

MARSHALL, THOMAS A. shooting: b. Mississippi; d. Aug. 18, 1922. The only man to win two Grand American Handicaps, in 1897 and 1899, he tied for the title in 1900 but lost the shootoff. He accomplished both victories without a miss.

American Trapshooting Hall of Fame.

MARSHMANN, "BOBBY" (Robert A.) auto racing: b. Sept. 24, 1936, Pottstown, Pa.; d. Dec. 3, 1964. Marshmann set an unofficial 1-lap speed record of 157.178 miles per hour at the Indianapolis Speedway in 1964. He was leading the race when forced out after 97 miles. During the year he qualified for every USAC championship race.

He died of burns suffered during a tire test run at the Phoenix International Raceway on Nov. 27, 1964.

MARTIN, "PEPPER" (John L.) baseball: b. Feb. 29, 1904, Temple, Okla.; d. March 5, 1965. Bat, throw R; outfield, third base. St. Louis NL, 1928, 1930–40, 1944. Thirteen years, 1,189 games, .298 BA; hit .300 in 1931, .316 in 1933, .309 in 1936. Led NL in runs (122) and stolen bases (26) in 1933; in stolen bases, 1934 (23) and 1936 (23). Three World Series, 1928, 1931, 1934: 15 games, 7 doubles (4th), 7 stolen bases (5th), .418 BA (1st), .636 slugging percentage (5th), 14 runs, 8 RBI. In 1931, he led the Cardinals to a 7-game triumph over Philadelphia by hitting .500 with 4 doubles, a home run, 5 stolen bases, 5 runs scored, and 5 RBI. In the 7-game victory over Detroit in 1934, he hit .355 and scored 8 runs.

"The Wild Hoss of the Osage" was twenty-seven before he really made it in the majors, but he almost immediately became a symbol of the St. Louis "Gashouse Gang." A kind of transplanted hobo, he spent his first few seasons riding freight cars to spring training so he could keep the expense money. His uniform was usually dirty and often tattered. As a third baseman, he fielded balls by stopping them with his chest, then picking them up and throwing to first. He wasn't graceful, but he was aggressive and he won games.

MASTERSON, BERNARD E. football: b. Aug. 10, 1911, Shenandoah, Iowa; d. May 16, 1963. Nebraska quarterback, Chicago Bears, 1934–40. In seven pro seasons he attempted 408 passes, completing 155, or 38 percent, for 3,372 yards and 33 TDs, averaging 8.26 yards per attempt.

MATHEWS, "BOBBY" (Robert T.) baseball: b. Nov. 21, 1851, Baltimore; d. April 17, 1898. Bat, throw R; pitcher. National Association, Ft. Wayne, 1871; Lord Baltimores, 1872; New York Mutuals, 1873–75. Five years, 132–111; 25–16 in 1872, 29–22 in 1873, 42–23 in 1874, 29–38 in 1875.

New York NL, 1876; Cincinnati NL, 1877; Providence NL, 1879, 1881; Boston NL, 1881–82; Philadelphia AA, 1883–87. Ten years, 166–136, 3.00

ERA; 21–34 in 1876, 30–13 in 1883, 30–18 in 1884, 30–17 in 1885. Occasionally played the outfield.

MATHEWSON, "CHRISTY" (Christopher) baseball: b. Aug, 12, 1880, Factoryville, Pa.; d. Oct. 7, 1925. Bat, throw R; pitcher. New York NL, 1900–16; Cincinnati NL, 1916. Seventeen years, 367 wins (4th), 186 losses, .664 percentage (8th), 2.13 ERA (5th), 634 games, 551 starts, 434 complete, 4,777⅓ innings (9th), 838 walks, 2,502 strikeouts (6th), 77 shutouts (3rd); 20–17 in 1902, 29–12 in 1904, 21–12 in 1906, 24–13 in 1911, 23–12 in 1912, 25–11 in 1913, and 24–13 in 1914. In relief, 26–9, 2.41 ERA, 27 saves. No-hitters, July 15, 1901, against St. Louis NL (5–0); June 13, 1905, against Chicago NL (1–0). Led NL in shutouts, 1902 (8); in strikeouts, 1903 (267); in victories (34–12) and strikeouts (212) in 1904; in victories and percentage (32–8, .800), ERA (1.27), strikeouts (206), and shutouts (8) in 1905; in victories (35–11), ERA (1.43), complete games (34), strikeouts (259), and shutouts (11) in 1908; in percentage (24–6, .800) and ERA (1.14) in 1909; in victories (27–9) and complete games (27) in 1910; in ERA, 1911 (1.99) and 1913 (2.06). Four World Series, 1905, 1911–13: 5 wins (4th), 5 losses (2nd), 1.15 ERA (7th), 11 starts (2nd), 10 complete (1st), 101⅔ innings (2nd), 10 walks, 48 strikeouts (8th), 4 shutouts (1st). In 1905, "Big Six" climaxed a great season by pitching 3 shutouts in the World Series, giving up just 14 hits and a walk while striking out 18 in his 27 innings, as the Giants beat Philadelphia 4 games to 1.

Mathewson was known for his "fadeaway" pitch—what would now be called a screwball—and for a "dry spitball," probably a knuckleball. He was also an excellent control pitcher: He set an NL record in 1913 by pitching 68 consecutive innings without issuing a walk. He holds the ML record for most years pitching 300 or more innings, 11. His 37 victories in 1908 is the modern NL record. In 1907 he shut out every other team in the league.

He managed Cincinnati NL, 1916 (part)–18 (part): 164–176, .482.

Serving in World War I, Mathewson was gassed, which helped cause his early death, from tuberculosis. He served as president of the Boston Braves from 1923 until his death, just before the 1925 World Series. During that series, players on both teams wore black armbands in mourning for him. Baseball Hall of Fame.

MATISI, "TONY" (Anthony F.) football: b. 1915(?); d. Aug. 26, 1969. Pittsburgh center; All-American, 1937. Detroit Lions, 1938.

MATTHEWS, "MATTY" (William R.) boxing: b. July 13, 1873, New York City; d. Dec. 6, 1948. His record: 47 wins, 14 by KO; 13 losses, 1 by KO; 17 draws, 17 no-decisions. Matthews lost his first attempt to win the welterweight title, Aug. 25, 1898, when he lost a 25-round decision to champion Mysterious Billy Smith. On Oct. 16, 1900, he won the title from Jim "Rube" Ferns in 15 rounds. He lost a rematch to Ferns on a 10th-round KO, May 24, 1901.

MATTHEWS, WID C. baseball: b. Oct. 20, 1896, Raleigh, Ill.; d. Oct. 5, 1965. Bat, throw L; outfield. Philadelphia AL, 1923; Washington AL, 1924–25. Three years, 192 games, .284 BA.

Matthews became well known as chief scout for Branch Rickey during the Dodgers' successful search for young talent in the 1940s.

He later became general manager of the Cubs and was the first general manager of the New York Mets.

MAUL, ALBERT J. ("Smiling Al") baseball: b. Oct. 9, 1865, Philadelphia; d. May 3, 1958. Bat, throw R; pitcher. Philadelphia UA, 1884; Philadelphia NL, 1887; Pittsburgh NL, 1888–89; Pittsburgh PL, 1890; Pittsburgh NL, 1891; Washington NL, 1893–97; Baltimore NL, 1897–98; Brooklyn NL, 1899; Philadelphia NL, 1900; New York NL, 1901. Fifteen years, 84–79, 4.43 ERA. Led NL in ERA, 1895 (2.45); in percentage, 1898 (20–6, .769).

MAULDIN, STANLEY H. football: b. Dec. 27, 1920, Amarillo, Tex.; d. Sept. 24, 1948. Texas tackle. Chicago Cardinals, 1946–48. Mauldin died of a heart attack shortly after a game.

MAUTHE, "PETE" J. L. football: b. July 8, 1890, DuBois, Pa.; d. Jan. 1, 1967. Penn State halfback. A fine kicker, Mauthe had a 51-yard field goal, by dropkick, in 1912.

National Football Foundation Hall of Fame.

MAY, GEORGE W. horseshoes: b. Feb. 21, 1889, Ironton, Ohio; d. June 5, 1969. May revolutionized horseshoe pitching when he decided there must be a way of getting ringers consistently. Previously, the idea had been simply to get near the stake, and a ringer was purely a matter of chance. May developed the so-called open style of pitching and won the national tournament in 1920, with 50 percent ringers, an unheard-of average at the time. He was also champion in the summer of 1923.

MAY, "JAKIE" (Frank S.) baseball: b. Nov. 25, 1895, Youngville, N.C.; d. June 3, 1970. Bat R. throw L; pitcher. St. Louis NL, 1917–21; Cincinnati NL, 1924–30; Chicago NL, 1931–32. Fourteen years, 72–95, 3.88 ERA. In relief, 24–22, 3.85 ERA, 19 saves. One World Series, 1932: 0–1, 11.57 ERA in 4⅔ innings.

MAYBURY, WILLIAM T. harness racing: b. 1894(?); d. Jan. 9, 1964. Maybury owned Maybury Farms, Dexter, Maine, which produced one of the great trotters of recent years, Galophone. Racing from 1954 through 1957, Galophone won $286,807. Major victories were in the 1954 Horseman's Stake and Arthur S. Tompkins Memorial, the 1956 American Trotting Championship and Gotham Free-for-All Trot, and the 1957 American Classic Invitational, Cleveland Trotting Derby, and Transylvania Free-for-All Trot.

MAYER, ERSKINE baseball: b. James Erskine, Jan. 16, 1891, Atlanta, Ga.; d. March 10, 1957. Bat, throw R; pitcher. Philadelphia NL, 1912–18; Pittsburgh NL, 1918–19; Chicago AL, 1919. Eight years, 91–70, 2.96 ERA; 12 shutouts; 21–19 in 1914, 21–15 in 1915. Two World Series, 1915, 1919: 0–1, 2.19 ERA.

MAYER, LOUIS B. horse racing: b. July 4, 1885, Minsk, Russia; d. Oct. 29, 1957. Better known as a movie producer, Mayer also owned horses that won a total of $2,404,240, and as a breeder he produced horses that won well over $8 million. When his stable of 60 was auctioned in 1947, it brought a record price, $1,553,500. His greatest horse was a filly, Busher, Horse of the Year in 1945, when she was top money-winner.

MAYS, REX auto racing: b. 1913(?), Glendale, Calif.; d. Nov. 6, 1949. Mays was national driving champion, 1940–41, Midwest champion, 1936–37. He finished second at Indianapolis in 1940 and 1941. During his career, he won about $20,000.
   Mays died in a crash at Del Mar, California, Race Track.
   Auto Racing Hall of Fame, Helms Hall of Fame.

McALEER, JAMES R. baseball: b. July 10, 1864, Youngstown, Ohio; d. April 29, 1931. Bat, throw R; outfield. Cleveland NL, 1889; Cleveland PL, 1890; Cleveland NL, 1891–98; Cleveland AL, 1901; St. Louis AL, 1902, 1907. Thirteen years, 1,021 games, .253 BA.
   McAleer managed Cleveland AL, 1901; St. Louis AL, 1902–09; Washington AL, 1910–11: 736–889, .453.

McAULIFFE, JACK boxing: b. March 24, 1866, Cork, Ireland; d. Nov. 5, 1937. His record: 41 wins, 9 by KO; 9 draws, 2 no-decisions. McAuliffe won 26 consecutive fights before KOing Billy Frazier in the 21st round, Oct. 29, 1886, for the American lightweight title. He fought Englishman Jem Carney for the vacant world title on Nov. 16, 1887. The fight was declared a draw after 74 rounds, when the crowd broke into the ring and made it impossible to continue. McAuliffe never fought for the world championship again but held the U.S. title until 1886, when he retired undefeated.
   Boxing Hall of Fame.

McCARTHY, "CAL" (Charles, Jr.) boxing: b. 1869, McClintockville, Pa.; d. Nov. 27, 1895. His record: 25 wins, 22 by KO; 2 losses, 1 by KO; 6 draws. After winning the amateur 110-pound title in 1887, McCarthy turned professional and was soon considered a strong claimant to the featherweight title, but his first loss, to George Dixon in 22 rounds on March 31, 1891, gave Dixon the vacant title.

McCARTHY, "CLEM" (Charles L.) broadcasting: b. Sept. 9, 1882, E. Bloomfield, N.Y.; d. June 4, 1962. After several years reporting races for newspapers, McCarthy became a broadcaster. He broadcast every Kentucky Derby, in his unmistakable gravel voice, from 1928 through 1950, first for NBC and later for CBS. McCarthy also did a number of major fights.

McCARTHY, "JACK" (John A.) baseball: b. March 26, 1869, Gilbertsville, Mass.; d. Sept. 11, 1931. Bat, throw L; outfield. Cincinnati NL, 1893–94; Pittsburgh NL, 1898–99; Chicago NL, 1900; Cleveland AL, 1901–03; Chicago NL, 1903–05; Brooklyn NL, 1906–07. Twelve years, 1,091 games, .287 BA; hit .305 in 1899.

McCARTHY, "TOMMY" (Thomas F. M.) baseball: b. July 24, 1864, Boston; d. Aug. 5, 1922. Bat, throw R; outfield. Boston UA, 1884; Boston NL, 1885; Philadelphia NL, 1886–87; St. Louis AA, 1888–91; Boston NL, 1892–95; Brooklyn NL, 1896. Thirteen years, 1,275 games, 467 stolen bases (3 years not included), .292 BA; hit .350 in 1890, .310 in 1891, .346 in 1893, .349 in 1894. Led league in stolen bases, 1890 (83).

A clever, aggressive player, McCarthy was one of the first to develop techniques of stealing signs, and he was a master of the hit-and-run. One of McCarthy's tricks resulted in a rule change: The sacrifice-fly rule originally said that a runner couldn't leave the base until the ball was held in the fielder's hand. With a runner on third, McCarthy, instead of catching the ball firmly, would juggle it from hand to hand while he ran into the infield with it.

His 53 assists in 1893 is an ML record for outfielders.

Baseball Hall of Fame.

McCARTY, GEORGE S. shooting: b. Dec. 9, 1868; d. March 18, 1945. McCarty was instrumental in building the Amateur Trapshooting Association's permanent home at Vandalia, Ohio, as ATA president, 1923–24. He spent nine months away from home, supervising the construction, and $5,000 of his own money on travel expenses while the work was going on. He was also instrumental in having the maximum handicap distance increased from 23 to 25 yards and in introducing the shooters' classification system still in use.

During his active shooting years, he won the New York Athletic Club amateur title in 1908–09 and 1921–22.

American Trapshooting Hall of Fame.

McCARTY, LUTHER boxing: b. March 20, 1892, Driftwood Creek, Nebr.; d. May 24, 1913. His record: 16 wins, all by KO; 1 loss, by KO; 8 no-decisions. The search for a "white champion" during Jack Johnson's exile from the United States revealed that McCarty was undoubtedly the best white heavyweight around. He easily won a 1912 tournament in California, designed to find a white hope, and on Jan. 1, 1913, he KOed Al Palzer, winner of a similar New York tournament, in the 18th round.

McCarty died in the ring less than five months later after being hit a light blow by Arthur Pelkey in the 1st round. Death was caused by a brain hemorrhage; an earlier injury probably contributed to the cause.

McCLUNG, "BUM" (Thomas Lee) football: b. March 26, 1870, Knoxville, Tenn.; d. April 25, 1936. Yale halfback; All-American, 1890–91; captain, 1891. A runner and kicker, he is credited with 150 TDs and more than 1,000 points in his career (a TD and a field goal each counted 5 points then). He was U.S. Treasurer, 1909–12.

National Football Foundation Hall of Fame.

McCORMICK, JAMES baseball: b. 1856, Paterson, N.J.; d. March 10, 1918. Bat, throw R; pitcher. Indianapolis NL, 1878; Cleveland NL, 1879–84; Cincinnati UA, 1884; Providence NL, 1885; Chicago NL, 1885–86; Pittsburgh NL, 1887. Ten years, 263–214, 2.43 ERA; 466 complete games (10th); 33 shutouts; 26–30 in 1881, 40–25 in 1884, 21–7 in 1885, 29–11 in 1886. Led NL in losses, 1879 (20–40); in wins, 1880 (45–28) and 1882 (36–30); in percentage (28–12, .700) and ERA (1.84) in 1883; in ERA, 1884 (2.37); in complete games, 1880 (72), 1881 (57), and 1882 (65).

He managed Cleveland NL, 1879–80: 74–92, .446.

McCORMICK, JAMES B. football: b. March 21, 1884, Boston; d. Jan. 7, 1959. Princeton fullback; All-American, 1905, 1907; 2nd team, 1906.

National Football Foundation Hall of Fame.

McCOY, AL boxing: b. Albert Rudolph, Oct. 23, 1894, Rosenhayn, N.J.; d. Aug. 29, 1966. His record: 50 wins, 22 by KO; 5 losses, 2 by KO; 8 draws, 83 no-decisions. McCoy won the middleweight title, April 7, 1914, by KOing George Chip in the 1st round. He held it until Nov. 14, 1917, when he was KOed by Mike O'Dowd in 6.

McCOY, "KID" (Charles) boxing: b. Norman Selby, Oct. 13, 1873, Rush County, Ind.; d. April 18, 1940. His record: 81 wins, 35 by KO; 6 losses,

2 by KO; 9 draws, 9 no-decisions. McCoy, Philadelphia Jack O'Brien, and Tommy Ryan were claimants for the middleweight title vacated by Bob Fitzsimmons in 1894, but they never fought one another at that weight, and there was no recognized champion until 1908. In the meantime, McCoy had fought Jack Root for the light-heavyweight title in the first championship fight after that division was created. Root beat him, April 22, 1903.
Helms Hall of Fame, Boxing Hall of Fame.

McCRACKEN, BRANCH basketball: b. June 9, 1908, Monrovia, Ind.; d. June 4, 1970. McCracken was Big Ten scoring champion, with 147 points in 12 games, in 1930 and was named an All-American forward.

That fall he became head coach at Ball State Teachers College, where he compiled a 93–41 record in seven seasons.

He then went to Indiana, where his teams became known as the Hurrying Hoosiers because of their running style of play. They won national championships in 1940 and 1953, with McCracken named Coach of the Year both times, and they were Big Ten champs in 1953–54 and 1958, co-champs in 1957. His record at Indiana, through the 1964–65 season, was 364–174.
Basketball Hall of Fame, Helms Hall of Fame

McCRACKEN, JACK D. basketball: b. June 11, 1911, Chickasha, Okla.; d. Jan. 5, 1958. "Jumping Jack," after starring at Northwest Missouri State (1933), played ten years of AAU basketball with the Denver Piggly-Wigglys, the Phillips 66ers, and the Denver Nuggets. He was named an AAU All-Star 7 times.
Basketball Hall of Fame, Helms Hall of Fame

McCUTCHEON, FLORETTA bowling: b. Doty, July 22, 1888, Ottumwa, Iowa; d. Feb. 2, 1967. Mrs. McCutcheon didn't start bowling until she was thirty-five. By the time she retired, she had rolled ten 300 games, eleven 800 series, and more than a hundred 700-plus series. What makes her record even more remarkable is the fact that most of her games, rolled in exhibitions or match play, were on alleys that were unfamiliar to her. From 1927 through 1936 she went on annual instructional-exhibition tours, averaging 201 for more than 8,000 games. She then settled down to teach in New York, later Chicago. She taught more than 250,000 men, women, and children.
Women's International Bowling Congress Hall of Fame.

McDONALD, "BABE" (Patrick J.) track: b. 1878(?), County Clare, Ireland; d. May 16, 1954. The 6'4", 250-pound McDonald was one of the several New York Police Department "whales" who competed in weight events. His list of championships spans more than two decades. He was Olympic shotput champion in 1912 and 56-pound-weight champion in 1920. He won the AAU outdoor shotput, 1911–12, 1914, 1919–20, 1922, and the indoor title, 1916–17 and 1919–21; he was outdoor 56-pound-weight titlist, 1911, 1914, 1919–21, 1926–29, and 1933.

Helms Hall of Fame.

McEWAN, JOHN J. football: b. 1893(?), Alexandria, Minn.; d. Aug. 9, 1970. Army center; All-American, 1914; 3rd team, 1915; 2nd team, 1916. Captained Army's unbeaten team in 1916.

McEwan coached Army, 1923–25, Holy Cross, 1926, and Oregon, 1927–29. He coached the Brooklyn Dodgers, 1933–34 (9–11–1).

National Football Foundation Hall of Fame.

McFARLAND, EDWARD W. baseball: b. Aug. 3, 1874, Cleveland; d. Nov. 28, 1959. Bat, throw R; catcher. Cleveland NL, 1893, St. Louis NL, 1896–97; Philadelphia NL, 1897–1901; Chicago AL, 1902–07; Boston AL, 1908. Fourteen years, 887 games, .275 BA; hit .333 in 1899, .305 in 1900. One World Series, 1906: 1 game, .000 BA.

His 7 assists in a 9-inning game, May 7, 1901, tied the AL record for catchers.

McFARLANE, WILLIE golf: b. June 29, 1889, Aberdeen, Scotland; d. Aug. 15, 1961. MacFarlane, who came to the United States permanently in 1921, won the U.S. Open in 1925 in one of the most dramatic battles that tournament has ever seen. Deadlocked with Bobby Jones at the end of the regulation 72 holes, MacFarlane beat him by one stroke in the 36-hole playoff.

McGANN, "DAN" (Dennis L.) baseball: b. July 15, 1872, Shelbyville, Ky.; d. Dec. 13, 1910. First base. Louisville NL, 1895; Boston NL, 1896; Baltimore NL, 1898; Brooklyn NL, Washington NL, 1899; St. Louis NL, 1900–01; Baltimore AL, 1902; New York NL, 1902–07; Boston NL, 1908. Thirteen years, 1,456 games, .284 BA; hit .301 in 1898, .300 in 1899, .308 in 1902. One World Series, 1905: 5 games, .235 BA.

McGann set the modern ML record by stealing 5 bases in a game on May 27, 1904.

McGEARY, MICHAEL H. baseball: b. 1851, Philadelphia; d. ?. Infield, catcher. National Association, Troy, 1871; Philadelphia As, 1872–74; Philadelphias, 1875. Five years, 250 games, .309 BA; hit .344 in 1872, .362 in 1874.

St. Louis NL, 1876–77; Providence NL, 1879–80; Cleveland NL, 1880–81; Detroit NL, 1882. Six years, 297 games, .243 BA.

McGeary managed Cleveland NL, 1881: 36–48, .429.

McGILL, "WILLIE" (William V.) baseball: b. Nov. 10, 1873, Atlanta, Ga.; d. Aug. 29, 1944. Throw L; pitcher. Cleveland PL, 1890; Cincinnati-Milwaukee AA, St. Louis AA, 1891; Cincinnati NL, 1892; Chicago NL, 1893–94; Philadelphia NL, 1895–96. Seven years, 71–74, 4.59 ERA; 20–15 in 1891.

McGINNITY, JOSEPH J. baseball: b. March 19, 1871, Rock Island, Ill.; d. Nov. 14, 1929. Bat, throw R; pitcher. Baltimore NL, 1899; Brooklyn NL, 1900; Baltimore AL, 1901–02; New York NL, 1902–08. Ten years, 242–142, 2.66 ERA; 465 games, 381 starts, 314 complete, 3,441 innings, 3,276 hits, 812 walks, 1,068 strikeouts, 23 shutouts; 24–20 in 1901, 20–18 in 1902, 21–15 in 1905. Led league in wins, 1899 (28–16); in wins and percentage, 1900 (28–8, .778); in complete games, 1901 (39); in wins (32–18) and complete games (44) in 1903; in percentage (33–8, .805) and ERA (1.61) in 1904; in wins, 1906 (26–12).

One World Series, 1905: 1–1, 0.00 ERA in 17 innings. McGinnity lost the 2nd game on 3 unearned runs but won the 4th, 1–0. He and Christy Mathewson pitched all but one inning of the 5-game series against Philadelphia without issuing an earned run.

It is ironic that McGinnity got his nickname, Iron Man, from the fact that he worked in an iron foundry before becoming a major-leaguer, because it fits his career so well. He's the only pitcher to win complete games in both ends of a doubleheader 3 times—and he did it in a single month, on Aug. 1, Aug. 8, and Aug. 31, 1903, giving up a total of just 10 runs in those 6 games. He holds the ML record for most years leading in games, 8; the modern NL record for most starts (48) and most innings pitched in a season (434), both set in 1903. In nine consecutive seasons he pitched more than 300 innings, twice more than 400.

Baseball Hall of Fame.

McGOVERN, JOHN E. football: b. 1890(?), Arlington, Minn.; d. Dec. 14, 1963. Minnesota quarterback; All-American, captain, 1909; 3rd team, 1910.

National Football Foundation Hall of Fame.

McGOVERN, "TERRY" (John Terrence) boxing: b. March 9, 1880, Johnstown, Pa.; d. Feb. 26, 1918. His record: 59 wins, 34 by KO; 4 losses, 2 by KO; 4 draws, 10 no-decisions. McGovern won the vacant world bantamweight title on Sept. 12, 1899, when he KOed Pedlar Palmer in the 1st round. By the end of the year, he had outgrown the class. In his first fight as a featherweight, he won that title, KOing George Dixon in the 8th round,

Jan. 9, 1901; it was his 9th consecutive KO, and he added 3 more to the string before it ended.

McGovern lost the title on Nov. 28, 1901, when Young Corbett KOed him in the 2nd round.

Helms Hall of Fame, Boxing Hall of Fame.

McGRATH, MATTHEW J. track: b. Dec. 20, 1876, Nenagh, Tipperary, Ireland; d. Jan. 29, 1941. McGrath came to the United States when he was twenty-one. He became one of the country's top weight-throwers, his career starting when he discovered Central Park and began throwing boulders around, until threatened with arrest. He won the 16-pound hammer throw in the 1912 Olympics. He was AAU hammer-throw champion in 1908, 1910, 1912, 1918, 1922, 1925–26, and 56-pound-weight champion in 1913, 1916, 1918, and 1922–25. His hammer throw of 173'7", in 1907, was a world record until 1909; in 1911, McGrath set another record of 187'4", which stood until 1913.

Helms Hall of Fame.

McGRAW, JOHN J. baseball: b. April 7, 1873, Truxton, N.Y.; d. Feb. 25, 1934. Bat L, throw R; third base, shortstop. Baltimore AA, 1891; Baltimore NL, 1892–99; St. Louis NL, 1900; Baltimore AL, 1901–02; New York NL, 1902–06. Sixteen years, 1,099 games, 1,024 runs, 436 stolen bases, .334 BA; hit .321 in 1893, .340 in 1894, .369 in 1895, .325 in 1897, .342 in 1898, .391 in 1899, .344 in 1900. Led the NL in runs, 1898 (143) and 1899 (140), and in walks, 1898 (112) and 1899 (124).

Voted baseball's greatest manager in a poll taken during baseball's centennial year, McGraw was a scrapper who fought with umpires and tongue-lashed players at times, but he inspired a fierce loyalty. Chief Meyers, the great Indian catcher, said of him, "What a great man he was! Oh, we held him in high esteem. We respected him in every way. . . . He fought for his ballplayers and protected them."

McGraw managed Baltimore NL in 1899 and Baltimore AL in 1901–02 (part) without much success. In the middle of the 1902 season, he was traded to the New York Giants, and he started a dynasty. With New York until ill health forced him to retire partway through the 1932 season, he won 10 pennants, 1904–05, 1911–13, 1917, and 1921–24, tying an ML record; his teams were 2nd 11 times and finished in the 2nd division only once. The 4 straight pennants is an NL record.

His overall record: 2,840 wins (2nd), 1,984 losses (3rd), a percentage of .589 (7th). He wasn't so successful in World Series play, winning only 3 (1905, 1921–22) in 9 tries, with a record of 26 wins (3rd) and 28 losses (1st).

Baseball Hall of Fame.

McGUGIN, DANIEL E. football: b. July 29, 1879, Tingley, Iowa; d. Jan. 19, 1936. Drake, Michigan guard. After getting his law degree from Michigan, McGugin became head coach at Vanderbilt, 1904–17 and 1919–34. He produced three unbeaten teams, 1904 (8–0–0), 1910 (8–0–1), and 1922 (8–0–1). His overall record was 196–55–19. He was Vanderbilt athletic director, 1921–34.

Helms Hall of Fame, National Football Foundation Hall of Fame.

McGUIRE, "DEACON" (James T.) baseball: b. Nov. 18, 1863, Youngstown, Ohio; d. Oct. 31, 1936. Bat, throw R; catcher. Toledo AA, 1884; Detroit NL, 1885; Philadelphia NL, 1887–88; Detroit NL, Cleveland AA, 1888; Rochester AA, 1890; Washington NL, 1892–99; Brooklyn NL, 1899–1901; Detroit AL, 1902–03; New York AL, 1904–07; Boston AL, 1907–08; Cleveland AL, 1910; Detroit AL, 1912. Twenty-six years, 1,781 games, .278 BA; hit .303 in 1891, .306 in 1894, .336 in 1895, .321 in 1896, .343 in 1897.

McGuire's twenty-six years of service is an ML record, and his 1,835 assists is an ML record for catchers. He was one of two players to see service with twelve different teams.

He managed Washington NL, 1898 (part); Boston AL, 1907 (part)–08 (part); Cleveland AL, 1909 (part)–11 (part): 208–289, .419.

McGUNNIGLE, WILLIAM H. baseball: b. Jan. 1, 1855, E. Stoughton, Mass.; d. March 9, 1899. Bat, throw R; outfield, pitcher. Buffalo NL, 1879–80; Worcester NL, 1880; Cleveland NL, 1882. Three years, 56 games, .173 BA; as pitcher, 11–8, 2.81 ERA.

He managed Buffalo NL, 1880 (part); Brooklyn AA, 1888–90; Pittsburgh NL, 1891 (part); Louisville NL, 1896 (part): 324–244, .570. Pennants, 1889–90.

McINNIS, "STUFFY" (John P.) baseball: b. Sept. 19, 1890, Gloucester, Mass.; d. Feb. 16, 1960. Bat, throw R; first base. Philadelphia AL, 1909–17; Boston AL, 1918–21; Cleveland AL, 1922; Boston NL, 1923–24; Pittsburgh NL, 1925–26; Philadelphia NL, 1927. Nineteen years, 2,128 games, 2,405 hits, 312 doubles, 172 stolen bases, .307 BA; hit .321 in 1911, .327 in 1912, .324 in 1913, .314 in 1914, .314 in 1915, .303 in 1917, .305 in 1919, .307 in 1921, .305 in 1922, .315 in 1923. Five World Series, 1911, 1913–14, 1918, 1925: 20 games .200 BA.

McInnis was a great glove man. His .999 fielding average in 1921, with only 1 error, is an ML record for first basemen, and during 1921–22 he had a streak of 163 games and 1,700 chances—both ML records—without an error. Also in 1921, he set an ML record for right-handed hitters by striking out only 9 times in 152 games and 584 at-bats. He was a member of the Philadelphia Athletics' "$100,000 Infield."

McINTIRE, "HARRY" (John R.) baseball: b. Jan. 11, 1879, Detroit; d. Jan 9, 1949. Bat, throw R; pitcher. Brooklyn NL, 1905–09; Chicago NL, 1910–12; Cincinnati NL, 1913. Nine years, 71–117, 3.23 ERA. No-hitter, Aug. 1, 1906, against Pittsburgh NL (10⅔ innings; lost 1–0 in 13 innings). One World Series, 1910: 0–1, 6.75 ERA in 5⅓ innings.

McINTYRE, MATTHEW W. baseball: b. June 12, 1880, Stonington, Conn.; d. April 2, 1920. Bat, throw L; outfield. Philadelphia AL, 1901; Detroit AL, 1904–10; Chicago AL, 1911–12. Ten years, 1,068 games, .269 BA; hit .323 in 1911. Led AL in runs, 1908 (105). Two World Series, 1908–09; 9 games, .190 BA.

McJAMES, "DOC" (James McC.) baseball: b. Aug. 27, 1873, Williamsburg, S.C.; d. Sept. 23, 1901. Throw R; pitcher. Washington NL, 1895–97; Baltimore NL, 1898; Brooklyn NL, 1899, 1901. Six years, 79–80, 3.43 ERA; 27–15 in 1898. Led NL in shutouts (3) and strikeouts (158) in 1897.

McKEAN, EDWIN J. baseball: b. June 20, 1868, Cleveland; d. Aug. 16, 1919. Bat L, throw R; shortstop. Cleveland AA, 1887–88; Cleveland NL, 1889–98; St. Louis NL, 1899. Thirteen years, 1,653 games, 323 stolen bases, .303 BA; hit .318 in 1889, .310 in 1893, .357 in 1894, .342 in 1895, .338 in 1896.

McKECHNIE, WILLIAM B. baseball: b. Aug. 7, 1886, Wilkinsburg, Pa.; d. Oct. 29, 1965. Sw. hit, throw R; third-second base. Pittsburgh NL, 1907, 1910–12; New York AL, Boston NL, 1913; Indianapolis Fed L, 1914; Newark Fed L, 1915; New York NL, 1916; Cincinannati NL, 1916–17; Pittsburgh NL, 1918, 1920. Eleven years, 845 games, .251 BA; hit .304 in 1914.

McKechnie managed Newark Fed L, 1915 (part); Pittsburgh NL, 1922–26; St. Louis NL, 1928–29 (part); Boston NL, 1930–37; Cincinnati NL, 1938–46: 1,898 wins (6th), 1,724 losses (5th), .524. Pennants, 1925, 1928, 1939–40, world championships, 1925, 1940.

McKechnie, who was particularly skillful at handling pitchers, tied NL records for most teams managed, 4, and most teams managed to pennants, 3.

Baseball Hall of Fame.

McLAREN, "TANK" (George W.) football: b. ?; d. Nov. 13, 1967. Pittsburgh halfback-fullback; 2nd team All-American, captain, 1918. Massillon Tigers, 1919.

National Football Foundation Hall of Fame.

McLEAN, "SCOOTER" (Raymond) football: b. Dec. 6, 1915, Lowell, Mass.; d. March 4, 1964. St. Anselm's (New Hampshire) halfback. Chicago Bears,

1940–47. As a pro, McLean caught 103 passes for 1,222 yards and 21 TDs He scored 30 TDs and 45 conversions for a career total of 225 points. He coached the Green Bay Packers, 1958: 1–10–1.

McLOUGHLIN, MAURICE tennis: b. Jan. 7, 1890, Carson City, Nev.; d. Dec. 10, 1957. "The California Comet" burst into prominence by winning the national singles and doubles (with Thomas C. Bundy) in 1912, repeating in both events in 1913, and he and Bundy again won the doubles in 1914. The red-haired, dynamic McLoughlin changed tennis dramatically with his style of play. He pioneered the serve as an offensive weapon and inspired others to play an aggressive version of tennis.

Tennis Hall of Fame, Helms Hall of Fame.

McMAHON, "SADIE" (John J.) baseball: b. Sept. 19, 1867, Wilmington, Del.; d. Feb. 20, 1954. Throw R; pitcher. Philadelphia AA, 1889–90; Brooklyn-Baltimore AA, 1890; Baltimore AA, 1891; Baltimore NL, 1892–96; Brooklyn NL, 1897. Nine years, 174–127, 3.51 ERA; 20–25 in 1892, 23–18 in 1893, 25–8 in 1894. Led league in wins (36–21), complete games (55), and strikeouts (291) in 1890; in wins (35–24), complete games (53), and shutouts (5) in 1891; in shutouts, 1895 (4).

McMANUS, MARTIN J. baseball: b. March 14, 1900, Chicago; d. Feb. 18, 1966. Bat, throw R; second-third base. St. Louis AL, 1920–26; Detroit AL, 1927–31; Boston AL, 1931–33; Boston NL, 1934. Fifteen years, 1,830 games, .289 BA; hit .312 in 1922, .309 in 1923, .333 in 1924, .320 in 1930. Led AL in doubles, 1925 (44); in stolen bases, 1930 (23).

He managed Boston AL, 1932 (part)–33: 95–151, .386.

McMILLIN, "BO" (Alvin N.) football: b. Jan. 12, 1895, Prairie Hill, Tex.; d. March 31, 1952. In 1921 tiny Centre College stunned Harvard with an amazing 6–0 upset; McMillin scored the winning TD on a 35-yard run. He was an All-American in 1919; 2nd team, 1920–21. Usually listed as a quarterback, he normally played singlewing tailback but also called signals. In 1920, he completed 119 of 170 passes, a remarkable percentage for the time.

After a brief pro career with the Milwaukee Badgers, 1922–23, and Cleveland Indians, 1923, he went into college coaching at Centenary, Louisiana; Geneva, Pennsylvania; and Kansas State, compiling an 81–29–5 record. In 1934, he went to Indiana, which had won only 27 conference games in thirty-four years; he turned the Hoosiers into a Big Ten power. Coaching them through 1947, he had a 63–48–11 record. His 1945 team was undefeated, bringing him the Coach of the Year award.

He coached the Detroit Lions, 1948–50, with a 12–24 record. In 1951, he took over the Philadelphia Eagles but resigned after they lost their first two games.

A devout Roman Catholic, McMillin was fond of the slogan, "You can be tough as nails and still be a gentleman," which was always seen on the walls of his locker rooms.

Helms Hall of Fame, National Football Foundation Hall of Fame.

McNAIR, ERIC (Donald Eric) baseball: b. April 12, 1890, Meridian, Miss.; d. March 11, 1949. Bat, throw R; shortstop, second-third base. Philadelphia AL, 1929–35; Boston AL, 1936–38; Chicago AL, 1939–40; Detroit AL, 1941–42; Philadelphia AL, 1942. Fourteen years, 1,251 games, .274 BA; hit .324 in 1939. Led AL in doubles, 1934 (47). Two World Series, 1930–31: 3 games, .000 BA.

McNAMEE, GRAHAM broadcasting: b. July 10, 1888, Washington, D.C.; d. May 9, 1942. McNamee once estimated that he had used ten times the number of words in an unabridged dictionary during his broadcasting career. He launched the career in 1923, when he did the Harry Greb–Johnny Wilson middleweight title fight. He also broadcast the World Series that fall. McNamee was best known for his fight announcing, but he handled every major sport. In 1926 he broadcast the first Rose Bowl game to be carried coast to coast.

McPHEE, "BID" (John A.) baseball: b. Nov. 1, 1859, Massena, N.Y.; d. Jan. 3, 1943. Bat, throw R; second base. Cincinnati AA, 1882–89; Cincinnati NL, 1890–99. Eighteen years, 2,135 games, 2,249 hits, 303 doubles, 188 triples, 1,678 runs, 528 stolen bases, .271 BA; hit .304 in 1894, .305 in 1896. Led league in home runs, 1886 (7); in triples, 1887 (19).

His 11 putouts on April 21, 1894, tied the NL record for second basemen. He managed Cincinnati NL, 1901–02 (part): 79–124, .389.

McQUILLAN, GEORGE W. baseball: b. May 1, 1885, Brooklyn; d. March 30, 1940. Bat, throw R; pitcher. Philadelphia NL, 1907–10; Cincinnati NL, 1911; Pittsburgh NL, 1913–15; Philadelphia NL, 1915–16; Cleveland AL, 1918. Ten years, 84–89, 2.38 ERA; 17 shutouts; 23–17 in 1908. Led NL in ERA, 1910 (1.60).

McQUILLAN, HUGH A. baseball: b. Sept. 15, 1897, New York City; d. Aug. 26, 1947. Bat, throw R; pitcher. Boston NL, 1918–22; New York NL, 1922–27; Boston NL, 1927. Ten years, 89–64, 3.83 ERA. Three World Series, 1922–24: 1–1, 3.60 ERA.

McTIGUE, MICHAEL F. boxing: b. Nov. 26, 1892, County Clare, Ireland; d. Aug. 12, 1966. His record: 81 wins, 57 by KO; 22 losses, 10 by KO; 6

draws, 36 no-decisions. McTigue won the light-heavy championship with a 20-round decision over Battling Siki on March 17, 1923. He lost it to Paul Berlenbach on May 30, 1925, on a 15-round decision. On Oct. 7, 1927, he lost in 15 rounds to Tommy Loughran for the then-vacated title.

McVEY, CALVIN A. baseball: b. Aug. 30, 1850, Montrose Lee County, Iowa; d. Aug. 20, 1926. Bat, throw R; all positions, most often first or third base or catcher. National Association, Boston, 1871–72; Baltimore, 1873; Boston, 1874–75. Five years, 262 games, .362 BA; hit .419 in 1871, .306 in 1872, .369 in 1873, .382 in 1874, .352 in 1875.

Chicago NL, 1876–77; Cincinnati NL, 1878–79. Four years, 265 games, .328 BA; hit .347 in 1876, .368 in 1877, .306 in 1878.

In the history of the major leagues, 102 players have collected 6 hits in a game; 5 players have done it twice. McVey not only did it twice but also did it in consecutive games, July 22 and 25, 1876, going 6-for-7 in each and scoring a total of 8 runs.

He was one of the "Big Four" hired away from Boston by William Hulbert, of Chicago, in 1876 in what turned out to be the first move toward formation of the National League.

He managed Cincinnati NL, 1878–79 (part): 72–52, .581.

McWHORTER, ROBERT L. football: b. June 4, 1891, Lexington, Ga.; d. June 29, 1960. Georgia halfback; captain, 1913.

National Football Foundation Hall of Fame.

MEADOWS, LEE (Henry Lee) baseball: b. July 12, 1894, Oxford, N.C.; d. Jan. 29, 1963. Bat L, throw R; pitcher. St. Louis NL, 1915–19; Philadelphia NL, 1919–23; Pittsburgh NL, 1923–29. Fifteen years, 189–180, 3.38 ERA; 25 shutouts. Led NL in losses, 1916 (13–23), 1919 (12–20); in wins, 1926 (20–9); in complete games, 1927 (25). Two World Series, 1925, 1927: 0–2, 6.28 ERA.

MEANWELL, WALTER E. basketball: b. Jan. 26, 1884, Leeds, England; d. Dec. 2, 1953. A 1909 graduate of Maryland, Meanwell never played basketball, but he coached it successfully. "The Little Doctor"—he was an M.D. —guided Wisconsin to 4 Western Conference (Big Ten) titles and 5 title ties in twenty years of coaching, 1911–17 and 1921–34. In three years at the University of Missouri, 1917–20, he won 2 Missouri Valley Conference titles. His teams won 290 games overall.

Basketball Hall of Fame.

MEEKIN, JOUETT baseball: b. Feb. 21, 1867, New Albany, Ind.; d. Dec. 14, 1944. Bat, throw R; pitcher. Louisville AA, 1891; Louisville NL, 1892;

Washington NL, 1892–93; New York NL, 1894–99; Boston NL, 1899; Pittsburgh NL, 1900. Ten years, 153–133, 4.07 ERA; 26–14 in 1896, 20–11 in 1897. Led NL in percentage, 1894 (33–9, .786).

MEINE, "HEINIE" (Henry W.) baseball: b. May 1, 1896, St. Louis; d. March 18, 1968. Bat, throw R; pitcher. St. Louis AL, 1922; Pittsburgh NL, 1929–34. Seven years, 66–50, 3.95 ERA. Led NL in wins, 1931 (19–13).

MELILLO, OSCAR D. ("Ski") baseball: b. Aug. 4, 1899, Chicago; d. Nov. 14, 1963. Bat, throw R; second base. St. Louis AL, 1926–35; Boston AL, 1935–37. Twelve years, 1,377 games, .260 BA; hit .306 in 1931. He holds the AL record for most assists in a season by a second baseman, 572 in 1930.

MELLODY, "HONEY" (William) boxing: b. Jan. 15, 1884, Charlestown, Mass.; d. March 15, 1919. His record: 56 wins, 36 by KO; 13 losses, 6 by KO; 13 draws, 13 no-decisions. Mellody won the welterweight title with a 15-round decision over Joe Walcott on Oct. 16, 1906. He lost the crown to Mike "Twin" Sullivan on April 23, 1907.

MENDELSON, HERBERT A. motorboat racing: b. 1897(?); d. June 24, 1950. Mendelson's boat, *Notre Dame,* won the Gold Cup in 1937 with an average time of 68.645 miles per hour, a record for the race until 1946. He also won the President's Cup in 1935, 1937, and 1940 and the Silver Cup in 1947.

MERCER, E. LEROY football: b. Oct. 30, 1888, Kennett Sq., Pa.; d. July 3, 1957. Pennsylvania; All-American fullback, 1910, 1912; 3rd team halfback, 1911; captain, 1911–12. Mercer won the IC4A broad-jump championship in 1912–13.

He was athletic director at Swarthmore College, 1914–31.

Helms Hall of Fame, National Football Foundation Hall of Fame.

MERCER, "WIN" (George B.) baseball: b. June 20, 1874, Chester, W.Va.; d. Jan. 12, 1903. Throw R; pitcher. Washington NL, 1894–99; New York NL, 1900; Washington AL, 1901; Detroit AL, 1902. Nine years, 131–164, 3.98 ERA; 25–18 in 1896, 20–20 in 1897. Led NL in shutouts 1897 (3).

MEREDITH, "TED" (James E.) track: b. Nov. 14, 1892, Chester Heights, Pa.; d. Nov. 2, 1957. In winning the 800-meter run in the 1912 Olympics, Meredith set a world record of 1:51.9 that stood until 1926. It was one of four records that he held for periods ranging from twelve to sixteen years. His 400-meter record of 47.4, set in 1916, was not broken until 1928; his 440-yard record, also 47.4, stood from 1916 until 1932; and his half-mile mark of 1:52.5, set in 1912, was broken by Meredith himself, at 1:52.2, in 1916. The latter record stood until 1926.

Representing Penn, he won the IC4A 440-yard title, 1914–16, the half-mile, 1915–16. He also won the AAU outdoor 440, 1914–15.

Helms Hall of Fame.

MERKLE, FREDERICK C. baseball: b. Dec. 20, 1888, Watertown, Wis.; d. March 2, 1956. Bat, throw R; first base. New York NL, 1907–16; Brooklyn NL, 1916–17; Chicago NL, 1917–20; New York AL, 1925–26. Sixteen years, 1,637 games, 271 stolen bases, .273 BA; hit .309 in 1912. Five World Series, 1911–13, 1916, 1918: 27 games, .239 BA.

Merkle tied an ML record by getting 6 RBI in one inning, on May 13, 1911. A steady player and fine base-runner, Merkle doesn't deserve to be remembered only for the "bonehead" play that lost the pennant for the Giants in 1908. (For the full story, see Johnny Evers.)

MERRILL, GRETCHEN (Mrs. Gay) figure skating: b. 1921(?); d. April 16, 1965. Miss Merrill was U.S. women's figure-skating champion six consecutive years, 1943–48.

MERTES, SAMUEL B. baseball: b. Aug. 6, 1872, San Francisco; d. March 11, 1945. Bat, throw R; outfield, second base. Philadelphia NL, 1896; Chicago NL, 1898–1900; Chicago AL, 1901–02; New York NL, 1903–06; St. Louis NL, 1906. Ten years, 1,190 games, 396 stolen bases, .279 BA. Led NL in doubles (32) and RBI (104) in 1903. One World Series, 1905: 5 games, .176 BA.

Mertes's 35 assists in 1902 is an AL record for outfielders.

MEUSEL, "IRISH" (Emil F.) baseball: b. June 9, 1893, Oakland, Calif.; d. March 1, 1963. Bat, throw R; outfield. Washington AL, 1914; Philadelphia NL, 1918–21; New York NL, 1921–26; Brooklyn NL, 1927. Eleven years, 1,294 games, .310 BA; hit .305 in 1919, .305 in 1920, .343 in 1921, .331 in 1922, .310 in 1924, .328 in 1925. Led NL in RBI, 1923 (125). Four World Series, 1921–24: 23 games, .276 BA; 3 doubles, 2 triples, 3 home runs, 10 runs, 17 RBI. Meusel hit .345, scoring 4 and driving in 7, in the Giants' 5-game-to-3 win over the Yankees in 1921.

MEYER, "BILLY" (William A.) baseball: b. Jan. 4, 1892, Knoxville, Tenn.; d. March 31, 1957. Bat, throw R; catcher. Chicago AL, 1913; Philadelphia AL, 1916–17. Three years, 113 games, .236 BA.

He managed Pittsburgh NL, 1948–52: 317–452, .412.

MILAN, J. CLYDE ("Deerfoot") baseball: b. March 25, 1887, Linden, Tenn.; d. March 3, 1953. Bat, throw R; outfield. Washington AL, 1907–22. Sixteen years, 1,981 games, 2,100 hits, 1,004 runs, 495 stolen bases (6th), .285 BA; hit .315 in 1911, .306 in 1912, .301 in 1913, .322 in 1920. Led AL in stolen bases, 1912 (88), 1913 (74).

Usually a centerfielder, Milan had exceptional speed and a very strong arm. He was also durable: He set an AL record for outfielders with 511 consecutive games.

He managed Washington AL, 1922: 69–85, .448.

MILBURN, DEVEREUX polo: b. 1881, Buffalo, N.Y.; d. Aug. 16, 1942. Milburn was rated at 10 goals twelve consecutive years, 1917–28. He was a member of the "Big Four" led by Harry P. Whitney and considered the greatest combination ever assembled. They gained the first U.S. victory over England in Westchester Cup play, in 1909. Milburn played in 7 of the cup matches between then and 1927, and the U.S. won 6 of them. He also played for the Meadowbrook team that won the National Open in 1916, 1919–20, and 1923 and the Monte Waterbury Memorial Cup in 1923 and 1926. Milburn was the first polo player who could hit the ball as far and accurately with his backhand as with his forehand.

MILES, KENNETH auto racing: b. 1919, England; d. Aug. 17, 1966. After starting in 1938 as a motorcycle racer in England, Miles came to the United States as an auto racer in 1951. In 1966 he won the Daytona 24-hour (with Lloyd Ruby) and the Sebring 12-hour. He also finished first at Le Mans but lost on a technicality.

He was killed in a car crash at Riverside, California.

MILEY, MARION golf: b. 1914(?), Danvers, Mass.; d. Sept. 28, 1941. Miss Miley won the Women's Western Amateur in 1935 and 1937, the Trans-Mississippi Amateur, 1935–36, and the Southern Amateur, 1938–39.

She was killed by an intruder in her home.

MILLER, "BING" (Edmund J.) baseball: b. Aug. 30, 1894, Vinton, Iowa; d. May 7, 1966. Bat, throw R; outfield. Washington AL, 1921; Philadelphia AL, 1922–26; St. Louis AL, 1926–27; Philadelphia AL, 1928–34; Boston AL, 1935–56. Sixteen years, 1,820 games, 389 doubles, .312 BA; hit .336 in 1922, .342 in 1924, .319 in 1925, .322 in 1926, .325 in 1927, .329 in 1928, .335 in 1929, .303 in 1930. Three World Series, 1929–31: 18 games, .258 BA. Miller doubled home the winning run in the final game when the As beat the Cubs, 4 games to 1, in 1929.

MILLER, "BING" (John E.) football: b. Dec. 6, 1903, Syracuse, N.Y.; d. Oct. 12, 1964. New York University tackle. Staten Island Stapletons, 1929–31.

He was general manager of the NYU department of athletics from 194
until his death.

MILLER, CHESTER J. auto racing: b. July 19, 1902, Detroit; d. May 15
1953. Miller's greatest success was in the Pike's Peak Hill Climb, which h
won in 1932 and 1933.

MILLER, "DOGGIE" (George F.) baseball: b. Aug. 15, 1864, Brooklyn ; d
April 6, 1909. Bat, throw R; catcher, outfield, third base. Pittsburgh AA
1884–86; Pittsburgh NL, 1887–93; St. Louis NL, 1894–95; Louisville NL
1896. Thirteen years, 1,317 games, 225 stolen bases, .267 BA; hit .339 i
1894.

Miller managed St. Louis NL, 1894: 56–76, .424.

MILLER, "DOTS" (John B.) baseball: b. Sept. 9, 1886, Kearny, N.J.; d. Sept
5, 1923. Bat, throw R; first-second base. Pittsburgh NL, 1909–13; St. Loui
NL, 1914–17, 1919; Philadelphia NL, 1920–21. Twelve years, 1,589 games
.263 BA. One World Series, 1909: 7 games, .250 BA.

MILLER, FREDDIE boxing: b. April 3, 1911, Cincinnati; d. May 8, 1962
His record: 201 wins, 43 by KO; 26 losses, 1 by KO; 5 draws, 4 no-decisions
1 no-contest. Miller had 237 bouts in thirteen years, winning 201 of them
He won the NBA version of the featherweight title by outpointing Tommy
Paul in 10 rounds, Jan. 13, 1933, and won recognition as world champ with
a 15-round decision over Ned Tarleton on Sept. 21, 1934. He lost the title
to Petey Sarron on May 11, 1936, in 15 rounds.

MILLIGAN, "JOCKO" (John) baseball: b. Aug. 8, 1861, Philadelphia; d
Aug. 30, 1923. Bat, throw R; catcher, first base. Philadelphia AA, 1884–87
St. Louis AA, 1888–89; Philadelphia PL, 1890; Philadelphia AA, 1891
Washington NL, 1892; Baltimore NL, New York NL, 1893. Ten years, 772
games, .286 BA; hit .302 in 1887, .366 in 1889, .303 in 1891. Led AA ir
doubles, 1891 (35).

His 3 assists in an inning, July 26, 1887, tied an ML record for catchers

MILSTEAD, CENTURY A. football: b. Jan. 1, 1901, Rock Island, Ill.; d. June
1, 1963. Yale tackle; All-American, 1923. New York Giants, 1925, 1927–
28; Philadelphia Quakers (AFL), 1926.

MILTON, "TOMMY' (Thomas) auto racing: b. 1893, Mt. Clemens, Mich.
d. July 10, 1962. Milton was the first man to win the Indianapolis 500 twice
he did it in 1921 and 1923. He was national driving champion, 1920–21
He retired in 1925, having made an estimated $500,000.

Auto Racing Hall of Fame, Helms Hall of Fame.

Connie Mack

"Christy" Mathewson

Rocky Marciano
(*New Bedford* Standard-Times)

"Tommy" McCarthy
(*Boston Public Library*)

Steve J. Nagy
(Bowling Magazine)

James A. Naismith
(Basketball Hall of Fame)

"Kid" Nichols
(Boston Public Library)

Annie Oakley
*(Amateur Trapshooting
Association Hall of Fame)*

"Barney" Oldfield
(Indianapolis Motor Speedway)

Melvin T. Ott

James H. O'Rourke
(Boston Public Library)

Stephen Owen (*Professional Football Hall of Fame*)

"Charlie" Paddock

Knute K. Rockne
(*Courtesy
University of Notre Dame*)

Abraham Saperstein
(*Basketball Hall of Fame*)

Wilbur Shaw
(*Indianapolis Motor Speedway*)

"Bucketfoot Al" Simmons   **Tristram E. Speaker**

Harry D. Stovey
(*Boston Public Library*)

Amos Alonzo Stagg
(*Basketball Hall of Fame*)

John L. Sullivan (Ring Magazine)

James F. Thorpe
*(Professional Football
Hall of Fame)*

"Big Bill" Tilden

Joseph B. Tinker
(Boston Public Library)

"Rube" Waddell

"Honus" Wagner

Edward A. Walsh
(*Boston Public Library*)

"Hurry Up" Yost
(*Courtesy
University of Michigan*)

"Babe" Zaharias
(*New Bedford* Standard-Times)

MINDS, "JACK" (John H.) football: b. 1871, Clearfield County, Pa.; d. Dec. 31, 1963. Pennsylvania fullback; All-American, 1897; 2nd team, 1895–96. Minds captained the 1897 team that won all 16 of its games. National Football Foundation Hall of Fame.

MISKE, BILLY boxing: b. April 12, 1894, St. Paul, Minn.; d. Jan. 1, 1924. His record: 45 wins, 34 by KO; 2 losses, 1 by KO; 2 draws, 54 no-decisions. Miske, who began as a middleweight and eventually became a heavyweight, compiled an outstanding record before being forced to retire in mid-1919 because of illness. He needed money and returned to the ring in 1920. He fought Jack Dempsey for the heavyweight title on Sept. 6, but Dempsey KOed him in the 3rd round. Miske retired in 1923.
He died of Bright's disease less than two months after his last fight.

MITCHELL, CLARENCE E. baseball: b. Feb. 22, 1891, Franklin, Nebr.; d. Nov. 6, 1963. Bat, throw L; pitcher. Detroit AL, 1911; Cincinnati NL, 1916–17; Brooklyn NL, 1918–22; Philadelphia NL, 1923–28; St. Louis NL, 1928–30; New York NL, 1930–32. Eighteen years, 125–139, 4.12 ERA. Led NL in shutouts, 1921 (3). Two World Series, 1920, 1928: 0–0, 0.87 ERA in 10⅔ innings of relief.

MITCHELL, MICHAEL F. baseball: b. Dec. 12, 1879, Springfield, Ohio; d. July 16, 1961. Bat, throw R; outfield. Cincinnati NL, 1907–12; Chicago NL, 1913; Pittsburgh NL, 1913–14; Washington AL, 1914. Eight years, 1,133 games, .278 BA; hit .310 in 1909. Led NL in triples, 1909 (17), 1910 (18).

MITCHELL, YOUNG boxing: b. John L. Herget, Jan. 30, 1868, San Francisco; d. Sept. 3, 1945. In 1885, Jack Keenan claimed the U.S. featherweight title, but Mitchell KOed him in 35 rounds on June 22 and became recognized as champion. Within two years, he had outgrown the class. Fighting as a middleweight, he was never beaten, but he never got a title bout either.
His record: 35 wins, 31 by KO; no losses; 6 draws.

MOGRIDGE, GEORGE A. baseball: b. Feb. 18, 1889, Rochester, N.Y.; d. March 4, 1962. Bat, throw L; pitcher. Chicago AL, 1911–12; New York AL, 1915–20; Washington AL, 1921–25; St. Louis AL, 1925; Boston NL, 1926–27. Fifteen years, 134–129, 3.20 ERA, 19 shutouts. In relief, 22–21, 2.56 ERA, 17 saves. No-hitter, April 24, 1917, against Boston AL (2–1). One World Series, 1924: 1–0, 2.25 ERA.

MOLESWORTH, KEITH F. ("Rabbit") football: b. Oct. 20, 1906, Washington, D.C.; d. March 12, 1966. Monmouth College quarterback. Chicago Bears, 1931–37. In seven pro seasons, he gained 1,705 yards and scored 9

TDs in 426 attempts, a 4.0 average; he completed 83 of 213 passes for 39 percent, 1,591 yards, and 11 TDs.

Molesworth returned a total of 8 punts in championship games, second to Willie Wood; his 4 in one game ties the NFL record. His total of 101 yards in returns is second to Charlie Trippi; so is his one-game high of 67 yards.

He coached the Baltimore Colts, 1953: 3–9.

MOLINEAUX, TOM boxing: b. 1784, Georgetown, S.C., or Washington, D.C.; d. Aug. 4, 1818. A Negro, Molineaux was the first American to fight for the London Prize Ring championship. He was born a slave, but he won a fight with a bully on a neighboring plantation and his owner was so pleased that he gave him not only his freedom but also passage money in order to go to England and try his fist at prizefighting. He won 8 fights before meeting champion Tom Cribb on Dec. 10, 1810. For 30 rounds, Molineaux was beating him badly. But in the 31st round Molineaux slipped and banged his head against a ring post right after he had knocked Cribb down. Both men were unconscious. After they were revived, they fought on groggily until Cribb KOed Molineaux in the 33rd round.

It was later found that the American had fractured his skull when he hit the post. He was never the same. In a rematch on Sept. 28, 1911, Cribb broke Molineaux's jaw in the 10th and KOed him in the 11th before a record crowd of 40,000.

Molineaux fought only sporadically after that. He went into a rapid physical decline and was found dead in a British Army barracks in Ireland.

Boxing Hall of Fame.

MOONEY, JAMES football: b. ?; d. Aug. 12, 1944. Georgetown end, tackle. Newark Tornadoes, 1930; Brooklyn Dodgers, 1930–31; Cincinnati Reds, 1933–34; Chicago Cardinals, Chicago Bears, 1935; New York Yanks (AFL), 1936–37.

Mooney was killed by a sniper while serving in France.

MOORE, DAVEY boxing: b. Nov. 1, 1933, Lexington, Ky.; d. March 25, 1963. His record: 56 wins, 28 by KO; 7 losses, 2 by KO; 1 draw. AAU bantamweight champion in 1952, Moore turned pro briefly but with so little success that he quit. After being talked out of retirement, he became known as invincible. On March 18, 1959, he KOed Kid Bassey, of Nigeria, in the 13th round to win the featherweight title. He lost it on March 21, 1963, when Sugar Ramos KOed him in 10 rounds. Moore collapsed shortly after the fight, went into a coma, and died of brain injuries four days later.

MOORE, EARL A. baseball: b. July 29, 1878, Pickerington, Ohio; d. Nov. 28, 1961. Bat, throw R; pitcher. Cleveland AL, 1901–07; New York AL, 1907; Philadelphia NL, 1908–13; Chicago NL, 1913; Buffalo Fed L, 1914. Fourteen years, 159–153, 2.78 ERA; 1,397 strikeouts, 34 shutouts in 2,767 innings; 21–15 in 1910. Led AL in ERA, 1903 (1.77); in strikeouts, 1910 (185); in losses, 1911 (15–19).

MOORE, W. WILCY baseball: b. May 20, 1897, Bonita, Tex.; d. March 29, 1963. Bat, throw R; pitcher. New York AL, 1927–29; Boston AL, 1931–32; New York AL, 1932–33. Six years, 51–44, 3.69 ERA. In relief, 39–26, 3.52 ERA, 49 saves. Two World Series, 1927, 1932: 2–0, 0.56 ERA, 1 save in 3 appearances.

Moore, as a rookie, was the premier relief pitcher for the 1927 New York Yankees, called by many the greatest team ever assembled. He was 19–7, with a 2.28 ERA that year. In relief, he was 13–3, with a 1.95 ERA, and had 13 saves.

MOORE, WILBUR ("Little Indian") football: b. April 22, 1916, Austin, Minn.; d. Sept. 9, 1965. Minnesota halfback. Washington Redskins, 1939–47. A fast, breakaway back, Moore was a spot player with Washington in those one-platoon days. He was particularly dangerous as a pass receiver. His over-the-head catch of a Sammy Baugh pass for a 25-yard TD put the Redskins ahead to stay in their 14–6 title victory over the Bears in 1942.

MORAN, PATRICK J. baseball: b. Feb. 7, 1876, Fitchburg, Mass.; d. March 7, 1924. Throw R; catcher. Boston NL, 1901–05; Chicago NL, 1906–09; Philadelphia NL, 1910–14. Fourteen years, 817 games, .235 BA. Two World Series, 1906–07: 0-for-2 as a pinchhitter.

Moran managed Philadelphia NL, 1915–18; Cincinnati NL, 1919–23: 748–586, .561. Pennants, 1915 and 1919; World Series, 1919. Both Philadelphia and Cincinnati won their first NL pennants under his leadership.

MORAN, "UNCLE CHARLIE" (Charles B.) football, baseball: b. Feb. 22, 1879, Nashville, Tenn.; d. June 13, 1949. Uncle Charlie had an interesting sports career; he was a major-league pitcher and catcher, a major-league umpire for twenty-four seasons, and a college and professional football coach. He won his greatest fame with the "Praying Colonels" of Centre College. Coaching them, 1919–23, he had a 42–6–1 record, including a shocking 6–0 upset of Harvard in 1921. A Tennessee graduate, he also coached Texas A & M, 1909–14 (38–8–4), and Bucknell, 1924–26 (19–10–2). He was co-coach of the Frankford Yellowjackets in 1927 (6–9–3). Moran pitched briefly for St. Louis NL in 1903, hurt his arm, and returned to the same team as a catcher in 1908 for twenty-one games. He was an NL umpire, 1916–39.

MORGAN, "CY" (Harry R.) baseball: b. Nov. 10, 1878, Pomeroy, Ohio; d. June 28, 1962. Bat, throw R; pitcher. St. Louis AL, 1903–05, 1907; Boston AL, 1907–09; Philadelphia AL, 1909–12; Cincinnati NL, 1913. Ten years, 76–75, 2.51 ERA; 667 strikeouts, 15 shutouts in 1,445⅓ innings.

MORGAN, JUSTIN R. horse racing: b. 1747, West Springfield, Mass.; d. March 22, 1798. It seems strange that a music teacher should enter into sports history, but Justin Morgan was also an innkeeper in Vermont, and one day a patron paid a debt by giving him a small stallion named Figure. Morgan used Figure to service mares, and Figure's grandchildren produced children who were true trotters. A few were raced, but most went to work hauling stagecoaches and buggies. Figure was renamed Justin Morgan posthumously for his former owner, and from his strain came the highly prized Morgan horse.

MORGAN, RALPH basketball: b. March 9, 1884, Philadelphia; d. Jan. 5, 1965. A founding member of the Collegiate Rules Committee, he served until 1931. He was also a founder of the Eastern Intercollegiate Basketball League (now the Ivy League) in 1910 and for many years was its secretary-treasurer.
Basketball Hall of Fame.

MORGAN, WILLIAM G. volleyball: b. Jan. 24, 1870, Lockport, N.Y.; d. Dec. 28, 1942. Like basketball, volleyball was invented as an addition to the YMCA physical program. Morgan, physical director of the YMCA in Holyoke, Massachusetts, invented the sport in 1895. He decided it might be as much fun for players to bat a large ball back and forth over a net as to try to throw it into a basket. Although volleyball has never become the spectator sport basketball is, its popularity as a participant sport has proven Morgan right.

He originally set up a lawn-tennis net, using a basketball bladder as the ball. The original name, mintonette, was changed to volleyball in 1896. Largely through the YMCA, volleyball gradually spread through the East. When it moved outdoors, at about the same time the public-playground movement was growing, it became immensely popular with people of all ages, and U.S. soldiers helped spread it around the world during World War II.

The U.S. Volleyball Association was formed in 1928 to govern the sport. In 1947, the International Volleyball Federation was established; nearly fifty countries now belong to it.
Helms Hall of Fame.

MORGENWECK, FRANK basketball: b. July 15, 1875; d. Dec. 8, 1941. A long-time team manager, Morgenweck began his career in 1901 in the National League. From 1912 to 1931, he managed several championship teams in various leagues. Basketball Hall of Fame.

MORIARTY, GEORGE J. baseball: b. July 7, 1884, Chicago; d. April 8, 1964. Bat, throw R; third base. Chicago NL, 1903–04; New York AL, 1906–08; Detroit AL, 1909–15; Chicago AL, 1916. Thirteen years, 1,071 games, .251 BA. One World Series, 1909: 7 games, .273 BA. Moriarty managed Detroit AL, 1927–28: 150–157, .489.

MORRILL, JOHN F. baseball: b. Feb. 19, 1855, Boston; d. April 2, 1932. Bat, throw R; first-third-second base. Boston NL, 1876–88; Washington NL, 1889; Boston PL, 1890. Fifteen years, 1,265 games, .260 BA. He managed Boston NL, 1882–83 (part), 1884–88; Washington NL, 1889 (part): 396–376, .513. Pennant, 1883.

MORRIS, EDWARD ("Cannonball") baseball: b. Sept. 29, 1859, Brooklyn; d. April 12, 1937. Bat R, throw L; pitcher. Columbus AA, 1884; Pittsburgh AA, 1885–86; Pittsburgh NL, 1887–89; Pittsburgh PL, 1890. Seven years, 171–123, 2.82 ERA; 307 starts, 297 complete; 1,217 strikeouts, 28 shutouts in 2,678 innings; 34–13 in 1884, 39–24 in 1885, 29–24 in 1888. Led league in complete games (63), shutouts (6), and strikeouts (298) in 1885; in victories (41–20) and shutouts (12) in 1886; in complete games (54) in 1888. His 12 shutouts in 1886 is an ML record for left-handers.

MORRISON, JOHN D. baseball: b. Oct. 22, 1895, Pelleville, Ky.; d. March 20, 1966. Bat, throw R; pitcher. Pittsburgh NL, 1920–27; Brooklyn NL, 1929–30. Ten years, 103–80, 3.65 ERA; 25–13 in 1923. In relief, 28–12, 3.34 ERA, 23 saves. Led NL in shutouts in 1921 (3), 1922 (5). One World Series, 1925: 0–0, 2.89 ERA in 9⅓ innings of relief.

MORRISSEY, JOHN C. horse racing, boxing: b. Feb. 12, 1831, Templemore, Tipperary, Ireland; d. May 1, 1878. Brought to the United States as a toddler, Morrissey as a teen-ager joined the 1849 Gold Rush. He won some mining-camp brawls and claimed the American bareknuckle championship. In 1852, he fought a visiting English prizefighter, Yankee Sullivan, and beat him in 37 rounds, mainly because Sullivan jumped from the ring to fight some hecklers and didn't get back fast enough to suit the referee.

In 1858, Morrissey fought John C. Heenan, later recognized as U.S. champ. Heenan broke his hand in the 1st round and quit in the 11th. Morrissey then retired from the ring and went to Saratoga Springs, N.Y., and entered politics. Many wealthy people visited Saratoga Springs, so

Morrissey built a racetrack. His first meeting lasted an entire month; until then, race meetings had generally lasted only a few days. His success inspired the establishment of racetracks elsewhere.

MORTON, GUY, SR. baseball: b. June 1, 1893, Vernon, Ala.; d. Oct. 18, 1934. Bat, throw R; pitcher. Cleveland AL, 1914–24. Eleven years, 97–88, 3.13 ERA; 830 strikeouts, 20 shutouts in 1,629⅔ innings. In relief, 18–15, 3.87 ERA, 6 saves.

MUDERSBACH, ALLEN auto racing: b. 1933(?); d. Feb. 11, 1966. Mudersbach was national drag-racing champion in 1957. He was killed during a practice run at Irwindale, California, Raceway.

MULDOON, WILLIAM A. wrestling, boxing: b. May 24, 1845, Belfast, N.Y.; d. June 9, 1933. For a time physical instructor for the New York police force, Muldoon became a professional wrestler, claimed the world championship, and went as far as Japan to take on all comers and prove his claim.

Next he took the job of training John L. Sullivan, who was badly out of shape. The first day of training, Muldoon awoke Sullivan at daybreak. Sullivan complained. A fight resulted, and Muldoon easily pinned the man who would soon be bareknuckle champion.

The health-farm idea was basically Muldoon's; two Presidents, Teddy Roosevelt and William Howard Taft, and many prominent businessmen joined him at Purchase, New York, to work out under his instruction, hoping to overcome the results of sedentary life.

Muldoon was a member of the New York State Athletic Commission, 1921–33, and frequently its chairman during the period. The rules he set down were copied almost verbatim by many such commissions across the country.

MULLANE, ANTHONY J. baseball: b. Feb. 20, 1859, Cork, Ireland; d. April 26, 1944. Sw. hit and sw. pitch. Detroit NL, 1881; Louisville AA, 1882; St. Louis AA, 1883; Toledo AA, 1884; Cincinnati AA, 1886–89; Cincinnati NL, 1890–93; Baltimore NL, 1893–94; Cleveland NL, 1894. Thirteen years, 285–220, 3.12 ERA; 469 complete games (9th), 31 shutouts; 30–24 in 1882, 37–26 in 1884, 33–27 in 1886, 31–17 in 1887, 26–16 in 1888, 23–26 in 1891, 21–13 in 1892. No-hitter, Sept. 11, 1882, against Cincinnati AA (2–0; first pitched from 50-foot distance). Led AA in strikeouts, 1882 (170); in percentage, 1883 (35–15, .700); in shutouts, 1884 (8) and 1887 (6).

MULLER, "BRICK" (Harold J.) football: b. June 12, 1901, Dunsmuir, Calif.; d. May 17, 1962. California end; All-American, 1921–22; 3rd team, 1920.

Los Angeles Buccaneers, 1926 (player, co-coach: 6–3–1). The California "Wonder Teams" brought Pacific Coast football into the national spotlight, and Brick Muller—so nicknamed because of his bright-red hair—was a major reason for the wonder. At 6'3" and 195 pounds, fast and powerful, an Olympic high jumper, Muller could snare the fat ball of the day with one hand and throw it great distances as well.

In California's 28–0 upset of previously undefeated Ohio State in the 1921 Rose Bowl, Muller completed 3 passes, one of which traveled 53 yards in the air for a TD, caught 5, recovered 3 fumbles, came up with 2 interceptions, and got downfield so fast on punts that Ohio State called fair catches all day.

Muller became a doctor; he was head physician for the U.S. Olympic team in 1956.

Helms Hall of Fame, National Football Foundation Hall of Fame.

MULLIN, GEORGE J. baseball: b. July 4, 1880, Toledo, Ohio; d. Jan. 7, 1944. Bat, throw R; pitcher. Detroit AL, 1902–13; Washington AL, 1913; Indianapolis Fed L, 1914; Newark Fed L, 1915. Fourteen years, 227–195, 2.82 ERA, 35 shutouts; 22–21 in 1905, 21–18 in 1906, 21–20 in 1907, 21–12 in 1910. No-hitter, July 4, 1912, against St. Louis AL (7–0). Led AL in complete games, 1905 (35); in wins and percentage, 1909 (29–8, .784). Three World Series, 1907–09: 3–3, 2.02 ERA; 6 starts, 6 complete (5th), 1 shutout.

MUNDORF, ROY M. basketball: b. Feb. 20, 1900, Gettysburg, Pa.; d. Dec. 2, 1966. Mundorf coached Georgia Tech basketball, 1925–42, compiling a 164–129 record. He helped to found the National Association of Basketball Coaches. Mundorf also coached Georgia Tech baseball, 1940–45, and was athletic director at Louisville, 1951–53.

MURPHY, DANIEL F. baseball: b. Aug. 11, 1876, Philadelphia; d. Nov. 22, 1955. Bat, throw R; second base, outfield. New York NL, 1900–01; Philadelphia AL, 1902–13; Brooklyn Fed L, 1914–15. Sixteen years, 1,518 games, .288 BA; hit .301 in 1906, .300 in 1910, .329 in 1911. Three World Series, 1905, 1910–11: 16 games, 7 doubles (4th), 10 runs, 10 RBI, .288 BA.

On July 8, 1902, he went 6-for-6, scoring 3 runs.

MURPHY, ISAAC horse racing: b. 1856, Lafayette County, Ky.; d. Feb. 12, 1896. Murphy was one of many Negro jockeys during the nineteenth century. Negroes rode 13 of the first 27 Kentucky Derby winners; Murphy rode 3, in 1884 (Buchanan), 1890 (Riley), and 1891 (Kingman). That was a record until Eddie Arcaro rode his 4th Derby winner in 1948. Murphy began riding in 1873, in the South, then moved to the Midwest. In 1879, he had 35 winners of 75 mounts. During his career, he had 1,412 mounts and 628 of them were winners. Among his major victories were 4 in the American Derby, including 3 in a row, 1884–86.

Jockey Hall of Fame, National Racing Hall of Fame.

MURPHY, "JIMMY" (James) auto racing: b. ?; d. Sept. 15, 1924. Originally a mechanic, Murphy moved over to the other seat when his driver was injured, and he was virtually an instant success. In 1920 he won a purse in every race he entered, in 1921 he became the first American to win the French Grand Prix, and in 1922 he won the Indianapolis 500 and was national driving champion. He was also national champion in 1924.

He was killed in a crash at the Syracuse Speedway.

Helms Hall of Fame, National Racing Hall of Fame.

MURPHY, JOHN J. baseball: b. July 14, 1908, New York City; d. Jan. 14, 1970. Bat, throw R; pitcher. New York AL, 1932, 1934–43, 1946: Boston AL, 1947. Thirteen years, 93–53, 3.50 ERA. In relief, 73 wins (5th), 42 losses, .635 percentage (5th), 3.25 ERA, 107 saves (6th). Six World Series, 1936–39, 1941, 1943: 8 games, 2–0, 1.10 ERA in 16⅓ innings of relief, 4 saves (1st).

Murphy was the New York Mets' chief scout from their first year, 1961, until 1967, when he became general manager. He was named Baseball Executive of the Year after the Mets won the World Series in 1969.

MURRAY, R. LINDLEY tennis: b. San Francisco; d. Jan. 17, 1970. A left-hander, Murray won the U.S. indoor singles title in 1916, the 1917 "Patriotic Tournament" held in lieu of the usual outdoor tourney, and the 1918 outdoor singles, when he beat young Bill Tilden in the finals.

Helms Hall of Fame, Tennis Hall of Fame.

MURRAY, "RED" (John J.) baseball: b. March 4, 1884, Arnot, Pa.; d. Dec. 4, 1958. Bat, throw R; outfield. St. Louis NL, 1906–08; New York NL, 1909–15; Chicago NL, 1915; New York NL, 1917. Eleven years, 1,263 games, .270 BA. Led NL in home runs, 1909 (7). Three World Series, 1911–13: 19 games, .206 BA. He hit .323, with 4 doubles, 5 runs, and 5 RBI, in the 1912 Series.

MUTRIE, JAMES J. baseball: b. June 13, 1851, Chelsea, Mass.; d. Jan. 24, 1938. Managed New York AA, 1883–91: 658–419, .611 (2nd). Pennants, 1884, 1888–89.

MYATT, GLENN C. baseball: b. July 9, 1897, Argenta, Ark.; d. Aug. 9, 1969. Bat L, throw R; catcher. Philadelphia AL, 1920–21; Cleveland AL, 1923–

35; New York NL, 1935; Detroit AL, 1936. Sixteen years, 1,004 games, .270 BA.

MYERS, "HY" (Henry H.) baseball: b. April 27, 1889, East Liverpool, Ohio; d. May 1, 1965. Bat, throw R; outfield. Brooklyn NL, 1909, 1911, 1914–22; St. Louis NL, 1923–25; Cincinnati NL, 1925. Fourteen years, 1,310 games, .281 BA; hit .307 in 1919, .304 in 1920, .317 in 1922. Led NL in triples, 1919 (14), 1920 (22); in RBI, 1919 (73); in slugging, 1919 (.436). Two World Series, 1916, 1920: 12 games, .208 BA.

MYERS, "LON" (Lawrence E.) track: b. Feb. 16, 1858, Richmond, Va.; d. Feb. 15, 1899. As a youth, Myers was told by a doctor to try running to improve his health. It worked so well that he won 15 national titles in 4 different running events. His greatest accomplishment came in the 1880 AAU championships, when he entered 7 events and won 4 of them, the 100-, 220-, 440-, and 880-yard runs. He also won the 100 in 1881, the 220 in 1879 and 1881, the 440 in 1879 and 1881–84, and the 880 in 1879 and 1884. At one time he held world records in both the 440 and the 880.

Helms Hall of Fame.

MYERS, "POP" (Theodore E.) auto racing: b. 1874, Williamsburg, Ind.; d. March 14, 1954. Myers took charge of ticket sales at the newly opened Indianapolis Motor Speedway in 1909. He became general manager in 1914, treasurer in 1915, and a vice-president of the Speedway Corporation in 1927, serving until his death.

Auto Racing Hall of Fame, Helms Hall of Fame.

N

NAGY, STEVE J. bowling: b. Aug. 10, 1913, Shoaf, Pa.; d. Nov. 10, 1966. Bowler of the Year in 1952 and 1955 and named to *Bowling Magazine*'s All-Star team in 1956 and 1958, Nagy became well known to TV fans when he rolled 300 in a 1954 film series, the first to do so. He won the ABC tournament all-events and doubles in 1952 and belonged to the all-events champion team. In 1958, he was on the team that won the team and all-events titles. He holds ABC records for the best two-, three-, and ten-year averages, 224, 221, and 208, respectively. His twenty-four-year tourney average was 197. He rolled six sanctioned 300s and four 299s. American Bowling Congress Hall of Fame.

NAISMITH, JAMES A. basketball: b. Nov. 6, 1861, Almonte, Ontario, Canada; d. Nov. 28, 1939. An instructor at the YMCA Training School in Springfield, Massachusetts, in 1891, Naismith was asked by his supervisor to devise a new game for winter—one that could be played indoors by small teams and that would combine good exercise with the fun of competition. The result was basketball. As Dr. Naismith described his invention of the game, he started with three basic principles, all intended to limit body contact: prohibiting a player from running with the ball, in order to eliminate tackling; using a high horizontal goal, since an upright goal, as in soccer or hockey, put a premium on using force to score; and penalizing a player guilty of excessive body contact.

The original game used a soccer ball and two peach baskets, which were fastened to the gym balcony. It was instantly popular. Introduced into virtually every YMCA in the country, it quickly spread beyond. Seven years after its invention, it was being played on a professional level. By 1940, the rules had been translated into thirty languages and the game was being played with some frequency by about twenty million people in seventy-five countries. It spread even further after World War II.

Dr. Naismith, who had taken his M.D. degree at McGill University in 1887 and taught there for a short time before going to Springfield, became a professor of physical education at the University of Kansas in 1898 and remained there until retiring in 1937, a few months after he saw basketball introduced to the Olympic Games in Munich, Germany.

The YMCA Training School, now Springfield College, is the site of the Naismith Memorial Basketball Hall of Fame.

Basketball Hall of Fame, Helms Hall of Fame.

NARDIELLO, VINCENT J. boxing: b. 1888(?), New York City; d. Jan. 18, 1965. As physician for the New York Athletic Commission and for Madison Square Garden for twenty-five years, Nardiello became familiar to millions of fight fans. He was introduced to the public before virtually every major fight in the Garden between 1932 and 1957, and his name was for a long time heard weekly by national radio and TV audiences. Dr. Nardiello, who worked his way through medical school by boxing, made many contributions to the safety of boxers: He pioneered the use of prefight electroencephalograms to detect brain damage, and he was instrumental in getting New York State to switch from 6-ounce to 8-ounce gloves. He won the James J. Walker Award in 1953.

NASH, WILLIAM M. baseball: b. June 24, 1865, Richmond, Va.; d. Nov. 16, 1929. Bat, throw R; third base. Richmond AA, 1884; Boston NL, 1885–89; Boston PL, 1890; Boston NL, 1891–95; Philadelphia NL, 1896–98. Fifteen years, 1,549 games, 1,072 runs, 249 stolen bases (three years not included), .275 BA.

He managed Philadelphia NL, 1896: 62–68, .477.

NEHF, ARTHUR N. baseball: b. July 31, 1892, Terre Haute, Ind.; d. Dec. 18, 1960. Bat, throw L; pitcher. Boston NL, 1915–19; New York NL, 1919–26; Cincinnati NL, 1926–27; Chicago NL, 1927–29. Fifteen years, 182–120, 3.20 ERA; 30 shutouts; 21–12 in 1920, 20–10 in 1921. Led NL in complete games, 1918 (28). Five World Series, 1921–24, 1929: 12 games (4th), 4–4 (3rd), 2.16 ERA, 9 starts (4th), 6 complete (5th), 79 innings (7th), 50 hits, 32 walks (2nd), 28 strikeouts, 2 shutouts (3rd).

NELSON, "BATTLING" (Oscar M.) boxing: b. June 5, 1882, Copenhagen, Denmark; d. Feb. 7, 1954. His record: 58 wins, 37 by KO; 19 losses, 2 by KO; 19 draws, 35 no-decisions. Nelson won the lightweight title, July 4, 1908, by KOing Joe Gans in 17 rounds. He lost it to Ad Wolgast, Feb. 22, 1910, on a TKO after the 40th round.

Helms Hall of Fame, Boxing Hall of Fame.

NELSON, "JACK" (Jackson W.) baseball: b. March 14, 1849, Brooklyn; d. Sept. 5, 1910. Bat L, throw R; infield. National Association, Brooklyn, Troy, 1872; New York Mutuals, 1873–75. Four years, 193 games, .230 BA.

Indianapolis NL, 1878; Troy NL, 1879; Worcester NL, 1881; New York AA, 1883–87; New York NL, 1887; Baltimore-Brooklyn AA, 1890. Nine years, 624 games, .254 BA; hit .305 in 1883.

NESSER, ALFRED football: b. ?; d. March 12, 1967. Guard, Akron Pros, 1919–26; Cleveland Bulldogs, 1925; Cleveland Panthers (AFL), 1926; New York Giants, 1926–28; Cleveland Indians, 1931. There were at one time six Nesser brothers playing pro football. Before the founding of the NFL, the six played together with the Columbus Panhandles; in 1921, all but Al were again playing for the Panhandles, who were then in the NFL. Al had by far the longest career of the six.

NEWELL, "MA" (Marshall) football: b. April 2, 1871, Clifton, N.J.; d. Dec. 24, 1897. Harvard tackle; All-American, 1890–93. Built like a fire hydrant, at 5'7" and 170 pounds, Newell was a powerful blocker who handled larger players with ease. He was also a member of the Harvard crew and was Cornell's first paid football coach, 1893–94.

Helms Hall of Fame, National Football Foundation Hall of Fame.

NEWSOM, "BOBO" (Norman Louis, "Buck") baseball: b. Aug. 11, 1907, Hartsville, S.C.; d. Dec. 7, 1962. Bat, throw R; pitcher. Brooklyn NL, 1929–30; Chicago NL, 1932; St. Louis AL, 1934–35; Washington AL, 1935–37; Boston AL, 1937; St. Louis AL, 1938–39; Detroit AL, 1939–41; Washington AL, Brooklyn NL, 1942; Washington AL, Brooklyn NL, St. Louis AL, 1943; Philadelphia AL, 1944–46; Washington AL, 1946–47; New York AL, 1947; New York NL, 1948; Washington AL, 1952; Philadelphia AL, 1952–53. Twenty years, 211–222, 3.98 ERA; 1,732 walks (3rd); 20–16 in 1938, 20–11 in 1939, 21–5 in 1940. Led the league in walks (149) and losses (16–20) in 1934; in losses, 1935 (18); in walks, 1937 (167); in complete games (31) and innings (329⅔) in 1938; in complete games (24) in 1939; in losses (12–20) in 1941; in strikeouts (134) in 1942; in losses (8–20) in 1945. Two World Series, 1940, 1947: 2–2, 2.86 ERA.

During his up-and-down career, Newsom won 20 three times and lost 20 three times. It seems typical that he pitched a no-hitter, Sept. 18, 1934, against Boston AL but lost it, 2–1, in 10 innings on 1 hit, largely because of his own wildness.

NEYLAND, ROBERT R. football: b. Feb. 17, 1892, Greenville, Tex.; d. March 28, 1962. Knute Rockne called General Neyland the best defensive coach in the country, and in a poll of coaches taken during football's centennial year, he was runner-up to Rockne as greatest college coach. During much of his twenty-one-year career, all at Tennessee, he combined coaching with work for the Army Corps of Engineers. Army duty twice called him away from coaching. His years at Tennessee: 1926–34, 1936–40, 1946–52. His Volunteers had a 173–31–12 record for an .829 percentage, 5th on the all-time list.

Neyland took over at Tennessee in 1926; that year the Volunteers started a 33-game unbeaten streak that stretched into 1930. He also had undefeated teams in 1938, 1939, 1940, and 1951, winning the national championship the latter year. His team shared a Southern Conference title in 1932 and won or shared five Southeastern Conference championships. They won the 1939 Orange Bowl, 17–0, over Oklahoma; lost the 1940 Rose Bowl, 14–0, to Southern California; lost the 1941 Sugar Bowl, 19–13, to Boston College; and lost the 1953 Cotton Bowl, 16–0, to Texas.

Neyland's dedication to solid defense and fundamental football produced a number of successful coaches, including Bobby Dodd, Murray Warmath, Bob Woodruff, and Bowden Wyatt.

Helms Hall of Fame, National Football Foundation Hall of Fame.

NICHOLS, GEORGE yachting: b. 1878, Boston; d. Aug. 14, 1950. Nichols was largely responsible for a revolution in yachting with his intensive study of jib-headed rigs. His jib-headed *Carolina* won a number of races in 1921 and, as a result, the rig was formally recognized. *Carolina* won the Astor Cup, 1921–22 and 1926, the King's Cup, 1921.

NICHOLS, "KID" (Charles A.) baseball: b. Sept. 14, 1869, Madison, Wis.; d. April 11, 1953. Bat, throw R; pitcher. Boston NL, 1890–91; St. Louis NL, 1904–05; Philadelphia NL, 1905–06. Fifteen years, 362 wins (6th), 208 losses, 2.95 ERA; 562 starts (9th), 533 complete (4th), 5,061⅓ innings (6th), 4,912 hits (4th), 1,265 walks, 1,868 strikeouts, 48 shutouts; 27–19 in 1890, 31–17 in 1891, 35–16 in 1892, 34–14 in 1893, 32–13 in 1894, 26–16 in 1895, 21–19 in 1899, 21–13 in 1904. Led NL in victories, 1896 (30–14), 1897 (31–11), 1898 (32–12); in shutouts, 1890 (7), 1894 (3), 1900 (4). He holds ML records for most seasons winning 30 or more games, 7, and most consecutive years winning 20 or more from beginning of career, 10.

He managed St. Louis NL, 1904–05 (part): 94–108, .465.

Baseball Hall of Fame.

NICHOLSON, LEO basketball: b. Feb. 28, 1901, Harrisburg, Ore.; d. June 11, 1967. As coach at Central Washington State College, 1931–64, Nicholson compiled a 505–270 record.

Helms Hall of Fame.

NICOL, HUGH N. baseball: b. Jan. 1, 1858, Campsie, Scotland; d. June 27, 1921. Bat, throw R; outfield. Chicago NL, 1881–82; St. Louis AA, 1883–86; Cincinnati AA, 1887–89; Cincinnati NL, 1890. Ten years, 888 games, 345 stolen bases (6 years not included), .235 BA. Led AA in stolen bases, 1887 (138).

NIEMI, LAURIE ("Finn") football: b. March 19, 1925, Red Lodge, Nebr.; d. Feb. 19, 1968. Washington State tackle. Washington Redskins, 1949–53.

NIGGELING, JOHN A. baseball: b. July 10, 1903, Remsen, Iowa; d. Sept. 16, 1963. Bat, throw R; pitcher. Boston NL, 1938; Cincinnati NL, 1939; St. Louis AL, 1940–43; Washington AL, 1943–46; Boston NL, 1946. Nine years, 64–69, 3.22 ERA; 620 strikeouts, 12 shutouts in 1,250⅔ innings.

NORRIS, JAMES D., JR. boxing, hockey: b. Nov. 6, 1906, Chicago; d. Feb. 25, 1966. Norris inherited from his father a financial interest in several sports but became best known as a kind of czar of boxing after 1949, when he bought Mike Jacobs's 20th Century Sporting Club and changed its name to the International Boxing Club. The IBC's major promotions were Rocky Marciano's championship fights. Alleged links with gangsters and the threat of federal antitrust action forced the breaking up of the IBC in 1958.

Norris became major owner of the Chicago Blackhawks hockey team in 1952 and retained control until his death.

NUNAMAKER, LESLIE G. baseball: b. Aug. 25, 1889, Aurora, Nebr.; d. Nov. 14, 1938. Bat, throw R; catcher. Boston AL, 1911–14; New York AL, 1914–17; St. Louis AL, 1918; Cleveland AL, 1919–22. Twelve years, 715 games, .268 BA. As pinch-hitter, 28-for-78, .359 BA. One World Series, 1920: 1-for-2 as pinch-hitter.

Nunamaker tied the ML record for catchers with 3 assists in an inning, Aug. 3, 1914.

O

OAKLEY, ANNIE shooting: b. Annie Moses, Aug. 13, 1860, Greenville, Ohio; d. Nov. 3, 1926. At eight, she was shooting game that could be bartered at a country store to help support her family. When she was fifteen, she was matched in Cincinnati against Frank Butler, a champion shot, and she beat him. He married her a year later, and she joined his traveling show. In 1884, the Butlers joined Buffalo Bill Cody's Wild West Show, remaining with it for seventeen years. Annie Oakley won world fame during a lengthy tour of Europe as the show's featured attraction.

Though basically a trick shot, she ran her first 100 straight at trap in 1887 and she did it for the last time in 1922, when she was sixty-two years old. During one two-year period, she won $9,000 trapshooting.

From 30 paces, she could split a playing card held on edge, hit a dime thrown into the air, or shoot a cigarette from her husband's lips. One of her most spectacular tricks was to lie on her back and have someone throw six glass balls into the air at once. Using three double-barreled shotguns, she would break all six before they hit the ground.

American Trapshooting Hall of Fame.

OBERLANDER, "SWEDE" (Andrew J.) football: b. Feb. 17, 1905, Chelsea, Mass.; d. Jan. 1, 1968. Dartmouth halfback; All-American, 1925. Oberlander threw 12 TD passes in 1925, when Dartmouth was undefeated.

Helms Hall of Fame, National Football Hall of Fame.

O'BRIEN, JOHN J. basketball: b. Nov. 4, 1888, Brooklyn; d. Dec. 9, 1967. O'Brien played pro basketball and officiated at all levels, but his major contribution was as an organizer and administrator. He helped organize the Interstate Professional League in 1914 and was its president, 1915–17. In 1921 he was the major force in organizing the Metropolitan Basketball League, serving as president and treasurer, 1922–28. He was also long-time president of the American Basketball League, which was formed in 1925. Basketball Hall of Fame.

O'BRIEN, PHILADELPHIA JACK boxing: b. Joseph F. Hagen, Jan. 17, 1878, Philadelphia; d. Nov. 12, 1942. His record: 91 wins, 36 by KO; 7 losses, 4 by KO; 16 draws, 57 no-decisions. O'Brien won the light-heavyweight title with a 13-round KO of Bob Fitzsimmons on Dec. 20, 1905. Twice he fought Tommy Burns for the heavyweight championship; on Nov. 28, 1906, the result was a 20-round draw, but on May 8, 1907, Burns won a 20-round decision. O'Brien was still light-heavy champion when he retired in 1912.

Helms Hall of Fame, Boxing Hall of Fame.

O'CONNELL, DANIEL F. baseball: b. Jan. 21, 1927, Paterson, N.J.; d. Oct. 2, 1969. Bat, throw R; second-third base, shortstop. Pittsburgh NL, 1950, 1953; Milwaukee NL, 1954–57; New York NL, 1957; San Francisco NL, 1958–59; Washington AL, 1961–62. Ten years, 1,143 games, .260 BA. He tied the NL record for most triples in a game, 3, in 1956.

He was killed in an auto accident.

O'CONNOR, "JACK" (John J.) baseball: b. March 3, 1867, St. Louis; d. Nov. 14, 1937. Bat, throw R; catcher, outfield, first base. Cincinnati AA, 1887–88; Columbus AA, 1889–91; Cleveland NL, 1892–98; St. Louis NL, 1899–1900; Pittsburgh NL, 1900–02; New York AL, 1903; St. Louis AL, 1904, 1906–07, 1910. Twenty-one years, 1,454 games, .263 BA; hit .324 in 1890.

He managed St. Louis AL, 1910: 47–107, .305.

O'CONNOR, PATRICK J. auto racing: b. Oct. 9, 1928, North Vernon, Ind.; d. May 30, 1958. O'Connor was Midwest driving champion, 1953–54 and 1956.

He was killed in a crash during the Indianapolis 500.

O'DAY, "HANK" (Henry F.) baseball: b. July 8, 1863, Chicago; d. July 2, 1935. Throw R; pitcher. Toledo AA, 1884; Pittsburgh AA, 1885; Washington NL, 1886–89; New York NL, 1889; New York PL, 1890. Led NL in losses, 1888 (16–29). Seven years, 70–110, 3.29 ERA.

Managed Cincinnati NL, 1912; Chicago NL, 1914: 153–154, .498.

O'DEA, PATRICK J. football: b. March 17, 1872, Melbourne, Australia; d. April 4, 1962. Wisconsin fullback; 2nd team All-American, 1898; 3rd team, 1899. One of the great kickers, O'Dea dropkicked a 62-yard field goal against Northwestern in 1898, 1 AL,as a record by some writers; he had an 87-yard punt in the same game. He also had a 50-yard field goal in 1897. O'Dea was a rugby star in Australia before coming to this country in 1896. He attended Wisconsin because his brother was track coach there. After graduating, O'Dea coached football at Notre Dame, 1900–01, and at Missouri, 1902.

Helms Hall of Fame, National Football Foundation Hall of Fame.

O'DOUL, "LEFTY" (Francis J.) baseball: b. March 4, 1897, San Francisco; d. Dec. 7, 1969. Bat, throw L; pitcher, outfield. New York AL, 1919–20, 1922; Boston AL, 1923; New York NL, 1928; Philadelphia NL, 1929–30; Brooklyn NL, 1931–33; New York NL, 1933–34. Eleven years, 970 games, .349 BA; hit .319 in 1928, .383 in 1930, .336 in 1931 and .316 in 1934. Led NL in hits (254), BA (.398) in 1929; in BA (.368) in 1932.

After developing a sore arm, O'Doul switched from the mound to the outfield and returned to the majors at the age of thirty-one. In his one World Series, 1933, he pinch-hit just once and drove in 2 runs with a single, then scored, sparking a rally that led the Giants from a 1–0 deficit to a 6–1 win in the second game; they went on to beat Washington in 5 games.

O'Doul was active in the 1930s in starting organized baseball in Japan, and after World War II he went back to Japan to help reorganize the sport.

O'DOWD, MIKE boxing: b. April 5, 1895, St. Paul, Minn.; d. July 28, 1957. His record: 52 wins, 35 by KO; 8 losses, 1 by KO; 3 draws, 52 no-decisions. O'Dowd won the middleweight title on Nov. 14, 1917, by KOing Al McCoy in 6 rounds. He lost it to Johnny Wilson on May 6, 1920, in a 12-round decision, which wasn't popular. O'Dowd got a rematch on March 17, 1921, and lost to Wilson again, this time in 15 rounds.

OLDFIELD, "BARNEY" (Berna E.) auto racing: b. Jan. 29, 1878, Wauseon, Ohio; d. Oct. 4, 1946. When Henry Ford needed a driver for his first racing car in 1902, a professional bike racer named Oldfield was recommended. Oldfield had never even driven a car, but he spent two weeks learning, then won the Detroit 5-mile classic in 5 minutes, 28 seconds. Ford later recalled, "While I was cranking the car for the start, Oldfield remarked cheerfully, 'Well, the chariot may kill me, but they will say after that I was going like hell when she took me over the bank.' "

In the same car, the "999," Oldfield became the first man to travel a mile a minute, in 1903. It was a 2,800-pound monster with a handlebar type of steering control. It took a lot of muscle, as well as nerve, to take such cars through turns. Oldfield, who always drove with a cigar clenched between his teeth, won so consistently that long after his records were broken his name was still synonymous with reckless speed. He considered his biggest victory the Los Angeles-to-Phoenix road race in 1914; it took three days.

Auto Racing Hall of Fame, Helms Hall of Fame.

OLDRING, REUBEN H. baseball: b. May 30, 1884, New York City; d. Sept. 9, 1961. Bat, throw R; outfield. New York AL, 1905; Philadelphia AL, 1906–16; New York AL, 1916; Philadelphia AL, 1918. Thirteen years, 1,237 games, .270 BA; hit .308 in 1910, .301 in 1912. Three World Series, 1911, 1913–14: 15 games, .194 BA.

OLIN, ROBERT boxing: b. July 4, 1908, New York City; d. Dec. 16, 1956. His record: 53 wins, 25 by KO; 27 losses, 4 by KO; 5 draws. After 35 consecutive wins as an amateur Olin turned professional, and on Nov. 16, 1934, he won the light-heavyweight title by decisioning Maxie Rosenbloom in 15 rounds. He lost it on Oct. 31, 1935, to John Henry Lewis on a 15-round decision.

OLIVER, "PORKY" (Edward S.) golf: b. Sept. 6, 1916, Wilmington, Del.; d. Sept. 21, 1961. Oliver, who was 5'9" and weighed 225 pounds in his prime, won his only major victory in the 1941 Western Open. He had some bad luck: Apparently tied for first place in the 1940 U.S. Open, he was disqualified for teeing off ahead of schedule in the last round. In the 1946 PGA, then match play, he led Ben Hogan by 3 halfway through the 36-hole final, but Hogan fired a 33 on the front 9 in the 2nd round and went on to win. Oliver's 279 in the 1953 Masters tied the previous record, but Hogan won with a 275, a new record.

Oliver died of lung cancer. Told he had six months to live, he helped raise $20,000 for cancer research before his death.

OLSEN, "OLE" (Harold G.) basketball: b. May 10, 1895, Rice Lake, Wis.; d. Oct. 29, 1953. Twice All-Conference at Wisconsin when the team won Western Conference titles, 1916–17, Olsen coached at Ripon College, 1919–21, Ohio State, 1922–46, and Northwestern, 1950. At Ohio State, he had a 263–180 record and won five Western Conference (Big Ten) titles. He also coached the professional Chicago Stags, 1946–49 (95–63).

Basketball Hall of Fame.

OLSON, "IVY" (Ivan M.) baseball: b. Oct. 14, 1885, Kansas City, Mo.; d. Sept. 1, 1965. Bat, throw R; infield. Cleveland AL, 1911–14; Cincinnati NL, 1915; Brooklyn NL, 1915–24. Led NL in hits, 1919 (164). Fourteen years, 1,572 games, .258 BA. Two World Series, 1916, 1920: 12 games, .293 BA.

O'NEILL, "BUCK" (Frank J.) football: b. 1875(?); d. April 21, 1958. After playing fullback at Williams College, O'Neill coached at Colgate, 1902, 1904–05; Syracuse, 1906–07, 1913–15, 1917–19; Columbia, 1920–22. His best years were at Syracuse, 1915 (9–1–2) and 1917 (8–1–1). National Football Foundation Hall of Fame.

O'NEILL, STEPHEN F. baseball: b. July 6, 1891, Minooka, Pa.; d. Jan. 26, 1962. Bat, throw R; catcher. Cleveland AL, 1911–23; Boston AL, 1924; New York AL, 1925; St. Louis AL, 1927–28. Seventeen years, 1,586 games, .263 BA; hit .321 in 1920, .322 in 1921, .311 in 1922. One World Series, 1920: 7 games, .333 BA.

He managed Cleveland AL, 1935 (part)–37; Detroit AL, 1943–48; Boston AL, 1950 (part)–51; Philadelphia NL, 1952 (part)–54 (part): 1,039–819, .559. Pennant, World Series, 1945.

O'NEILL, "TIP" (James E.) baseball: b. May 25, 1858, Woodstock, Ontario, Canada; d. Dec. 31, 1915. Bat, throw R; outfield. New York NL, 1883; St. Louis AA, 1884–89; Chicago PL, 1890; St. Louis AA, 1891; Cincinnati NL, 1892. Ten years, 1,054 games, .326 BA; hit .328 in 1886, .335 in 1889, .302 in 1890, .321 in 1891. Led league in hits (225), doubles (52), triples (19), home runs (14), runs (167), BA (.435), and slugging (.691) in 1887; in hits (177) and BA (.335) in 1888.

O'Neill is the only player ever to lead a league in doubles, triples, and home runs in the same season.

O'ROURKE, JAMES H. ("Orator Jim") baseball: b. Aug. 24, 1852, Bridgeport, Conn.; d. Jan. 8, 1919. Bat, throw R; outfield, catcher, infield. National Association, Middletown, 1872; Boston, 1873–75. Four years, 225 games, .317 BA.

Boston NL, 1876–78; Providence NL, 1879; Boston NL, 1880; Buffalo NL, 1881–84; New York NL, 1885–89; New York PL, 1890; New York NL, 1891–92; Washington NL, 1893; New York NL, 1904. Nineteen years, 1,774 games, 2,304 hits, .310 BA; hit .327 in 1876, .362 in 1877, .348 in 1879, .302 in 1881, .328 in 1883, .347 in 1884, .300 in 1885, .309 in 1886, .360 in 1890, .340 in 1892. Led league in hits, 1884 (162); home runs, 1880 (6); triples, 1885 (16); walks (20) and runs (68) in 1877.

He managed Buffalo NL, 1881–84; Washington NL, 1893: 246–258, .488. Baseball Hall of Fame.

ORSATTI, ERNESTO R. baseball: b. Sept. 8, 1903, Los Angeles; d. Sept. 4, 1968. Bat, throw L; outfield, first base. St. Louis NL, 1927–35. Nine years, 709 games, .306 BA; hit .332 in 1929, .336 in 1932, .300 in 1934. Four World Series, 1928, 1930–31, 1934: 13 games, .273 BA.

ORTH, ALBERT L. baseball: b. Sept. 5, 1872, Danville, Ind.; d. Oct. 8, 1948. Bat L, throw R; pitcher. Philadelphia NL, 1895–1901; Washington AL, 1902–04; New York AL, 1904–09. Fifteen years, 202–189, 3.37 ERA; 28 shutouts; 21–12 in 1901. Led league in ERA, 1899 (2.49); in shutouts, 1901 (6); in wins (25–17) and complete games (36) in 1906; in losses, 1907 (13–21).

ORTIZ, MANUEL, boxing: b. ?, Corona, Calif.; d. May 31, 1970, His record: 89 wins, 44 by KO; 27 losses, 1 by KO; 3 draws. Ortiz won the bantam-weight title, Aug. 7, 1942, by outpointing Lou Salica in 12 rounds. He lost it to Harold Dade in 15 rounds on Jan. 7, 1947, regained it by outpointing Dade in 15 rounds on March 11, 1947, and lost it for good to Vic Toweel on May 31, 1950, another 15-round decision.

ORTON, GEORGE W. track: b. 1872, Ontario, Canada; d. June 26, 1958. Orton won the 2,500-meter steeplechase at the 1900 Olympics. He was AAU 1-mile champion, 1892–96 and 1900, and the 10-mile champion in 1899. He won the AAU 2–mile steeplechase, 1893–94, 1896–99, and 1901. Representing Pennsylvania, he won the IC4A mile in 1895 and 1897. He was also AAU cross-country champion, 1897–98.

Helms Hall of Fame.

OSTERMUELLER, "FRITZ" (Frederick R.) baseball: b. Sept. 15, 1907, Quincy, Ill.; d. Dec. 17, 1957. Bat, throw L; pitcher. Boston AL, 1934–40; St. Louis AL, 1941–43; Brooklyn NL, 1943–44; Pittsburgh NL, 1944–48. Fifteen years, 114–115, 3.99 ERA. In relief, 15–17, 3.87 ERA, 15 saves.

OTT, MELVIN T. baseball: b. March 2, 1909, Gretna, Ill.; d. Nov. 21, 1958. Bat L, throw R; outfield, third base. New York NL, 1926–47. Twenty-two years (7th), 2,732 games (6th), 9,456 at-bats, 2,876 hits, 488 doubles, 72 triples, 511 home runs (8th), 1,859 runs (6th), 5,041 total bases (8th), 1,860 RBI (6th), 1,708 walks (4th), .304 BA; hit .322 in 1928, .328 in 1929, .349 in 1930, .318 in 1932, .326 in 1934, .322 in 1935, .328 in 1936, .311 in 1938, .308 in 1939, .308 in 1945. Led NL in runs, 1938 (116), 1942 (118); home runs, 1932 (38), 1934 (35), 1936 (33), 1937 (31), 1938 (36), 1942 (30); RBI, 1934 (135); walks, 1929 (113), 1931 (80), 1932 (100), 1933 (75), 1937 (102), 1942 (109); slugging, 1936 (.588).

Ott arrived in the majors as a baby-faced seventeen-year-old. Only 5'9" and about 170 pounds, he had quick, strong wrists and was a vicious pull-hitter. On Aug. 4, 1934, and April 30, 1944, he scored 6 runs in a game, the only player to do it twice. On the latter date, he had 2 singles and 5 walks, tying the ML record for most times reaching base safely without being put out. Twice in 1944 he scored 5 or more runs in a game, tying the ML record, and he did it 3 times in his career, a modern record. Ott also set an ML record in 1929 with an 11-game RBI streak. On June 19 of that year, he got 6 extra-base hits (4 doubles and 2 home runs) in a doubleheader, tying the ML record. He is also coholder of the ML record for most times getting 5 walks in a game, 4.

He is holder or coholder of NL records for most years leading in walks, 6, most consecutive, 3; most years 100 or more walks, 10, most consecutive, 7; most consecutive years 100 or more RBI, 8; most double plays in a season, outfielder, 12 in 1929.

Three World Series, 1933, 1936–37: 16 games, .295 BA; 2 doubles, 4 home runs, 8 runs, 10 RBI.

He managed New York NL, 1942–48 (part): 454–530, .461.

Baseball Hall of Fame.

OUIMET, FRANCIS D. golf: b. May 8, 1893, Brookline, Mass.; d. Sept. 2, 1967. Two top British golfers, Harry Vardon and Ted Ray, came to Brookline to compete in the 1913 U.S. Open, and it seemed certain one of them would win it. But at the end of the regulation 72 holes, a twenty-year-old former caddy named Ouimet was tied with them. In the playoff, the young American amateur shot his best round, a 72, to Vardon's 77 and Ray's 78, and for the first time a golf tournament was headlined across the country. Ouimet was an instant hero, and golf had a new popularity.

Ouimet went on to become a three-time winner of the U.S. Amateur, in 1914, 1920, and 1931, and also won the Western Amateur in 1917 and the North and South Amateur in 1920. He was a member of the Walker Cup team, 1921–49, and its captain six times, and he never did turn professional to cash in on his fame.

In 1951, he became the only non-British member of the Royal and Ancient Golf Club of St. Andrew's. Scotland.

Helms Hall of Fame, Professional Golfers Association Hall of Fame.

OVERALL, ORVAL baseball: b. Feb. 2, 1881, Visalia, Calif.; d. July 14, 1947. Sw. hit, throw R; pitcher. Cincinnati NL, 1905–06; Chicago NL, 1906–10, 1913. Seven years, 110–69, 2.24 ERA (8th); 933 strikeouts, 30 shutouts in 1,532⅓ innings; 21–11 in 1909. Led NL in victories (23–7) and shutouts (8) in 1907; in strikeouts (205) and shutouts (9) in 1909. Four World Series, 1906–08, 1910: 3–1, 1.58 ERA, 1 shutout; 35 strikeouts in 51⅓ innings.

OVERLIN, KEN boxing: b. 1910, Decatur, Ill.; d. July 21, 1969. His record: 126 wins, 23 by KO; 13 losses, 1 by KO; 7 draws, 1 no-contest. Overlin challenged Freddy Steele for the middleweight title but lost on a 4th-round KO, Sept. 11, 1937. He won the New York version of the title with a 15-round decision over Ceferino Garcia on May 24, 1940, only to lose it to Billy Soose on May 9, 1941, in another 15-round decision.

OWEN, BENJAMIN G. football: b. July 24, 1875, Chicago; d. Feb. 26, 1970. A Kansas graduate, Owen coached Oklahoma, 1905–26, compiling a 122–54–16 record, with four undefeated teams, in 1911, 1915, 1918, and 1920. His best season record was 10–0–0 in 1915, but the 1918 team had an awesome record, winning all six of its games while outscoring the opposition 278–7. Owen had previously coached at Washburn College and Bethany of Kansas.

Helms Hall of Fame, National Football Foundation Hall of Fame.

OWEN, FRANK M. baseball: b. Dec. 23, 1879, Ypsilanti, Mich.; d. Nov. 27, 1942. Throw R; pitcher. Detroit AL, 1901; Chicago AL, 1903–09. Eight years, 79–68, 2.55 ERA; 16 shutouts; 21–15 in 1904, 21–13 in 1905. One World Series, 1906: 0–0, 3.00 ERA in 6 innings of relief.

OWEN, LAURENCE figure skating: b. 1944, Winchester, Mass.; d. Feb. 15, 1961. Coached by her mother, Maribel Vinson Owen, Miss Owen looked like the successor to an American skating dynasty that had been established by Tenley Albright and Carol Heiss. She had won the 1961 U.S. and North American championships and was en route to Europe with other members of the American team when the plane crashed in Belgium. She, her mother, her older sister, and fifteen members of the team were killed.

OWEN, STEPHEN football: b. April 21, 1898, Cleo Springs, Okla.; d. May 17, 1964. After graduating from Phillips College, Owen played tackle for the Kansas City Cowboys, 1924–25, and the New York Giants, 1926–31, 1933. He began to coach the Giants in 1931, while still a player. He stayed for twenty-two years, through the 1952 season. His teams compiled an overall mark of 150–100–17; they won division titles, 1933–35, 1938–39, 1941, 1944, and 1946, and NFL titles in 1934 and 1938. Owen holds the record for most times coached in a championship game, 8. The Giants also tied for divisional titles in 1943 and 1950 but lost both playoffs.

Owen was skilled at designing defenses. His greatest contribution to the game was the "umbrella" defense, which he developed in 1950, mainly to stop the Cleveland Browns' passing attack. He had one linebacker and four defensive backs behind a six-man line, but the ends frequently dropped off to cover shallow receivers, making an alignment very similar to today's standard 4–3–4 defense.

In the famed "Sneakers" championship game of 1934, the Giants were trailing the Bears, 10–3, at half time on an icy field. Owen had his players change to basketball shoes to get better traction in the second half, and the Giants won going away, literally, 30–13, with 4 TDs in the final quarter. Professional Football Hall of Fame.

P

PACKARD, "GENE" (Eugene M.) baseball: b. July 13, 1887, Colorado Springs, Colo.; d. May 19, 1959. Bat, throw L; pitcher. Cincinnati NL, 1912–13; Kansas City Fed L, 1914–15; Chicago NL, 1916–17; St. Louis NL, 1917–18; Philadelphia NL, 1919. Eight years, 86–67, 3.01 ERA; 15 shutouts; 21–13 in 1914, 20–11 in 1915.

PADDOCK, "CHARLIE" (Charles W.) track: b. Aug. 11, 1900, Gainsville, Tex.; d. July 21, 1943. Paddock at one time held three sprint records and was coholder of a fourth. He was AAU 100-yard champion in 1921 and 1924 and 220-yard champion, 1920–21 and 1924. He won the Olympic 100 in 1920.

In 1921 Paddock set records of 20.8 seconds in the 220 and 200 meters and 10.4 seconds in the 100 meters. He also became the third man to run 100 yards in 9.6. It had been done twice before; he did it four times in 1921 and twice more during his career.

A Marine captain, Paddock was killed in a plane crash.
Helms Hall of Fame.

PAGE, "PAT" (Harlan O.) basketball: b. March 20, 1887, Chicago; d. Nov. 23, 1965. Page was a four-sport star at the University of Chicago—in 1908, he completed 21 passes in one game, more than most football teams would complete in a season at that time—but basketball was his outstanding sport. While he was playing, Chicago won three Western Conference (Big Ten) titles; the team was undefeated in 1909 and Page was named College Player of the Year in 1910. He later coached football at Indiana and basketball at Butler and Idaho.
Basketball Hall of Fame, Helms Hall of Fame.

PALIN, SEPTER F. harness racing: b. 1878(?), Iroquois, Ill.; d. Oct. 3, 1952. At his death Palin led in 2-minute performances, with 64. He twice won the Hambletonian, in 1935, with Greyhound, and in 1947, with Hoot Mon.

With Palin driving, Greyhound set records for the 1-mile trot on both 1-mile and ½-mile tracks. Hoot Mon set a Hambletonian record of 2 minutes flat.

Harness Hall of Fame.

PAPKE, "BILLY" (William H.) boxing: b. Sept. 17, 1886, Spring Valley, Ill.; d. Nov. 26, 1936. His record: 39 wins, 29 by KO; 9 losses, 1 by KO; 7 draws, 9 no-decisions. Papke won the middleweight title on Sept. 7, 1908, with a 12th-round KO of Stanley Ketchel. The enraged Ketchel beat him badly before KOing him in the 11th to regain the title on Nov. 26. They had another fight, July 5, 1909, and Ketchel won a 20-round decision.

After Ketchel's death, Papke claimed the championship but quickly lost it on a 20-round decision to Johnny "Cyclone" Thompson on Feb. 11, 1911. When Thompson vacated the title in October, Papke claimed it again. He lost a 20-round decision to Frank Mantell on Feb. 22, 1912, but Mantell was recognized only in California. Papke finally lost the crown, on a foul in the 15th round, on March 5, 1913, to Frank Klaus.

Helms Hall of Fame.

PARSHALL, H. M. A. harness racing: b. 1899(?); d. Oct. 30, 1950. A veterinarian, Dr. Parshall drove to 25 two-minute performances, 21 of them with pacers. Among his 32 major victories were two in the Hambletonian, with Lord Jim in 1934 and with Peter Astra in 1939.

Harness Hall of Fame.

PASKERT, "DODE" (George H.) baseball: b. Aug. 28, 1881, Cleveland; d. Feb. 12, 1959. Bat, throw R; outfield. Cincinnati NL, 1907–10; Philadelphia NL, 1911–17; Chicago NL, 1918–20; Cincinnati NL, 1921. Fifteen years, 1,715 games, .268 BA; hit .300 in 1910, .315 in 1912. Two World Series, 1915, 1918: 11 games, .175 BA.

PATTERSON, ROY L. baseball: b. Dec. 17, 1876, Stoddard, Wis.; d. April 14, 1953. Bat, throw R; pitcher. Chicago AL, 1901–07. Seven years, 82–69, 2.75 ERA; 17 shutouts; 20–16 in 1901.

PECK, ROBERT D. football: b. May 30, 1891, Lock Haven, Pa.; d. June 19, 1932. Pittsburgh center; All-American, 1915–16. Peck weighed only 180 pounds but was solidly built at 5'8", and he was an aggressive player who never retreated from anyone. Because of his great speed, he frequently made two or three blocks on a single play, and as a linebacker he had great range.

Helms Hall of Fame, National Football Foundation Hall of Fame.

PEDEN, DONALD C. football: b. 1899, Kewanee, Ill.; d. Feb. 23, 1970. A halfback at Illinois (1922), Peden coached at Ohio University, 1924–42, 1945–46, compiling a 121–46–11 mark. He produced two consecutive un-

beaten, untied teams, 1929–30, and had another unbeaten team in 1935. As baseball coach for twenty-five years, he had a 261–142 record. Ohio University's stadium is named for him.
Helms Hall of Fame.

PEITZ, "HEINIE" (Henry C.) baseball: b. Nov. 28, 1870, St. Louis; d. Oct. 23, 1943. Bat, throw R; catcher, third base. St. Louis NL, 1892–95; Cincinnati NL, 1896–1904; Pittsburgh NL, 1905–06; St. Louis NL, 1913. Sixteen years, 1,234 games, .271 BA; hit .315 in 1902.

PELL, CLARENCE C. racquets: b. 1885(?); d. Nov. 4, 1964. Pell in 1927 became the first American to win the British amateur championship. He won U.S. singles titles, 1915, 1917, 1920–22, 1924–25, 1927–28, and 1931–33; with Stanley G. Mortimer, he won the doubles 9 times. He also won the Tuxedo Gold Racquet, 1914–17, 1921–23, 1925–27, 1929–30, 1932–33, and 1936.

PELL, THEODORE R. tennis: b. 1878(?); d. Aug. 18, 1967. Pell won the U.S. indoor singles championship in 1907, 1909, and 1911, and the indoor doubles in 1905 (with Harry F. Allen), 1909 (with Wylie C. Grant), and 1911–12 (with Frederick B. Alexander).
Tennis Hall of Fame.

PELTY, BARNEY baseball: b. Sept. 10, 1880, Farmington, Mo.; d. May 24, 1939. Bat, throw R; pitcher. St. Louis AL, 1903–12; Washington AL, 1912. Ten years, 91–116, 2.62 ERA; 23 shutouts.

PENNOCK, HERBERT J. baseball: b. Feb. 10, 1894, Kennett Square, Pa.; d. Jan. 20, 1948. Sw. hit, throw L; pitcher. Philadelphia AL, 1912–15; Boston AL, 1915–17, 1919–22; New York AL, 1923–33; Boston AL, 1934. Twenty-two years, 240–162, 3.61 ERA; 35 shutouts. In relief, 24–17, 3.49 ERA, 32 saves; 21–9 in 1924, 23–11 in 1926. Led AL in percentage, 1923 (19–6, .760); in shutouts, 1928 (5). Five World Series, 1914, 1923, 1926–27, 1932: 4 complete games, 5 wins (4th), 0 losses, 1.95 ERA; 5 starts. In relief, 3 saves (2nd), 1.59 ERA.

A great clutch pitcher, as his World Series record indicates, Pennock retired the first 22 men he faced en route to a 3-hit, 8–1 victory in the 3rd game in 1927, when the Yankees won 4 straight from Pittsburgh.
Baseball Hall of Fame.

PENNOCK, STANLEY B. football: b. June 15, 1892, Syracuse, N.Y.; d. Nov. 27, 1916. Harvard guard; All-American, 1912–14.
Helms Hall of Fame, National Football Foundation Hall of Fame.

PERRITT, "POL" (William D.) baseball: b. Aug. 30, 1892, Arcadia, La.; d. Oct. 15, 1947. Bat, throw R; pitcher. St. Louis NL, 1912–14; New York NL, 1915–21; Detroit AL, 1921. Ten years, 91–78, 2.89 ERA; 23 shutouts. One World Series, 1917: 0–0, 2.16 ERA in 8⅓ innings of relief.

PERRY, H. SCOTT baseball: b. April 17, 1892, Corsicana, Tex.; d. Oct. 27, 1959. Bat L, throw R; pitcher. St. Louis AL, 1915; Chicago NL, 1916; Cincinnati NL, 1917; Philadelphia NL, 1919–21. Seven years, 41–68, 3.07 ERA. Led AL in losses (21–19) and complete games (30) in 1918; in losses, 1920 (11–25).

PETERSON, CHARLES C. billiards: b. 1880, Milwaukee, Wis.; d. June 26, 1962. Peterson's slogan was, "Show me a shot that I can't make." After an auto accident, he realized his nerves were no longer good enough for tournament play, so he became a trick-shot artist. He entertained millions and helped to make billiards respectable with thousands of appearances on college campuses and for the armed forces.

PETTITT, THOMAS tennis: b. 1860(?), Beckenham, Kent, England; d. Oct. 17, 1946. Pettitt was America's first world champion in court tennis. He challenged Englishman George Lambert in 1885; trailing 5 sets to 1, he won 6 in a row for a 7–5 victory. In 1890 he defended against Charles Saunders and again won, 7–5. He then resigned the title but returned in 1898 to challenge Peter Latham but lost, 7–0. For more than fifty years, Pettitt was the professional tennis instructor at the Newport, Rhode Island, Casino, first home of lawn tennis in the United States.

PFEFFER, "FRED" (Nathaniel Frederick) baseball: b. March 17, 1860, Louisville, Ky.; d. April 10, 1932. Bat, throw R; second base, shortstop. Troy NL, 1882; Chicago NL, 1883–89; Chicago PL, 1890; Chicago NL, 1891; Louisville NL, 1892–95; New York NL, 1896; Chicago NL, 1896–97. Sixteen years, 1,670 games, 1,094 runs, 352 stolen bases (five years not included), .255 BA; hit .308 in 1894.

Pfeffer tied an NL record for most years leading second basemen in putouts, 7. His 3 hits (2 singles and a double) in one inning, Sept. 6, 1883, tied an ML record.

PFEISTER, "JACK" (John T. J.) baseball: b. Pfiestenberger, May 24, 1878, Cincinnati; d. Sept. 3, 1953. Bat R, throw L; pitcher. Pittsburgh NL, 1903–04; Chicago NL, 1906–11. Eight years, 70–45, 2.04 ERA, 503 strikeouts, 17 shutouts in 1,058⅓ innings. Led NL in ERA, 1907 (1.15). Four World Series, 1906–08, 1910: 5 games, 1–3, 3.97 ERA.

PHILLIPPE, "DEACON" (Charles L.) baseball: b. May 23, 1874, Rural Retreat, Va.; d. March 30, 1952. Bat, throw R; pitcher. Louisville NL, 1899; Pittsburgh NL, 1900–11. Thirteen years, 186–109, 2.59 ERA, 27 shutouts. In relief, 25–4, 2.10 ERA, 12 saves; 21–17 in 1899, 20–13 in 1900, 21–13 in 1901, 20–9 in 1902, 24–9 in 1903. He won 13 consecutive games in 1910, when he had a 14–2 record. No-hitter, May 25, 1899, against New York NL (7–0). Two World Series, 1903, 1909: 5 starts, 5 complete (6th), 3–2, 2.88 ERA. Phillippe was virtually the only healthy pitcher Pittsburgh had in the 1903 Series against Boston, the first in history. He beat Cy Young in the opener, then won the third and fourth games to give Pittsburgh a commanding lead, but they couldn't win another. He was the loser, 7–3, in the seventh game and 3–0 in the eighth game.

PHILLIPS, HENRY D. football: b. Jan. 16, 1882, Philadelphia; d. June 29, 1955. University of the South guard, 1905.
 He was Episcopal bishop of the Diocese of Southwest Virginia, 1938–54. National Football Foundation Hall of Fame.

PHILLIPS, WILLIAM C. baseball: b. Nov. 9, 1868, Allenport, Pa.; d. Oct. 25, 1941. Throw R; pitcher. Pittsburgh NL, 1890; Cincinnati NL, 1895, 1899–1903. Seven years, 71–77, 4.10 ERA.
 He managed Indianapolis Fed L, 1914; Newark Fed L, 1915 (part): 114–92, .553. Pennant, 1914.

PIATT, WILEY H. baseball: b. July 13, 1874, Blue Creek, Ohio; d. Sept. 20, 1946. Bat, throw L; pitcher. Philadelphia NL, 1898–1900; Philadelphia AL, 1901; Chicago AL, 1901–02; Boston NL, 1903. Six years, 85–78, 3.61 ERA; 12 shutouts; 24–14 in 1898, 23–15 in 1899. Led NL in shutouts, 1898 (6).

PICCOLO, BRIAN football: b. Oct. 21, 1943, Pittsfield, Mass.; d. June 16, 1970. Wake Forest halfback, Chicago Bears, 1965–69. Piccolo led collegiate rushers in 1964 with 1,044 yards. In five pro seasons he gained 927 yards on 257 carries, a 3.5 average, and caught 58 passes for 537 yards.
 He died of cancer.

PICINICH, VALENTINE J. baseball: b. Sept. 8, 1896, New York City; d. Dec. 5, 1942. Bat, throw R; catcher. Philadelphia AL, 1916–17; Washington AL, 1918–22; Boston AL, 1923–25; Cincinnati NL, 1926–28; Brooklyn NL, 1929–23; Pittsburgh NL, 1933. Eighteen years, 1,048 games, .258 BA; hit .302 in 1928.

PIERCE, DONALD football: b. Feb. 7, 1919, Topeka, Kan.; d. Jan. 2, 1965. Kansas center; captain, 1940. Brooklyn Dodgers, 1942; Chicago Cardinals, 1943.

PIEROTTI, "AL" (Albert F.) football: b. Oct. 24, 1895, Boston; d. Feb. 12, 1964. Washington and Lee center, Cleveland Panthers, 1919–20; Milwaukee Badgers, 1922–24; Boston Bulldogs (AFL), 1926; Providence Steamrollers, 1927–28; Boston Braves, 1929.
He also pitched briefly for Boston NL, 1920–21.

PIKE, "LIP" (Lipman E.) baseball: b. May 25, 1845, New York City; d. Oct. 10, 1893. Bat, throw L; outfield, second base. National Association, Troy, 1871; Baltimore, 1872–73; Hartford, 1874; St. Louis, 1875. Five years, 260 games, .321 BA.
St. Louis NL, 1876; Cincinnati NL, 1877–78; Providence NL, 1878; Worcester NL, 1881; New York AA, 1887. Five years, 163 games, .304 BA. Led NL in home runs, 1877 (4).
Pike was also a professional sprinter; he once won $250 in a 100-yard race against a horse. Twice he was clocked in under 10 seconds for 100 yards, which was then the U.S. amateur record.

PILGRIM, PAUL H. track: b. 1883, New York City; d. Jan. 7, 1958. Pilgrim won both the 400-meter and 800-meter runs in the 1906 Olympics. He was manager of athletics at the New York AC from 1914 until his death.

PINCKNEY, GEORGE B. baseball: b. Jan. 11, 1862, Peoria, Ill.; d. Nov. 9, 1926. Bat, throw R; third-second base. Cleveland NL, 1884; Brooklyn AA, 1885–89; Brooklyn NL, 1890–91; St. Louis NL, 1892; Louisville NL, 1893. Ten years, 1,163 games, 264 stolen bases (3 years not included), .263 BA; hit .309 in 1890. Led league in walks, 1886 (70); in runs, 1888 (134).
Pinckney went 6-for-6, scoring 5 runs, on June 25, 1885.

PIPP, "WALLY" (Walter C.) baseball: b. Feb. 17, 1893, Chicago; d. Jan. 11, 1965. Bat, throw L; first base. Detroit AL, 1913; New York AL, 1915–25; Cincinnati NL, 1926–28. Fifteen years, 1,872 games, .281 BA; hit .329 in 1922, .304 in 1923. Led AL in triples, 1924 (19); in home runs, 1916 (12) and 1917 (9). Three World Series, 1921–23: 19 games, .224 BA.
Pipp is well known, unfortunately, only as the man who "temporarily" yielded first base to Lou Gehrig, only to see the "Iron Horse" play 2,130 consecutive games. He was the Yankee slugger before Babe Ruth and the live ball arrived, and he holds AL records for most years leading first basemen in chances, 4, and most years leading in putouts, 4.

PITTINGER, "TOGIE" (Charles R.) baseball: b. 1871, Greencastle, Pa.; d. Jan. 14, 1909. Throw R; pitcher. Boston NL, 1900–04; Philadelphia NL, 1905–07. Eight years, 116–114, 3.10 ERA; 20 shutouts; 27–16 in 1902, 23–14 in 1905. Led NL in losses, 1903 (19–23).

PLAISTED, FREDERICK A. rowing: b. 1849(?), Maine; d. May 1, 1946. Plaisted won his first professional race at seventeen; he won his last (but not for money) at eighty-nine, beating John B. Kelly, the former Olympic champion, who was only fifty. In his most famous race he was seventy-four and matched against two other professional oarsmen, Jim Ten Eyck and Jim Riley. There were one thousand spectators at Saratoga and the purse was $3,000. Plaisted won going away.

PLANK, "EDDIE" (Edward S.) baseball: b. Aug. 31, 1875, Gettysburg, Pa.; d. Feb. 24, 1926. Bat, throw L; pitcher. Philadelphia AL, 1901–14; St. Louis Fed L, 1915; St. Louis AL, 1916–17. Seventeen years, 325 wins (10th), 190 losses, 2.34 ERA; 2,246 strikeouts, 67 shutouts, in 4,505⅓ innings; 20–15 in 1902, 23–16 in 1903, 26–16 in 1904, 24–16 in 1907, 22–8 in 1911, 25–6 in 1912, and 21–11 in 1915. In relief, 23–14, 2.35 ERA, 25 saves. Led league in wins (26–12) and complete games (35) in 1905; in percentage, 1906 (19–5, .792); in shutouts, 1907 (8) and 1911 (6). Four World Series, 1905, 1911, 1913–14: 7 games, 2–5, 1.32 ERA (9th), 6 starts, 6 complete (5th), 32 strikeouts in 54⅔ innings, Plank had very bad luck in the Series. Four times the opposing pitcher threw a shutout against him.

Plank had more complete games and more shutouts than any other left-hander in history, and his 304 AL victories is a league record for left-handers. He holds the AL record for most consecutive years 100 or more strikeouts, 13.

Baseball Hall of Fame.

PLATAK, JOSEPH handball: b. 1909(?); d. Nov. 7, 1954. "The Blond Panther" dominated the U.S. four-wall softball singles for eleven years, winning the title, 1935–41, 1943, and 1945. He also shared the doubles title in 1937.

POE, ARTHUR football: b. March 22, 1879, Baltimore; d. April 15, 1951. Princeton end; All-American, 1899; 2nd team, 1898. Brother of Edgar A.

National Football Foundation Hall of Fame.

POE, EDGAR A. football: b. Sept. 15, 1871, Baltimore; d. Nov. 29, 1961. Princeton quarterback; All-American, captain, 1889.

PORES, CHARLES track: b. 1897(?); d. May 24, 1951. Pores won the AAU outdoor 5-mile run, 1917–19, the 10-mile in 1918.

POSEY, "CUM" (Cumberland W.) baseball: b. June 20, 1891, Homestead, Pa.; d. March 28, 1946. A journeyman outfielder, Posey was one of the outstanding organizers and managers in Negro baseball. After starring in basketball at Duquesne and Penn State, he joined a team known as the Murdock Grays, playing out of Homestead, Pennsylvania, near Pittsburgh.

In 1916, he became manager of the team, now known as the Homestead Grays, and quickly built it into one of the outstanding Negro teams in the country.

The Grays were a barnstorming team until 1929, when they joined the American Negro League. In 1932, Posey organized a new league, but the Depression killed it quickly, and the Grays went back to barnstorming. In 1935 they joined the Negro National League; they finished in first place, 1937–45. During the period, they won 2 of the 4 Negro World Series in which they appeared, in 1943 and 1944.

POWELL, "JACK" (John J.) baseball: b. July 9, 1874, Bloomington, Ill,; d. Oct. 17, 1944. Bat, throw R; pitcher. Cleveland NL, 1897–98; St. Louis NL, 1899–1901; St. Louis AL, 1902–03; New York AL, 1904–05; St. Louis AL, 1905–12. Sixteen years, 246–253, 2.97 ERA; 47 shutouts; 23–15 in 1898, 23–19 in 1899, 21–17 in 1902, 23–19 in 1904. In relief, 16–7, 2.59 ERA, 13 saves. Led league in shutouts, 1898 (6); in complete games, 1899 (40); in losses, 1911 (8–18).

POWELL, "JAKE" (Alvin Jacob) baseball: b. July 15, 1908, Silver Spring, Md.; d. Nov. 4, 1948. Bat, throw R; outfield. Washington AL, 1930, 1934–36; New York AL, 1936–40; Washington AL, 1943–45; Philadelphia NL, 1945. Eleven years, 688 games, .271 BA; hit .312 in 1935. Three World Series, 1936–38: 8 games, .435 BA.

He hit .455 in 1936, with 8 runs and 5 RBI.

PREISS, EMIL K. gymnastics: b. 1898, Kircheim-Tech, Germany; d. Feb. 15, 1962. Preiss came to the United States in 1924. He won the American Turner all-around championship in 1926, the AAU free calisthenics title in 1925.

He was gymnastics coach at the University of Pennsylvania from 1930 until his death.

Helms Hall of Fame.

PRINSTEIN, MYER track: b. 1880; d. March 10, 1925. Representing Syracuse, Prinstein won the IC4A broad-jump title in 1898 and 1900 and the AAU outdoor event, 1898, 1902, 1904, and 1906. His jump of 24'7½ " in 1900 was a world record at the time.

Prinstein won 4 Olympic titles, the hop, step, and jump in 1900 and 1904 and the broad jump in 1904 and 1906.

Helms Hall of Fame.

PROCTOR, CHARLES A. skiing: b. Sept. 15, 1878, Hanover, N.H.; d. April 14, 1961. A 1900 graduate of Dartmouth, Proctor became a professor of physics at his alma mater. He was one of the founders of the Intercollegiate Ski Association, and he helped set up rules for judging competitive jumping. Skiing Hall of Fame.

PYLE, "CASH AND CARRY" (Charles C.) promoter: b. 1881, Van Wert, Ohio; d. Feb. 3, 1939. The P. T. Barnum of sports, Pyle was Red Grange's business manager in 1925, when Grange signed with the Chicago Bears for a reported $125,000 immediately after graduating from Illinois. He played the rest of that season with the Bears, but in 1926 Pyle formed the American Football League, with Grange as chief box-office attraction. (It was the first of four pro-football leagues with that name.)

The AFL folded after one season and Grange went back to the Bears without his business manager. In the meantime, Pyle had organized the first professional tennis tour. Again, he had a top box-office name, the spectacular Suzanne Lenglen. She was guaranteed $50,000. Pyle also signed Mary K. Browne, Vincent Richards, Howard O. Kinsey, Harvey Snodgrass, and Paul Peret. He not only made a profit of $80,000 on the tour but also paid Miss Lenglen a $25,000 bonus. His success led to the formation of the U.S. Professional Lawn Tennis Association in 1927.

Another Pyle idea didn't work out so well. The "Bunion Derby" of 1928 was a 2,500-mile marathon from Los Angeles to Passaic, New Jersey. There were 241 starters, and public interest ran high at first. But the event lasted eighty-four days and it had become a public joke long before it was over. Pyle lost an estimated $50,000 on it; it was his last major venture in sports.

Q

QUIGLEY, ERNEST C. basketball: b. March 22, 1880, Newcastle, New Brunswick, Canada; d. Dec. 10, 1960. For forty years an official of collegiate and AAU basketball games after being a four-sport star at Kansas (1904), Quigley also coached for ten years at St. Mary's of Kansas, was a National League baseball umpire for many years, working in five World Series, and officiated at football games in his spare time. During several of his seasons he traveled more than 100,000 miles getting from one game, and from one sport, to another.

Basketball Hall of Fame.

QUINN, "JACK" (John P.) baseball: b. John Quinn Picus, July 5, 1884, Jeanesville, Pa.; d. April 17, 1946. Bat, throw R; pitcher. New York AL, 1909–12; Boston NL, 1913; Baltimore Fed L, 1914–15; Chicago AL, 1918; New York AL, 1919–21; Boston AL, 1922–25; Philadelphia AL, 1925–30; Brooklyn NL, 1931–32; Cincinnati NL, 1933. Twenty-three years, 242–217, 3.27 ERA; 755 games (5th), 3,934⅔ innings, 859 walks, 1,329 strikeouts, 28 shutouts. In relief, 51–35, 3.17 ERA, 59 saves. Led league in losses, 1915 (9–22); in saves, 1931 (15), 1932 (8). Three World Series, 1921, 1929–30: 0–1, 8.44 ERA.

Quinn was one of the established spitball pitchers exempted from the 1920 rule forbidding the spitball and other strange pitches. When he retired at the age of forty-nine there was only one legal spitballer left, Burleigh Grimes, who lasted one more season.

QUINN, JOSEPH J. baseball: b. Dec. 25, 1864, Sydney, Australia; d. Nov. 12, 1940. Bat, throw R; second base. St. Louis UA, 1884; St. Louis NL, 1885–86; Boston NL, 1888–89; Boston PL, 1890; Boston NL, 1891–92; St. Louis NL, 1893–96; Baltimore NL 1896–98; St. Louis NL, 1898; Cleveland NL, 1899; Cincinnati NL, St. Louis NL, 1900; Washington AL, 1901. Seventeen years, 1,768 games, .261 BA; hit .301 in 1890, .311 in 1895.

R

RADBOURN, "OLD HOSS" (Charles G.) baseball: b. Dec. 11, 1854, Rochester, N.Y.; d. Feb. 5, 1897. Bat, throw R; pitcher. Buffalo NL, 1880; Providence NL, 1881–85; Boston NL, 1886–89; Boston PL, 1890; Cincinnati NL, 1891. Twelve years, 309–195, 2.67 ERA; 503 starts, 489 complete (7th), 4,535⅓ innings, 875 walks, 1,830 strikeouts, 34 shutouts. No-hitter, July 25, 1883, against Cleveland NL (8–0).

It's hard to believe, but there it is in the record books: In 1884, Radbourn won 60 games, an all-time record, while losing 12. (Providence, winning the pennant, had only 84 victories.) He also led the league in percentage (.833), ERA (1.38), games (75), starts (73), complete games (also 73), innings (678⅔), and strikeouts (441). He won 19 in a row that season, a record. When he didn't pitch, he played four other positions, for 15 games.

He led the league in percentage in 1881 (25–11, .694); in strikeouts (201)

and shutouts (5) in 1882. He was 33–20 in 1882, 28–21 in 1885, 27–31 in 1886, 24–23 in 1887, 27–12 in 1890.
Baseball Hall of Fame.

RADCLIFF, "RIP" (Raymond A.) baseball: b. Jan. 19, 1906, Kiowa, Okla.; d. May 23, 1962. Bat, throw L; outfield. Chicago AL, 1934–39; St. Louis AL, 1940–41; Detroit AL, 1941–43. Ten years, 1,081 games, .311 BA, hit .335 in 1936, .325 in 1937, .330 in 1938, .342 in 1940, .311 in 1941. Led league in hits, 1940 (200).
Radcliff went 6-for-7, scoring 4 runs, on July 18, 1936.

RADFORD, PAUL R. baseball: b. Oct. 14, 1861, Roxbury, Mass.; d. Feb. 21, 1945. Bat, throw R; outfield, shortstop. Boston NL, 1883; Providence NL, 1884–85; Kansas City NL, 1886; New York AA, 1887; Brooklyn AA, 1888; Cleveland NL, 1889; Cleveland PL, 1890; Boston AA, 1891; Washington NL, 1892–94. Twelve years, 1,361 games, 307 stolen bases (4 years not included), .242 BA.

RAGAN, "PAT" (Don Carlos Patrick) baseball: b. Nov. 15, 1888, Blanchard, Iowa; d. Sept. 4, 1956. Bat, throw R; pitcher. Chicago NL, Cincinnati NL, 1909; Brooklyn NL, 1911–15; Boston NL, 1915–19; New York NL, Chicago AL, 1919; Philadelphia NL, 1923. Eleven years, 75–104, 2.99 ERA, 13 shutouts. In relief, 12–13, 2.13 ERA, 5 saves.

RAMSEY, "TOAD" (Thomas A.) baseball: b. Aug. 8, 1864, Indianapolis; d. March 27, 1906. Bat R, throw L; pitcher. Louisville AA, 1885–89; St. Louis AA, 1889–1900. Six years, 114–124, 3.29 ERA; 1,515 strikeouts in 2,100⅔ innings; 38–27 in 1886, 37–27 in 1887. No-hitter, July 29, 1886, against Baltimore AA. Led AA in strikeouts, 1887 (355). Ramsey pitched two consecutive 1-hitters, July 29 and 31, 1886. The second game went 12 innings.

RAY, "SHORTY" (Hugh L.) football: b. Sept. 21, 1884, Highland Park, Ill.; d. Sept. 16, 1956. Probably the least-known member of the Pro Football Hall of Fame, Ray was important to the development of the modern game. As NFL supervisor of officials and technical adviser from 1938 until his death, he was responsible for much rule interpretation and for studying films of teams and officials in action to suggest ways of improving the game. Many of his recommendations resulted in rules changes; probably the most important change he inspired was that from the one-platoon system to unlimited substitution.
Professional Football Hall of Fame.

REID, WILLIAM A. basketball: b. Sept. 26, 1893, Detroit; d. Oct. 30, 1955. After starring for three years at Colgate (1915–18), Reid became director of athletics at Detroit University for a year, then returned to Colgate to coach baseball and basketball. During his ten years, Colgate's basketball teams won 151 games. He became associate professor of physical education in 1928 and athletic director in 1935, serving until his death.

Basketball Hall of Fame.

REILLY, JOHN G. baseball: b. Oct. 5, 1858, Cincinnati; d. May 31, 1937. Bat, throw R; first base. Cincinnati NL, 1880; Cincinnati AA, 1883–89; Cincinnati NL, 1890–91. Ten years, 1,142 games, .289 BA; hit .311 in 1883, .339 in 1884, .309 in 1887, .321 in 1888, .300 in 1890. Led league in home runs (11) and slugging (.551) in 1884; in home runs (13), RBI (103), and slugging (.501) in 1888; in triples, 1890 (26).

Reilly went 6-for-7, with a double, a triple, a home run, and 6 runs scored, on Sept. 12, 1883.

REULBACH, EDWARD M. baseball: b. Dec. 1, 1882, Detroit; d. July 17, 1961. Bat, throw R; pitcher. Chicago NL, 1905–13; Brooklyn NL, 1913–14; Newark Fed L, 1915; Boston NL, 1916–17. Thirteen years, 185–105, 2.28 ERA; 20–10 in 1915. Led NL in percentage, 1906 (20–4, .833), 1907 (17–4, .810), 1908 (24–7, .774).

Reulbach set an NL record by leading the league three consecutive years in percentage. On Sept. 25, 1908, he became the only pitcher ever to throw shutouts in both games of a doubleheader, 5–0 and 3–0. That season he tied an ML record by beating one team, Brooklyn, nine times without a loss.

Four World Series, 1906–08, 1910: 2–0, 3.03 ERA. He pitched a 1-hitter in the second game in 1906, winning 7–1; the one run was unearned.

RHEM, FLINT (Charles Flint) baseball: b. Jan. 24, 1901, Rhems, S.C.; d. July 30, 1969. Bat, throw R; pitcher. St. Louis NL, 1924–32; Philadelphia NL, 1933; St. Louis NL, 1934; Boston NL, 1934–35; St. Louis NL, 1936. Twelve years, 105–97, 4.20 ERA. Led NL in victories, 1926 (20–7). Four World Series, 1926, 1928, 1930–31: 0–1, 6.10 ERA.

Rhem was the star of a celebrated drama during the 1930 season. Scheduled to pitch an important game against Brooklyn late in the season, Rhem disappeared. When he reappeared after two days, he explained to manager Gabby Street that two men had kidnapped him, taken him to a house and forced him, at gunpoint, to drink cups full of whiskey until he passed out. Those who knew him doubted the story.

RHINES, WILLIAM P. baseball: b. March 14, 1869, Ridgway, Pa.; d. Jan. 30, 1922. Bat, throw R; pitcher. Cincinnati NL, 1895–97; Pittsburgh NL, 1898–99. Nine years, 114–103, 3.47 ERA; 13 shutouts; 28–17 in 1890, 21–15 in 1897. Led NL in ERA, 1890 (1.95) and 1896 (2.45).

RHOADS, ROBERT B. baseball: b. Oct. 4, 1879, Wooster, Ohio; d. Feb. 12, 1967. Bat, throw R; pitcher. Chicago NL, 1902; St. Louis NL, 1903; Cleveland AL, 1903–09. Eight years, 97–81, 2.61 ERA; 21 shutouts; 21–10 in 1906. No-hitter, Sept. 18, 1908, against Boston AL (2–1).

RICE, GRANTLAND (Henry Grantland) sportswriting: b. Nov. 1, 1880, Murfreesboro, Tenn.; d. July 13, 1954. "The drama of sport is a big part of the drama of life and the scope of this drama is endless. Sport has its triumphs and its tragedies, its great joys and heavy sorrows with more spectacular effect than most dramas may ever know." This feeling expressed by Grantland Rice was the heart of his fame as a sportswriter. During the Golden Age of Sports, when every game could be viewed as an epic struggle, Rice was America's Homer. It was he who named the Notre Dame backfield of 1924–25 the Four Horsemen and who named Jack Dempsey the Mannassa Mauler.

He often celebrated sports in poetry. His most often quoted—and misquoted—lines are, "When the Last Great Scorer comes/ To mark against your name,/ He'll write not 'won' or 'lost'/ But how you played the game."

At Vanderbilt University, Rice captained the baseball team. After graduating in 1901, he couldn't decide whether to become an athlete or a poet; so he became a sportswriter, first in Nashville, then in New York, with the *Evening Mail* and the *Tribune*, 1914–30, with a year off for World War I. After 1930 he was writing only a syndicated column and narrating many short movie features. During his career, he saw virtually every major sports event in the United States. In one year alone, he estimated that he traveled 16,000 miles and wrote a million words.

RICHARDS, ALMA W. track: b. ?; d. April 3, 1963. Richards was Olympic high-jump champion in 1912. He won the AAU outdoor title in 1913. In 1918, he won the AAU shotput title.

RICHARDS, VINCENT tennis: b. March 20, 1903, New York City; d. Sept. 28, 1959. Overshadowed by Bill Tilden as a singles player, Richards was outstanding in doubles. He won major titles with a variety of partners: At Wimbledon, 1924, with Francis T. Hunter; the U.S. Outdoor, 1919, 1921–22, with Tilden, 1925–26, with R. Norris Williams II; the U.S. mixed doubles in 1919 with Marion Zinderstein; and in 1924 with Helen K. Wills.

He won the U.S. indoor singles in 1919 and 1923–24 and the indoor doubles in 1919–20 with Tilden, 1921 with S. Howard Voshèll, and 1923–24 with Hunter.

Richards joined the first pro-tennis tour in 1926, and the following year he and Howard O. Kinsey led in the establishment of the U.S. Professional

Lawn Tennis Association. Richards was pro singles champion, 1927–28, 1930, and 1933, and doubles champ in 1929 with Karel Kozeluh, in 1930–31 with Kinsey, in 1933 with Charles Wood, in 1937 with George M. Lott, Jr., in 1938 with Fred J. Perry, and in 1945 with Tilden. Helms Hall of Fame, Tennis Hall of Fame.

RICHARDSON, DANIEL baseball: b. Jan. 25, 1863, Elmira, N.Y.; d. Sept. 12, 1926. Bat, throw R; second base, shortstop, outfield. New York NL, 1884–89; New York PL, 1890; New York NL, 1891; Washington NL, 1892; Brooklyn NL, 1893; Louisville NL, 1894. Eleven years, 1,131 games, .254 BA.
Richardson handled 19 chances on June 20, 1892, the ML record for shortstops in a 9-inning game. On June 11, 1887, he went 6-for-7.

RICHARDSON, "HARDY" (Abram Harding) baseball: b. April 21, 1855, Clarksboro, N.J.; d. Jan. 14, 1931. Bat, throw R; second base, outfield, third base. Buffalo NL, 1879–85; Detroit NL, 1886–88; Boston NL, 1889; Boston PL, 1890; Boston AA, 1891; New York NL, Washington NL, 1892. Fourteen years, 1,331 games, .299 BA; hit .311 in 1883, .301 in 1884, .319 in 1885, .351 in 1886, .328 in 1887, .304 in 1889, .326 in 1890. Led league in hits, 1886 (189); in RBI, 1890 (143).

RICHIE, LEWIS A. baseball: b. Aug. 23, 1883, Ambler, Pa.; d. Aug. 15, 1936. Bat, throw R; pitcher. Philadelphia NL, 1906–09; Boston NL, 1909–10; Chicago NL, 1910–13. Eight years, 75–64, 2.54 ERA, 20 shutouts. One World Series, 1910: 0–0, 0.00 ERA in 1 inning of relief.

RICHMOND, BILL boxing: b. Aug. 5, 1763, Staten Island, N.Y.; d. Dec. 29, 1829. Richmond, a Negro, was the first American to gain any kind of athletic fame elsewhere. When very young, he won a number of fights, privately staged by Gen. Earl Percy, of the British Army, against British soldiers. Percy took him back to England when he was fourteen. After winning several fights, Richmond took on Tom Cribb for the London Prize Ring title on Oct. 8, 1805. Cribb was in much better shape—he was twenty-four years old, to Richmond's forty-two—and he won on a KO in 90 minutes.
Boxing Hall of Fame.

RICHMOND, LEE (John Lee) baseball: b. May 5, 1857, Sheffield, Ohio; d. Sept. 30, 1929. Throw L; pitcher. Boston NL, 1879; Worcester NL, 1880–82; Providence NL, 1883; Cincinnati AA, 1886. Six years, 75–100, 3.06 ERA; 8 shutouts; 32–32 in 1880; 25–26 in 1881. Led NL in losses, 1882 (14–33).

Richmond pitched the first perfect game in ML history, beating Cleveland NL 1–0 on June 12, 1880.

RICKARD, "TEX" (George L.) boxing: b. Jan. 2, 1870, Kansas City, Mo.; d. Jan. 6, 1929. A dreamer full of practical ideas, an often flamboyant showman with a kind heart, a gambler who made and lost fortunes with ease, a shrewd operator who was respected as a man of his word in a business not known for high ethical standards—that was Tex Rickard. He discovered boxing rather late in life, at thirty-four. He had been a cowboy and town marshal; he had joined the Yukon gold rush of 1895, struck it rich, built a gambling hall with his $60,000 profit, and been wiped out by a band of miners who hit a lucky streak. With $35 in capital, he built another saloon-casino and made $500,000 in four years but lost most of it in worthless mining claims. In 1903, he opened another casino in Goldfield, Nevada.

In order to promote Goldfield, Rickard promoted a boxing match there, in 1906. He guaranteed a purse of $30,000 for the lightweight title fight between Joe Gans and Battling Nelson. He made a profit of $30,000. At the time, promoters usually offered fighters a cut of the gate receipts. Rickard's method, for most of his career, was to guarantee them definite sums. And at a time when fighters often had trouble collecting their money, Rickard established the policy of paying them with certified checks the day before the fight.

Rickard paid $101,000 for the Jack Johnson–Jim Jeffries fight in Reno in 1910. A decade later, an established promoter, he went east to take over Madison Square Garden, generally considered a white elephant, and proceeded to turn boxing into a big business—and a much more respectable business than it had been. One of his ploys was to stage fights for charities backed by society leaders, insuring their attendance at ringside and making boxing a socially acceptable sport.

Besides using ballyhoo and showmanship to sell tickets, Rickard also used the practical approach. He spent hours on seating plans, developed a corps of efficient ushers well trained in the art of handling large crowds, and practiced the slogan, "A seat for every customer and every customer in his seat."

Rickard promoted the first fight to have a million-dollar gate, the Jack Dempsey–Georges Carpentier bout on July 2, 1921, and the only one ever to have a two-million-dollar gate, the second Dempsey-Tunney fight, Sept. 22, 1927. It was largely because of Rickard's promotional abilities that Dempsey and Tunney both retired from fighting as rich men. But many an unknown or washed-up fighter was indebted to him, too. He never refused money to a former boxer who needed it, and widows of fighters also often received financial help from him.

RICKEY, W. BRANCH baseball: b. Dec. 20, 1881, Stockdale, Ohio; d. Dec. 9, 1965. Bat L, throw R; catcher, outfield. St. Louis AL, 1905–06. New York AL, 1907; St. Louis AL, 1914. Four years, 119 games, .239 BA.

Rickey's major-league career was ended by tuberculosis, but it would probably have been brief, anyway. In 1907, Rickey set a modern record by giving up 13 stolen bases in a single game.

After receiving his law degree from the University of Michigan, where he coached baseball, Rickey managed the St. Louis AL team, 1913 (part)– 15, then became president of the St. Louis NL team, 1917–20, managing the team, 1919–25 (part). His overall record was 597–664, .473.

The Cardinals had little money with which to outbid other teams for established players, so Rickey decided on the idea of a farm system. The Cardinals bought minor-league franchises and young players and let the players get their experience and prove themselves in the minors before coming up to the major-league team. The system helped the Cardinals win their first pennant, in 1926; in the next twenty-seven seasons, they won 8 more pennants and finished in the 2nd division only 4 times.

In 1942, Rickey became general manager of the Brooklyn Dodgers, who had adopted the farm-club idea, like most teams. But most of them had virtually stopped signing young players, with World War II going on. Rickey kept signing them, even if they were going to be in the service for some time. As a result, Brooklyn had loads of young talent when the war ended. In an eleven-year period starting with 1946, the Dodgers won six pennants, finished second four times, and third the other year.

But Rickey's greatest fame came in 1947, when Jackie Robinson joined the Dodgers after a fine season with their Montreal farm team. Rickey originally disguised his intention to bring a Negro into the majors by buying the Brooklyn Brown Dodgers, a Negro League team, and sending scouts out to find Negro players, ostensibly for the new team. Rickey wanted to make sure that the player chosen to break the color barrier was, first, a genuinely outstanding prospect and, second, a man who could put up with the abuse from players and fans alike until he was established. Rickey decided Robinson was the right choice, after a long interview in which he warned Robinson of all the problems ahead.

Rickey moved from the Dodgers to the Pittsburgh Pirates, then became president of the proposed Continental League, which was to be a third major league. It was killed when the established major leagues added teams in some of the cities in which the Continental League had planned to have franchises.

RIDDLE, SAMUEL D. horse racing: b. July 1, 1861, Glen Riddle, Pa.; d. Jan. 9, 1951. Riddle owned Glen Riddle Farm, whose fame was achieved in 1920 with Man O'War, considered by many the greatest thoroughbred in history; certainly his is the most legendary name in racing. Man O'War, racing for only two years before being retired to stud, won 20 of 21 starts, including the 1920 Belmont and Preakness. (He didn't run in the Kentucky Derby.) He also made Glen Riddle Farm one of the great breeding farms; his offspring have won more than $5 million.

The greatest of them, War Admiral, won the Triple Crown in 1937; Glen Riddle Farm was breeder and owner. The stable led in money-winning in 1925 with $199,143.

RING, JAMES J. baseball: b. Feb. 15, 1895, Brooklyn; d. July 6, 1965. Bat, throw R; pitcher. Cincinnati NL, 1917–20; Philadelphia NL, 1921–25; New York NL, 1926; St. Louis NL, 1927; Philadelphia NL, 1928. Twelve years, 118–149, 4.06 ERA. One World Series, 1919: 1–1, 0.64 ERA.

RIPPLE, JAMES A. baseball: b. Oct. 14, 1909, Export, Pa.; d. July 16, 1959. Bat L, throw R; outfield. New York NL, 1936–39; Brooklyn NL, 1939–40; Cincinnati NL, 1940–41; Philadelphia AL, 1943. Seven years, 554 games, .282 BA; hit .317 in 1937. Three World Series, 1936–37, 1940: 17 games, .320 BA. Ripple was the unexpected hero for Cincinnati in the 1940 Series. A spot starter and pinch-hitter for most of his career, he went to the Reds in a late-season trade but played in every Series game, hitting .333, with 3 runs and 6 RBI. His two-run homer won the second game with Detroit, and he doubled home the tying run, then scored the winner in the Reds' 2–1 victory in the seventh and deciding game.

RISKO, EDDIE "BABE" boxing: b. Henry Pylkowski, 1911, Syracuse, N.Y.; d. March 7, 1957. His record: 27 wins, 7 by KO; 18 losses, 9 by KO; 6 draws. Risko won the American middleweight title with a 15-round decision over Teddy Yarosz on Sept. 19, 1935, knocking Yarosz down three times. He held the title until July 11, 1936, when Freddie Steele won a 15-round decision.

RITCHEY, CLAUDE C. baseball: b. Oct. 5, 1873, Emlenton, Pa.; d. Nov. 8, 1951. Sw. hit, throw R; second base, shortstop. Cincinnati NL, 1897; Louisville NL, 1898–99; Pittsburgh NL, 1900–06; Boston NL, 1907–09. Thirteen years, 1,671 games, .273 BA; hit .300 in 1899. One World Series, 1903: 8 games, .111 BA.

Ritchey holds the NL record for most consecutive years leading second basemen in fielding, 6. He tied an ML record for second basemen with two unassisted double plays on July 9, 1899.

RIXEY, EPPA baseball: b. May 3, 1891, Culpeper, Va.; d. Feb. 28, 1963. Bat R, throw L; pitcher. Philadelphia NL, 1912–17, 1919–20; Cincinnati NL, 1921–33. Twenty-one years, 266–251, 3.15 ERA; 552 starts (10th), 290 complete, 4,494⅔ innings, 1,082 walks, 1,350 strikeouts, 39 shutouts; 22–10 in 1916, 20–15 in 1923, 21–11 in 1925. Led NL in losses, 1917 (16–21) and 1920 (11–22); in wins (25–13), starts (38), and innings (313⅓) in 1922; in shutouts, 1924 (4).

When Warren Spahn broke his record for most career wins by a left-hander, Rixey told an interviewer, "I'm glad he broke it, otherwise people wouldn't know I set it." He had a point, because Spahn's feat did help revive the name of a man whose misfortune was to have spent most of his career with mediocre teams. He would have had 300 victories, except that he pitched for 2nd-division teams in 13 of his twenty-two seasons; the year he lost 21 games, he had an ERA of 2.27.

Baseball Hall of Fame.

ROBERTS, "FIREBALL" (Glenn) auto racing: b. 1927(?), Apopka, Fla.; d. July 1, 1964. At his death, Roberts was the biggest money-winner in the history of stock-car racing; he had won 32 late-model races and more than $400,000 in fifteen years. He had driven in all 14 of the Southern 500-mile races, winning the event in 1958 and 1963.

He died of burns suffered May 24, 1964, at Charlotte, N.C.

ROBERTS, FLOYD auto racing: b. ?; d. May 30, 1939. Roberts won the Indianapolis 500 and was national driving champion in 1938. His average speed of 117.20 miles per hour was a record until 1948.

He was killed at Indy the year after his victory.

ROBERTSON, GEORGE H. auto racing: b. 1885(?); d. July 3, 1955. One of the real pioneers in racing, Robertson began on the tracks in 1904; he won the prestigious Vanderbilt Cup Race in 1908 and was national driving champion in 1909.

Auto Racing Hall of Fame, Helms Hall of Fame.

ROBERTSON, LAWSON N. track: b. 1883(?), Aberdeen, Scotland; d. Jan. 22, 1951. Robertson, who won the AAU outdoor 100-yard-dash title in 1904, became coach in 1908 of the Irish-American AC in New York, one

of the outstanding track teams of the time. He became University of Pennsylvania track coach, 1916–47, and was head coach of the U.S. Olympic teams in 1924, 1928, 1932, and 1936.
Helms Hall of Fame.

ROBINSON, "UNCLE ROBBIE" (Wilbert) baseball: b. June 2, 1863, Bolton, Mass.; d. Aug. 8, 1934. Bat, throw R; catcher. Philadelphia AA, 1886–90; Baltimore-Brooklyn AA, Philadelphia AA, 1890; Baltimore AA, 1891; Baltimore NL, 1892–99; St. Louis NL, 1900; Baltimore AL, 1901–02. Seventeen years, 1,371 games, .273 BA; hit .334 in 1893, .353 in 1894. He's the only player ever to collect 7 hits in 7 times at bat; he did it on June 10, 1892.

Despite his long career as a player, Robinson is better known as a well-liked manager—the "Uncle" nickname came from his players—who preferred to laugh people out of slumps instead of shouting at them. He managed Baltimore AL, 1902 (part); Brooklyn NL, 1914–31: 1,397–1,395 (7th), .500. Pennants, 1916, 1920.
Baseball Hall of Fame.

ROBY, THOMAS steeplechase: b. 1911(?); d. Jan. 9, 1965. Roby was the country's leading steeplechase jockey in 1941 with 13 victories in 55 mounts. Among his wins that year was the Grand National Steeplechase. On June 1, 1942, he suffered head and spinal injuries in a fall from his horse; he was completely paralyzed for 22½ years, until his death.

ROCKNE, KNUTE K. football: b. March 4, 1888, Voss, Norway; d. March 31, 1931. Rockne was chosen the greatest all-time coach during college football's centennial year, which surprised no one. With 105 wins, 12 losses, and 5 ties, all at Notre Dame, he had the best record ever compiled by a coach with 10 or more seasons (Rockne had 13). He never had a losing year. His teams were undefeated in 1919–20, 1924, 1929–30; he had national champions in 1924, 1929–30. His teams scored an average of 23 points per game to 5 for the opposition. In 1925, Notre Dame beat Stanford 27–10 in the Rose Bowl.

Rockne's family came to the United States when he was five. He grew up in Chicago, starred in track in high school, then went to work. In 1910, he entered Notre Dame, a balding, overage freshman and, as he later described himself, "a lone Norse Protestant on the Irish Catholic campus." He quickly excelled in many things: as a science student, musician, actor, school-newspaper editor, track captain—and as a football player, though he was only 5'8" and 145 pounds. He was 3rd team All-American in 1913, partly because he and quarterback Gus Dorais had practiced the forward pass while working at an Ohio resort that summer and then had used it as a basic weapon in beating a heavily favored Army team, 35–13, and establishing Notre Dame as a football power.

Rockne taught chemistry and helped Jess Harper coach football after graduation. In 1918, he succeeded Harper as athletic director and football coach.

Rockne is given major credit for two football innovations. His defensive linemen were taught to charge diagonally, one way or the other, to confuse blocking assignments ("stunting" or "looping," we say today), and he often used "shock troops," sending in a second team to tire the opposition for a while before bringing in a fresh first unit to win the game.

Many of Rockne's pupils became outstanding coaches—Sleepy Jim Crowley, Frank Leahy, Frank Thomas, Eddie Anderson, Buck Shaw, and others.

As an athletic director, Rockne did a great deal for college football. He believed in playing a game in a nearby big city, when necessary, to draw bigger crowds of football fans in general, instead of relying on students and alumni to fill the stands. He liked to play teams from all over the country instead of looking for those within easy traveling distance, and he invented the "suicide schedule," taking on seven or eight tough opponents every year, instead of spotting breathers here and there.

Rockne died in a private-plane crash in Kansas.

Helms Hall of Fame, National Football Foundation Hall of Fame.

RODGERS, "RAT" (Ira E.) football: b. May 26, 1895, Bethany, W.Va.; d. Feb. 15, 1963. West Virginia fullback; All-American, 1919. Rodgers was one of the best passers of his day; his 51-yard pass in 1917 was the second longest of the season.

Helms Hall of Fame, National Football Foundation Hall of Fame.

ROEHNELT, WILLIAM football: b. June 4, 1936, Peoria, Ill.; d. July 19, 1968. Bradley linebacker. Chicago Bears, 1958–59; Washington Redskins, 1960; Denver Broncos (AFL), 1961–62.

ROGAN, "BULLET JOE" (Wilbur) baseball: b. 1893, Kansas City, Kan.; d. March 4, 1967. Bat, throw R; pitcher. Negro leagues: Kansas City Monarchs, 1919–38. Rogan's nickname came from his fast ball, but he also had a fine curve. He was an excellent fielder, a good hitter who was often in the cleanup spot, and during his professional career he played every position but catcher.

In his first start for the Monarchs, Rogan threw a 1-hitter against the strong Chicago American Giants, and from then on he was their top pitcher for 20 seasons. Monarch owner J. L. Wilkinson once said that during the thirties, Rogan never had to be relieved.

He managed the Monarchs for several years during the end of his playing career.

ROLFE, "RED" (Robert A.) baseball: b. Oct. 17, 1908, Penacook, N.H.; d. July 8, 1969. Bat, throw R; third base, shortstop. New York AL, 1931, 1934–42. Ten years, 1,175 games, .289 BA; hit .300 in 1935, .319 in 1936, .311 in 1938, 329 in 1939. Led AL in triples, 1936 (15); in runs (139), hits (213), and doubles (46) in 1939. Six World Series, 1936–39, 1941–42: 28 games, .284 BA, 17 runs.

Managed Detroit, 1949–52 (part): 278–256, .521.

Called by Connie Mack "the greatest team player in the game," Rolfe set an ML record in 1939 by scoring a run in each of 18 consecutive games.

He coached baseball and basketball at Yale, 1942–46. In 1954 he became athletic director at Dartmouth, retiring in 1967.

ROOT, CHARLES H. baseball: b. March 17, 1899; d. Nov. 5, 1970. Bat, throw R; pitcher. St. Louis AL, 1923; Chicago NL, 1926–41. Seventeen years, 201–160, 3.58 ERA. Led NL in losses, 1926 (18–17); in wins, 1927 (26–15); in percentage, 1929 (19–6, .760); in shutouts, 1930 (4). Four World Series, 1929, 1932, 1935, 1938: 0–3, 5.96 ERA.

Root's fine record has been overshadowed by the fact that in the 1932 Series he was the pitcher when Babe Ruth supposedly pointed to the center-field stands and then hit a home run to the spot he had indicated. Root always denied the story, and most baseball historians agree with him.

ROOT, JACK boxing: b. Janos Ruthaly, May 26, 1876, Austria; d. June 9, 1963. His record: 44 wins, 24 by KO; 3 losses, all by KO; 5 draws, 1 no-decision. When Root outgrew the middleweight class, his manager, Lou Houseman, suggested there should be a new weight division, between middleweight and heavyweight. So the light-heavyweight class was born, and Root became its first champion by decisioning Kid McCoy in 10 rounds on April 22, 1903. He lost it to George Gardner on a 12th-round KO, July 4, 1903.

Root fought Marvin Hart for the heavyweight title, which had been vacated by Jim Jeffries, in 1905, but Hart won on a 12-round KO.

Helms Hall of Fame, Boxing Hall of Fame.

ROPER, WILLIAM W. football: b. Aug. 22, 1880, Philadelphia; d. Dec. 10, 1933. After playing football at Princeton (1903), Roper coached at Virginia

Military Institute, 1903–04; Princeton, 1906–08, 1910–11, 1919–30; Missouri, 1909; and Swarthmore, 1915–16. His 1922 Princeton team won all 8 of its games; his one Missouri team had a 7–0–1 record.
Helms Hall of Fame, National Football Foundation Hall of Fame.

ROSS, BARNEY boxing: b. Barnet Rasofsky, Dec. 23, 1909, Chicago; d. Jan 18, 1967. His record: 74 wins, 24 by KO; 4 losses, none by KO; 3 draws, 1 no-decision. Ross was the first boxer to hold the lightweight and welterweight titles simultaneously. He became lightweight champion, June 23, 1933, winning a 10-round decision from Tony Canzoneri. On May 28, 1934, he outpointed Jimmy McLarnin in 15 rounds for the welterweight title. McLarnin won it back with a decision on Sept. 17, 1934.

Ross then resigned the lightweight title and went after McLarnin again, winning the welterweight title, May 28, 1935, with a 15-round decision. He lost it, May 31, 1938, to Henry Armstrong.

He and Canzoneri shared the Fighter of the Year award in 1934 and Ross won it outright in 1935. He was given the Edward J. Neil trophy in 1942.
Helms Hall of Fame, Boxing Hall of Fame.

ROSS, DONALD J. golf: b. 1872(?), Scotland; d. April 26, 1948. Ross won the North and South Open in 1903 and 1905–06 but is better known as a designer of courses. He came to the United States in 1899, became a pro in Boston, and there got his first experience in designing. Among his courses are the three that have made Pinehurst, North Carolina, a famous golfing city. He also designed Belaire in Florida, Brae Burn in Boston, and many courses in the Chicago area.

ROSS, NORMAN swimming: b. 1896(?), Portland, Ore.; d. June 19, 1953. Ross won three Gold Medals in the 1920 Olympics, in the 400-meter and 1,500-meter freestyles and as a member of the 800-meter freestyle relay team. He won the U.S. outdoor 440-yard freestyle in 1917 and 1920, the 1-mile freestyle in 1917. In national indoor competition he won the 100-yard freestyle in 1921, the 220-yard freestyle in 1917–18 and 1921, and the 150-yard backstroke in 1917. He also won five medals at the 1919 Allied War Games.

When his career ended, he became the country's first classical disc jockey, with a Chicago radio station.
Helms Hall of Fame, Swimming Hall of Fame.

ROWE, "JACK" (John J.) baseball: b. Dec. 8, 1857, Harrisburg, Pa.; d. April 26, 1911. Bat L, throw R; shortstop, catcher, outfield. Buffalo NL, 1879–85;

Detroit NL, 1886–88; Pittsburgh NL, 1889; Buffalo PL, 1890. Twelve years, 1,044 games, .286 BA; hit .315 in 1884, .303 in 1886, .318 in 1887. Led league in triples, 1881 (11).
He managed Buffalo PL, 1890: 36–96, .273.

ROWE, "SCHOOLBOY" (Lynwood T.) baseball: b. Jan. 11, 1910, Waco, Tex.; d. Jan. 8, 1961. Bat, throw R; pitcher. Detroit AL, 1933–42; Brooklyn NL, 1942; Philadelphia NL, 1943, 1946–49. Fifteen years, 158–101, 3.87 ERA, 22 shutouts. In relief, 22–10, 3.47 ERA, 12 saves. Led AL in shutouts, 1935 (6); in percentage, 1940 (16–3, .842). Three World Series, 1934–35, 1940: 2 wins, 5 losses (2nd), 3.91 ERA.
Rowe tied an AL record in 1934 with 16 consecutive wins.
An excellent hitter, he had a .279 career average as a pinch-hitter; his career BA was .263 with 18 home runs.

ROWLAND, "PANTS" (Clarence H.) baseball: b. Feb. 12, 1879, Platteville, Wis.; d. May 17, 1969. Managed Chicago AL, 1915–18: 339–247, .578. Pennant, World Series, 1917.
After umpiring in the AL for many years, Rowland became president of the Pacific Coast League and fought to have it recognized as a third major league. He won a partial victory in 1951, when the PCL was placed in an "open" classification, one step above the minors but still below the major leagues.

RUDOLPH, RICHARD baseball: b. Aug. 25, 1887, New York City; d. Oct. 20, 1949. Sw. hit, throw R; pitcher. New York NL, 1910–11; Boston NL, 1913–23, 1927. Thirteen years, 121–108, 2.66 ERA; 26 shutouts. Led NL in wins, 1914 (27–10); in losses, 1915 (21–19).
He was the Braves' pitching star in their 1914 Series sweep over Philadelphia, pitching two complete-game victories, in the first and fourth games, giving up just 1 earned run while striking out 15.

RUEL, "MUDDY" (Herold D.) baseball: b. Feb. 20, 1896, St. Louis; d. Nov. 13, 1963. Bat, throw R; catcher. St. Louis AL, 1915; New York AL, 1917–20; Boston AL, 1921–22; Washington AL, 1923–30; Boston AL, 1931; Detroit AL, 1931–32; St. Louis AL, 1933; Chicago AL, 1934. Nineteen years, 1,469 games, .275 BA; hit .316 in 1923, .310 in 1925, .308 in 1927. Two World Series, 1924–25: 14 games, .200 BA.
He managed St. Louis AL, 1947: 59–95, .383.

RUETHER, "DUTCH" (Walter H.) baseball: b. Sept. 13, 1893, Alameda, Cal.; d. May 16, 1970. Bat, throw L; pitcher. Chicago NL, 1917; Cincinnati NL, 1917–20; Brooklyn NL, 1921–24; Washington AL, 1925–26; New

York AL, 1926–27. Eleven years, 137–95, 3.50 ERA; 17 shutouts. Led NL in percentage, 1919 (19–6, .760). Two World Series, 1919, 1926: 1–1, 3.93 ERA.

RUSIE, AMOS W. baseball: b. May 30, 1871, Mooresville, Ind.; d. Dec. 6, 1942. Bat, throw R; pitcher. Indianapolis NL, 1889; New York NL, 1890–95, 1897–98; Cincinnati NL, 1901. Ten years, 245–174, 3.07 ERA; 1,934 strikeouts, 30 shutouts, in 2,769⅔ innings; 33–30 in 1891, 31–31 in 1892, 33–21 in 1893, 23–23 in 1895, 28–10 in 1897, 20–11 in 1898. No-hitter, July 31, 1891, against Brooklyn NL (6–0). Led NL in losses, 1890 (29–34); in wins (36–13), ERA (2.78), strikeouts (195), and shutouts (3) in 1894; in ERA, 1897 (2.54); in complete games, 1893 (50); in strikeouts, 1890 (341), 1891 (337), 1893 (208), and 1895 (201); in shutouts, 1891 (6), 1893 (4), and 1895 (4).

"The Hoosier Thunderbolt" tied an ML record by striking out 300 or more in three different seasons. Four consecutive times he won more than 30 games. His 276 walks in 1890 is an ML record and his 1,637 career walks is the NL record.

RUTH, "BABE" (George H.) baseball: b. Feb. 6, 1895, Baltimore; d. Aug. 16, 1948. Bat, throw L; pitcher, outfield. Boston AL, 1914–19; New York AL, 1920–34; Boston NL, 1935. Twenty-two years (7th), 2,502 games (10th), 8,399 at-bats, 2,873 hits, 506 doubles, 136 triples, 714 home runs (1st), 2,174 runs (2nd), 5,793 total bases (3rd), 2,174 RBI (2nd), 2,056 walks (1st), 1,330 strikeouts (3rd), .342 BA (9th), .690 slugging percentage (1st). As a pitcher: ten years (primarily 1914–19), 94–46, 2.28 ERA, 17 shutouts. Led AL in ERA (1.75) and shutouts (9) in 1916; in complete games, 1917 (35); 23–12 in 1916, 24–13 in 1917.

The Babe Ruth story has become an American legend. When he was seven, Ruth, a slum child, was sent to St. Mary's Industrial Home in Baltimore. He stayed there almost continuously until he was eighteen, and there he developed his baseball skills. He signed a contract with the Boston Red Sox and spent most of the 1914 season with a farm club before coming up to the parent team as a left-handed pitcher, and a good one. He won the second game of the 1916 World Series, 2–1, in 14 innings, as Boston beat Brooklyn in 5 games. In the 1918 Series, he won the opening game 1–0, and then won 3–2 in the fourth as Boston beat Chicago 4 games to 2. In the two Series combined, he set a record with 29⅔ consecutive scoreless innings.

But he could also hit. In 1918 manager Ed Barrow began using him in the outfield and at first base on occasion. Ruth led the league in home runs with 11, though he appeared in only 95 games. In 1919, he played 111 games in the outfield, pitched in 20, and was at first base in 13. The result was an unheard-of 29 home runs, a record at the time. Then he was sold to the New York Yankees for $125,000, and he became a full-time outfielder, setting a new record with 54 home runs in 1920, raising it to 59 in 1921 and finally to 60 in 1927, the famous mark that stood until 1961, Roger Maris, and the 162-game season.

Ruth led the AL in hitting, 1924 (.378); runs, 1919 (103), 1920 (158), 1921 (127), 1923 (151), 1924 (143), 1926 (139), 1927 (158), 1928 (163); home runs, 1919 (29), 1920 (54), 1921 (59), 1923 (41), 1924 (46), 1926 (47), 1927 (60), 1928 (54), 1929 (46), 1930 (49), 1931 (46); RBI, 1919 (114), 1920 (137), 1921 (170), 1923 (130), 1926 (155), 1928 (142); walks, 1920 (148), 1921 (144), 1923 (170), 1924 (142), 1926 (144), 1927 (138), 1928 (135), 1930 (136), 1931 (128), 1932 (130), 1933 (114); slugging, 1919 (.657), 1920 (.847), 1921 (.846), 1922 (.672), 1923 (.764), 1924 (.739), 1926 (.737), 1927 (.772), 1928 (.709), 1929 (.697), 1930 (.732), 1931 (.700).

He is holder or coholder of ML records for highest season slugging percentage, .847, in 1920; most years led in slugging, 11; most runs, season, 177; most years leading in runs, 8; most years 150 or more runs, 6; most years led in home runs, 12; most seasons more than 50 home runs, 4; most seasons more than 40, 11; most consecutive, 7; most years 30 or more, 13; most consecutive years 20 or more, 16; most times 2 or more home runs in game, 72; most seasons hit home runs in every park in the league, 11; most total bases, season, 457, in 1921; most extra-base hits in season, 119, in 1921; most years led in RBI, 6; most consecutive, 3; most years 100 or more runs, 13; most consecutive years, 150 or more runs, 3; most walks in season, 170, in 1923; most years led in walks, 11; most years 100 or more walks, 13.

He is holder or coholder of AL records for lowest ERA (1.75) and most shutouts (9) for left-handed pitcher, both in 1916; most extra-base hits, career, 1,356; most consecutive years leading in home runs, 6; most years led in total bases, 6.

Ten World Series, 1915–16, 1918, 1921–23, 1926–28, 1932: 41 games (3rd), 129 at-bats, 42 hits (8th), 5 doubles, 2 triples, 15 home runs (2nd), 37 runs (3rd), 33 RBI (4th), 33 walks (2nd), 30 strikeouts (4th), .326 BA, .744 slugging percentage (1st). In 1923 Ruth hit .368, with 3 home runs, 8 runs, and 3 RBI. He set a record with 3 home runs in the fourth game in 1926, and in 1927 he hit .400, with 2 home runs, 4 runs, and 7 RBI, during a 4-game sweep of Pittsburgh. His greatest series came in 1928, when the Yankees again won in a sweep, this time against the Cardinals: He hit .625, a record, with 10 hits, a 4-game record; he again hit 3 home runs in a game, the fourth, and he had 3 doubles, 9 runs, and 4 RBI. In 1932, he hit .333, with 6 runs and 6 RBI.

The Ruth legend has become so enormous that certain facts are almost forgotten. Ruth could be troublesome: Barrow was brought from Boston to New York as general manager because he knew how to handle the young slugger. Ruth was a frequently heavy drinker and could be very uncouth. A Boston teammate of his, Harry Hooper, has told how Ruth was known as the big baboon in his early years. "Sometimes," Hooper said, "I still can't believe what I saw: This nineteen-year-old kid, crude, poorly educated, only lightly brushed by the social veneer we call civilization, gradually transformed into the idol of American youth and the symbol of baseball the world over." In fairness to Ruth, Hooper also pointed out, "He had never been anywhere, didn't know anything about manners or how to behave among people," largely because he had grown up in an orphanage. That was also the main reason for Ruth's fondness for children, his willingness to sign autographs for them, chat with them in the bleachers, or visit them in hospitals.

Ruth's last season in baseball was a sad one and yet it had its dramatic moment. He had hoped to become manager of the Yankees, but Joe McCarthy was firmly established in that job, so the Babe went to the Boston Braves as player, vice-president, and assistant manager. He was heavy and slow now, and he hit only .118. But on May 25, 1935, he hit 3 home runs in a game, becoming the first player ever to do it in both leagues. He made a few more appearances, then announced his retirement, on June 3.

Baseball Hall of Fame.

RUTHSTROM, RALPH football: b. July 12, 1921, Schenectady, N.Y.; d. March 29, 1962. Sam Houston College, Southern Methodist back. Cleveland Rams, 1945; Los Angeles Rams, 1946; Washington Redskins, 1947; Baltimore Colts (AAFC), 1949.

RYAN, JAMES E. baseball: b. Feb. 11, 1863, Clinton, Mass.; d. Oct. 26, 1923. Bat R, throw L; outfield. Chicago NL, 1885–89; Chicago PL, 1890; Chicago NL, 1891–1900; Washington AL, 1902–03. Eighteen years, 2,012 games, 1,642 runs, 408 stolen bases, .306 BA. Led league in hits (182), doubles (33), home runs (16), and slugging (.515) in 1888.

Ryan holds the NL record for most career assists by an outfielder, 356. He is coholder of the ML record for most times scoring 5 or more runs in a game, 6, and the NL record for most runs in a game, 6, on July 25, 1894.

RYAN, PADDY boxing: b. March 15, 1853, Thurles, Ireland; d. 1901. The first American to hold the London Prize Ring title won it in his first recorded fight. Ryan KOed visiting English champion Joe Goss in 87 rounds either May 30 or June 1, 1880. He lost it to John L. Sullivan two years later in the first recorded defense of his title. So far as is known, Ryan had only 4 fights, with 1 victory, 2 losses, and 1 stopped by police.

RYAN, PATRICK J. track: b. 1882(?), Ireland; d. Feb. 15, 1964. The Irish hammer-throw champion at nineteen, Ryan dominated the event in the United States for years. He was AAU champion, 1913–17 and 1921, and his record of 189′6½″, set in 1913, wasn't broken for twenty-five years. He won the Olympic event in 1920. Ryan also won the AAU 56-pound-weight title in 1912 and 1917. In 1924 he returned to Ireland to take over the family farm.

Helms Hall of Fame.

RYAN, TOMMY boxing: b. Joseph Youngs, Jr., March 31, 1870, Redwood, N.Y.; d. Aug. 3, 1949. His record: 86 wins, 45 by KO; 3 losses, 1 by KO; 8 draws, 11 no-decisions. Ryan won the welterweight title from Mysterious Billy Smith in 20 rounds in 1894. He vacated the title in 1897 to become one of three claimants for the middleweight title but never fought either of the other two, Kid McCoy and Philadelphia Jack O'Brien. Ryan was generally considered the champ because he had held the title in the lower division before moving up.

Helms Hall of Fame, Boxing Hall of Fame.

S

SACHS, "EDDY" (Edward) auto racing: b. May 28, 1927, Detroit; d. May 30, 1964. Sachs was Midwest driving champion in 1958, after having been runner-up three straight years. In 1957, he set a number of rookie records in the Indianapolis 500 but was forced out by car failure after 105 laps. In 1958 he was leading the race when his car again failed. In 1960 and 1961, he was the fastest qualifier. Trouble forced him out in 1960, and in 1961 he was leading with two laps to go when he had to have a tire changed and lost the lead. He finished 3rd at Indy in 1962.

On the first lap in 1964, rookie driver Dave MacDonald hit the wall and his car burst into flames, and Sachs crashed into it. Both drivers were killed.

SACHS, LEONARD basketball, football: b. Aug. 7, 1897, Chicago; d. Oct. 27, 1942. A football and basketball star at Loyola of Chicago, Sachs played end for the Chicago Cardinals, 1920–23; Milwaukee Badgers, 1923–24; Hammond Pros, 1924–25; Chicago Cardinals, 1925; Louisville Colonels, 1926.

He coached basketball at his alma mater, 1924–42, compiling a 224–129 record. His teams won 31 straight, 1928–30, and in 1939 won 21 in a row but lost the last game of the season.

Basketball Hall of Fame, Helms Hall of Fame.

ST. JOHN, LYNN W. basketball, college sports: b. Nov. 18, 1876, Union City, Pa.; d. Sept. 30, 1950. An Ohio State graduate (1900), St. John coached basketball at the College of Wooster, Ohio Wesleyan, and his alma mater. As OSU athletic director, 1915–47, he guided the school to prominence in all major sports. For twenty-five years he was a member of the NCAA Rules Committee, eighteen of them as its chairman.

Basketball Hall of Fame.

SALING, GEORGE J. track: b. July 24, 1909, Memphis, Mo.; d. April 15, 1933. Saling set a world record of 14.4 seconds in the 110-meter hurdles trials at the 1932 Olympics, then set the Olympic record of 14.6 in winning the finals. The world record stood until 1934, the Olympic mark until 1936. Saling won the NCAA championship in the event in 1932 and won the AAU outdoor 220-yard low-hurdle event the same year.

He died in a car crash less than a year after his Olympic victory.

SALLEE, "SLIM" (Harry F.) baseball: b. Feb. 3, 1885, Higginsport, Ohio; d. March 22, 1950. Bat, throw L; pitcher. St. Louis NL, 1908–16; New York NL, 1916–18; Cincinnati NL, 1919–20; New York NL, 1920–21. Fourteen years, 172–143, 2.57 ERA; 25 shutouts; 21–7 in 1919. Two World Series, 1917, 1919: 1–3, 3.14 ERA.

SALMON, "RED" (Louis J.) football: b. 1880, Syracuse, N.Y.; d. Sept. 27, 1965. Notre Dame fullback; captain, 1902–03; 3rd team All-American, 1903. Salmon was the first Notre Dame player to receive All-America mention.

He coached at his alma mater in 1904.

SANDE, EARL H. horse racing: b. Nov. 13, 1898, Groton, S.D.; d. Aug. 19, 1968. The great jockey of the Golden Age of Sports, Sande began as a broncobuster and quarter-horse rider in Idaho before riding thoroughbreds. At his peak, he rode for Harry Sinclair's Rancocas Stable and William Woodward's Bel Air Stud Farm. He won three Kentucky Derbies, with Zev in 1923, Flying Ebony in 1925, and Gallant Fox in 1930; he rode Gallant Fox to the Triple Crown. In all, Sande rode 967 winners for purses of $3 million. His best year was 1923, when his 39 stakes winners collected a half-million dollars.

Sande turned to training after retiring as a jockey and in 1938 was the nation's top money-winning trainer, with 15 stakes winners for purses of $226,495. He attempted a comeback as a jockey in 1953, but a series of knee infections forced him back into retirement.

Jockey Hall of Fame, National Racing Hall of Fame.

SANDERS, "RED" (Henry R.) football: b. March 7, 1905, Asheville, N.C.; d. Aug. 14, 1958. Sanders won twelve letters in three sports at Vanderbilt, 1926, and coached football there, 1940–43, 1946–48, compiling a 36–22–2 record. Then he moved to UCLA, 1949–57, compiling a 66–19–1 record. His 1954 team was national champion and he was Coach of the Year. His Uclans were twice beaten by Michigan State in the Rose Bowl, 28–0 in 1954 and 17–14 in 1956.

Helms Hall of Fame.

SAPERSTEIN, ABRAHAM basketball: b. July 4, 1901, London, England; d. March 15, 1966. Though he was only 5′ tall, Saperstein played baseball, basketball, and track while a high-school student in Chicago but wasn't allowed to go out for basketball at the University of Illinois.

In 1927 he founded what was to become the most famous basketball team in the world, the Harlem Globetrotters. Asked later how he named the team, Saperstein said the "Harlem" part was easy, since all the players were black. As for the "Globetrotters," he explained, "We had high hopes." Those hopes were more than fulfilled. Originally there were only five players who rode with Saperstein in a dilapidated car. But, with a unique blend of basketball skill and clowning, the Globetrotters have lived up to their name, traveling more than six million miles and visiting nearly one hundred countries through the years. The total number of spectators who have seen them can't even be estimated.

Saperstein was also founder of the short-lived American Basketball League; he lost more than a million dollars on the league, but he said he never regretted it.

Basketball Hall of Fame.

SCANLAN, "DOC" (William D.) baseball: b. March 7, 1881, Syracuse, N.Y.; d. May 29, 1949. Bat L, throw R; pitcher. Pittsburgh NL, 1903–04; Brooklyn NL, 1904–07, 1909–11. Eight years, 66–72, 3.00 ERA, 15 shutouts.

SCHAEFER, "GERMANY" (Herman A.) baseball: b. Feb. 4, 1878, Chicago; d. May 16, 1919. Bat, throw R; second-first-third base. Chicago NL, 1901–02; Detroit AL, 1905–09; Washington AL, 1909–14; Newark Fed L, 1915;

New York AL, 1916; Cleveland AL, 1918. Fifteen years, 1,143 games, .257 BA; hit .334 in 1911. Two World Series, 1907–08: 10 games, .135 BA.

One of baseball's great characters, Schaefer one day went to second base on what was supposed to be the first half of a double steal, but no throw was made. On the next pitch he stole first! Again there was no throw, and after checking the rule book, the umpires decided it was perfectly legal. Schaefer then headed for second again; this time the throw was made, he was safe, and the other runner went home to complete the double steal.

SCHAEFER, JACOB, SR. billiards: b. Feb. 2, 1855, Milwaukee, Wis.; d. March 9, 1909. "The Wizard" was largely responsible for the development of modern billiards because no one could beat him at the old style of play, in which a player could "nurse" the balls near a cushion. Schaefer won so consistently that the 14.2, 18.1, and 18.2 balkline games were introduced to give others a chance to win. In 1890, against J. F. B. McCleery at straight-rail billiards, a 3,000-point match, Schaefer ran 3,000 on his fourth turn, winning 3,004 to 15. Probably his greatest victory came in 1908, when the much younger Willie Hoppe was acknowledged champion at 18.2 balkline. Schaefer won the title from Hoppe, 500–423, then retired.

His son, Jacob, Jr., was Hoppe's chief competitor from the early twenties through the thirties.

SCHALK, RAYMOND W. ("Cracker") baseball: b. Aug. 12, 1892, Harvel, Ill.; d. May 19, 1970. Bat, throw R; catcher. Chicago AL, 1912–28; New York NL, 1929. Eighteen years, 1,760 games, .253 BA. Two World Series, 1917, 1919: 14 games, .286 BA.

Schalk holds ML records for most no-hit games caught, 4 (including a perfect game); most years leading catchers in fielding average, 8, and most consecutive, 5; most years leading in putouts, 9; most assists in an inning, 3, on Sept. 30, 1921; most years leading catchers in chances accepted, 8. He also holds the AL record for most career assists by a catcher, 1,810.

He managed Chicago AL, 1927–28 (part): 102–125, .449.

Baseball Hall of Fame.

SCHANG, "WALLY" (Walter H.) baseball: b. Aug. 22, 1889, South Wales, N.Y.; d. March 26, 1965. Sw. hit, throw R; catcher, outfield, third base. Philadelphia AL, 1913–17; Boston AL, 1918–20; New York AL, 1921–25; St. Louis AL, 1926–29; Philadelphia AL, 1930; Detroit AL, 1931. Nineteen years, 1,839 games, .284 BA; hit .306 in 1919, .305 in 1920, .316 in 1921, .319 in 1922, .330 in 1926, .319 in 1927. Six World Series, 1913–14, 1918, 1921–23: 32 games, .287 BA.

Schang set modern ML records for catchers with 8 assists in a 9-inning game, May 12, 1920; five years before, to the day, he had set an AL record for most runners caught stealing, 6, in a 9-inning game.

SCHMELZ, GUSTAVUS H. baseball: b. Sept. 26, 1850, Columbus, Ohio; d. Oct. 14, 1925. Managed Columbus AA, 1884; St. Louis NL, 1886; Cincinnati AA, 1887–89; Cleveland NL, 1890 (part); Columbus AA, 1890 (part)–91; Washington NL, 1894–97 (part): 623–703, .470.

SCHNEIDER, HANNES skiing: b. 1890, Stuben, Austria; d. April 26, 1955. Schneider developed the so-called Arlberg technique of skiing and instruction, which was eventually adopted almost universally. Up until about 1920, skiers usually used an upright stance. Developed in Norway, it wasn't suited for the steep, irregular Alpine slopes. Schneider began to use, instead, a crouch, with knees bent and weight forward. By 1920, he was regarded as the Alps' outstanding ski master and is said never to have lost a downhill or slalom event. He became well known in the United States in 1936, when he was the chief attraction at a ski show in Madison Square Garden.

In 1938, he defied the Nazis by refusing to fire a Jew who worked at his school. That ultimately led to his emigration to the United States in 1939, where he opened a school in Conway, New Hampshire, a major factor in bringing advanced European methods to American skiing.

Skiing Hall of Fame.

SCHNEIDER, PETER J. baseball: b. Aug. 20, 1895, Los Angeles; d. June 1, 1957. Bat, throw R; pitcher. Cincinnati NL, 1914–18; New York AL, 1919. Six years, 57–86, 2.62 ERA; 11 shutouts; 20–19 in 1917. Led NL in losses, 1915 (13–19).

SCHOMMER, JOHN J. basketball: b. Jan. 29, 1884, Chicago; d. Jan. 11, 1960. The first University of Chicago athlete to win 12 letters, Schommer was particularly outstanding in basketball. He led the Western Conference (Big Ten) in scoring three years in a row, 1907–09, and captained the team that won the 1909 national championship.

Basketball Hall of Fame.

SCHULTE, "WILDFIRE" (Frank) baseball: b. Sept. 17, 1882, Coschocton, N.Y.; d. Oct. 2, 1949. Bat L, throw R; outfield. Chicago NL, 1904–16; Pittsburgh NL, 1916–17; Philadelphia NL, 1917; Washington AL, 1918. Fifteen years, 1,805 games, 233 stolen bases, .270 BA; hit .301 in 1910, .300 in 1911. Led league in triples, 1906 (13); in home runs, 1910 (10); in home runs (21), RBI (107), and slugging (.534) in 1911. Four World Series, 1906–08, 1910: 21 games, 6 doubles, 11 runs, 9 RBI, .309 BA.

SCHULZ, "GERMANY" (Adolph G.) football: b. April 19, 1883, Ft. Wayne, Ind.; d. April 14, 1951. Michigan center; All-American, 1907; captain, 1908. Walter Camp's biggest mistake in selecting All-American teams was probably leaving Schulz off the team in 1908. Later, Camp included him on an All-Time team, and Grantland Rice felt that he was better than even the great Mel Hein, a member of the Professional Football Hall of Fame.

Even today he would be big enough to play center, at 6'4" and 245 pounds, and he might well be used as a linebacker because of his strength and mobility. He was one of the first centers to use the one-hand spiral snap and one of the first to play as a "rover" on defense, moving a yard behind the line and playing much like a modern linebacker. Schulz was also very durable: He played every minute of 50 games during his career at Michigan, which spanned 51 games. While in high school, he worked part time in a steel mill and played three football games every weekend, with the high-school team, the town team, and a semipro team.

The "center eligible" play was legal in 1907–08, and Michigan used it several times with great effectiveness. The other six linemen would all line up on one side of Schulz, making him an end as well as a center, so he could receive a pass. (Under today's rules, the man who centers the ball can't ever be eligible to receive.)

Helms Hall of Fame, National Football Foundation Hall of Fame.

SCHWAB, "DUTCH" (Frank J.) football: b. 1895, Madera, Pa.; d. Dec. 12, 1965. Lafayette guard; All-American, 1921–22.

Helms Hall of Fame, National Football Foundation Hall of Fame.

SCOTT, "DEACON" (L. Everett) baseball: b. Nov. 19, 1892, Bluffton, Ind.; d. Nov. 2, 1960. Bat, throw R; shortstop. Boston AL, 1914–21; New York AL, 1922–25; Washington AL, 1925; Chicago AL, Cincinnati NL, 1926. Thirteen years, 1,654 games, .249 BA. Five World Series, 1915–16, 1918, 1922–23: 27 games, .156 BA.

Scott holds the ML record for most consecutive games by a shortstop, 1,307, from June 20, 1916, to May 5, 1925. He tied the AL record for most years leading shortstops in fielding, 8.

SCOTT, "JACK" (John W.) baseball: b. April 18, 1892, Ridgeway, N.C.; d. Nov. 30, 1959. Bat L, throw R; pitcher. Pittsburgh NL, 1916; Boston NL, 1917, 1919–21; Cincinnati NL, 1922; New York NL, 1922–23, 1925–26; Philadelphia NL, 1927; New York NL, 1928–29. Twelve years, 103–109, 3.85 ERA. In relief, 19–24, 3.98 ERA, 19 saves. Led NL in losses, 1927 (9–21). Two World Series, 1922–23: 1–1, 3.00 ERA.

SCOTT, JAMES baseball: b. April 23, 1888, Deadwood, S.D.; d. April 7, 1957. Bat, throw R; pitcher. Chicago AL, 1909–17. Nine years, 111–113, 2.32 ERA; 26 shutouts. No-hitter, May 14, 1914, against Washington AL (9 innings; lost 1–0 in tenth on 2 hits). Led AL in losses, 1913 (20–21); in shutouts, 1915 (7).

SEARS, ELEONORA R. squash, tennis, and others: b. Sept. 28, 1881, Boston; d. March 26, 1968. An attractive, well-dressed member of Boston and Newport society, Miss Sears was a remarkable all-round athlete who won more than 240 trophies on tennis and squash courts and in horse-show rings and was also active and accomplished in a number of sports in which she didn't formally compete. Four times she was national doubles tennis champion, with Hazel Hotchkiss Wightman in 1911 and 1915 and with Molla Bjurstedt Mallory in 1916–17; she was mixed doubles champion with Willis E. Davis in 1916; and twice she was a national singles finalist. In 1928, when she was forty-six, she won the national squash racquets championship.

She was one of the first women to drive a car, one of the first to ride in an airplane, and one of the most fearless ever to ride thoroughbreds in steeplechases and hunting meets. She once skippered a yacht that beat Alfred Vanderbilt's *Walthra.* At one time or another she also played baseball, football, and golf, skated, and raced speedboats. She was an accurate shot with either rifle or pistol. She often swam distances of from 3 to 6 miles and in her late forties she took up long-distance walking. Her Newport-to-Boston walk became an annual news story. She once covered the 50 miles in less than 10 hours.

Miss Sears also loved dancing. When the Prince of Wales went to a party in Boston during his 1924 visit to the United States, he did most of his dancing with her.

SEARS, RICHARD D. tennis: b. 1861(?), Boston; d. April 8, 1943. Sears was the first U.S. outdoor singles champion, and he won the title seven consecutive years, 1881–87. He also won the doubles championship six consecutive times, 1882–87, with Dr. James Dwight as his partner each time except 1885, when he teamed with Joseph S. Clark. Like Dwight, Sears had learned to play on the second court built in the United States, at Nahant, Massachusetts.

He won the first U.S. court tennis championship in 1892.

Helms Hall of Fame, Tennis Hall of Fame.

SEATON, THOMAS G. baseball: b. Aug. 30, 1889, Blair, Nebr.; d. April 10, 1940. Bat L, throw R; pitcher. Philadelphia NL, 1912–13; Brooklyn Fed L, 1914–15; Newark Fed L, 1915; Chicago NL, 1916–17. Six years, 93–64,

3.14 ERA; 644 strikeouts, 16 shutouts in 1,340 innings; 25–13 in 1914. Led NL in wins (27–12) and strikeouts (168) in 1913.

SEDRAN, BARNEY basketball: b. Jan. 28, 1891, New York City; d. Jan. 14, 1969. Sedran was only 5'4", but he led City College of New York in scoring three seasons and captained the team during his senior year, 1910–11. He then went on to play for a number of pro teams during a fifteen-year career, among them the Cleveland Rosenblums, the Carbondale team that won 35 straight in 1914–15, and the New York Whirlwinds. He led the Whirlwinds in scoring for two seasons, and his 31-point performance in one game was the pro record for a long time. Nat Holman said of him, "He was the greatest little man who ever played the game. He could do everything." Basketball Hall of Fame.

SELBACH, "KIP" (Albert K.) baseball: b. March 24, 1872, Columbus, Ohio; d. Feb. 17, 1956. Bat, throw R; outfield. Washington NL, 1894–98; Cincinnati NL, 1899; New York NL, 1900–01; Baltimore AL, 1902; Washington AL, 1903–04; Boston AL, 1904–06. Thirteen years, 1,613 games, 1,064 runs, 334 stolen bases, .293 BA; hit .306 in 1894, .322 in 1895, .304 in 1896, .313 in 1897, .303 in 1898, .337 in 1900, .320 in 1902. Led league in triples, 1895 (22).

Selbach went 6-for-7, with 4 runs, on June 9, 1901.

SELEE, FRANK G. baseball: b. Oct. 26, 1859, Amherst, N.H.: d. July 5, 1909. Managed Boston NL, 1890–1901; Chicago NL, 1902–05: 1,299–872, .598 (4th). Pennants, 1891–93, 1897–98.

Selee was one of the first major-league managers to come to his job with little experience as a player. He was a quiet man, skillful at handling players. After his great success at Boston, he molded the Cub team that was to win 3 straight pennants, but tuberculosis forced him to quit; Frank Chance replaced him.

SEVAREID, "HANK" (Henry L.) baseball: b. June 1, 1891, Story City, Iowa; d. Dec. 17, 1968. Bat, throw R; catcher. Cincinnati NL, 1911–13; St. Louis AL, 1915–25; Washington AL, 1925–26; New York AL, 1926. Fifteen years, 1,389 games, .289 BA; hit .324 in 1921, .321 in 1922, .308 in 1923, .308 in 1924. Two World Series, 1925–26: 8 games, .280 BA.

On July 13, 1920, Sevareid set an ML record for catchers by handling 27 chances in a doubleheader.

SEWARD, EDWARD W. baseball: b. Sourhardt, July 29, 1867, Cleveland; d. July 30, 1947. Throw R; pitcher. Providence NL, 1885; Philadelphia AA, 1887–90; Cleveland NL, 1891. Six years, 88–72, 3.40 ERA; 13 shutouts;

25–25 in 1887, 35–19 in 1888, 21–15 in 1889. No-hitter, July 26, 1888, against Cincinnati AA (12–2). Led AA in strikeouts (272) and shutouts (6) in 1888.

SEYBOLD, "SOCKS" (Ralph O.) baseball: b. Nov. 23, 1870, Washington-ville, Ohio; d. Dec. 22, 1921. Bat, throw R; outfield. Cincinnati NL, 1899; Philadelphia AL, 1901–08. Nine years, 996 games, .294 BA; hit .334 in 1901, .316 in 1902, .316 in 1906. Led AL in doubles, 1903 (45); in home runs, 1902 (16). One World Series, 1905: 5 games, .125 BA.

Seybold tied an ML record for outfielders with 2 unassisted double plays in 1907 (Aug. 15 and Sept. 10).

SEYMOUR, "CY" (James B.) baseball: b. Dec. 9, 1872, Albany, N.Y.; d. Sept. 20, 1919. Bat, throw L; pitcher, 1896–1900; outfield, 1901–13. New York NL, 1896–1900; Baltimore AL, 1901–02; Cincinnati NL, 1902–06; New York NL, 1906–10; Boston NL, 1913. Sixteen years, 1,528 games, .303 BA. Led NL in hits (219), doubles (40), triples (21), RBI (121), BA (.377), and slugging (.559) in 1905.

As a pitcher: five years, 61–57, 3.76 ERA. Led NL in strikeouts in 1898 (239); 25–19 in 1898.

SHANKS, "HANK" (Howard S.) baseball: b. July 21, 1890, Chicago; d. July 30, 1941. Bat, throw R; outfield, infield. Washington AL, 1912–22; Boston AL, 1923–24; New York AL, 1925. Fourteen years, 1,663 games, .253 BA; hit .302 in 1921. Led AL in triples, 1921 (19).

SHARKEY, THOMAS J. boxing: b. Nov. 26, 1873, Dundalk, Ireland; d. April 17, 1953. His record: 40 wins, 37 by KO; 6 losses, 2 by KO; 5 draws, 3 no-decisions. Despite a fine record as a heavyweight in the early days of the Marquis of Queensbury rules, Sharkey was never a champion.

Helms Hall of Fame, Boxing Hall of Fame.

SHAUGHNESSY, CLARK D. football: b. March 6, 1892, St. Cloud, Minn.; d. May 15, 1970. Shaughnessy played fullback and tackle at the University of Minnesota; he was 3rd-team All-American as a tackle in 1912.

He coached in college for a quarter of a century before winning fame by reviving the T-formation and turning what had appeared to be a mediocre Stanford team into a national champion, in 1940, winning the Coach of the Year award.

Shaughnessy had coached Tulane, 1915–20, 1922–25; Loyola of the South, 1926–32, and Chicago, 1933–39. His 1919 Tulane team had a 6–0–1 record, and his 1926 Loyola team was 10–0–0. When he moved to Stanford and saw game films of a left-handed tailback named Frankie Albert, he decided Albert's ball-handling ability could be put to better use in the T than in the single wing, and Stanford won all 9 of its regular-season games, then beat Nebraska 21–13 in the Rose Bowl. That record spurred college and pro teams alike to shift over to the T. Shaughnessy, a close friend of Chicago Bear Coach George Halas, also acted as a consultant to the Bears, who had been using the T fairly regularly, but without much success, for years. It was largely Shaughnessy's expert play design and development of precise terminology that helped to make it a successful formation.

After a 6–3 season in 1941 at Stanford, Shaughnessy coached at Maryland in 1942 and 1946 and at Pittsburgh, 1943–45. He coached the Los Angeles Rams, 1948–49, winning the divisional title in 1949 but losing the NFL championship to the Philadelphia Eagles, 14–0.

As an assistant to Halas in the fifties, Shaughnessy also did a great deal to develop the modern sophisticated pro-football defenses that give each player a specific assignment on every play.

Helms Hall of Fame, National Football Foundation Hall of Fame.

SHAUGHNESSY, "SHAG" (Frank J.) baseball: b. April 8, 1883, Amboy, Ill.; d. May 15, 1969. While business manager of the Montreal team in the International League in 1933, Shaughnessy came up with the idea of a postseason championship playoff system. Because of the fan interest it stirred, the "Shaughnessy playoff" system was adopted by many minor leagues in various forms, and it's now also used in professional hockey and basketball.

Shaughnessy, an alumnus of Notre Dame, coached football there in 1904. He briefly played major-league baseball, a total of 9 games in 1905 and 1908.

SHAUTE, JOSEPH B. baseball: b. Aug. 1, 1899, Peckville, Pa.; d. Feb. 21, 1970. Bat, throw L; pitcher. Cleveland AL, 1922–30; Brooklyn NL, 1931–33; Cincinnati NL, 1934. Thirteen years, 99–109, 4.15 ERA. In relief, 20–14, 4.23 ERA, 18 saves. Led AL in losses, 1924 (20–17).

SHAW, "DUPEE" (Frederick L.) baseball: b. May 31, 1859, Charlestown, Mass.; d. June 11, 1938. Throw L; pitcher. Detroit NL, 1883–84; Boston UA, 1884; Providence NL, 1885; Washington NL, 1886–88. Six years, 83–121, 3.10 ERA; 950 strikeouts, 13 shutouts in 1,762 innings. No-hitter, Oct. 7, 1885, against Buffalo NL (4–0; 5 innings).

SHAW, JAMES A. baseball: b. Aug. 13, 1893, Pittsburgh; d. Jan. 27, 1962. Bat, throw R; pitcher. Washington AL, 1913–21. Nine years, 83–98, 3.07 ERA; 767 strikeouts, 17 shutouts in 1,600⅓ innings.

SHAW, WILBUR (Warren Wilbur) auto racing: b. Oct. 31, 1902, Shelbyville, Ind.; d. Oct. 30, 1954. Because of a string of bad luck, Shaw didn't win the Indianapolis 500 until he was thirty-five; then he won it twice more. Overall, he finished in the top four 7 times. His victories came in 1937, 1939, and 1940, and he was second in 1933, 1935, and 1938 and fourth in 1927. He was national driving champion in 1937 and 1939.

Shaw built his own car when he was eighteen and became a frequent winner at midwestern tracks, setting many records in the process. He pioneered use of the crash helmet after suffering a skull fracture in a 1923 crash. He took a lot of needling from other drivers, but helmets were made mandatory after Shaw survived a crash in which he was thrown from his car and landed on his head.

After World War II, during which auto racing had been suspended because of gas rationing, Shaw became president and general manager of the Indianapolis Speedway Corporation.

He died in the crash of a private plane.

Auto Racing Hall of Fame, Helms Hall of Fame.

SHECKARD, "JIMMY" (Samuel J. T.) baseball: b. Nov. 23, 1878, Upper Chanceford, Pa.; d. Jan. 15, 1947. Bat L, throw R; outfield. Brooklyn NL, 1897–98; Baltimore NL, 1899; Brooklyn NL, 1900–01; Baltimore AL, 1902; Brooklyn NL, 1902–05; Chicago NL, 1906–12; Cincinnati NL, St. Louis NL, 1913. Seventeen years, 2,121 games, 1,295 runs, 465 stolen bases (7th), .274 BA. Led league in triples, 1901 (19); in home runs, 1903 (9); in runs (121) and walks (147), 1911; in walks, 1912 (122); in stolen bases 1899 (77), 1903 (67); in slugging, 1901 (.534). Four World Series, 1906–08, 1910: 21 games, .182 BA.

Sheckard tied an ML record by hitting grand-slam home runs in consecutive games, Sept. 23 and 24, 1901.

SHEELY, EARL H. baseball: b. Feb. 12, 1893, Bushnell, Ill.; d. Sept. 16, 1952. Bat, throw R; first base. Chicago AL, 1921–27; Pittsburgh NL, 1929; Boston NL, 1931. Nine years, 1,234 games, .300 BA; hit .304 in 1921, .317 in 1922, .320 in 1924, .315 in 1925.

Sheely collected 7 consecutive extra-base hits, 6 doubles, and a home run on May 20 and 21, 1926, tying the ML record.

SHELDON, JAMES M., SR. football: b. 1880(?); d. July 7, 1965. He captained Chicago's teams, 1901–02. As head coach at Indiana, 1905–12, he had a 34–26–3 record. His first team was his best, with an 8–1–1 record. Sheldon is generally credited with inventing the "Statue of Liberty" play.

SHELLOGG, "ALEC" (Frederick) football: b. Feb. 8, 1916, Newcastle, Pa.; d. July 13, 1968. Notre Dame tackle. Brooklyn Dodgers, Chicago Bears, 1939; Buffalo Indians (AFL), 1940; Buffalo Tigers (AFL), 1941.

SHEPHERD, WILLIAM L. football: b. Dec. 4, 1911, Clearfield, Pa.; d. March 9, 1967. Western Maryland halfback. Boston Redskins, 1935; Detroit Lions, 1935–40. Shepherd led college scorers in 1934 with 133 points. In six years of pro ball, he gained 1,984 yards in 519 carries, a 3.8 average.

SHEPPARD, MELVIN W. track: b. 1884(?); d. Jan. 4, 1942. Sheppard won the 800-meter and 1,500-meter runs in the 1908 Olympics. He was AAU outdoor champion in the 880 in 1906–08 and 1911–12.
Helms Hall of Fame.

SHERDEL, "WEE WILLIE" (William H.) baseball: b. Aug. 15, 1896, McSherrystown, Pa.; d. Nov. 14, 1968. Bat, throw L; pitcher. St. Louis NL, 1918–30; Boston NL, 1930–32; St. Louis NL, 1932. Fifteen years, 165–146, 3.72 ERA. In relief, 39–32, 3.25 ERA, 26 saves; 21–10 in 1928. Led league in percentage in 1925 (15–6, .714). Two World Series, 1926, 1928: 0–4, 3.26 ERA.

SHERRILL, CHARLES H., JR. track: b. April 13, 1867, Washington, D.C.; d. June 25, 1936. Sherrill originated the crouch start while at Yale (Class of 1889). He won the IC4A 100-yard dash, 1887–90, the 220 in 1888–90; he was U.S. outdoor champion in the 100 in 1887. Sherrill also organized a series of international interuniversity track meets, the first of which, between Yale and Oxford, was held in 1894. He directed the New York Athletic Club team in the 1900 Olympics. Later, he served as U.S. ambassador to Turkey.

SHEVLIN, THOMAS L football: b. March 1, 1883, Muskegon, Mich.; d. Dec. 29, 1915. Yale end; All-American 1902, 1904–05; 2nd team, 1903. Big for his time, at 5'10" and 195 pounds, Shevlin frequently played tackle and was a good enough runner to appear in several games at fullback in his sophomore year. In 1903 he returned one kickoff 95 yards for a TD and returned another 85 yards.
    The wealthy son of a lumber tycoon, Shevlin was a student of football. He assisted Dr. H. L. Williams at the University of Minnesota, helping him to come up with a tricky double shift. He brought the shift to Yale in 1910, helping the Bulldogs upset a heavily favored Princeton team, 5–3. Called upon to coach Yale for its two most important games in 1915, he came up with another upset of Princeton, 13–7, but Yale was whipped, 41–0, by Harvard. On the sidelines during the latter game, he caught a bad cold which turned into a fatal case of pneumonia.
    Helms Hall of Fame, National Football Foundation Hall of Fame.

SHILLING, CARROL H. horse racing: b. Paris, Tex.; d. Jan. 12, 1950. Shilling rode Worth to victory in the 1912 Kentucky Derby. During his career, he rode 969 winners of 3,838 mounts, with 631 seconds and 536 thirds. Among his major victories were the Alabama Stakes, Belmont Futurity, Blue Grass Stages, Dwyer Handicap, Saratoga Special, and Travers Stakes.

SHINDLE, WILLIAM baseball: b. Dec. 5, 1863, Gloucester City, N.J.; d. 1920. Bat, throw R; third base, shortstop. Detroit NL, 1886–87; Baltimore AA, 1888–89; Philadelphia PL, 1890; Philadelphia NL, 1891; Baltimore NL, 1892–93; Brooklyn NL, 1894–98. Thirteen years, 1,422 games, 316 stolen bases, .269 BA; hit .314 in 1889, .322 in 1890. He went 6-for-6, with 2 doubles and a triple, on Aug. 26, 1890.

Shindle holds the NL record (154-game schedule) for assists by a third baseman in a season, 384, in 1892. On Sept. 28, 1893, he tied an ML record for third basemen by handling 13 chances in a 9-inning game.

SHIVELY, BION harness racing: b. 1878(?); d. Feb. 24, 1970. In 1953, Shively, then seventy-five, became the oldest man ever to drive to victory in the Hambletonian, with Sharp Note. He had previously won the event in 1948–49. During his career, which ended with retirement in 1959, he won more than 60 major races.

Harness Hall of Fame.

SHOCKER, URBAN J. baseball: b. Urbain J. Schockeor, Aug. 22, 1890, Cleveland; d. Sept. 9, 1928. Bat, throw R; pitcher. New York AL, 1916–17; St. Louis AL, 1918–24; New York AL, 1925–28. Thirteen years, 188–117, 3.17 ERA; 28 shutouts; 20–10 in 1920, 24–17 in 1922, 20–12 in 1923. Led AL in wins, 1921 (27–12); in strikeouts, 1922 (149). One World Series, 1926: 0–1, 5.87 ERA.

SHOTTON, BURTON E. baseball: b. Oct. 18, 1884, Brownhelm, Ohio; d. July 29, 1962. Bat L, throw R; outfield. St. Louis AL, 1909, 1911–17; Washington AL, 1918; St. Louis NL, 1919–23. Fourteen years, 1,388 games, 294 stolen bases, .270 BA. Led league in walks, 1913 (99) and 1916 (111).

Managed Philadelphia NL, 1928–33; Cincinnati NL, 1934 (part); Brooklyn NL, 1947–50: 698–764, .477. Pennants, 1947, 1949.

SHOUN, "HARDROCK" (Clyde M.) baseball: b. March 29, 1912, Mountain City, Tenn.; d. March 20, 1968. Bat, throw L; pitcher. Chicago NL, 1935–37; St. Louis NL, 1938–42; Cincinnati NL, 1942–44, 1946–47; Boston NL, 1947–49; Chicago NL, 1949. Fourteen years, 73–59, 3.91 ERA. In relief, 41–25, 3.53 ERA, 29 saves. No-hitter, May 15, 1944, against Boston NL (1–0).

SIELAFF, LOUIS A. bowling: b. Dec. 10, 1915, Detroit; d. May 1, 1964. Sielaff captained the only team to win three ABC tournaments, 1952–53 and 1955; they also won four team all-events titles, 1949, 1950, 1953, and 1955. His twenty-nine year ABC tournament average was 193. He had two sanctioned 300 games.

American Bowling Congress Hall of Fame.

SIEVER, EDWARD T. baseball: b. April 2, 1878, Lewistown, Ill.; d. Feb. 5, 1920. Bat, throw L; pitcher. Detroit AL, 1901–02; St. Louis AL, 1903–04; Detroit AL, 1906–08. Seven years, 80–84, 2.60 ERA; 14 shutouts. Led AL in ERA, 1902 (1.91). One World Series, 1907; 0–1, 4.50 ERA.

SIMMONS, "BUCKETFOOT AL" (Aloysius H.) baseball: b. Szymanski, May 22, 1902, Milwaukee; d. May 26, 1956. Bat, throw R; outfield. Philadelphia AL, 1924–32; Chicago AL, 1933–35; Detroit AL, 1936; Washington AL, 1937–38; Boston NL, Cincinnati NL, 1939; Philadelphia AL, 1940–41; Boston AL, 1943; Philadelphia AL, 1944. Twenty years, 2,215 games, 8,761 at-bats, 2,927 hits, 539 doubles, 149 triples, 307 home runs, 1,507 runs, 1,827 RBI (8th), .334 BA. Led AL in hitting, 1930 (.381), 1931 (.390); in runs, 1939 (152); in hits, 1925 (253) and 1932 (216); in RBI, 1929 (157). Four World Series, 1929–31, 1939: 19 games, 15 runs, 17 RBI, .329 BA, .658 slugging percentage (3rd).

His unusual batting style, in which he violated a basic principle of hitting by stepping away from home plate—"putting his foot in the bucket"—gave Simmons his nickname. He hit .308 in 1924, .384 in 1925, .343 in 1926, .392 in 1927, .351 in 1928, .365 in 1929, .322 in 1932, .331 in 1933, .344 in 1934, .327 in 1936, .302 in 1938. He tied the modern ML record by getting more than 200 hits 5 consecutive seasons, and his 253 hits in 1925 is an ML record for right-handers; his 174 singles that year is the AL record for right-handers. On July 15, 1932, Simmons hit 3 consecutive home runs. He also tied the ML record for most assists in one inning by an outfielder, 2, Sept. 28, 1933.

Baseball Hall of Fame.

SINGER, AL boxing: b. Sept. 6, 1907, New York City; d. April 19, 1961. His record: 60 wins, 24 by KO; 8 losses, 4 by KO; 2 draws. Singer began one of the shortest reigns in boxing history, July 17, 1930, winning the lightweight title with a KO of Sammy Mandell at 1:32 of the 1st round. He lost it Nov. 14, when Tony Canzoneri KOed him at 1:06 of the 1st round.

SLAGLE, JAMES F. baseball: b. July 11, 1873, Worthville, Pa.; d. May 10, 1956. Outfield. Washington NL, 1899; Philadelphia NL, 1900–01; Boston NL, 1901; Chicago NL, 1902–08. Ten years, 1,297 games, 273 stolen bases,

.268 BA; hit .315 in 1902. One World Series, 1907: 5 games, 6 stolen bases (6th), .273 BA.

SLATER, "DUKE" (Frederick E.) football: b. Dec. 9, 1898, Normal, Ill.; d. Aug. 14, 1966. Iowa tackle, 2nd team All-American, 1921; 3rd team, 1919. Milwaukee Badgers, 1922; Rock Island Independents, 1922–25; Rock Island (AFL), 1926; Chicago Cardinals, 1926–31.
National Football Foundation Hall of Fame.

SLATTERY, JIMMY boxing: b. Aug. 25, 1904, Buffalo, N.Y.; d. Aug. 30, 1960. His record: 109 wins, 45 by KO; 14 losses, 5 by KO; 1 draw, 2 no-decisions, 2 no-contests. Slattery won the NBA version of the light-heavyweight title on Aug. 30, 1927, decisioning Maxie Rosenbloom in 10 rounds. He lost it to Tommy Loughran on Dec. 12, on a 15-round decision. Loughran resigned the title in 1929 to become a heavyweight, and Slattery won a New York Commission tournament with a 15-round decision over Lou Scozza on Feb. 10, 1930. But he lost that bit of the title to Rosenbloom, who won a 15-round decision on June 25, 1930.

SLOAN, "TOD" (James F.) horse racing: b. Aug. 10, 1874, Bunker Hill, Ind.; d. Dec. 21, 1933. Sloan's nickname was a corruption of "Toad," given him in childhood because of his unusually short legs. Those legs led him to revolutionize the art of riding thoroughbreds: He adopted short stirrups and the so-called monkey crouch, which brought him ridicule for a time. But his success led other jockeys to start using the crouch. Sloan was an expert strategist and technician, one of the first to study other horses as well as his own in order to plan his races carefully.
He made several extended trips to England, eventually becoming a rider for King Edward VII. In 1901, the English Jockey Club refused to give him a license, accusing him of "conduct detrimental to the sport," without further specification. As a result, he was ultimately banned from riding all over the world.
Jockey Hall of Fame, Racing Hall of Fame.

SLOCUM, HENRY W., JR. tennis: b. ?; d. Jan. 22, 1949. Slocum was U.S. outdoor singles champion, 1888–89, and doubles champion, with Howard A. Taylor, in 1889.
Tennis Hall of Fame.

SLOSSON, GEORGE F. billiards: b. 1854, DeKalb, N.Y.; d. June 21, 1949. In 1884, Slosson won the first world championship at 14.2 balkline, and in 1897 he won the first 18.1 balkline title. He also won the 18.2 championship in 1906 and 1908 and the 18.1 championship in 1908.

SMITH, ALEX golf: b. 1872, Carnoustie, Scotland; d. April 20, 1930. Five Smith brothers, including Alex and MacDonald, came to the United States in the 1890s. Alex was the most successful of them, in terms of major tournaments won. He finished second in the U.S. Open in 1898, his first year in the states, and he won the Open in 1906 and 1910, after losing a playoff to Willie Anderson in 1901 and finishing second in 1905. He also won the Western Open in 1903 and 1906.
Professional Golfers Association Hall of Fame.

SMITH, BRUCE P. football: b. Feb. 8, 1920, Faribault, Minn.; d. Aug. 28, 1967. Minnesota halfback; captain, All-American, 1941. Heisman Trophy, 1941. With Great Lakes in 1942, Smith was sixth in the nation in rushing, with 849 yards on 144 carries for a 5.9 average. Green Bay Packers, 1945–48; Los Angeles Rams, 1948.

SMITH, DWIGHT basketball: b. 1944, Princeton, Ky.; d. May 14, 1967. Smith, a 6'5" forward who averaged 14.4 points in three seasons at Western Kentucky, was the second draft choice of the Los Angeles Lakers in 1967. He died in an auto accident.

SMITH, EARL S. baseball: b. Feb. 14, 1897, Sheridan, Ark.; d. June 9, 1963. Bat L, throw R; catcher. New York NL, 1919–23; Boston NL, 1923–24; Pittsburgh NL, 1924–28; St. Louis NL, 1928–30. Twelve years, 860 games, .303 BA; hit .313 in 1925, .346 in 1926. As pinch-hitter, 41-for-129, .318 BA. Five World Series, 1921–22, 1925, 1927–28: 17 games, .239 BA.

SMITH, ELMER E. baseball: b. March 28, 1868, Pittsburgh; d. Nov. 5, 1945. Bat, throw L; pitcher, 1886–89; outfield, 1892–1901. Cincinnati AA, 1886–89; Pittsburgh NL, 1892–97; Cincinnati NL, 1898–1900; New York NL, 1900; Boston NL, Pittsburgh NL, 1901. Fourteen years, 1,235 games, 232 stolen bases, .310 BA; hit .346 in 1893, .356 in 1894, .302 in 1895, .362 in 1896, .310 in 1897, .342 in 1898. As pitcher: led AA in ERA in 1887 (2.94); 34–17 in 1887, 22–17 in 1888. Arm trouble forced him into the outfield.

SMITH, FRANK E. baseball: b. Oct. 28, 1879, Pittsburgh; d. Nov. 3, 1952. Bat, throw R; pitcher. Chicago AL, 1904–10; Boston AL, 1910–11; Cincinnati NL, 1911–12; Baltimore Fed L, 1914–15; Brooklyn Fed L, 1915. Eleven years, 132–112, 2.59 ERA; 1,051 strikeouts, 27 shutouts, in 2,273 innings; 23–11 in 1907, 24–17 in 1909. No-hitters, Sept. 6, 1905, against Detroit AL (15–0) and Sept. 20, 1908, against Philadelphia AL (1–0). Led AL in complete games (37) and strikeouts (177) in 1909.

SMITH, "GERMANY" (George J.) baseball: b. April 21, 1863, Pittsburgh; d. Dec. 1, 1927. Bat, throw R; shortstop. Cleveland NL, Altoona UA, 1884;

Brooklyn AA, 1885–89; Brooklyn NL, 1890; Cincinnati NL, 1891–96; Brooklyn NL, 1897; St. Louis NL, 1898. Fifteen years, 1,710 games, 213 stolen bases (3 years not included), .243 BA; hit .300 in 1895.

Smith holds the NL record for most consecutive years leading shortstops in assists, 4.

SMITH, HORTON golf: b. May 22, 1908, Springfield, Mo.; d. Oct. 15, 1963. On his twenty-first birthday, Smith won the French Open, the first of 33 major titles. He won the first Masters ever held, in 1934, and repeated in 1936. He also won the North and South Open in 1929 and 1937. Smith, who suffered from Hodgkin's disease, won the 1960 Ben Hogan Award for coming back to play in his 23rd consecutive Masters after having had a lung and two ribs removed because of his illness.

Helms Hall of Fame, Professional Golfers Association Hall of Fame.

SMITH, JAMES bowling: b. Mellilo, 1880(?), Brooklyn; d. April 21, 1946. At a time when there were match-game "champions" all over the country, rolling on their home lanes, Smith traveled around the United States taking on all challengers and usually beating them. In tours from 1910 to 1915 and late 1916 to 1924, he averaged 205 and was considered match-game champion until the World Open in 1922, won by Jimmy Blouin. Smith was the first man to win two ABC all-events titles, in 1911 and 1920, and the first to roll four 1900s in ABC tourneys. His twenty-five-year tournament average was 192.

American Bowling Congress Hall of Fame.

SMITH, JEFF boxing: b. Jerome Jeffords, Aug. 23, 1891, New York City; d. Feb. 3, 1962. His record: 101 wins, 46 by KO; 10 losses, 1 by KO; 3 draws, 65 no-decisions, 1 no-contest. Smith claimed the world middleweight title after Stanley Ketchel's death but never won recognition. He never even got a title fight, despite his record. He twice traveled around the world, boxing wherever he went, and he made seven trips to Europe for extended stays.

SMITH, MacDONALD golf: b. March 18, 1890. Carnoustie, Scotland; d. Aug. 31, 1949. In a three-way tie for the U.S. Open in 1910, Smith finished third to his brother Alex and John McDermott in the 18-hole playoff. He won the Western Open in 1912, 1925, and 1933, the North and South Open in 1925, and the Canadian Open in 1926.

Helms Hall of Fame, Professional Golfers Association Hall of Fame.

SMITH, "MYSTERIOUS BILLY" (Amos) boxing: b. May 15, 1871, Eastport, Maine; d. Oct. 15, 1937. His record: 30 wins, 13 by KO; 18 losses, 4 by KO (10 by fouls); 28 draws, 6 no-decisions. Smith was the first genuine American welterweight champ, winning the title with a 14th-round KO of

Danny Needham on Dec. 14, 1892. He lost it to Tommy Ryan in 20 rounds on July 20, 1894. After Ryan became a middleweight in 1896, Smith claimed the title again. He lost it to Rube Ferns on a foul in the 21st round on Jan. 15, 1900.

SMITH, OWEN P. dog racing: b. ?; d. January, 1929. Smith revived dog racing in the United States in 1919. The sport had been banned because it had involved a live rabbit, chased by the pack and caught and killed by the winner. Smith realized that a greyhound has virtually no sense of smell and responds to visual impressions, so he designed a mechanical rabbit that ran on an electric track. He opened a 3/16-mile track in Emeryville, California. His success there led him to build the first electrically lighted track, at Tulsa, the following year. He later opened tracks in East St. Louis, Chicago, and Miami.

SMITH, "POP" (Charles M.) baseball: b. Oct. 12, 1856, Digby, Nova Scotia, Canada; d. April 18, 1927. Bat, throw R; second base, shortstop. Cincinnati NL, 1880; Buffalo NL, Cleveland NL, Worcester NL, 1881; Baltimore AA, Louisville AA, 1882; Columbus AA, 1883–84; Pittsburgh AA, 1885–86; Pittsburgh NL, 1887–89; Boston NL, 1889–90; Washington AA, 1891. Twelve years, 1,093 games, .224 BA. Led league in triples, 1883 (17). He was one of two players to see action with 12 different teams.

SMITH, "RED" (James C.) baseball: b. April 6, 1890, Greenville, S.C.; d. Oct. 10, 1966. Bat, throw R; third base. Brooklyn NL, 1911–14; Boston NL, 1914–19. Nine years, 1,117 games, .278 BA. Led NL in doubles, 1913 (40).

SMITH, "SHERRY" (Sherrod M.) baseball: b. Feb. 18, 1891, Monticello, Ga.; d. Sept. 12, 1949. Bat, throw L; pitcher. Pittsburgh NL, 1911–12; Brooklyn NL, 1915–17, 1919–22; Cleveland AL, 1922–27. Fourteen years, 113–118, 3.32 ERA. In relief, 22–17, 3.32 ERA, 20 saves. Two World Series, 1916, 1920: 3 starts, 3 complete, 1–2, 0.89 ERA.

SMITH, "SILENT TOM" horse racing: b. 1878(?), Georgia; d. Jan. 23, 1957. Smith was a horse breaker and ranch foreman in Texas until he began training rodeo racehorses in 1921. At the Century of Progress Exposition in Chicago in 1934, his horses won 16 of the 18 races. Later that year, he was hired by Charles S. Howard, a wealthy California auto dealer who was trying to build up a stable. One of the first horses Smith asked Howard to buy was an undersized three-year-old with a bad knee and a worse temper. The horse's name was Seabiscuit; his only recommendation was that he was a grandson of Man O'War.

Smith's remarkable patience and his skill as a veterinarian made Seabiscuit one of the great champions. He was Horse of the Year in 1938; Handicap Division Horse of the Year, 1937–38; top money-winner among horses four years and older in 1937–38 and 1940; and when he retired after the 1940 season he had won more money than any other horse in history, $437,730, a record broken by Whirlaway in 1942.

Smith was top money-winning trainer in 1940, with $269,200, and in 1945, with $510,655. In 1947 he trained Kentucky Derby winner Jet Pilot for Maine Chance Farm.

SMITH, SOLLY boxing: b. 1871, Los Angeles; d. 1929. His record: 20 wins, 6 by KO; 6 losses, 1 by KO; 17 draws, 2 no-decisions. Smith won the featherweight title from George Dixon in 20 rounds on Oct. 4, 1897. In his first defense, Sept. 26, 1898, against Dave Sullivan, he broke an arm and had to quit. He had only five more fights before retiring in 1899.

SNYDER, FRANK E. baseball: b. May 27, 1893, San Antonio, Tex.; d. Jan. 5, 1962. Bat, throw R; catcher. St. Louis NL, 1912–19; New York NL, 1919–26; St. Louis NL, 1927. Sixteen years, 1,392 games, .265 BA; hit .320 in 1921, .343 in 1922, .302 in 1924. Four World Series, 1921–24: 17 games, .273 BA.

SNYDER, "POP" (Charles N.) baseball: b. Oct. 6, 1854, Washington, D.C.; d. Oct. 29, 1924. Bat, throw R; catcher. National Association, Washington, 1873; Baltimore, 1874; Philadelphia, 1875. Three years, 133 games, .228 BA.

Louisville NL, 1876–77; Boston NL, 1878–81; Cincinnati AA, 1882–86; Cleveland AA, 1887–88; Cleveland NL, 1889; Cleveland PL, 1890; Washington AA, 1891. Fifteen years, 797 games, .236 BA.

He managed Cincinnati AA, 1882–84 (part); Washington AA, 1891 (part): 164–124, .569. Pennant, 1882.

SONNENBERG, GUSTAVE football, wrestling: b. March 6, 1898, Ewen, Mich.; d. Sept. 12, 1944. Dartmouth, Detroit tackle. Guard, Columbus Tigers, 1923; Detroit Panthers, 1925–26; Providence Steamrollers, 1927–28, 1930.

After retiring from football, Sonnenberg introduced the flying tackle to professional wrestling, winning the heavyweight championship from Strangler Lewis in 1932.

SOTHORON, ALLEN S. baseball: b. April 29, 1893, Laura, Ohio; d. June 17, 1939. Sw. hit, throw R; pitcher. St. Louis AL, 1914–15, 1917–21; Boston AL, 1921; Cleveland AL, 1921–22; St. Louis NL, 1924–26. Eleven years, 92–100, 3.31 ERA; 17 shutouts; 21–13 in 1919. Led AL in losses, 1917 (14–19); led NL in shutouts, 1924 (4).

SOUTHWORTH, "BILLY" (William H.) baseball: b. March 9, 1893, Harvard, Nebr.; d. Nov. 15, 1969. Bat L, throw R; outfield. Cleveland AL, 1913, 1915; Pittsburgh NL, 1918–20; Boston NL, 1921–23; New York NL, 1924–26; St. Louis NL, 1926–27, 1929. Thirteen years, 1,192 games, .297 BA; hit .308 in 1921, .319 in 1923, .320 in 1926, .301 in 1927. Led NL in triples, 1919 (14). Two World Series, 1924, 1926: 12 games, 7 runs, 4 RBI, .333 BA.

He managed St. Louis NL, 1929 (part); 1940 (part)–45; Boston NL, 1946–51 (part): 1,064–729, .593 (5th). Pennants, 1942–44, 1948; World Series, 1942 and 1944.

SPALDING, ALBERT G. baseball: b. Sept. 2, 1850, Bryan, Ill.; d. Sept. 9, 1915. Bat, throw R; pitcher. National Association, Boston, 1871–75. Five years, 207–56, .320 BA.

Chicago NL, 1876–78. Three years, 47–12, 1.78 ERA, .287 BA. Led NL in victories and percentage (46–12, .793) and shutouts (8) in 1876. He was primarily a first baseman the next two years.

During the five years he was with the old Boston Red Stockings, Spalding pitched virtually every game, collecting 207 of the team's 227 victories during the period. He won 24 in a row during the 1875 season.

He managed Chicago NL, 1876–77: 78–47, .624. Pennant, 1876.

In 1876 Spalding formed the sporting-goods company that still bears his name and retired at the age of twenty-eight to devote full time to the company. He also founded a number of sports publications, the most influential of them the annual *Spalding's Baseball Guide*.

He was owner and president of the Chicago NL team, 1882–91.

Spalding was also an important figure in the formation of the National League as a replacement for the old National Association. He was one of the "Big Four" Boston stars lured to Chicago by John A. Hulbert in 1876. Baseball Hall of Fame.

SPARKS, TULLY F. baseball: b. April 18, 1877, Monroe, La.; d. July 15, 1937. Bat, throw R; pitcher. Philadelphia NL, 1897; Pittsburgh NL, 1899; Milwaukee AL, 1901; Boston AL, New York NL, 1902; Philadelphia NL, 1903–10. Twelve years, 120–138, 2.79 ERA; 19 shutouts; 21–8 in 1907.

SPEAKER, TRISTRAM E. baseball: b. April 4, 1888, Hubbard, Tex.; d. Dec. 8, 1958. Bat, throw L; outfield. Boston AL, 1907–15; Cleveland AL, 1916–26; Washington AL, 1927; Philadelphia AL, 1928. Twenty-two years (7th), 2,789 games (4th), 10,205 at-bats (4th), 3,514 hits (3rd), 2,383 singles (5th), 793 doubles (1st), 224 triples (6th), 115 home runs, 1,881 runs (5th), 5,100 total bases (6th), 433 stolen bases (10th), .344 BA (6th); hit .309 in 1909,

.340 in 1910, .327 in 1911, .383 in 1912, .363 in 1913, .338 in 1914, .322 in 1915, .352 in 1917, .318 in 1918, .388 in 1920, .362 in 1921, .378 in 1922, .380 in 1923, .344 in 1924, .389 in 1925, .304 in 1926, .327 in 1927. Led AL in hitting, 1916 (.386); in hits, 1914 (193), 1916 (211); in doubles, 1912 (53), 1914 (46), 1916 (41), 1918 (33), 1920 (50), 1921 (52), 1922 (48), 1923 (59); RBI, 1923 (130); in slugging, 1916 (.502). Three World Series, 1912, 1915, 1920: 20 games, 3 doubles, 4 triples (1st), 12 runs, .306 BA.

"The Gray Eagle" was a great defensive outfielder. He played an exceptionally shallow centerfield but was great at going back on long drives. He holds the ML record for most unassisted double plays by an outfielder, 4, and his 2 in 1918 ties the season record. He also holds the following AL records for outfielders: most career putouts, 6,706; most years led in putouts, 7; most career assists, 449; most assists, season, 35 (in 1909 and 1912); most years led in assists, 4; most years led in chances, 8. He led the AL in doubles 8 seasons, 4 consecutive, and 5 times he hit 50 or more, all ML records, and he holds the AL record for most seasons playing 100 or more games, 19.

He managed Cleveland AL, 1919 (part)–26: 616–520, .542. Pennant, World Series, 1920.

Baseball Hall of Fame.

SPEARS, "DOC" (Clarence W.) football: b. July 24, 1894, DeWitt, Ark.; d. Feb. 1, 1964. Dartmouth guard; All-American, 1915.

Spears coached at his alma mater, 1917, 1919–20, winning the Ivy League title and compiling a 7–2–0 record in his last year there. He moved on to West Virginia, 1921–24, Minnesota, 1925–29, Oregon, 1930–31, and Wisconsin, 1932–35, before retiring to practice medicine.

National Football Foundation Hall of Fame.

STAGG, AMOS ALONZO football: b. Aug. 16, 1862, West Orange, N.J.; d. March 17, 1965. Yale end; All-American, 1889.

In 1892, Stagg went to the University of Chicago to coach football. He stayed there for forty-one seasons. He also coached other sports; one year he handled football, baseball, basketball, and track. His Chicago football teams won six Western Conference (Big Ten) titles and tied for another; five of his teams were undefeated and he had an over all record of 268–141 at Chicago.

Forced by a school rule to retire at seventy, Stagg turned College of the Pacific into a football power. In 1943, at the age of eighty-one, he was named Coach of the Year. He retired—voluntarily this time—in 1946, after fifty-seven seasons of coaching, but went to Susquehanna College as an adviser to his son, who was coaching there.

Stagg designed plays such as the end around, the hidden-ball trick, the double reverse, and the "flea flicker." More down to earth, he also invented the tackling dummy.

Basketball Hall of Fame, Helms Hall of Fame, National Football Foundation Hall of Fame.

STAHL, "CHICK" (Charles S.) baseball: b. Jan. 10, 1873, Ft. Wayne, Ind.; d. March 28, 1907. Brother of Jake. Bat, throw L; outfield. Boston NL, 1897–1900; Boston AL, 1901–06. Ten years, 1,304 games, .305 BA; hit .354 in 1897, .308 in 1898, .351 in 1899, .303 in 1901, .323 in 1902. Led AL in triples, 1904 (19). One World Series, 1903: 8 games, .303 BA, 3 triples (2nd), 8 runs.

Stahl went 6-for-6, scoring 4 runs, on May 31, 1899.

STAHL, "JAKE" (Garland) baseball: b. April 13, 1879, Elkhart, Ill.; d. Sept. 18, 1922. Bat, throw R; first base. Boston AL, 1903; Washington AL, 1904–06; New York AL, 1908; Boston AL, 1908–10, 1912–13. Nine years, 981 games, .260 BA. Led AL in home runs, 1910 (10). One World Series, 1912: 8 games, .281 BA.

He managed Washington AL, 1905–06; Boston AL, 1912–13 (part): 263–270, .493. Pennant, World Series, 1912.

STAHLMAN, RICHARD F. football: b. 1902(?); d. May 11, 1970. DePaul, Northwestern tackle. Hammond Pros, Kenosha Maroons, 1924; Akron Pros, 1924–25; Rock Island Independents (AFL), Chicago Bulls (AFL), 1926; New York Giants, 1927–28, 1930; Green Bay Packers, 1931–32; Chicago Bears, 1933.

STALEY, "HARRY" (Henry E.) baseball: b. Nov. 3, 1866, Jacksonville, Ill.; d. Jan. 12, 1910. Bat, throw R; pitcher. Pittsburgh NL, 1888–89; Pittsburgh PL, 1890; Pittsburgh NL, 1891; Boston NL, 1891–94; St. Louis NL, 1895. Eight years, 137–119, 3.80 ERA; 21–25 in 1890, 24–13 in 1891, 22–10 in 1892. Led NL in losses, 1889 (21–26).

STALLINGS, GEORGE T. baseball: b. Nov. 17, 1867, Augusta, Ga.; d. May 13, 1929. Bat, throw R; catcher. Brooklyn NL, 1890; Philadelphia NL, 1897–98. Three years, 7 games, .100 BA.

He managed Philadelphia NL, 1897–98 (part); Detroit AL, 1901; New York AL, 1909–10 (part); Boston NL, 1913–20: 880–900, .494. Pennant, World Series, 1914. In 1914, Stallings' Braves were in last place, 11 games out of first, on July 19; they ended up winning the NL pennant by 6½ games and then further astounded baseball fans by beating the powerful Philadelphia Athletics in 4 straight games in the World Series.

STANAGE, OSCAR H. baseball: b. March 17, 1883, Tulare, Calif.; d. Nov. 11, 1964. Bat, throw R; catcher. Cincinnati NL, 1906; Detroit AL, 1909–20, 1925. Fourteen years, 1,094 games, .234 BA. One World Series, 1909: 2 games, .200 BA. Stanage holds the AL record for most assists by a catcher, 212 in 1911.

START, JOSEPH baseball: b. Oct. 14, 1842, New York City; d. March 27, 1927. Bat, throw L; first base. National Association, New York, 1871–75. Five years, 273 games, .282 BA.

New York NL, 1876; Brooklyn NL, 1877; Chicago NL, 1878; Providence NL, 1879–85; Washington NL, 1886. Eleven years, 798 games, .300 BA; hit .332 in 1877, .351 in 1878, .319 in 1879, .328 in 1881, .329 in 1882. Led NL in hits, 1878 (100).

STEERS, GEORGE yachting: b. July 20, 1820, Washington, D.C.; d. Sept. 25, 1856. Steer designed the 101-foot schooner *America,* which won one of England's most prized yachting trophies, the Hundred Guinea Cup, in 1851. Renamed the America's Cup, it is still in competition; challenges have been received from England, Canada, and Australia through the years, but the cup has remained in American hands ever since.

Steers designed many other racing yachts, as well as the steamship *Adriatic* and the warship *Niagara,* which helped lay the first transatlantic cable. When he was only eighteen, he built the prototype of the modern racing shell, a 30-foot, 140-pound vessel with outriggers, powered by four oars.

STEERS, HARRY H. bowling: b. Oct. 3, 1880, Dunlap, Iowa; d. Feb. 13, 1963. Twice winner of the ABC doubles, in 1902 and 1918, and once of all-events, 1918, Steers bowled in a record total of 57 ABC tournaments for a 181 average. He also won the first Petersen Classic, in 1921.

American Bowling Congress Hall of Fame.

STEFFEN, WALTER P. football: b. ?; d. March 9, 1937. Chicago quarterback; captain, All-American, 1908. Steffen had TD runs of 75 and 100 yards during the 1908 season.

He coached at Carnegie Tech, 1914–32, inventing the spinner play in 1924.

National Football Foundation Hall of Fame.

STEIN, EDWARD F. baseball: b. Sept. 5, 1869, Detroit; d. May 10, 1928. Pitcher. Chicago NL, 1890–91; Brooklyn NL, 1892–96, 1898. Eight years, 110–78, 3.96 ERA; 12 shutouts; 27–16 in 1892, 27–14 in 1894.

STEIN, RUSSELL F. football: b. April 21, 1896, Warren, Ohio; d. June 1, 1970. Washington and Jefferson tackle; All-American, 1921. Toledo Maroons, 1922; Frankford Yellowjackets, 1924; Pottsville Maroons, 1925; Canton Bulldogs, 1926.

STEINBACK, LAURENCE J. football: b. Dec. 23, 1900, New Rockford, N.D.; d. June 29, 1967. St. Thomas (Minn.) tackle. Chicago Bears, 1930–31; Chicago Cardinals, 1931–33; Philadelphia Eagles, 1933.

STEINFELDT, HARRY M. baseball: b. Sept. 27, 1876, St. Louis; d. Aug. 17, 1914. Bat, throw R; third base. Cincinnati NL, 1898–1905; Chicago NL, 1906–10; Boston NL, 1911. Fourteen years, 1,645 games, .267 BA; hit .312 in 1903, .327 in 1906. Led NL in hits (176) and RBI (83) in 1906; in doubles, 1903 (32). Four World Series, 1906–08, 1910: 21 games, .260 BA. He hit .471 during the Cubs' 4-game sweep of Detroit in 1907.

STEINMETZ, CHRISTIAN W. basketball: b. June 28, 1882, Milwaukee; d. June 11, 1963. The first collegiate player to score more than 1,000 career points, Steinmetz played at Wisconsin, 1903–05. He captained the team in his senior year and scored 462 points, including 50 in one game—twice as much as the average team scored in a game in those days of ball control. Basketball Hall of Fame.

STENZEL, JACOB C. baseball: b. Stelzle, June 24, 1867, Cincinnati; d. Jan. 6, 1919. Bat, throw R; outfield. Chicago NL, 1890; Pittsburgh NL, 1892–96; Baltimore NL, 1897–98; St. Louis NL, 1898–99; Cincinnati NL, 1899. Nine years, 766 games, 292 stolen bases, .339 BA; hit .354 in 1894, .374 in 1895, .361 in 1896, .353 in 1897. Led NL in doubles, 1897 (43).
   Stenzel tied an ML record with 2 home runs in an inning, June 6, 1894. He went 6-for-6 on May 14, 1896.

STEPHENS, "JUNIOR" (Vernon D.) baseball: b. Oct. 23, 1920, McAlister, N.M.; d. Nov. 3, 1968. Bat, throw R; shortstop, third base. St. Louis AL, 1941–47; Boston AL, 1948–52; Chicago AL, St. Louis AL, 1953; Baltimore AL, 1954–55; Chicago AL, 1955. Fifteen years, 1,720 games, 307 doubles, 247 home runs, 1,001 runs, 1,174 RBI, .286 BA; hit .307 in 1946, .300 in 1951. Led AL in home runs, 1945 (24); in RBI, 1944 (109), 1949 (159), and 1950 (144). One World Series, 1944: 6 games, .227 BA.

STEVENS, "HUB" (J. Hubert) bobsledding: b. 1890(?); d. Nov. 26, 1950. Stevens drove the two-man sled that won the North American championship in 1931 and 1933 and the AAU title in 1931, 1933 and 1935. He and his brother Curtis won the two-man event in the 1932 Winter Olympics. He also drove the four-man North American champion sled in 1933.

STEVENS, JOHN COX yachting: b. 1785, Hoboken, N.J.; d. June 10, 1857. At Stevens' suggestion, a group of men formed the New York Yacht Club in a meeting aboard his yacht in 1844, and he was chosen its first commodore. In that position, he received a letter in 1851 suggesting that the club bring a schooner to England for the Great Exhibition, the first modern world's fair. The club had already formed a five-man syndicate, headed by Stevens, to build "the fastest yacht afloat." She was named *America*.

America arrived in England on Aug. 1, 1851. Her owners hoped to regain some of their $20,000 investment by betting on match races, but she was too fast; no one accepted the challenge. Finally, *America* was entered in the Royal Yacht Squadron's Aug. 22 regatta round the Isle of Wight, for the Hundred-Guinea Cup.

It was a confused race. *America* got off to a poor start, quickly passed ten other yachts, but found herself behind four more, sailing so close together that she couldn't get by them. But the squadron had made an error in issuing instructions for the race. Most of the entrants had been told to go outside Nab Light, but *America*'s instructions didn't carry that stipulation. She sailed inside the light and finished 20 minutes ahead of the second-place boat. The unusual route brought some criticism from the British, and there was even a rumor that *America* was driven by a well-concealed propellor.

The Hundred-Guinea Cup, brought back to the New York Yacht Club, is now known as the America's Cup.

STEVENSON, MALCOLM polo: b. 1887(?); d. July 9, 1953. Stevenson was rated at 10 goals in 1925 and 1928. He played for the National Open champions, 1912–13 (Cooperstown), 1925 (Orange County), and 1928 (Meadow Brook). He was also a member of the U.S. teams that beat England in Westchester Cup play in 1924 and 1927 and of the team that beat Argentina in 1928.

STEVENSON, "STEVE" (Vincent M.) football: b. 1884, Livingston, Ky.; d. Aug. 7, 1962. Pennsylvania quarterback; All-American, 1904.
National Football Foundation Hall of Fame.

STEWART, WILLIAM baseball, hockey: b. Sept. 20, 1895, Fitchburg, Mass.; d. Feb. 18, 1964. At various times a minor-league manager, professional wrestler, and boxing referee, Stewart was a National League umpire, 1933–55.
He coached the Chicago Black Hawks to the Stanley Cup in 1938, his only season of coaching major-league hockey.

STILLMAN, LOUIS boxing: b. ?; d. Aug. 14, 1969. Stillman opened his famous New York gymnasium in 1921. For nearly four decades it was almost synonymous with boxing. Famous fighters trained at Stillman's, famous managers hung around looking for new talent, and hoodlums dropped in to listen for the latest inside information. Stillman sold the gym in 1959, complaining, "The racket is dead. All these fighters today are a bunch of sissies."

STIRNWEISS, "SNUFFY" (George H.) baseball: b. Oct. 26, 1918, New York City; d. Sept. 15, 1958. Bat, throw R; second-third base, shortstop. New York AL, 1943–50; Cleveland AL, 1950–52. Ten years, 1,028 games, .268 BA; hit .319 in 1944. Led AL in runs (125), hits (205), triples (16), and stolen bases (55) in 1944; in hitting (.309), runs (107), hits (195), triples (22), and stolen bases (33) in 1945. Three World Series, 1943, 1947, 1949: 9 games, .250 BA.

STIVETTS, "JACK" (John E.) baseball: b. March 31, 1868, Ashland, Pa.; d. April 18, 1930. Bat, throw R; pitcher, outfield. St. Louis AA, 1889–91; Boston NL, 1892–98; Cleveland NL, 1899. Eleven years, 198–132, 3.74 ERA, 1,223 strikeouts in 2,886⅔ innings. He also played five other positions and had a lifetime BA of .297. No-hitters, Aug. 6, 1892, against Brooklyn NL (11–0) and Oct. 15, 1892, against Washington NL (6–0; 5 innings). Led AA in ERA, 1889 (2.25), and in strikeouts, 1891 (259).

STOEFEN, LESTER R. tennis: b. 1911(?); d. Feb. 8, 1970. Stoefen teamed with George M. Lott, Jr., to win the U.S. outdoor doubles in 1933–34, the indoor doubles in 1934. He also won the indoor singles in 1934.

STOKES, MAURICE basketball: b. June 17, 1933, Pittsburgh; d. April 6, 1970. When Stokes, a graduate of little St. Francis College, Pennsylvania, became a member of the Cincinnati Royals in 1955, he was one of a new breed—a big but quick center who could shoot from the outside, drive to the basket, grab rebounds, play defense, and pass off. Some called him the greatest all-around player of the time, but Stokes unfortunately didn't get a chance to prove it. During his third season in the NBA, he suddenly lost consciousness while aboard the team plane. He was in a coma for months, and when he finally regained consciousness, he was almost totally paralyzed.

Stokes was named NBA Rookie of the Year in 1956. He had averaged 16.8 points a game and had set a league record with 1,356 rebounds (since broken). In his second year, he averaged 15.6 points and was 2nd team All-NBA. He was averaging 16.9 points when stricken with encephalitis, caused by brain damage suffered when he banged his head on the floor during a game.

A Royal teammate, Jack Twyman, became Stokes's legal guardian. He not only worked raising funds to pay for Stokes's treatment, which eventually cost more than $200,000, but also helped with his physical therapy and offered him badly needed encouragement and cheer. In turn, Twyman was impressed by Stokes's determination in his attempts to master simple tasks like brushing his teeth or pecking at an electric typewriter. "Maury really did a lot for me," Twyman said. "I'm so much a better person for having known him."

Stokes died of a heart attack.

STONE, GEORGE R. baseball: b. Sept. 3, 1876, Clinton, Iowa; d. Jan. 5, 1945. Bat, throw L; outfield. Boston AL, 1903; St. Louis AL, 1905–10. Seven years, 848 games, .301 BA; hit .320 in 1907. Led AL in hits, 1905 (187); in hitting (.358) and slugging (.501) in 1906.

STONE, JOHN T. ("Rocky") baseball: b. Oct. 10, 1905, Lynchburg, Tenn.; d. Nov. 11, 1955. Bat L, throw R; outfield. Detroit AL, 1928–33; Washington AL, 1934–38. Eleven years, 1,198 games, .310 BA; hit .313 in 1930, .327 in 1931, .315 in 1934, .315 in 1935, .341 in 1936, .330 in 1937.

STOVALL, GEORGE T. baseball: b. Nov. 23, 1878, Independence, Mo.; d. Nov. 5, 1951. Bat, throw R; first base. Cleveland AL, 1904–11; St. Louis AL, 1912–13; Kansas City Fed L, 1914–15. Twelve years, 1,412 games, .265 BA.

Stovall had 7 assists in a 9-inning game, Aug. 7, 1912, tying the ML record for first basemen.

Managed Cleveland AL, 1911 (part); St. Louis AL, 1912 (part), 1913 (part); Kansas City Fed L, 1914–15: 313–376, .454.

STOVEY, HARRY D. baseball: b. Dec. 20, 1856, Philadelphia; d. Sept. 20, 1937. Bat, throw R; outfield, first base. Worcester NL, 1880–82; Philadelphia AA, 1883–89; Boston PL, 1890; Boston NL, 1891–92; Baltimore NL, 1892–93; Brooklyn NL, 1893. Fourteen years, 1,486 games, .288 BA; hit .302 in 1883, .326 in 1884, .315 in 1885, .308 in 1889. Led league in triples (14) and home runs (6) in 1880; in runs (110), home runs (14), doubles (31), and slugging (.504) in 1883; in triples (23) and runs (124) in 1884; in home runs (13) and runs (130) in 1885; in home runs, 1886 (7); in triples, 1888 (20); in home runs (19), runs (152), RBI (119), and slugging (.525) in 1889; in stolen bases, 1890 (97); in triples, 1891 (20).

STRADER, "RED" (Norman) football: b. 1902(?), Newton, N.J.; d. May 26, 1956. St. Mary's (Calif.) fullback; 3rd team All-American, 1924. Chicago Bulls (AFL), 1926; Chicago Cardinals, 1927.

Strader coached St. Mary's, 1940–41. He guided the New York Yankees to a 21–17 record, 1948–50 (they were in the AAFC the first two years, the NFL in 1950). With the San Francisco 49ers in 1955, he was 4–8.

STRATTON, C. SCOTT baseball: b. Oct. 2, 1869, Campbellsburg, Ky.; d. March 8, 1939. Throw R; pitcher. Louisville AA, 1888–91; Pittsburgh NL, 1891; Louisville NL, 1892–94; Chicago NL, 1894–95. Eight years, 97–115, 3.88 ERA; 21–19 in 1892. Led AA in percentage (34–14, .708) and ERA (2.36) in 1890.

STREET, "GABBY" (Charles E.) baseball: b. Sept 30, 1882, Huntsville, Ala.; d. Feb. 6, 1951. Bat, throw R; catcher. Cincinnati NL, 1904–05; Boston NL, 1905; Washington AL, 1908–11; New York AL, 1912; St. Louis NL, 1931. Eight years, 503 games, .208 BA.

In 1909 Street set an AL record for catchers in a 154-game season by accepting 924 chances.

He managed St. Louis NL, 1929 (part)–33 (part); St. Louis AL, 1938: 368–339, .521. Pennants, 1930–31; World Series, 1931.

STULDREHER, HARRY A. football: b. Oct. 14, 1901, Massillon, Ohio; d. Jan. 22, 1965. Notre Dame quarterback, 1922–24; All-American, 1924. Brooklyn Lions, Brooklyn Horsemen (AFL), 1926.

One of the famed "Four Horsemen," Stuldreher coached Villanova, 1925–36, and Wisconsin, 1937–47, with an overall record of 110–87–15.

Helms Hall of Fame, National Football Foundation Hall of Fame.

SUGGS, GEORGE F. baseball: b. July 7, 1883, Kinston, N.C.: d. April 4, 1949. Bat, throw R; pitcher. Detroit AL, 1908–09; Cincinnati NL, 1910–13; Baltimore Fed L, 1914–15. Eight years, 100–88, 3.11 ERA; 16 shutouts. In relief, 14–10, 3.18 ERA, 14 saves; 25–12 in 1914.

SULLIVAN, BARTHOLOMEW J. track: b. Feb. 12, 1879, Boston; d. Feb. 24, 1968. A versatile runner, Sullivan won the 220- and 440-yard dashes and the 5-mile run in the 1906 Scottish Games, competing against New England's top trackmen, and was 2nd in the 100-yard dash. After a year each at Colby College and Boston College, he went to Holy Cross in 1912 as athletic trainer and track coach. He spent fifty-two years there, retiring in 1964.

In 1962, the IC4A dropped its traditional salute to twenty-five-year track coaches to honor Sullivan on his fiftieth anniversary. During tenure at Holy Cross, he produced a number of Olympic competitors and several world record holders.

Helms Hall of Fame.

SULLIVAN, "BILLY" (William J., Sr.) baseball: b. Feb. 1, 1875, Oakland, Wis.; d. Jan. 28, 1965. Bat, throw R; catcher. Boston NL, 1899–1900; Chicago AL, 1901–12, 1914; Detroit AL, 1916. Sixteen years, 1,146 games, .212 BA. One World Series, 1906: 6 games, .000 BA.

Sullivan is credited with inventing the modern style of catching by getting very close to the plate and the hitter. Naturally, he also invented the chest protector.

Managed Chicago AL, 1909: 78–74, .513.

SULLIVAN, JAMES E. track, amateur sports: b. Nov. 18, 1860, New York City; d. Sept. 16, 1914. Each year since 1930 the AAU has presented the James E. Sullivan Memorial Trophy to the outstanding amateur athlete of the year. Sullivan was a kind of benevolent despot of amateur sports for more than a quarter-century. He was one of the founders of the AAU in 1888; he was its secretary, 1889–96, its president, 1906–09. As secretary-treasurer, 1909–14, he virtually ruled many amateur sports. Under his guidance, the AAU gained control of a number of sports.

He was editor of the *Spalding Sports Library* for many years.

Helms Hall of Fame.

SULLIVAN, JOHN L. boxing: b. Oct. 15, 1858, Boston; d. Feb. 2, 1918. His record: 30 wins, 16 by KO; 1 loss, by KO; 3 draws, 1 no-decision. After dropping out of college, "the Boston Strong Boy" just drifted into boxing, as he put it later. In 1880, he challenged Paddy Ryan, the heavyweight champion, through a newspaper ad. Ryan didn't accept until 1882. They fought on Feb. 7, 1882, in Mississippi City, Mississippi, for $5,000 and the London Prize Ring championship of the world. Sullivan KOed Ryan in the 8th round. He quickly became world-famous, touring the United States, England, and Ireland, taking on all comers. In the last bare-knuckle fight of any importance, Sullivan defended his title against Jake Kilrain, with a 75-round KO on July 8, 1889.

In the first heavyweight championship fight under Marquis of Queensbury rules, Sullivan was KOed in 21 rounds by James J. Corbett on Sept. 7, 1892. It was his only defeat.

Sullivan had become a heavy drinker during his tempestuous career, but after retiring from the ring, he became a teetotaler and a temperance lecturer.

Helms Hall of Fame, Boxing Hall of Fame.

SULLIVAN, MIKE "TWIN" boxing: b. Sept. 23, 1878, Cambridge, Mass.; d. 1937. His record: 35 wins, 18 by KO; 7 losses, 4 by KO; 14 draws, 13 no-decisions. Sullivan won the welterweight title, April 23, 1907, with a 20-round decision over Honey Mellody. Late in 1908 he suffered an eye

injury and gave up the title, though he returned to the ring later for five more years.

SUMMA, HOMER W. baseball: b. Nov. 3, 1898, Gentry, Mo; d. Jan. 29, 1966. Bat L, throw R; outfield. Pittsburgh NL, 1920; Cleveland AL, 1922–28; Philadelphia AL, 1929–30. Ten years, 840 games, .302 BA; hit .328 in 1923, .330 in 1925, .308 in 1926. One World Series, 1929; 1 at-bat, no hits.

SUMMERS, "ED" (Oren Edgar) baseball: b. Dec. 5, 1884, Ladoga, Ind.; d. May 12, 1953. Sw. hit, throw R; pitcher. Detroit AL, 1908–12. Five years, 68–45, 2.42 ERA. Two World Series, 1908–09: 0–4, 5.32 ERA.

He set an AL record for most victories by a rookie with a 24–12 mark in 1908. On July 16, 1909, he tied an ML record for longest shutout, pitching all 18 innings of an 0–0 tie.

SUSOEFF, NICHOLAS football: b. April 15, 1921, Umapine, Ore.; d. Jan. 30, 1967. Washington State end. San Francisco 49ers (AAFC), 1946–49. In four years, he caught 61 passes for 610 yards and 4 TDs.

He graduated from college in 1942; his pro career was delayed by service in World War II.

SUTHERLAND, "JOCK" (John B.) football: b. March 21, 1889, Cooper Angus, Scotland; d. April 11, 1948. "The Dour Scot" came to the United States at eighteen, enrolled at Pittsburgh when he was twenty-five, and became a starting guard on one of Pop Warner's greatest teams. Pitt lost only one game during Sutherland's three seasons. He also won the IC4A hammer throw in 1918.

He coached Lafayette, 1919–23, compiling a 33–8–2 record, including wins over Pitt in 1921 and 1922.

He took over at Pittsburgh in 1924. His first team was his poorest, with a 5–3–1 mark; during the next fourteen years, no Pitt team ever lost two games in a row. His record was 111–20–12. Seven of his teams won Lambert Trophies as eastern champions and four of them went to the Rose Bowl, winning once, 21–0, over Washington in 1937. His 1929 team was 9–0–0 but lost to Southern California in the Rose Bowl; his 1937 team was 9–0–1.

Sutherland's collegiate coaching percentage of .812 is 8th on the all-time list.

He coached the Brooklyn Dodgers, 1940–41 (15–7) and the Pittsburgh Steelers, 1946–47 (13–9–1).

Helms Hall of Fame, National Football Foundation Hall of Fame.

SUTTON, EZRA B. baseball: b. Sept. 17, 1850, Seneca Falls, N.Y.; d. June 20, 1907. Bat, throw R; third base, shortstop. National Association, Cleveland Forest Citys, 1871–72; Philadelphia As, 1873–75. Five years, 231 games, .327 BA.

Philadelphia NL, 1876; Boston NL, 1877–88. Thirteen years, 1,031 games, .288 BA; hit .324 in 1883, .346 in 1884, .313 in 1885. Led NL in hits, 1884 (162).

Sutton scored 6 runs in a game, Aug. 27, 1887, tying an NL record.

SWEENEY, CHARLES J. baseball: b. April 13, 1863, San Francisco; d. April 4, 1902. Throw R; pitcher. Providence NL, 1882–84; St. Louis UA, 1884; St. Louis NL, 1885–86; Cleveland AA, 1887. Six years, 64–52, 2.87 ERA, 505 strikeouts in 1,030⅔ innings. Sweeney also played every other position but catcher, hitting .251 in 233 games. In 1884, he won 17 games for Providence, had an argument with his manager, and jumped to St. Louis, where he won 24 more for an overall record of 41–15, with an ERA of 1.70, 6 shutouts, and 337 strikeouts in 492 innings.

Sweeney holds the all-time record for strikeouts in a 9-inning game, 19, on June 7, 1884.

SWEENEY, WILLIAM J. baseball: b. March 6, 1886, Covington, Ky.; d. May 26, 1948. Bat, throw R; infield. Chicago NL, 1907; Boston NL, 1907–13; Chicago NL, 1914. Eight years, 1,039 games, .272 BA; hit .314 in 1911, .344 in 1912.

SWIFT, ROBERT V. baseball: b. March 6, 1915, Salina, Kan.; d. Oct. 17, 1966. Bat, throw R; catcher. St. Louis AL, 1940–42; Philadelphia AL, 1942–43; Detroit AL, 1944–53. Fourteen years, 1,001 games, .231 BA. One World Series, 1945: 3 games, .250 BA.

Managed Detroit, 1966 (part): 32–25, .561.

A heart attack forced him to quit managing.

T

TABOR, JAMES R. baseball: b. Nov. 5, 1913, Owens Crossroads, Ala.; d. Aug. 22, 1953. Bat, throw R; third base. Boston AL, 1938–44; Philadelphia NL, 1946–47. Nine years, 1,005 games, .270 BA. Tabor had a glorious Fourth of July in 1939: He hit a home run in the first game of a double-header and three more in the second game, including 2 grand slams. That tied the ML record for grand slams in a game and AL records for most home runs, 4, most total bases, 19, and most RBI, 11, in a doubleheader.

TANNEHILL, JESSE N. baseball: b. July 14, 1874, Dayton, Ohio; d. Sept. 22, 1956. Sw. hit, throw L; pitcher. Cincinnati NL, 1894; Pittsburgh NL, 1897–1902; New York AL, 1903; Boston AL, 1904–08; Washington AL, 1908–09; Cincinnati NL, 1911. Fifteen years, 194–118, 2.79 ERA; 34 shutouts; 25–13 in 1898, 24–14 in 1899, 20–6 in 1900, 20–6 in 1902, 21–11 in 1904, 21–9 in 1905. No-hitter, Aug. 17, 1904, against Chicago AL (6–0). Led AL in ERA, 1901 (2.18).

TATUM, "GOOSE" (Reece) basketball: b. 1919(?), Eldorado, Ark.; d. Jan. 18, 1967. After two seasons playing Negro League baseball, Tatum joined the Harlem Globetrotters in 1942 and was with the team until 1954, when he formed his own barnstorming group, the Harlem Roadkings, later the Magicians. Tatum was one of the Globetrotters' major attractions. A brilliant ball-handler, he averaged 25 points a game as well. Tatum was only 6'3" but had an incredible 84-inch arm-span and large hands that made it simple for him to palm the ball.

TATUM, JAMES M. football: b. July 22, 1913, McColl, S.C.; d. July 23, 1959. An All-South tackle at North Carolina (1935), Tatum began his head coaching career there in 1942. After Navy duty during World War II, he coached at Oklahoma, 1946, then went to Maryland. In nine seasons, 1947–55, his Terrapins never had a losing season. In 1953 they won the national title with a 10–0–0 record and Tatum was named Coach of the Year. His teams won the 1952 Sugar Bowl, 28–13, over Tennessee but lost the Orange Bowl to Oklahoma twice, in 1954 and 1956. His record at Maryland was 73–15–4. He coached at North Carolina, 1956–58.

Tatum's overall record was 100–35–7.

Helms Hall of Fame.

TAYLOR, "BUD" (Charles B.) boxing: b. July 22, 1903, Terre Haute, Ind.; d. March 8, 1962. His record: 70 wins, 35 by KO; 23 losses, 4 by KO; 6 draws, 60 no-decisions. Taylor won the NBA version of the bantamweight title on June 24, 1927, with a 10-round decision over Tony Canzoneri. He resigned in 1928 because he couldn't make the weight. In 1931 he retired to become a manager.

TAYLOR, "CHUCK" (Charles H.) basketball: b. June 24, 1901, Brown County, Ind.; d. June 22, 1969. "The Ambassador of Basketball" played professionally for eleven years, then became interested in designing a better shoe for the sport. Working for the Converse Rubber Co., he presented the first basketball clinic in 1922. It was the first of thousands he conducted all over the world. In 1922 he began editing the authoritative *Converse Yearbook of Basketball,* for which he chose All-American teams until his death. Basketball Hall of Fame, Helms Hall of Fame.

TAYLOR, C. I. baseball: b. 1872, North Carolina; d. March 2, 1922. Taylor owned and managed a Negro team, the Birmingham Giants, 1904–14; he moved the team to West Baden, Indiana, in 1914 and to Indianapolis the following year. With financial help from the American Brewing Co., he built it into a powerhouse. In 1916, the ABCs played the American Giants for the Negro title; each won 4 games and the 9th and deciding game ended in a protest, without decision.

Taylor played occasionally, usually as a pinch-hitter. He was one of the first managers in baseball history to hold clubhouse meetings before and after games to discuss strategy.

TAYLOR, "DUMMY" (Luther H.) baseball: b. Feb. 21, 1875, Oskaloosa, Kan.; d. Aug. 22, 1958. Bat, throw R; pitcher. New York NL, 1900–02; Cleveland AL, 1902; New York NL, 1903–08. Nine years, 113–109, 2.75 ERA; 21 shutouts; 22–15 in 1904. Led NL in losses, 1901 (17–27).

Because Taylor was a deaf mute, most of the New York Giants learned the hand alphabet, and John McGraw often used it to give his signs.

TAYLOR, "JACK" (John B.) baseball: b. May 27, 1873, Staten Island, N.Y.; d. Feb. 7, 1900. Bat, throw R; pitcher. New York NL, 1891; Philadelphia NL, 1892–97; St. Louis NL, 1898; Cincinnati NL, 1899. Nine years, 120–117, 4.23 ERA; 23–13 in 1894, 26–14 in 1895, 20–21 in 1896. Led NL in losses (15–29) and complete games (42) in 1898.

TAYLOR, "JACK" (John W.) baseball: b. Sept. 13, 1873, Straightville, Ohio; d. March 4, 1938. Bat, throw R; pitcher. Chicago NL, 1898–1903; St. Louis NL, 1904–06; Chicago NL, 1906–07. Ten years, 150–139, 2.67 ERA; 19 shutouts; 22–11 in 1902, 21–14 in 1903, 20–19 in 1904, 20–12 in 1906. Led NL in ERA, 1902 (1.33); in complete games, 1904 (39). His 39 consecutive complete games in 1904 is an ML record.

TAYLOR, WILLIAM H. sportswriting: b. May 31, 1901, New Bedford, Mass.; d. Jan. 6, 1966. Taylor became the first sportswriter to win the Pulitzer Prize when he was honored for his coverage of the 1934 America's Cup races. He was, at the time, yachting editor of the New York *Herald-Tribune,* a position he held, 1927–41. After World War II, he became associate editor of *Yachting* magazine; he was later managing editor. Taylor coauthored *Story of American Yachting* and *America's Cup Races.*

TEBEAU, "PATSY" (Oliver W.) baseball: b. Dec. 5, 1864, St. Louis; d. May 15, 1918. Bat, throw R; first-third base. Chicago NL, 1887; Cleveland NL, 1889; Cleveland PL, 1890; Cleveland NL, 1891–98; St. Louis NL, 1899–1900. Thirteen years, 1,167 games, .280 BA; hit .300 in 1890, .329 in 1893, .302 in 1894.

Managed Cleveland PL, 1890 (part); Cleveland NL, 1891 (part)–98; St. Louis NL, 1899–1900 (part): 732–575, .560.

TEMPLETON, "DINK" (Robert L.) track: b. 1897(?), Helena, Mont.; d. Aug. 7, 1962. Templeton was a track and football star at Stanford—he once dropkicked a field goal from 55 yards—and he coached track in his senior year, 1917. He returned to Stanford as track coach, 1922–41; his teams won 77 percent of their dual meets during that period. They were NCAA champions in 1925, 1928, and 1934. Templeton believed in continuous daily practice, a heresy at the time. Most coaches felt the method would "burn out" their athletes.

Helms Hall of Fame.

TEN EYCK, JAMES A. rowing: b. Oct. 16, 1851, Tompkins Cove, N.Y.; d. Feb. 11, 1938. At thirteen Ten Eyck won his first race and at sixteen he started a long string of victories against all challengers on the Hudson near Sing Sing, New York (now Ossining). In 1884 he was a member of a four-man crew that won the world championship in England. Ten Eyck began coaching boat-club crews in the eighties. In 1903 he went to Syracuse to set up that college's rowing program. The following year both his varsity and freshman crews won their events at the Intercollegiate Rowing Association regatta. His varsity crews also won at Poughkeepsie in 1908, 1913, 1916, and 1920. During the summer of 1910, he coached Ottawa Boat Club crews that won Canadian and American titles, and from 1918 to 1920—his only absence from Syracuse until his death—he coached the Duluth, Minnesota, Boat Club.

Helms Hall of Fame.

TEN EYCK, "NED" (Edward H.) rowing: b. Aug. 7, 1879, Peekskill, N.Y.; d. Sept. 9, 1956. Coached by his father, James A., Ten Eyck became the first American to win the Diamond Sculls at the Henley Regatta in 1897, when he was seventeen. He was never defeated. He won the Association Singles Sculls in 1898, the U.S. championship in 1899 and 1901, and the doubles championship, 1898–1901. After graduating from Pennsylvania, he coached crew at Wisconsin, Syracuse, and Rutgers. He returned to Syracuse in 1938 to succeed his father as coach.

Helms Hall of Fame.

TENNEY, FRED baseball: b. Nov. 26, 1871, Georgetown, Mass.; d. July 3, 1952. Bat, throw L; first base, catcher. Boston NL, 1894–1907; New York NL, 1908–09; Boston NL, 1911. Seventeen years, 1,994 games, 2,231 hits, 1,278 runs, 285 stolen bases, .294 BA; hit .318 in 1897, .328 in 1898, .347 in 1899, .315 in 1902, .313 in 1903. Led NL in runs, 1908(101).

Tenney invented the claw-type glove for first basemen. He holds NL records for first basemen of most career assists, 1,365; most assists in a season, 152, in 1905; and most years leading in assists, 8. He went 6-for-8 on May 31, 1897.

He managed Boston NL, 1905–07, 1911: 202–402, .334.

TERRY, "ADONIS" (William J.) baseball: b. Aug. 7, 1864, Westfield, Mass.; d. Feb. 24, 1915. Bat, throw R; pitcher, outfield. Brooklyn AA, 1884–89; Brooklyn NL, 1890–91; Baltimore NL, 1892; Pittsburgh NL, 1892–94; Chicago NL, 1894–97. Fourteen years, 197–195, 3.72 ERA; 20–35 in 1884, 22–15 in 1889, 26–16 in 1890, 21–14 in 1895. No-hitters, July 24, 1886, against St. Louis AA (1–0); May 27, 1888, against Louisville AA (4–0).

Terry frequently played the outfield when not pitching.

TESRAU, "JEFF" (Charles M.) baseball: b. March 5, 1889, Ironton, Mo.; d. Sept. 24, 1946. Bat, throw R; pitcher. New York NL, 1912–18. Seven years, 118–72, 2.43 ERA; 880 strikeouts, 27 shutouts, in 1,679 innings; 22–13 in 1913, 26–10 in 1914. No-hitter, Sept. 6, 1912, against Philadelphia NL (3–0). Led NL in ERA, 1912 (1.96); in shutouts, 1914 (8). Three World Series, 1912–13, 1917: 1–3, 3.62 ERA.

TEWKSBURY, J. W. B. track: b. March 21, 1876, Tunkhannock, Pa.; d. Aug. 23, 1967. Tewksbury was a double winner for the United States in the 1900 Olympics, in the 200-meter dash and 400-meter hurdles. He finished 2nd by inches in the 110-meter hurdles and was 3rd in the 200-meter hurdles. Representing the University of Pennsylvania, he won both the 100- and 220-yard dashes in IC4A competition in 1898–99.

THEVENOW, THOMAS J. baseball: b. Sept. 6, 1903, Madison, Ind.; d. July 29, 1957. Bat, throw R; shortstop, second-third base. St. Louis NL, 1924–28; Philadelphia NL, 1929–30; Pittsburgh NL, 1931–35; Cincinnati NL, 1936; Boston NL, 1937; Pittsburgh NL, 1938. Fifteen years, 1,229 games, .247 BA. Two World Series, 1926, 1928: 8 games, .417 BA.

THOMAS, FRANK W. football: b. Nov. 15, 1898, Muncie, Ind.; d. May 10, 1954. Thomas played quarterback at Notre Dame, 1921–22, while working for his law degree.

He coached Chattanooga, 1928–31, then went to Alabama, 1932–42 and

1944–46, taking teams to bowl games 6 times. His 1934 team was 10–0–0. In the Rose Bowl, Alabama beat Stanford 29–13 in 1935, lost to California 13–0 in 1938, and beat Southern Cal 34–14 in 1946. Thomas's teams won the 1942 Cotton Bowl, 29–21, over Texas A & M, beat Boston College 37–21 in the 1943 Orange Bowl, and lost the 1945 Sugar Bowl, 29–26, to Duke.

His overall percentage of .795 on a 141–33–9 record is 9th best in history. Helms Hall of Fame, National Football Foundation Hall of Fame.

THOMAS, ROY A. baseball: b. March 24, 1874, Norristown, Pa.; d. Nov. 20, 1959. Bat, throw L; outfield. Philadelphia NL, 1899–1908; Pittsburgh NL, 1908; Boston NL, 1909; Philadelphia NL, 1910–11. Thirteen years, 1,471 games, 1,011 runs, 1,042 walks, 244 stolen bases, .290 BA; hit .325 in 1899, .316 in 1900, .309 in 1901, .327 in 1903, .317 in 1905. Led NL in runs (132) and walks (115) in 1900; in walks, 1901 (100), 1902 (107), 1903 (107), 1904 (102), 1906 (107), and 1907 (83).

Thomas scored 137 runs in 1899, an NL record for rookies.

THOMPSON, "CHUCK" (Charles) motorboat racing: b. 1912(?), St. Clair, Mich.; d. July 3, 1966. Thompson won the President's Cup three straight years, 1950–52; he also won the Silver Cup in 1951 and was unlimited high-point winner in 1951–52. Thompson had won the first two heats of the Gold Cup in 1966 but was killed when his boat disintegrated shortly after the start of the third heat.

THOMPSON, "CYCLONE" (John) boxing: b. June 20, 1876, Ogle County, Ill.; d. May 28, 1951. His record: 84 wins, 47 by KO; 24 losses, 1 by KO; 20 draws, 11 no-decisions. After nearly twenty years in boxing, Thompson won the middleweight title with a 20-round decision on Feb. 11, 1911, over Billy Papke. However, by October he had outgrown the class and he resigned.

THOMPSON, "HANK" (Henry C.) baseball: b. Dec. 8, 1925, Oklahoma City, Okla.; d. Sept. 20, 1969. Bat L, throw R; third base, outfield. Nine years, 933 games, .267 BA; hit .302 in 1953. St. Louis AL, 1947; New York NL, 1949–56. Two World Series, 1951, 1954: 9 games, .240 BA. Thompson set a record by walking 7 times in the 4 games of the 1954 Series.

THOMPSON, L. FRESCO baseball: b. June 6, 1902, Centreville, Ala.; d. Nov. 20, 1968. Bat, throw R; second base. Pittsburgh NL, 1925; New York NL, 1926; Philadelphia NL, 1927–30; Brooklyn NL, 1931–32; New York NL, 1934. Nine years, 669 games, .298 BA; hit .303 in 1927, .324 in 1929. After scouting for the Dodgers, 1947–48, Thompson moved into the team's front office as farm director, 1949–68. He became executive vice-president and general manager in June of 1968.

THOMPSON, SAMUEL L. baseball: b. March 5, 1860, Danville, Ind.; d. Nov. 7, 1922. Bat L; outfield. Detroit NL, 1885–88; Philadelphia NL, 1889–98; Detroit AL, 1906. Fifteen years, 1,407 games, 1,256 runs, 1,300 RBI, .331 BA; hit .310 in 1886, .313 in 1890, .305 in 1892, .370 in 1893, .407 in 1894, .392 in 1895. He went 6-for-7, with a double, a triple, a home run, and 4 runs scored, on Aug. 17, 1894. Led NL in hits (203), BA (.372), and triples (23) in 1887; in home runs, 1889 (20); in hits (172) and doubles (41) in 1890; in hits (222) and doubles (37) in 1893; in triples (18), RBI (165), and slugging (.654) in 1895.

THOMPSON, "YOUNG JACK" (Cecil L.) boxing: b. 1904, San Francisco; d. April 19, 1946. His record: 46 wins, 31 by KO; 16 losses, none by KO; 3 draws, 1 no-decision. Thompson won the welterweight title from Jackie Fields with a 15-round decision on May 9, 1930. He lost it in 15 to Tommy Freeman on Sept. 5, 1930, won it back with a 12th-round KO on April 14, 1931, then lost the crown for good to Lou Brouillard on a 15-round decision, Oct. 23, 1931.

THORNHILL, "TINY" (Claude E.) football: b. April 14, 1893, Richmond, Va.; d. June 29, 1956. Pittsburgh tackle. Massillon Tigers, 1919; Buffalo All-Americans, Cleveland Panthers, 1920.

Coaching at Stanford, 1933–39, Thornhill took teams to three consecutive Rose Bowls; they lost to Columbia, 7–0, in 1934 and to Alabama, 21–13, in 1935, then beat SMU, 7–0, in 1936.

THORPE, JAMES F. football, track, baseball: b. May 28, 1888, Prague, Okla.; d. March 28, 1953. "Sir, you are the greatest athlete in the world," the King of Sweden told Jim Thorpe in 1912, presenting him with Olympic Gold Medals for record-breaking victories in both the decathlon and penthathlon. Thirty-eight years later, Thorpe was voted the greatest athlete of the first half of the twentieth century. And in 1969 he was named to the all-time all-pro team, on the fiftieth birthday of the NFL.

In 1913 Thorpe had to return his Olympic medals and other trophies; the AAU had learned that Thorpe had played pro baseball while attending college—not unusual in those days—and therefore couldn't be considered a true amateur.

Despite his Olympic triumphs and his six years in major-league baseball, Thorpe is remembered chiefly as a football player who could do everything well. Of mixed ancestry—Irish, French, and Sac and Fox Indian—he starred in football at Carlisle Indian School in 1908 and 1911–12 and was named an All-American halfback in his last two years. Thorpe combined size, strength, and speed with a competitive savagery, when he was aroused, that could frighten opponents. He could run, pass, punt, dropkick, block, tackle, and catch passes or defend against them.

He played pro football as early as 1915, with Canton. When the National Football League was organized in 1919, Thorpe was player-coach for Canton. His field goal gave his team a 3–0 victory over Massillon and the first league championship. In 1920, he served as president of the league, largely because of the publicity value of his name. He played for the Cleveland Indians in 1921 and then organized his own team, the Oorang Indians, with many former Carlisle players. In two seasons, that team won only 3 of 19 games. Thorpe played with Toledo at the end of the 1923 season, went to Rock Island in 1924, and to the New York Giants in 1925. He made a brief comeback with the Chicago Cardinals in 1929, when he was forty-one.

His major-league record: bat, throw R; outfield. New York NL, 1913–15; Cincinnati NL, 1917; New York NL, 1917–19; Boston NL, 1919. Six years, 289 games, .252 BA.

Like many other professional athletes of his time, Thorpe wasn't equipped to succeed after retiring from sports. He began drinking heavily and virtually disappeared for a time. With his wife, he organized a touring show of Indian dances, which he narrated, but he developed cancer of the lip and was forbidden to talk for some time, which ended that project. He died of a heart attack in his house trailer near Lomita, California.

Helms Hall of Fame, National Football Foundation Hall of Fame, Professional Football Hall of Fame.

TIERNAN, MICHAEL J. baseball: b. Jan. 21, 1867, Trenton, N.J.; d. Nov. 9, 1918. Bat, throw L; outfield. New York NL, 1887–99. Thirteen years, 1,476 games, .311 BA; hit .335 in 1889, .304 in 1890, .306 in 1891, .309 in 1893, .347 in 1895, .369 in 1896, .330 in 1897. Led NL in runs, 1889 (147); in slugging, 1890 (.495); in home runs (17) and slugging (.500) in 1891.

Tiernan tied an NL record by scoring 6 runs in a game on June 15, 1887.

TILDEN, "BIG BILL" (William T., II) tennis: b. Feb. 10, 1893, Germantown, Pa.; d. June 5, 1953. Early in his career, he was known as One Round Tilden because, despite his great potential, he often played sloppily against inferior opponents and was defeated in the first round of many major tournaments. He teamed with Mary K. Browne to win the national outdoor mixed doubles in 1913 and 1914 but didn't come into his own as a singles player until 1920, when he was twenty-seven.

But that was a great year: He became the first American to win the Wimbledon singles, led the U.S. Davis Cup team to victory over Australia, and came home to win the U.S. singles title, the first of six in a row. He finally lost it in 1926 to René LaCoste, of France, but won it for a seventh time in 1929, when he was thirty-six. He won the Wimbledon singles again in 1921 and 1930, the doubles (with Francis T. Hunter) in 1927. He also won the U.S. clay-court title, 1922–27, the indoor singles in 1920, the world hard-court title at Paris in 1921, the U.S. outdoor doubles in 1918, 1921–23, and 1927, the indoor doubles in 1919–20, 1926, and 1929, and the outdoor mixed doubles in 1922–23.

In Davis Cup play, he won 17 matches and lost 5 in eleven years of competition, sparking seven straight U.S. victories, 1920–26.

Having lost his fortune in the stock-market crash, Tilden turned professional in 1931. He made his debut on Feb. 18 against Karel Kozeluh, the Czech champion, before a crowd of 13,600. Tilden won the pro singles title that year and again in 1935, when he was forty-two. He teamed with Bruce Barnes to win the pro doubles title in 1932, and he and Vincent Richards won it in 1945. Though he turned professional at an age when most tennis players are thinking of retiring, his overall record was 340 matches won, 147 lost.

Though famed for his cannonball service, Tilden's strength was an outstanding all-around game; he had no real flaw, except a tendency to play lackadaisically in the early stages of a match. Many critics thought he did it deliberately, to build up the drama, before rallying to win.

Tilden acted on Broadway stages several times, once in a play of his own; he wrote several technical books about tennis, a number of short stories, and a novel and was at one time owner and editor of *Racquet*, a tennis magazine.

Helms Hall of Fame, Tennis Hall of Fame.

TINKER, JOSEPH B. baseball: b. July 27, 1880, Muscotah, Kan.; d. July 27, 1948. Bat, throw R; shortstop. Chicago NL, 1902–12; Cincinnati NL, 1913; Chicago Fed L, 1914–15; Chicago NL, 1916. Fifteen years, 1,802 games, 336 stolen bases, .262 BA; hit .317 in 1913. Four World Series, 1906–08, 1910: 21 games, .235 BA; 12 runs, 6 stolen bases (6th).

Tinker was a scrappy ballplayer who had to be appreciated for his intangibles. He was a fine base-runner—on June 28, 1910, he tied an ML record by stealing home twice; a good fielder—he tied the NL record for most years leading shortstops in fielding; and a good clutch hitter. He was known for hitting Christy Mathewson better than anyone else could. In the pennant playoff game against the Giants in 1908, Tinker hit a triple off Mathewson to start the Cubs' winning rally.

He managed Cincinnati NL, 1913; Chicago Fed L, 1914–15; Chicago NL, 1916: 304–308, .497.

Baseball Hall of Fame.

TITUS, JOHN F. baseball: b. Feb. 21, 1876, St. Clair, Pa.; d. Jan. 8, 1943. Bat, throw L; outfield. Philadelphia NL, 1903–12; Boston NL, 1912–13. Eleven years, 1,401 games, .282 BA; hit .308 in 1905, .309 in 1912.

TOBIN, JAMES A. baseball: b. Dec. 27, 1912, Oakland, Calif.; d. May 19, 1969. Bat, throw R; pitcher. Pittsburgh NL, 1937–39; Boston NL, 1940–45; Detroit AL, 1945. Nine years, 105–112, 3.44 ERA; 12 shutouts. In relief, 10–11, 3.32 ERA, 5 saves. No-hitter, April 27, 1944, against Brooklyn NL (2–0). Led NL in losses (12–21) and complete games (28) in 1942; in complete games (28) in 1944. One World Series, 1945: 6.00 ERA in 3 innings of relief.

Tobin set a modern ML record for pitchers by hitting 3 home runs on May 13, 1942.

TOBIN, JOHN T. baseball: b. May 4, 1892, St. Louis; d. Dec. 10, 1969. Bat, throw L; outfield. St. Louis Fed L, 1914–15; St. Louis AL, 1916, 1918–25; Washington AL, 1926; Boston AL, 1926–27. Thirteen years, 1,618 games, .308 BA; hit .327 in 1919, .341 in 1920, .352 in 1921, .331 in 1922, .317 in 1923, .310 in 1927. Led league in hits, 1915 (184). Tobin was a great drag bunter and a fine place hitter.

TOKLE, TORGER skiing: b. Norway; d. March 19, 1945. In his brief jumping career, Tokle won 42 of the 48 tournaments he entered and set 24 hill records. In 1941 he set an American record of 273 feet at Leavenworth, Washington; he raised it to 288 feet the same year at Hyak, Washington, and to 289 feet at Iron Mountain, Michigan, in 1942. He was U.S. Class A Jump champion in 1941.

Tokle was killed while serving with the U.S. Army Ski Patrol in the Italian mountains.

Skiing Hall of Fame.

TOLAN, EDWARD track: b. 1909(?); d. Jan. 30, 1967. Only 5′4″, Tolan was known as the Midnight Express because of his speed and his color. His 10.3 clocking in the Olympic 100-meter dash in 1932 was a world record until 1935 and an Olympic record until Armin Hary broke it in 1960. He also won the 200-meter dash in the 1932 Games.

Representing Michigan, he was NCAA champion in the 220 in 1931 and won the IC4A title the same year; he was AAU outdoor champion in the 100 in 1929–30 and in the 220 in 1929 and 1931. His 9.5 in the 100 yards in 1929 was briefly a world record.

Helms Hall of Fame.

TONEY, FREDERICK A. baseball: b. Dec. 11, 1887, Nashville, Tenn.; d. March 11, 1953. Bat, throw R; pitcher. Chicago NL, 1911–13; Cincinnati

NL, 1915–18; New York NL, 1918–22; St. Louis NL, 1923. Twelve years, 137–102, 2.69 ERA; 28 shutouts; 24–16 in 1917, 21–11 in 1920. One World Series, 1921: 0–0, 23.63 ERA in 2⅔ innings.

Toney was the winning pitcher in the only double no-hitter in history, May 2, 1917. He and Hippo Vaughn, of Chicago, both pitched no-hitters for 9 innings; Toney continued to stop the Cubs without a hit in the tenth, while Cincinnati got 2 hits and 1 run off Vaughn for the victory.

TOPPERWEIN, "PLINKY" (Mrs. Ad) shooting: b. Elizabeth Servanty; d. Jan. 15, 1945. Even Annie Oakley thought Mrs. Topperwein was the greatest female shooter of all time. She was the first woman to break 100 straight traps, in 1904, and she went on to do it more than 200 times; she broke 200 straight 14 times. In an endurance contest in 1916, she broke 1,952 of 2,000 targets in 5 hours, 20 minutes, without a moment's rest. The heat of the gun blistered her hand, but she still broke 98 of the last 100.

American Trapshooting Hall of Fame.

TORRANCE, JACK track, football: b. 1913(?); d. Nov. 10, 1970. LSU tackle. Chicago Bears, 1939–40. In 1934 Torrance broke the world shotput record 3 times, raising the mark from 54′ 1″, to 57′ 1″, a record that stood until 1948. He was AAU outdoor champion, 1933–35, indoor champion, 1935, and NCAA champion, 1933–34. He was a member of LSU's "Fabulous Five" track team, a group of five athletes who won the NCAA team title in 1933, against many schools that had twenty or twenty-five entrants.

Helms Hall of Fame.

TORRENCE, WALTER basketball: b. 1937(?); d. Sept. 21, 1969. UCLA captain, All-American, 1959. He was one of the top ten scorers in the school's history.

He died in a car crash.

TOWER, OSWALD basketball: b. Nov. 23, 1883, North Adams, Mass.; d. May 28, 1968. Little known outside basketball circles, Tower was the sport's official rules interpreter for forty-four years, 1915–59, as editor of the influential *Basketball Guide*. A 1907 graduate of Williams College, he was a member of the Rules Committee, 1910–59, and officiated games for more than thirty-five years.

Basketball Hall of Fame.

TRAUTMAN, GEORGE M. baseball: b. Jan. 11, 1890, Bucyrus, Ohio; d. June 24, 1963. Trautman played baseball and football at Ohio State, then coached basketball and baseball there, 1916–29. He was president of the American Association, 1936–45, briefly worked in the front office of the

Detroit Tigers, and in 1947 became president of the National Association of Professional Baseball Leagues, comprising all minor leagues. He held that job until his death.

TRAVERS, JEROME D. golf: b. May 19, 1887, New York City; d. March 29, 1951. Travers and Bobby Jones are the only golfers to win 4 U.S. Amateur titles; Travers won his in 1907–08, 1912–13; in 1914 he lost to Francis Ouimet in the finals. He is one of 5 amateurs to win the U.S. Open. Known as a great match player who never had much success in stroke play, he surprised observers with his victory in the 1915 Open.
Helms Hall of Fame, Professional Golfers Hall of Fame.

TRAVIS, WALTER J. golf: b. Jan. 10, 1862, Victoria, Australia; d. July 31, 1927. Travis didn't begin to play golf until he was nearly thirty-five, yet he won three U.S. Amateur titles, 1900–01 and 1903, and was the first American to win the British Amateur, in 1904. He also won the North and South Amateur, 1904, 1910, and 1912. The "Schenectady putter," of his own design, helped make him an expert on the greens. The British banned it after his 1904 victory; Travis's temperament, taciturn to the point of being surly, was probably a contributing factor.
Helms Hall of Fame, Professional Golfers Hall of Fame.

TRESTER, ARTHUR L. basketball: b. June 10, 1878, Pecksburg, Ind.; d. Sept. 18, 1944. A high-school teacher, coach, and principal, Trester became secretary of the Indiana High School Athletic Association in 1913 and became commissioner in 1922, holding that position until his death. Under his leadership, the association became a model for similar state groups all over the United States, and the famous Indiana high-school basketball tournament similarly set an example for many other states to follow.
Basketball Hall of Fame.

TUCKER, THOMAS J. baseball: b. Oct. 28, 1863, Holyoke, Mass.; d. Oct. 22, 1935. Sw. hit, throw R; first base. Baltimore AA, 1887–89; Boston NL, 1890–97; Washington NL, 1897; Brooklyn NL, St. Louis NL, 1898; Cleveland NL, 1899. Thirteen years, 1,687 games, .290 BA; hit .330 in 1894, .304 in 1896. Led AA in hits (196) and BA (.372) in 1889. He went 6-for-6 on July 15, 1897.

TURNER, "TERRY" (Terrence L.) baseball: b. Feb. 28, 1881, Sandy Lake, Pa.; d. July 18, 1960. Bat, throw R; shortstop, third-second base. Pittsburgh NL, 1901; Cleveland AL, 1904–18; Philadelphia AL, 1919. Seventeen years, 1,685 games, 256 stolen bases, .253 BA; hit .308 in 1912. Turner holds the AL record for most assists by a shortstop in a season, 570, in 1906.

TURPIE, MARION (Mrs. Lake, Mrs. McNaughton) golf: b. ?; d. Feb. 27, 1967. She won the Women's Southern Amateur in 1926, 1928, and 1931, the Eastern Amateur in 1941.

TYLER, "LEFTY" (George A.) baseball: b. Dec. 14, 1889, Derry, N.H.; d. Sept. 29, 1953. Bat, throw L; pitcher. Boston NL, 1910–17; Chicago NL, 1918–21. Twelve years, 125–119, 2.95 ERA; 1,003 strikeouts, 31 shutouts in 2,230 innings. Led NL in losses, 1912 (11–22); in complete games, 1913 (28); in shutouts, 1918 (8). Two World Series, 1914, 1918: 1–1, 1.91 ERA.

U

UNSER, JERRY H. auto racing: b. Nov. 15, 1932, Colorado Springs, Colo.; d. May 17, 1959. One of three brothers in racing, Unser was national stock-car champion in 1957. He died during a practice run at the Indianapolis Speedway.

UPSON, RALPH HAZLETT balloon racing: b. June 21, 1888, New York City; d. Aug. 13, 1968. Early in the century, balloon and air races were popular sporting events. Upson, basically a designer and engineer, won the International Balloon Race in 1913, the U.S. races in 1913, 1919, and 1921. Later he concentrated on heavier-than-air craft, and he designed a pioneer streamlined train for Union Pacific in 1933.

V

VANCE, "DAZZY" (Clarence Arthur) baseball: b. March 4, 1891, Orient, Iowa; d. Feb. 16, 1961. Bat, throw R; pitcher. Pittsburgh NL, 1915; New York AL, 1915, 1918; Brooklyn NL, 1922–32; St. Louis NL, 1933–34; Cincinnati NL, 1934; Brooklyn NL, 1935. Sixteen years, 197–140, 3.24 ERA; 2,045 strikeouts, 30 shutouts in 2,967 innings; 22–10 in 1925. No-hitter, Sept. 13, 1925, against Philadelphia NL (10–1). Led NL in strikeouts (134) and shutouts (5) in 1922; in strikeouts, 1923 (197); in victories (28–6), ERA (2.16), complete games (30), and strikeouts (262) in 1924; in victories (22–9), strikeouts (221), and shutouts (4) in 1925; in strikeouts, 1926 (140); in complete games (25) and strikeouts (184) in 1927; in ERA (2.09), strikeouts (200), and shutouts (4) in 1928; in ERA (2.61) and shutouts (4) in 1930. One World Series, 1934: 0–0, 0.00 ERA in 1⅓ innings of relief.

Though he was thirty-one when he pitched his first full season in the majors (1922), he set an NL record by leading in strikeouts 7 consecutive seasons, and on Sept. 14, 1924, he became one of eleven pitchers to strike out three men in an inning with only 9 pitches.

Baseball Hall of Fame.

VANDERBILT, HAROLD S. yachting: b. July 6, 1884, Oakdale, N.Y.; d. July 4, 1970. The youngest child of William K. Vanderbilt, he was skippering his own fourteen-foot sloop when he was twelve. In 1910, he won the Bermuda race in his schooner, *Vagrant*. He won the major trophies in American yachting a total of 14 times: the Astor Cup for sloops, 1927 and 1934–37, for schooners, 1921–22 and 1925, and the King's Cup, 1922, 1925, 1934–35, 1937–38.

He was one of two men to skipper three America's Cup defenders: the *Enterprise* in 1930, the *Rainbow* in 1934, and the *Ranger* in 1937. He belonged to syndicates that built the first two; he paid all expenses of building the *Ranger*. He was also a member of the syndicate that built *Intrepid,* the 1967 defender.

His major revision of yachting rules was adopted throughout the world after World War II. Vanderbilt also, in effect, invented contract bridge in 1925 when he developed a set of revisions in the rules for auction bridge to give a player credit only for the tricks that he had contracted to win.

VANDERBILT, WILLIAM K. yachting, horse racing, and auto racing: b. Dec. 12, 1849, Staten Island, N.Y.; d. July 22, 1920. The heir to a fortune built on boating and railroads, Vanderbilt enjoyed sports that involved means of travel. He owned and raced yachts and several times belonged to syndicates that built America's Cup defenders. He also owned a racing stable in France, where his horses won several Grand Prix. But he was probably most important to American sports as the sponsor of the first major auto races held here. The Vanderbilt Cup was put up as the trophy for a 1904 race on Long Island, the first of five. There were so many accidents and deaths in the races that Vanderbilt withdrew the cup after 1908. Nevertheless, enthusiasm for the new sport had been developed, and auto racing remained popular.

VAN HALTREN, GEORGE E. M. baseball: b. March 30, 1866, St. Louis; d. Sept. 2, 1945. Bat, throw L; outfield, pitcher. Chicago NL, 1887–89; Brooklyn PL, 1890; Baltimore AA, 1891; Baltimore NL, 1892; Pittsburgh NL, 1892–93; New York NL, 1894–1903. Seventeen years, 1,984 games, 2,532 hits, 285 doubles, 1,639 runs, 1,014 RBI, 583 stolen bases, .316 BA; hit .309 in 1889, .355 in 1890, .318 in 1891, .338 in 1893, .331 in 1894, .340 in 1895, .351 in 1896, .330 in 1897, .312 in 1898, .301 in 1899, .315 in 1900, .335 in 1901. As pitcher, 40–31, 4.05 ERA. Led NL in triples, 1896 (21); in stolen bases, 1900 (45).

VAUGHAN, "ARKY" (Joseph Floyd) baseball: b. March 9, 1912, Clifty, Ark.; d. Aug. 30, 1952. Bat L, throw R; shortstop, third base. Pittsburgh NL, 1932–41; Brooklyn NL, 1942–43, 1947–48. Fourteen years, 1,817 games, 2,103 hits, 356 doubles, 128 triples, 1,173 runs, 118 stolen bases, .318 BA; hit .318 in 1932, .314 in 1933, .333 in 1934, .335 in 1935, .322 in 1937, .322 in 1938, .306 in 1939, .300 in 1940, .316 in 1941, .305 in 1943. Led NL in triples, 1933 (19); in walks, 1934 (94); in BA (.385), slugging (.607), and walks (97) in 1935; in walks (118) and runs (122) in 1936; in triples, 1937 (17); in triples (15) and runs (113) in 1940; in runs (112) and stolen bases (20) in 1943.

Vaughan's .385 BA in 1935 is a modern NL record for shortstops. He tied NL records for most consecutive years leading in walks, 3, and most years leading shortstops in games played, 6.

VAUGHN, "HIPPO" (James L.) baseball: b. April 9, 1888, Weatherford, Tex.; d. May 29, 1966. Sw. hit, throw L; pitcher. New York AL, 1908, 1910–12; Washington AL, 1912; Chicago NL, 1913–21. Thirteen years, 176–137, 2.49 ERA; 1,416 strikeouts, 40 shutouts in 2,730 innings; 21–13 in 1914, 23–13 in 1917, 21–14 in 1919. Led NL in wins (22–10), ERA (1.74), shutouts (8), and strikeouts (148) in 1918; in strikeouts, 1919 (141). One World Series, 1918: 1–2, 1.00 ERA; 3 starts, 3 complete, 1 shutout, 17 strikeouts in 27 innings.

On May 2, 1917, Vaughn pitched a no-hitter for 9⅓ innings against Cincinnati, only to lose in 10 innings, 1–0, to Fred Toney, who had a no-hitter all the way.

VEACH, ROBERT H. baseball: b. June 29, 1888, Island, Ky.; d. Aug. 7, 1945. Bat L, throw R; outfield. Detroit AL, 1912–23; Boston AL, 1924–25; Washington AL, New York AL, 1925. Fourteen years, 1,820 games, 2,061 hits, 393 doubles, 147 triples, 1,163 RBI, 195 stolen bases, .310 BA; hit .313 in 1915, .306 in 1916, .319 in 1917, .355 in 1919, .307 in 1920, .338 in 1921, .327 in 1922, .321 in 1923. Led AL in doubles (40) and RBI (112) in 1915;

in RBI, 1917 (103) and 1918 (78); in hits (191), doubles (45), and triples (17) in 1919. One World Series, 1925: 1 at-bat, no hits.

Veach went 6-for-6, with a double, a triple and a home run, on Sept. 17, 1920.

VIAU, LEON baseball: b. July 5, 1866, Corinth, Vt.; d. Dec. 31, 1947. Bat, throw R; pitcher. Cincinnati AA, 1888–89; Cincinnati NL, 1890; Cleveland NL, 1890–92; Boston NL, Louisville NL, 1892. Five years, 83–77, 3.33 ERA; 27–14 in 1888, 22–20 in 1889.

VILLA, PANCHO boxing: b. Francisco Guilledo, Aug. 1, 1901, Iloilo, Philippines; d. July 14, 1925. His record: 71 wins, 22 by KO; 5 losses; 4 draws, 23 no-decisions. Villa won Oriental flyweight and bantamweight titles before starting his U.S. campaign. He won the American flyweight championship with an 11th-round KO of Johnny Buff on Sept. 14, 1922. He lost it to Frankie Genaro on a 15-round decision, March 1, 1923, but was generally recognized as world champ after KOing Jimmy Wilde in the 7th round on June 18, 1923. He held the title until his death, from blood poisoning caused by an infected tooth.

Helms Hall of Fame, Boxing Hall of Fame.

VINSON, MARIBEL (Mrs. Owen) figure skating: b. 1918(?), Winchester, Mass.; d. Feb. 15, 1961. In a ten-year period, she won 9 U.S. singles championships, 1928–33 and 1935–37. She also shared the pairs title in 1928–29, 1933, and 1935–37. She was North American singles champion in 1937 and shared the pairs title in 1935. In 1961, one of her daughters, Laurence, won the U.S. singles title, and another daughter, Maribel, shared the pairs title.

They and fifteen other American skaters died in a plane crash en route to Belgium.

VITT, "OSSIE" (Oscar J.) baseball: b. Jan. 4, 1890, San Francisco; d. Jan. 31, 1963. Bat, throw R; third-second base. Detroit AL, 1912–18; Boston AL, 1919–21. Ten years, 1,062 games, .238 BA.

He managed Cleveland AL, 1938–40: 262–198, .570.

VON ELM, GEORGE golf: b. 1900(?); d. May 1, 1961. Von Elm lost the longest playoff the U.S. Open has ever seen, in 1931. He and Billy Burke were tied at 292 after the regulation 72 holes. They went into a 36-hole playoff, each shooting a 149. Burke won the second 36-hole playoff by one stroke, 148–149. In the USGA Amateur, Von Elm lost to Bobby Jones in the finals in 1924 but beat Jones in 1926. He also won the Pacific Northwest Amateur in 1921 and 1922.

VOSMIK, JOSEPH F. baseball: b. April 4, 1910, Cleveland; d. Jan. 27, 1962. Bat, throw R; outfield. Cleveland AL, 1930–36; St. Louis AL, 1937; Boston AL, 1938–39; Brooklyn NL, 1940–41; Washington AL, 1944. Thirteen years, 1,414 games, .307 BA; hit .320 in 1931, .312 in 1932, .341 in 1934, .348 in 1935, .325 in 1937, .324 in 1938. Led AL in hits (216), doubles (47), and triples (20) in 1935; in hits (201) in 1938.

VUKOVICH, WILLIAM auto racing: b. Dec. 13, 1918, Fresno, Calif.; d. May 30, 1955. "The Mad Russian" was national midget champion in 1950. He set a qualifying record in the Indianapolis 500 in 1952 and led through most of the race but was forced out by mechanical failure with 20 miles to go. In 1953, he won the 500 by more than 7 miles, having led for 195 of the 200 laps. He repeated in 1954, one of only two drivers to win at Indy two years in a row. Leading after 57 laps in his bid for a third straight victory, he was killed in a crash in 1955.

Auto Racing Hall of Fame. Helms Hall of Fame.

W

WACHTER, EDWARD A. basketball: b. June 30, 1883, Troy, N.Y.; d. March 12, 1966. Wachter began playing basketball in the Troy YMCA when it was still a brand-new sport, and he didn't retire from pro basketball until 1924. His twenty-two-year pro career included stints in the New England, Central Pennsylvania, New York State, and Hudson River Leagues, and he led every league in scoring at least one season. He played a total of 1,800 professional games. In a 1928 poll, he was chosen basketball's greatest center up to that point.

Basketball Hall of Fame.

WADDELL, "RUBE" (George E.) baseball: b. Oct. 13, 1876, Bradford, Pa.; d. April 1, 1914. Bat R, throw L; pitcher. Louisville NL, 1897, 1899; Pittsburgh NL, 1900–01; Chicago NL, 1901; Philadelphia AL, 1902–07; St. Louis AL, 1908–10. Thirteen years, 191–141, 2.16 ERA (6th); 407 games, 2,961⅓ innings, 803 walks, 2,316 strikeouts, 50 shutouts (10th); 25–7 in 1902, 21–16 in 1903, 21–16 in 1904, 24–11 in 1905. Led league in strikeouts, 1900 (130), 1902 (210), 1903 (302), 1904 (349), 1905 (287), 1906 (196), 1907 (232); in ERA, 1900 (2.37), 1905 (1.48); in complete games, 1903 (34).

He set an ML record for most years 200 or more strikeouts, 7, and the AL record for most years 300 or more, 2. His 349 strikeouts in 1904 is also an AL record. On July 1, 1902, he struck out the side on 9 pitches to tie an ML record.

Waddell was a big kid who chased fire engines, often disappeared for days, frequently drank before games, and never took baseball quite seriously. It was only a game to him. Once, during an exhibition game, he ordered his fielders to the dugout and then struck out the side; another time, having had a few drinks before a game, he gave up a home run and got so dizzy watching the hitter circle the bases that he fell down and was taken out of the game.

While playing minor-league baseball in 1912, he volunteered to help fight floods in Minneapolis, badly damaging his health and contributing to his early death.

Baseball Hall of Fame.

WAGNER, "HONUS" (John P.) baseball: b. Feb. 24, 1874, Mansfield (now Carnegie), Pa.; d. Dec. 6, 1955. Bat, throw R; shortstop. Louisville NL, 1897–99; Pittsburgh NL, 1900–17. Twenty-one years, 2,787 games (5th), 10,430 at-bats (3rd), 3,415 hits (4th), 2,422 singles (4th), 252 triples (3rd), 101 home runs, 1,736 runs, 1,732 RBI (9th), 722 stolen bases (4th), .327 BA; led NL in hitting, 1900 (.381), 1903 (.355), 1904 (.349), 1906 (.339), 1907 (.350), 1908 (.354), 1909 (.339), 1911 (.334); runs, 1902 (105), 1906 (103); hits, 1908 (201), 1910 (178); doubles, 1900 (45), 1902 (30), 1904 (44), 1906 (38), 1907 (38), 1908 (39), 1909 (39); triples, 1900 (22), 1903 (19), 1908 (19); RBI, 1901 (126), 1902 (91), 1908 (109), 1909 (100), 1912 (102); stolen bases, 1901 (49), 1902 (42), 1904 (53), 1907 (61), 1908 (53); slugging, 1900 (.573), 1902 (.463), 1904 (.520), 1907 (.513), 1908 (.542), 1909 (.489); hit .338 in 1897, .336 in 1899, .353 in 1901, .330 in 1902, .363 in 1905, .320 in 1910, .324 in 1912, .330 in 1913. Two World Series, 1903, 1909: 15 games, 3 doubles (3rd), 7 runs, 6 RBI, 9 stolen bases, .275 BA.

Ed Barrow, who made an outfielder of Babe Ruth and was general manager of the Yankees when Ruth was playing for them, felt that Wagner was the greatest player ever; so did Sam Crawford, who played next to Ty Cobb at Detroit for many years. Wagner was the complete player. His versatility was well displayed with the great Pittsburgh team of 1902, which won the pennant by 27½ games. He wasn't even considered a starter, yet he played 136 games, in the outfield, at shortstop, at first base, at second base, and even made one appearance on the mound. He led the NL that year in doubles, runs scored, RBI, stolen bases, and slugging percentage. A big man at 5'11" and 200 pounds, he was remarkably fast and had extra-large hands. A teammate recalled that when Wagner scooped up a grounder and threw to first, the ball was usually accompanied by pebbles and bits of dirt. He is coholder of ML records for most consecutive years leading league in hitting, 4; most consecutive years leading in total bases, 4; most years led in extra base hits, 7. He holds NL records for most years led in hitting, 8; most career singles, 2,422; most career triples, 252; most times stole way from 1st to home, 2.

The 1909 World Series brought a much-heralded confrontation between Cobb and Wagner; Wagner won hands down as he led the Pirates to a 7-game victory over the Tigers. He hit .333, with 2 doubles, 1 triple, 4 runs, 6 RBI, and 6 stolen bases.

Baseball Hall of Fame.

WALCOTT, JOSEPH boxing: b. March 13, 1873, Barbados, West Indies; d. October, 1935. His record: 81 wins, 34 by KO; 24 losses, 4 by KO; 30 draws, 15 no-decisions. Walcott came to the United States when he was fourteen. After a couple of years as an amateur boxer and wrestler, he turned professional. On Dec. 18, 1901, he became welterweight champion by KOing Jim "Rube" Ferns in the 5th round. He lost on a foul in the 20th round to Dixie Kid on April 30, 1904. On May 12, he and Dixie Kid fought a 10-round draw. When Dixie Kid outgrew the division, Walcott reclaimed the title but lost it to Honey Mellody in 15 rounds on Oct. 16, 1906.

Helms Hall of Fame, Boxing Hall of Fame.

WALKER, "CURT" (William Curtis) baseball: b. July 3, 1896, Beeville, Tex.; d. Dec. 9, 1955. Bat L, throw R; outfield. New York AL, 1919; New York NL, 1920–21; Philadelphia NL, 1921–24; Cincinnati NL, 1924–30. Twelve years, 1,359 games, .304 BA; hit .337 in 1922, .318 in 1925, .306 in 1926, .313 in 1929, .307 in 1930.

WALKER, "PEAHEAD" (Douglas C.) football: b. 1901, Birmingham, Ala.; d. July 16, 1970. A graduate of Howard College, Alabama, Walker was head football coach at Wake Forest for fourteen seasons, compiling a 77–51–6 record. He also coached at Atlantic Christian and Elon Colleges and with the Montreal Alouettes, of the Canadian professional league. He was probably more famous as the teller and the subject of anecdotes. He was a minor-league baseball player and manager for more than a decade, but he explained, "I decided it was time to quit when the Yankees made Casey Stengel manager. That was the job I shoulda had."

WALKER, "TILLY" (Clarence W.) baseball: b. Sept. 4, 1889, Telford, Tenn.; d. Sept. 20, 1959. Bat, throw R; outfield. Washington AL, 1911–12; St. Louis AL, 1913–15; Boston AL, 1916–17; Philadelphia AL, 1918–23. Thirteen years, 1,418 games, .281 BA; hit .304 in 1921. One World Series, 1916: 3 games, .273 BA.

Walker tied the AL record for most years leading outfielders in assists, 4.

WALKER, WILLIAM H. baseball: b. Oct. 7, 1903, E. St. Louis, Ill.; d. June 14, 1966. Bat R, throw L; pitcher. New York NL, 1927–32; St. Louis NL, 1933–36. Ten years, 98–77, 3.59 ERA; 15 shutouts. In relief, 14–7, 4.04 ERA, 8 saves. Led NL in ERA, 1929 (3.09); in ERA (2.26) and shutouts (6) in 1931. One World Series, 1934: 0–2, 7.11 ERA in 6⅓ innings of relief.

WALLACE, "BOBBY" (Roderick J.) baseball: b. Nov. 4, 1873, Pittsburgh; d. Nov. 3, 1960. Bat, throw R; shortstop, third base. Cleveland NL, 1894–98; St. Louis NL, 1899–1901; St. Louis AL, 1902–16; St. Louis NL, 1917–18. Twenty-five years, 2,380 games, 2,309 hits, 391 doubles, 1,057 runs, 1,121 RBI, 201 stolen bases, .268 BA; hit. 335 in 1897, .324 in 1901.

Wallace set an AL record for most chances accepted by a shortstop in a 9-inning game with 17 on June 10, 1902.

He managed St. Louis AL, 1911–12 (part); Cincinnati NL, 1937 (part): 62–154, .287.

Baseball Hall of Fame.

WALLARD, LEE auto racing: b. Sept. 7, 1910, Schenectady, N.Y.; d. Nov. 29, 1963. Wallard won the Indianapolis 500 in 1951 and was the first driver to finish in less than 4 hours. Four days later, he was badly burned in an accident and had to retire.

WALSH, EDWARD A. baseball: b. May 14, 1881, Plains, Pa.; d. May 26, 1959. Bat, throw R; pitcher. Chicago AL, 1904–16; Boston NL, 1917. Fourteen years, 194–130, 1.82 ERA (1st); 430 games, 315 starts, 250 complete, 2,964⅓ innings, 617 walks, 1,736 strikeouts, 57 shutouts (7th). In relief, 16–15, 1.85 ERA; 25–18 in 1907, 27–17 in 1912; 36 saves. No-hitters, Aug. 27, 1911, against Boston AL (5–0); May 26, 1907, against New York AL (5 innings; 8–1). Led AL in shutouts, 1906 (10); in ERA (1.60) and complete games (37) in 1907; in wins (39–15), complete games (42), strikeouts (269), and shutouts (11) in 1908; in shutouts (8) in 1909; in losses (16–20) and ERA (1.27) in 1910; in losses (26–18) and strikeouts (255) in 1911. One World Series, 1906: 2–0, 1.80 ERA, 17 strikeouts in 15 innings. He had a 2-hitter in the third game.

Walsh had an ERA of under 2.00 for 5 consecutive years and had an ERA under 3.00 in thirteen of his fourteen seasons. He developed arm trouble in 1913 and from then until the end of his career had a 13–8 record.

He holds the modern ML record for most innings in a season (464 in 1908) and tied an ML record by twice throwing 10 or more shutouts in a season. He tied an AL record for most shutouts in a month, 6, and was the only AL pitcher to do it twice, in August 1906 and September 1908. He also holds the AL record for most complete-game doubleheaders won, 2, and on Sept, 29, 1908, he won both games in a doubleheader, giving up 7 hits and 1 run.

Baseball Hall of Fame.

WALSH, JIMMY boxing: b. 1886, Newton, Mass.; d. Nov. 23, 1964. His record: 52 wins, 12 by KO; 9 losses, 1 by KO; 18 draws, 41 no-decisions. Walsh was generally recognized as U.S. bantamweight champ and he claimed the world title after beating English champion Digger Stanley in 15 rounds, Oct. 20, 1905. On Dec. 7, 1906, he fought Abe Attell for the featherweight crown and was KOed in the 8th round. He resigned the bantam title and continued fighting as a featherweight. His 12-round title bout with Johnny Kilbane, then champion, on May 21, 1912, ended in a draw.

WANER, PAUL G. baseball: b. April 16, 1903, Harrah, Okla.; d. Aug. 29, 1965. Bat, throw L; outfield. Pittsburgh NL, 1926–40; Brooklyn NL, 1941; Boston NL, 1941–42; Brooklyn NL, 1943–44; New York AL, 1944–45. Twenty years, 2,549 games (8th), 9,459 at-bats (10th), 3,152 hits (7th), 2,247 singles (11th), 603 doubles (6th), 190 triples (9th), 112 home runs, 1,626 runs, 1,309 RBI, 1,091 walks, 376 strikeouts, .333 BA; hit .336 in 1926, .370 in 1928, .336 in 1929, .368 in 1930, .322 in 1931, .341 in 1932, .309 in 1933, .321 in 1935, .354 in 1937, .328 in 1939. Led NL in hitting, 1927 (.380), 1934 (.362), 1936 (.373); runs, 1928 (142), 1934 (122); hits, 1927 (237), 1934 (217); doubles, 1928 (50), 1932 (62); triples, 1926 (22), 1927 (17); RBI, 1927 (131).

Waner was called Big Poison because at 5'8" and 155 pounds he was an inch taller and ten pounds heavier than his younger brother, Lloyd, "Little Poison," who had a lifetime average of .316, mostly with the Pirates. They had developed quick, strong wrists as youngsters, swinging at corncobs with broomsticks.

On Aug. 26, 1926, Paul went 6-for-6, with 2 doubles and a triple. He set a modern ML record for most triples by a rookie, 22 in 1926, and he holds NL records for most years 50 or more doubles, 3; most consecutive years leading in triples, 2; and most doubles by a left-handed hitter, 62 in 1932.

One World Series, 1927: 4 games, 3 RBI, .333 BA.

Baseball Hall of Fame.

WARD, AARON L. baseball: b. Aug. 28, 1896, Booneville, Ala.; d. Jan. 30, 1961. Bat, throw R; second-third base. New York AL, 1917–26; Chicago AL, 1927; Cleveland AL, 1928. Twelve years, 1,059 games, .268 BA; hit .306 in 1921. Three World Series, 1921–23: 19 games, .286 BA. He hit .417 in 1923 as the Yankees beat the Giants in 6 games.

WARD, ARCH sportswriting: b. Dec. 27, 1896, Irwin, Ill.; d. July 8, 1955. As sports editor of the Chicago *Tribune,* Ward proposed the idea of a major-league All-Star baseball game to be held as one of the attractions of the Chicago Centennial Exposition of Progress in 1933. It was so popular that it is now an annual event. He also promoted the first College All-Star game between the pro-football champions and a collection of recently graduated college stars, and the first Golden Gloves tournament, which was held in Chicago in 1926.

WARD, "BUD" (Marvin) golf: b. May 1, 1913, Olympia, Wash.; d. Jan. 2, 1968. An amateur throughout his career, Ward won his biggest victory in 1939, beating W. B. McCullough 11-and-9 for the U.S.G.A. Amateur title. He also won the Western Amateur in 1940–41 and 1947 and the Pacific Northwest Amateur in 1941.

WARD, HOLCOMBE tennis: b. Nov. 23, 1878, New York City; d. Jan. 23, 1967. Representing Harvard, Ward won the intercollegiate doubles in 1899 with Dwight F. Davis. He won the U.S. outdoor singles, 1904, and the indoor singles, 1901, but was most prominent as a doubles player. He and Davis won the U.S. outdoor doubles, 1899–1901, and he and Beals C. Wright won it, 1904–06. He was president of the U.S. Lawn Tennis Association, 1937–48.

Helms Hall of Fame, Tennis Hall of Fame.

WARD, "MONTE" (John Montgomery) baseball: b. March 3, 1860, Bellefonte, Pa.; d. March 4, 1925. Bat L, throw R; shortstop, second base, pitcher. Providence NL, 1878–82; New York NL, 1883–89; Brooklyn PL, 1890; Brooklyn NL, 1891–92; New York NL, 1893–94. Seventeen years, 1,825 games, 2,105 hits, 1,408 runs, 504 stolen bases (nine years not included), .275 BA; hit .338 in 1887, .337 in 1890, .328 in 1893. As pitcher: 163–102, 2.10 ERA (4th), 24 shutouts; 22–13 in 1878. Led league in ERA, 1878 (1.51); in victories and percentage (47–19, .712) in 1879; in shutouts, 1880 (8); in stolen bases, 1887 (111) and 1892 (88).

It would be easy to think there were several John M. Wards. He is the only player to collect more than 1,000 hits and to win more than 100 games. He was a shortstop in 1887, when he stole 111 bases, and he was a playing manager in 1892, when he set an ML record for second basemen with 12 assists in a 9-inning game. He pitched the second perfect game in history on June 27, 1880, beating Buffalo, 5–0. He won both games of a double-header on Aug. 9, 1878. On Aug. 17, 1882, he tied an ML record for the longest shutout, 18 innings.

He was also a leader of the Brotherhood of Professional Baseball Players and was its president during the battle over salaries and working conditions that led to formation of the Players League in 1890.

He managed Brooklyn PL, 1890; Brooklyn NL, 1891–92; New York NL, 1893–94: 388–299, .565.

Baseball Hall of Fame.

WARNER, "POP" (Glenn S.) football: b. April 5, 1871, Springville, N.Y.; d. Sept. 7, 1954. A forty-six-year college coaching career, second longest in history, began when Warner coached Georgia to an undefeated season in 1896. He had played football and won his law degree at Cornell, and he returned to his alma mater to coach for two seasons before going to Carlisle Indian School. His fourteen years there, in two stints—1899–1903 and 1907–14 (he coached at Cornell again in between)—made both Carlisle and Warner famous. He had the players to work with, of course, including Jim Thorpe, but Warner was an inventive coach who discarded the old-fashioned T and short-punt formations in favor of his own developments, the single- and double-wings. Another Warner idea was to have players start from a three-point stance.

In 1915 Warner went to Pittsburgh for nine seasons, during which he produced three undefeated teams, including two generally acknowledged as national champions. During one stretch, his Pitt teams won 33 in a row. At Stanford, 1924–32, Warner turned out three Rose Bowl teams, losing to Notre Dame 27–10 in 1925, tying Alabama 7–7 in 1927, and beating Pittsburgh 7–6 in 1928. He rounded out his coaching career at Temple, 1933–38, but was an advisory coach at San Jose State for two years after that.

Helms Hall of Fame, National Football Foundation Hall of Fame.

WATKINS, GEORGE A. baseball: b. June 4, 1902, Palestine, Tex.; d. June 1, 1970. Bat L, throw R; outfield. St. Louis NL, 1930–33; New York NL, 1934; Philadelphia NL, 1935–36; Brooklyn NL, 1936. Seven years, 904 games, .288 BA; hit .373 in 1930, .312 in 1932. Two World Series, 1930–31: 9 games, .231 BA. His 2-run home run gave the Cardinals a 4–2 win over the Athletics in the seventh and deciding game of the 1931 Series.

Watkins hit 3 home runs in a game on June 25, 1931.

WATKINS, WILLIAM H. baseball: b. May 5, 1859, Brantford, Ontario, Canada; d. June 9, 1937. Infield. Indianapolis AA, 1884. Thirty-four games, .205 BA.

Managed Indianapolis AA, 1884 (part); Detroit NL, 1885 (part)–88 (part); Kansas City AA, 1888 (part)–89; St. Louis NL, 1893; Pittsburgh NL, 1898–99 (part): 437–433, .502. Pennant, 1887.

WEATHERLY, JOSEPH motorcycle racing, auto racing: b. 1922(?); d. Jan. 20, 1964. As a motorcyclist, Weatherly was the national 100-mile road-racing champion, 1948–49, and 10-mile dirt-track champion in 1950. Then he switched to cars. He was NASCAR national modified champ in 1953, grand national champ in 1962–63.

He was killed in a crash during the Riverside 500.

WEAVER, "BUCK" (George D.) baseball: b. Aug. 18, 1890, Stowe, Pa.; d. Jan. 31, 1956. Bat, throw R; shortstop, third base. Chicago AL, 1912–20. Nine years, 1,254 games, .272 BA; hit .300 in 1918, .333 in 1920. Two World Series, 1917, 1919: 14 games, 5 doubles, 7 runs, .327 BA.

Weaver hit .324 in the 1919 Series, with 4 doubles and a triple, and scored 4 of his team's 20 runs. But that was the year of the Black Sox Scandal, and Weaver was one of eight White Sox banned from baseball for life after the 1920 season.

WEAVER, JAMES A. football: b. 1898(?); d. 1968. Centre College center; All-American, 1919. Columbus Tigers, 1923; Cleveland Panthers (AFL), 1926. Weaver set a college record in 1919 by dropkicking 53 of 53 extra-point attempts. He also holds the college record for most consecutive conversions, 95.

WEAVER, SAMUEL H. baseball: b. July 20, 1855, Philadelphia; d. Feb. 1, 1914. Throw R; pitcher. Milwaukee NL, 1878; Philadelphia AA, 1882; Louisville AA, 1883; Philadelphia UA, 1884; Philadelphia AA, 1886. Five years, 69–80, 3.23 ERA; 26–15 in 1882, 26–22 in 1883. No-hitter, May 9, 1878, against Indianapolis NL. Led NL in losses, 1878 (12–31).

WEBB, W. EARL baseball: b. Sept. 17, 1898, Bon Air, Tenn.; d. May 23, 1965. Bat L, throw R; outfield. New York NL, 1925; Chicago NL, 1927–28; Boston AL, 1930–32; Detroit AL, 1932–33; Chicago AL, 1933. Seven years, 649 games, .306 BA; hit .301 in 1927, .323 in 1930, .333 in 1931. Webb's 67 doubles in 1931 is an all-time ML record.

WEED, "CY" (Randolph W.) rowing: b. 1883(?); d. Feb. 2, 1964. Weed was stroke for the outstanding Cornell crew of 1909, which won the 4-mile Poughkeepsie race for the Varsity Challenge Cup and set a new American Henley record at Philadelphia.

Helms Hall of Fame.

WEEKES, HAROLD H. football: b. April 2, 1880, Oyster Bay, N.Y.; d. July 26, 1950. Columbia halfback; All-American, 1901; 2nd team, 1900; 3rd team, 1899; captain, 1902. Weekes was just a freshman substitute until the 1899 Yale game, when he ran 45 yards for the game's only TD. From that point on, he was a star. A speedster, he was also very strong; he could sidestep people or run over them when he had to. In 1901 he gained 230 yards against Pennsylvania, scoring all of Columbia's points in a 10–0 victory, with TD runs of 75 and 18 yards. In 1902 he scored 6 TDs against Fordham, on runs ranging from 35 to 75 yards, then returned a kickoff 107 yards against Hamilton, but an injury kept him below par for the rest of the season.

He coached Kansas to a 6–1 record in 1903.

Helms Hall of Fame, National Football Foundation Hall of Fame.

WEFERS, BERNARD J. track: b. 1873(?); d. April 18, 1957. Wefers held both world sprint records for a long time. His 21.2 in the 220-yard dash, set in 1896, stood until 1921, and his 9.8 in the 100, set in 1895, was the record until 1906. Representing Georgetown, he was IC4A champion in the 100 in 1896–97 and 220 champion in 1896. He won the AAU titles in both the 100 and 220 in 1895–97.

Helms Hall of Fame.

WEIDMAN, "STUMP" (George) baseball: b. Feb. 17, 1861, Rochester, N.Y.; d. March 3, 1905. Bat, throw R; pitcher. Buffalo NL, 1880; Detroit NL, 1881–85; Kansas City NL, 1886; Detroit NL, New York AA, 1887; New York NL, 1887–88. Nine years, 102–156, 3.61 ERA; 25–20 in 1882, 20–24 in 1883. Led NL in ERA, 1881 (1.80); in losses, 1886 (12–36).

WEILL, AL boxing: b. ?; d. Oct. 20, 1969. Once a matchmaker at Madison Square Garden, Weill was more famous as manager of world champions in four different weight classes: heavyweight Rocky Marciano, welterweight Marty Servo, lightweight Lou Ambers, and featherweight Joey Archibald.

WEILMAN, CARL W. baseball: b. Weilenmann, Nov. 29, 1889, Hamilton, Ohio; d. March 26, 1924. Bat, throw L; pitcher. St. Louis AL, 1912–17, 1919–20. Eight years, 84–94, 2.67 ERA; 14 shutouts.

WEIMER, JACOB ("Tornado Jake") baseball: b. Nov. 29, 1873, Ottumwa, Iowa; d. June 17, 1928. Bat, throw L; pitcher. Chicago NL, 1903–05; Cincinnati NL, 1906–08; New York NL, 1909. Seven years, 97–72, 2.23 ERA, 21 shutouts.

WELCH, CURTIS B. baseball: b. Feb. 11, 1862, East Liverpool, Ohio; d. Aug. 29, 1896. Bat, throw R; outfield. Toledo AA, 1884; St. Louis AA, 1885–87;

Philadelphia AA, 1888–90; Brooklyn-Baltimore AA, 1890–91; Baltimore NL, Cincinnati NL, 1892; Louisville NL, 1893. Ten years, 1,107 games, 394 stolen bases (three years not included), .263 BA. Led league in doubles, 1889 (39).

WELCH, FRANCIS G. track, football: b. Aug. 21, 1895, near Hartford, Kan.; d. June 19, 1970. Welch won 11 letters at Kansas State Teachers College, Emporia, 1918. He coached football at his alma mater, 1928–42, 1946–55, compiling a 116–81–15 record, but was better known as a track coach during the same period. His track teams won 18 Central Conference titles. He trained Archie San Romani for the 1936 Olympics and he coached the women's Olympic track team in 1960.

National Association of Intercollegiate Athletes Hall of Fame.

WELCH, "MICKEY" (Michael F.) baseball: b. July 4, 1859, Brooklyn; d. July 30, 1941. Bat, throw R; pitcher. Troy NL, 1880–82; New York NL, 1883–92. Thirteen years, 309–211, 2.71 ERA; 564 games, 549 starts, 525 complete (6th), 4,802 innings (8th), 4,587 hits (8th), 1,850 strikeouts, 40 shutouts; 34–30 in 1880, 21–18 in 1881, 25–23 in 1883, 39–21 in 1884, 33–23 in 1886, 22–15 in 1887, 26–19 in 1888, 27–12 in 1889. Led NL in percentage, 1885 (44–11, .800).

On Aug. 28, 1884, he struck out 9 hitters in a row, tying the ML record.

WELSH, FREDDY boxing: b. Frederick H. Thomas, March 5, 1886, Pontypridd, Wales; d. July 29, 1927. His record: 77 wins, 24 by KO; 4 losses, 1 by KO; 7 draws, 79 no-decisions. "The Welsh Wizard" began boxing in Philadelphia in 1905. He won the British lightweight title on Nov. 8, 1909, with a 20-round decision over John Summers. On July 7, 1914, he took the world title by beating Willie Ritchie in 20 rounds. He lost the title on a 9th-round KO by Benny Leonard on May 28, 1917.

Boxing Hall of Fame.

WENCK, FREDERICK A. swimming: b. 1879(?); d. July 26, 1946. Wenck won both the U.S. half-mile and 1-mile freestyle titles, 1898–99.

WERNER, "BUDDY" (Wallace) skiing: b. 1935(?); d. April 12, 1964. Werner was the first American male skier to represent a serious challenge to Europeans in international competition. He was U.S. downhill champion in 1957, and in 1959 he won three North American titles, the downhill, slalom, and combined Alpine. In the 1964 Olympics he finished 17th in the downhill, 8th in the slalom. Shortly afterward, he was one of several skiers killed by an avalanche in the Swiss Alps while filming a ski-fashion movie.

WESTON, EDWARD PAYSON walking: b. March 15, 1839, Providence, R.I.; d. May 13, 1929. Weston first drew public notice in 1861, when he walked from Boston to Washington to see Abraham Lincoln's inauguration. In 1867, he went from Portland, Maine, to Chicago, 1,326 miles, in less than 26 days; forty years later, when he was sixty-eight, he did it 29 hours faster than his previous try.

In 1909, now seventy, Weston walked from New York to San Francisco, 3,985 miles, in 104 days, 7 hours. As if to show that he improved with age, he walked the return trip in just under 77 days. Weston's last great trip by foot brought him from New York to Minneapolis to lay the cornerstone for a new athletic club. After covering 1,546 miles in 51 days, he was greeted by thousands of cheering Minnesotans, led by the mayor of Minneapolis. Helms Hall of Fame.

WESTROPE, "JACKIE" (John) horse racing: b. Jan. 27, 1918, Baker, Mont.; d. June 19, 1958. When he was only fifteen, Westrope was national champion jockey, riding 301 victories on a total of 1,224 mounts in 1933. It was his best year, largely because of daredevil tactics, which caused injuries that kept him from riding a good deal of the time. In 1957, he broke a leg in a fall. Shortly after he returned, he was killed when a mount threw him at Hollywood Park.

WEYHING, "GUS" (August) baseball: b. Sept. 29, 1866, Louisville, Ky.; d. Sept. 3, 1955. Bat, throw R; pitcher. Philadelphia AA, 1887–89; Brooklyn PL, 1890; Philadelphia AA, 1891; Philadelphia NL, 1892–95; Pittsburgh NL, 1895; Louisville NL, 1895–96; Washington NL, 1898–99; Brooklyn NL, St. Louis NL, 1900; Cleveland NL, Cincinnati NL, 1901. Fourteen years, 264 wins, 232 losses (9th), 3.89 ERA; 28 shutouts; 26–28 in 1887, 28–18 in 1888, 30–21 in 1889, 30–16 in 1890, 31–20 in 1891, 32–21 in 1892, 23–16 in 1893.

WHARTON, "BUCK" (Charles M.) football: b. 1868, Magnolia, Del.; d. Nov. 15, 1949. Pennsylvania guard; All-American, 1895–96; 2nd team, 1894; captain, 1896. Wharton played for the great Penn teams that compiled a 52–4 record from 1893 to 1896.
National Football Foundation Hall of Fame.

WHEELER, ARTHUR L. ("Beef") football: b. May 12, 1872, Philadelphia; d. Dec. 20, 1917. Princeton guard; All-American, 1892–94.
National Football Foundation Hall of Fame.

WHITE, BENJAMIN F. harness racing: b. Feb. 5, 1873, Whiteville, Ontario, Canada; d. May 20, 1958. The first driver to win 4 Hambletonians, White accomplished it in 1933, 1936, 1942–43. He won the Kentucky Futurity 7 times, the Matron Stakes (trot) 6 times. Other major races he won included the Trotting Derby, Arthur S. Tompkins Memorial, and the Horseman's Stake.

Harness Hall of Fame.

WHITE, "DEACON" (James L.) baseball: b. Dec. 7, 1847, Caton, N.Y.; d. July 7, 1939. Brother of Will. Bat L, throw R; third base, catcher, first base, outfield. National Association, Cleveland Forest Cities, 1871–72; Boston, 1873–75. Five years, 259 games, .347 BA.

Chicago NL, 1876; Boston NL, 1877; Cincinnati NL, 1878–80; Buffalo NL, 1881–85; Detroit NL, 1886–88; Pittsburgh NL, 1889; Buffalo PL, 1890. Fifteen years, 1,299 games, .303 BA; hit .343 in 1876, .314 in 1878, .330 in 1879, .310 in 1881, .325 in 1884, .303 in 1887. Led league in hits (103), triples (11), RBI (49), BA (.387), and slugging (.545) in 1877; in RBI, 1876 (60).

White tied an ML record for third basemen with 11 assists in a 9-inning game on May 16, 1884.

He was one of the "Big Four" who jumped from Boston to Chicago in 1876, precipitating the formation of the National League. A farmer and Sunday-school teacher who didn't smoke, drink, or swear, he firmly believed that the earth was flat, and spent a good part of his time trying to convince teammates that he was right. He convinced at least one of them.

WHITE, WILLIAM H. baseball: b. Oct. 11, 1854, Caton, N.Y.; d. Aug. 31, 1911. Brother of Deacon. Sw. hit, throw L; pitcher. Boston NL, 1877; Cincinnati NL, 1878–80; Detroit NL, 1881; Cincinnati AA, 1882–86. Ten years, 229–166, 2.28 ERA (10th); 36 shutouts, 394 complete games in 401 starts; 30–21 in 1878, 43–31 in 1879, 34–18 in 1884. Led NL in complete games, 1879 (75); in losses, 1880 (18–42); led AA in wins (40–12), percentage (.769), complete games (52), and shutouts (8) in 1882; in wins (43–22), ERA (2.09), and shutouts (6) in 1883. His 76 starts and 75 complete games in 1879 are ML records.

WHITEHEAD, JOHN H. baseball: b. April 27, 1909, Coleman, Tex.; d. Oct. 20, 1964. Bat, throw R; pitcher. Chicago AL, 1935–39; St. Louis AL, 1939–40, 1942. Seven years, 49–54, 4.60 ERA. No-hitter, Aug. 5, 1940, against Detroit AL (4–0; 6 innings).

WHITEHILL, EARL O. baseball: b. Feb. 7, 1899, Cedar Rapids, Iowa; d. Oct. 22, 1954. Bat, throw L; pitcher. Detroit AL, 1923–32; Washington AL, 1933–36; Cleveland AL, 1937–38; Chicago NL, 1939. Seventeen years,

218–185, 4.36 ERA; 22–8 in 1933. One World Series, 1933; he pitched a 5-hit, complete-game shutout in his one start.

WHITMAN, MALCOLM D. tennis: b. 1877; d. Dec. 28, 1932. Representing Harvard, Whitman won the intercollegiate singles title in 1896. He was U.S. outdoor singles champion, 1898–1900, and, with L. E. Ware, won the indoor doubles title, 1897–98. A member of the first two Davis Cup teams, 1900 and 1902, he was undefeated in cup competition.

Tennis Hall of Fame.

WHITNEY, HARRY PAYNE polo, horse racing: b. April 29, 1872, New York City; d. Oct. 26, 1930. Whitney was an ardent lover of sports and invested a large share of his inherited fortune in polo ponies and thoroughbreds. As leader of the "Big Four," he revolutionized polo by developing the long passing and hitting game. Whitney led his team to victory over Great Britain in Westchester Cup matches in 1909, 1911, and 1913. He was rated at 10 goals five years in a row, 1917–21.

In racing, he was the top money-winning owner in 1920, 1924, 1926–27, 1929–30, and the top money-winning breeder in 1924, 1926–30. He had 3 Kentucky Derby winners, 4 Preakness winners, and 4 Belmont winners.

WHITNEY, "LONG JIM" (James E.) baseball: b. 1856, Binghamton, N.Y.; d. May 21, 1891. Pitcher, outfield. Boston NL, 1881–85; Kansas City NL, 1886; Washington NL, 1887–88; Indianapolis NL, 1889; Philadelphia AA, 1890. Ten years, 550 games, .261 BA; hit .323 in 1882. As pitcher, 190–204, 2.97 ERA; 26 shutouts; 24–21 in 1882, 37–21 in 1883, 22–14 in 1884, 24–21 in 1887. Led NL in both wins and losses (31–33) and complete games (57) in 1881; in strikeouts, 1883 (345); in losses, 1885 (18–32).

Whitney tied an NL record by scoring 6 runs on June 9, 1883.

WHITTED, "POSSUM" (George B.) baseball: b. Feb. 4, 1890, Durham, S.C.; d. Oct. 16, 1942. Bat, throw R; outfield, third base. St. Louis NL, 1912–14; Boston NL, 1914; Philadelphia NL, 1915–19; Pittsburgh NL, 1919–21; Brooklyn NL, 1922. Eleven years, 1,021 games, .270 BA. Two World Series, 1914–15: 9 games, .138 BA.

WICKER, ROBERT K. baseball: b. May 25, 1878, Lawrence County, Kan.; d. Jan. 22, 1955. Bat, throw R; pitcher. St. Louis NL, 1901–03; Chicago NL, 1903–06; Cincinnati NL, 1906. Six years, 64–53, 2.73 ERA; 10 shutouts. No-hitter, June 11, 1904, against New York NL (9⅓ innings; won 1–0 on 1 hit in 12 innings).

WILCE, JOHN W. football: b. May 12, 1888, Rochester, N.Y.; d. May 17, 1963. Wisconsin fullback; captain, 1909.

He coached Ohio State, 1913–28, compiling a 78–33–9 record and winning Western Conference (Big Ten) titles in 1916–17 and 1920. His team lost 28–0 to California in the 1921 Rose Bowl. He resigned because, he said, "They're taking the game away from the boys."

Helms Hall of Fame, National Football Foundation Hall of Fame.

WILHELM, "KAISER" (Irvin K.) baseball: b. Jan. 26, 1874, Wooster, Ohio; d. May 21, 1936. Bat, throw R; pitcher. Pittsburgh NL, 1903; Boston NL, 1904–05; Brooklyn NL, 1908–10; Baltimore Fed L, 1914–15; Philadelphia NL, 1921. Nine years, 57–105, 3.44 ERA; 12 shutouts.

He managed Philadelphia NL, 1921 (part)–22: 77–128, .376.

WILLARD, JESS boxing: b. Dec. 29, 1883, Pottawotamie, Kan.; d. Dec. 15, 1968. His record: 23 wins, 20 by KO; 6 losses, 2 by KO; 1 draw, 5 no-decisions. One of boxing's first giants, at 6'7" and about 240 pounds, Willard was the "great white hope" who finally took the heavyweight title from Jack Johnson. He didn't turn pro until 1911, when he was twenty-eight. He KOed Johnson in the 26th round on April 5, 1915, in Havana, Cuba, receiving nothing more than his training expenses for the trouble. He lost his title to Jack Dempsey on July 4, 1919, and retired. Dempsey beat him badly, knocking him down seven times in the 1st round, and his seconds threw in the towel after 3 rounds.

WILLETT, "ED" (Edgar R.) baseball: b. March 7, 1884, Norfolk, Va.; d. May 10, 1934. Bat, throw R; pitcher. Detroit AL, 1906–13; St. Louis Fed L, 1914–15. Ten years, 101–99, 3.22 ERA; 21–11 in 1909. One World Series, 1909: 0–0, 0.00 ERA in 7⅔ innings of relief.

WILLIAMS, HENRY L. football: b. July 26, 1869, Hartford, Conn.; d. June 14, 1931. Williams was a halfback at Yale; he also won the IC4A title in the 110-yard high hurdles in 1890 and 1891 and the 220-yard lows in 1891. His 15.8 time in the high hurdles in 1891 was a world record at the time.

He coached football at Army in 1891 and his team beat Navy; Williams is credited with inventing the crossbuck during that season. He then got his M.D. degree and from 1900 to 1921 he coached at Minnesota, producing undefeated teams in 1900, 1903–04, 1911, and 1915. He won two Western Conference (Big Ten) titles and tied for six others. Williams's twenty-three-season percentage of .788, on a 143–34–12 record, is tenth best in history.

Helms Hall of Fame, National Football Foundation Hall of Fame.

WILLIAMS, JAMES T. baseball: b. Dec. 20, 1876, St. Louis; d. Jan. 16, 1965. Bat, throw R; second-third base. Pittsburgh NL, 1899–1900; Baltimore AL, 1901–02; New York AL, 1903–07; St. Louis AL, 1908–09. Eleven years,

1,456 games, .275 BA; hit .355 in 1899, .317 in 1901, .313 in 1902. Led league in triples, 1899 (27), 1901 (21), 1902 (21).

Williams' 27 triples in 1899 is an ML record for a rookie, and his 219 hits that year is second highest for a rookie. On Aug. 25, 1902, he went 6-for-6.

WILLIAMS, KENNETH R. baseball: b. June 28, 1890, Grant's Pass, Ore.; d. Jan. 22, 1959. Bat L, throw R; outfield. Cincinnati NL, 1915–16; St. Louis AL, 1918–27; Boston AL, 1928–29. Fourteen years, 1,397 games, .319 BA; hit .307 in 1920, .347 in 1921, .332 in 1922, .357 in 1923, .324 in 1924, .331 in 1925, .323 in 1927, .303 in 1928. Led league in home runs (39) and RBI (155) in 1922; in slugging, 1925 (.613).

Williams was the first AL player to hit 3 home runs in a game, on April 22, 1922. He tied an ML record by hitting 2 home runs in an inning on Aug. 7, 1922. Just before that, July 28–Aug. 2, he had tied an AL record by hitting at least 1 home run in each of 6 consecutive games.

WILLIAMS, KID boxing: b. John Gutenko, Dec. 5, 1893, Copenhagen, Denmark; d. Oct. 18, 1963. His record: 87 wins, 43 by KO; 12 losses, 1 by KO; 8 draws, 72 no-decisions. Williams won the bantamweight title on June 9, 1914, by KOing Johnny Coulon in the 3rd round. Although he lost on a foul to Johnny Ertle on Sept. 10, 1915, in 5 rounds, he was generally considered the champion until Pete Williams KOed him in 20 rounds, Jan. 9, 1917.

Helms Hall of Fame.

WILLIAMS, "LEFTY" (Claude P.) baseball: b. March 9, 1893, Aurora, Mo.; d. Nov. 4, 1959. Bat R, throw L; pitcher. Detroit AL, 1913–14; Chicago AL, 1916–20. Seven years, 82–48, 3.13 ERA; 23–11 in 1919, 22–14 in 1920. Two World Series, 1917, 1919: 0–3, 6.75 ERA.

Williams was banned from baseball for life because of his implication in the Black Sox World Series scandal of 1919. He lost three games in that series, including the final game, in which he gave up 4 runs while retiring just 1 hitter in the 1st inning.

WILLIAMS, R. NORRIS, II tennis: b. Jan. 29, 1891, Geneva, Switzerland; d. June 3, 1968. Williams and his father were returning to the United States aboard the *Titanic* in 1912. When the ship sank, his father drowned, but young Williams was rescued after swimming for more than an hour in icy water.

He won the national intercollegiate singles title for Harvard in 1913 and 1915 and, with Richard Harte, the doubles title in 1914–15. He also won the U.S. outdoor singles in 1914 and 1916. Williams and Charles S. Garland won the Wimbledon doubles in 1920 and he and Vincent Richards won the U.S. outdoor doubles, 1925–26.

Helms Hall of Fame, Tennis Hall of Fame.

WILLIAMSON, "IVY" (Ivan) football: b. Feb. 4, 1911, Wayne, Ohio; d. Feb. 19, 1969. Michigan end; captain, 1932, when the team won the national championship.

In two years of coaching at Lafayette, he had a 13–5 record. At Wisconsin, 1948–54, he had a 41–19–4 record. His team lost to Southern California in the 1953 Rose Bowl, 7–0. He was athletic director at Wisconsin from 1955 until shortly before his death.

WILLIAMSON, "NED" (Edward N.) baseball: b. Oct. 24, 1857, Philadelphia; d. March 3, 1894. Bat, throw R; third base, shortstop. Indianapolis NL, 1878; Chicago NL, 1879–89; Chicago PL, 1890. Thirteen years, 1,201 games, .255 BA. Led league in doubles, 1883 (49), home runs, 1884 (27), walks, 1885 (75).

Williamson was the first player to hit 3 home runs in a game; he did it May 30, 1884. On June 6, 1883, he set an NL record by scoring 3 runs in an inning and tied an ML record by getting 3 hits in an inning.

WILLIS, VICTOR G. baseball: b. April 12, 1876, Wilmington, Del.; d. Aug. 3, 1947. Bat, throw R; pitcher. Boston NL, 1898–1905; Pittsburgh NL, 1906–09; St. Louis NL, 1910. Thirteen years, 248–206, 2.63 ERA; 50 shutouts (10th); 24–13 in 1898, 27–8 in 1899, 20–17 in 1901, 22–13 in 1906, 21–12 in 1907, 24–11 in 1908, 23–11 in 1909. Led NL in shutouts, 1899 (5) and 1901 (6); in losses (27–20), complete games (45), and strikeouts (225) in 1902; losses (18–25) and complete games (39) in 1904; in losses, 1905 (11–29). One World Series, 1909: 0–1, 4.76 ERA.

His 45 complete games in 1902 is a modern NL record.

WILLS, HARRY boxing: b. May 15, 1890, New Orleans; d. Dec. 21, 1958. His record: 62 wins, 45 by KO; 8 losses, 4 by KO; 2 draws, 27 no-decisions, 3 no-contests. Wills is considered one of the top heavyweights of his time, but he never fought for the title. He wanted to fight Jack Dempsey but didn't get the chance, largely because promoters were afraid of a "mixed match" after the controversy that had surrounded Negro champion Jack Johnson.

WILMAN, "BUCK" (Joseph) bowling: b. Dec. 20, 1905, Fontanet, Ind.; d. Oct. 22, 1969. Wilman was the first man to roll two 2,000 series in the ABC tournament all-events and the second to win four ABC titles. He won the all-events in 1939 and 1946 and was on the winning teams in 1942 and 1954.

He tied a record, with eight straight 1,800 series, and holds the highest five-year average, 214. His thirty-six year ABC tourney average was 197; he had 3 sanctioned 300 games.

American Bowling Congress Hall of Fame.

WILMOT, WALTER R. baseball: b. Oct. 18, 1863, Stevens Point, Wis.; d. Feb. 1, 1929. Sw. hit, throw L; outfield. Washington NL, 1888–89; Chicago NL, 1890–95; New York NL, 1897–98. Ten years, 960 games, .275 BA; hit .301 in 1893, .330 in 1894. Led NL in triples, 1889 (19); in home runs, 1890 (14). He tied an ML record by drawing 6 walks in a game, Aug. 22, 1891.

WILSON, GEORGE football: b. 1903(?); d. Dec. 27, 1963. Washington half-back; All-American, 1925; 2nd team, 1924. Los Angeles Wildcats (AFL), 1926; Providence Steamrollers, 1927–29.

Helms Hall of Fame, National Football Foundation Hall of Fame.

WILSON, "HACK" (Lewis R.) baseball: b. April 26, 1900, Elwood City, Pa.; d. Nov. 23, 1948. Bat, throw R; outfield. New York NL, 1923–25; Chicago NL, 1926–31; Brooklyn NL, 1932–34; Philadelphia NL, 1934. Twelve years, 1,348 games, 244 home runs, 1,062 RBI, .307 BA; hit .321 in 1926, .318 in 1927, .313 in 1928, .345 in 1929, .356 in 1930. Led NL in home runs (21) and walks (69) in 1926; in home runs, 1927 (30) and 1928 (31); in RBI, 1929 (159); in home runs (56), RBI (190), walks (105), and slugging (.723) in 1930. Two World Series, 1924, 1929: 12 games, .319 BA. He hit .471 in the 1929 Series but became the goat by losing two fly balls in the sun during the seventh inning of the fourth game, when the As scored 10 runs to win after being behind, 8–0; they won in 5 games.

Wilson's 190 RBI in 1930 is an ML record, and his 56 home runs the same year is the NL record. He was the only NL player to have more than 150 RBI two consecutive seasons. On July 1, 1925, he hit 2 home runs in an inning, tying the ML record.

A short, thickset, no-necked player at 5' 6" and 190 pounds, Wilson won his nickname in a contest among fans while playing in New York. "Hack" is an abbreviation of Hackenschmidt, for the great Russian strongman and wrestler.

WILSON, JAMES ("Ace") baseball: b. July 23, 1900, Philadelphia; d. May 31, 1947. Bat, throw R; catcher. Philadelphia NL, 1923–28; St. Louis NL, 1928–33; Philadelphia NL, 1934–38; Cincinnati NL, 1939–40. Eighteen years, 1,525 games, .284 BA; hit .305 in 1926, .325 in 1929, .318 in 1930. Four World Series, 1928, 1930–31, 1940: 20 games, .242 BA.

Wilson managed Philadelphia NL, 1934–38 (part); Chicago NL, 1941–44 (part): 493–735, .401.

WILSON, J. OWEN baseball: b. Aug. 21, 1883, Austin, Tex.; d. Feb. 22, 1954. Bat L, throw R; outfield. Pittsburgh NL, 1908–13; St. Louis NL, 1914–16. Nine years, 1,276 games, .269 BA; hit .300 in 1911 and 1912. Led league in RBI, 1911 (107); in triples, 1912 (36). One World Series, 1909: 7 games, .154 BA.

His 36 triples in 1912 is the ML record for a season; he also set an ML record by hitting 6 triples in 5 consecutive games, June 17–20, 1912.

WILTSE, "HOOKS" (George L.) baseball: b. Sept. 7, 1880, Hamilton, N.Y.; d. Jan. 21, 1959. Bat R, throw L; pitcher. New York NL, 1904–14; Brooklyn Fed L, 1915. Twelve years, 142–90, 2.48 ERA; 27 shutouts. In relief, 20–13, 2.54 ERA; 23–14 in 1908; 29 saves. One World Series, 1911: 0–0, 18.90 ERA in 3⅓ innings of relief.

WINGO, IVEY B. baseball: b. July 8, 1890, Gainesville, Ga.; d. March 1, 1941. Bat L, throw R; catcher. St. Louis NL, 1911–14; Cincinnati NL, 1915–26, 1929. Seventeen years, 1,326 games, .260 BA. One World Series, 1919: 3 games, .571 BA.

WINN, MATT J. horse racing: b. June 30, 1861, Louisville, Ky.; d. Oct. 5, 1949. At thirteen, Winn watched the first Kentucky Derby, in 1875; it was the first of 75 consecutive Derbies he was to see. Only death ended the string. But he wasn't formally associated with racing until 1902, when Churchill Downs was having financial difficulty and Winn, a successful businessman, was asked to take over the operation. His first year in charge was the track's first profitable year. He turned the Derby into a spectacle, demonstrated a genius for publicity, and established the policy of having seats available at a wide range of prices.

He also did a great deal to make racing respectable. He installed pari-mutuel machines in 1908, when Louisville banned track bookmakers. He lured millionaires to the track by setting up $100 box seats featuring $2 mint juleps and $5 sandwiches, and though he had previously been a heavy bettor, he never placed a bet on a horse after taking over, to avoid any chance of scandal.

WINTER, GEORGE L. ("Sassafrass") baseball: b. April 27, 1878, New Providence, Pa.; d. May 26, 1951. Throw R; pitcher. Boston AL, 1901–08; Detroit AL, 1908. Eight years, 82–102, 2.87 ERA. One World Series, 1908: 0–0, 0.00 ERA in 1 inning of relief.

WISE, SAMUEL W. baseball: b. Aug, 18, 1857, Akron, Ohio; d. Jan. 23, 1910. Bat L, throw R; shortstop, second base. Detroit NL, 1881; Boston NL, 1882–88; Washington NL, 1889: Buffalo PL, 1890; Baltimore AA,

1891; Washington NL, 1893. Twelve years, 1,175 games, .272 BA; hit .334 in 1887, .311 in 1893. Led NL in RBI, 1884 (104).

Wise went 6-for-7, with a double, a triple, and 5 runs, on June 20, 1883. His 11 putouts on May 9, 1893, tied an NL record for second basemen in a 9-inning game.

WITHINGTON, PAUL W. football: b. Jan. 25, 1888, Escondido, Calif.; d. April 2, 1966. Harvard center; 2nd team All-American, 1909. He coached Wisconsin, 1916, and assisted Percy Haughton at Harvard and Columbia, taking over the Columbia team in 1924, when Haughton became ill. Dr. Withington was a member of the Union Boat Club that rowed in the 1914 Henley Regatta and he coached the Army crews that rowed at Henley and at the Inter-Allied Games in Paris in 1919.

WOLF, PHIL bowling: b. Nov. 2, 1869, Germany; d. July 7, 1935. Wolf was on the ABC tournament champion team in 1909 and 1920 and won the all-events in 1928. His twenty-five year ABC tourney average was 198. American Bowling Congress Hall of Fame.

WOLGAST, AD boxing: b. Feb. 8, 1888, Cadillac, Mich.; d. April 14, 1955. His record: 60 wins, 38 by KO; 12 losses, 2 by KO; 14 draws, 49 no-decisions. Wolgast won the lightweight title on Feb. 22, 1910, KOing Battling Nelson in the 40th of a scheduled 45 rounds. He held it until Nov. 28, 1912, when he lost it to Willie Ritchie on a foul in the 16th round.

WOLGAST, MIDGET boxing: b. Joseph R. Loscalzo, July 18, 1910, Philadelphia; d. Oct. 19, 1955. His record: 96 wins, 11 by KO; 35 losses, 6 by KO; 15 draws, 1 no-decision. After outpointing Black Bill in 15 rounds on March 21, 1930, Wolgast was recognized as New York flyweight champion, and on May 16 he KOed Willie LaMorte, New Jersey champion, in the 6th round. On Dec. 26, he fought a 15-round draw with Frankie Genaro, NBA titleholder, for the vacant world championship. He was considered U.S. champion after Genaro's retirement in 1934 but lost a title fight to Small Montana, on a 10-round decision, Sept. 16, 1935.

WOOD, "BARRY" (William Barry) football: b. May 4, 1910, Milton, Mass.; d. March 9, 1971. Harvard quarterback; All American, captain, 1931. Also a baseball and hockey star, Wood was chosen for the U.S. Davis Cup squad in 1932. He became an outstanding bacteriologist and teacher at Johns Hopkins.

WOOD, CRAIG golf: b. Nov. 18, 1901, Lake Placid, N.Y.; d. May 8, 1968. Wood was known as the bridesmaid because he finished second so often, most dramatically in 1939, when he ended the U.S. Open in a tie with Byron

Nelson and Denny Shute. He shot a 68 in the first playoff round to tie Nelson, while Shute was eliminated, but Nelson beat him, 70–73, in the second playoff round. However, Wood in 1941 became one of the few golfers ever to win the Open and the Masters in a single year.

Helms Hall of Fame, Professional Golfers Association Hall of Fame.

WOOD, GEORGE A. ("Dandy") baseball: b. Nov. 9, 1858, Boston; d. April 4, 1924. Bat L, throw R; outfield. Worcester NL, 1880; Detroit NL, 1881–85; Philadelphia NL, 1886–89; Baltimore AA, 1889; Philadelphia PL, 1890; Philadelphia AA, 1891; Baltimore NL, Cincinnati NL, 1892. Thirteen years, 1,280 games, .273 BA; hit .302 in 1883, .309 in 1891. Led NL in home runs, 1882 (7).

WOODRUFF, GEORGE W. football: b. Feb. 22, 1864, Dimock, Pa.; d. March 23, 1934. After playing football at Yale, 1889, Woodruff went to Pennsylvania to get his law degree and stayed on to coach football, 1892–1901. His 1895 team was 14–0–0; his 1897 team won all 16 of its games. He had winning streaks of 34 games, 1894–96, and 32 games, 1896–98. Woodruff extended the principle of the flying wedge to give his runners "flying interference." He also coached Illinois, 1903, and Carlisle, 1905. His overall record, for twelve seasons, was 142–25–2.

Woodruff left coaching for a distinguished legal career, including four years as Pennsylvania attorney-general.

Helms Hall of Fame, National Football Foundation Hall of Fame.

WOODWARD, WILLIAM F., SR. horse racing: b. April 7, 1876, New York City; d. Sept. 26, 1953. Woodward's Belair Stud Farm produced two Triple Crown winners, Gallant Fox, 1930, and Omaha, 1935. In addition, his Johnstown won the Kentucky Derby and the Belmont in 1939, and Faireno, 1932, and Granville, 1936, were also Derby winners. Another great Belair horse, Nashua, won the Preakness and Belmont in 1955, nearly two years after Woodward's death.

WOOLF, GEORGE horse racing: b. 1906(?); d. Jan. 4, 1946. Woolf rode Bold Venture to victory in the 1936 Preakness. He won both the American Derby and Belmont Futurity, 1942–44, and he also won the Hollywood Gold Cup three straight years, 1938–40. Other major races he won include the Arlington Classic, Carter Handicap, Dwyer Handicap, Hawthorne Gold Cup, Jockey Club Gold Cup, Metropolitan Handicap, Pimlico Special, and Santa Anita Derby.

National Racing Hall of Fame, Jockey Hall of Fame.

WORKMAN, "SONNY" (Raymond) horse racing: b. 1909(?); d. Aug. 21, 1966. Workman was the top money-winning jockey in 1932, with 87 winners that brought in $385,070. He led in percentage of victories in 1930, 1933, and 1935. Riding from 1926 to 1940, he had a total of 1,152 winners in 5,751 mounts. He rode Victorian to a win in the 1928 Preakness.

National Racing Hall of Fame, Jockey Hall of Fame.

WRAY, "LUD" (James R. Ludlow) football: b. Feb. 7, 1894, Philadelphia; d. July 24, 1967. Pennsylvania center. Massillon Tigers, 1919; Buffalo Bisons, 1920–21; Rochester Jeffersons, 1922.

Wray coached the Boston Redskins to a 4–4–2 record in 1932. The following year, he and Bert Bell bought the Frankford Yellowjacket franchise and moved it to Philadelphia, where Wray coached, 1933–35, compiling a 9–21–1 record.

WRENN, ROBERT D. tennis: b. Sept. 20, 1872, Highland Park, N.J.; d. Nov. 12, 1925. A lefthander, Wrenn won the intercollegiate doubles title in 1891, with F. H. Hovey, and in 1892, with F. D. Winslow. He was U.S. outdoor singles champion in 1893–94 and 1896–97. In 1895, he and Malcolm G. Chace won the outdoor doubles title.

Helms Hall of Fame, Tennis Hall of Fame.

WRIGHT, BEALS C. tennis: b. 1879(?); d. Aug. 23, 1961. The son of baseball player George Wright, he was U.S. outdoor singles champion in 1905 and teamed with Holcombe Ward to win the doubles title, 1904–06.

Tennis Hall of Fame.

WRIGHT, "CHALKY" (Albert) boxing: b. Feb. 10, 1912, Durango, Mexico; d. Aug. 12, 1957. His record: 102 wins, 57 by KO; 32 losses, 5 by KO; 5 draws, 1 no-contest. Wright won the featherweight title by KOing Joey Archibald in the 11th round on Sept. 11, 1941. He lost it to Willie Pep on a 15-round decision, Nov. 20, 1942.

WRIGHT, GEORGE baseball: b. Jan. 28, 1847, Yonkers, N.Y.; d. Aug. 21, 1937. Bat, throw R; shortstop. National Association, Boston, 1871–75. Five years, 262 games, .353 BA.

Boston NL, 1876–78; Providence NL, 1879; Boston NL, 1880–81; Providence NL, 1882. Seven years, 329 games, .256 BA.

Managed Providence NL, 1879: 59–25, .702. Pennant.

Wright played for a number of semipro baseball teams, for which statistics are not available, before joining the Cincinnati Red Stockings in 1869. This was the first real professional team, organized and managed by his brother, Harry. The Red Stockings won 56 and tied 1 game in 1869. George scored 339 runs, had 304 hits, 49 home runs, and a BA of .629. (Baseball was somewhat different then; the Red Stockings, despite their amazing record, gave up nearly 10 runs a game that year, but they scored nearly 40 a game.)

Baseball Hall of Fame.

WRIGHT, "HARRY" (William Henry) baseball: b. Jan. 10, 1835, Sheffield, England; d. Oct. 3, 1895. The son of a professional cricket player, Wright was brought to the United States when he was a year old. In 1866 he went to Cincinnati as pro at a cricket club. However, he also organized the Cincinnati Red Stockings baseball team that year. In 1868 he gave up cricket to become full-time manager of the Red Stockings, who became the first fully professional baseball team the following year. They won 93 games in a row before finally losing to the Brooklyn Atlantics.

Wright played for and managed the Boston team in the National Association, 1871–75, winning pennants, 1872–75; in 179 games, he hit .263. He also managed Boston NL, 1876–81; Providence NL, 1882–83; Philadelphia NL, 1884–93: 1,042–848, .551. Pennants, 1877–78.

Baseball Hall of Fame.

WRIGHT, IRVING C. tennis: b. May 13, 1882, Boston; d. June 23, 1953. Wright teamed with Molla Bjurstedt Mallory in 1917 and with Hazel Hotchkiss Wightman in 1918 to win the U.S. mixed-doubles title.

WRIGHT, "TENNESSEE" (V. Richard) horse racing: b. 1921(?), Gallatin, Tenn.; d. July 24, 1966. Wright led all trainers in winners saddled in 1956–57, 1959, and 1961. During his career, he saddled more than 1,800 winners, who won more than $5 million.

WRIGHT, WILLIAM C., JR. tennis: b. ?; d. Feb. 6, 1970. Wright was national court-tennis champion, 1931–32, and teamed with Jay Gould, Jr., to win the court doubles title, 1927–29 and 1931–32.

WYANT, ANDREW R. E. football: b. ?; d. June 17, 1964. Wyant played four years of football at Bucknell, then three years at Chicago, captaining the team in 1893.

National Football Foundation Hall of Fame.

WYATT, BOWDEN football: b. Nov. 4, 1917, Loudon, Tenn.; d. Jan. 21, 1969. Tennessee end; captain, All-American (Rice), 1938.

Wyatt was the first coach to win titles in three major conferences. He coached Wyoming, 1947–52, Arkansas, 1953–54, and Tennessee, 1955–62, winning the Skyline Conference, 1949–50, the Southwest Conference in 1954, and the Southeastern Conference in 1956. His Arkansas team lost the 1955 Cotton Bowl, 14–6, to Georgia Tech, and his Tennessee team lost the 1957 Sugar Bowl, 13–7, to Baylor.

Y

YDE, EMIL O. baseball: b. Jan. 28, 1900, Great Lakes, Ill.; d. Dec. 5, 1968. Sw. hit, throw L; pitcher. Pittsburgh NL, 1924–27; Detroit AL, 1929. Five years, 49–25, 4.02 ERA. Led NL in percentage (16–3, .842) and shutouts (4) in 1924. One World Series, 1925: 0–1, 11.57 ERA.

YORK, RUDOLPH P. baseball: b. Aug. 17, 1913, Ragland, Ala.; d. Feb. 5, 1970. Bat, throw R; first base, catcher. Detroit AL, 1934, 1937–45; Boston AL, 1946–47; Chicago AL, 1947; Philadelphia AL, 1948. Led AL in home runs (34), RBI (118), and slugging (.527) in 1943. Thirteen years, 1,603 games, 277 home runs, 1,152 RBI, .275 BA; hit .307 in 1937, .307 in 1939, .316 in 1940. Three World Series, 1940, 1945–46: 21 games, .221 BA.

York, who was part Cherokee Indian, holds the ML records for most home runs in a month, 18 in August 1937, and for most grand slams in a month, 3 in May 1938. On July 27, 1946, he hit 2 grand slams in a game, tying the ML record. He hit 3 home runs on Sept. 1, 1941.

YORK, THOMAS J. baseball: b. July 13, 1848, Brooklyn; d. Feb. 17, 1936. Bat L; outfield. National Association, Troy, 1871; Baltimore, 1872–73; Philadelphia, 1874; Hartford, 1875. Five years, 269 games, .269 BA.

Hartford NL, 1876; Brooklyn NL, 1877; Providence NL, 1878–82; Cleveland NL, 1883; Baltimore AA, 1884–85. Ten years, 690 games, .271 BA; hit .309 in 1878, .310 in 1879, .304 in 1881. Led NL in triples, 1878 (10).

YOST, "HURRY UP" (Fielding H.) football: b. April 30, 1871, Fairview, W.Va.; d. Aug. 20, 1946. Yost played tackle at both Lafayette and West Virginia, then began his coaching career at Ohio Wesleyan with a 7–1–1 record in 1897. He moved on to Nebraska in 1898, Kansas in 1899, Stanford in 1900, and then settled down at Michigan, where he was head coach for a quarter of a century and athletic director from 1921 until his death.

Yost produced the great "point-a-minute" teams at Michigan, 1901–05. They had a 56-game unbeaten streak until losing to Chicago, 2–0, in the last game of 1905—and those 2 points were the only points scored against them all season. During that span, Michigan scored 2,821 points to 42 for the opposition, including a 550–0 spread in 1901.

Overall, in twenty-nine years of coaching, Yost had 196 wins, 36 losses, and 12 ties, for an .828 percentage. His Michigan teams won Western Conference (Big Ten) titles in 1902 and 1925 and shared the title in 1901, 1903–04, and 1922–23. Michigan beat Stanford 49–0 in the first Rose Bowl game in 1902.

Helms Hall of Fame, National Football Foundation Hall of Fame.

YOUNG, CHARLES A. ("Sparrow") shooting: b. Sept. 10, 1865, Springfield, Ohio; d. May 15, 1951. In 1916, Young became the first man to break 100 straight traps from 23 yards, then the maximum distance in handicap shooting. In 1926, he won the Grand American Handicap with another perfect score from 23 yards, the first time it had been done at the GAH. He was then sixty-one years old. It was 1966 before anyone duplicated his feat. Young entered every GAH from its inception in 1900 through 1950.

YOUNG, "CY" (Denton T.) baseball: b. March 29, 1867, Gilmore, Ohio; d. Nov. 4, 1955. Bat, throw R; pitcher. Cleveland NL, 1890–98; St. Louis NL, 1899–1900; Boston AL, 1901–08; Cleveland AL, 1909–11; Boston NL, 1911. Twenty-two years, 509 wins (1st), 316 losses (1st), 2.63 ERA; 906 games (2nd), 816 starts (1st), 750 complete (1st), 2,803 strikeouts (2nd), 77 shutouts (3rd) in 7,377 innings (1st); 27–22 in 1891, 34–16 in 1893, 26–21 in 1894, 28–15 in 1896, 21–19 in 1897, 25–13 in 1898, 26–16 in 1899, 27–16 in 1904, 21–12 in 1908. In relief, 28–18, 3.21 ERA, 17 saves. Perfect game, May 5, 1904 against Philadelphia AL (3–0; first perfect game in modern era); no-hitters, Sept. 18, 1897, against Cincinnati NL (6–0); June 30, 1908, against New York AL (8–0).

Young was an incredibly tireless pitcher with excellent control. When he finally retired, at forty-four, his arm was still good, but he had gained so much weight that he could no longer bend over to field bunts. His victory total will never be matched. He is the only pitcher to win more than 200 games in each of the two major leagues. He won more than 20 games 16 times, an ML record, and more than 30 games 5 times. He also holds ML records for most years pitching 300 or more innings, 16; most years pitching 200 or more innings, 19; most seasons struck out 100 or more, 18; and most consecutive hitless innings, 23, in 1904.

On Oct. 4, 1890, he won two complete games in a doubleheader, and in 1904 he shut out every other team in the AL. He holds AL records for longest game without issuing a walk, 20 innings, on July 4, 1905, and for fewest walks in a season, 250 or more innings, 1904 (28 walks in 380 innings).

Young led the NL in percentage (36–12, .750), ERA (1.93), and shutouts (9) in 1892; in wins (35–10) and shutouts (4) in 1895; in strikeouts (140) and shutouts (5) in 1896; in complete games, 1899 (40). He led the AL in wins (33–10), ERA (1.62), strikeouts (158), and shutouts (5) in 1901; in wins (32–11) and complete games (41) in 1902; in wins and percentage (28–9, .757), complete games (39), and shutouts (7) in 1903; in shutouts, 1904 (10); in losses, 1906 (13–21.)

One World Series, 1903: 2–1, 1.59 ERA; 17 strikeouts, 4 walks in 34 innings.

Baseball Hall of Fame.

YOUNG, GEORGE bowling: b. Oct. 3, 1909, Omega, Ga.; d. Aug. 30, 1959. The holder of the highest lifetime average for 20 or more ABC tourneys (202 in 20 years), Young was a member of three ABC title teams, in 1952–53 and 1955, and three all-events champion teams, 1949, 1953, and 1955. He rolled better than 1800 nine straight times, a record, and had five 1900s. He had two sanctioned 300 games.

American Bowling Congress Hall of Fame.

YOUNG, GEORGE D. football: b. May 10, 1924, Wilkes-Barre, Pa.; d. Sept. 21, 1969. Georgia end. Cleveland Browns, 1946–53.

YOUNG, IRVING M. baseball: b. July 21, 1876, Columbia Falls, Maine; d. Jan. 14, 1935. Bat R, throw L; pitcher. Boston NL, 1905–08; Pittsburgh NL, 1908; Chicago AL, 1910–11. Six years, 62–94, 3.12 ERA; 19 shutouts; 20–21 in 1905. Led NL in complete games, 1905 (41) and 1906 (37).

YOUNG, "WADDY" (Walter R.) football: b. Sept. 4, 1916, Ponca City, Okla.; d. Jan. 9, 1945. Oklahoma end; All-American, 1938 (Rice, AP). Brooklyn Dodgers, 1939–40.

Young died when his B-29 was shot down during the first bombing raid on Tokyo.

YOUNGS, ROSS M. baseball: b. Royce Youngs, April 10, 1897, Shiner, Tex.; d. Oct. 22, 1927. Bat L, throw R; outfield. New York NL, 1917–26. Ten years, 1,211 games, .322 BA; hit .302 in 1918, .311 in 1919, .351 in 1920, .327 in 1921, .331 in 1922, .336 in 1923, .356 in 1924, .306 in 1926. Led NL in doubles, 1919 (31); in RBI, 1923 (121). Four World Series, 1921–24: 26 games, .286 BA; 10 runs, 9 RBI.

Z

ZABEL, "ZIP" (George W.) baseball: b. Feb. 18, 1891, Wetmore, Kan.; d. May 31, 1970. Bat, throw R; pitcher. Chicago NL, 1913–15. Three years, 14–14, 2.71 ERA. Zabel set a record for most innings by a relief pitcher finishing a game, with 18⅓ on June 17, 1915. Called into the game with 2 out in the 1st, he ended up as the winning pitcher in 19 innings.

ZACHARY, "TOM" (Jonathan Thomas W.) baseball: b. May 7, 1896, Graham, N.C.; d. Jan. 24, 1969. Bat, throw L; pitcher. Philadelphia AL, 1918; Washington AL, 1919–25; St. Louis AL, 1926–27; Washington AL, 1927–28; New York AL, 1928–30; Boston NL, 1930–34; Brooklyn NL, 1934–36; Philadelphia NL, 1936. Nineteen years, 185–191, 3.72 ERA; 23 shutouts. In relief, 17–20, 3.13 ERA, 22 saves. Three World Series, 1924–25, 1928: 3–0, 2.86 ERA.

Zachary is best known as the pitcher who gave up Babe Ruth's 60th home run in 1927.

ZAHARIAS, "BABE" (Mildred [Didrikson]) golf, track: b. June 26, 1914, Pt. Arthur, Tex.; d. Sept. 27, 1956. Voted the greatest woman athlete of the first half of the twentieth century, she might as well be acknowledged as the greatest of the first seven-tenths of the century now. Early in her career, she starred on touring basketball, softball, and baseball teams.

She came to national and international fame in track and field. She won these U.S. outdoor titles: 80-meter hurdles, 1931–32; high jump, broad jump, 8-pound shot put, 1932; javelin, 1930, 1932; baseball throw, 1930–32. In the 1932 Olympics, she won the 80-meter hurdles and the javelin; her 1st-place finish in the high jump was disallowed because judges said she used the "Western roll."

She turned professional after the Olympics, concentrating on golf. The Women's Golf Association eventually returned her to amateur status and she won the U.S. Amateur and Trans-Mississippi Amateur in 1946 and the North and South Amateur in 1947. She was the first American to win the British Women's Amateur, in 1947.

In 1948, she joined the professional tour, winning the U.S. Women's Open; she repeated that victory in 1950 and in 1954, despite an operation for cancer in 1953. She was the women's titleholder at Augusta, Georgia, in 1947, 1950, and 1952, and she won the Western Open in 1940, 1944–45, and 1950. She was the leading money-winner four straight years, 1948–51, and she won the Vare Trophy, for lowest strokes-per-round, in 1954, with a 75.48 average. She was chosen Woman Athlete of the Year by the Associated Press in 1932, 1945–47, 1950, and 1954.

ZIMMER, "CHIEF" (Charles L.) baseball: b. Nov. 23, 1860, Marietta, Ohio; d. Aug. 22, 1949. Bat, throw R; catcher. Detroit NL, 1884; New York AA, 1886; Cleveland AA, 1887–88; Cleveland NL, 1889–99; Louisville NL, 1899; Pittsburgh NL, 1900–02; Philadelphia NL, 1903. Nineteen years, 1,280 games, .269 BA; hit .340 in 1895, .316 in 1897, .307 in 1899.
  Zimmer went 6-for-6, with 2 doubles and 3 runs, on July 11, 1894.
  He managed Philadelphia NL, 1903: 49–86, .363.

ZINN, RONALD L. walking: b. May 10, 1937, Chicago; d. July 7, 1965. Zinn was the top American finisher in the Olympic 20-kilometer walk in both 1960 and 1964, placing 19th and 6th, respectively, and he led all Americans by finishing 3rd in the Pan-American Games in 1963. He won the following AAU titles: 35-kilometer, 1960; 1-mile, 1961–63 and 1965; 2-mile, 1961–64; 10-kilometer, 1961–64; 15-kilometer, 1961; 20-kilometer, 1961–62.
  He was killed in Vietnam.

ZUNKER, GILBERT bowling: b. 1899, Milwaukee, Wis.; d. Dec. 16, 1938. The first man to roll two 700s in one ABC tournament, 1933, Zunker won doubles and all-events that year, with a 2060, then a record, in the latter. His thirteen-year ABC tourney average was 199.
  American Bowling Congress Hall of Fame.

ZUPPKE, ROBERT C. football: b. July 12, 1879, Berlin, Germany; d. Dec. 22, 1957. Despite a 131–80–12 record compiled at Illinois, which included 5 Western Conference (Big Ten) titles and shares of 2 others, the "little Dutchman" will probably be remembered best for the upsets his teams came up with. The greatest occurred in 1939. The University of Michigan, led by Tom Harmon, had won all 8 of its games; Illinois had won only 1. Michigan was favored by 30 or 40 points, but Illinois won, 16–7.
  Zuppke was a year old when his family moved to the United States and settled in Milwaukee. He lettered in basketball at the University of Wisconsin, 1906, then became a high-school coach. He became head coach at Illinois in 1913. In the next sixteen years, Illinois won or shared the conference title 7 times. The 1927 team, with a 7–0–1 record, won the national championship.
  In 1928, Illinois won its last conference title under Zuppke, though he coached for thirteen more seasons. He retired, under pressure, after the 1941 season, in which Illinois lost all five conference games.
  Helms Hall of Fame, National Football Foundation Hall of Fame.